The Cluniac priory and abbey of St Saviour Bermondsey, Surrey

Excavations 1984–95

MOLA Monograph Series

For more information about these titles and other MOLA publications visit the publications page at www.museumoflondonarchaeology.org.uk

The Cluniac priory and abbey of St Saviour Bermondsey, Surrey

Excavations 1984–95

Tony Dyson, Mark Samuel, Alison Steele
and Susan M Wright

MOLA MONOGRAPH 50

MUSEUM OF LONDON ARCHAEOLOGY

Published by Museum of London Archaeology

Copyright © Museum of London 2011

A CIP catalogue record for this book is available from the British Library

Production and series design by Tracy Wellman
Typesetting and design by Sue Cawood
Reprographics by Andy Chopping
Copy editing by Wendy Sherlock
Series editing by Sue Hirst/Susan M Wright

Printed by the Lavenham Press

*Front cover: cast copper-alloy, hollow-backed appliqué figure of Christ crucified
<S25>, decorated with champlevé enamel (Fig 98) (height 157mm)*

CONTRIBUTORS

Principal stratigraphic author	Alison Steele
Documentary evidence	Tony Dyson
Architectural reconstruction and fragments	Mark Samuel
Additional text	Susan M Wright
Decorative brickwork	Terence P Smith
Stone roofing and paving, ceramic building material	Ian M Betts
Saxon pottery	Lyn Blackmore
Medieval and post-medieval pottery	Jacqui Pearce
Window glass	Geoff Egan
Accessioned finds	Geoff Egan
Animal bone	Alan Pipe, Kevin Rielly, with Charlotte Ainsley
Human remains	Brian Connell, William White
Conservation	Elizabeth Barham
Photography	Andy Chopping, Maggie Cox (finds), excavation staff (site photographs)
Graphics	Carlos Lemos, with † Susan Banks, Peter Hart Allison, Jane Sandoe (maps and plans), Julia Jarrret, Sandra Rowntree (accessioned finds), Jacqui Pearce (medieval pottery), Lyn Blackmore (Saxon pottery)
Academic advisers	Glyn Coppack, Roberta Gilchrist
Project management	David Bowsher, Richard Malt, Barney Sloane
Editor	Susan M Wright with David Bowsher

CONTENTS

FIGURES

TABLES

SUMMARY

Excavations by Museum of London Archaeology (MOLA) on the site of the Cluniac priory and later abbey of St Saviour Bermondsey took place between 1984 and 1995. The site, formerly in Surrey and now part of the London Borough of Southwark, is a Greater London Scheduled Ancient Monument (GLSAM 165). Work by W F Grimes in 1956 and 1962–3 uncovered the north side of the east end of the monastic church, while recent excavations by Pre-Construct Archaeology Ltd (PCA) have revealed masonry in the area of the south transept, north-east corner of the main cloister and east range (BYQ98; WBP07); data from these excavations have been incorporated into the publication. Drawings and survey work undertaken by the antiquarian J C Buckler have also been used to complement and inform the evidence supplied by modern excavation.

The archaeological evidence is set out in a chronological sequence (Chapters 2, 3 and 5), beginning with the evidence for Middle Saxon and Late Saxon settlement, following a brief summary of prehistoric and Roman activity in the study area. The first buildings on the site were a small apsidal chapel, constructed in the Late Saxon/early Norman period and enclosed within ditches, and a timber latrine which spanned the ditch to the south. By the mid 12th century work had advanced on the priory church and some of the major conventual buildings. These included the structures around the principal cloister with its free-standing lavabo – the east dormitory range, the reredorter and possible bathhouse, and refectory. The east end of the priory church is reconstructed with an asymmetric apse echelon scheme comprising five parallel apses. The monastic cemetery developed between the church and the earlier chapel. In the later 12th century, the east range undercroft was revaulted and a new stone reredorter built across the south end of the east range. To the east the first infirmary complex was constructed with its own latrine building and a hall or lodgings to the south. A new drainage system was built. An additional apsidal chapel was added to the north aisle of the priory church, while the Saxo-Norman chapel was retained and enlarged. A masonry wall enclosed the south-west part of the monastic precinct.

In the first half of the 13th century the second or infirmary cloister was expanded and the hall/lodgings developed with a new kitchen and hall. The second half of the 13th and early 14th century saw major changes to the infirmary, with the disuse of the infirmary latrine and new structures and another courtyard to the east, and expansion and renovation of the chapel to the north of the infirmary. In the 14th century (from c 1330) the eastern arm of the priory church was extended with a square east end and a second north aisle was added. The main cloister and the chapter house were remodelled, and there was considerable rebuilding elsewhere – in the south range, around the second cloister and to its immediate east where a large courtyard and new chambers were built. In the pre-Dissolution period this eastern area was disused. The evidence for the Dissolution period suggests a prompt surrender and systematic stripping. Evidence for the private Tudor mansion constructed by Thomas Pope around the former main cloister is described.

Particular aspects of the medieval priory are addressed thematically (Chapter 4). A section on the foundation addresses some of the complexities surrounding the priory's beginnings, including the Anglo-Saxon minster located on the Bermondsey eyot. The small apsidal chapel, a structure spanning the crucial, transitional Late Saxon/early Norman years, is the focus of much interest. The reconstructed plans of the 12th-century and c 1400 phases of the priory church dedicated to the Holy Saviour are discussed in the context of contemporary English and Continental examples. The local topography and early landscape, and their influence on the subsequent plan and development of the monastery and home grange are examined, including various buildings in the precinct known only from documentary evidence. The infirmary and its continuing development throughout the life of the priory is considered, with particular reference to the evidence for segregation in the early periods. A section about the people of the monastery discusses the inhabitants and attempts to define some of the more complex social processes at work within the precinct: the demography and health of those buried in the monastic cemetery, and burial practices; the material culture and diet of the inhabitants; food preparation, hygiene and the supply of clean water to the house; and the priory's economic base and evidence for industrial activities taking place within the precinct. A large and uniquely informative assemblage of artefacts and materials discarded from the conventual buildings is illustrated and discussed.

The results and wider conclusions that can be drawn from this study of the Cluniac monastery of Bermondsey are considered (Chapter 6), along with to what extent the research project's original aims have been attained and what questions remain to be answered. Specialist appendices (Chapter 7) include detailed studies of the evidence provided by the 19th-century survey work of John Chessell Buckler and the surviving architectural fragments, and by the other stone and ceramic building materials, window glass and pottery, together with catalogues and supporting data for the accessioned finds, and analysis of the animal bone assemblage and the remains of 193 individuals buried here.

ACKNOWLEDGEMENTS

This publication is the product of a joint venture between English Heritage and Museum of London Archaeology (MOLA) (prior to 2009 known as MoLAS, ie the Museum of London Archaeology Service) to publish backlog sites identified in the London post-excavation review (Hinton and Thomas 1997). MOLA would like to thank English Heritage for their generous funding of the post-excavation analysis that has resulted in this publication. The post-excavation phase of this project was monitored on behalf of English Heritage by Brian Kerr and Barney Sloane, and the post-excavation programme was managed for MOLA by Gordon Malcolm.

MOLA excavations on the principal site (BA84) were funded by the then Greater London Council. Archaeological investigations of other sites and post-excavation reports were funded by Swinhoe Measures Partnership, the Wandle Housing Association Limited, Bellway Homes plc and Countryside Homes plc. David Beard, with the assistance of Richard Bluer, Carrie Cowan, Eric Norton and Kevin Wooldridge, supervised the principal site (BA84); subsequent excavations were supervised by Simon Blatherwick (BER88), Alison Steele (TRE91 and TOB95), Portia Askew (TWB94) and Helen Jones (LWK92). Results have been incorporated from additional excavations by MOLA, supervised by Kieron Heard (VIY97) and David Saxby (JAC96), and from the 1950s–70s excavations by D Corbett and W F Grimes. The digital drawings on which the phased site plans were based were the work of the late David Bentley.

The post-excavation assessment report and updated project design were completed in 1997, by Alison Steele and Barney Sloane. A complete draft text was refereed in 2003 and revised in 2004 (mainly by two of the principal authors, AS and MS), with the editorial assistance of David Bowsher. In the final stage of publication (2008–), with the support of English Heritage, it was agreed to incorporate structural evidence recently recorded by Pre-Construct Archaeology Ltd (PCA) in the area of the south transept and east range. PCA generously provided computer aided drawing (CAD) data and preliminary phasing from their excavations at Bermondsey Square (BYQ98) in 1998 (for London Borough of Southwark; supervisors David Divers and Kevin Wooldridge), 2002 (for Urban Catalyst (Bermondsey) Ltd; consultant Richard Hughes; supervisor Chris Mayo), and 2004–8 (for Urban Catalyst (Bermondsey) Ltd (2004–5) and Igloo Regeneration (GP) Limited (2005–8); consultant Peter Mills (Mills Whipp); supervisor Alistair Douglas), and at the former White Bear public house (WBP07) in 2007–8 (for Commodore Developments (UK); supervisors Alistair Douglas and Ireneo Grosso). We are particularly grateful to Alistair Douglas of PCA for his advice and assistance.

Incorporation of PCA data required substantial reworking of the medieval chronological narrative and accompanying period plans (Chapter 3), with consequent implications for the thematic discussion and conclusions (Chapters 4 and 6), in particular the plan and architectural development of the monastery and graphic reconstructions (Chapter 4.2). This work was undertaken by the monograph's editor, Susan M Wright, with the assistance of Mark Samuel. Other sections were revised, including the context and significance of the window glass, and of the reredorter ceramic and accessioned finds assemblages, and the interpretation of the precinct as a whole and the home grange, together with limited updating of some parts of the text, for example Chapter 2 (all by SMW). Particular thanks are due to Stephen Humphrey (Archivist, Southwark Local History Library) and Bruce Watson (MOLA), together with Graham Dawson, for information and discussions about Southwark topography and archaeology, and to Carlos Lemos (MOLA) for his integration of the new graphic data and preparation of the revised plans and reconstructions.

Alison Steele would like to thank Stephen Priestley who very kindly contributed both his knowledge and enthusiasm in the course of discussions about the documentary sources for St Saviour Bermondsey. Mark Samuel gratefully acknowledges the role played by the late Freda Anderson in the study of the Romanesque sculpture. Roland Harris and John Crook provided invaluable information and advice on the Romanesque buildings. Lindy Grant (Reading University, formerly of the Courtauld Institute) and Jeffrey West (Church Buildings Council) offered much useful advice on the assemblage of architectural fragments. David Park (Courtauld Institute) advised on the surviving paint on stone and its conservation requirements, and David F Williams (then of Southampton University) advised on and identified geological samples. John Shepherd brought unpublished material in the Grimes archive connected with the 1950s excavation of the presbytery to the attention of AS and MS.

Terence P Smith, who kindly contributed an analysis of the patterning of the brick garden walls, would like to thank the staff of the British Library and the Guildhall Library for their help. Geoff Egan thanks John Blair (The Queen's College, Oxford) for advice on the tomb-inscription letters, Marian Campbell (Victoria and Albert Museum) for discussion of some of the metalwork, John Cherry (British Museum) for advice on the seal matrix, Michael Hammerson for advice on the numismatic finds, John Shepherd for help with the glassware, Gabor Thomas (Reading University) for advice on the strapends, David Williams (Southampton University) for advice on the petrology of quernstones and Sue Youngs (British Museum) for help with the Saxon strapends, together with Richenda Goffin, Roy Stephenson and Angela Wardle.

Dedicated to the memory of

Geoff Egan
1951–2010

and

William ('Bill') White
1944–2010

1

Introduction

1.1 The Cluniac Order, the English priories and St Saviour Bermondsey: introduction and background

The Cluniac priory of Bermondsey was dedicated to the Holy Saviour and commonly known as St Saviour Bermondsey; it was founded in the 1080s from La Charité-sur-Loire, and was the only Cluniac house in Surrey, the nearest major house of the Order being Lewes in Sussex (Fig 1). The two nearest religious houses were Augustinian, St Mary Overie (or Overy) in Southwark (founded *c* 1106) and St Mary Merton, Surrey (founded on its final site *c* 1117; Blair 1991, 99–102). The first colony of monks arrived at Bermondsey in 1089 (*Ann Monast*, iii, 427–8).

The Cluniac Order, based on its mother house of Cluny (Saône-et-Loire) in Burgundy, was founded early in the 10th century. Enjoying a remarkable degree of royal and aristocratic support, it was increasingly called upon to found new religious houses and restore older foundations that had fallen into disrepair or disorder, and its influence soon spread throughout France to Italy and Spain. The Order reached its high point under Abbot Hugh (1049–1109), and in Normandy even the great abbeys of Jumièges and Fécamp (both in Seine-Maritime), though not themselves Cluniac, were reformed under its influence. The Conqueror's first intention was to use Cluniac monks to reform the English church (Knowles and Hadcock 1953, 11–12), and Archbishop Lanfranc's Constitutions, compiled for the guidance of the monks of Christchurch Canterbury (Kent) and adopted by several of the older monasteries, were largely derived from the customs of Cluny (Poole 1955, 185–6). The first, and therefore senior, English house of the Order was Lewes Priory, founded *c* 1081 (1077–82: Lyne 1997, 6–7), and by 1108 Cluny was also responsible for Montacute (Somerset) and Lenton (Nottinghamshire). Lewes founded daughter houses of its own at Heacham, Castle Acre and Thetford (all in Norfolk); Stansgate (Essex), Clifford (Herefordshire) and Monks Horton (Kent) by 1142 (Fig 1). In England, Henry I's foundation at Reading (Berkshire) (1121) and later King Stephen's at Faversham (Kent) (1148) were strongly influenced by Cluny but remained autonomous (Burton 1994, 36).

Apart from Cluny, a small number of other French houses of the Order established daughter houses in England, notably La Charité-sur-Loire which by 1100 was responsible for Bermondsey, Wenlock (Shropshire), Pontefract (Yorkshire West Riding), Preston Capes (later to Daventry) and Northampton (Northamptonshire) (Knowles and Hadcock 1953, 95–101; Fig 1). La Charité-sur-Loire, on the Loire, itself refounded in 1059, had already supplied the first monks for Wenlock, refounded by the earl of Shrewsbury in 1081–2. Bermondsey excepted, the founders were major Norman nobles. One of Bermondsey's early 20th-century historians, Rose Graham, suggested that it was the first monks from La Charité-sur-Loire, passing through London on their way to Shropshire in the early 1080s, who inspired Alwyn Childe (or Alwin Child), the accredited founder of Bermondsey, to

Fig 1 Map of Cluniac foundations in England and Wales (after Knowles and Hadcock 1974, map 'The black monks') (scale 1:5,000,000)

endow the French house with rents in London in 1082 with a view to helping establish a Cluniac house near London (Graham 1926, 159).

The Cluniacs formed the first wave of foundations in England after the Conquest, an expression of a newly found sense of Anglo-Norman rather than Norman identity (Burton 1994, 35–9). Cluniac monasticism also had its own particular features. We know that the Cluniacs had a significant impact on both the liturgy as practised by the Benedictines and the *horarium* or timetable. The Benedictine liturgy had developed since the 6th century AD, when the Eucharist or Mass was celebrated only once a week (ibid, 161). Cluny (and other 10th-century AD reform movements) added two daily Masses: the morrow or Chapter Mass and a sung High Mass. Processions came to be of increasing importance and in Cluniac ritual those celebrating Mass on principal feasts were clothed in rich vestments (ibid, 162). The constitutions drawn up by Archbishop Lanfranc of Canterbury between 1079 and 1089 were heavily influenced by Cluny and were followed not only at Christchurch Canterbury but also at Durham (Durham), St Albans (Hertfordshire), St Peter's Westminster (London) and probably elsewhere. In line with Cluniac custom, the constitutions elaborate the recitation of psalms. The design and layout of monastic churches was affected by liturgical practice: Continental liturgy, transmitted through the *Decreta* of Lanfranc, concentrated worship in the east end (ibid, 42).

In terms of the daily round, Cluniac monasticism had all

but expunged physical labour from the timetable, partly because of the proliferation of services and partly because of developing attitudes which regarded work as fit for peasants and not monks (Burton 1994, 164). The daily work of the monastery gradually fell to hired servants. The Cistercians were later to restore manual work to its place in the monastic timetable and the Cluniac inspired liturgy was pruned and simplified.

It has been pointed out that Cluniac houses remained part of an organised family in a way quite unfamiliar to the completely autonomous abbeys of England and Normandy, that the relation between Cluny and her dependencies was more feudal than canonical, although 'it did not make of the Cluniacs a religious order in the sense later made familiar by Cîteaux and still more by the orders of friars' (Knowles and Hadcock 1953, 12). St Saviour Bermondsey owed direct allegiance to the abbot of Cluny who exercised a control over the Cluniac congregation throughout Europe that was monarchical in scale. Each Cluniac house was retained in absolute dependence on the mother house at Cluny and the superiors of each house were not the elect of their own communities as is the normal Benedictine custom. The Cluny constitution required the priors of daughter houses to be nominated by the heads of the mother house, the priors of Bermondsey, like those of Wenlock, Northampton and Pontefract being preferred by La Charité-sur-Loire, and the prior of Wenlock, as the head of the eldest daughter house, being occasionally authorised to act as vicar-general for the mother house and to nominate priors to other houses. The king would agree the chosen candidate via letters patent and, when the newly appointed prior had done fealty to him, would restore to the prior the monastic estates which had been in crown hands during the vacancy. The position of the English church and its diocesan bishops was relatively weak a propos the 'alien' houses, whose authority came directly from their mother houses abroad and from the pope.

English Cluniacs were a loosely organised group in the period from the late 11th to the first part of the 13th century and one which played no outstanding part in public life. Not until after 1231 when Pope Gregory introduced the general chapter and visitations was more direct control over Cluniac houses sought (Burton 1994, 38). Thus in the 13th century all the priors of the English houses were bound to go to Cluny once in two years to attend the chapter general, which met on the third Sunday after Easter, and the prior of Bermondsey was also obliged to attend the chapter general at La Charité-sur-Loire (Graham 1926, 165–7).

Like the other houses of the Order, St Saviour Bermondsey owed spiritual and financial allegiance to a foreign institution. It is evident from the history of debt and dispute throughout the pages of this volume that the position was not an easy one to occupy. The priory had to pay money on all sides at various times and, at times, the inherent tensions in the political situation came to the surface; it was taxed by the king as a foreign priory, by Cluny as a dependent house and was also liable for the payment of a special papal subsidy.

In the 14th century, a natural development following on from the economic burdens, the war with France and seizures of French property was a move towards denization, a move supported by the alien houses themselves. The senior house of the Order, Lewes, secured its denization as early as 1351 (and that of its subordinate priories) and it was the first Englishman to hold the office of prior at Bermondsey who achieved the denization of that house in 1380. At the time of the *Valor Ecclesiasticus* in 1535, Bermondsey (with £474) was the second richest house of the Order in England, after Lewes (with £920) (*Val Eccl* [B] ii, 60; *Val Eccl* [Lewes] i, 332; *VCH* 1967, 64–77; 1973, 64–71).

1.2 A note on the documentary and graphic sources

As with other religious houses, the contemporary documentary sources for Bermondsey consist of the standard sources generated by central and local government, and those produced by (and surviving from) the house itself. In the first category, coverage is generally better for Bermondsey than for many of its sister houses in the area. The Patent Rolls and Close Rolls, recording day-to-day royal decisions and directives, the Fine Rolls and Miscellaneous Inquisitions are all particularly full: the Patent Rolls contain an exceptionally large body of material for the late 13th and 14th centuries, as do the Close Rolls for the 15th century. In the case of the Patent Rolls the explanation for this richness is not hard to find: during the period in question Bermondsey Priory was a matter of recurrent concern and trouble to the crown. As an alien priory, belonging to an alien Order and a foreign mother house, it had little effective control over its finances, resources or inmates, and throughout the wars with France it was in the king's hands as enemy property. To add to the burden, the priory and its surrounding lands were frequently flooded by the Thames. In each of these respects it was constantly coming to the king's attention for special treatment of one kind or another. On the evidence of the subsequent decrease in mentions in the Patent Rolls, these problems all but vanished overnight once the priory was removed from foreign possession and supervision and became an abbey. Even the flooding episodes feature less prominently.

Another way in which Bermondsey appears especially favoured by the Patent Rolls, and even more so by the Close Rolls, lies in the detail these provide of the corrodies that the house was regularly called upon to provide for retired servants of the royal household. This may be explained by the fact that Bermondsey was closer to the City and Westminster than many of the other male regular houses and, therefore, much more sought after. In practically every other respect, however, the records of central government are disappointing during the period before the Dissolution.

The registers of the diocesan bishops of Winchester provide less topographical information about Bermondsey than about other houses, largely because visitations were more often undertaken by Cluny than by the bishops. No doubt also the institutional and financial problems that the visitors encountered claimed more of their attention than the state of the fabric.

As if by way of compensation, an unusual amount of detail concerning the precinct, its buildings and surrounding lands, is available from the period immediately after the Dissolution. Particulars for grants (especially those relating to Sir Robert Southwell in 1540–1 and Sir Thomas Pope in 1543) along with royal grants, Chancery decrees and proceedings (these last two sources are exceptionally full for the abbey site in the later 16th century) refer in greater or lesser detail to almshouses or hospice, infirmary, bakehouse, brewhouse, larder, kitchen, monks' cemetery, cloister, bell tower, dormitory, prior's/abbot's house and refectory. They also mention several tenements within the close, the precinct's gates and adjoining pastures, meadows, orchards and gardens. Stow's (1603) coverage of Bermondsey is exceptionally good, again clearly on account of its proximity to the City.

The sources generated by Bermondsey itself are equally variable in quantity and quality. In the first place, a few fragments apart, there is no surviving cartulary comparable with those for St Mary Merton or St Mary Clerkenwell (Islington), nor any priory rentals or accounts to compare with those for St John Clerkenwell or St Mary Clerkenwell. Among the survivals from the abbey's archives may be noted a single sheet of expenses incurred during a vacancy in 1418 (TNA: PRO, SC6/1107/11) and concerned only with the house's City properties, and an account roll at the British Library detailing priory expenditure during the period Easter 1391 to Michaelmas 1392 (Graham 1937, 148–9). One survival (albeit indirect) of the abbey's records unrivalled by any of its fellow houses in the area is the collection of priory deeds preserved in the Exchequer's Ancient Deeds series: these are particularly rich in material relating to local Bermondsey and Rotherhithe topography. Two recent articles list surviving leases, deeds, court rolls and other documents relating to the priory's manors, generally of 14th-century and later date – in particular, a substantial number of court rolls for the manors of Dulwich and Leigham Court (both Surrey), Paris Garden in Southwark, East Chalk (Kent), and court rolls from 1274–81 for the manors of Widford (Hertfordshire) and Quickbury (in Sheering) and Monkbury (in Little Hallingbury) in Essex (Jurkowski 2006; 2007, 8).

In the early 19th century, John Buckler, senior (1770–1851), and his son John Chessell Buckler (1793–1894) compiled three volumes of notes, sketches and topographic plans relating to Sir Thomas Pope's mansion house and elements of the earlier monastic building at Bermondsey. This extraordinary resource has been used in the reconstruction of the monastic layout and the later mansion house and has been incorporated into the relevant plans and discussions in this report. The history of the Buckler plans and a catalogue of the material relevant to Bermondsey is given in Chapter 7.1.

1.3 Circumstances of excavation

The study area

This report describes the genesis and development of part of the precinct of the priory of St Saviour Bermondsey. The extent of the study area is *c* 600m east–west by *c* 1000m north–south and its centre lies at Ordnance Survey (OS) grid reference 533650/179650 (Fig 2). The focus of the study area is the eastern ranges of the monastic complex, located some 750m from the south bank of the Thames, almost directly opposite the Tower of London, and just over 1km to the south-east of London Bridge. The area covered by excavation, evaluation or watching brief within the study area totals 7732m².

This analysis and publication project concerns the medieval and post-medieval history and archaeology of the sites, up to *c* 1650. The earlier evidence from the sites in the study area is only briefly summarised here (Chapter 2). The prehistoric and the Roman evidence were considered as part of two separate studies, of prehistoric Southwark and Lambeth (Sidell et al 2002) and Roman Southwark (Cowan et al 2009).

History of archaeological investigations in the study area before the 1950s

The ancient priory and later abbey of St Saviour Bermondsey first became a subject of serious study between the years 1808 and 1820, when John Buckler, senior, and his son John Chessell Buckler compiled three volumes of notes and sketches relating to the site (Chapter 7.1). The first archaeological discoveries in the study area came in 1902 when two large chalk-lined graves were observed during the construction of 'workmen's cottages' for rail workers on the south side of Abbey Street (Fig 3). A body of material relating to chance finds over the succeeding 20 years, principally during works by the railway company, includes written descriptions of wall foundations and architectural fragments and one or two photographs (all filed under the English Heritage London Division file HB92). In 1922, foundations underlying Bermondsey Square were observed by G Topham Forrest during the construction of Tower Bridge Road. In 1923, building works on the Anglo-American Oil Company's petrol station in the square led to the uncovering of several foundations and moulded capitals.

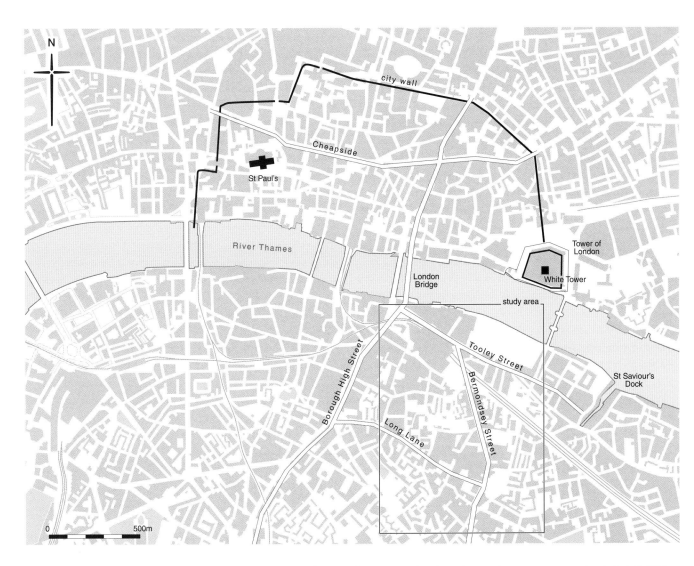

Fig 2 Location of the study area in relation to the medieval walled city and main roads, superimposed on the modern, Ordnance Survey, street plan (scale 1:20,000)

Archaeological investigations in the study area since the 1950s

In recent years, a number of archaeological sites have been investigated within the curtilage of the historic monastic precinct. It has been possible to incorporate the results of seven of these into the present volume; for the purpose of clarity, these individual sites have been allocated a letter prefix (sites A–G, Table 1; Fig 3). Site codes are used for sites which are referred to but which remain outside the scope of this study.

Observations were made by F H Healey in 1955 on the western side of Tower Bridge Road (Jones 1993, 1.2). The first modern excavations took place on the north side of Abbey Street in 1956 and 1962–3, where D Corbett and W F Grimes uncovered the north part of the eastern arm of the priory church (site G, Fig 3). The Corbett and Grimes sites, funded by the Ministry of Public Building and Works (MOPBW), and the Corporation of Bermondsey, were briefly published (Grimes 1968, 210–17). Some further work by Grimes took place in the 1970s within the perimeters of what was later to become the principal excavation site (site A, Fig 3). An undated MOPBW report by Corbett, filed in the Grimes archive in the London Archaeological Archive and Research Centre (LAARC), stems from 'the 1956 season's work' (Grimes 1968, 210, n 1); a plan is dated 1960 suggesting Corbett's text was written before Grimes's 1962 excavation. Grimes mentions Corbett as having excavated the eastern part of the site directly for the MOPBW. Interestingly, Corbett describes areas of possible survival outside the excavation. The western part of the site was separately excavated in 1962–3 by Grimes's 'Excavation Council' (ibid). The relationship between Grimes's published plan (ibid, fig 52; published here as Fig 23) and Corbett's sketch plans is not clear, and there are some differences. Grimes's preparatory plan of the western transept excavation survives in the Grimes archive and is directly reused in the published plan with some simplifications.

Between 1984 and 1988 the former Department of Greater London Archaeology (DGLA), under the aegis of the Museum of London (MOL, formerly MoL), carried out large-scale excavations over the east part of site A (Fig 4), with more limited excavation and recording of foundations on the west part. Site A, the largest single excavated area, was c 65m by 65m and revealed the infirmary of the medieval monastery. This was one of the largest excavations carried out in Southwark in the 1980s; and metal detectors were used systematically, possibly accounting, for example, for the high number of 4th-century AD coins recovered (Cowan et al 2009, 119).

As a result of the Grimes excavations of the priory church and of the Museum of London (DGLA) excavations which identified the infirmary, it was possible to assess the accuracy of the Buckler drawings of the site (Chapters 5.2, 7.1). These drawings had been, until Grimes, the sole record of the lost medieval monument. With the integrity of the Buckler records confirmed by excavation and the likely location of surviving archaeological remains established, it was possible to schedule the site. This was done in 1988 (GLSAM 165).

Sites B–F (1988–95) within the study area were responses to piecemeal commercial development of plots within the former monastic precinct. The status of the archaeological recording from these sites ranges from watching brief notes (sites B and E) through to single context recording in evaluation and full excavation (sites C and F). Site D, so crucial in its contribution of evidence for the main cloister and south cloister range, was almost completely unexcavated but was cleaned and recorded at the level where the first archaeological features and foundations were revealed. This area, and the adjacent area of site A, the south end of the east cloister range, have been backfilled and preserved in situ, in accordance with the legislation that was brought into force in 1990 (Department of the Environment 1990).

Site Z, on the south bank of the Thames near Tower Bridge was the subject of rescue excavations in 1988 at Vine Lane (Southwark; VIN88; Table 1; Fig 3); it was the site of a 17th-century tin-glazed ware pothouse (Pickleherring: Tyler et al 2008). Architectural fragments recovered there were identified as having come from the medieval monastery. Some further observation and recording was carried out in adjacent areas to the west in 1992 (ABO92; Abbots Lane, Southwark), the site of the medieval moated residence known as Fastolf Place (Blatherwick and Bluer 2009). The architectural fragments from site Z have been added to the archive for St Saviour Bermondsey and their analysis and interpretation have made an important contribution to this report.

Excavation at Harp Lane, City of London (HL74), near Lower Thames Street, on the north bank of the Thames east of London Bridge, produced a number of medieval architectural fragments in 17th-century contexts (Lea 1981). The Harp Lane mouldings were attributed to a City church but are more likely to have come from St Saviour Bermondsey; they are not included in detail here but reference is made to them, principally in Chapter 7.2.

Two other archaeological sites excavated by MOLA at Mill Street/Bermondsey Wall West, Jacob's Island (Southwark; JAC96; Saxby 1997) and at Vinegar Yard, Tanner Street (Southwark; VIY97; Heard 1998) since the analysis and publication programme for this volume began in earnest in 1995, have not been included but reference to their findings has been made (Fig 3; Fig 81).

Table 1 Sites investigated within the study area at St Saviour Bermondsey and described in this report

Prefix	Site code	Site address	Site type
A	BA84	Abbey Street/Tower Bridge Road	excavation
B	BER88	39–45 Bermondsey Street	watching brief
C	TRE91	Bermondsey Street/Tower Bridge Road	evaluation
D	LWK92	Long Walk/Tower Bridge Road	evaluation
E	TWB94	Long Walk/Tower Bridge Road roadworks	watching brief
F	TOB95	Bermondsey Street/Tower Bridge Road	excavation
G	WFG54	Abbey Street	excavation
Z*	VIN88	Vine Lane	excavation

* architectural fragment assemblage only

Fig 3 The location within the study area of the individual archaeological investigations described in this report (sites A–G and Z: see Table 1 for details) and other sites referred to in the text (scale 1:5000; inset 1:2500)

Fig 4 View of Bermondsey Square across site A from the north-east (Grange Walk is to the left of the picture)

A further archaeological evaluation by PCA in 1998 was conducted in order to determine viable development options for Bermondsey Square (BYQ98; Divers 1998; Fig 3); this evaluation revealed deposits and structures related to the western part of the priory complex. Excavation by PCA of the west part of the church and north-west part of the cloister, and the area west of that, and of the south transept, continued under the site code BYQ98 in subsequent years, in 2002 and 2004–8 (A Douglas, pers comm 2008; interim report in Gaimster and O'Connor 2006). In 2007–8 excavation by PCA on the site of the former White Bear public house (WBP07; Fig 3, inset) revealed remains of the east range of the main cloister. All these sites are the subject of separate assessment and publication programmes. However, with the kind permission and cooperation of PCA, their recording and preliminary interpretation of structural evidence revealed in the south transept, north-east corner of the cloister and west side of the east range have been included here (A Douglas, pers comm 2008); the evidence incorporated on the period plans in this volume comprises PCA's main medieval phase, a later medieval phase (their phases 4B and 4C) and a post-medieval (probably mansion) phase (their phase 5), in these two areas.

1.4 Organisation of this report

This report follows the integrated structure adopted by earlier volumes in the MOLA monograph series where the research

and interpretation in this volume are presented in three ways, the chronological narrative, thematic sections and specialist appendices, with a fourth form of data remaining unpublished, as described below. In accordance with the principles laid out in *Management of archaeological projects* (English Heritage 1991), analysis of the material from the sites resulted in a series of research archives, one for each specialist discipline. Much of the detailed data and all the major themes from each specialist research archive have been integrated into this volume.

The archaeological data have been organised chronologically into dated periods (Table 2) grouped into three chapters, Chapters 2, 3 and 5; these describe the pre-priory (pre-Saxon, and periods M1 and M2), medieval priory and later abbey (periods M3–M9), and post-medieval, that is, post-Dissolution

Table 2 The chronological periods used in this report

Period	Description	Date range AD (approx)
M1	Middle Saxon settlement	650–850
M2	Late Saxon settlement	850–1050
M3	priory: foundation and earliest buildings	1050–1100
M4	priory: church and cloister	1100–50
M5	priory: further expansion of the conventual buildings	1150–1200
M6	priory: modifications to the domestic conventual buildings	1200–50
M7	priory: changes around the infirmary courtyard	1250–1330
M8	priory and abbey: remodelling of the conventual buildings and cloisters	1330–1430
M9	abbey: change and dissolution	1430–1538
P1	after the Dissolution: the development of Bermondsey House	1538–1650

and later up to *c* 1650 (period P1), sequences. These periods have been formed from the stratigraphic phasing combined with other evidence for clear changes to the layout or function of elements within the study area and the available dating evidence, primarily ceramic. Each period section (M1–M9, P1) begins with the documentary evidence for that period. Archaeological activity is described in terms of land-use elements (Buildings, Open Areas and Drains). Artefactual and environmental material that resulted from such activity are described (in summary form if appropriate) as they relate to a particular land-use element. The narrative for each period section concludes with a period discussion and summary. Each period description is accompanied by a plan showing the major features (period M2, Fig 10; period M3, Fig 14; period M4, Fig 21; period M5, Fig 33 and Fig 47; period M6, Fig 49; period M7, Fig 53; period M8, Fig 57; period M9, Fig 65; period P1, Fig 111).

The chronological narrative combines the available strands of evidence. The priory narrative reveals aspects of its development and character over time and the themes that have emerged from the narrative find wider expression in Chapter 4. This comprises a series of essays presenting aspects of the priory, highlighting patterns, comparisons and particular points of interest and debate. Chapter 6 presents general conclusions, summarising the achievements of the project, and suggests potential research avenues.

Specialist data where appropriate, including the necessary technical support and justification for conclusions and interpretations, are gathered together in the specialist appendices in Chapter 7. There remains, however, a large corpus of material that is inappropriate for publication in the present format, including detailed identification, quantification, measurement and description of the various assemblages, stored in research archives (selected references are included in the bibliography). They are publicly accessible in the archive of the Museum of London and may be consulted by prior arrangement at the Museum's London Archaeological and Research Centre (LAARC), Mortimer Wheeler House, 46 Eagle Wharf Road, London N1. Elements of the Bermondsey archive are available digitally on the Archaeology Data Service (nd) website (http://ads.ahds.ac.uk/catalogue/resources.html?stsaviour_eh_ 2009). Note that periods and land uses recorded in the various databases were revised during final analysis and publication; a concordance table is available.

The study and the publication project thus set out to unify the records both chronologically and spatially and to unite them with the archaeological finds and materials from the sites, and to address a series of questions – the research aims – as set out in the post-excavation assessment report and updated project design of 1997 (Steele and Sloane 1997). The pre-priory use of the site and whether archaeology was able to tell us anything about the inception processes of a monastic establishment were two such questions. Similarly, was there any archaeological support for the documentary evidence, which indicates a high-status site in the Middle Saxon period? One consideration was the need to produce definitive phase plans for the

conventual layout which would inform any subsequent work or development in the vicinity of the Scheduled Ancient Monument. A further aim was to compare St Saviour Bermondsey with other Cluniac houses, mainly in England but also in France, with a view to identifying and interpreting any similarities or differences, including an assessment of the architecture and material culture of the house, and whether any Cluniac element (as opposed to, for example, Benedictine) was identifiable in the archaeological and artefactual record. The extent to which those research aims were achieved is discussed in Chapter 6.

As a major monastic cemetery excavation, Bermondsey data formed part of the database created as part of a research project analysing evidence for demography, burial practice and cemetery use from London's religious houses and elsewhere in the country (Gilchrist and Sloane 2005). Differences in criteria, and occasionally interpretation (the result in some cases of subsequent revision of the Bermondsey phasing and periods), mean that details may vary between the two publications. Note that the inhumed human bone data presented here are those produced by Brian Connell and William (Bill) White during the preparation of the published report; the assemblage has been reanalysed and recorded as part of its transfer to the Centre for Human Bioarchaeology, Museum of London.

1.5 Textual and graphical conventions used in this report

The priory of St Saviour Bermondsey was raised to the status of an abbey in 1399 (Chapter 3.6, 'Documentary evidence'). Weights and measures quoted in the text are, where appropriate, in the units used before metrication, for example, the imperial measurements of yards, feet and inches (the latter abbreviated to ft and in) along with conversions when appropriate (1ft equals 0.305m; 12in to 1ft, 3ft to 1 yard). A perch is equivalent to 5.03m. A mile is equivalent to 1.61km. An acre is 0.4 hectare (abbreviated to ha), or alternatively a hectare equals about 2.5 acres. Sums of money are quoted in the text as cited in £, s and d, where 12 pence (d) made one shilling (s) and 20 shillings (or 240d) a pound (£), since modern equivalents would be misleading. A mark was worth 13s 4d and 3 marks made £2. Dyer (1989, xv) provides the following reminder on which to base an approximation to current values: 'a skilled building worker earned 2d per day in 1250, 4d per day in 1400 and 6d in 1500'. County names in the text refer to historic counties.

Kentish limestone ragstone and Hassock sandstone, from the Maidstone area of Kent, identified on site as Kentish ragstone are referred to as 'ragstone' in the text. Most of the architectural fragments from St Saviour Bermondsey were dressed from one building stone type, here termed 'Reigate' stone. The potential sources of building stone and the basis of their identifications are detailed in Chapter 7.2 ('Methodology').

The basic unit of cross reference throughout the publication and research archive is the context number. This is a unique number given to each archaeological event identified in excavation (such as a layer, wall, grave cut or pit fill). Each context in this volume is prefixed by a single letter (A–G, Z; Table 1). For example, A[1146] representing context 1146 is from site BA84. All sites referred to by their site codes are MOLA sites unless stated otherwise. During assessment and analysis it is standard MOLA practice to group contexts together into 'subgroups' (abbreviated as subgp) and to aggregate subgroups into 'groups' (abbreviated as gp) on the basis of interpretation. Where relevant and applicable here, the archaeological sequence is expressed in terms of group and land use/type of activity.

The chronological periods are labelled M1–M9 (medieval) and P1 (post-medieval). The land-use entities are described as Buildings (B1–B14), Open Areas (OA1–OA14) and Drains (D1–D4). Where a burial is recorded in Grimes's archive and, therefore, has no context number, a subgroup number is given, prefixed G, for example subgroup G[48].

This publication employs standard Museum of London reference codes for ceramics; these codes were developed by the MOL for recording purposes. A fabric number system is used to record building materials (tile and brick); these numbers relate to detailed fabric descriptions. Pottery is recorded using codes (alphabetic or a combination of alphabetic and numeric) for fabrics, forms and decoration. Expansions of pottery codes are given at the first mention in a text section. Detailed descriptions of the building material fabrics and complete lists of the pottery codes, their expansions and date ranges are available from the LAARC as part of the research archive and are also posted on the LAARC and MOLA pages of the MOL (nd a) website (www.museumoflondonarchaeology.org.uk). Pottery is quantified by sherd count (SC), weight (in g), estimated number of vessels (ENV) and/or estimated vessel equivalents (EVEs; the total of the proportion of rims present by fabric and form) as appropriate.

There are several categories of finds that have been numbered within the volume. As the finds are drawn from all the sites as a single corpus of material, they do not use a site code prefix. The catalogue is divided by material and an appropriate letter prefix used as follows:
<G10> glass object
<P10> illustrated pottery sherd(s)
<S10> accessioned find
<T10> illustrated ceramic building material

Catalogue entries (Chapter 7.6, 7.7) are arranged as follows: (first line) catalogue number, brief description and, where illustrated, Fig no.; (second line) accessioned find number, context number, period found, and, lastly land use. Only illustrated pottery sherds have been catalogued in this report (<P1> to <P65>, Table 17).

For non-catalogued accessioned finds and the architectural fragments, site accession numbers are used with the site letter prefix thus:
A<241> representing accessioned find 241 from site BA84.

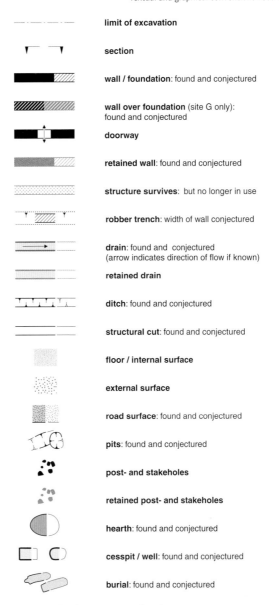

Fig 5 Graphical conventions used in this report

Environment sample numbers appear within curly brackets, for example {491}.

The following abbreviations are used throughout the volume and catalogues:
D depth
Diam diameter
H height
L length
Th thickness
W width
Wt weight

Because of the synthetic nature of the integrated report, the precise details of truncation and horizontal stratigraphy (such as dumps and layers) have not been included in the site plans. The archive holds the original site plans and also a series of interpretative plans that developed into the present sequence. The graphical conventions used in this report are shown on Fig 5.

2

Pre-priory land use: prehistoric to Late Saxon

2.1 Topography and geology

The natural topography of the area of what is now north Southwark and Bermondsey has a complex history and has been the subject of a number of studies based on data from borehole surveys and archaeological fieldwork (eg Sidell et al 2002). The model of the local topography has been recently reviewed and revised to the west of Bermondsey Priory by Cowie and Corcoran (2008) in the light of fieldwork at Rephidim Street (RS76) and the former Hartley's Jam Factory (GEN00) (located on Fig 3).

The Holocene landscape was one of low gravel islands, fen, mudflats and channels. The sites lie on Pleistocene gravel, part of the Kempton Park River Terrace (the first terrace above the flood plain) on what is known as Bermondsey eyot (Cowie and Corcoran 2008, 162, fig 3). The eyot (meaning island or land partly surrounded by water or marsh) was, on the basis of the recent fieldwork, not a gravel island but a peninsula, connected at the north-west corner to the mainland by a neck of land or 'land bridge' (Fig 6). Between the south-west part of Bermondsey eyot and the mainland lay a broad shallow channel in the gravel. The postulated land bridge appears to have been high enough to form a barrier between the tidal channels to the north and the valley of this relict channel to the south. Bermondsey eyot was approximately 2km square, with the gravel surface rising to a maximum potential height of +2.2m OD (Cowie and Corcoran 2008).

A freshwater stream flowed in the valley. It probably would have been unaffected by the tidal Thames in the prehistoric and Roman periods, and up to at least the second half of the 9th century AD, and possibly later. The valley was probably water meadows during the lifetime of Bermondsey Priory and the stream was part of the drainage system which fed the watercourse to the south and east later known as 'Earl's Sluice' (Cowie and Corcoran 2008; Fig 6).

Bermondsey eyot was separated from Horselydown eyot to the north by a large channel (Fig 6); evidence for this was found at Vinegar Yard, Tanner Street (VIY97, located on Fig 3; Heard 1998; Sidell et al 2002, 64, gazetteer nos 160 and 163). The channel carried a stream that later became known as the Neckinger (Chapter 4.1, 'Topography and early landscape', 4.2, 'The precinct and home grange').

2.2 Prehistoric background

Evidence for prehistoric activity has been recovered from excavation sites on the eyots of Southwark, and also in or on the edges of the wetter channels (Sidell et al 2002; Cowie and Corcoran 2008, 163, fig 4). Prehistoric peat deposits with finds of struck flints and pottery were recorded at Jacob's Island (JAC96; Fig 81; Saxby 1997; Sidell et al 2002, 66, gazetteer no. 201). At Vinegar Yard, Tanner Street, a Bronze Age cooking pit was dug into the alluvial sand to the north of the stream.

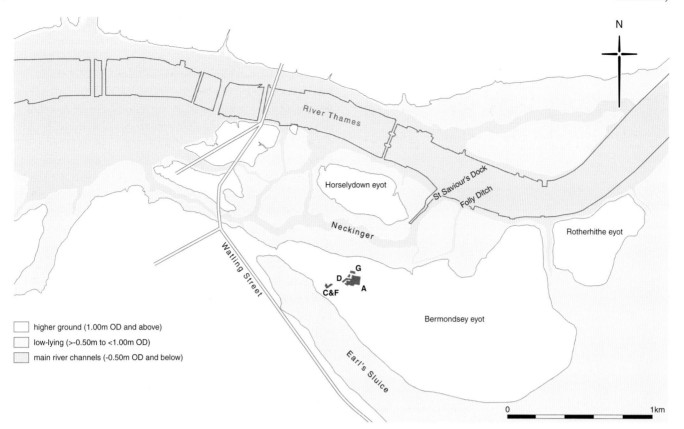

Fig 6 Reconstruction of the early topography of Bermondsey, showing the outline of the modern Thames shoreline and bridges, and sites A, C, D, F and G (scale 1:25,000)

Sealing the pit was a Bronze Age/Iron Age peat deposit, over which a series of clay silt layers indicated that the site had been subject to flooding over the course of several centuries (VIY97, Fig 3; Heard 1998; Sidell et al 2002, 64, gazetteer nos 160 and 163). Neolithic–Bronze Age material is reported from 110 Grange Road (Cowie and Corcoran 2008, 163, fig 4; for location of Grange Road see Fig 3).

Evidence for prehistoric activity on site A was entirely residual; no pits or ditches could be assigned with certainty to the period. A significant amount of Late Bronze Age–Iron Age and Middle Iron Age and Late Iron Age–early Romano-British pottery, as well as prehistoric struck flints were found as residual finds in Roman and later features and in deposits immediately overlying weathered sand and gravel. This material and its significance is described in detail elsewhere (Sidell et al 2002, 40–2, 64, gazetteer no. 159; Cowan et al 2009, 14, 38). Iron Age material is also reported from 41–45 Grange Walk and 170–176 Grange Road (Cowan et al 2009, 38–40, site 93). The evidence indicates small-scale pre-Roman activity, including settlement sites such as farmsteads, with activity concentrated on the islands, especially the Bermondsey eyot.

2.3 Roman activity

In the Roman period, most of Bermondsey was open land under agricultural use, linked to Londinium by water and the road

from London to Canterbury in Kent. The sites were located to the east of Watling Street and about 1km from the Roman settlement in north Southwark, south of the Roman bridgehead (Cowan et al 2009). A minor road, perhaps a precursor of Long Lane, was recorded at 5–27 Long Lane and it has been suggested may have led to Bermondsey eyot (ibid, 65; cf Fig 3; Fig 6).

Roman burials have been found mainly alongside Watling Street, south of its junction with Stane Street, but two were found at site F (Fig 7). A north-east to south-west aligned burial had a roughly squared slab of ragstone placed over the knees. It was succeeded by a north-west to south-east aligned inhumation, which was dated by two pottery sherds to *c* AD 120–60. Five regularly spaced nails close to the body indicated that it may have been in a coffin, or placed on a bier. Some Roman features and deposits were identified at Bermondsey Square (BYQ98; Fig 3) including a truncated burial. Overlying these was a ploughsoil deposit up to 1.2m thick, which contained a significant amount of Roman pottery but also sherds from the Late Iron Age, Saxon and medieval periods (Divers 1998, 15; Cowie and Corcoran 2008, 163).

There were Roman buildings in the vicinity of Watling Street, including religious and/or funerary structures; two 2nd-century AD Romano-Celtic temples have been recorded at Tabard Square, Long Lane (Heard 1996; Cowan et al 2009, 19–24, 90–9). Perhaps from these, or from the settlement to the north-east, came the large amount of ceramic building material later brought to the priory site. A considerable number of (mainly residual) Roman tile fragments were found at site A (Fig 3) and comprise mainly roof tile (almost all tegula) and

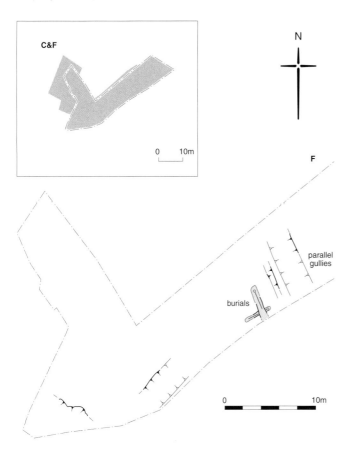

Fig 7 Plan of principal Roman archaeological features on site F (scale 1:400; inset 1:1500)

brick, with smaller quantities of other types such as box-flue tile with combed and roller stamped keying, tessera, tegula mammata and possibly wall tile and voussoir tile (Brodribb 1987). A Roman roof tile found in a Late Saxon (period M2) ditch (A[3940]) had part of a PBRILON stamp; the lettering of the stamp translates as 'the procurators of the province of Britain at London'. Fragments of eight tiles with PBRILON stamps have been found in Southwark; they were produced for the procurator for use in public buildings c AD 75–125 (Betts 1995a, 209; Cowan et al 2009, 195, 200–1). (For a discussion of the reuse of Roman material, see Chapter 3.3, 'Discussion'.)

Agricultural activity is suggested by ditches found on the Bermondsey eyot, which could have served as field boundaries and/or drainage channels (Cowie and Corcoran 2008, 163; Cowan et al 2009, 117). On site A, Roman activity took the form of six widely scattered pits and three ditches. The relative scarcity of Roman remains probably indicates poor survival rather than absence. Site A, the location for many of the major buildings of the medieval priory, was naturally the focus of much more construction, robbing, digging and quarrying than elsewhere on the eyot before the post-medieval period. Pre-monastic remains, therefore, were more likely to have suffered truncation, disturbance or complete obliteration.

On site F, the truncated bases of two parallel gullies yielded pottery dated c AD 160–300 (Fig 7). The north ditch contained 20 fragments of animal bone representing at least two large mammals, cattle and horse. Two other ditches and five pits

contained pottery almost entirely from the late Roman period. Roman features have been found to the south on Grange Road (GGA92; GNU04; GGO06), including pits containing pig burials at 161 Grange Road (Cowie and Corcoran 2008, 163; Mackinder in prep; GGO06, Fig 3). All the evidence indicates Bermondsey eyot was a managed rural landscape, with ditches and possibly animal enclosures, and was occupied throughout the Roman period (Cowan et al 2009, 117).

2.4 Middle Saxon settlement, c AD 650–850 (period M1)

Documentary evidence

The place-name Bermondsey – Beornmund's island or land partly surrounded by water or marsh (derived from the Old English *ēg*) – denotes the site's modest elevation above the low-lying Thames flood plain (Mills 2001, 20; Cowie and Blackmore 2008, 134). It was first recorded in the early 8th century: the *Liber Niger* of Peterborough (Northamptonshire) includes a papal privilege of AD 708 x 715 in which Pope Constantine addresses Haedda as abbot of *Vermundsei* (Bermondsey) and *Wocchingas* (Woking, Surrey), founded in the name of St Peter. There was also a tradition in the 12th century that dependencies of Peterborough monastery in c AD 690 had included Bermondsey and Woking minsters (Blair 1991, 102–3). This suggests that a minster church occupied the site in the Middle Saxon period.

Archaeological evidence

A total of seven pottery sherds from site A (Fig 3; Table 1) were recorded as being of Middle Saxon date (327g/0.25 EVE), all of which were residual in later contexts. In addition, there are four sherds which are atypical for both the Saxon and prehistoric periods. Two of these were from Dissolution and later contexts, A[2917] and A[3519] (period P1). The remaining two were from A[1838], a deposit over the natural subsoil (perhaps the only *in situ* Saxon pottery sherd), and from A[3945], the fill of a north–south ditch (Late Saxon, period M2). The amount of Saxon pottery originally recovered was reportedly higher than these 11 sherds subsequently presented for specialist work. While this might have been inflated by misidentification of prehistoric or Roman material, the fact that five fabric types are present in this small group testifies both to the early date and importance of the site.

Four sherds are of chaff-tempered ware (CHAF), while one is of a finer variant; these include the rim of a small jar or bowl (Fig 8, <P1>). This ware is present in the Early Saxon period, becoming more common in the 6th and 7th centuries AD and declining in the mid 8th century AD (Blackmore 1988, 84–5, 101–8; 1989, 73–7, 104–7; 2008, 179–81). On the basis of parallels within the emporium of Lundenwic, the Bermondsey sherds are typical for the Middle Saxon period.

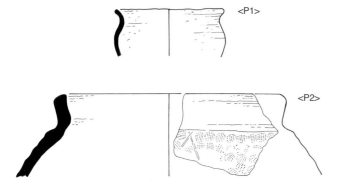

Fig 8 Middle Saxon pottery: small chaff-tempered ware jar or bowl <P1> and an Ipswich fine ware storage jar <P2> (scale 1:4)

The largest and most impressive sherd is from a large storage jar in Ipswich fine ware (IPSF), which is profusely decorated with gridded circle stamps in combination with incised diagonal lines (Fig 8, <P2>). The surface of this sherd, found in the cemetery soil A[2752] (OA6, period M4; Chapter 3.2, 'Archaeological evidence'), is abraded and damaged in places, indicating that it had probably been redeposited more than once. Ipswich ware is currently dated to c AD 730–850 in London (Blackmore 1988, 85–7, 101–8; 1989, 77–80, 104–7; 2008, 181). It is unclear exactly how early the stamped designs were introduced but they may be most typical of the later 8th and earlier 9th centuries AD. Stamped Ipswich wares, both jars and spouted pitchers, are now relatively common within the market area of Lundenwic, but the gridded circle motif has so far only been recorded at the Peabody site (PEA87, Westminster; Blackmore 1989, fig 30 no. 40), and so far no other piece has the same degree of ornamentation as the Bermondsey find.

One sherd is of shell-tempered ware (MSS); the fabric is similar to that of the Lundenwic type MSSB (Blackmore 1988, 88). Work currently in progress on the analysis of these shelly wares suggests that they are not imported, as has been speculated; most are probably from Kent (Blackmore 2008, 181–2).

Finally, there is one sherd from an imported greyware spouted pitcher in a distinctive fabric with a 'sandwich' effect which belongs to the original Hamwic group 'Class 13' (Hodges 1981, 21; Timby 1988, 92–3) and the Lundenwic group of 'north French/east Belgium hard greyware' (NFEBB; Blackmore 1988, 91; 1989, 87; 2008, 182). This ware is most common in 8th-century AD contexts within Lundenwic, although it seems to be part of a long tradition of greywares.

As a group, these few sherds indicate activity on the site in the mid 8th century AD (the Ipswich ware (IPSF) and imported pitcher in NFEBB). The chaff-tempered ware (CHAF) may be slightly older, but could represent the end of this industry c AD 730–50. The shell-tempered ware (MSS) indicates continuing occupation in the area in the late 8th or 9th century AD. Secondly, the range of wares is wider than that first indicated (Vince 1990, 65) and the non-local and imported wares demonstrate that Bermondsey was not merely a rural/farming settlement (ibid, 13) but part of the international trade network

of the day. It is likely, however, that, together with Westminster Abbey (Westminster) (Blackmore 1995, 85), Bermondsey was a consumer site supplied via the emporium of Lundenwic, rather than directly visited by traders, as may have been the case at Barking Abbey in Essex (Redknap 1991; 1992).

The three 'sceatta' coins of the 7th to early 8th century AD – probably the early 8th century – were residual in later contexts (<S22> period M2, <S23> and <S24> period M4). This small group of coins suggests the Saxon presence in Bermondsey coincided with the renewed presence just across the Thames inside the old Roman city walls at Bull Wharf (even if the range of coins from each location is of a completely different series; Chapter 7.7; Fig 168).

A small, but diverse, assemblage of Saxon accessioned finds were all from period M2 or later contexts (<S1>–<S24>); they range in date from strapends (<S5>, <S7>) broadly datable to the 9th century AD up to the late 11th/early 12th century. The Continental glass vessel <S12> (Fig 166) may be as early as the 8th century AD. The accessioned finds include double-sided combs, bun-shaped loom weights and lumps of waste from iron- and lead working (although these last may be residual from the Roman period). A selection is shown on Fig 9. Two decayed fragments of window glass were also catalogued from period M2 (OA1) and would imply the existence of a high-status building in the area (Chapter 7.6, 'The context and character of the catalogued window glass').

Discussion

By the late 7th century AD, an international trading port was established north of the Thames in London at Lundenwic and the Church was firmly established in the London region, north and south of the Thames (Cowie and Blackmore 2008, 6). In Surrey, a minster church was founded at Chertsey c AD 666, and there were probably others at Southwark and Lambeth, just north-east of Bermondsey, but both of these were later (late 9th and 11th century respectively) foundations than Bermondsey (Blair 1991, 91–108). Documentary evidence attests to the presence of a Middle Saxon minster church somewhere on the Bermondsey eyot. The site was typical in several ways for a Thames-side minster: it was on a gravel island or peninsula and close to important road crossings and the waterfront (Blair 1996).

The archaeological evidence for this period is based entirely on, mainly residual, Middle Saxon pottery, 7th to early 8th-century AD sceatta coins and other Saxon accessioned finds; nevertheless, it does indicate that there existed in the vicinity a significant and prosperous Middle Saxon settlement. Whether this was occupation directly associated with the minster or not is unknown, but likely. The four isolated burials on the site of the later priory of St Saviour (Chapter 3.1, 'Archaeological evidence', 'Quarry site, burials and ?boundary ditches (OA2)') may perhaps be a relic from the Saxon minster, but the bodies could have been interred any time up to the mid 12th century; they were exhumed in the 12th century. So far, adjacent sites in Bermondsey do not appear to have produced any similar concentration of material of comparable Middle Saxon date.

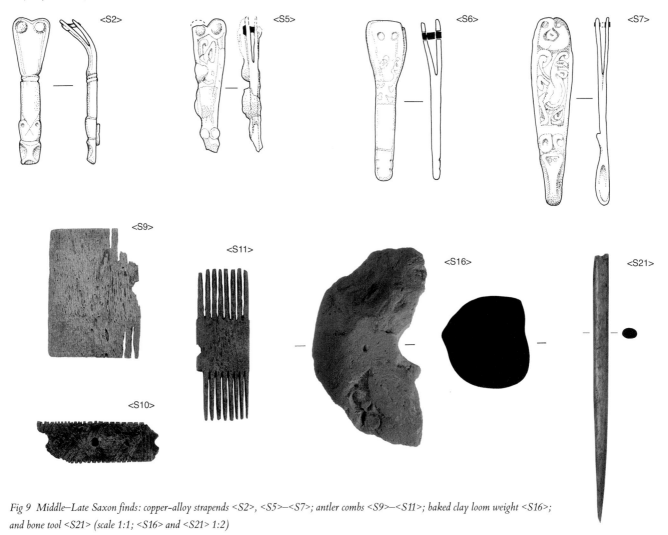

Fig 9 Middle–Late Saxon finds: copper-alloy strapends <S2>, <S5>–<S7>; antler combs <S9>–<S11>; baked clay loom weight <S16>; and bone tool <S21> (scale 1:1; <S16> and <S21> 1:2)

2.5 Late Saxon settlement, c AD 850–1050 (period M2)

Documentary evidence

Bermondsey was a royal manor in the Late Saxon period. The manor was held before the Conquest by Earl Harold, in 1086 by the king. It covered a larger area than that encompassed by the late 11th-century manor granted to the priory (*VCH* 1912, 19).

Archaeological evidence

Open ground with ditches (OA1)

In the Late Saxon period site A was open land (OA1) intersected by large ditches (Fig 3; Fig 10) and characterised by an extensive ploughsoil deposit. There is no direct evidence for its specific agricultural use, other than the worked ploughsoil itself, which was found to contain pottery from the Late Iron Age through to the post-medieval periods.

The proximity of human habitation is signified by the presence of large boundary and enclosure ditches, the most impressive of which was a large, east–west aligned ditch at the northern limit of site A (Fig 10). The ditch had near-vertical sides and a flat base (Fig 11; Fig 12). It was 17.3+m long and 3.2m wide, slightly curving, and continued beyond the west and north limits of excavation. Silt deposits on the north and south sides of the cut were considered to be evidence for the accumulation of silts behind a wattle lining. A single sherd of Late Saxon shelly ware (LSS) dated these silts to c AD 900–1050. A bent and incomplete copper-alloy strapend (<S2>, Fig 9) with an animal-head terminal was also recovered from the silt deposits. This strapend (like strapend <S6>, residual in period M7) is a type which was current from the 9th century AD through until the 11th century (G Thomas, pers comm 2009; Chapter 7.7, 'Pre-monastic house period').

The ditch was recut at least once, and in its final stages became something like a watercourse or unmanaged channel. The fill of the channel A[2969] yielded the largest pottery group for this period (M2), a total of 38 sherds from a minimum of 21 vessels. The only fabric present is Late Saxon shelly ware (LSS), the wheel-thrown, shell-tempered pottery which was used in London throughout most of the 10th century AD, to the virtual exclusion of all but a very limited range of imports. LSS predominated until the last quarter of the century when local, handmade coarsewares began to be made

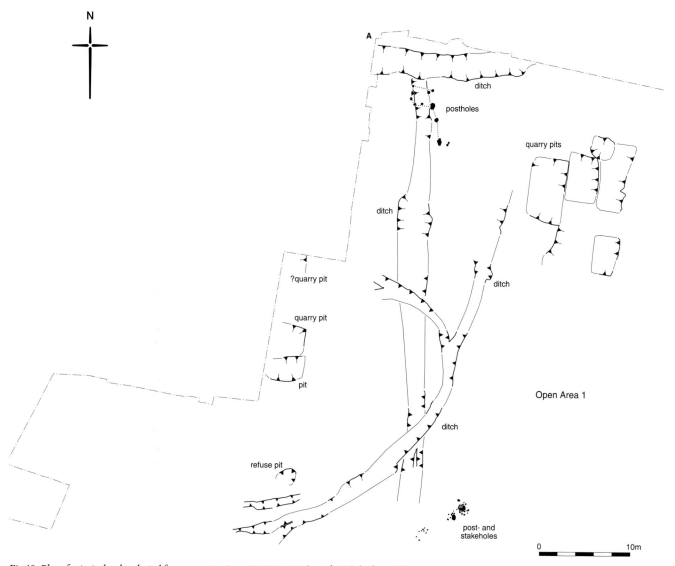

N

A

ditch

postholes

quarry pits

ditch

?quarry pit

ditch

quarry pit

pit

Open Area 1

ditch

refuse pit

post- and
stakeholes

0   10m

Fig 10 Plan of principal archaeological features at site A, c AD 850–1050 (period M2) (scale 1:400)

and used in the region (Vince and Jenner 1991, 49–54). The
source of LSS has not yet been identified but on petrological
grounds it appears to lie to the west of London, along the
Thames valley. The pottery has affinities with Late Saxon shelly
ware used in Oxford, Oxfordshire (Mellor 1994, 37), although
the sources are probably different. Cooking pots with a simple
everted rim are the main form found in Late Saxon ware
although other vessel types were also made. The two main
forms are both represented in the channel fill: there are sherds
from three shallow bowls and from two spouted pitchers (cf
Vince and Jenner 1991, fig 2.24 nos 14–24, fig 2.25). Given the
absence of any other 10th-century AD or later pottery, a date in
the 10th century seems likely. An incomplete plain shale finger
ring was also recovered from the channel fill (<S1>, Fig 13).

To the south of the channel was a ditch 46.4m long and
aligned north–south (Fig 10). The ditch was 3.85m wide but
had suffered much, later, truncation. It was associated with a
timber structure (evidenced by postholes) and a fence line. The
fence line extended 6.0m along the east bank of the ditch.
Timber uprights straddled the ditch, forming a structure 2.4m
east–west by 1.3m north–south. The structure may have been

a small bridge, or a device for trapping debris or regulating
water flow. Overlying the north–south ditch, a large,
curvilinear ditch described a flattened oval (Fig 10). This ditch
had a total extent of c 44m with a parallel, perhaps
contemporary, channel 1.5m to the north.

To the east of the ditches, a complex of intercutting quarry
pits covered an area c 14.5m north–south by c 10m east–west
(Fig 10). Pottery recovered from the backfill of these pits
included residual Roman wares and a single sherd of Late Saxon
shelly ware (LSS) dated to c AD 900–1050. A pit in this area
(A[3827]) yielded 20 sherds in LSS from a minimum of three
cooking pots and shares a probable 10th-century AD date with
the east–west channel to the north.

The animal bone assemblage from this period was
dominated by the major mammalian domesticates – cattle,
sheep/goat and a substantial proportion of pig – with minor
representations of other species including domestic poultry,
particularly chicken and goose, plus two fragments from a game
species, roe deer; the horse bones recovered may all derive from
the same carcass (Chapter 7.8; Table 18).

A few accessioned items are potentially 11th century (Late

Fig 11 View of Late Saxon ditch at the northern limit of site A (period M2), from the west (1.0m and 2.0m scales)

Fig 12 View of section through Late Saxon ditch at the northern limit of site A (period M2), from the east (1.0m scale)

Saxon to very early Norman) rather than earlier (eg copper-alloy strapend <S4> and copper-alloy brooch <S8>, Fig 13; lead ingot <S20>, Fig 167; Chapter 7.7).

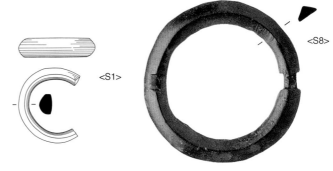

Fig 13 Late Saxon/Saxo-Norman finds (OA1, period M2): shale finger ring <S1>; copper-alloy brooch <S8> (scale 1:1)

Discussion

The large east–west aligned ditch in Open Area 1 was probably a feature of some permanence judging by the changes in its profile, although the ceramic evidence fails to confirm this; its fill was dated to the 10th century AD. Its depth of over 1.5m and original square profile imply that it was more than a simple field boundary. Large quantities of burnt daub were recovered from both the east–west and north–south ditches (15.2kg from the east–west ditch). Many of the daub fragments have wooden wattle and lath impressions, indicating that they derive from a timber building with wattle and daub walls. Late Saxon structures may well have been located to the north and west of the boundaries/field systems in Open Area 1 (Fig 10). The excavation of large quarry pits in this period is testament to construction of some sort. This evidence, taken together with the accessioned finds, ceramics and animal bone, implies a significant permanent settlement in the vicinity. Ongoing work by PCA is providing more evidence for Saxon activity (Gaimster and O'Connor 2006, 316; Cowie and Blackmore 2008, 134).

Following the abandonment of Lundenwic and reoccupation of Londinium in the late 9th century, a bridge was re-established: exactly when in the period c AD 900–1100 is not known, but probably in the 10th century AD (Watson et al 2001, 52–60). The evidence for settlement around the Southwark bridgehead in the 10th–11th centuries AD is reviewed in Watson et al (2001, 56–7). To the south-east, the combined evidence indicates settlement of the Bermondsey eyot in the Middle Saxon and Late Saxon periods. This settlement may have been continuous, but not necessarily so. The Middle Saxon occupation at least appears from the archaeological evidence to have been of relatively high status (above, 2.4). The Late Saxon large, east–west aligned ditch at the north end of site A (Fig 10) could have been both defence and drain round a building or buildings to the north and west of the principal excavation area, possibly the minster church and its associated buildings. This ditch may have gone out of use at the end of the 10th century AD, but it was not necessarily the latest feature identified on the site in this period.

The '?pre-monastic foundations' and 'early wall' recorded by Grimes under the north-east side of the 12th-century (period M4) priory church – that is, to the north of the east–west ditch – could be 12th century or earlier, and may be significant (Chapter 3.2, 'Archaeological evidence', 'Priory church (B3)'; Fig 23). Further evidence is needed, however. The possibly early masonry remains reported by PCA in the area of the priory's south transept (BYQ98; A Douglas, pers comm) – that is, to the west of the ditches – and fieldwork further to the west may contribute to our assessment of this period and the minster.

A small group of burials which were exhumed in the 12th century may originally have been made in this period, in which case they would have been located to the east of the ditch systems (in OA1) – perhaps associated with the minster, or part of a field cemetery (Chapter 3.1, 'Archaeological evidence', 'Quarry site, burials and ?boundary ditches (OA2)'; Fig 14).

It is not possible to provide a direct link between the documented Anglo-Saxon minster of Bermondsey and the Cluniac priory of St Saviour Bermondsey. It is still the case that survival of the minster through the troubled times of the late 9th and 10th centuries AD and into the 11th century cannot be proved, nor should the minster be identified with the 'Ibi nova et pulchra aecclesia' of Domesday (Blair 1991, 92, 102–3). Blair's comment may be correct: 'Bermondsey may therefore be one genuine case of a minster totally destroyed by the Vikings' (1991, 103); and Southwark may have been the post-Danish successor to Bermondsey (Blair 1991, 104). This would make Bermondsey the single exception to the pattern where the Surrey Domesday churches on former demesne of King Edward can be identified as old minsters and suggest an explanation as to why (ibid, 113). The substantial Late Saxon ditches, together with the wattle and daub structures and quarry pits, are the best indication we have at present of the possible continuation of the minster at least into the late 10th century AD.

3

The priory and (later) abbey of Bermondsey

3.1 Foundation and earliest buildings: the priory *c* 1050–*c* 1100 (period M3)

Documentary evidence

Before the Norman Conquest, the manor of Bermondsey was held by Earl Harold. In 1086 it was held by the king, at which time there was land for eight ploughs, of which one was on the demesne and four were held by 25 villeins and 33 bordars. There were 20 acres (8.1ha) of meadow and the wood was worth five hogs from the pannage. Thirteen London burgesses paid 44d in rent to the royal manor (*VCH* 1902, 296; 1912, 19). The property granted to the monastery and later confirmed by William II (known as William Rufus) and by Henry I included Bermondsey itself, part of Camberwell, Rotherhithe, the hide of Southwark and Dulwich, Waddon and Leigham in Streatham (all in Surrey). These places had all originally been part of the manor of Bermondsey which was part of the ancient demesne of the crown. All lands and tenements held of the manor were pleadable in the manor court by writ of right according to custom of the manor and not at common law (*Mon Angl*, v, 100). One hide in the manor, worth 8s, was held in 1086 by the count of Mortain and must have been acquired from William I by his half-brother, Robert of Mortain, Earl of Cornwall. Robert's successor, Earl William, who had been imprisoned in the Tower in 1106, upon his release took the habit at the priory of St Saviour in 1140 and there died without heirs. It is possible that by his gift to the house his holding was united to Bermondsey manor (*VCH* 1912, 18–20).

The foundation of the priory of St Saviour appears to have been a complex and lengthy process. The picture is not clarified by the notorious unreliability of the Bermondsey annals. These were compiled in *c* 1432 long after the events in question (Graham 1926, esp 159–60), but do contain materials collected in the period up to the mid 13th century (Brett 1992). According to the annals, the wealthy citizen Alwyn Childe endowed a new Cluniac house in 1082 with his London rents, several years before the donation of the royal manor by William II (1087–1100, William Rufus), and encouraged various lords temporal and spiritual to contribute property, churches and manors (*Ann Monast*, iii, 425–6). Four French monks from La Charité-sur-Loire, Peter, Richard, Osbert and Umbald, arrived in 1089, a detail confirmed by the annals of Lewes Priory (Graham 1926, 161; see Brett 1992, 297). The mention in Domesday Book of a 'nova et pulchra ecclesia' (new and beautiful church) at the royal manor of Bermondsey suggests the presence of a noteworthy church as early as 1086 (*VCH* 1967, 64); the Domesday statement is quoted by the Bermondsey annals, although they antedate it by at least four years from its actual date, adding that this was built in honour of St Saviour. All this presents several difficulties concerning the origin and early chronology of the priory as known from the documentary sources, not least the Domesday entry. Another possibility is that William I, known to be sympathetic to Cluny, had harboured similar plans of his own.

Other gifts followed quickly in the early 1090s. William II's foundation charter, surviving in a late 16th- or early 17th-century transcript made by John Selden, has been dated 1093–7 (Davis and Whitwell 1913, no. 398; Golding 1981, 75). It is addressed to the monks of La Charité-sur-Loire and confirms the grants to them of the church of St Saviour Bermondsey, the manor of Bermondsey and the gifts of Robert, Bishop of Lincoln, Winebald of Baalun, Odo of Tiron, Walter son of Ansgar and Peter of St Olave. The charter included some London gifts, possibly those donated by Alwyn Childe, who died in 1094 and whom the annals describe as 'fundator Bermund' (*Ann Monast*, iii, 425–6; Paris, *Flores*, ii, 21, 26; Brett 1992, 298).

The written sources provide little by way of direct topographical information for the earliest periods of the priory, c 1050–c 1150. The main access to the monastery by land was west–east via Long Lane, which led to the priory's west gate at the junction with Bermondsey Street, or north–south by Bermondsey Street, originally an artificial causeway across the marshy ground (Fig 2; Fig 3; cf Fig 6).

Archaeological evidence

A chapel (B1) and a timber latrine (B2) were the first buildings found on the site of the priory by the excavations reported here. Two large boundary ditches enclosed these buildings and the intervening open land.

Chapel (B1)

A chapel (B1, Fig 14) was built over a network of quarry pits which had been backfilled in the 10th century AD (period M2; Chapter 2.5; Fig 10) and consisted of a simple nave and apsidal

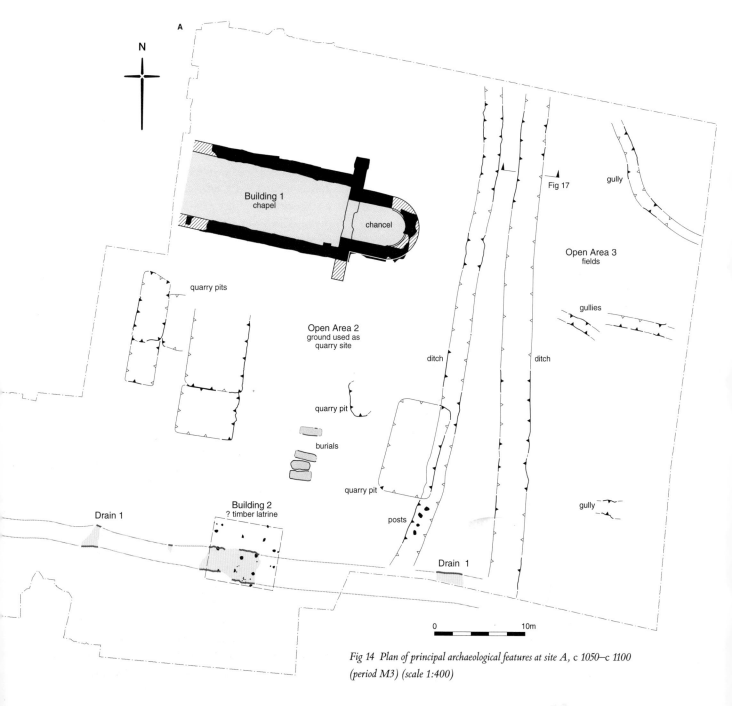

Fig 14 Plan of principal archaeological features at site A, c 1050–c 1100 (period M3) (scale 1:400)

Fig 15 A typical wall foundation with alternating layers of compacted gravels and chalk boulders (1.0m scales)

Fig 16 View of section through Drain 1 (period M3), from the west (0.2m and 0.5m scales)

east end or chancel. The nave was 6.9m wide and at least 16.9m long. Evidence for the west ends of both north and south nave walls was ambiguous. The small apsidal chancel was 6.3m east–west by 4.25m north–south and a sleeper foundation carried the chancel arch. The apse foundations were not continuous with the north and south walls of the nave. A rectangular robber trench against the north-east corner of the nave may have been an additional buttress. The foundations for the chapel consisted of alternating layers of compacted gravels and chalk boulders (Fig 15). This construction method was widely used among the conventual buildings and reflects both the absence of a nearby source of suitable building materials and the relative cheapness and availability of the local subsoil gravels. Four fragments of incised decorated floor tiles (all residual) are paralleled by a set of 11th-century incised tiles in the Pyx chamber in Westminster Abbey (Chapter 7.4; Fig 149).

Monastic sewer (D1) and timber latrine (B2)

The first monastic sewer (D1) was an east–west aligned ditch that ran under the south side of the timber latrine (B2) (Fig 14; Fig 16). Drain 1 probably connected with one or both of the inner and outer ditches that defined Open Area 2 (below). It was c 54+m long and between 2.3m and 3.3m wide. The direction of flow could not be established. Before c 1100 a timber structure (B2) was erected across the drain (D1), c 10m from the south-east corner of Open Area 2. The structure comprised 14 postholes, 0.40m in diameter and up to 0.45m deep and seven smaller postholes with diameters of c 0.15m. The posts formed a structure c 6.3m square, which has been interpreted as a timber-built latrine. The latrine was presumably in use contemporaneously with the chapel (B1), and before the construction of the first stone reredorter (B8; below, 3.2). The lower fills of the drain (D1) were brown-green silts with a high cess content and included oyster shell, copper-alloy waste and pottery dated to c 1080–c 1200.

Quarry site, burials and ?boundary ditches (OA2)

The monastic precinct in which lay the chapel and latrine (OA2) was enclosed to the east of the chapel (B1) by two large roughly parallel ?boundary ditches which lay a minimum of 2.16m apart (Fig 14). The western ditch was c 46.8+m long and c 1.8 to 2m wide. Its surviving depth varied between 0.7m and 1.55m and the base sloped down from north to south (1.6m OD at the north to between 0.8m and 1.08m OD at the south). Towards the south, the western ditch changed course slightly towards the south-west. Before this point, on its west bank, four large postholes may have provided the uprights for some sort of revetment or fence. The east ditch was 51.36m long and between c 2m and 4m wide (Fig 17). Both ditches probably connected at their south ends with the east–west aligned ditch (the first monastic sewer; D1). If the east ditch drained north to south as the west ditch appears to have done, then the east ditch's south end could have formed with Drain 1 the south-east corner of a rectangular enclosure, and Drain 1 drained from east to west. From the east ditch A[1046] came 34 sherds from a single spouted pitcher in early medieval grog-tempered ware (EMGR; date range c 1050–1150), a relatively uncommon fabric in London

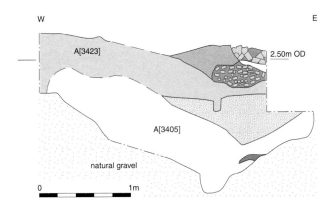

Fig 17 North-facing section through fills of the northern section of the east boundary ditch in Open Area 2 (period M3) (scale 1:40)

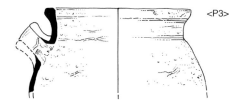

Fig 18 A spouted pitcher <P3> in early medieval grog-tempered ware from the east boundary ditch in Open Area 2 (period M3) (scale 1:4)

(Fig 18, <P3>; Vince and Jenner 1991, 80–1, fig 2 no. 69). The vessel had clearly been discarded as unwanted or newly broken.

To the south of the chapel (B1), the land (OA2) was characterised by the digging of quarry pits (Fig 14). The zone of quarrying lay c 6m south of the chapel (B1) and extended over an area 30.4m east–west by 16.5m north–south. The fills of quarry pits adjacent to the west boundary ditch included pottery in widespread, everyday use in the London area from c AD 900 until the mid 12th century: Late Saxon shelly ware (LSS), early medieval sand- and shell-tempered ware (EMSS), early medieval shell-tempered ware (EMSH) and early medieval grog-tempered ware (EMGR). One sherd from a bowl in shelly-sandy ware (SSW; A[1525]) suggests a final backfill during the second half of the 12th century. A similar dating (c 1140–c 1220) for the backfill of a quarry pit to the south of the chapel (B1) is indicated by the presence of SSW. Once again, a date in the second half of the 12th century, derived from

coarse London-type ware (LCOAR) and London-type ware with early-style decoration (LOND EAS), is given to the backfill of quarry pits in the centre of Open Area 2. A large amount of residual Roman and prehistoric pottery was also recovered from the pits in this area.

A north–south row of four graves where the burials had been exhumed was located c 18m south of the chapel (B1) (Fig 14; Fig 19). Three of the grave cuts were closely spaced; the fourth was isolated at the north end of the row, with an intervening gap sufficient for two burials. All the grave cuts were regular, with vertical sides and flat bases. They were east–west aligned, c 2m long and up to 0.6m deep. A wood stain recognised on the south side of the southernmost grave cut may have been the remains of a coffin. Some human skeletal remains had been left *in situ* in one of the graves, but there was not enough bone to enable the ageing or sexing of the individual. Shelly-sandy ware (SSW) gave an exhumation backfill date of c 1140–c 1220 (A[1094]). The bodies may have been interred before c 1100 or as late as the early 12th century (period M4; Chapter 3.2, 'Archaeological evidence', 'Priory church (B3)'); they were exhumed in the 12th century, prior to the redevelopment in this area in the second half of the 12th century (period M5; Chapter 3.3, 'Archaeological evidence', 'Infirmary courtyard (OA2)'). Thus these burials may possibly even date from the Middle Saxon or Late Saxon periods, perhaps associated with the Anglo-Saxon minster (Chapter 2.4, 2.5, 'Discussion'). However, they would appear to be at some

Fig 19 View of empty graves in Open Area 2 (period M3), from the south-east (0.5m scale)

distance from it (wherever it was located) and so perhaps even part of a Saxon, 'traditional lay' or 'field' cemetery (Blair 2005, 243–4). Equally, however, these burials may be contemporary with the chapel, although not clustered around it.

Fields (OA3)

To the east of the chapel (B1) and the eastern boundary ditches lay open land probably used as fields (OA3, Fig 14). The area extended c 18m east–west by 46.5m north–south and was the site of several gullies. The least truncated of these features was a north-west–south-east aligned, curving gully, 15.12m long and 1.6m wide. A 2.8m length of gully c 13m to the south shared roughly the same alignment. These gullies may indicate a field system. The features in Open Area 3 contained pottery dated between c 1050 and c 1220, mainly cooking pots in handmade coarsewares current during the 11th to early 12th centuries: early medieval sand- and shell-tempered ware (EMSS), early medieval shell-tempered ware (EMSH), early Surrey ware (ESUR) and London-area greyware (LOGR). The latest pottery comes from the secondary fill of the long gully, which yielded five sherds from two shelly-sandy ware (SSW) cooking pots, datable to c 1140–c 1220. The pottery dates suggest that Open Area 3 was possibly being exploited as agricultural land before c 1140.

Open ground to the south-west (OA4)

The land to the south and west of Drain 1 was unexcavated on site A. On sites C and F (Fig 3) gravel extraction (OA4) was taking place (not illustrated). The quarry pits were regular in shape and up to 4m square, with near-vertical sides. They had evidently been dug as part of an organised construction campaign (compare activity in OA2 for this period, above). Two pits contained fragments of cooking pots in early medieval shell-tempered ware (EMSH).

Discussion

The archaeological evidence for the pre-monastic period clarifies a little the period of the foundation of the priory of St Saviour. No direct link between the documented Anglo-Saxon minster of Bermondsey and the Cluniac priory of St Saviour has yet been established (Chapter 2.4, 2.5). The archaeological evidence attests to occupation in the Middle Saxon and Late Saxon periods, with the focus of Saxon occupation apparently to the north and west of the main excavation area.

The date of construction of the chapel (B1) rests on the *terminus post quem* provided by pottery dated to the 10th century from the backfilled quarry pits (OA1) of period M2 (Chapter 2.5, 'Archaeological evidence'). A Saxo-Norman/early Norman date for the chapel is entirely consistent with its simple ground plan. In his extensive survey of Saxon church architecture, H M Taylor identified the two-cell linear plan as occurring at both extremes of the Saxon period: the plan was recorded at Escomb

(Durham) at the beginning of the era and at Deerhurst (Odda's chapel, Gloucestershire) at its end (Taylor and Taylor 1978, 1042). The tradition of the apsidal east end was almost entirely confined to south-east England. Of 19 churches with apsed chancels from the entire Saxon period only one, Hexham (Northumberland), lies in the north of the country. The revival of this architectural feature in the south most probably owes its renewed vigour in the second half of the 11th century to the alliance with the early Anglo-Norman Romanesque. Building 1 can readily be identified as one among a group of Saxo-Norman/early Norman churches located in northern Surrey, at Wisley, Pyrford and Farleigh, and in the Wealden parts of northern Sussex, at Selham, Stopham, Hardham and Buncton (Service 1982, 61–3).

The external appearance of the chapel (B1) was probably very simple, if not rather austere; internally, the chapel would have been equally plain. The superstructure is presumed to be of stone. As an unaisled, relatively small-scale structure, it would have been built mostly with plain walls and rubble masonry that would be impossible to distinguish from later plain work. A close parallel for the interior of an early Norman church, though one with avowedly more sophisticated architecture and complex spaces, is the chapel in the Tower of London, built in the last quarter of the 11th century.

The apparent absence of architectural fragments dating from the 11th century (even though it survived until the end of the medieval period) does not necessarily undermine the proposed dating and interpretation of Building 1. A general lack of adornment of the chapel may be one explanation for this. Relatively plainly dressed stone may go unidentified and uncollected. It may have been reused in the post-medieval period and subsequently been more widely scattered. Stone from the priory was widely robbed and taken to distant sites (as the stone assemblage found on site Z (Fig 3; Table 1), on the south bank of the Thames, testifies). The early construction history of the priory also demonstrates the severe lack of building materials available locally: large-scale gravel quarrying took place in the period up to c 1140 to provide aggregates for wall foundations and Roman tiles were widely reused in the first phase conventual buildings (below 3.2, 3.3, 'Discussion'). The chapel in particular may have been constructed using Roman building materials.

One of only three pieces of figure sculpture from the priory, however, does provide a clue as to the possible appearance of the chapel (B1). A fragment of sculpted relief was found amongst robbing debris (A[928]) subsequent to the demolition in period M6 of a wall associated with the nearby infirmary. The panel consisted of a single piece of oolitic limestone, c 0.36m x 0.27m (14in x 10½in), and depicts a large central figure holding a book, with a group of seven smaller (distant) standing figures to the right (Fig 20). To the left, three kneeling figures are grouped. The figures on the right are bowed beneath an overreaching arch (or vault), which is also the border of the panel. The left of the panel is defined by a vertical, square-section border in high relief. The piece is very worn and no detail is discernible. It could have

Fig 20 Eleventh-century sculpted panel, perhaps indicating the raising of Lazarus and used in the early chapel (B1, period M3) (scale c 1:3)

come from a tympanum or been part of a relief at string course level. The sculpture has been dated to the 11th century (G Zarnecki, pers comm in Beard 1986, 191) and may represent the raising of Lazarus (R Morris, pers comm in Beard 1986, 191). The chapel (B1), with its presumed 11th-century origins, is the only known building to which such a panel could have belonged.

The Domesday entry for Bermondsey describes a new church on the manor, giving a pre-1086 date for completion of this structure. Alwyn Childe may have contributed his rents in 1082 towards the construction of this church. It is also feasible that a chapel was commissioned by William I himself (d 1087) for his new royal manor at Bermondsey after 1066; and it is conceivable the chapel was built prior to 1066. The Domesday entry simply states there is a 'new and beautiful church' there. The survival of the Anglo-Saxon minster into the 11th century has not so far been demonstrated (Chapter 2.4, 2.5). At present we know too little about the possibly early masonry remains recorded by Grimes (below, 3.2, 'Archaeological evidence', 'Priory church (B3)'; Fig 23), or those reported by PCA, in the area of the priory church (BYQ98; Fig 3; A Douglas, pers comm), to assess their significance or to speculate on whether these could be associated with the minster.

Whoever the initiative came from, it is reasonable to suggest that the chapel (B1) might be the 'new church' of 1086; at least, it is the only structure so far of the right type and date for which we have firm archaeological evidence.

The chapel (B1) was most probably used as a place of worship during the construction to the north-west of the priory church and until that church was sufficiently complete to be consecrated. The timber latrine (B2) would have been in use during the construction of the conventual buildings. These two first-phase buildings were in a sense temporary, but the chapel was a substantial masonry building. The latrine was replaced in the first half of the 12th century by a stone reredorter (B8; below, 3.2, 'Archaeological evidence'). The chapel was retained and altered when the principal church was fully functional (period M5; below, 3.3, 'Archaeological evidence', 'Chapel (B1)'). The small group of former burials apparently isolated from the chapel may be a relict from the Anglo-Saxon minster, but the focus of Anglo-Saxon activity seems to lie to the north of the chapel not to its south (Chapter 2.4, 'Discussion'). These burials could have taken place as late as the first half of the 12th century.

Precedents exist for similar free-standing small churches, which later became subsidiary chapels within monastic complexes, most notably at Lewes Priory in Sussex and at Jumièges in Normandy (below, 3.3, 'Discussion'). At Lewes, the infirmary chapel may originally have been built as the first monastic church. This late 11th-century building, it is suggested, was itself constructed to replace the Norman nobleman William de Warenne I's rebuild between 1066 and 1077 of the earlier Saxon church on the site, undertaken in anticipation of establishing a Cluniac priory at Lewes. William I (d 1087) and his wife Gundrada (d 1085) were said to have been buried there (Lyne 1997, 11–23). The 12th-century church was constructed to the north. Bermondsey appears to be another example of a shift of site.

The foundation and construction history of another English Cluniac house provides an interesting comparison. At Wenlock, the 13th-century priory church overlay two earlier churches. The monks' church of the double monastery of St Milburge, founded *c* AD 680, was sited in the area of the later priory crossing. Leofric's minster church was constructed *c* 1040 on the site of St Milburge; Leofric's church was itself reused by the first Cluniac monks and a new priory church constructed after 1200 (Pinnell 1999, 15–18). At Bermondsey, the presence of the chapel south-east of the (later) priory church shows there was not the same degree of locational continuity.

3.2 Church and cloister: the priory *c* 1100–50 (period M4)

Documentary evidence

Royal interest in St Saviour Bermondsey was maintained in the reign of Henry I (1100–35), who was a generous benefactor of Cluny and its daughter houses and refounded Reading Abbey (Berkshire) with monks drawn from Lewes Priory. Henry's 'charter' to Bermondsey confirmed to the bishop of Winchester (as diocesan for Surrey) and the barons and lieges of Surrey the gift of Balham (Surrey) by Nigel de Mandeville to the prior and monks of the priory. Also confirmed were the endowments made earlier by William Rufus and his contemporaries: Hallingbury (Essex), given by Geoffrey Martel, Widford and Broxbourne (Hertfordshire) given by Ivo de Grantmesnil (Grandmesnil), Hardwick church (Buckinghamshire) given by Winebald de Baalun (Ballon) and Preston (Somerset) given by Ansgar Brito on condition that St Saviour Bermondsey maintain two chaplains at the chapel there. In addition, Mary, Countess of Boulogne, gave Kingweston (Somerset) and one Walter Brito gave Stone (Kent). From his own demesne, Henry gave the manors of Rotherhithe and Dulwich (Surrey), a hide of land in Southwark (Surrey), the manor of Waddon near Croydon (Surrey) and the churches of Shorne and Cobham (Kent) (Graham 1926, 164; *VCH* 1967, 65). The date of Henry's charter has been assigned with diffidence to March 1103 on the basis of the Bermondsey annals (*Cal Chart R*, iv, 182; *Mon Angl*, v, 100, no. III; Johnson and Cronne 1956, no. 639).

Important benefactors are among the earliest documented burials at the priory. In 1115, Queen Matilda's mother, Mary, Countess of Boulogne, was buried at the priory (*Ann Monast*, iii, 432). Leofstan, the domesman of London, died in 1115 and was buried at Bermondsey (Brett 1992, 298). Among other notable Normans who were buried at the priory of St Saviour was William Count of Mortain who retired to Bermondsey and received the monastic habit in 1140 (*VCH* 1967, 74; Brett 1992, 299) and Adelaide or Adelize, wife of Hugh de Grantmesnil and the mother of Ivo, who gave properties in Hertfordshire (BL, Cotton MS Claudius A.viii, fos 110–18v; *VCH* 1967, 75).

Bermondsey had acquired much of its endowment in the first two decades of its existence. Most of the gifts made or confirmed by Henry I date from early in his reign. His successor, Stephen, did maintain royal interest in Bermondsey but the favour he showed was possibly strongly influenced by his wife Matilda, given her mother, Mary, Countess of Boulogne, was buried there. According to the annals, in 1141 King Stephen granted to the priory various liberties, including exemption from local courts – shire, hundred and husting (or court of the City of London) – for the monks and their men (*Ann Monast*, iii, 436). He also granted lands at *Grava* in 1142 (ibid, 436–7) and the church of Writtle (Essex) in 1143 (ibid, 437). As well as grants to Bermondsey itself during the period *c* 1140 to 1154 (Cronne and Davis 1968, nos 89–97), a number of Stephen's and also Queen Matilda's charters – in favour of Faversham Abbey, Holy Trinity Priory Aldgate (London), St Martin le Grand (London) and Winchester Cathedral (Hampshire) – were issued from Bermondsey priory within the period *c* 1140 to 1154 (Cronne and Davis 1968, nos 300, 507, 512, 514, 549–50, 957). A mark of royal favour in 1148 was the transferral by Stephen of the prior and 12 monks of Bermondsey to found Faversham Abbey, a venue preferred by him as his burial place (Graham 1926, 162–3).

Archaeological evidence

The priory church (B3) and buildings in the principal cloister (B5–B7) were revealed in plan on sites A and D but largely unexcavated (Fig 21). D Corbett and W F Grimes investigated the church (B3) in the 1950s and 60s. The main claustral range of buildings (B5–B7) was preserved *in situ* under the terms of the planning legislation of the early 1990s. The first burials were made in the cemetery (OA6), in the chapel (B1) and around the church (B3). There was no evidence of activity in the open ground to the south-west of the conventual buildings (OA4) in period M4.

Chapel (B1)

In period M4 three people were buried in the chancel of the chapel (B1, Fig 21). The head end of one of the graves A[3798] had partly cut through the sleeper foundation to the chancel arch. The hunched shoulders and ribs of the skeleton suggested that this individual might have been buried in a shroud. A second burial on the south side of the chancel had a very regular tapering cut. The recovery of four nails from either side of the head and shoulders indicated that the burial may have been made within a coffin or on a bier. Rubble backfill in the grave and the presence of fragments of 13th-century decorated floor tiles of 'Westminster' type confirm this interpretation; debris from subsequent refurbishment of the chapel appears to have been used to make up sinkage over the burial after the coffin lid had rotted or collapsed (below, 3.5, 'Archaeological evidence', 'Chapel (B1)'). Both individuals were male, aged 26 to 45 years, and one A[3798] had suffered a fractured clavicle (Fig 22). On the north side of the chancel, a chalk and plaster-lined grave A[3804] had only partially survived and had no remaining skeletal material.

Priory church (B3)

The foundations uncovered by D Corbett and W F Grimes in 1956 and 1962–3 and interpreted as the east arm of the priory church (Fig 23) lay on the north side of modern Abbey Street (site G, Fig 3). An apsidal foundation located at the northern limit of site A and excavated in 1989 has for the first time been interpreted as part of the south presbytery wall of the church and beginning of an apsidal end. The width of the presbytery (the eastern arm of the church, including aisles) as revealed by excavation was nearly c 18m, and its length, from the eastern apse of the north aisle to the apsidal chapels of the north transept, was c 33+m (all measurements are internal).

The bulk of the evidence for the priory church has come from the Grimes archive. The methods of the time involved clearing, digging by workmen, and multi-context planning, with rare observations on perceived relationships, but otherwise no stratigraphic recording or Ordnance Datum heights. In addition, much of the recovered evidence is for unexcavated robber trenches with uncertain limits. The location of Corbett and Grimes's excavation trenches is itself a 'best fit' rather than exact siting; it uses Grimes's 1962 draft plan of the western, transept, excavation which shows 'angle of modern building' twice and these points have been related to the contemporary (and still standing, 2009) building identifiable on current OS mapping. These limitations have meant that it has been difficult to establish a conclusive plan of the east end of the church. The period plans (M4–M9; Fig 21; Fig 33; Fig 49; Fig 53; Fig 57; Fig 65) show outlines of robber trenches and foundations recorded by Grimes where interpreted as appropriate (cf Fig 23). Grimes's preparatory plan of the western transept excavation survives in the Grimes archive and is directly reused in the published plan with some simplifications.

The Grimes data for the north side and the south apsidal foundation excavated on site A are combined with evidence for the south transept from more recent PCA excavations. This comprises masonry wall foundations located by PCA on the 'Island' site (BYQ98; located on Fig 3); preliminary phasing of the site assigns these to the main medieval phase of the priory. (Possibly earlier masonry remains on this site are not included here.) The asymmetry between the north aisle and the south aisle, and between the eastern apses, is discussed further below ('Discussion'), and in Chapter 4.2 ('The 12th-century priory church'; Fig 69) where a possible reconstruction of the east arm of the church in the 12th century (periods M4 and M5) and c 1400 (period M8) is suggested.

The archaeological evidence for the eastern part of the church (B3) in the first half of the 12th century is presented on Fig 21. Elements of the church plan which do seem clear indicate that the building had an aisled presbytery. A large, east–west robber trench and a fragment of surviving foundation represented the sleeper foundation for the north arcade of the presbytery north aisle. There were apsidal terminations to both

north and south aisles and Grimes identified a second apse south of the north aisle apse and projecting east of it. The eastern side of the north transept took the form of two apsidal chapels, the internal dimensions of which were c 3m east–west by 2.8m north–south. The exposed north–south length of the transept and part of the crossing was 12.8m.

Grimes's plan of the north side of the eastern part of the church (Fig 23) identified a further apsidal chapel on the north side of the north aisle as forming part of the 12th-century church. The evidence is slightly ambiguous: Grimes records a roughly rectangular, external north-east foundation whose line is continued south by a robber trench; Grimes assumed, however, that the chapel formed an external absidiole rather than being externally rectilinear and this is what his reconstruction shows. He also recorded a number of graves, including four outside the north presbytery wall of the church, each of which had a chalk lining and three had an anthropomorphic head niche (subgroups G[48], G[49], G[53]*, G[54]). The most easterly of the three with a head niche was subsequently truncated by the apsidal foundation. If any skeletal remains were recovered from these burials at the time of the Corbett and Grimes excavations, their whereabouts is no longer known. These burials have been assigned to this period, M4, on the basis that they were positioned externally in relation to the foundations of the earliest identified church phase; and the northern apsidal chapel is interpreted as having been added to the north aisle in period M5 (below, 3.3, 'Archaeological evidence', 'Priory church (B3)'; Fig 33).

It is possible, however, that these burials relate to an earlier structure. Grimes identified '?pre-monastic foundations (robber trench)' on the north edge of his excavation, and an 'early wall' extending north and south of the line of the west wall of the northern apsidal chapel (Fig 23). The southern of the two adjacent burials just north of the north aisle wall is shown by Grimes as truncated by a foundation (Fig 23; not shown on Fig 21) which is itself earlier than the north wall foundation. Future evaluation of the evidence recovered by PCA excavations to the west, and of evidence for early masonry remains (north–south walls and a curving west–east wall) found within the main body of the later (here M4, 12th-century) south transept (BYQ98; A Douglas, pers comm), may allow reinterpretation of the earliest phases of the priory church, and possibly of the Anglo-Saxon minster (cf above, 3.1, 'Discussion').

The apsidal foundation excavated on site A was 6.27m long and was at least 1.33m wide (it continued beyond the north limit of excavation). It was built out of alternate layers of gravel, chalk and ragstone, the sole example of this construction on site A (Fig 24). Thin gravel and sand layers in the foundation functioned as bedding joints, sealing some gaps around the chalk blocks and levelling up the chalk courses. Roughly hewn chalk blocks, between 200mm and 400mm long, overlay courses of ragstone, which varied in size between 100mm and 500mm in length. The foundation survived to a height of 2.4m OD and its base was at 0.65m OD. It had not been tightly packed, so that voids were present within the construction. Where the foundation overlay the Late Saxon ditch (OA2,

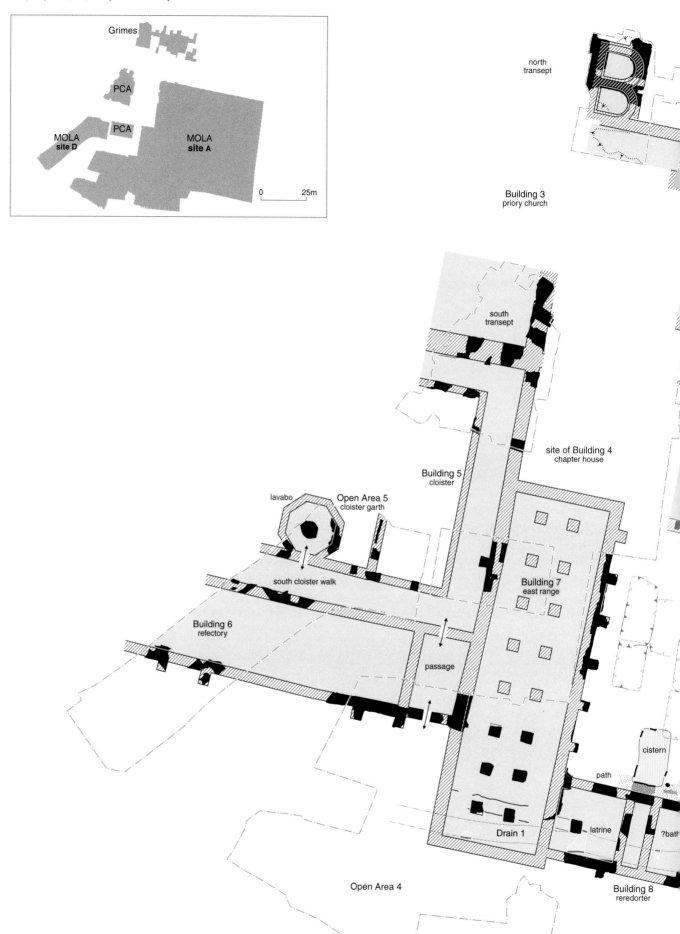

Grimes

PCA

PCA

MOLA
site D

MOLA
site A

0   25m

north
transept

Building 3
priory church

south
transept

site of Building 4
chapter house

Building 5
cloister

lavabo

Open Area 5
cloister garth

south cloister walk

Building 7
east range

Building 6
refectory

passage

cistern

path

Drain 1

latrine

?bath

Open Area 4

Building 8
reredorter

Fig 21 Plan of principal archaeological features at sites in the study area,
c 1100–50 (period M4) (scale 1:400; inset 1:2000)

N

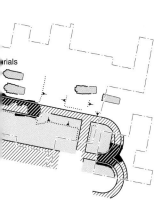

rials

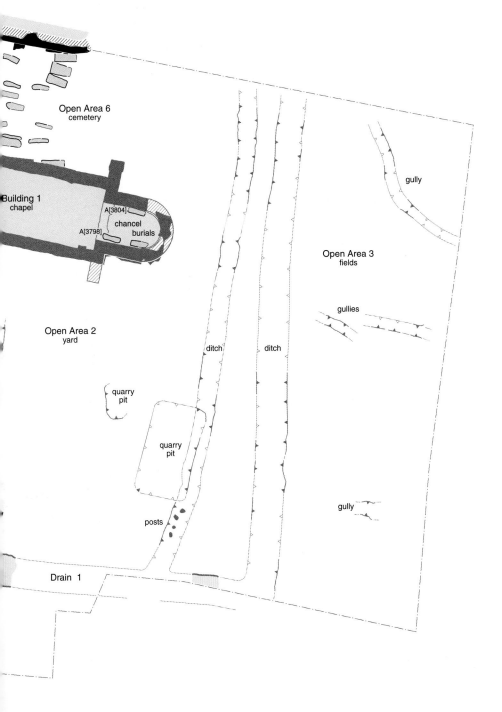

Open Area 6
cemetery

gully

Building 1
chapel

A[3804]

chancel
burials

A[3798]

Open Area 3
fields

gullies

Open Area 2
yard

ditch   ditch

quarry
pit

quarry
pit

gully

posts

Drain 1

female burial

0   10m

Fig 22 View of skeleton A[3798] with a fractured clavicle, in the chapel (B1, period M4), from the north (1.0m scale)

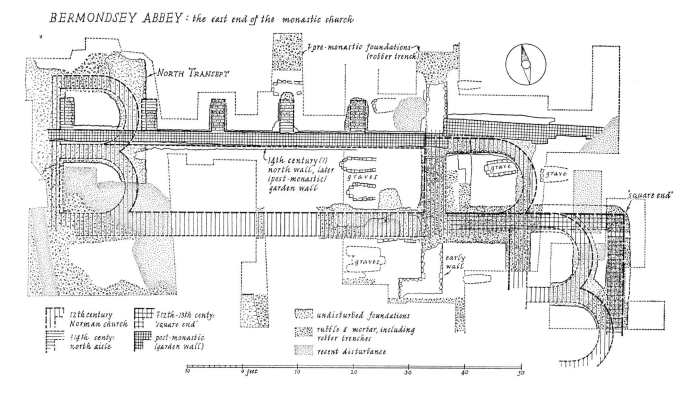

Fig 23 W F Grimes's plan of the east end of the church as excavated (reproduced in Grimes 1968, 215, fig 52) (scale 1:200)

period M2; Chapter 2.5; Fig 10) it had been made deeper to counteract the soft ditch fill, a construction technique noted elsewhere on site.

The construction of the south wall of the presbytery over the backfilled Late Saxon ditch (period M2) gives a *terminus post quem* for the priory church of the 10th century (strictly AD post-900; Chapter 2.5, 'Discussion'). The dating otherwise relies on the documentary evidence, the analysis of architectural elements, on stylistic and tooling arguments and on comparisons of the ground plan with contemporary Anglo-Norman Benedictine and Cluniac churches (Chapter 4.2, 'The 12th-century priory church').

Fig 24 View of the apsidal foundation of the south side of the priory church (B3, period M4), from the east (0.5m scale)

Some architectural fragments recovered during the excavation of site A and from the assemblage found on site Z (Fig 3) have been tentatively linked with the church. The earliest datable elements are associated with Taynton stone wall responds, plinths, pier bases and an example of figurative sculpture. The nave arcade piers were of simple round form. A simple hollow-chamfered plinth (A<3150>, Fig 25), found reused in a later context as part of the bridge across Drain 2 (period M5; below, 3.3, 'Archaeological evidence', 'Stone-built drain (D2)'; Fig 33) indicates that Taynton stone was not used exclusively for a single structure but was also employed at or near floor level where resistance to abrasion was important. The single element A<3150> was perhaps one of eight such hollow-chamfered blocks which together formed the base of a circular pier. The composite base formed part of a ?nave arcade that was otherwise faced with Caen stone. It is probable that the base rested on a plain or chamfered square base as at Reading Abbey (BL, Add MS 36400A xlv, fos 10 and 24) and at St Bartholomew Smithfield (extant) in the City of London. The

conjectural reconstruction (Fig 25) uses a bay width of 13ft 6in (4.115m), an average course height of 6in (152mm) in the elevation of typical pier bases, and for the aisle wall in plan at ground level the maximum width of 5ft 6in (1.676m) recorded by Buckler (Chapter 4.2, 'The 12th-century priory church'; BL, Add MS 24433, fo 58).

Distinctively 'compressed' scallop capitals embellished with slit and paper-dart ornament and representing at least four columnar piers of the ?nave arcade were also found; these would suggest, however, a construction date in the third quarter of the 12th century (ie period M5), rather than earlier (below, 3.3, 'Archaeological evidence', 'Priory church (B3)' and Chapter 4.2, 'The 12th-century priory church'; Fig 71).

Very little evidence survives for the arcade arch itself. A solitary broken voussoir A<3082> (Fig 71) can be recognised as the minor order of a large arch, which, if semicircular, was c 3.07m wide. Another voussoir type is possibly from an arcade minor order and is reconstructed as an arch c 2.22m wide (Fig 71, Z<126>, Z<140>). The reconstructed elevation of the ?nave arcade employs both these minor orders and shows the apparent relation of pier to arch (Chapter 4.2; Fig 74). A single ribstone (A<3125>; CP1.2.1; Fig 126; below, 'Discussion' and Chapter 7.2), found in a post-Dissolution context, was directly comparable to a rib used in the choir aisle cross arches at Peterborough, c 1120s (Clapham 1934, fig 42 3).

elevation

plan

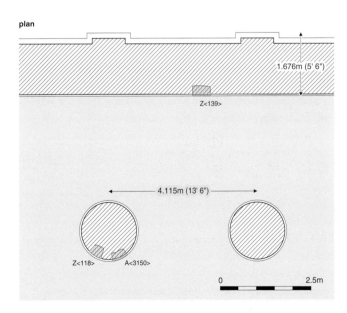

Fig 25 The 12th-century nave, a conjectural reconstruction detail of the aisle and nave arcade, showing the probable employment of common typestones from sites A and Z (A<3150>, Z<118>, Z<139>): upper – elevation of typical pier bases; lower – plan of a typical bay at ground level (scale 1:100)

Chapter house (B4)

The presumed location of the chapter house is shown on Fig 21; a reconstruction of its form is suggested in Chapter 4.2 ('The cloister').

Cloister walk (B5) and cloister garth (OA5)

The evidence for the main cloister (B5, Fig 21) was drawn initially from records of unexcavated foundations exposed on site D (Fig 3). On site A the east part of the refectory (B6), the east range (B7) and the area to the south (OA4) were first partially cleared and recorded by W F Grimes in 1972. Some preliminary work took place when the area was reopened in 1985, but the focus of the modern excavation was on the infirmary and cemetery and the area was largely left until the decision was made to record, reduce and backfill it in 1988. Consequently, the east part of the refectory (B6) and the greater part of the east range (B7) have as many as three sets of records apiece. The small pottery groups recovered during the limited works to reduce the area in 1988 show a high degree of disturbance and do not support the allocation of the main claustral range to the first period (M3) of priory construction. Some rudimentary phasing was possible where some foundations were obviously abutting or overlying others.

This evidence has been supplemented by the preliminary results from excavations by PCA (pers comm). Masonry wall foundations in the area of the south transept (B3) and north-east corner of the cloister (on the 'Island' site, BYQ98; located on Fig 3) are assigned as part of preliminary phasing of the site to the main medieval phase of the priory. The pentise walls of the north and east cloister walks have two phases of foundations, indicating the cloister alley was rebuilt during the lifetime of the priory (below, 3.6, 'Archaeological evidence', 'Chapter house (B4) and cloister (B5)'). A mortar surface survived in the north cloister walk, adjacent to the south wall of the south transept. Excavation by PCA to the south, at the site of the former White Bear public house (WBP07; located on Fig 3), revealed the remains of a north–south wall foundation with a buttress on its west side; this is interpreted as part of the west wall of the east range (B7).

The main cloister was on the south side of the priory church but their precise relationship is not certain. The location of the east range (B7, below) is not in doubt but the south transept was apparently not aligned with the east range: the west wall of the east range could not align with the west wall of the south transept as conjectured from a combination of the PCA evidence and mirror imaging of Grimes's north transept. This is discussed further below ('Discussion') and in Chapter 4.2 ('The 12th-century priory church') where a possible (and partly schematic) reconstruction of the 12th-century church and cloister is suggested (Fig 69).

The north and east cloister walks at their junction are respectively c 3.0m and c 3.6m wide (Fig 21). The pentise wall of the south cloister walk (B5) was identified on site D; it consisted of insubstantial fragments of chalk foundation. The cloister walk thus formed was c 3.5m wide.

Enclosed by the cloister walks was the cloister garth (OA5, Fig 21). On the south side of the cloister garth, c 12m from the (conjectured) south-east corner, the remains of a lavabo or washing place were recorded. The structure had been heavily robbed but part of the flagged base and rubble core of the central foundation survived. On the east and south sides of the lavabo were the chalk and gravel foundations of a surrounding wall. Further fragments of chalk foundation recorded to the east may be part of another garth structure adjacent to the south cloister walk, perhaps associated with the lavabo.

The location of the lavabo (where the monks washed their hands before eating) on the south side of the cloister garth (OA5) suggests the entrance to the refectory (B6) was close by. The simplest and most usual form of lavabo is a basin and fountain built into the cloister wall, often in a recess, but this is an independent structure standing in the cloister garth. The lavabo building at St Saviour Bermondsey could have been either round or octagonal; it is shown reconstructed as octagonal on Fig 21. It is probable that it broadly resembled the example at the Cluniac priory of Wenlock (Morley 1990, 8; Coppack 1999; Pinnell 1999, 10; Coppack 2006, 152–3; below, 'Discussion' and Chapter 4.2, 'Water supply and sanitation'; Fig 82; Fig 83). With a rubble core foundation diameter of c 2m, the Bermondsey central structure could have been very similar to that at Wenlock; there a circular central fountain or cistern on deep foundations was encircled by a basin and water flowed out of the basin into a circular shallow trough. At Bermondsey, the walkway or paved access around where the trough would have been was in the region of c 1m wide and bordered by an outer wall that would have provided support for some form of roofing. The lavabo building at St Saviour Bermondsey would have had a total diameter of c 7m, again very like that at Wenlock.

Refectory (B6)

The east–west aligned building on the south side of the cloister has been identified as the refectory (B6, Fig 21) on the basis of its position. The refectory was 7.9m wide and at least 30m long. The north wall of the building consisted of the fragmented remains of a chalk and gravel foundation. The south wall foundations were also chalk and gravel, over which elements of the superstructure had survived to a height of 0.20m. The walls had a chalk rubble core and were faced with Reigate stone, Kentish rag and ?Caen stone blocks. The foundation offset level was 3.5m OD.

Found in demolition rubble overlying the south refectory wall was a sculpted stone head (A<703> A[2059]; Fig 32) that, perhaps, may originally have formed part of the sculptural detail of the building (below, 'Discussion').

At the east end of the building, a separate room or passage was indicated by the robber trench for a north–south wall. This room was nearly 5m long west–east. At Cluny, a similarly placed room but with a fireplace has been identified as the calefactory or warming room (Conant 1959, 112, fig 31; 1968, plan 6 [Cluny c 1157]; G Coppack, pers comm). Here at Bermondsey, as at

Castle Acre and Thetford priories (Raby and Reynolds 1979, 13 and plan; Coad and Coppack 1998, 21, 33), it is interpreted as a passage, linking the cloister (B5) and south exterior (OA4) adjacent to the south end of the east range (B7). The width could have accommodated a stair to an upper floor room, as at Castle Acre where the north and south doors are offset.

East range (B7)

A north–south aligned building (B7, Fig 21) occupied the east side of the cloister. The evidence for this east range was limited to largely unexcavated deposits and robber trenches with some surviving *in situ* wall and square pier foundations. With the exception of the east wall, the majority of the building lay outside the area of excavation. Parts of two wall foundations were observed in section during a watching brief in 1994 (site E, Fig 3): two discontinuous fragments of a north–south wall foundation, built of mortared chalk blocks but with no facings, survived to a height of 3.87–3.89m OD and a fragment of east–west return wall built of unworked ragstone survived to a height of 3.77m OD (Askew 1995, 45–51, trench 9). The north–south foundation was on a similar alignment to the east wall of the east range but neither wall can be interpreted on this evidence as indicating the northern end of the east range; both appear to lie within the site of the chapter house. Part of the west wall foundation, with a buttress on its west side, was excavated by PCA at the site of the former White Bear public house (WBP07; PCA, pers comm). The width of the east range, therefore, was *c* 13m (measured externally, *c* 10.5m internally).

The overall north–south length of the east range is more difficult to establish. It was at least *c* 36m long, and possibly more – *c* 40m – if the east range extended south over (the pre-existing) Drain 1. It is reconstructed thus on Fig 21. However, the detail of the building at the south end, where it formed an L-shaped complex with the latrine (B8), is not clear from the largely unexcavated evidence. The west wall of the east range may have continued south, perhaps overarching Drain 1 and returning to meet the south wall of the reredorter (B8). The continuation in this way of the west wall may equally have belonged to period M5, when the building is known to have had this extended form. The two square pier foundations in an east–west robber trench at the south end of the building may have supported originally the ribs of a barrel-vaulted bridge spanning the drain rather than supporting the range's vault. The positioning of the east range over Drain 1 would have allowed for privies at the south end of the range, in addition to those in the reredorter.

The internal arrangements in the east range reveal a building vaulted in three bays and at least eight bays (nine if it extended over D1) long. External buttresses to the east wall reflected the internal bay divisions, each bay being 4.3m long, north–south (Fig 26). The east range undercroft was almost certainly ceiled with a stone vault, carried on two rows of piers. Excavated, *in situ* and loose, base elements indicate a late 12th-century or slightly later vault, suggesting possible rebuilding then (period M5; below, 3.3, 'Archaeological evidence', 'East range (B7)'). This would have been a two-storey building, where the upper floor presumably functioned as the monks' dorter or dormitory

Fig 26 View of external face of the east wall of the east range (B7) in period M4, from the east (1.0m and 2.0m scales)

<S121>

Fig 27 Copper-alloy scourer <S121> (from B7, period M4) (scale c 2:1)

as in the standard Cluniac, and monastic, plan. The ground floor may have been divided internally and have had several functions (eg stairs to the upper floor, a warming room, a day room, a parlour: cf Castle Acre: Coad and Coppack 1998, plans 20, 21, 29–31). The internal width of this building is similar to that of the first, early 12th-century, phase of the Thetford east range (G Coppack, pers comm); the ground floor of the north part of the east range at Battle Abbey (Sussex) is vaulted in three bays (Hare 1985, 17, fig 3).

From the building came three copper-alloy items: a (residual) strapend <S4>, a small padlock <S56> and an unusual scourer (Fig 27, <S121>), a brush made out of a group of wires presumably originally mounted into a wooden handle. This robust brush could have had a number of uses including everyday cleaning, and was possibly made for use on metal vessels.

Reredorter (B8)

The earlier timber latrine (B2, period M3) was replaced in the first half of the 12th century by a stone reredorter (B8; Fig 21). It adjoined, and was contemporary with, the east range (B7). This reredorter (B8) was *c* 17.5m long and 7m wide; it had been greatly truncated by modern concrete footings and so evidence was very fragmentary. That which survives, however, indicates that the building lay at right angles to the east wall of the east range (B7) (rather than across the south end of the east range as

at, for example, Castle Acre, Thetford and Lewes priories) and that the buildings were separate. The north wall of the reredorter (B8) was a continuation of the southernmost buttress to the east wall of the east range (B7), indicating the reredorter was a secondary addition. South of the buttress the foundation to the east wall of the east range continued south a further 3.75m, at which point it had been truncated by an east–west robber trench left as a result of the later robbing of three pier bases (two in B7 and one in B8).

The reredorter (B8) straddled Drain 1 and though evidence is lacking owing to later robbing and modern truncation, it is likely that the north–south walls were carried over the drain on arched culverts. The building was divided on the ground floor into three rooms, two of almost equal proportions either side of a much narrower chamber. The west room was 7.25m long (east–west) with an off-centre pier on the north side of the drain. The west room is interpreted as a ground-floor latrine; the pier probably separated at least two privies. The latrine blocks at both Castle Acre and Thetford priories had privies on the ground floor for daytime use (Raby and Reynolds 1979, 12; Coad and Coppack 1998, 31–2). The surviving pier also would have supported an upper floor; this would have connected with the first-floor dorter in the east range. The first floor of the reredorter (B8) would have allowed provision for a larger number of closets along its full length; these would have emptied into the drain below.

The central room in Building 8 was only 2m wide. It and the adjacent east room must have been screened somehow from the drain, perhaps by wooden partitions for which no evidence survived; the drain, however, was below ground level and simply may have been covered. A foundation stub midway along the inside of the south wall of the east room could have supported a cover, partition or other structure. The foundation trench to the east wall of the central room was 0.6m wider than the footing itself and the foundation had been aligned along the east side of the cut (Fig 28). The channel left within the foundation trench on its west side had been lined with mortar and faced with ragstone and it would have carried a water pipe (G Coppack, pers comm). The room at the east end of the reredorter (B8) was *c* 6.8m long (east–west) and there is no internal evidence for its function in this period.

Outside the north wall of the reredorter (B8) and separated from the central room by a gravel path was a large, rectangular pit (5.9m long north–south by 2.8m wide). The pit had been carefully dug: it had straight, vertical sides, postholes in its north-west and south-west corners and was 1.2m deep. The upper backfill included lumps of burnt mud-brick and clay, indicating that the pit had been clay-lined. It could have functioned as a cistern. Between the pit and the north wall of the building there was a crushed chalk surface. This was defined, to the north and east, by two postholes in line with the south edge of the pit; these may have supported a lean-to structure against the north wall of the reredorter. Sherds of early Surrey ware (ESUR) and shelly-sandy ware (SSW) (dated to *c* 1140–*c* 1220) were recovered from one of the postholes associated with the pit.

Fig 28 View of east wall foundation of the central room of the reredorter (B8) in period M4, from the south (0.5m scale)

The cistern outside the north side of the reredorter (B8) along with the evidence for a water pipe suggest that in the first half of the 12th century clean water was being stored and piped into the reredorter (B8). With the exception of the lavabo in the main cloister (OA5), this is the only evidence for piped water or the collection and routing of clean water anywhere on the site or indeed within the study area. The central and east rooms in the reredorter (B8), therefore, may have been used as a bathhouse. Water from the external cistern could have been piped into a tank in the central room, where it could have been heated by means of portable braziers. Bathing may have taken place in the room at the east end of the building. The central room may also have served as a passage, providing access from the exterior into the east and west ground-floor rooms.

The direction of flow in the underlying drain (D1, below) could not be established. A reasonable assumption would have been that at this developed stage of the monastery it was west to east, given the overall evidence for drainage channels on the south side of the main cloister (Chapter 4.2, 'The precinct and home grange'; Fig 81); if so, this would mean waste moved from the (west) latrine through the possible bathing area. It is possible that all of the ground floor of the reredorter block

served as a bathhouse, including the west room, with the drain presumably covered and the latrines confined to the upper floor (cf Lyne 1997, 38–9). However, Drain 1 still probably connected with the two ?boundary ditches to the east, at least one of which (the western) apparently drained north to south (above, 3.1, 'Archaeological evidence'). This might suggest Drain 1 was part of a drainage cum sewerage system which served the conventual buildings from the east side (Chapter 4.2, 'Water supply and sanitation').

Monastic sewer (D1)

The monastic sewer (D1, Fig 21) continued in use throughout period M4, now straddled by the reredorter (B8). The origins of Drain 1, however, lie in the earliest phase of the priory and it still probably connected with the two ?boundary ditches to the east, of which the western apparently drained north to south (above, 3.1, 'Archaeological evidence').

Quarry site and ?boundary ditches (OA2)

Dating evidence suggests that the quarry pits (OA2; above, 3.1; Fig 14; Fig 21) were finally backfilled in the second half of the 12th century (period M5) so it is likely that during this period Open Area 2 remained very much a working zone characterised by disused or partly backfilled quarry pits. The four burials to the south of the area (Fig 14; Fig 19) were removed some time after c 1140 (above, 3.1, 'Archaeological evidence'), presumably when a more suitable area for their interment, such as the cemetery (OA6), became available and prior to redevelopment here in the second half of the 12th century (period M5; below, 3.3). The ?boundary ditches were still open in this period and probably did mark the eastern boundary of the inner precinct (Fig 21). Animal bone from east ditch fill A[1045] was dominated by the major mammalian domesticates (cattle, sheep/goat and pig), but included four horse fragments, all from the lower hind legs of the same animal, cut so as to suggest at least a part of this carcass had been prepared for meat removal and consumption (Chapter 7.8). Fill A[1045] yielded a limestone hone (<S159>, Fig 29) and fill A[3405] in the northern part of the east ditch a quernstone (<S157>) in an uncommon, pink, coarse millstone grit.

Fig 29 Limestone hone <S159>
(from OA2, period M4) (scale: c 1:1)

Fields (OA3)

In period M4, land to the east of the boundary ditches continued in use as fields (OA3, Fig 21). The field gullies fell out of use some time after *c* 1140.

Cemetery (OA6)

The monastic cemetery lay between the priory church (B3) and chapel (B1). In period M4, the east limit of the cemetery (OA6, Fig 21) was the boundary ditches (OA2) which appear to have defined the east side of the inner monastic precinct. Thus, the extent of the cemetery as revealed by excavation was in the region of *c* 32m east–west by 11.5m north–south. The graves discovered by Grimes adjacent to the north side of the priory church (B3), *c* 21m to the north of the cemetery (OA6), may indicate more exactly the true north–south extent of the cemetery around the eastern end of the priory church.

The first burials in the monastic cemetery (OA6) were widely spaced in irregular north–south rows. Graves were dug across the full width of the land between the church (B3) and the chapel (B1). Eighteen burials in the cemetery (OA6) have been identified as belonging to period M4. At least four of the graves contained mortared stone cists (Fig 86) – three close to the south-east end of the priory church (B3) and one adjacent to the north wall of the chapel (B1) – while another had crushed chalk at the base (Table 5). Adult male A[2765] had a chalk stone cist with head niche and a mortar skin to the interior of the lining (Fig 30). This cist was constructed with an unmortared stone first course, including two head support elements; the second stone course was mortared on to the first, and the whole given a mortar wash or skin. A shallow, third course of mortar 'bricks' included slots, probably for wooden cross supports for a stone slab or wooden cover for the cist.

The 18 individuals available for osteological analysis from the cemetery were almost exclusively adult males (14 males/ ?males: namely two young adults 16–25 years, five mature adults 26–45 years, four old/elderly ≥46 years, and three 'adult' ie 16+ years), with three of indeterminate sex (one elderly adult, two adult) and a solitary female young adult A[2736] (the age and sex breakdown is detailed in Table 20; the location of the female is indicated on Fig 21).

The cemetery soil, a dark sandy silt, was homogeneous and without any apparent horizontal banding. It was treated as a single stratigraphic unit A[2752]. The difficulty of recognising grave cuts was such that these were often created arbitrarily, the body being located via a process of 'chasing' around the predicted skeletal outline. Later pit digging and modern foundations had, in their turn, caused a great deal of disturbance. The medieval pottery collected from the cemetery soil included several sherds from London-type ware (LOND) jugs dating between *c* 1180 and *c* 1350, as well as single sherds of Kingston-type ware (KING; date range *c* 1230–*c* 1400) and Mill Green ware (MG; date range *c* 1270–*c* 1350). The context also included four sherds of 16th- to 17th-century pottery and was, in terms of the ceramic content, chronologically very mixed with the latest medieval material, part of a lobed cup in coarse Surrey-Hampshire border ware (CBW), from the late 14th to 15th century. The bulk of the pottery from A[2752], however, belongs to the Late Saxon period and 11th to 12th centuries, and comprises 89.2% of all pottery from this period in Open Area 6 by sherd count (85.5% ENV/89.6% Wt/100% by EVEs). These figures are mainly derived from a minimum of 44 cooking pots in (residual) Late Saxon shelly ware (LSS; 63 sherds) dated to *c* AD 900–1050 and 17 in early medieval shell-tempered ware (EMSH), dated *c* 1050–*c* 1150 (51 sherds). Other 11th- and 12th-century fabrics common to the London area include early medieval sand- and shell-tempered ware (EMSS; *c* 1000–*c* 1150), early medieval sandy ware (EMS; date range *c* AD 970–1100), early medieval chalk-tempered ware (EMCH;

Fig 30 Stone cist in the cemetery (OA6), close to the south wall of the church (B3), from the north (burial A[2765], period M4): detail of the head niche and mortar skin to the interior of the chalk lining (0.5m scale)

date range *c* 1050–*c* 1150) and early medieval flint-tempered ware (EMFL; date range *c* 1000–*c* 1100+). All of these are cooking pots, undoubtedly the predominant form at this period. Apart from decorated jugs in LOND, there are few other forms, the exceptions being part of a pedestal lamp in LSS (Fig 155, <P32>), which is sooted internally (Vince and Jenner 1991, fig 2.26 nos 36–41; Pearce 1998, 128) and a spouted pitcher in the same fabric. The only imports are a sherd from a green-glazed jug or pitcher probably of north French origin (Vince and Jenner 1991, 106–8) and part of a pitcher in red-painted or Pingsdorf-type ware (REDP) from the Rhineland, a type generally associated with the wine trade. The scarcity of joining sherds and the broad chronological span of the pottery indicate a degree of disturbance which is not unexpected for cemetery soil.

A small quantity of animal bone from the cemetery soil consisted chiefly of the major mammalian domesticates, but also included a partial horse skeleton; butchery marks on the latter suggest this animal was used for meat although not necessarily for human consumption (Chapter 7.8; Table 18).

Discussion

The specific problems surrounding the evidence for the east part of the priory church (B3) concern the apparent size and location of the eastern apses (Fig 21). The foundation to the junction of two apses uncovered by Grimes falls short of the curving foundation excavated on site A on a north–south axis. The projected end of the south aisle of the presbytery, therefore, lies slightly further east than the equivalent north presbytery aisle. This presents a problem for any symmetrical solution to the east end of the church. It would, of course, be a relatively simple matter to assume a surveying anomaly in the Grimes archive, except that a ready resolution of the east end continues to be hampered by the size of the apse to the north aisle, the curve of which dictates that it apparently does not meet the east–west line of the north presbytery arcade. In addition, the conjectured line of the foundation curving south from the north aisle appears to delineate a tight half circle and thereby another small-sized apse.

One possibility is that the curving foundation of the south aisle is a later construction. But this possibility merely postpones the asymmetry, not resolves it. The problem of the small apse size and consequent disagreement with the aisle dimensions is solved to a degree by the presence of a north–south aligned foundation which must have acted as a sleeper wall for multi-apse openings. An apse echelon scheme, though apt owing to its use at the mother house of La Charité-sur-Loire originally in the 11th century (Fig 68) and at the famous Benedictine house of St Benoît-sur-Loire (Abbaye de Fleury, Loiret) (Conant 1959, 155), is marred by asymmetry at St Saviour Bermondsey. A possible (partly schematic) reconstruction of the 12th-century church and cloister from the available archaeological evidence is suggested in Chapter 4.2 ('The 12th-century priory church'; Fig 69).

A second problem area is the relationship between the priory church and the main cloister, specifically the lack of alignment of the south transept and the east range (above, 'Cloister walk (B5) and cloister garth (OA5)'). Such an unusual arrangement presents some difficulties of interpretation.

It would be normal for construction in stone of the main cloister and ranges to follow that of the permanent church, or at least for the construction of the east range to follow construction of the eastern arm of the church, rather than precede it. This misalignment in the layout of the period M4 church and east cloister range suggests different dates for their laying out, but the arrangement is so unusual that the full explanation may be more complex. The lack of alignment may be due to the location of pre-existing buildings, either the chapel (B1), constructed in the preceding period (M3) and retained in M4, and/or an earlier phase of the priory church (B3). No archaeological evidence was recovered in the excavations reported here for such an earlier phase (above, 3.1, 'Discussion'). (Analysis and publication of the recent excavations by PCA or future excavations may revise this view.)

A resolution of these problems is not helped by the sparse dating evidence outlined above for the priory church (B3) and for the main claustral buildings. A large pottery assemblage dated to the second half of the 12th century (*c* 1140–*c* 1200) from the primary fill of the new drain (D2) serving the second stone reredorter (B9) and infirmary latrine (B11) suggests those buildings were complete and in use by around 1200 (period M5; below, 3.3, 'Archaeological evidence', 'Stone-built drain (D2)'). A construction date in the second half of the 12th century for the infirmary (B10) and second reredorter range (B9) is consistent with an earlier 12th-century date for the first stone reredorter range (B8). Extensive quarrying (OA2) for building materials, indicative of the first phase of construction (period M3), could still have been taking place in this the next period.

The architectural fragments evidence suggests a slightly later date for the bulk of the construction work, that is, mid 12th century or later rather than earlier 12th century. Dating of any decorative motif or moulding in the English Romanesque (or Anglo-Norman) style is hindered by the lack of distinctive 11th-century forms. The earliest typestone on site was the single ribstone (A<3125>; CP1.2.1; Fig 126). It is probable that, if Clapham's (1934, fig 42 3) dating is still correct for the Peterborough parallel, that this dates to the second quarter of the 12th century. Construction phase 1, as defined in this volume (Chapter 7.2, 'Methodology'; Table 11), is centred on build numbers 10–13, which give an average early date of not before *c* 1140. Therefore, although there are ten stone groups with an average early date before *c* 1140, the peak of construction as evidenced by the architectural fragments assemblage falls after that date.

The apparent inconsistencies of the architectural fragments and stratigraphic dating are discussed further in Chapter 4.2, but they can be seen as more apparent than real. It seems probable that the ongoing major building work after *c* 1140 included substantial work on the priory church (below, 3.3, 'Discussion'). An initial burst of building activity followed by a slower and more drawn-out programme to complete the works would be consistent with the documentary evidence for a flood of grants in the first two decades after the priory's foundation, endowments which slackened thereafter (above). The description in the annals of how Henry I 'the glorious king enlarged the priory church and endowed it with possessions at the same time' (*Ann Monast*, iii, 435) suggests there was significant building work during his reign; the east end of the church was presumably sufficiently complete for Mary, Countess of Boulogne, to be interred there (ibid, 432).

A fine, carved lion was the only surviving piece of animal sculpture in the architectural fragments assemblage (found reused in a unphased but post-medieval wall A[1572]; A<3118>; Conway Library, Courtauld Institute negative no. A98/308; Fig 31). It has parallels with the lions carved at the base of the jambs of the west cloister door at Ely Cathedral (Cambridgeshire) (L Grant, pers comm). The lion in oolitic limestone (probably Taynton stone of Oxfordshire: D F Williams, pers comm) was executed in high relief and was held in place by a stone projection at the back, while his hind leg overhung the stone plinth on which it rested. The style of the carving is naturalistic; the lion lies on his belly, with his curled tail passing beneath his leg. The pose is stereotypical and has been encountered in other examples: a displaced pinnacle from Old Sarum (Wiltshire) is flanked by two crouching lions in this pose (Salisbury and South Wiltshire Museum no. 270/1945; L Grant, pers comm); a tympanum from the Cluniac priory at Thetford (Lockett 1971, pl xiv.1) has a less naturalistic but similarly posed lion. The symbolic significance of the lion in Christian art is dependent on context (Hulme 1899, 171). The lion is the symbol of the Evangelist Mark and of Christ; a 12th-century manuscript, the *Book of Beasts*, firmly identifies the lion with Christ and describes the symbolism of the lion's physical attributes. The lion also figured in the arms of St Saviour 'passant gardant, holding in his paw a pastoral staff erect, surmounted with a mitre' (Clarke 1901, 10), and it is conceivable that the lost part of the sculpture included this detail.

The second piece of figure sculpture in the architectural fragments assemblage studied is also 12th century. A stone head was found in demolition debris over the south wall of the refectory (B6) (A[2059] A<703>; period P1; H 192mm, W 160mm, D 100mm; Fig 32); it may perhaps have originally been part of the internal decoration of that building. The head was fashioned from Upper Greensand, probably Reigate stone and is that of a clean-shaven youth carved in the round. The intended viewpoint was frontal, as is shown by the incomplete finishing of the stone behind the jowls. The outline of the head is naturalistic but the face, in particular the nose, is relatively elongated with wide-set eyes and a low brow. The chin, now damaged, was originally prominent. The neatly arranged hair is shown schematically by uniform locks radiating from the crown, leaving the ears free. The small mouth frowns sharply and the undrilled eyeballs are prominent and appear to look upward. The chin is sharply undercut and is supported by a tongue of stone; and there is no certain evidence of a neck connecting the head to a body. The reverse of the head has sheared off a greater mass of stone; this was probably an

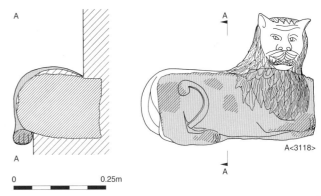

Fig 31 Sculpted lion A<3118> found reused in wall A[1572]: right – conjectural reconstruction of frontal view; left – sectional elevation (scale 1:10)

Fig 32 Sculpted stone head A<703> found in destruction debris (A[2059], period P1) over south wall of the refectory (B6) (scale c 1:2)

ashlared tail allowing the whole block to be set in an ashlared wall surface. If the face were isolated, it would probably have formed a label stop. The apparent absence of weathering (as opposed to abrasion occurring at the time of demolition) shows that the mask had an internal location, perhaps ornamenting the meeting of the label mouldings of arcade arches.

It is often supposed that such masks record the appearance of masons and others concerned in the construction of the church or other buildings of which they form part. The bland idealised nature of the face, however, may identify the individual as a saint or historic personage and it is worth commenting that St John the Evangelist was usually shown as a youthful clean-shaven figure (Wilson 1984, 204). The stylised nature of the head is perhaps more indicative of date than would be the case were this a carving in a rustic church. A marked increase in sculptural naturalism occurred in England during the period c 1150–80 (ibid, 181), which would place this head in the earlier part of the 12th-century time bracket.

The ceramic dating evidence for the majority of the land uses in period M4 is far from convincing. Since four out of six of the buildings assigned to this period (B3–B8) were not excavated but merely uncovered, and in some cases (B6 and B7) had their walls/foundations reduced, the lack or unreliability of the dating evidence is understandable. Where other land uses (OA2, OA3, D1, B8) benefited from full excavation, the quality and reliability of the ceramic dating is considerably enhanced. The exception is the cemetery soil (OA6) which produced a ceramic assemblage that ranged in date from the Late Saxon period to the 17th century. This degree of disturbance is not unexpected in a reworked deposit of this kind. The construction of the main cloister in stone probably took place in stages and the west and possibly south ranges, like the priory church, may have only been completed in the second half of the 12th century (period M5) rather than the first.

The ceramic assemblage for period M4 (discussed in detail in Chapter 7.5, 'Period M4, c 1100–50') consists entirely of fabrics commonly found throughout the London area, but the range is less varied than that found on City sites across the river. There are no East Anglian imports and imported wares are extremely rare, suggesting that 11th-century Southwark may have had well-established trade networks to the south-east of London which tended to dominate supply. Cooking pots or jars are overwhelmingly the predominant form in this period, as with 10th- to 12th-century assemblages throughout the London area. Kitchen wares are much more common than serving vessels (jugs and pitchers). The assemblage's domestic character seems entirely in keeping with the domestic nature of the areas excavated. Apart from one residual vessel, the pedestal lamp (<P32>, Fig 155), all other pottery of this period can be related to cooking, food preparation, serving beverages and possibly storage. There is nothing industrial nor is there any high-status pottery or a concentration of imported wares.

There are two structures, however, in the areas excavated worthy of particular comment. The independent lavabo or lavatorium was more common in Continental Europe and the relative scarcity of this building form in medieval Britain, particularly in the 12th century, adds further interest to the Bermondsey example (Godfrey 1952, 91; Bond 2001, 115–16, 124; Coppack 2006, 149–54). Coppack (2006, 149) considered that the detached laver standing in its own building first appears in the mid 12th century. There are a number of examples in England of the independent lavabo building standing in a cloister garth which date from the 12th and 13th centuries, but the 12th-century examples are primarily in the older Benedictine houses, such as Durham and Battle, and Battle's cell of St Nicholas in Exeter (Devon), and in Cluniac houses, such as

Lewes and Wenlock. (Bermondsey's own Benedictine 'daughter house' of Faversham is suggested to have had such a lavabo building in the cloister garth: Philp 1968, fig 4 opp 7.) The great fountain from Westminster Palace Yard (Westminster), as a virtual replica of the first phase lavabo at Wenlock, is a monastic lavabo in a lay context (G Coppack, pers comm; Coppack 1999, 40). Both the great abbey of Cluny and its daughter house La Charité-sur-Loire possessed free-standing lavabos of this type (Virey 1910, 236–7 and pl XI; Godfrey 1952, 92). The form of the Bermondsey lavabo remains ambiguous; the building is shown reconstructed as octagonal (Fig 21), like the Wenlock example (Chapter 4.2, 'Water supply and sanitation'; Fig 82; Fig 83). Given that the cloister itself is unlikely to have been built until the adjacent stone ranges were complete, the lavabo may be part of this final building phase or even a secondary addition; as such it may date to after c 1150 (period M5) rather than before (period M4).

The second structure is the potentially outstanding feature in this period. Although the evidence was extremely fragmented, the water pipe and external cistern suggest that the east part at least of the reredorter (B8) may have been used for bathing. A few English bathhouses are known from documentary sources, at Benedictine Abingdon Abbey (Oxfordshire) and Christchurch Cathedral Priory Canterbury (Kent), and at Cistercian Rievaulx Abbey (Yorkshire North Riding) (Fergusson and Harrison 1999, 127; Bond 2001, 101; Coppack 2006, 144–6). Although by the later 12th or 13th century bathing in monasteries was looked upon as a sensual indulgence, a return to the original intentions of the Benedictine Rule included a reassertion of the belief that baths were especially intended for the sick (Gilchrist 1995, 48; Bond 2001, 101). Bathhouses tend to be associated with the infirmary hall; at Rievaulx, for example, the bathhouse probably lay on the infirmary's south side, adjacent to the main drain and latrines (Fergusson and Harrison 1999, 110, fig 72, 120, 127; Bond 2001, 101). Bathhouses are well attested from Cluniac sites. The *Farfa customary* of c 1000 describes the 'bathroom' or bathhouse attached to the west end of the Cluny latrine block; it had 12 rooms each containing a wooden bathtub, but no dimensions are given (Lyne 1997, 39; Bond 2001, 119). The western end of the first reredorter range at Lewes has an enclosed room. The discovery of a slate slab with a faucet perforation outside the west wall of the room and a fragment of a Tournai marble double column base, possibly the support for a cistern, may be evidence for a bathhouse there (Lyne 1997, 38). At Thetford the 12th-century reredorter range also had a separate room at its west end (Raby and Reynolds 1979, plan; Lyne 1997, 39). The evidence certainly suggests a tradition of bathhouses at Cluniac establishments. However, the Lewes room measures internally c 8m by 6m (excluding the drain), and is rather larger than the Bermondsey east room which is internally c 6.8m by 7.6m, with roughly half of the area occupied by the drain.

In the medieval monastery, Christian notions of baptism and rebirth combined with medical ideas regarding bathing and healing (Gilchrist 1995, 47). The connection between water and healing became linked in popular medicine and religion. Healing cults centred upon holy wells were associated especially with female saints, such as that of St Milburge of Wenlock. Monastic medicine was also able to draw upon the classic tradition with the new availability, in the 11th and 12th century of Greek, Arab and Jewish medical texts. Benedictine abbeys, in particular, housed these texts in their libraries.

Bloodletting may have taken place in the monastic bathhouse. In large Benedictine monasteries, the practice of letting blood was carried out up to eight times a year, often outside the infirmary (Harvey 1993, 96–7). Excavation of the large infirmary complex at Augustinian Merton Priory recovered the remains of several buildings which might have acted as wash rooms or bloodletting houses: Building 7 between the reredorter and the infirmary hall, Building 10 south of the infirmary, and Building 12 on the east side of the infirmary hall (Miller and Saxby 2007, 53, fig 57, 61, 62, 69, fig 71, 92). At Bermondsey there is no archaeological evidence for a specific infirmary building before the creation of the infirmary complex in the second half of the 12th century (period M5; below, 3.3).

Both the lavabo and the possible Bermondsey bathhouse evidently fit into what would have been a fairly complex and extensive system of water management at the priory (Chapter 4.2, 'Water supply and sanitation').

3.3 Further expansion of the conventual buildings: the priory c 1150–c 1200 (period M5)

Documentary evidence

Henry II's charters from the 1150s and 1160s confirmed gifts from a number of individuals: the manor and church of Birling (Kent) given by Walchelin de Maminot, the manor of Camberwell (Surrey) given by William Earl of Gloucester, Bengeo church (Hertfordshire) given by Reginald de Taney, Warlingham manor and church (Surrey) given by Robert de Waterville, Fifield church (Essex) given by Matilda de Tany and Beddington church (Surrey) given by Sibil de Waterville and Ingelram de Funteines (*Mon Angl*, v, 89, 100–1). Little is known of the individual benefactions in the City of London which, by the end of the 13th century, made up a quarter of the priory's total taxable income (Chapter 4.4, 'The monastic economy'). One individual benefactor in the City of London was Peter, son of Henry fitz Ailwin, mayor of London in 1189–1212 and perhaps a descendent of Alwyn Childe; Peter's wife was buried in the priory church (Graham 1926, 165).

In general, however, Henry II (1154–89) seems to have shown little interest in Bermondsey. On 25 December 1154 the king's court convened at Bermondsey to consider the state of the kingdom and the expulsion of foreign persons (Gervase, i, 160). Henry II was obliged to choose an alternative as the council venue because his '*palatium regium*' at Westminster was

uninhabitable, having been sacked and burnt down when Matilda was ejected in 1141. The implication is that by this date the monastic premises were at least sufficiently complete to play host to the royal court. The occasion was also significant in that it was the first of many on which the priory served as a venue for large-scale assemblies and conventions (below, 3.4, 'Discussion'). All this suggests the priory was looking for donations from new benefactors as well as from the descendants of previous donors to supplement the grants obtained in its early years from the royal family and courtiers.

Much of the additional information relating to Bermondsey Priory during the second half of the 12th century derives from the annals (above, 3.1, 'Documentary evidence'). They largely consist of notes of the elections, deaths or departures of successive priors, which Graham (1926, 166) thought particularly unreliable, and of grants of property, many of which are corroborated in charter and other sources but whose dating cannot be trusted.

Archaeological evidence

Major developments took place within the monastic precinct (Fig 33), around at least part of which a wall was constructed (Fig 47). A completely new reredorter (B9) was built, with an integrated drainage system (D2) that skirted all the domestic buildings on the south side of the priory church (B3). The east arm of the church was modified and the chapel (B1) underwent extensive rebuilding and enlargement. An infirmary hall (B10) with its own latrine block (B11) was built on the east side of a second cloister (OA2).

The chapter house (B4), cloister walk (B5), cloister garth (OA5) and refectory (B6) were all retained in period M5 with no evidence for any changes.

Chapel (B1)

The apse superstructure of the chapel (B1, Fig 33) was torn down to make way for a much extended east end with a square termination. Mortared chalk foundations were butted on to the outsides of the existing apse foundations to form an extended chancel c 5m wide and c 19m long. There was no evidence for the vault or ceiling of the chapel (B1), which was now a long, narrow building of two rectangular cells.

A linear robber cut 2.25m south of the chapel terminated in a butt end to the east. It may have been the pentise wall to a covered passage between the chapel and courtyard (OA2), although the width of the robbing trench implies a fairly substantial foundation. The buttress conjectured at the south-east corner of the chapel in period M3 to match evidence for one at the north-east corner (Fig 14) could have restricted movement between the two-cell chapel, the newly constructed infirmary (B10) and courtyard (OA2); it would probably have been removed during the construction work in this period, or at least in the next when a new passage continued the line to the east (period M6; Fig 49). If buttressing was required, this could have been provided by an arched support or flying buttress.

Priory church (B3)

The north side of the presbytery was altered by the addition of a northern apsidal chapel to the north aisle (B3, Fig 33). This chapel was identified by Grimes as part of the 12th-century church (above, 3.2; Fig 23); he shows a roughly rectangular foundation but reconstructs an apsidal chapel internally and externally. The projecting chapel may have resembled the extant north chapel at St Benoît-sur-Loire, creating, in effect, a minor transept arm. The Loire example is thought to be 11th century in date (Conant 1959, 154–5). The 12th-century priory church of Lewes also had (rectangular) side chapels (Lyne 1997, 12, fig 2), as did Holy Trinity Priory Aldgate (Schofield and Lea 2005, 85).

A typestone Z<141> (CP2; Chapter 7.2) represents about one sixth of the circumference of a Reigate stone-cased round pier which was 1.61m wide, significantly wider than the 12th-century Taynton stone ?nave pier (period M4; Fig 25). *Ex situ* fragments show two basic types of scallop ornament were employed on the capitals of the ?nave arcade, of which the outstanding feature was the paper dart and slit ornament (Fig 71). A larger and rarer capital element suggests a rectilinear abacus on a round pier; it also employed the paper dart motif (Z<121>, Fig 71). The date of this phase is probably third quarter of the 12th century (ie period M5), rather than earlier. The rectilinear abacus elements probably do not represent a distinct capital form. It is more probable they represent local extensions of an otherwise round capital. Their purpose was probably to support the arcade arch minor order (Chapters 4.2, 'The 12th-century priory church', 7.2, 'Construction phase 1, c 1140–90 (periods M4 and M5): important stone groups from the 12th-century priory church (B3)'; Fig 71). Architectural elements probably or possibly associated with the church and dated to after c 1140 (CP1, c 1140–90) are discussed in Chapter 4.2; they include the intersecting triforium arcading (Chapters 4.2, 'The 12th-century priory church', 7.2 'Construction phase 1, c 1140–90 (periods M4 and M5): important stone groups from the 12th-century priory church (B3)'; Fig 73; Fig 130).

Three graves, two with stone linings (subgroups G[63], G[65]), excavated by Grimes outside the north wall of the church are assigned to this period, although the burials could have taken place at any time between the 12th and 14th centuries; the most westerly of the three graves is shown by Grimes as cut by a buttress of the later (period M8) north wall (Fig 23; cf Fig 33). (The whereabouts of any skeletal remains is not known.)

East range (B7)

In this period, M5, the new reredorter (B9) lay adjacent to the south end of the east range. As discussed in period M4, it is not clear from the archaeological evidence whether the east range was extended south in period M5 or existed in this form in period M4 (above, 3.2, 'Archaeological evidence'; Fig 21). The east range appears in this period to have been a building of (at least) nine bays. New piers, 0.8m further south, replaced two

piers at the south end of the period M4 building, giving a north–south dimension of c 4.10m to the new enlarged south bay. The east wall of the east range was possibly rebuilt, depending on the interpretation of this range in period M4, and extended south by the insertion of a shallow foundation, 1.32m wide. The two pier bases between the sixth and seventh bays of the east range (B7) survived *in situ* (Fig 34). These unmoulded octagonal bases, on the basis of technical similarities – distinctive tooling on Reigate stone – with an (unstratified) octagonal moulded base A<3067> and column shaft A<3164>, have been dated within the period c 1185–c 1210. The moulded base A<3067> and column shaft A<3164> would have fitted on the *in situ* bases. This could effectively place the whole of the east range (B7) in (architectural fragments) construction phase 2 (c 1190–c 1220; Chapter 7.2), given the very limited evidence available to us. The interpretation preferred here, however, is that the east range undercroft received a new vault in period M5, or possibly early in period M6.

The undercroft columns then were represented by base and shaft elements: the base occurred in moulded and *in situ* plain chamfered varieties (A<3067> and A[4439]); a shaft element was also recovered (A<3164>; Fig 35). The wall respond base (unmoulded; A[1567]) was also recorded *in situ*; it is simply half of the plain chamfered base. The moulded base retains a complex of setting-out lines and these were probably also used to allow the accurate positioning of the base. An arrow was cut into one side, presumably to allow the base to be correctly aligned over a tightly pulled marker string. The first drum of the shaft was held in place by a tenon secured in a mortice cut into the base. The simple proportions of the base are: width A = 1, the shaft B = 4/5, and the base height C = 1/4 of the width (Fig 35). The neo-attic base moulding dates it to c 1175–c 1200.

Machine clearance on site A in the southernmost part of the east range revealed not only base and pier fragments but also simple chamfered ribstones (A<3131>; CP2.1.1; not illustrated; Fig 3). The rib (if semicircular) was c 4.12m in span and probably derived from the east range undercroft vault. The rib resembles the undercroft of Boothby Pagnell manor house (Lincolnshire) which Wood (1965, pl xvi:a) dates c 1200.

The east range and reredorter buildings may have been directly linked via the first floor only.

Hall/lodgings (B8)

Extensive works took place within the ground floor of the former reredorter range (B8, Fig 33) in tandem with the completion, by c 1200, of the new reredorter (B9). Drain 1 was backfilled and replaced by a new stone-built drain (D2) and the east end of Building 8 extended to adjoin the south wall of new Building 10 (Fig 36). The extension was 2.8m wide and subdivided so that the north room (D) measured c 2m north–south and the south room (E) c 4m north–south. In the southern room, a hearth was installed in a central position along the west wall. The hearth comprised a slab of orange brickearth (c 2m x 1m), which incorporated large numbers of peg tiles set on edge and a fragment of Caen stone. The foundations to the extended

*Fig 33 Plan of principal archaeological features at sites in the study area,
c 1150–c 1200 (period M5) (scale 1:400; inset 1:2000)*

N

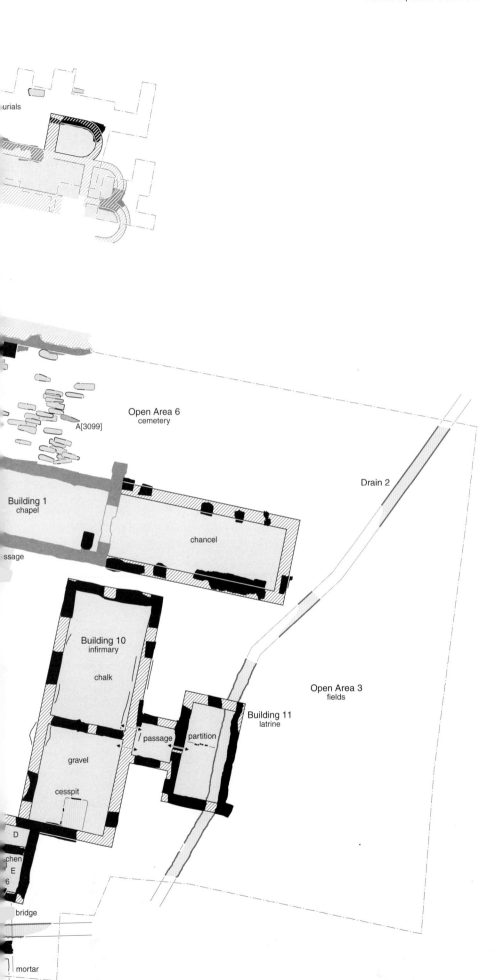

urials

Open Area 6
cemetery

A[3099]

Drain 2

Building 1
chapel

chancel

ssage

Building 10
infirmary

chalk

Open Area 3
fields

Building 11
latrine

passage   partition

gravel

cesspit

D

chen
E
6

bridge

mortar

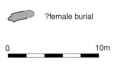
?female burial

0   10m

Fig 34 View of the pier bases between the sixth and seventh bays in the east range (B7, period M5), from the south (1.0m scale)

building included peg tiles and roofing slate, and a single fragment of plain-glazed 'Westminster' floor tile presumed to be intrusive.

Two fragmentary (west and south) wall foundations indicate some sort of structure adjacent to the south wall of Building 8, between the hall (room C) and Drain 2, and aligned with the drain. A large group of medieval pottery from a silt deposit A[4134] dumped outside and south of Building 8, within this structure, yielded 101 sherds from a minimum of 34 vessels, including a number of joining sherds and complete vessel profiles and dates to *c* 1140–*c* 1200. This suggests that the material had been cleared out over a short period. Shelly-sandy ware (SSW) and coarse London-type ware (LCOAR) are the chief fabrics represented, including 29 sherds from a cooking pot with thumbed rim in coarse London-type ware with shell inclusions (LCOAR SHEL; Fig 37, <P4>) and 12 sherds from a rounded jug with thumbed base and early style decoration (LCOAR EAS; Fig 37, <P5>). The only other fabric found is early medieval shell-tempered ware (EMSH), in use between *c* 1050 and *c* 1150. Cooking pots are the most common form in all fabrics (84% of the group by SC/85% ENV) suggesting that the assemblage came from a kitchen. The deposit could be interpreted, therefore, as representing a clear-out from room E Building 8 which had a hearth and could have served as a kitchen.

The silt dump also yielded a well-made key <S62> and a lead/tin seal with a gemstone setting of ?jet and a Latin legend which translates as 'I retain the secret' (<S47>, Fig 38; Fig 169; Chapter 7.7). The legend draws attention to the security of the contents of a document sealed with this stamp; it was presumably held by one of the senior members of the monastery and was possibly used as a counterseal for further security. The seal matrix (surely an accidental loss) may argue against an interpretation of the deposit as representing a clear-out from Building 8, in particular its kitchen. The location of the context between Building 8 and Drain 2 renders its origins ambiguous. The deposit could have resulted from the clearing out of Drain 1 prior to the changes in the building. It is also possible that it represents some early clearing of Drain 2 immediately to the south. The presence in the pottery assemblage of large numbers of joining sherds and complete vessel profiles, however, does suggest a clear-out from Building 8.

In room C of Building 8 two mortar floors were laid which then slumped into the underlying, now backfilled sewer (D1). A tile floor superseded the mortar surfaces and comprised peg tiles and small pieces of slate with ragstone rubble set in sand. In the centre of the room, and overlying the tiled floor, was a hearth made out of peg tiles set on edge, aligned east–west in a clay and mortar bedding; it stood proud of the surrounding tiled floor by *c* 100mm. The presence of a central hearth in this chamber suggests that this part of the building was a hall open to the roof, with a louvre opening allowing the smoke to escape.

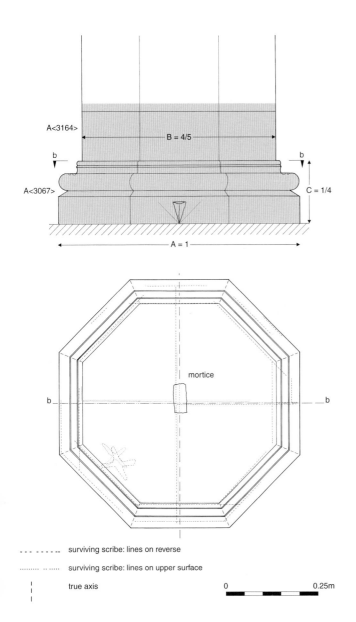

A<3164>

B = 4/5

b   b

A<3067>

C = 1/4

A = 1

mortice

b   b

- - - - - - -   surviving scribe: lines on reverse

....   surviving scribe: lines on upper surface

true axis

0   0.25m

Fig 35 Octagonal pier base A<3067> and column shaft A<3164>: upper –
elevation showing position marker; lower – plan showing completion marks and
corrected orientation lines (scale 1:10)

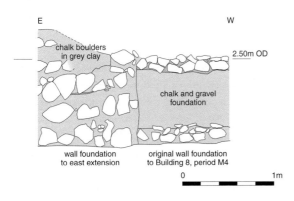

E   W

chalk boulders
in grey clay

2.50m OD

chalk and gravel
foundation

wall foundation
to east extension

original wall foundation
to Building 8, period M4

0   1m

Fig 36 North-facing elevation of south wall foundations of hall/lodgings (B8),
showing new extension to the east built in period M5 (scale 1:40)

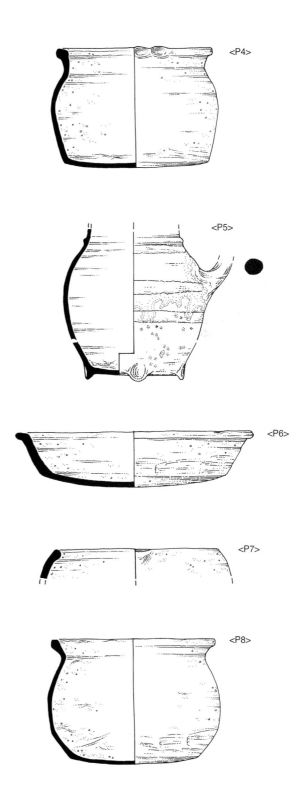

<P4>

<P5>

<P6>

<P7>

<P8>

Fig 37 Pottery from period M5: cooking pot <P4> in coarse London-type ware
with shell inclusions; rounded jug <P5> in coarse London-type ware with early
style decoration; flared bowl <P6> and a cooking pot <P7>, both in coarse
London-type ware with gritty inclusions; and cooking pot <P8> in south
Hertfordshire-type greyware (scale 1:4)

43

<S47>

Fig 38 Lead/tin seal with gemstone (?jet) setting <S47>, from a silt deposit outside Building 8 in period M5 (scale c 2:1)

The cistern on the north side of the building remained in use in the second half of the 12th century, suggesting that piped water continued to be supplied either to or via the narrow room B. The gravel surface A[1156] between the cistern and Building 8 yielded three sherds of shelly-sandy ware (SSW), with a date range of c 1140–c 1200.

Contemporary with the changes to the south end of Building 7 were some radical alterations to the western room, room A, of Building 8. The square base was robbed out and the ground floor of the building refurbished. A tiled floor was laid, at the same level as the tiled floor in the hall. It is not known whether the western room was receiled and had an upper floor or whether it was now open to the roof as was the hall room C on the other side of room B.

The pottery associated with the foundations and construction deposits of this phase of Building 8 dates largely to the 12th century, in particular the second half of the century. There is a relatively low proportion of 11th- to 12th-century handmade coarsewares, which are probably residual (a total of 4.6% by SC/13.9% ENV). London-type ware (LOND) and, to a lesser extent, coarse London-type ware (LCOAR) together account for 60.9% of all period M5 pottery from Building 8 by sherd count (55.6% ENV). This includes sherds from several jugs, many of which have an overall white slip under a green or clear glaze and only one of which is decorated in the early style (based on painted white slip designs) typical of the late 12th century. The other jug sherds in London-type ware, rather than coarse London-type ware (which was not made after c 1200), could conceivably come from later jug forms, although the general make-up of the contexts suggests a 12th-century date. Both medium-sized contexts date to c 1140–c 1200/20, giving a more reliable date than the smaller contexts.

The presence of several sherds from two vessels in a relatively uncommon gritty variant of coarse London-type ware (LCOAR GRIT) in A[4393] is of interest. The fabric is very coarse with frequent voids from leached-out calcareous

inclusions and abundant grit tempering, as well as irregular, ill-sorted, iron-stained, clear and white quartz and rare freshwater shell inclusions comparable to those in London-area greyware (LOGR), suggesting a similar clay source. Both vessels are oxidised throughout and are unglazed. A shallow flared bowl (Fig 37, <P6>) has a reconstructable profile and a cooking pot (Fig 37, <P7>), which is sooted externally, has an evenly rounded, shallow profile and an unusual, simple, inturned rim with a pouring lip, suggesting a more specialised function than was served by the standard form of cooking pot. Perhaps it was used as a pipkin with a single straight handle, now missing (cf Pearce et al 1985, fig 68 no. 352). Pipkins are not at all common in London-type wares before the early 13th century (ibid, 42). The presence of a probable example in a 12th-century fabric, therefore, is most interesting. The bowl has an externally thickened rim and a pronounced, convex or sagging base, with external knife-trimming (cf ibid, fig 72 nos 385, 388, 390).

The question of the function of Building 8 in period M5 is of great interest. The changes made are suggestive of the development of private quarters. The quarters are strongly reminiscent of a hall (room C) with perhaps an attached kitchen (in room E) and buttery or store (room D). Access via the bridge over Drain 2 would have meant that the kitchen was accessible from the south. It could be directly serviced, therefore, from a more public part of the monastery; it would not have been necessary to pass through the cloister in order to reach it. Given its proximity to the new infirmary range (B10 and B11), it is possible that in period M5 Building 8 became accommodation for the infirmarer.

Reredorter (B9)

A replacement, second, masonry reredorter (B9, Fig 33) was built at the south end of the extended east range (B7) at the end of the 12th century. The second reredorter (B9) was part of the expansion of the domestic buildings of the priory, which included the construction of the new infirmary range (B10 and B11). It was built on open ground to the south and west of the conventual buildings (OA4). The second reredorter was an east–west aligned building of six bays, 17.5m long and c 8.5m wide. The north part of the bay at the east end of the building was excavated, but the west end and most of the south part were either only partially recorded or beyond the excavation trench limits.

The second reredorter was constructed on a raft or platform of unbonded ragstones in a construction trench lined with timber (Fig 39). The exploratory excavation of a narrow trench through the construction deposits revealed the presence of a ?natural gully beneath the building, which may have necessitated the additional foundations (Fig 40). The standard chalk and gravel foundations used elsewhere for monastic foundations may have been thought too liable to erosion and collapse here. Deposits of crushed chalk and gravel were laid as levelling over the ragstone base, followed by a mortar bedding layer for the tiled floor A[4187].

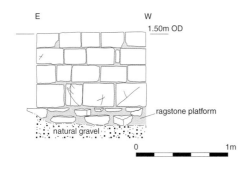

Fig 39 *North-facing elevation of wall of Building 9 in period M5, showing ragstone construction raft (scale 1:40)*

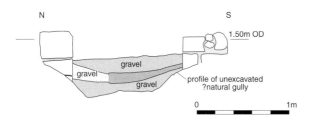

Fig 40 *West-facing section across east opening of Building 9 in period M5, showing ?natural gully beneath (scale 1:40)*

The floor of the reredorter was covered with large, unglazed floor tiles, which were between 284mm and 293mm square and 28–34mm thick (Fig 41). They were excavated in an area 5m east–west by 3.6m north–south at the east end of B9. The tiles were made from the same distinctive sandy clay (fabric type 2273) which was used to make the earliest roofing tile found at the priory. In London, roof tiles made from this clay date from the mid 12th to the early 13th centuries (Betts 1990, 221–3; Chapter 7.4). Unlike later floor tiles, the reredorter tiles from A[4187] were not cut to a bevel but had straight sides covered by moulding sand. None of them were glazed but some appeared to incorporate a thin, pale clay slip on their upper surface. The significance of the tiles lies in their early date. With the exception of a few Saxon tiles, probably used as flooring (Betts et al 1995), these unglazed

floor tiles and the incised examples (period M3; Chapter 7.4; Fig 149) are some of the earliest used in medieval Britain. The only other floor tiles of comparable date are the late 12th-century decorated relief tiles from St Albans Abbey, Hertfordshire (Eames 1992, 18–21), which are quite unlike the plain and incised Bermondsey examples.

The construction of Drain 2 was integral with that of Building 9; the large, plain floor tiles extended through the east opening into the base of Drain 2; the tiled base of Building 9 and the base of the drain (D2) were both at 1.55m OD. This was then a sub-basement, with no evidence for a ground floor. The flow of water in the first stone drain (D2) entered and left the reredorter range via central openings in the west and east walls of the building. The openings consisted of well-constructed arch responds built out of limestone and Reigate stone ashlar blocks (Fig 40).

The upper, latrine, floor of the second reredorter (B9) was supported by a central row of five circular piers, each with a diameter of c 1m. The piers were constructed out of large ragstones laid in rough courses, the gaps between being filled with pebbles and fragments of Reigate stone.

Infirmary (B10) and latrine (B11)

The infirmary (B10) and latrine (B11, Fig 33) were built over the earlier monastic boundary ditches (OA2). The infirmary lay parallel to and c 20m to the east of the east range (B7) and at right angles to the chapel (B1) and hall/lodgings (B8), creating a courtyard or second cloister. The hall was 24.65m long and 8.5m wide. The ground floor was subdivided internally by an east–west wall, which created a north room 13.50m long and a south room 10.20m long. The infirmary (B10) was constructed on levelling deposits over the earlier quarry pits (OA2, periods M3 and M4). The latest of these deposits A[1768], was dated c 1170–c 1220 by a sherd of early Rouen ware (ROUE) from northern France, part of a finely decorated whiteware jug with applied bosses in red clay or slip and ring-and-dot stamps.

A thin, compact chalk and mortar floor at 2.75m OD was located at the north end of Building 10 and extended 3.36m

Fig 41 *View of tiled floor in reredorter (B9), period M5, from the north-east (0.5m scale)*

north–south by 1.96m east–west. At the south end of the building, at 3.08m OD, a gravel surface abutted the building's south foundation. It was 2.53m north–south by 2.70m east–west and had been truncated by a large cesspit. The cesspit was 3.16m north–south by 1.83m east–west and at least 1.76m deep. A fill of the cesspit A[1389] was dated c 1080–c 1200 and included 17 sherds from an unglazed cooking pot in coarse London-type ware (LCOAR). It had a squared rim typical of contemporary shelly-sandy ware (SSW) forms (cf Pearce et al 1985, fig 67 no. 347). The same context also included 16 sherds from two cooking pots in early Surrey ware (ESUR). With the exception of two chicken bones, the animal bones from the cesspit were those of the major mammalian domesticates (Chapter 7.8).

A passage linked the infirmary (B10) to a latrine building (B11), to the east. Two successive floors were excavated within the passage, at approximately the same height as those in the adjacent infirmary. The floors were of crushed chalk and mortar and sloped down to the north, the first floor from 2.79m OD to 2.72m OD in the north. The floor surfaces in the infirmary (B10) were lower than in the other monastic buildings. The foundation offset level in the east range (B7) indicated a floor level up to 0.5m higher.

The latrine (B11, Fig 33) was a rectangular building, externally c 12m north–south by c 6.8m east–west. It was built over the former western boundary ditch (OA2). The new stone drain (D2) passed internally along the length of the building on its east side, and chutes would have emptied into

the drain (below, 'Stone-built drain (D2)'). Where the drain passed under the north and south walls of the latrine, the openings were faced with limestone ashlar blocks, upon which the arched drain culvert was carried. An external buttress was added against the south-east corner of the building. A worn mortar floor (at 2.6m OD) was punctuated by a line of seven stakeholes which divided the building laterally, forming a north room 4.3m long and a south room 5.6m long (Fig 42). The latrine (B11) was of comparable size with the infirmary latrine excavated at St Mary Spital (Tower Hamlets) (Thomas et al 1997, fig 32), which was c 4m wide and c 11m long.

Disuse of first monastic sewer (D1)

The disuse of Drain 1 appears to have taken place at the end of period M4 or the beginning of period M5. A deposit of lime A[4307] sealing the sewer and a backfill of the sewer A[4306] both contained pottery post-dating c 1140. A use fill A[4308] from Drain 1 under the west end of the first stone reredorter (B8) contained two sherds giving the complete profile of a cooking pot in south Hertfordshire-type greyware (SHER; Fig 37, <P8>) dating to the second half of the 12th or early 13th century. It may be that a section of the sewer was kept open to function as a cesspit, while the second stone reredorter (B9) was under construction in period M5. The animal bone (84 fragments) dumped within the drain was dominated by cattle and sheep.

Fig 42 Remains of the internal partition, represented by a line of stakeholes, within the infirmary latrine (B11, period M5), from the north-west (1.0m scale)

Stone-built drain (D2)

The construction of the new latrine buildings (reredorter B9 and infirmary latrine B11) and the disuse of the original monastic sewer (D1) required a new drain to be built. The new east–west drain (D2, Fig 33) was substantially built in stone. It ran along the south side of the monastic complex, south of the refectory (B6) and passing under the new reredorter (B9). One would expect such a sewer to have been a deliberately built leat that diverted a source of flowing water and the direction of flow in this section might be presumed to have been west to east, coming from the direction of the kitchens (Chapter 4.2, 'Water supply and sanitation'). However, the form of the new reredorter (B9) makes the flow of water in this drain section not straightforward. Moreover, having skirted the east end of what was now the hall/lodgings (B8), this south drain most likely connected with a north–south aligned length of drain to the north-east (also D2).

For a short stretch, the north–south aligned section occupied the exact position of the earlier western ?boundary ditch (periods M3 and M4; Fig 14; Fig 21), at this point also passing through the new infirmary latrine along its east side (B11). North of the north wall of the new infirmary latrine, the stone drain eventually became a simple (apparently uncovered) ditch, whose course changed direction, to the north-east, and continued beyond the north limits of site A (Fig 3). The new stone drain was recorded over a length of c 114m and its width was 1.3m. The form of a secondary (period M6; below, 3.4; Fig 49) east–west drain which would have emptied into Drain 2 near the south wall of later (period M6) Building 12 may suggest the north-east, north–south aligned, section of Drain 2 drained north to south, as had the earlier western ?boundary ditch (above, 3.2; Fig 21). How the north-east, north–south aligned, drain section worked with the south section is not clear; any junction lay outside the excavated area. It is possible the south section drained west–east, connected with the north-east section, and continued east or south, eventually connecting with the 'ancient drain' and 'moat' recorded by Buckler (Fig 78; Chapter 4.2, 'Water supply and sanitation').

The drain sides were constructed of mortared chalk blocks internally faced with ragstone and its base was a mixture of ragstone flags with some flint cobbles. In the north-east, north–south aligned, section of the drain, the base was compact gravel with chalk fragments and occasional ragstone cobbles. Where the drain (D2) ran beneath the infirmary latrine (B11) the base was at c 0.8m OD; elsewhere, the base was some 0.35m higher. A layer of ragstone had been laid in the deeper area, to consolidate the drain base in the relatively soft fills of the former boundary ditch (Fig 43). The masonry on the west side of the drain (D2) where the drain ran beneath the infirmary latrine (B11) was 0.6m wide and on the east side it was c 1m wide. There was probably some kind of superstructure on the west side of the drain, pierced by arched openings for cubicles, possibly with chutes at the base of each cubicle through the thickness of the wall into the drain (Fig 44). Given the

dimensions of the latrine (B11) there may have been four or perhaps five cubicles in total with chutes over the drain (D2). The unequal division of the latrine by a partition may indicate a north room with two cubicles and a south room with three.

A small bridge crossed the drain (D2) south of the hall/lodgings (B8, Fig 33) as indicated by two masonry pads on either side of the drain. The bridge would have afforded access from the south and west parts of the precinct to the hall/lodgings (B8) and infirmary range (B10, B11).

Fig 43 View of Drain 2 running under the infirmary latrine (B11, period M5), from the north-east (2.0m scales)

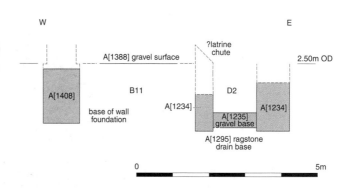

Fig 44 A reconstruction of a south-facing section through the infirmary latrine (B11) and associated drain (D2) in period M5 (scale 1:100)

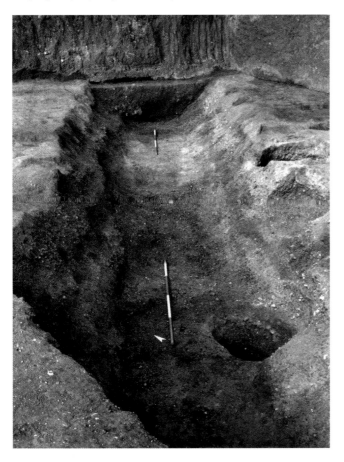

Fig 45 *View of Drain 2 crossing Open Area 3 in period M5, from the south-west (2.0m scales)*

The pottery from Drain 2 amounted to a total of 222 sherds from a minimum of 68 vessels. In the larger contexts there are several reconstructable vessel profiles and a number of complete pots, with relatively frequent joining sherds, suggesting that much of the pottery recovered from the drain was discarded over a relatively short period, with little subsequent disturbance. This is not the case where the drain, in the form of a ditch, crosses Open Area 3 (Fig 45). Here, similar quantities of 12th-century and early 17th-century pottery were found in the fills, suggesting that parts of the uncovered drain/ditch remained at least partially open until the post-medieval period.

The primary fill of the drain (D2) under the latrine (B11) yielded a large pottery assemblage A[1125] dated to *c* 1140– *c* 1200 and includes three complete, though fragmentary, vessels as well as two complete vessel profiles. One vessel is a complete *kugeltöpfe* or handled cooking pot in blue-grey or Paffrath-type ware (BLGR) (Fig 46, <P9>) of the kind imported from the Rhineland *c* 1040–*c* 1200 (Vince and Jenner 1991, 103–4). This is the only imported pottery recovered from the drain fills in period M5. There are also two complete early squat jugs in London-type ware (LOND), each one similar in form and detail, with overall green splash glaze, strap handle, collar rim and convex base (Fig 46, <P10>; cf Pearce et al 1985, 24, fig 46). A large rounded jar or cooking pot (Fig 46, <P11>) in coarse London-type ware with gritty inclusions (LCOAR GRIT) has the squared rim typical of contemporary shelly-sandy ware (SSW) cooking pots and vertical, applied, thumbed strips at intervals around the body. There are also sherds from at least

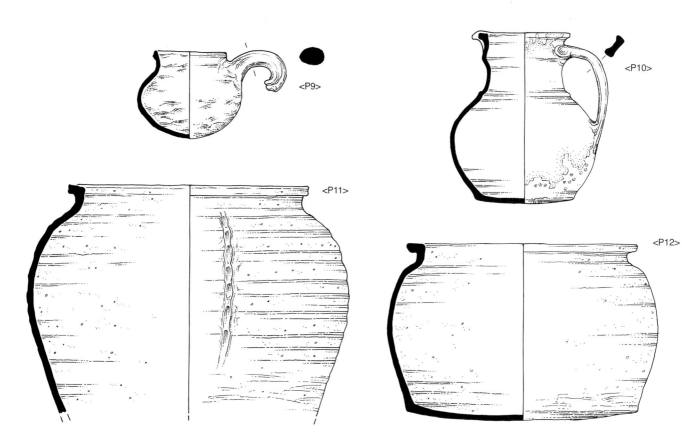

Fig 46 *Pottery from the primary fill A[1125] of Drain 2 in the infirmary latrine (B11), period M5: a handled cooking pot in blue-grey ware <P9>; London-type ware jug <P10>; coarse London-type ware with gritty inclusions cooking pot <P11>; and a shelly-sandy ware cooking pot <P12> (scale 1:4)*

ten shelly-sandy ware (SSW) cooking pots, including one with a complete profile (Fig 46, <P12>). The context includes a small amount of residual Late Saxon pottery (five sherds in all) but the remaining pottery could have been in contemporary use during the mid to late 12th century. A single sherd from the secondary fill of the drain A[1020], part of an early style coarse London-type ware (LCOAR EAS) jug with green glaze, has been dated to c 1140–c 1200.

A silt deposit A[517] which had accumulated to the south of Building 8 and subsequently been cut through by the construction trench for Drain 2 includes pottery typical of the 11th to late 12th century (EMFL, EMSS, ESUR, LCOAR, LSS, SSW), with a sizeable proportion of 11th- to 12th-century handmade coarsewares (61% SC/76% ENV). Much of this would have been residual by the time the drain was in use, and it is accordingly more fragmentary than the material from the primary fill A[1125].

Infirmary courtyard (OA2)

The construction of the new infirmary (B10) created an enclosed courtyard (OA2, Fig 33) surrounded by buildings on all four sides – a second or infirmary cloister. It extended 24.35m north–south (measured internally, excluding the north passage) by c 20m east–west. A passage and partially covered walkway bordered the courtyard on its north side (above, 'Chapel (B1)'). Otherwise, routes to and from the courtyard must have been through the ground floors of adjacent buildings. It is likely that there was at least one route from the main cloister via a passage through the east range, possibly through the north part of the range and connecting with the new courtyard passage. Twelve sherds of medieval pottery came from a silt deposit in Open Area 2. These included a sherd from

a London-type ware jug decorated in the north French-inspired Rouen style (LOND ROU), introduced c 1180. Most of the remaining pottery was typical of the 12th century and was a mixture of both cooking pots and jugs.

Open ground to the east and south-west of the conventual buildings (OA3 and OA4) and the precinct wall

In period M5 new conventual buildings began to encroach into former open land (OA3 and OA4). To the east, the boundary ditches (OA2) that had formerly defined the inner court or core of the priory in periods M3 and M4 were backfilled and the new infirmary latrine (B11) and associated new stone drain (D2) built over them. To the north of Building 11, the drain/ditch turned north-east and truncated the earlier field system. To the south of the refectory (B6) the land (OA4) was bisected by the new drain (D2).

A wall, located during excavation on site F, now enclosed parts of the monastic precinct for the first time (Fig 3; Fig 47). The excavated section of wall was aligned approximately east–west (east-south-east to west-north-west), c 13.2+m long and 1.20m wide. The foundations were the standard chalk and gravel and the superstructure, chalk rubble core with ragstone facing. The wall had survived to a height of 2.95m OD, not much below modern street level at c 3.2m OD. Precinct walls generally do not appear on rural monastic sites much before 1200 and St Saviour Bermondsey accords with the national pattern in this respect (Coppack 2006, 133–4).

The presence of the wall (Fig 47) at the corner of modern Bermondsey Street and Grange Road (Fig 3) confirms the line on Buckler's survey of the precinct at this point (Fig 78) and explains much of the later street plan. Post-medieval mapping (eg Rocque 1746; Fig 79) demonstrates that, until the 19th

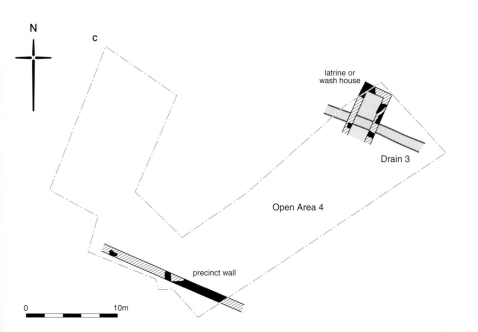
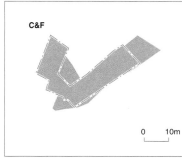

Fig 47 Plan of principal archaeological features at sites C and F, c 1150–c 1200 (period M5) (scale 1:400; inset 1:1500)

century, the street map in this part of Bermondsey was broadly that dictated by the western and southern boundaries of the medieval priory and home grange (Chapter 4.2, 'The precinct and home grange').

Stone-built drain (D3) and possible latrine or wash house

Another stone-built drain (D3) crossed Open Area 4 some 19m north of the precinct wall (Fig 47). The drain was 10.2+m long, continued east and west beyond the trench limits and shared the same alignment as the precinct wall (above). It was built of mortared chalk blocks, internally faced with ragstones. The base of the drain was a compact mixture of small chalk and ragstone fragments in a gravel and mortar matrix, which yielded a few sherds of early medieval sand- and shell-tempered ware (EMSS) dated to c 1000–c 1150. A small, square structure spanned the drain on arches of well-cut limestone voussoirs. The structure was 3.7m north–south by c 2m east–west and may have been a latrine or wash house, or possibly a conduit house.

It is possible that the stone-built Drain 3 continued east to connect with the 'ancient drain' (along the north side of Grange Walk) which ran west–east south of the claustral ranges and eventually joined a moat to the east, as shown by Buckler (Chapter 4.2, 'The precinct and home grange'; Fig 78).

Cemetery (OA6)

In period M5, c 50 individuals were buried in the cemetery (OA6, Fig 33) between the chapel (B1) and the priory church (B3). These occupied the same general area as the burials from the preceding period (M4) and, for the most part, completed the south ends of rows begun in that period. The distinction, however, between rows was already becoming less clear. The 50 individuals analysed from the cemetery were mainly adult males (34 males/?males: three young adults, 15 mature adults, nine old/elderly adults, seven defined only as adult), with 15 adults

of indeterminate sex and a single ?female, an elderly adult (the age and sex breakdown is detailed in Table 20; the ?female A[3099] is located on Fig 33).

The occurrence of congenital and developmental disorders in members of the population in this period is noteworthy. Of the two cases of spina bifida occulta, where the posterior arches of the sacrum are open from S1 to S5, one A[3200] comes from period M5. In A[3200], spina bifida occulta was associated with spondylolysis. Five period M5 burials out of a total of 14 individuals from the population as a whole had partial spina bifida occulta (below, 'Discussion', and Chapter 7.9, 'Congenital and developmental disorders'). Four of these six burials formed a cluster c 2.5m north of Building 1, with the other two a little further to the north (Fig 48). Two were adjacent in the same row, another was in the neighbouring row; the fourth was in the same row as the first two but 1.4m distant to the north, with the fifth in the same row but some distance to the north and the sixth to the north-west. It is possible that some form of related grouping was taking place when these individuals were buried; all occur in the east part of the burying area in period M5 (Fig 33). Of the six, four were mature adult males, one an elderly adult male and one (A[3099]) an elderly adult ?female.

One of the individuals buried in this period, A[2701], had suffered a fractured ribcage. His was one of five cases, the others all occurring in individuals from period M7. This elderly adult was also one of the four, possibly five, burials made in stone cists in this period; another burial had a chalk lining to the base of the grave (Table 5). Three of the stone cists lay close to the priory church (B3), and two north of the chapel (B1).

Discussion

The dating evidence for the construction of new buildings (and the alteration of existing buildings) is better for period M5 than for the first phase of the conventual buildings (periods M3 and M4). The dating framework for the period rests in particular on large pottery groups associated either with the use of the stone-built drain (D2) or with the change of use of the hall/lodgings (B8). The ceramics from the primary fill of Drain 2 inside the

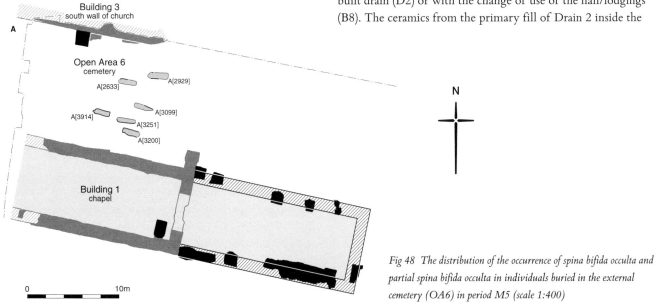

Fig 48 The distribution of the occurrence of spina bifida occulta and partial spina bifida occulta in individuals buried in the external cemetery (OA6) in period M5 (scale 1:400)

infirmary latrine and from a silt deposit outside the hall/lodgings (B8) give the date for this period as c 1140–c 1200. Since the construction of the drain is integral with that of the second reredorter (B9) and the infirmary latrine (B11), these buildings seem securely placed in the second half of the 12th century. The dating is refined by the construction of the new infirmary (B10) over quarry pits (OA2) finally backfilled between c 1170 and c 1220. This gives a construction date for the new infirmary range within the last quarter of the 12th century. A medium-sized pottery assemblage dated to c 1080–c 1200 from the use fills of a cesspit inside the infirmary (B10) may indicate that old ceramics were being used there. However, the more complete pots found in the drain (D2) fill would have been contemporary in the late 12th and early 13th century.

In period M5 the chapel (B1) was not only retained but dramatically extended. The apsidal chancel was replaced by a squared off chancel which was now of equal proportions to the nave. The existence of a free-standing chapel in such close proximity to the priory church and chapter house is unusual, but is known at Cluny in the 11th and 12th centuries (respectively, Cluny II and III: Conant 1968, plans 4–6) and at the great Norman monastery of Jumièges and at Lewes.

At Jumièges, the Carolingian church of St Pierre was the only church on the site until the consecration of the abbey church in 1067 (Aubertin 1973, 19). In the course of the 12th, 13th and 14th centuries, St Pierre became incorporated into the east cloister range. The church of St Pierre is believed to be part of the ancient monastery founded on the site by Duke William (Longue-Epée) of Normandy in AD 930–40 (ibid, 6). It had served, in AD 993, as the burial place for Ensulbert, the abbot of St Wandrille (Normandy). The church no doubt owed its continuance to this circumstance, as well as to its institution by a royal figure. The retention of the chapel at Bermondsey could perhaps be viewed in a similar light, whether it is identified as the 'new and beautiful church' of 1086, founded on a manor held by the king, or its history is more closely linked with that of the Anglo-Saxon minster (above, 3.1, 'Discussion').

An English example of an early chapel retained and included throughout the development of a monastic site can be found at the priory of St Pancras Lewes, foremost among the English Cluniac houses. There, what became the infirmary chapel was built in the late 11th century as the first monastic church, before the great 12th-century priory church (to the north) was consecrated or complete. It reused the site of the earlier Saxon church (Lyne 1997, 11–23).

A second reason for the chapel's retention and extension may have been that the priory church was incomplete, although the extension itself could have caused some limited disruption. The construction of a major church would always have been a project of some duration. Battle Abbey, begun in 1070/1 was completed within a relatively short time, in 1094 (Coad 2003, 10). The church of the Cluniac priory of St Milburge Wenlock begun after 1200 took over 40 years to complete (Pinnell 1999, 4). Documentary evidence for the construction of the great priory church at Lewes, begun in the 1140s, intimates that the west end of the church remained unfinished in 1268, although

work done at that time may have been as a result of damage caused during the Battle of Lewes in 1264. The dedication of the priory church in 1147 marked the beginning of construction work, not completion; work continued, it is argued, into the 13th century (Lyne 1997, 8, 13).

It is very likely, therefore, that the priory church of St Saviour was still under construction in the 1160s–70s (above, 3.2, 'Discussion'). A number of architectural elements which can be suggested as probably or possibly associated with the church and are dated after c 1140 are discussed in Chapter 4.2 ('The 12th-century priory church'). If the building programme lasted 40 years, not an unreasonable conjecture given a slower rate of benefactions in the 12th century and the paucity even of readily available building stone, the church would not have been completed before the 1180s. According to the annals, on 9 June 1206 the body of Peter, first prior of Bermondsey, was translated into the priory church. Two days later the 'matutinal' or morning altar, generally the altar located between the high altar and the choir, was dedicated in honour of the Virgin Mary and All Saints, the first recorded dedication (*Ann Monast*, iii, 450; Martin 1926, 210–11). These two events could suggest that an important stage had been reached, at least, and that the church was not finished until after c 1200, which implies a building programme of 50 or more years' duration.

If the chapel was still needed to accommodate the religious community, then it also had a new function, as the infirmary chapel. The development immediately to the south of the chapel (B1) of the new infirmary range (B10, B11) suggests that in this period the chapel almost certainly came to be used as the infirmary chapel. A doorway in the north wall of the infirmary (B10) and another in the south wall of the chapel chancel (B1) could have given ready access between the two. The passage identified south of the chapel could have continued east and the space between the two buildings covered over (Fig 33).

It has been suggested that the chapel nave was adapted as an infirmary hall and that the extended chancel alone served as the infirmary chapel (G Coppack, pers comm). Examples of this arrangement of (interconnecting) western hall and eastern chapel from the second half of the 12th century may be seen at Thetford and Castle Acre priories (Raby and Reynolds 1979, 12 and plan; Coad and Coppack 1998, 32). This view is supported by the tendency of Benedictine infirmaries to lie west–east, with the chapel expressed as an eastern extension, as at Christchurch Cathedral Priory Canterbury. The same arrangement can be seen elsewhere, at Augustinian Lesnes (Kent) and Cistercian Furness (Lancashire), and at the hospital of St Mary Chichester (Sussex) (Fergusson and Harrison 1999, 125; Miller and Saxby 2007, 124–5). However, perhaps the topography of this part of the inner court at Bermondsey, where two pre-existing buildings (B8 and in particular B1) were incorporated into the infirmary scheme, allied to the desire to utilise the existing ditch system for Drain 2 for the infirmary latrines, dictated a departure in plan? This arrangement is itself not without parallels: at Augustinian Merton Priory the infirmary chapel was located across the north end of the north–south aligned infirmary hall, while at St Augustine

Canterbury the chapel projected east from the south part of the north–south infirmary hall (Fergusson and Harrison 1999, 126; Miller and Saxby 2007, 124–5). Whatever the case, the infirmary range and associated buildings came to be neatly grouped around its own courtyard (OA2) by *c* 1200.

Although the surviving evidence for the infirmary latrine (B11) and associated drain (D2) was entirely at foundation level, the ground plan of the structures enables parallels to be drawn from other 12th- and 13th-century examples. The ground-floor latrine section of the first 11th-century (monastic) reredorter range at Lewes had the remains of four latrine chutes and space for ten cubicles in all (Lyne 1997, 33–6; Bond 2001, 120). This Lewes section was over twice the length and width of Bermondsey Building 11. At Lewes, openings in the longitudinal wall separating the main part of the building from the sewer gave on to chutes that discharged directly into the drain beneath. The wall openings were round-headed and dressed with limestone voussoirs. It is likely that the cubicles did not go through the thickness of the wall, but were more like recesses walled in behind. Those at Castle Acre did go through the wall and were boarded in behind. At Bermondsey, given the relative narrowness of the west wall of the drain (D2) inside the latrine (at 0.60m wide compared to the Lewes example at over 1m wide), it is probable that the cubicles at St Saviour Bermondsey went through a partition wall on the west side of the drain (Fig 44). Such an arrangement would imply that the Bermondsey latrine block was single storey, with cubicles only at ground level. With the base of the sewer some 0.35m lower inside the infirmary latrine than outside, despite the flushing action of water passing through the drain, solid matter may have accumulated and had to be dug out.

The exact function of the infirmary building (B10) remains ambiguous. The low floor levels to the ground floor suggest that this building was entered down short flights of stairs. The south part of the building with its gravel floor and cesspit may have been little more than a cellar or storage space. The larger north end of the building could have been a room used for eating and as the resort of day-patients and the walking convalescent. The operation of bloodletting, or the seyney, was very probably performed by the barber and usually took place outside the infirmary. Only those monks who were too ill to be moved might have undergone the ritual there. The infirmarer, however, was obliged to provide convalescent beds and a fortified diet for sick monks to whom the seyney had been prescribed (Harvey 1993, 96–7). This implies that some sort of parlour or resting place in the infirmary would have been necessary, over and above the long-term requirements of the permanently resident sick.

Both ends of the building could have had access to the latrines (B11) through the passage (Fig 33). The cesspit at basement level suggests that Building 10 had an upper floor served by a garderobe and chute in the south wall. There was no archaeological evidence for piers and a vault. The first-floor space above may have housed the infirmary dormitory for in-patients, with latrine provision for those who could not easily access the latrine cubicles on the ground floor. If this building

did function as the infirmary hall, then it was, at 24.65m by 8.5m, comparable in size to that at Merton Priory (*c* 30m by *c* 9.5m; Miller and Saxby 2007, 124–5), and considerably larger than the chapel nave (B1) (at least 16.9m by 6.9m).

A range of people would have frequented the infirmary. As well as sick monks and their attendants, there would of course have been the infirmarer, very probably a visiting physician and an apothecary, a barber, laundresses, and some permanent inhabitants of the infirmary, such as elderly religious and elderly non-religious males or females. The divisions in the infirmary (B10) and its latrine (B11) might indicate that separate social groups were being catered for inside the infirmary complex at St Saviour Bermondsey; however, as we have seen, there was only one passage (although this might have been partitioned) to the latrine building, and the south part of the infirmary may have been little more than a cellar or storage space. The use of latrines throughout the monastic complex at Benedictine Westminster Abbey was socially segregated (Harvey 1993, 78); there were separate latrines for the monks, for monastic officials and for lay brethren, as well as some latrines for common use.

The new reredorter (B9) at Bermondsey, serving the monks and attached to the east range, was a highly unusual design. In the majority of medieval monastic reredorters, the underlying drain or sewer was located on one side and flushed waste through and away, although some sites had particular problems and adopted unusual solutions to dispose of their waste (Bond 2001, 104–5, 119–22). The sub-basement of the new reredorter (B9), however, appears to have been designed as a single, large sewer or cess pool. Water could have flowed in and out of the reredorter through the single opposed openings but it is unlikely to have been very effective at flushing out the bulk of the waste from this rectangular structure with its central line of piers. Like most reredorters, the drain openings are at the base of the reredorter's east and west walls, and the reredorter's tiled floor extended into the drain. The openings, therefore, are not positioned to act as overflows. The drain (D2) – presumably with the aid of sluices, a head of water and/or gradient – could have achieved some limited flushing but possibly primarily served to maintain a certain level of water in the basement, thus keeping down the smell. The insertion of possible cutwaters in the next period, M6, does suggest that the piers needed protection, and so perhaps that there was some 'flow' (below, 3.4. 'Archaeological evidence', 'Reredorter (B9)'). There may of course have been other outlets, higher up in the south wall for example, for which no evidence has survived and these outlets may have enabled fluid waste to drain off. Perhaps the sub-basement functioned in both these ways, having a constant level of water ensured by the drain (D2) and sluices while the basement filled up with solid matter, and a number of overflow holes higher in the walls, in addition to the drain openings, to take off the liquid, when the level was too high or when the basement was due to be emptied.

Human excrement was a valuable commodity in the medieval period. Cesspits built of stone were common on house plots in London from the 14th century, for example (Schofield 1984, 76, 96). These permanent pits, like the new reredorter at

St Saviour Bermondsey, were designed to be periodically cleaned out by gong fermours. The mid 13th-century reredorter at Battle Abbey seems to have been built with similar methods in mind. Although the reredorter was outwardly of conventional design, the south or outer wall of the drain consisted of an arcade of large, round-headed arches, such that the sewer channel itself was not enclosed (Hare 1985, 33; Bond 2001, 122). Socket holes on the arch jambs indicate that the arched openings may have been shut off by sets of wooden gates. The site of Battle Abbey was on top of a narrow ridge without a regular water supply, hence the need for a reredorter built to a 'non-flushing' design. The sewer or drain would have allowed liquids to drain off and access to clear out the channel would have been available via the shuttered arcade on the drain's south side. Regular payments were recorded for scouring and cleaning out Battle's latrines.

Changes to and expansion of the priory buildings between c 1150 and 1200 signal a growth in the community in this period (M5). A further half-dozen grants to the house of manors and churches had been confirmed in the early years of the period by Henry II and these must indicate new sources of income (above, 'Documentary evidence'). St Saviour's status may have been raised by its choice as a venue for a meeting of the king's court in 1154. The new buildings involved a more elaborate system of water management and, for the first time, one at least of the principal drains (D2) was built in stone. If the 'ancient drain' recorded by Buckler and shown on Fig 81 was linked to Drain 3, in the south-west corner of the precinct (Fig 81, sites C and F), there is a strong likelihood that it too was stone built for at least some of its length.

The priory's latrine provision was greatly enhanced. The new reredorter (B9) with internal measurements of c 17.5m x 8.5m was not a large reredorter by comparison with some of its contemporaries. The first reredorter at Lewes was 28.8m long overall and 7.5m wide; at Castle Acre the first reredorter was nearly 30m long. Lewes provided a maximum of 18 closets at ground-floor level (over the whole length of the building; Bond 2001, 120) and there was sufficient space for at least 25 at Castle Acre, with 12 on the ground floor and the rest at dormitory level (Coad and Coppack 1998, 21, 31). Given the Bermondsey reredorter's design, however, and the fact that latrine chutes or holes did not have to be positioned in a single linear arrangement over a drain along one side of the building, it may have had two rows of cubicles on the first floor, so that as a building with six bays, it could have provided 12 latrines. Additional provision was also provided by a new latrine (B11), with perhaps four or five ground-floor cubicles. This latrine served the particular community of the infirmary, for which a whole new range of buildings was made available in the second half of the 12th century.

The large quantity of Roman brick, roof tile and combed box-flue tile found amongst the debris from the later robbing of Building 10 raises interesting questions concerning the building materials used for some of the early priory buildings. The majority of the Roman building material found was roof tile and brick, but other types of material such as *tessera*, tegula

mammata, some wall tile and voussoir tile were also present. A significant feature of the Roman tile assemblage is the almost total lack of curved imbrex roof tile. If the material represents demolition debris from former Roman buildings in Bermondsey then there should be a considerable number of such tiles, as they were used on roofs together with tegula. The almost complete absence of such tile suggests that certain types of Roman tile were selected from long-abandoned Roman structures elsewhere and brought on to the site for use in the priory buildings. Since imbrex tiles were curved, they were not suitable for reuse in walls hence their rarity. Roman ceramic building material may have been used extensively in the earliest masonry buildings at the priory. Ryan (1996, 18–20) has already drawn attention to the widespread reuse of Roman brick in post-Conquest parish churches and monastic buildings throughout Essex until the first half of the 12th century. In London, the reuse of Roman brick was common in buildings until the 13th century. At the church of St Nicholas Shambles (City of London) Roman tile is extensively used in the early construction periods (c 1050–c 1250) but is much less frequent in the same building after c 1340 (Betts 1997, 127–8). If some of the early priory buildings were (partly) constructed of reused Roman material, it might help to explain the paucity of structural stonework from St Saviour Bermondsey before c 1140. In particular, the early chapel (B1) could have been partially constructed using Roman building materials.

Small quantities of grey roofing slate were found among the domestic buildings of the priory complex. The slate was probably brought in from quarries in Cornwall and Devon, which were exporting slate on a large scale by the late 12th century (Betts 1990, 221). The presence of the slate indicates that at least one of the priory buildings had a slate roof, but the evidence is inconclusive as to which. Slate was also used for purposes other than roofing. The earliest fragment was used as a levelling course in the foundations of the east range (B7) in period M4. In the hall/lodgings (B8), slate was used in wall construction and as part of a tiled surface. Certainly the presence of large numbers of peg tiles suggests that most of the conventual buildings were roofed in ceramic tile rather than slate. The scarcity of slate suggests it can only have been used for a short period and on no more than one or two buildings.

The occurrence in the cemetery (OA6) of six individuals with spina bifida occulta or partial spina bifida occulta indicates that there *may* have been some grouping of burials (Fig 48). Of the six, five were adult males and one an adult ?female. The disorder is congenital.

The ceramic assemblage for period M5 (discussed in detail in Chapter 7.5, 'Period M5, c 1150–c 1200') continues the pattern seen in the preceding period (M4) whereby potteries in the London area and south-east supplied the bulk of the priory's ceramic needs. Glazed wheel-thrown pottery (coarse London-type ware (LCOAR)) is the most common type represented in late 12th- to early 13th-century contexts, as elsewhere in London. Wheel-thrown coarsewares are the other main type at this period, predominantly cooking pots in shelly-sandy ware (SSW), with 11th- to 12th-century handmade coarsewares present in some quantity. There are very few imported Continental ceramics. Cooking pots predominate generally, outnumbering jugs, and particularly in groups from the infirmary (B10) and outside the hall/lodgings (B8). The ceramic assemblage is again utilitarian in character.

The breakdown of kitchen wares indicates a continuation of cooking methods, and thus probably of dietary trends, into the 13th century. The range of forms is the same as in period M4: jar-shaped cooking pots, bowls and the handled cooking pot or *kugeltöpfe*, while the growing number of jugs shows the importance of communal serving at mealtimes. These serving vessels were functional and plain, rather than decorative.

The number of blue-grey ware (BLGR) *kugeltöpfe* in larger contexts dated to the 12th century is noteworthy, many of them substantially complete. Most are sooted externally from use. They are not large vessels and were undoubtedly made for specialised use, probably in the kitchen for heating components of meals or heating and serving individual portions. They are too small to hold a substantial meal, such as a potage or stew for several people, and their integral handle implies a usage akin to a modern saucepan which can be taken on and off the heat as required, rather than left to cook for some time. Alternatively, they might be used to ladle food. No obvious industrial or other recognisable residues have been found on the Bermondsey examples to suggest a usage other than culinary, although involvement with medicinal preparations for use in the infirmary cannot be ruled out. Blue-grey ware (BLGR) vessels were identified among the pottery assemblage at the hospital and priory of St Mary Spital and recovered from around the infirmary hall at Merton Priory; subsurface residue analysis of a vessel from Merton indicated the presence of fats/oil and cereal (?wheat) (Thomas et al 1997, 59; Miller and Saxby 2007, 55, 128).

There are no other ceramics at this date that can readily be associated with the specific functions either of the infirmary or with industrial processes, without embarking on a programme of residue analysis (as was done at Merton Priory: above; Miller and Saxby 2007, 218–19). In the main, the forms recovered are those in widespread use for cooking and serving and these are the functions they probably fulfilled in the early priory. As regards what may have been cooked, the relatively small number of vertebrate remains from this period comprised, with few exceptions, the ubiquitous major mammalian domesticates (Chapter 7.8; Table 18).

3.4 Modifications to the domestic conventual buildings: the priory *c* 1200–50 (period M6)

Documentary evidence

Much of the documentary material for the 13th century as a whole from sources such as the Patent Rolls, Close Rolls and other state papers concerns the relations of the priory with successive monarchs, including the appointment of new priors.

On 25 March 1227 Henry III inspected and confirmed Henry II's charter of legal immunities to Bermondsey, made in 1154–5 (*Cal Chart R*, i, 25). No other confirmations of the kind were issued during this period. In 1229, general letters of protection were issued to the prior and monks of Bermondsey, without time limit (*sine termino*) or further explanation (*Cal Pat R Hen III*, 1225–32, 275). Inasmuch as the monks were included with the prior, this safeguard was clearly unrelated to the prior's routine visits abroad and must have been concerned with the well-being of the house as a whole. A similar protection until the following Easter was given to numerous houses including Bermondsey on 17 August 1265 (*Cal Pat R Hen III*, 1258–66, 440), perhaps arising from the contest between the king and Simon de Montfort.

Henry's sympathy for religious houses generally did not always extend to their overseas affiliations. The French mother house of La Charité-sur-Loire continued to be active in its management role. On 10 June 1238, Henry III assented to the ordination by Prior Theobald of La Charité-sur-Loire, of Brother Guichard to be prior of Bermondsey, with a mandate *de intendendo* addressed to the priory tenants (*Cal Pat R Hen III*, 1232–47, 223). In due course the new prior would do fealty to the king, and was authorised to receive full possession of all the priory estates. On 1 January 1246, however, the constable of the Tower and the sheriffs of London were ordered to accompany the bailiffs of Surrey to Bermondsey to ensure that any money collected for the use of the abbot of Cluny against the king's prohibition and deposited in a chest or coffers (*in archa vel cofinis*) be sealed with the bailiff's seal, and the prior forbidden 'as he valued his English tenements' to move any of it without the king's knowledge (*Cal Close R*, 1242–7, 381).

It is the periods of crisis in the 13th century, however, arising from flooding, debt and incompetence which have attracted particular attention. From the 1230s onwards, the priory laboured under an ever-increasing burden of debt. When the prior of Bermondsey attended the chapter general at Cluny in 1238, he took a letter to the abbot of Cluny, as collector of a special papal subsidy, begging him to deal leniently with the poor house of Bermondsey. At about the same time, a delegate from a Cluniac visitation was ordered to return to Cluny from St Saviour Bermondsey in order to bring the deplorable conditions (unspecified), bordering on bankruptcy, of the priory before the chapter general for consideration and decision (Duckett 1888, ii, 194; Graham 1926, 166–7; *VCH* 1967, 69). Later reports indicate the insolvency of the house in the second half of the 13th century was partly owing to crises engendered by flooding and the consequent loss of revenue from lands, with a contributory factor said to be the alienation of priory lands and properties (Duckett 1890, 13–14, 16; below, 3.5, 'Documentary evidence'). The selling or leasing of lands by the head of a religious house to raise capital in the short-term exacerbated the problems for his successor.

Little direct evidence survives of the priory's leases and the handling of its tenants at this period, however. Prior Hugh in the early 13th century leased land in Bermondsey to his man,

John the cook (*Cat Anc Deeds*, iv, A7947). A dispute is recorded: on 13 December 1232 the justiciar Peter de Rivaux was called upon to repossess the priory of its mill at Querendon (Quarndon, Derbyshire), which was in the hands of the late earl of Chester at his death (*Cal Close R*, 1231–4, 173).

In 1208 the annals make the first reference to flooding of the Thames, by which the lands of Bermondsey were 'washed' (*mundate*) (*Ann Monast*, iii, 451). In 1230 repairs were being made: Bartholomew and John de Courtray were recorded as beginning to enclose one side of the breech of Rotherhithe, while John de Rokeford began to enclose the other side: *coeperunt includere terras de brecce de Retherhithe ex una parte, et dominus Johannes de Rokeford coepit ex altera parte* (ibid, 457). These appear to have been isolated incidents of no great severity, compared with what was to come at the end of the century and subsequently, though it is surprising that the annals make no reference to the great flood of 10 October 1253 when the Thames was reported as rising higher than ever it had before in the lifetime of contemporaries (*Liber Albus*, 502–3).

Notable occasions continued to take place at St Saviour Bermondsey, no doubt placing further strain on stretched resources. On 22 April 1250 the priory saw a great assembly of crusaders (*Chron Majora*, v, 102; *VCH* 1967, 75). The Benedictine chapter general of the province of Canterbury met there in 1249 and in 1258 the new bishop of Carlisle was consecrated there by the bishops of Salisbury and Bath (Graham 1926, 167; *VCH* 1967, 75). The monks of Bermondsey had sought exemption from subsidy in 1238, pleading that 'we have lately been burdened with fresh taxes due to the king, with the exactions of the papal legate Otho, and with heavy expenses of hospitality which we cannot reduce without scandal or commotion, since our house is set as a spectacle to the king and kingdom' (*Cluny*, 259; Graham 1929, 100). The heavy demands made on the priory's obligation to provide hospitality were in part owing to its location a short distance from the London to Dover road (Graham 1926, 167). The assizes were held there in 1241 and 1259 (*VCH* 1912, 18). Canterbury pilgrims as well as visitors from the Continent were no doubt frequent guests.

References to the fabric of the priory are still rare at this period. On 9 June 1206, according to the annals, the bishop of Carlisle translated the body of Peter, the first prior, to the priory church and two days later dedicated the morning altar in honour of the Blessed Virgin and All Saints (*Ann Monast*, iii, 450; above, 3.3, 'Discussion'). Mention is also made of the building by Prior Richard in 1213 of an almshouse or hospice (*eleemosynaria sive hospitale*) for converts and boys on the cellarer's ground against the priory wall. This was done in honour of St Thomas the martyr. The almoner was subsequently to pay the cellarer 10s 4d *per annum*, and, like the priory itself, the new hospice was to be exempt from episcopal authority (*Ann Monast*, iii, 452). A grant to the hospital is recorded at a somewhat earlier date when Agnes, sister of Thomas Becket, made an endowment of 10s rent to the 'hospital of St Mary Magdalene Bermondsey' from her property in the parish of Staining (City of London) (Manning and Bray 1804–14, i, 206). Henry III's benevolent attitude towards the priory is manifested

by his gift on 24 April 1234 of ten oaks from his forest of Essex to assist work in progress on the chapel of Holy Cross – *ad operationem capelle Sancti Crucis, quam construi facit* (*Cal Close R*, 1231–4, 409); such timbers may have been used for roofing. The chapel of St Cross was evidently being built to hold the miraculous rood which, according to the annals, had been found near the Thames in 1117 and the chapel indicates the priory's concern to attract pilgrims.

Archaeological evidence

Minor modifications were made to the hall/lodgings (B8): a fireplace and chimney were inserted in the south wall and a large assemblage of unwanted pottery was cleared from the building. The north range of the infirmary cloister was extended with a new building (B12). Building 11 ceased to function as a latrine, when the associated (internal) stone-built drain (D2) was blocked and partially backfilled (Fig 49). There was no evidence (surviving) for any change to the chapter house (B4), cloister walk (B5) and garth (OA5), refectory (B6), the east range (B7), the infirmary (B10), the courtyard (OA2) or in the open ground to the south-west of the conventual buildings (OA4) in the first half of the 13th century and all remained in use.

Chapel (B1)

There were three burials in the chapel chancel (B1, Fig 49). One A[3522] was an adult male of unknown age who had been buried in a cist or stone-lined grave. The lining consisted of squared and rough-hewn chalk blocks covered with a lime render. Another A[3596] was an adult female but the burial was very disturbed. The burial had a head niche, which consisted of two vertical blocks to either side of the head, with a flat central slab in the base. The third A[2527] was an adult of indeterminate sex, only the right leg and part of the left leg survived. The excavator noted a purple humic deposit under and over the legs of A[2527], perhaps the remains of clothing.

The chapel could have had a tiled floor at this time, composed of 'Westminster'-type tiles produced in the mid to late 13th century which were recovered in some quantity from later, demolition, contexts. However, the extensive remodelling of the chapel nave and chancel which took place in the next period would have required major repairs and/or the laying of a new floor and the residual material more likely derives from this, later, phase (below, 3.5, 'Archaeological evidence').

Priory church (B3)

There is no archaeological evidence for alterations to the priory church (B3, Fig 49) in period M6. From the architectural fragments assemblage, however, at least ten examples of the rib typestone A<3059> were allocated to this period or early in the next (CP3, c 1220–60; Fig 50). The size of the elements indicated a very large rib, even for a great church vault: the arch centre derived from the soffit and the 'bed convergence' is c 11m distant, although the curvature of the rib is barely perceptible to

Grimes

PCA

PCA

MOLA
site D

MOLA
site A

0   25m

north
transept

Building 3
priory church

south
transept

Open Area 5
cloister garth

Building 5
cloister

site of Building 4
chapter house

lavabo

south cloister walk

Building 6
refectory

passage

Building 7
east range

Oper
cou

Bui
hall/l

Open Area 4

Drain 2

Building 9
reredorter

chim

Drain 2

*Fig 49 Plan of principal archaeological features at sites in the study area,
c 1200–50 (period M6) (scale 1:400; inset 1:2000)*

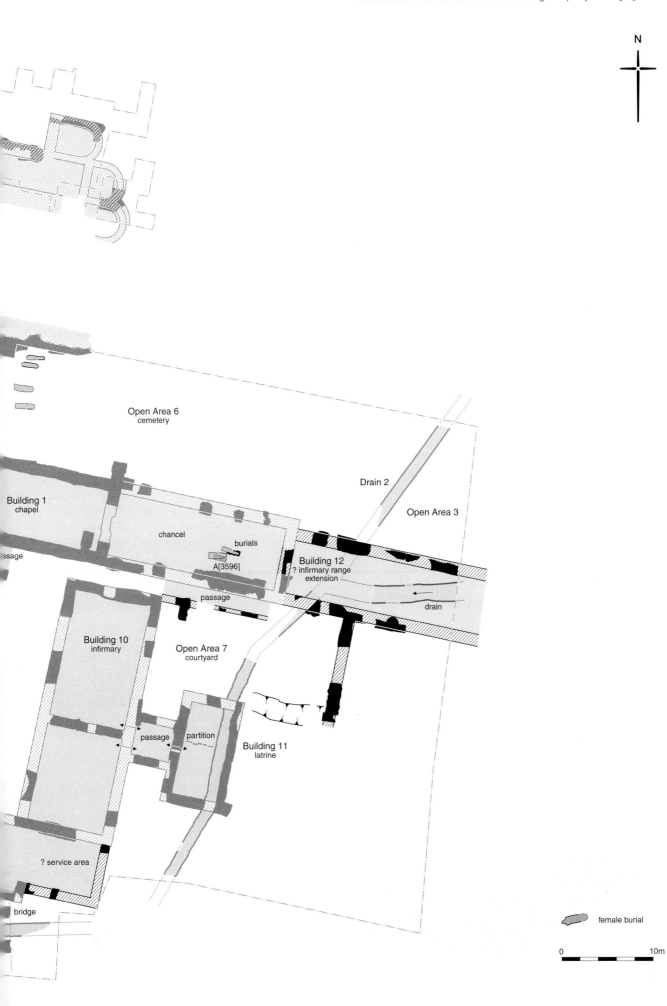

N

Open Area 6
cemetery

Drain 2

Open Area 3

Building 1
chapel

chancel

burials

A[3596]

ssage

Building 12
? infirmary range
extension

drain

passage

Building 10
infirmary

Open Area 7
courtyard

passage   partition

Building 11
latrine

? service area

bridge

female burial

0   10m

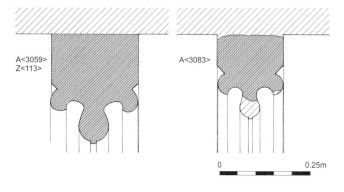

A<3059>
Z<113>

A<3083>

0   0.25m

Fig 50 Rib typestones (A<3059>, <Z113> and A<3083>) associated with the priory church (B3) and dating to period M6 (CP3, c 1220–60) (scale 1:10)

the eye. Such an element would have been suitable for the diagonal ribs of a quadripartite vault in the main vessel of the church. The masons perhaps used the same minutely curved ribs to create a variety of vault sizes, the mortar between the voussoirs accommodating any slight variations in arc.

Example A<3083> is a scaled down version of the A<3059> rib moulding (Fig 50). The axial termination was very likely the same, but at *c* 1.2m the arch centre was much smaller. The moulding is paralleled by the diagonal ribs of the nave aisles at Westminster Abbey, which are closely dated to 1260–9 (RCHM(E) 1924, 95). The rib form was very widespread and perhaps indicates Cistercian influence: similar ribs occur in the undercroft of the lay brothers' range at Cistercian Waverley Abbey (Surrey) (M Samuel, pers observation) and in Ireland at Corcomroe, Co Clare (*c* 1210) and Graiguenamanagh, Co Kilkenny (1210–30) (Stalley 1987, fig 74). The angular junction

between the fillet and the roll in the St Saviour Bermondsey example is indicative of an early date (Morris 1992, 14) and the rib is likely to have pre-dated the vault at Westminster.

The presence of these typestones suggests some changes took place to the vaulting of the priory church in the period before 1260. The size of the elements implies that it was parts of the nave itself and a nave aisle that may have undergone alteration.

Hall/lodgings (B8)

The hall/lodgings (B8) – postulated as possibly the infirmarer's own lodging – were extended eastwards by 7.0m, so that the east end of the building shared the same alignment as the east wall of infirmary Building 10 (Fig 49). The south wall of the extension was not in line with the original south wall, perhaps because of the proximity of the drain (D2) to the south, making the east extension of Building 8 5.5m north–south. The east wall of the former hall (period M5; Fig 33) was removed apparently and a large chimney inserted in the south wall of the enlarged room (Fig 51). The chimney was 2.5m wide and projected 0.7m from the south wall of Building 8. The drip-moulded base of a round chimney pot A<3137>, found reused in a later drain, has two mortices, perhaps for metal tenons for securing the bottom course of the chimney shaft. The diameter of the chimney pot was 0.65m and it was badly weathered, indicating that the building it adorned had stood for many years. Such chimney pots did not appear until the middle of the 12th century (Wood 1965, 281) and the moulding on the Bermondsey example indicates a date of *c* 1190–*c* 1220, in good agreement with the period M6 alterations to Building 8.

Fig 51 View of chimney foundations built against the south wall of the hall/lodgings (B8) in period M6, from the south-west (1.0m scale)

A tiled hearth 1.0m east–west by 0.65m north–south occupied the fireplace. The tiles, at 3.22m OD, were laid on edge in a north–south alignment and set in a lime mortar. Associated with the hearth at 3.29m OD was a compacted mortar floor, which extended 6.15m north–south by 4.5m east–west and overlay the robbed foundation to the former east wall.

The construction trench for the chimney foundation was 1.2m wider than the foundation itself. The chimney construction trench had been backfilled with large quantities of dumped pottery, animal bone and waste building material. The upper 50mm of backfill was excavated separately as A[1121], to avoid possible contamination of the assemblage. The remainder of the backfill was excavated as A[1122] and yielded a very large pottery group (619 sherds/58 ENV/9292g/6.09 EVEs) which was fully quantified, with weight and EVEs recorded. Sherd count and ENV alone were recorded for A[1121]. Figures derived from the fully quantified record are given here for A[1122], with the proviso that for the backfill as a whole (contexts A[1121] plus A[1122]) the figures are incomplete.

The discarded pottery from the chimney foundation dates to c 1140–c 1200 and consists predominantly of wheel-thrown coarsewares in use during this period, particularly shelly-sandy ware (SSW) (65.6% SC/54.8% ENV/68.4% Wt/57.5% EVEs). Interestingly, with such a high proportion of shelly-sandy ware (437 sherds/46 ENV for all pottery from Building 8; 410 sherds/34 ENV/6357g/3.50 EVEs in A[1122]) there is no south Hertfordshire-type greyware (SHER), which provided the other main contemporary source of wheel-thrown coarsewares in the City, principally for use in the kitchen. There are two complete, though fragmented SSW cooking pots in A[1122], as well as several rims and bases (Fig 52, <P13>–<P15>) and part of a concave-sided bowl (Fig 52, <P16>), sooted externally. One

cooking pot in A[1122] has at least one horizontal band of rouletting around the shoulder, an unusual decorative technique for SSW, which is generally embellished, if at all, with applied thumbed strips for strengthening. There is also a relatively high proportion of 11th- to 12th-century handmade coarsewares (EMSH, ESUR; 19.8% SC/10.7% ENV of all pottery; 20% Wt/13% EVEs of A[1122]) largely accounted for by 125 sherds of early Surrey ware (ESUR; date range c 1050–c 1150) in A[1122] from two cooking pots, one of which can be reconstructed as complete.

Both London-type ware (LOND) and coarse London-type ware (LCOAR) occur, as well as sherds from four cooking pots in the latter with shell inclusions including one base sherd (from A[1122]) with traces of glaze inside, an unusual feature for this fabric. All London-type wares are found in forms and styles of decoration typical of the late 12th century, together accounting for 9.9% by sherd count of all period M6 pottery from Building 8 or 25% ENV (6.6% Wt/2.5% EVEs of A[1122]). There are also 27 sherds from four *kugeltöpfe* or handled cooking pots in blue-grey ware (BLGR; date range c 1050–c 1200), one of which, in A[1122], is complete. These represent the only imported pottery from Building 8 during this period (4.2% SC/6% ENV of all pottery; 4.7% Wt/25% EVEs from A[1122]).

The animal bone group from the chimney construction backfill A[1122] was largely composed of unidentifiable fragments, indicative of a high level of redeposition (Chapter 7.8). It is, however, clearly dominated by sheep/goat and pig. In both this assemblage and another from a robber cut, the domesticate birds and a wide range of game species are represented, at a low level, with red and fallow deer, hare, rabbit, teal and partridge. The great diversity of species found identifies the assemblages as waste from a high-status diet.

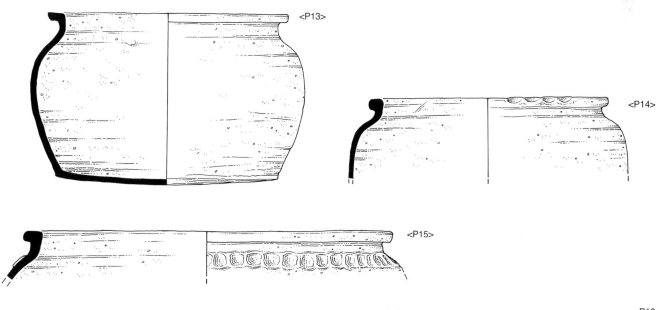

Fig 52 Shelly-sandy ware cooking pots <P13>–<P15> and bowl <P16>, all from the construction backfill around the chimney in Building 8, period M6 (scale 1:4)

Reredorter (B9)

A stretch of wall 4.3m long and 0.7m wide was inserted into the reredorter (B9) sub-basement floor between the eastern opening and the easternmost pier base (Fig 49). The masonry consisted of ragstone blocks mortared with hard orange mortar. The wall described an open V shape, enclosing the pier base and with its apex pointing east towards the drain opening. Behind the inserted wall was a dumped deposit of chalk, mortar and gravel, which was thicker around the pier base, where it also contained a few ragstones. At the west end of the reredorter, and occupying a similar position between the westernmost pier base and the west opening, was a surviving stub of masonry 1.26m long and 0.55m wide, interpreted as the counterpart of the V at the east end. There is no direct dating for these insertions. If they were intended to function as cutwaters, they must have been contemporary with an open and functioning drain (D2). The normal direction of flow in the drain itself prior to this is *presumed* to have been west to east, but there is no direct evidence (Chapter 4.2, 'Water supply and sanitation'); and indeed the flow in the rectangular reredorter with its central line of piers would have been considerably hampered (above, 3.3, 'Discussion'). Does the east V suggest the reredorter could also be flushed or filled from the east or would this east wall and infill have buttressed and protected the pier from water flowing in either direction? Maybe the piers in the reredorter (B9) were being undermined, aggravated in this period by episodes of flooding (above, 'Documentary evidence').

These masonry alterations could suggest problems with the drain and water management system at a relatively early stage after the construction of the second reredorter. The blocking of the drain (D2) at either end of the infirmary latrine (B11) towards the end of period M6 (below) indicates that water ceased to flow through the drain (D2) in the north-east, north–south aligned, section of its course. The reredorter (B9) could have continued in use as latrine and sewer (Chapter 4.2, 'Water supply and sanitation'; for its robbing, Chapter 5.2, 'Monastic buildings completely or largely demolished').

Infirmary latrine (B11) and stone-built drain (D2)

Towards the end of period M6, the drain (D2) under the infirmary latrine (B11) was backfilled with mortar and fragments of chalk, Reigate stone and ragstone. The arched culverts were blocked up with large mortared chalk and ragstone blocks. Building 11 must then have ceased to function as a latrine, following these major alterations to Drain 2.

? Infirmary range extension (B12)

A new building (B12, Fig 49) was constructed adjoining the east end of the chapel (B1) and this extension is thought to be possibly associated with the main north–south infirmary range to the south-west. It was aligned east–west, 6.0m wide and at least 18.25m long (it continued beyond the east limits of excavation). The chalk and gravel foundations of the south wall were carried over the stone-built drain (D2) on arches faced with dressed chalk voussoirs. An east–west drain, *c* 9+m long and 1.95m wide, lay under the floor. This drain was up to 0.55m deep and the base dropped by 200mm from east to west; it probably emptied into Drain 2 near the south wall of the building. There is no ceramic dating for Building 12 other than by inference from the disuse date of the underfloor drain (dated *c* 1230–*c* 1400 by two pottery sherds) and from the building's contemporaneity with the north-east part of Drain 2, in use throughout most of period M6 (below, 'Discussion').

Material from the robbing of the south wall of the ? infirmary range extension (B12) in period M7 suggests that the building had in the mid to late 13th century a decorated tiled floor, comprising plain and decorated 'Westminster' tile. The function of Building 12 is uncertain and the evidence only fragmentary, but it seems reasonable to assume, given its location, that it was associated in some way with the infirmary, and a decorated tiled floor is suggestive of status. Another possible linked building immediately to the south is described below ('Courtyard (OA7)').

Open ground to the east of the conventual buildings (OA3)

In periods M5 and M6 the open land (OA3) to the east of the chapel (B1) began to be encroached upon by the gradual spread eastwards of the monastic buildings (Fig 49). It is not known whether there were outlying buildings in the eastern part of the precinct in this period.

Cemetery (OA6)

Five additional interments were made in the cemetery (OA6) in period M6 (Fig 49). Two of these were buried over the chalk-lined graves from period M4 (Fig 86). These individuals were all adult males: two were elderly, 46 years old or more, two were mature adults, between 26 and 45 years old, while one was a young adult aged between 16 and 25 years (the age and sex breakdown is detailed in Table 20). One skeleton A[2692], a mature adult, had periosteal bone formations on his ribs; a second case was identified (also in OA6) in period M7. It is possible that these lesions may indicate tuberculosis (Chapters 4.3, 'Demography and health of the burial population', 7.9, 'Infectious disease', 'Non-specific infections').

Courtyard (OA7)

A new courtyard area (OA7, Fig 49) was created by the construction of new buildings in period M6. It was defined by the infirmary latrine (B11) to the south, to the west by the infirmary (B10) and to the north, by the uninterrupted line of the chapel and chancel (B1) and new ? infirmary range extension (B12). South of the chancel (B1) and abutting the north-east corner of Building 10, a narrow foundation represented the south wall of a gallery or covered passage. This passage may have formed a continuation of the passage on the north side of the large courtyard (OA2) to the west of the infirmary; if so it is likely that the south buttress of the chapel was modified to allow access between the passages.

A north–south wall, contiguous with the south wall of the ? infirmary range extension (B12) and at right angles to it, may have been evidence for another building east of the infirmary latrine (B11). The remains were extremely fragmentary owing to the presence of extensive modern concrete foundations and no associated internal surfaces were found which might render an interpretation more certain.

An east–west wall, 8.7m long (represented only by later robbing trenches), abutted the north-east corner of the infirmary latrine (B11). Its relationship with the north–south wall described above is not known, but it seems probable that the new area (OA7) was an enclosed court accessible only via the passage on the north side or through the infirmary (B10).

Discussion

The documentary sources for the period suggest the beginnings of what would be spiralling debt and a time of financial crisis, while the archaeological evidence shows continuing, though rather modest, expansion of the monastery buildings. More than a century after the foundation and the first flush of construction, patronage and money for building campaigns were more difficult to find.

The overwhelming message in the documentary sources for St Saviour Bermondsey is that this is the period when the priory began to slide into severe financial troubles, starting from around 1230. These troubles were aggravated by natural disaster in the form of repeated local flooding throughout the 13th century, which would have had a heavy impact on the priory's meadow and pasture (Chapter 4.2, 'The precinct and home grange'). In 1238, the priory is referred to as the 'poor' house of Bermondsey and said to be on the verge of bankruptcy by members of the Cluniac visitation. However, the sources do refer to two new structures: the hospice on the cellarer's ground against the priory wall in 1213, the construction of which may argue for the priory church itself being complete by that date; and the chapel of the Holy Cross in 1234, implying a desire to accommodate, and maximise revenue from, pilgrims.

The archaeological evidence does not indicate any changes to the east end of the priory church (B3) but evidence from the architectural fragments suggests that large vaults were under construction somewhere among the priory buildings in this period. It is possible that the west end of the church was still undergoing completion c 1200 (period M5; above, 3.3, 'Discussion'). The chapel of the Holy Cross, referred to in the documentary sources as under construction in 1234 (Cal Close R, 1231–4, 409), may well have been located in one of the nave aisles and the rib typestones allocated to this period could be associated with the chapel construction. There was considerable evidence for a very elaborate columnar structure of Purbeck marble in the 13th century (Chapter 7.2, 'Construction phase 3, c 1220–60 (periods M6 and beginning of M7)'). Architectural fragments recorded in Buckler's drawings (BL, Add MS 24433, fos 114–15) bear this out and additional fragments of this sort

have recently been found on PCA excavations (M Samuel, pers observation, courtesy of PCA). One possibility is the chapel of St Cross; also, a new chancel was constructed for the chapel (B1) in period M7 (c 1250–c 1330).

Dated to the early 13th century and from an altar or processional cross is the copper-alloy figure of Christ crucified, decorated with champlevé enamel and probably made at Limoges (Haute-Vienne) in France, which was found in a later period (M9; Fig 98, <S25>).

The archaeological evidence does demonstrate other building works in this period, namely in the infirmary area, in the form of the ? infirmary range extension (B12), the putative building to its south and alterations to the hall/lodgings (B8). The infirmary buildings were extended in the first half of the 13th century (M6) by the addition of Building 12. The true size and function of the building is not entirely clear, but the presence of an underfloor drain suggests that at least part of the ground floor was devoted to service areas. Part of the building was apparently tiled with 'Westminster'-type tiles in the mid to later 13th century, suggesting that it may have incorporated a hall in periods M6 and M7. To the south, the presence of a major wall may indicate another infirmary building, whose alignment is not known owing to the fragmentary nature of the evidence.

The possible infirmarer's lodging (B8) underwent further expansion. The hall was enlarged and improved with the addition of a new chimney, eliminating the smoky central hearth. The extension of the building east may have allowed the former offices (kitchen and ?store) to be retained in some form.

The large pottery group from the chimney construction trench outside the hall/lodgings (B8) seems most likely to have come from inside the building, given the number of complete profiles and joining sherds (discussed in detail in Chapter 7.5, 'Period M6, c 1200–50'). The group is essentially 12th century in composition and the ware breakdown is very similar to that in period M5. The great majority of the vessels are cooking pots and most of the more complete examples show signs of heating and external sooting. Jugs are far less common in the period M6 pottery and relatively few are decorated. Although cooking pots are subject to much heavier use and probably had a shorter life expectancy, the presence of so many strongly suggests that the pottery found in association with the construction of the chimney was derived from a kitchen. Unglazed, handmade and wheel-thrown coarsewares predominate as the favoured fabrics for these forms, although the blue-grey ware (BLGR) kugeltöpfe provide evidence for a more specialised cooking process. These handled vessels are smaller, with an evenly rounded profile which would make them difficult to stand on a flat surface. The form has more in common with a modern milk pan, designed to heat small quantities of food, such as sauces, as separate elements of a meal. Although kugeltöpfe are relatively common throughout the London area at this date, the presence of several in debris which appears to have been cleared out from a kitchen may indicate the adoption of more refined culinary techniques and diet; their presence in the pottery assemblage from period M5 has already been commented upon (above, 3.3, 'Discussion').

Both the pottery and animal bone assemblages suggest that the diet and cooking practices of the inhabitant(s) of Building 8 were becoming more sophisticated. Beef, mutton, pork, venison, hare, rabbit and game birds were being consumed and the fragments of blue-grey ware (BLGR) *kugeltöpfe* discarded outside the building are indicative of more specialised heating and/or serving practices.

This period, M6, then witnessed some limited expansion of the domestic and functional buildings of the priory, principally in the form of modifications and extensions to the (?infirmarer's) hall/lodgings (B8) and infirmary range (B12, OA7).

3.5 Changes around the infirmary courtyard: the priory *c* 1250–*c* 1330 (period M7)

Documentary evidence

The concerns apparent in the first half of the 13th century are also evident in the second half and into the 14th century. The priory's relations with successive kings loomed large in the documents and major concerns were the appointment of new priors and the management of priory estates during vacancies and during periods of crisis.

The issue of the management of the priory during vacancies seems often to have been a vexed one. It was royal practice to farm out the management of priory estates and the results were not always an unqualified success. On 13 May 1261 Geoffrey of Northampton, into whose hands Wenlock Priory had been committed during its last vacancy, was instructed to pay the prior of Bermondsey 20 marks in damages done during his tenure, on pain of a levy on his lands and chattels (*Cal Close R*, 1259–60, 477). On 5 August 1261, following the appointment of Gilbert de Bussa as prior, Richard Oysell, guardian of Bermondsey was instructed to give him seisin of the temporalities (*Cal Pat R Hen III*, 1258–66, 171). On 30 January 1266 Thomas de Rowell, king's clerk, was given the keeping of the priory during the king's pleasure, answering for its income at the exchequer (ibid, 542), but he was called upon to restore the temporalities to John de Chartres the new prior as soon as 5 February of that year (ibid, 544; *Cal Close R*, 1264–8, 172). On 13 December 1297 William de Carleton, keeper of the priory of Bermondsey, was called upon to restore the priory temporalities to Peter de Sancto Simphoriano, a monk of La Charité-sur-Loire, who had been preferred as prior (*Cal Pat R*, 1292–1301, 325).

The appointment of external officials to manage the priory estates could cause some friction with local, permanent officials. On 22 January 1276 the sheriff of Surrey, escheator in that county, was ordered not to interfere with the temporalities of the house of Bermondsey, which had been committed to the prior of Wenlock during the king's pleasure on account of its inability to meet its debts (*Cal Fine R*, i, [p] 64; *VCH* 1967, 69). On 27 November 1298 the royal escheator beyond Trent was

ordered to restore the temporalities of Bermondsey to Henry, former prior of St Helens, Isle of Wight, who had been appointed in succession to Prior Peter (*Cal Pat R*, 1292–1301, 386). In the 1270s priors or subpriors were called upon to pay a fine of £20 to the king for the restoration of their temporalities (*Cal Pat R Hen III*, 1266–72, 714; *Cal Fine R*, i, [p] 117; *Cal Pat R Edw I*, 1272–81, 325).

A royal writ of 22 September 1284 refers to the king's taking of Bermondsey under his protection at the insistence of Robert Prior of Coulanges and vicar-general of the priory of La Charité-sur-Loire. The king granted safe conduct until Christmas for Robert to visit and correct the excesses of the house (*Cal Pat R Edw I*, 1281–92, 134). This seems to have been a special case and by 5 October 1285 Prior Robert was given the custody of the priory during its vacancy (*Cal Pat R*, 1281–92, 194; *Cal Fine R*, i, [p] 221), perhaps as part of an effort to reform the house.

One royal prerogative that came into play during vacancies was the presentation of clergy to priory livings and in 1293 a curiously complex dispute arose over this question. On 9 August Prior Henry presented Geoffrey de Wyttleburi, chaplain to the bishop of Winchester, to the vicarage of Camberwell (*Cal Inq Misc*, i, 1633). Prior Henry himself died on 27 August, before he had instituted Geoffrey, and within days the king announced that he had presented John Esegar of Shoreham to the vicarage of Camberwell, in the king's gift on account of the priory vacancy (*Cal Pat R*, 1292–1301, 37). Later that year the new prior of Bermondsey claimed before parliament that the king, in substituting a clerk of his own choosing, had acted 'to the prejudice and disinheritance of the priory' and sought a revocation of the king's presentation. The king replied that it was his duty to fill a vacancy in these circumstances (*Rot Parlt*, i, 116 no. 24).

All this should be seen in the context of deteriorating relations between the English crown and Cluny in the second half of the 13th century and the separation early in the 14th century of the alien priories from their Continental mother house (Graham 1926, 172–3; Keen 1973, 30–57, 215; Burton 1994, 267). In 1289 Edward I forbade the priors and monks of the English houses to make payments of any kind to the abbot of Cluny until further order. Problems in France had grown since 1259 when Henry III as duke of Gascony formally recognised the feudal overlordship of the king of France. In the 1290s wars in Wales, Scotland and France were a huge financial burden for the crown. The outbreak of war between Edward I and Philip IV of France with the French invasion of Aquitaine in 1295 led to the seizure of the property of the alien priories, founded in the wake of the Norman Conquest. In each case, the temporalities were put in the charge of royal commissioners or keepers who collected the revenues, paying the proceeds into the exchequer while making a modest allowance for the monks and their servants. The lands were returned to their owners when the war ended, but the same procedure was to be routinely adopted with each new outbreak of hostilities in the following century, as in 1324, in 1337 and in 1369, and as also occurred during the severest floods. In 1307 parliament decreed that monks should send no taxes overseas and that foreign superiors might come to England to exercise their right of visitation on condition they carried nothing out of the country but reasonable expenses. Whether or not such actions were seen as such at the time, in hindsight they can be taken as the first signs of resentment against foreign rule and influence per se, a feeling much enhanced by the disastrous appointments of John of Chartres and his immediate successors at Bermondsey (below).

In December 1274 the earliest reference in this period is recorded to another of Bermondsey's repeated problems: insolvency. Simon, prior of La Charité-sur-Loire, wrote to Edward I about the house's burden of debt (TNA: PRO, SC1/16/26). Prior Simon's source of information appears to have been Wenlock Priory. On 22 January 1276, the prior of La Charité-sur-Loire appointed the prior of Wenlock as keeper of the house of Bermondsey 'which was in debt' (*Cal Pat R Edw I*, 1272–81, 131). In subsequent years it was to be the king who took the house into his hands at moments of particular crisis and then appointed keepers to administer the estates. On 27 April 1299 a precedent was set for future practice when the priors of Wenlock and Bermondsey acknowledged their debt of 390 marks to William de Hamelton, clerk, conceding that in default of payment the sum was to be levied from their lands and chattels in Shropshire and Surrey (*Cal Close R*, 1296–1302, 305).

By the 13th century the rate of recorded donations and benefactions had greatly decreased, although there was a marked upturn c 1270. On 10 February 1269 the crown granted the prior and convent a weekly Monday market at their manor of Charlton (Kent) together with an annual fair there on the vigil, feast and morrow of Holy Trinity (*Cal Chart R*, ii, 115), and in 1270–2 John de Burgh, son of the justiciar Hubert, gave the monks the manor of Chalk (Kent) and the advowson of the parish church (*Ann Monast*, iii, 464). The grant was confirmed by Henry III on 12 April 1272 (*Cal Pat R Hen III*, 1266–72, 643). According to the Bermondsey annals, in 1272 Reginald and Richard de Tany granted the manor of Bengeo (Hertfordshire), known as Richmond, and confirmed the advowson which the monks already held (*Ann Monast*, iii, 464). The appropriation of the churches of Chelsham and Beddington (both in Surrey) to Bermondsey in the first decade of the 14th century and subsequent licensing seem to be responses to the priory's plight (*Ann Monast*, iii, 474–5; *Reg Pontissara*, 1282–1304, i, 96; *Reg Woodlock*, 1305–16, 229–30; *Cal Pat R*, 1313–17).

Much more common in this period are disputes with tenants or problems arising from sub-letting. Three leases are recorded: Prior Henry's lease of the mill of Widford (also Wideford or Wydeford) (Hertfordshire) to William atte Milne for 13s 4d pa (*Ann Monast*, iii, 467–8); and confirmations in 1298 of two earlier leases by William de Carleton, keeper of the priory, of the priory's lands at Chalk and Birling (both in Kent) (*Cal Pat R*, 1292–1301, 224–5). Disputes reveal more extensive leasing. In 1290, for example, an agreement was reached between Prior Henry and Hamo, prior of Bilsington in Kent, to whom Bermondsey had leased property there and in *Osewardistone* for

29s 1³/₄d (*Ann Monast*, iii, 467). But Bermondsey Priory's most unwelcome tenant in this period was Adam de Stratton, clerk of the works at Westminster and chamberlain of the exchequer, and a notorious moneylender and profiteer. His special interest lay in monastic property, and he finally resorted to violence and forgery before he was brought to account (see Graham 1926, 168–71 for a full account of his dealings with Bermondsey).

Adam first appears in connection with Bermondsey in September 1269 as tenant for life of Winterbourne, Buketon and Swanwick in Dorset (*Cal Pat R Hen III*, 1266–72, 476). In April 1271 Prior John, who was already bound to him for £40, acknowledged a further debt of 700 marks and Adam was given powers of distraint on priory lands in Surrey and Kent (*Cal Close R*, 1268–72, 409–12). On 12 March 1274 he was leasing land in Stapleford (Essex) which he held by grant from the prior and convent of Bermondsey (*Cat Anc Deeds*, i, A816). On 15 November 1274 Prior Henry notified the priory's tenants in the manors of Widford, Richmond (Surrey), Cowick and Hallingbury (both in Essex) that Adam was to be put in possession of the manors and that they were to answer to him in future (ibid, A767). Adam subsequently sub-let portions of this property to tenants of his own, leasing to Oxbert of Waterford on 25 March 1275 land of the fee of Richmond in Bengeo which he claimed to hold by 'gift' of Bermondsey (ibid, A1008, A5451). On the same day he leased to the vicar of Hertford other lands held of the fee of the prior and convent (ibid, A1139). The Cluniac visitation of Bermondsey in December 1275, reporting the house's heavy debt of 1000 marks, referred in particular to a loss of income following the sale of the five estates 'by one of its priors', while a further visitation in July 1279 stated that Prior John had sold to Adam de Stratton a wood called Chavor for 700 marks, a transaction about which there was something 'underhand or not straightforward'. By now the priory's debt had increased to 1700 marks. Graham suggests that the episode which took place shortly before 14 April 1284 when certain persons broke the door of the prior's chamber, forced open chests and coffers there and carried away £68 in money, silver vessels and 'jewels of gold' to the value of £40, imprisoning the prior, his chaplain and yeoman (*Cal Pat R Edw I*, 1281–92, 141) represented a distraint on the part of Adam to recover the £100 per annum pledged to him and his heirs by the priory (Graham 1926, 170).

Adam's grip on Bermondsey had steadily tightened since 1272. By 1288, the usurer had got half its substance and was demanding a capital sum of £6000 (Graham 1926, 170). On 21 January 1290, the month when Adam was finally deprived of his lands and imprisoned, the king ordered the sheriff of Essex to deliver to Bermondsey Priory the manors of Widford, Cowick and Richmond, which the house had 'indiscreetly' leased to Adam and which had now come into the king's hands; a similar writ was issued to the sheriff of Berkshire in respect of the manor of Upton (*Ann Monast*, iii, 467; *Cal Close R*, 1288–96, 64). In the same year, evidently following Bermondsey's recovery of the lands at Richmond, Roger de Gardino, Adam's tenant there, complained that the prior had ejected him and his wife Joan (*Rot Parlt*, i, 58 no. 157). This particular claim was still being pursued by Joan's new husband, Geoffrey Scurlag, in 1304, when a petition to parliament led to the appointment of justices to discover the truth of the matter (*Rot Parlt*, i, 171 no. 100).

A good deal of the blame for the whole episode could be laid at the door of Prior John of Chartres (1266–72) whose short period of office coincided with the priory's first entanglement with Adam. This, however, did not prevent John being subsequently promoted to Northampton and then to Wenlock, where similar problems were soon to arise as a result of what the visitors of 1279 reported as his enthusiasm for selling and alienating everything he could. Nor did it prevent his appointment to Lewes, the senior English house of the Order, in 1285. Before long that house was indebted to Italian merchants (Graham 1926, 171).

It is clear that a still heavier responsibility for Bermondsey's financial problems lay with Cluny and La Charité-sur-Loire, both for their failure to react constructively to the priory's plight, as reported to them by their visitors, and even more for their continued patronage of the deplorable Prior John. As a result of these shortcomings Bermondsey was plunged into a prolonged period of grave financial difficulty (aggravated by severe flooding; below) which lasted for the greater part of a century.

The most direct form of supervision from Cluny took the form of visitations from there or from the mother house, La Charité-sur-Loire. One such visitation occurred in 1262, when it was reported that:

> having ascertained the exact truth as to the observance of the convent's statutes and rule, the result of such enquiry showed that all devotional offices and rites were most properly and becomingly performed; that silence, the correction of what is amiss or required reform rigidly obeyed, and that almsgiving and hospitality are there carried out according to established customs. (Duckett 1890, 13–14)

At that time in 1262 the indebtedness of the house amounted to 266 marks, and there were 32 monks and one lay brother (ibid, 14; *VCH* 1967, 69). The 'deplorable' problems first detected in 1237–8 seem to have resurfaced by the time of the next visitation on 29 December 1275, when the number of monks had fallen to 20. The house was now said to be burdened with a debt of 1000 marks silver owing to various creditors. It also paid an annuity of £100 to one of the king's chaplains in perpetuity, regardless of the fact that five of its estates – Cowick and Hallingbury, Bengeo, Widford and Richmond – had been alienated. The report concluded with the remark that La Charité-sur-Loire had already made its own visitation, and had corrected everything that was to be amended (Duckett 1890, 16), and this seems to suggest that the mother house was concerned more with the religious aspects of the priory than with its finances. In 1277 the abbot of Cluny himself visited Bermondsey, where a provincial chapter was held and a series of enactments issued against the alienation of property (Graham 1926, 170).

On 29 July 1279 a still more detailed inspection was carried out by the priors of Mont-Didier (Amiens) and Lenton (Nottinghamshire). They reported that 'the state of this house is simply deplorable' (*VCH* 1967, 69). Whereas there ought to be, as a rule, 32 brethren, there were at present no more than 18. The prior explained that the house was overwhelmed with debt so that 'by the orders of the diocesan and the wish of the abbot' some of the monks had withdrawn. The 'original' debt of the house was said to have been 1700 marks (whatever was meant by 'original': four years previously it had been only 1000 marks) but had now risen to 2300 marks. The priory admitted that it received more than 100 marks *per annum* from official receivers and rent collectors from properties, done with a view to reducing the debt 'a thing never heard of before'. The prior had sold property called *Ompton* (?Hampton), which the purchaser was to hold in fee, for which he had received upwards of 500 marks. The prior also received 600 marks for sale of other woods, £8 for sale of rents, and 600 marks for property at Richmond, and he had purchased a property called Bearmont (probably Beaumont, Essex), which he afterwards sold for 500 marks.

On 25 August 1279, in connection with Wenlock Priory, the visitors complained of difficulties in getting the truth about debts out of the English monks, and remarked that greater loss and complications would arise there and at Bermondsey if the present prior (apparently Peter of Mont St Vincent) remained at his post. He was reported as selling and alienating what he could, and 'in an underhand way is manoeuvring to get himself elected to Rochester and make himself independent of Cluny' (Duckett 1890, 30). At Bermondsey's own subordinate cell of St James Derby (whose gift to Bermondsey had been confirmed in 1140 and a priory and hospital established thereafter) the visitors reported there were a prior and two monks, of whom the prior was 'good and exemplary' and one of the monks chaste and honest. The visitors had expelled the other and sent him to do penance at Bermondsey, substituting another in his place. When the prior first came to Derby the debt was 40s but was subsequently £4 10s 'because the house had no assets of its own'. The priory was on the point of getting in the harvest, which would support it till next season; the conventual buildings were 'sufficiently good', but the roof of the church was in bad repair and the prior was told to get a new roof (Duckett 1890, 29–31; *VCH* 1907, 45).

The priory's problems were exacerbated by serious flooding. On 18 October 1294, according to the annals, the Thames exceeded its accustomed limits and caused a great breach at Rotherhithe, flooding the 'plain' of Bermondsey and the precinct of Tothill (*Ann Monast*, iii, 468). This report is corroborated before 1340 by a city chronicle which noted that the burst embankment was still known as *le Breche* (Riley 1863, 243). On 24 September 1295, the king, having taken the priory into his own hands, appointed David le Graunt as keeper. The appointee was instructed to apply the priory revenues 'to the stopping of the breach in its lands caused by a violent inundation of the Thames whereby the surrounding lands of the priory were submerged, and to other purposes as he thinks fit, saving reasonable sustenance for the house' (*Cal Pat R*, 1292–1301, 148). This commission was not finally discharged until November 1314, delayed possibly by at least one similar disaster in 1309 (*Cal Pat R*, 1307–13, 114, 173, 370; 1313–17, 56; *VCH* 1967, 70).

The priory buildings themselves had evidently not escaped damage: following the great flood of 1294, the Cluniac visitors of 1299 found the priory buildings were in poor shape and the bishop of Winchester's permission of 12 March 1308 for the prior to appropriate Beddington church in consideration of losses caused by flood referred to the ruinous state of the priory and its need of repair (*Reg Woodlock*, 1305–16, 229–30; Graham 1926, 177). Edward II (1307–27) made a number of concessions, deferring or exempting the priory from various contributions, including the tenth (by the mid 13th century, the standard fractional tax levied on clerical income from benefices – rectories and vicarages – and other ecclesiastical offices), and intervening on Bermondsey's behalf with its diocesan the bishop of Winchester whose attitude was sometimes a good deal less sympathetic to the priory's financial hardship (*Reg Woodlock*, 1305–16, 241, 245, 395, 902, 915–16; *Cal Pat R*, 1307–13, 114). Recorded business between Bermondsey and the bishop at this period centres on the priory's recurrent difficulty from the 1310s in collecting annual payments due from the bishop in respect of property in Southwark (*Ann Monast*, iii, 477–8; *Cal Pat R*, 1317–21, 321; *Cat Anc Deeds*, iii, A6112; *Cal Close R*, 1343–6, 619), as well as disputes over presentations to churches (*Reg Pontissara*, 1282–1304, i, 107; *Reg Woodlock*, 1305–16, 81, 212–13). The bishop, acting as royal tax collector, ironically encountered difficulties in extracting dues from the priory, and excommunicated the house on those grounds on several occasions (*Reg Pontissara*, 1282–1304, i, 107; *Reg Woodlock*, 1305–16, 241, 437, 954).

The king's efforts, however, were not always well directed. Edward in 1312 urged the abbot of Cluny successfully for the appointment of Brother Peter de Sancto Laurentio, monk and almoner of Bermondsey and brother of the king's yeoman John, as prior, and the priory's lands were restored the same year (*Cal Close R*, 1307–13, 207, 505, 548; *VCH* 1967, 70–1). This direct royal contact with the Cluniac Order over the election of a new prior marks the first recorded occasion when the king intervened in the internal affairs of the priory. It must reflect a measure of frustration and dissatisfaction with the running of the house – something with which the Order's own visitors themselves had been concerned since the 1280s. But Prior Peter proved no more capable than his predecessors: Peter leased priory property but was still unable to pay the priory's debts. Two allegations of housebreaking and theft were made against Prior Peter within 18 months in 1317–18 (*Cal Pat R*, 1317–21, 91, 182). In 1320 the house was taken again into the king's hands (ibid, 457, 513, 529; *Cal Close R*, 1318–23, 269). Edward asked the prior of Cluny to recall Peter, acknowledging he had been misled in his judgement of Peter and that the suspicions of La Charité-sur-Loire of Peter had been well founded; Edward notified La Charité-sur-Loire the value of lands, churches and rents demised for life and for terms of years during Peter's

prioracy amounted to £292, and that the income from this was now wholly exhausted, as revealed by a survey of the state of the priory (*Cal Close R*, 1318–23, 344; TNA: PRO, E135/3/33). In 1321 Edward nominated John de Cusancia, a monk of Lewes, as prior, appointed new keepers but then unexpectedly ordered that Peter was to have custody and rule of the priory's temporalities again (*Cal Close R*, 1318–23, 358, 403; *Cal Pat R*, 1321–4, 23). Edward appears reluctant to accept Peter's shortcomings and as late as 1327 Peter received royal protection (*Cal Close R*, 1327–30, 101).

Further extraordinary events followed. In 1322 Prior Peter was finally replaced by Walter de Diluiz (or de Lutz), who had been preferred by La Charité-sur-Loire and accepted by the king (*Cal Pat R*, 1321–4, 143). Walter proved an even more unsatisfactory appointment and in a much shorter space of time. It was alleged Prior Walter and others in 1322–3 received in the priory and aided 'adherents of the rebels' – the rebellion in question being presumably part of the general unrest in London and elsewhere that followed the death of Thomas of Lancaster (*Cal Inq Misc*, ii, 686; cf *Cal Pat R*, 1321–4, 358). Prior Walter's arrest was ordered in January 1324, he was detained in the Tower and resigned (*Cal Pat R*, 1321–4, 358, 361, 397). Subsequently, in 1327, Edward III explained to the prior of La Charité-sur-Loire that the accusation had been false and malicious (*Cal Close R*, 1327–30, 215–16).

The priory was committed to custodians until April 1324 when John de Cusancia, now prior, received back the temporalities (*Cal Fine R*, 1319–27, 261; *Cal Pat R*, 1321–4, 407). A dispute in 1327 betweeen Prior John and the former prior, Walter, saw the new king briefly taking the temporalities back again, declaring the waste and impoverishment of the house by the indiscreet rule of former heads, and requesting Walter's reinstatement (*Cal Close R*, 1327–30, 215–16; *Cal Pat R*, 1327–30, 136). An agreement was reached between Walter and Prior John in John's favour and the priory's possessions were restored to him in 1328 (*Cal Close R*, 1327–30, 288). Bermondsey's reviving fortunes under the priorate of John de Cusancia (1324–60) are described in more detail below (3.6, 'Documentary evidence') but the lack of good government of the house by his predecessors was the frequent refrain in this period. The repeated seizure of the priory's temporalities from the 1290s must have contributed to the house's difficulties. In addition, the English Cluniac houses generally showed themselves discontented with their internal system of government directed from France.

While the priory annals include numerous leases which must have been regarded as particularly interesting, in a novel departure from previous practice priory leases are to be found from the beginning of the 14th century in the Patent Rolls in the form of royal licences or confirmations and this would seem to reflect the increasingly direct role played by the crown in the priory's affairs (eg in 1302, *Cal Pat R*, 1301–7, 73). The leasing out of the larger priory estates under royal supervision is particularly noticeable from the late 1310s (in 1317: *Cal Pat R*, 1317–21, 49, 62; in 1318: ibid, 68; and in 1319 in favour of one of the king's clerks: ibid, 380).

The priory's continuing role as church and provider of care for its community and its obligations of hospitality could have put it under further pressure. In this area near London a tendency to split into smaller parishes requiring new churches can be seen and Bermondsey had a new church *c* 1270 (Blair 1991, 129, 206, n 169 citing *Reg Pontissara*, 608). The earliest reference to a parish church in the annals is 1291, to a chapel of St Mary Magdalene (Martin 1926, 199). Some visitors were encouraged. In 1287 the archbishop of York, staying at Bermondsey, granted an indulgence of 40 days to all in his diocese, and other dioceses where his indulgences were recognised, 'who came to pray in the church of St Saviour of Bermondsey, and to adore the venerable cross set up on high therein, or who made contributions to the fabric fund of the church' (Graham 1926, 177). Undated fragments of visitations made in the period after 1298 include the statements that five Masses were celebrated daily, as set forth in the table of lessons; three of them sung and two said, though there had once been six. Hospitality, almsgiving, silence, and all other monastic obligations and duties, as enjoined by the rule, were well observed (Duckett 1890, 39). The frequent resort of the poor and infirm to the priory was referred to in 1308, implying the existence of an infirmary (*Reg Woodlock*, 1305–16, 229–30). The earliest references to corrodies at Bermondsey for lay individuals come in the mid 13th century and from early in the 14th century successive kings were in the habit of sending at least one retired royal servant at a time, probably more, to enjoy a corrody at the priory's expense (Chapter 4.3 'The inhabitants: lay people'). In the same period, not only were the priory's buildings said to be in a poor state (above, in 1299, and again in 1308: Graham 1926, 177) but its own numbers were low: in 1331, Bermondsey was cited as an example of a house that ought to have had 30 to 40 monks but had less than a third of that number (*VCH* 1967, 72, n 5).

Archaeological evidence

In period M7 further developments took place within the infirmary complex. The infirmary chapel (B1) was enlarged and refurbished (Fig 53). There were also modifications to the ? infirmary range extension and adjacent areas (B12, OA3, OA7), and the north-east section of the stone-built drain (D2) was dismantled. There is no archaeological evidence for alterations to the priory church (B3), the chapter house (B4), the cloister walk (B5) and garth (OA5), the refectory (B6), the east range (B7) and the reredorter (B9) in period M7 and all remained in use. There is also no evidence for any change to land to the south-west of the conventual buildings (OA4) in period M7.

Chapel (B1)

In period M7 a significant expansion of the chapel (B1) took place, with a widening of the nave in conjunction with a more grandiose east end (Fig 53). The earlier (period M3) chapel nave was slightly shortened by the insertion of a new west wall on a broad chalk foundation. The south wall of the nave was demolished and replaced by a wall built in the former walkway on the north side of the courtyard (OA2) to the south. The presence of the monastic cemetery (OA6) on the north side of the chapel (B1) seems to have inhibited any widening of the nave to the north. The new nave was 8.0m wide and 22m long. The south-east corner of the nave abutted the north-east end of the infirmary (B10).

The chancel was also rebuilt in this period (Fig 53). Massive ragstone foundations, heavily buttressed to north and south, indicate that the chancel was probably vaulted. It was now 9.6m east–west by 5.8m north–south and had foundations between 1.66m and 2.5m wide. The south chancel wall shared the alignment of the rebuilt south nave wall, but the north chancel wall was inset from the line of the north nave wall, the alignment being shared instead by the ends of the north buttresses. The chapel (B1) had been widened and to achieve this, it had been necessary to move it to the south. The length of the whole building, nave and chancel, was 32.8m.

Aspects of the external appearance and internal decoration of the newly built chapel can be tentatively suggested from later demolition material. A huge quantity of building material was recovered from demolition debris (period P1) presumed to be in large part from the chapel. Evidence for the likely appearance of the chapel (B1) came from a number of large fragments of stone roofing tile, which were probably put on when the chapel was remodelled in period M7. The roofing tiles had been fashioned from a fine-grained laminated sandstone and most have a single circular nail hole in the centre of the tile near the top edge. The size of stone roof tile used at the priory varied widely, indicating that the stone was graded when laid on the roof (Table 3). The largest size was employed at the bottom of the roof and tiles of progressively smaller size were used up to the ridge. The line of the ridge was presumably covered by a layer of ceramic ridge tiles. This system of stone roofing can be seen today on the Guildhall in the City of London.

Demolition material included a large number of floor tiles, many of which were almost certainly originally part of the chapel floor. The vast majority of these are either plain Low Countries type (current *c* 1300 onwards) or mid–late 13th-century plain and decorated 'Westminster' tile (designs W35, W59, W61, ?W76, W77, W99, W103, W113, W130, W147, Fig 77). There are also a number of decorated tiles of uncertain source referred to as the fine clay group (design <T10>, Fig 144) which may be contemporary with the 'Westminster'

Table 3 Size (mm) of stone roof tiles from the chapel (B1)

Length (mm)	Breadth (mm)	Thickness (mm)
-	134	9–15
-	155	9–15
-	157–162	11–14
358	160–176	13
-	211–232	21–23
-	217	9–15
-	360	21–22

tiles, and a few mid–late 14th-century Penn tiles, suggesting subsequent repair work rather than replacement (below, 3.6, 'Archaeological evidence'). Ten fragments of 'Westminster' floor tile (both plain and decorated designs W83, W97, W99, W103, Fig 77), along with two very small fragments of peg roofing tile, were also recovered from the upper (later) grave fill of one of the burials originally made in the chancel in period M4 (above, 3.2, 'Archaeological evidence').

Furthermore, a large quantity of window glass was recovered from Dissolution and immediately post-Dissolution clearance and demolition contexts, mainly pit fills, in the (former) monastic cemetery area (OA6) north of the chapel (Chapter 5.2, 'Elements of the former monastery partly or wholly retained and adapted', 'Chapel (B1)'). Many of these fragments appear to be 'old' glass and the illustrated pieces suggest mainly a broadly 14th-century date (Chapter 4.2, 'Interior decoration of the monastic buildings: glazing and tiling'; Fig 164). Although the chapter house was modified in period M8 (below, 3.6, 'Archaeological evidence') and some of the glass may have come from there, much of this glass probably formed part of the glazing installed in the rebuilt chapel as the final stage in its completion, and perhaps after some delay (in periods M7 and M8).

Chapter house (B4)

There is no stratigraphic evidence for the chapter house in this period. There was, however, no dating evidence for the structural changes described under period M8 and it is possible that the rebuilding of the chapter house took place in the latter part of period M7 (below, 3.6, 'Archaeological evidence'; Fig 57).

Hall/lodgings (B8)

In the hall of Building 8, a foundation for a partition wall and traces of a parallel foundation 1.30m to the east may have created a through passage and stairs (Fig 53). The stair would have allowed access to a first-floor chamber or solar at the east end of the building over the ? service area. It is possible that first-floor chambers were inserted both here and over the former hall. A straight flight of stairs against the east wall of the passage could have led to a first-floor landing supported by timber or masonry corbels in the south, east and west passage walls.

In a make-up deposit for the stair foundation, a silver coin, a denier of Gui de Dampierre (1279–1305) for Flanders and Namur was found (Fig 54, <S176>).

Infirmary (B10)

At the south end of the infirmary (B10), a chalk and mortar floor was laid over the earlier cesspit (dug, and apparently backfilled, in period M5). The floor extended 1.1m east–west by a maximum 0.5m north–south. The pottery recovered from a possible make-up deposit A[1339] beneath the floor, was dated c 1080–c 1200, an early date for this period which may reflect some disturbance of the underlying cesspit fill A[1389] (also

dated c 1080–c 1200; period M5; above, 3.3, 'Archaeological evidence'). The physical proximity of these two contexts and the comparable size and date of the pottery assemblages either confirms some disturbance or intimates that A[1339] was itself part of the cesspit. Although the pottery has been dated to c 1080–c 1200, the absence of diagnostic fabrics and forms makes closer dating difficult, and it could have been deposited after c 1140 (Chapter 7.5, 'Period M7, c 1250–c 1330').

A hearth was built over the chalk floor; a deposit of pale yellow mortar formed a low surround on top of which was set the clay slab of the hearth. The clay, together with a layer of crushed scorched tile, formed the hearth structure. A second area of floor extended 1.54m north–south by 1m east–west to the south-east of the hearth. Both floors and hearth sloped down slightly to the east, slumping slightly into the soft fills of the underlying cesspit.

An external stone-built cesspit against the east wall of Building 10, south of the passage, replaced the earlier internal cesspit. The new cesspit was 1.85m x 0.92m east–west (Fig 55). A single sherd of Kingston-type ware (KING) from the primary silt fill was dated c 1230–c 1400.

Former infirmary latrine (B11)

The stone-built drain (D2), under the former infirmary latrine (B11), was blocked and backfilled at the end of period M6. It seems probable, therefore, that Building 11 ceased to be used as a latrine. In period M7 an additional west–east wall was added to the north-east corner of the building and the extremely fragmented remains of other foundations were recorded to the south and east (Fig 53). Modern truncation of archaeological features in this area of the site was extensive and it is difficult to elucidate a meaning from such evidence as survives.

? Infirmary range extension (B12)

The south wall of the ? infirmary range extension (B12) was robbed and a replacement wall inserted on its north side (Fig 53). Sixteen sherds of medieval pottery from a section of the south wall robbing trench A[3626] were dated c 1140–c 1200 (Chapter 7.5, 'Period M7, c 1250–c 1330'). Other finds from the robbing of the south wall were plain and decorated 'Westminster' tile (designs W83, W99, ?W103, W108, Fig 77) – possibly the remains of this building's floor, and perhaps laid in the preceding period – but there was also some plain Low Countries tile (current c 1300 onwards; possibly from floor repairs) and definitely intrusive material in the form of 15th-century or later red brick.

The new south wall was built across the now disused stone drain (D2; cf Fig 49). Backfill deposits in the (period M6) east–west ditch beneath the building were dated c 1230–c 1400 by two sherds of pottery. The foundation to a possible flight of external stone stairs was represented by a masonry pad 2.25m north–south by 1.2m east–west, located 0.7m south of the wall.

Found discarded as waste in post-Dissolution contexts were two fragments of green-glazed, circular roof finials. One finial was in coarse London-type ware (LCOAR) and could be dated

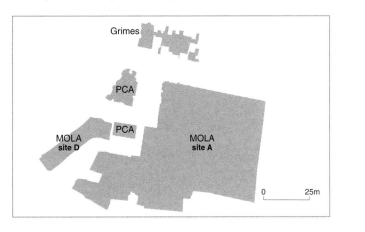

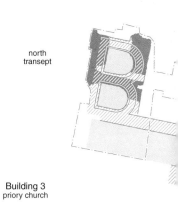

north transept

Building 3
priory church

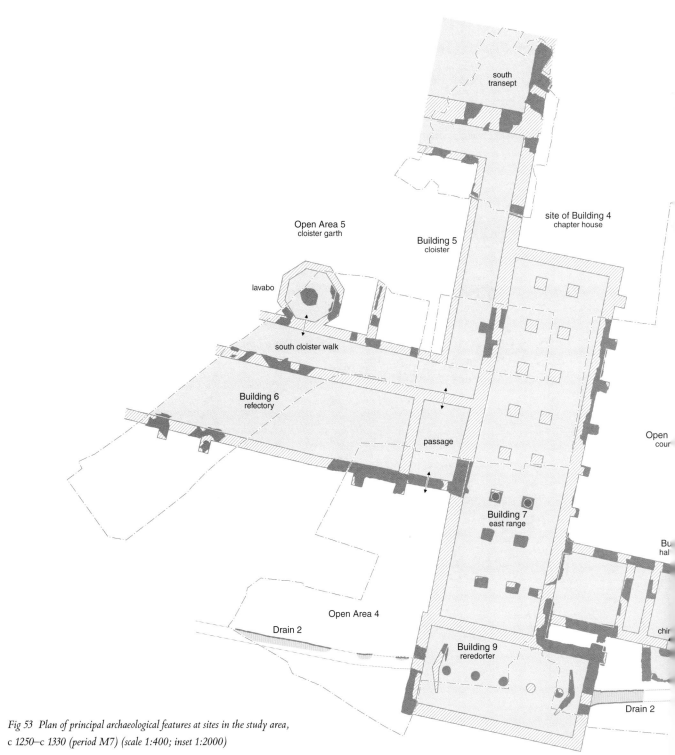

Open Area 5
cloister garth

Building 5
cloister

site of Building 4
chapter house

lavabo

south cloister walk

Building 6
refectory

passage

Building 7
east range

Open
cour

Bu
hal

Open Area 4

Drain 2

Building 9
reredorter

chir

Drain 2

*Fig 53 Plan of principal archaeological features at sites in the study area,
c 1250–c 1330 (period M7) (scale 1:400; inset 1:2000)*

N

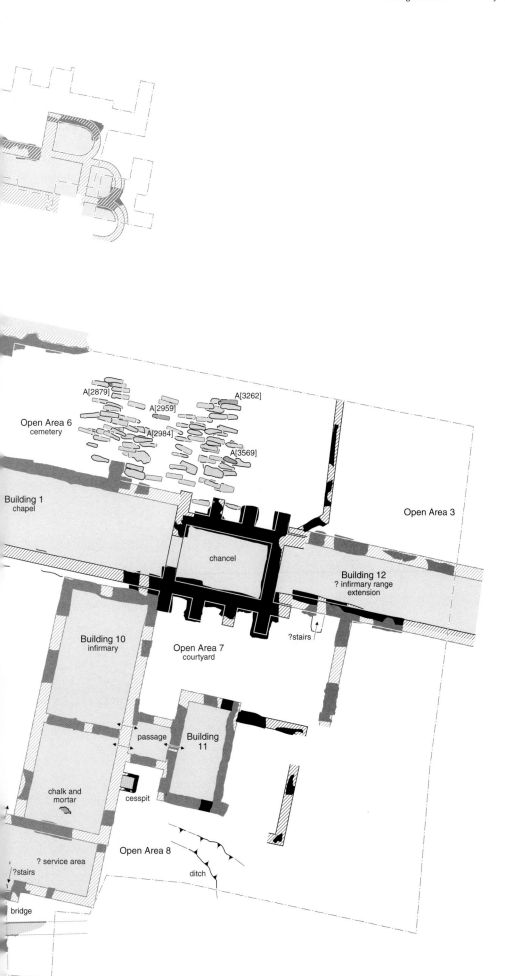

A[2879]

A[2959]

A[3262]

Open Area 6
cemetery

A[2984]

A[3569]

Building 1
chapel

Open Area 3

chancel

Building 12
? infirmary range
extension

Building 10
infirmary

Open Area 7
courtyard

?stairs

passage

Building
11

chalk and
mortar

cesspit

? service area

Open Area 8

?stairs

ditch

bridge

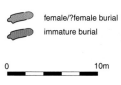

female/?female burial

immature burial

0   10m

to *c* 1080–*c* 1200 (Fig 152, <T37>); the second was in Kingston-type ware (KING) and dated to *c* 1230–*c* 1400 (Fig 152, <T38>). Finials of this type were placed on the ridge of a roof as decorative features but may also have acted as ventilators. Building 12 may have had its roofline enhanced in this way.

Stone-built drain (D2)

The later part of period M6 and beginning of period M7 witnessed the disuse of the north-east (north–south aligned)

<S176>

Fig 54 Silver denier <S176> of Gui de Dampierre (1279–1305) from hall/lodgings (B8), period M7 (scale c 2:1)

section of the stone drain (D2). The backfill in the ?tributary (period M6) east–west drain under Building 12 was dated *c* 1230–*c* 1400 by just two sherds. However, a much larger pottery assemblage was associated with the disuse and robbing of the main drain. A total of 246 sherds from a minimum of 137 vessels was recovered and fully quantified (discussed in detail in Chapter 7.5, 'Period M7, *c* 1250–*c* 1330'). The bulk of the pottery recovered from the various backfills of this part of Drain 2 comprises fabrics and forms in use during the 12th century, especially the second half. One large group from context A[548] (167 sherds) and one medium-sized group from A[270] are dated *c* 1180–*c* 1230. The latest readily identifiable medieval pottery in any of the period M7 backfills is a single sherd from a Kingston-type ware (KING) cooking pot, dated broadly to *c* 1230–*c* 1400, from backfill context A[583]. This excepted, the latest distinctive fabric introduced into London is London-type ware decorated in the Rouen style (LOND ROU), dating to *c* 1180–*c* 1270, together with several sherds possibly from jugs decorated in French-inspired styles of similar date. There were only two sherds of imported wares. Kitchen wares, mostly cooking pots, were most common, and some serving vessels.

Fig 55 View of the cesspit built against the outside face of the east wall of the infirmary (B10) in period M7, from the south (0.5m vertical scale, 1.0m horizontal scales)

While the composition of the total disuse assemblage suggests a deposition date at the end of the 12th century, the stratigraphic sequence proposed for the infirmary latrine (B11) and the ? infirmary range extension (B12) requires that the drain was at least partially open and functioning in some way in the first half of the 13th century (period M6). The backfill dumps must have been made over a period of time and contain a large proportion of residual material.

Also recovered from the drain robbing debris was a sheet domed octagon made out of copper alloy (Fig 56, <S83>). It was probably the lid to a shallow box of the kind used to hold folding scales for weighing. Close by in debris was found an incomplete bone handle with rivet holes, probably from a knife; it is decorated with single and paired, compass-engraved circle and dot motifs (Fig 56, <S116>). These items could have been employed in the infirmary, perhaps for weighing medical powders, liquids or dried herbal additives.

Infirmary courtyard (OA2)

Open Area 2 had evolved into an infirmary courtyard by the second half of the 12th century (period M5), and it continued so, but in a modified way, in the 13th century (Fig 53). The walkway or gallery across the north side of the courtyard (periods M5 and M6) was cut off by the extension and widening of the chapel (B1) to the south. The dimensions of the courtyard were now *c* 20m east–west by 25.4m north–south. There may have been access to and from the courtyard (OA2) in its south-east corner, via the through passage in Building 8, and through the ground floor of the east range, possibly through the north part of the range.

Cemetery (OA6)

Further burials in the cemetery (OA6) in this period numbered 91, arranged in fairly haphazard north–south rows (Fig 53). An area *c* 5.2m wide, considerably larger than the width of a burial row, was left vacant between the interments of the previous period and those of period M7. This broadly coincided with the apsidal termination of the south aisle of the priory church, but not otherwise with any other building alignments or developments. Throughout all periods, the cemetery did not extend beyond the current limits of contemporary buildings; one may assume, therefore, that the more easterly of the period M7 burials did not take place until after the completion of the vaulted chapel chancel (B1). The cemetery boundaries were formalised in this period by the construction of a north–south cemetery wall (Fig 53), which abutted the north-east corner of the chancel (B1).

The 90 individuals available for osteological analysis were in the main adult males (62 males/?males: ten young adults, 28 mature adults, 14 old/elderly adults, ten defined only as adult), with 23 adults of indeterminate sex (one young adult, one mature adult, one old/elderly adult, 20 defined only as adult), four females/?females (three mature adults A[2959], A[3262] and A[3569] and one adult A[2984]) and the only immature or adolescent individual (A[2879]) in the whole recorded population (the age and sex breakdown is detailed in Table 20); the location of the females/?females and immature individual is shown on Fig 53).

One skeleton A[3515], a mature adult male, had periosteal bone formation on his ribs. These lesions may indicate tuberculosis (Chapters 4.3, 'Demography and health of the burial population', 7.9, 'Infectious disease', 'Non-specific infections'). Four individuals among those buried in period M7 had sustained fractured ribs.

At least six burials were made in stone cists, forming a fairly

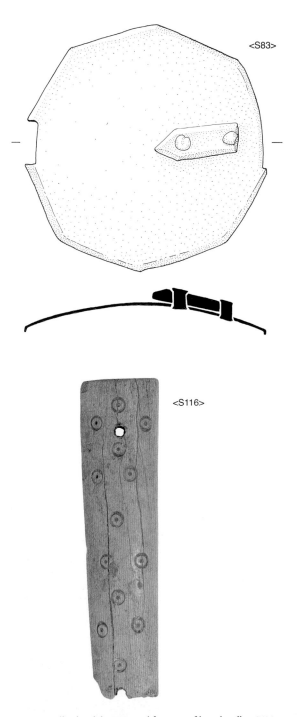

<S83>

<S116>

Fig 56 Copper-alloy box lid <S83> and fragment of bone handle <S116> from robbing of the north-east stone-built drain (D2), period M7 (scale 1:1; photo c 1:1)

tight group north of the infirmary chapel chancel (B1). Two other graves had a plaster lining: one of these burials was in a (wooden) coffin, the other was not (Table 5).

Courtyard/yard (OA7)

The buttresses of the new chancel of the infirmary chapel (B1) blocked the earlier (period M6) west–east gallery or passage that had crossed the north side of the courtyard (OA7, Fig 53). The wall on the east side of the area (OA7) was retained but there was no further evidence in this period to confirm whether or not it was part of a building. An east–west wall abutting the north-east corner of Building 11 (see period M6; Fig 49) was removed during this period and a new wall built. Fragmentary remains of another, possibly right-angled, wall foundation were recorded to the south-east.

The backfill in the wall-robbing trench produced 147 sherds from a minimum of 42 vessels. Two contexts A[1281] and A[937] from the robbing group (gp29) were fully quantified (125 sherds) and included several joining sherds (discussed in detail in Chapter 7.5, 'Period M7, c 1250–c 1330'). The pottery from A[1281] was dated c 1270–c 1350 on the presence of 51 sherds from at least six jugs in Mill Green ware (MG); a further three sherds from one Mill Green ware jug were present in the small backfill context A[937]. Only four sherds of coarse Surrey-Hampshire border ware (CBW; date range c 1270–c 1500) from a cooking pot were present. This argues strongly for a date of deposition before the mid 14th century, by which date, coarse border ware was by far the most common kind of pottery used in London.

The exact arrangement of the walls around the south-east corner of this area is not clear owing to lack of evidence. Nonetheless, the yard seems in this period to be an enclosed space, perhaps accessible only from infirmary Building 10, Building 11 or Building 12. Completely enclosed yards, where there is no through-traffic, tend to be used as rubbish dumps, for storage and as work zones; a testament to this statement are the two pits dug in this period in the yard (not shown on plan). The north-east section of the stone drain (D2) went out of use and was backfilled and robbed in the later part of period M6 and beginning of period M7 (above). The burial of waste here suggests a downgrading of the space. The pits contained pottery dated broadly to c 1080–c 1350 by two sherds from jugs in London-type ware (LOND).

Open ground to the south-east of the conventual buildings (OA8)

In the area beyond the south and east walls of the infirmary buildings (Fig 53, OA8), the north-east section of the stone drain (D2) was disused and robbed (above). A new ditch, aligned north-west to south-east and 7.3+m long and 2.5m wide, was dug south of Building 11 and may thus have served as an overflow channel to take fluid waste from the cesspit outside infirmary Building 10.

Discussion

By the close of period M7 in the second quarter of the 14th century, the chapel (B1) was without doubt an impressive structure: it was roofed in stone and the chancel had a stone-vaulted interior; it was decorated with magnificent tiled floors and (eventually) with stained glass in the windows. The chapel nave was widened while the infirmary (B10) was standing. The chancel was modified after the disuse of the north-east section of stone-built drain (D2) and in conjunction with the widening of the chapel nave. There was no direct dating evidence for these developments in period M7.

It is possibly surprising that such a development was undertaken in a period when the priory was suffering from debt, mismanagement during vacancies and loss of income owing to the sale and alienation of lands. There had been a general downturn in grants and benefactions during the 13th century, but this was relieved somewhat around 1270 when gifts of manors in Hertfordshire and Kent were confirmed. Income from these, or from cash generated by sales and alienations, may have funded the chapel (B1) building programme. On the west side of the precinct the parish church was also constructed in the later 13th century, presumably at the priory's expense.

A comparison with the Cluniac house of St John, Pontefract, also a dependency of La Charité-sur-Loire, reveals the seriousness of the plight in which St Saviour Bermondsey found itself in the latter years of the 13th century. The Cluniac visitation of 1262 found that the priory of St Saviour had debts of 266 marks and a population of monks numbering 32 (above, 'Documentary evidence'). In the same year, Pontefract Priory's debt was £666 and its population 17. By 1275, St Saviour's debt had risen to 1000 marks and the number of brothers was reduced to 20. Comparisons exist for the year 1279, in which Bermondsey's debt, at 2300 marks, had more than doubled and its population had again shrunk, now to only 18. The fortunes of the house at Pontefract, however, had steadily improved. There, the debt had been reduced to £233 and the number of monks had reached 27 (Bellamy 1965, xv–xvi). Bermondsey's population, however, does not seem to have recovered in the early 14th century: in 1331, it had less than a third of the 30 to 40 monks it should have had (VCH 1967, 72, n 5).

The south ground-floor room in infirmary Building 10 was apparently refurbished in the mid to late 13th century. The internal cesspit was backfilled and a new floor laid. A garderobe shaft in the thickness of the east wall would have probably emptied into the new external cesspit on the east side of the building. The upgrade of the ground floor may suggest a change of use for this part of the building, but the evidence is scant.

The lifespan of the north-east section of the stone-built drain (D2), from its construction in the last quarter of the 12th century (period M5) to disuse and robbing in the second quarter of the 13th century to mid 13th century (periods M6 and M7), appears relatively short for a major drain associated with two conventual buildings (B11 and B12). Whether Building 11 continued in use as a latrine after the backfilling of the drain is not known, but seems unlikely, although as the latrine had been a ground-floor facility, other arrangements may have been possible: waste may have been simply carried out of the building and emptied elsewhere, for example nearby in the cesspit adjacent to the infirmary Building 10 or in the ditch dug in Open Area 8.

The decline in numbers of the monastic population witnessed in the 20 years between 1260 and 1280 may have meant that the infirmary was less in demand. Certainly, the associated open area (OA7) appears to have a diminished status as more yard than courtyard. The possible external stair added to the south side of the ? infirmary range extension (B12) suggests that a first floor was inserted in the 13th or early 14th century and the building may have become more private accommodation. Individual apartments came to be more favoured during the course of the 14th century; they housed elderly lay people from benefactors' families as well as sick and infirm brothers (Greene 1992, 158). Possibly derived from the grave slabs or tombs of such benefactors are the copper-alloy letters <S26>–<S28> (Fig 88) of a type current from the 1280s to 1350s which testify to the presence of funerary structures at the priory in the 13th and 14th centuries. The needs of the poor and infirm who resorted to the priory, referred to in 1308, would have been met at the almonry close to the priory's west gate (above, 'Documentary evidence').

The total ceramic assemblage from period M7 (discussed in detail in Chapter 7.5, 'Period M7, *c* 1250–*c* 1330') includes a very high proportion of residual material, notably from the stone drain (D2). The group from the yard (OA7) presents a more typical picture of the late 13th to early 14th century, suggesting that the Thames continued to limit the distribution of wares from south-east England north of the Thames into Southwark. Good-quality Mill Green ware (MG) jugs from Essex were reaching Bermondsey; imports were still rare.

Cooking pots and jugs predominate in the total assemblage where the figures are biased by the large quantity of 12th-century pottery, but other forms used for cooking are present, such as bowls and a D-shaped dripping dish in coarse Surrey-Hampshire border ware (CBW) probably used to catch the juices from a spit-roasted joint. (This common method of preparing meat was in use earlier, from at least the 12th century, as is shown by a probable spit-support in shelly-sandy ware (SSW; Fig 89, <P23>).) Although the meat of quadrupeds was officially prohibited as a regular part of the monastic diet, from the 13th century onwards it was increasingly prepared and eaten, not only by the upper echelons of the monastic heirarchy and their guests, but eventually by all the brethren (Wilson 1973, 26). Poultry, however, was allowed and was most likely spit-roasted (ibid, 116). Otherwise, there is no evidence from the pottery to indicate major changes in culinary methods during this period, nor any analysis of vertebrate remains with which to compare.

3.6 Remodelling of the conventual buildings and cloisters: the priory and abbey *c* 1330–*c* 1430 (period M8)

Documentary evidence

The early decades of the 14th century had seen the culmination of the financial problems which had begun to afflict the priory from the 1270s, and which were described in some detail in the visitations of the 1270s and later (above, 3.5, 'Documentary evidence'). These difficulties, recognised at the time as the result of poor management, or worse, on the part of successive priors, had deprived the house of most of its income, and were compounded by the series of floods which had begun in 1294.

Under the exceptionally long and relatively competent priorate of John de Cusancia (1324–60) a steady and undramatic recovery appears to have been made. References to the priory's debts continue to occur frequently, but as these coincide with records of building work, it is possible that they reflect exceptional building costs rather than routine deficits. After John's tenure little more is heard of the priory's debts and indeed the priory features very much less frequently in the king's correspondence. A period of relative stability and tranquillity seems to have occurred during which two successive priors served as vicar-generals of the priory of La Charité-sur-Loire in England. The outstanding events during the remainder of the century were the denization of the priory and, in 1399, its promotion, at the king's urging, to the status of abbey.

Prior John de Cusancia, described as a monk of the Carthusian Order (*Cal Pat R*, 1321–4, 407), was the brother of James de Cusancia, the head of the Cluniac priory of Prittlewell (Essex) (*Cal Close R*, 1323–7, 310). On 30 October, Prior John was granted royal protection at the request of another of his brothers, William, king's clerk and treasurer of the earl of Chester (the future Edward III). This was on the basis that Prior John was of the power of the count of Burgundy and not of the king of France, 'although the priory is subject to the priory of La Charité-sur-Loire, within the dominion of the king of France' (*Cal Pat R*, 1324–7, 37). On 13 January 1327 the prior of Bermondsey, along with the priors of St Mary Southwark, Holy Trinity Aldgate and Westminster, was required to swear to safeguard Queen Isabella and her son Edward against Hugh le Despenser the younger (*Cal Plea and Mem R*, 1323–64, 14). And with the dispute between Prior John and the late Prior Walter settled in 1328 (*Cal Close R*, 1327–30, 288), a new era began. In July 1330, as if in acknowledgement of a new dawn in the priory's fortunes, Edward III confirmed no fewer than 22 of Bermondsey's charters, beginning with Henry I's privileges (*Ann Monast*, iii, 472 under 1329; *Cal Chart R*, iv, 177–86). There was to be no immediate recovery, however.

The series of floods beginning in 1294 repeatedly broke down the local river defences, rendering the area liable to inundation even in normal conditions. The effect of this was to deprive the priory of food and income from its extensive local estates in Bermondsey and Rotherhithe. On 24 October 1325, a fresh commission of walls and ditches had been appointed to inspect the breach in the bank of the Thames between Greenwich and Bermondsey (*Cal Pat R*, 1324–7, 232). In 1331–2 the priory was still affected by *la brekke* (TNA: PRO, C81/193/5746). On 11 September 1332 the situation was so bad that the priory and its possessions were taken back into the king's hand and entrusted to John Darcy, prior of Stonegate (Stansgate, Essex), and John de Ludelowe, monk of Bermondsey, while a protection was granted Prior John, 'now grievously burdened by debts incurred by the neglect and bad rule of late priors and other misfortunes' (*Cal Pat R*, 1330–4, 332). On 15 September 1337 the sheriffs of Surrey and Sussex were ordered to desist from making distraints on priory property (*Cal Close R*, 1337–9, 182) which they had presumably been doing in the interests of the priory's unpaid creditors. On 19 February 1338 the Thames had broken through the ditches and caused flooding to a depth of 5ft (1.52m) in the priory (TNA: PRO, SC8/33/1606 (dated on dorse)). In March 1338 the prior was given a nine-month respite for the £100 payable annually (the first mention of such a payment) for the custody of his priory 'in consideration of damage suffered by him suddenly and without his fault after he had the said custody' (*Cal Close R*, 1337–9, 335, 389).

Debts continued to be contracted more or less regularly throughout John's lengthy prioracy, and particularly in the years 1346–7 and 1350; there is little sign of any progressive reduction in the amounts during the period. The largest single debt was £500 (*Cal Close R*, 1341–3, 501) and the smallest £9 (*Cal Fine R*, 1354–60, 239). Sums of £40 were common, and those of £100 and £200 only slightly less so. With one exception (concerning Kent) all these were to be levied, in cases of default on repayment, on priory properties in Surrey; and in only one case was that liability shared with another county (Essex).

On 4 May 1338 there occurs the first reference to a new development: the king's custody of the prior of Bermondsey's temporalities (not because of financial problems but on account of the war between the king and France) manifested in the king's presentation of John de Waterton to the priory's vicarage of Birling (*Cal Pat R*, 1338–40, 55). This was the first of a long series of such presentations, reflecting Bermondsey's status during much of the Hundred Years' War as the alien house of a French order under a French prior appointed by a French religious house. The notion of the temporalities being in the king's hands was perhaps more a theoretical than an actual state of affairs, for the king's principal interest was in raising revenue, and he was prepared to farm back the property to the prior for a yearly sum of £100 (the same figure that was first exacted from the priory in 1337). In July 1338 the prior was being called upon to pay 314s of the £50 he still owed for custody until the following Easter, for which the king had previously given him respite till Michaelmas (29 September) (*Cal Close R*, 1337–9, 444); and on 13 November 1338 Bermondsey was among a number of religious houses (none of which was alien) holding land in London from whom money was being collected in lieu of tax ('scot and lot'): 5 marks were collected from St Saviour, St Bartholomew and St John of Jerusalem, as against 10 marks

each from the Dean and Chapter of St Paul and Holy Trinity Aldgate and 20 marks from the New Hospital without Bishopsgate (ie St Mary Spital) (*Cal Plea and Mem R*, 1323–64, 101). A further reflection of the war with France is to be seen in the king's notification of 20 April 1339 to John de Warenne, Earl of Surrey, and the keepers of maritime lands in Sussex that the prior of Bermondsey's obligation to find four men at arms or other armed men in respect of his lands in that county had been rescinded, in that he had shown the king that although his priory was taken into the king's hands as an alien priory, the prior holds the custody thereof at will for rendering a certain farm yearly, and the charge was included in the farm (*Cal Close R*, 1339–41, 79).

The £100 annual farm was soon to prove an excessive burden on top of the house's other commitments. On 12 June 1340 the prior and convent, unable to repay a large sum of money which they owed to the prior's brother, William de Cusancia, as a result of 'intolerable charges daily incumbent upon them in keeping in repair the breach of Bermondsey for the defence of their land there, as well as for other great sums which they pay yearly to the king for their farm with other aliens, they cannot pay', were authorised to lease their manor of Widford, for a sum to be paid in advance, or at a yearly farm (*Cal Pat R*, 1338–40, 543). On 16 June 1340 the priory and convent, in view of the yearly payment of £100, were finally excused from the payment of the tenth granted by the clergy of the realm for that year and the next, a petition having been made on behalf of the prior and convent to the effect that since they have suffered and still suffer many losses through floods of the Thames in the lands, meadows and pastures belonging to them, the king would release them from the tenth in return for a prompt render of the annual payment, now reduced to £50 (*Cal Fine R*, 1337–47, 177) and the holding of knights' fees and the advowsons of churches. This was reinforced on 6 March 1342 at the request of William de Cusancia, the king's treasurer and one of the priory's main creditors, with a further release from the payment of tenths, in view of the inability of the priory's possessions and goods to support the prior and monks (ibid, 277).

The priory's perennial problems continued. On 8 July 1346 a commission was appointed to investigate the prior's complaint that Alan Ferthyng of Southwark and 12 others had broken and thrown down his close and dykes in Bermondsey and dug so much in his soil there that 140 acres (56.7ha) of meadow were inundated by the Thames, depriving him of his profits there, felled his trees and carried them away with other goods, and assaulted his men and servants whose services were thus lost for some time (*Cal Pat R*, 1345–8, 176–7, 240–1). On 16 June 1351 the king noted that during Prior John's absence in Rome 'to further the business of his house', a certain monk of the house, appointed by John to govern the house and its goods on his behalf, had so wasted its rents and goods that a great part of the said annual farm payable to the king was in arrears: the king had therefore committed the keeping of the priory, its lands and goods to William de Cusancia, brother of the prior, two monks of the priory and one other during the prior's absence prior, to answer to the king touching his farm, find fitting sustenance for the monks, household and servants of the house, and support all the other charges incumbent on the priory and its lands (*Cal Fine R*, 1347–51, 301). The importance to the king of the receipt of his annual farm from the priory is underlined by the proviso, in relation to Prior John's lease of the church of Cobham on 20 April 1352 in return for specified quantities of wheat and barley, that where the farm fell into arrears the king's ministers would be liable to levy the 'fruits and profits' of that church as well as of other possessions of the priory (*Cal Pat R*, 1353–4, 252). In May 1359, and for reasons not explained, the £50 annual farm was granted to William de Grandisson to hold for life if the priory remains in the king's hands that long (ibid, 1358–61, 205). On 8 October 1360 Prior John resigned his office into the hands of the prior of Wenlock (HMC 1855, 423).

On 15 October 1360, Bermondsey Priory and all its lands, possessions and goods were committed by the king to Brother John de Cariloco, following the resignation of John de Cusancia and at the request of Henry, prior of Wenlock and vicar-general of the priory of La Charité-sur-Loire in England (*Cal Fine R*, 1356–68, 140–1). On 16 February 1361, following the peace treaty of Brétigny with France, a general restitution was made of the possessions of alien priories (*Cal Pat R*, 1358–61, 560). On 30 April William de Grandisson was granted an annuity of £60 for life in lieu of the £50 of the farm of the alien priory of Bermondsey, now restored to the prior by the peace with France (ibid, 1361–4, 10). On 30 January 1364 the treasurer and barons of the exchequer were instructed to stay their demands upon the priory for £20 16s 9d, being the arrears of £50 owing from the prior's annual farm of his alien house, pardoning them that sum 'out of compassion for the estate of the said priory' (*Cal Close R*, 1364–8, 2, 6).

By the time of the prioracy of Peter de Tenolio in 1367 the priory appears at last to have achieved some measure of stability and tranquillity, on the evidence of the great decrease in references to it in the Patent and Close Rolls and other sources. By February 1370 the prior had been appointed vicar-general in England of the prior of La Charité-sur-Loire, empowered to provide a new head of house for the Cluniac priory of Wenlock (*Cal Pat R*, 1367–70, 362). It is difficult to imagine the prior of Bermondsey exercising those high responsibilities 40 years earlier, and the role must reflect the restoration of much of the priory's good name. The king's interest in the matter, however, was in the alien status of the house and the fact that he had taken the new prior's fealty. By this date the war with France had been renewed, and from 1369 a series of some 20 royal presentations to benefices taken into the king's hands is recorded as a result.

Richard Dunton first appears as prior in October 1375; there are, however, references to him early in 1374 as keeper of Bermondsey Priory, then 'void by the death of the late prior and in the king's hand on that account and by reason of the war with France' (*Cal Fine R*, 1369–77, 232, 250). In this office he continued to serve as vicar-general in England of the prior of La Charité-sur-Loire (*Cal Pat R*, 1374–7, 354). On 12 October 1377 he received from the king the keeping of the priory, lands and

possessions for as long as they shall remain in the royal hand on account of the war with France (*Cal Fine R*, 1377–83, 23) and on 10 July 1378 the priory received an inspeximus and confirmation of Edward III's charter of 15 July 1330, confirming previous charters and letters patent (*Ann Monast*, iii, 480; *Cal Pat R*, 1381–5, 261). Stow (1603, ii, 67) pointed out that Richard was the first Englishman in this alien house to hold the office of prior, and not inappropriately it was Richard who achieved the denization of the house on 9 May 1380 for the payment of a fine of 200 marks (*Cal Pat R*, 1381–5, 18). This move, a natural development from the earlier seizures of French property before 1360 and after 1369, followed a general growth of anti-clericalism and even demands that all aliens, monks included, should be expelled on the grounds that they were spies. In 1376 the Commons had petitioned for measures to ensure that French priors and monks be banished and replaced by Englishmen (*Rot Parlt*, ii, 342–3). But the denization was also the result of lobbying by the alien houses themselves, for the annual payment to the crown for the custody of their own possessions had proved impossibly burdensome and Lewes Priory had secured its denization as early as 1351 (McKisack 1959, 293–5).

Prior Dunton has been seen as the priory's most successful administrator (*VCH* 1967, 72). Dunton's successor in 1390, Prior John (de) Attilburgh, would be accused of bad government and illicitly alienating property after his resignation in 1399 (ibid, 73). Before this, however, on 13 August 1399, according to the annals, Prior John was appointed the first abbot of the house, at the wish and request of Richard II (*Ann Monast*, iii, 482), and on 17 November 1399 the manors of Cluny were committed to Abbot John to be held for the duration of the wars with France (*Cal Fine R*, 1399–1405, 19).

Early in 1400 a short series of letters patent relating to the election of an abbot in succession to John Attilburgh reveal the changed procedure following the denization of the abbey in 1380, a procedure not documented at the time of John's own election in 1390. On 1 February 1400 the king issued a licence for the prior and convent of Bermondsey to elect an abbot in place of John Attilburgh resigned (*Cal Pat R*, 1399–1401, 191), and on 9 February 1400 notified the archbishop of Canterbury his assent to the election of Henry Tompston (Tomstone), monk of the house, as abbot (ibid, 185). The former role of La Charité-sur-Loire in preferring a new head of house, though often one of the king's choosing, had now entirely lapsed; instead, the king licensed the house to elect its own abbot, which had always been the normal procedure for 'native' houses. One long-standing arrangement remained unchanged. The temporalities of the house still came into the king's hand during a vacancy and had to be restored to the new abbot once his election was confirmed, as happened on 12 March (ibid, 244). On 2 April 1400 Henry IV confirmed royal charters to Bermondsey previously confirmed by King Richard, and also Richard's charter of denization (ibid, 304; *Ann Monast*, iii, 482 – where the annal is mistakenly dated 1399).

Restoration was short-lived, however. On 11 May 1400 a commission was issued for taking custody of the abbey and its possessions on the grounds that it had been overburdened by bad government in the time of John Attilburgh, the late abbot, along with a grant of protection for the abbot, convent and their possessions (*Cal Pat R*, 1399–1401, 284); instructions to arrest Attilburgh followed on 8 June 1400 (ibid, 315). On 21 November 1401 the king announced that he had taken the abbey and its possessions into his hand, on account of bad government under John Attilburgh who had charged the house with many pensions, corrodies and great debts, and 'indiscreetly demised' or otherwise alienated various of its estates; keepers had now been appointed to ensure that all issues beyond the necessary maintenance of abbot, monks and servants should be applied to the relief of the abbey, and the said pensions, corrodies and farms shall cease until the abbey be cleared of debt (ibid, 1401–5, 23). On 10 April 1402 the king permitted John Tournay to sue the abbey (though it was still under royal protection) for an annual rent of £20 granted by Abbot John from the manor of Bermondsey and which the abbey, after defaulting for 15 months, had now repudiated (ibid, 82). The former abbot last appeared in March 1406 when, as bishop of Ardfert (an office he held from 1405 to his death sometime before 1411), he surrendered to Bermondsey a pension of £20 from the abbey's lands in Surrey which had been granted to him for life while he was still in office (*Cal Close R*, 1405–9, 119).

Early in 1403 there arose a case, not uncommon for religious houses generally but rare for Bermondsey, where the title to its former royal property came under hostile scrutiny and had here resulted in confiscation. On 12 January 1403 the royal escheator in Somerset was ordered to restore the abbey's manors of Kingweston and Preston (Plucknett), and its revenues, as it had been found by inquisition that the manors were given to Bermondsey by one of the king's forefathers (which one was unknown) to find two monk resident chaplains at Preston to celebrate daily in the chapel of St Mary there for the souls of the faithful departed (*Cal Close R*, 1402–5, 241; *Cal Inq Misc*, vii, 238). A similar case occurred nearer home in April 1406, when a local inquest at Southwark found that for the previous 80 years the abbey had occupied without licence 22 acres (8.9ha) of land and 8 acres (3.2ha) of meadow called *Brokeshull*, formerly part of the common of the township of Rotherhithe (*Cal Fine R*, xii, [p] 45; *Cal Inq Misc*, vii, 322). In June, however, the king decided to restore the land to the abbey, though pointing out to the escheator that every acre was worth 6s per annum (*Cal Close R*, 1405–9, 45); the implication being that an annual payment would henceforth be required of the abbey.

After an apparently problematic decade, Bermondsey does seem to have returned to respectability in the first decade of the 15th century. In 1404 Abbot Henry was helping to oversee the affairs of the Cluniac priory of Montacute during its vacancy, and also acting as collector of the tenth in Surrey (*Cal Pat R*, 1401–5, 335; *Cal Close R*, 1402–5, 350, also 413, 415); a century earlier, Bermondsey had been excommunicated for its inability or unwillingness to pay up its own contribution to a similar levy (above, 3.5, 'Documentary evidence').

In the early 15th century, although Bermondsey was well established as a denizened house, formal links with Cluny were still maintained. On 12 June 1415 Thomas Elmham, prior of Lenton, was given two years' protection during his appointment by Raymond 'minister of Cluny' to 'hear, treat and determine all questions, spiritual and temporal belonging to him by right and custom, and to visit all places of the Order at their expense, when necessary or expedient.' Among these the abbey of Bermondsey was mentioned expressly (*Cal Pat R*, 1413–16, 333).

Following Abbot Henry's death in 1413, Thomas Thetford, monk of St Saviour, was elected abbot and the abbey's temporalities restored to the new abbot (*Ann Monast*, iii, 484; *Cal Pat R*, 1413–16, 19, 24, 47). On 2 June 1413 the king nominated Mr Nicholas Colnet, his physician, to receive the pension which the abbey was bound to pay, on the election of a new abbot, to one of the king's clerks until it provided him with a benefice (*Cal Close R*, 1413–19, 82). There is no earlier evidence of such a custom, which was quite separate from the regular royal corrody existing at this period (Chapter 4.3, 'The inhabitants: lay people').

Throughout this period, *c* 1330–*c* 1430, the documents reflect a preoccupation with the priory's financial affairs and difficulties and maximising income. Many more benefactions, concessions, gifts and wills are recorded for the 14th century than for the 13th. The annals state that in 1347 the king conceded that the prior and his successors should be able to acquire each year and forever lands, rents and tenements to a value of £20 in their own or others' fee, excepting lands held of the king in chief, the Statute of Mortmain notwithstanding, and this concession was entered on the Patent Rolls on 1349 (*Ann Monast*, iii, 474–5; *Cal Pat R*, 1348–50, 225). This relaxation of the mortmain provisions had been foreshadowed in May 1341 by a licence to acquire lands and rents to the value of 100s per annum (*Cal Pat R*, 1340–3, 225) and by 18 August of the same year the priory had received from Peter de Cusancia and John Lambyn of Colchester, citizen of London, a messuage and a toft in Rotherhithe in satisfaction of 30s of the 100s yearly (ibid, 1313–17, 254; *Ann Monast*, iii, 473–4). A further licence was granted on 24 May 1350 for the acquisition from William de Cherleton of a messuage and 65 acres (26.3ha) in Kynewardeston to the clear annual value of 11s 8d and within the same 100s quota (*Ann Monast*, iii, 475; *Cal Pat R*, 1348–50, 508). After a lengthy interval the king's clerk Guy Mone was licensed, on 6 July 1397, to grant the priory the advowson of Kemsing (Kent) (*Cal Pat R*, 1396–9, 291).

Wills proved in the City court of husting and favouring Bermondsey during this period include that of Roger de Euere, ironmonger, proved on 31 January 1334, who bequeathed to his son John, a monk of Bermondsey, an annuity of 6 marks for celebrating for the good of himself and family, and to the prior and convent his tenements in the City on the deaths of his daughters (*Cal Husting Wills*, i, 393). Smaller bequests were made to the priory by Henry Hale, a fishmonger, in his will proved in March 1376 (ibid, ii, 186) and Margaret Tonk, who left the monks 13s 4d in her will proved in 1378 (ibid, ii, 214–15). And Bermondsey was among a number of local religious houses which received a measure of red wine and money under the will of John de Oxenford, vintner, proved in

July 1342 in return for their prayers (ibid, i, 460).

Two major property transactions occurred at the end of the 14th century. On 16 February 1390, Prior Richard Dunton, with the king's prior consent, exchanged the manor of Waddon for the church of Croydon (worth £24 per annum in 1535) with William Courtenay, Archbishop of Canterbury (*Ann Monast*, iii, 481; *Cal Pat R*, 1388–92, 367). Waddon lay near Croydon, close to one of the archbishop's most important manors, and the exchange consolidated Canterbury's estates in the district. The second transaction concerned a much nearer property and was set in train on 8 March 1397 when the abbot and convent of St Mary Graces by the Tower were authorised to lease in perpetuity to Bermondsey Priory at a yearly fee-farm rent of £20 the 'place and manor' of Rotherhithe, with all its houses and garden, together with a messuage hard by called *le Grange*, acquired by the late king from Walter Forester, citizen of London, and granted by the said king's feoffees and executors to the St Mary's as part of its endowment (*Cal Pat R*, 1396–9, 108; TNA: PRO, E326/4529). In the late 1360s Walter Forester and later Robert Crull had leased the property (known at one point as *la Daierie*) to Bermondsey, and by 1373 the rent was payable to the exchequer (*Cal Fine R*, 1369–77, 237). The present arrangement was plainly a continuation, or reinstatement, of that lease, and was plainly of advantage to both houses. It survived until the Dissolution, by which date the site had come to be regarded as actually belonging to Bermondsey. This included, and was probably centred upon, Edward III's 'manor house' at Platform Wharf, Rotherhithe (references to which are contained in a survey of the manor of Rotherhithe 'once pertaining to the monastery of Bermondsey' in 1632 (TNA: PRO, E178/5672; see Blatherwick and Bluer 2009). The lease of the Rotherhithe estate to Bermondsey was ratified in 1398 and again in 1399 (*Cal Pat R*, 1396–9, 330; 1399–1401, 326).

A series of legal actions during the time of Abbot Thomas Thetford (1413–32), especially those relating to distant Somerset, give the impression that Bermondsey had learnt the lessons of its former negligence and was now far more zealous in defence of its rights and income. In 1417, according to the Bermondsey annals, the abbot recovered from the king in Chancery the 'manors of Preston, Bermondsey [*sic*] and Stone in Somerset' (*Ann Monast*, iii, 485); this was evidently a recrudescence of the dispute over the abbey's title to its Somerset manors that had arisen 14 years before (see also *Cal Close R*, 1413–19, 411; *Cal Inq Misc*, vii, 546). In 1419, again according to the annals, Abbot Thomas proceeded against the parson of Beddington, recovering from him an annual pension of 100s payable from the church (*Ann Monast*, iii, 485). The same source also records Abbot Thomas's recovery of a messuage, dovecot, 60 acres (24.3ha) of land and 12 acres (4.9ha) of pasture in Kingweston in 1426 (ibid, 486), while two years later he came to an agreement with the master of the Hospital of St Thomas in Southwark, concerning lands and tenements held of the abbot in Southwark and elsewhere, and an ancient rent payable to the abbey (ibid). In 1429 Walter Wolley of the town of Derby (Derbyshire), yeoman, was fined for not appearing before the king to answer Abbot Thomas

concerning a plea of debt of 20 marks (*Cal Pat R*, 1422–9, 509).

Leasing out, under royal supervision, of the larger priory estates so evident from the late 1310s continued in this period. The manors and advowsons of Charlton (Kent) and Widford, leased in 1317, were leased again in, respectively, 1354 for £20 per annum (*Cal Pat R*, 1353–8, 49) and in 1340 (ibid, 1338–40, 543). Similarly, Upton by Blewbury (Berkshire) for example continued to be leased (ibid, 1317–21, 380; 1324–7, 2; 1334–8, 388; 1345–8, 193–4; 1353–8, 43). In 1342 Prior John was licensed to lease his manor of Cowick (Essex) to whomsoever he would for a term of life or years 'for the more prompt payment of his debts and farm of his priory, custody whereof has been committed to him by the king at a rent' (ibid, 1340–3, 432).

Local properties leased under royal licence include in 1357 *Druetesmarsh* and 3 acres (1.2ha) of meadow of Bermondsey, to be enclosed with a dyke by *Danyeleswalle*, in favour of Thomas de Habyndon for life, and the manor of Dulwich in favour of Thomas Dolsaly for life at 20 marks annually (*Cal Pat R*, 1353–8, 489, 513). A highly unusual arrangement (as far as the record goes) was Walter Forester's 30-year lease of 6 April 1369 to the priory of land in Bermondsey in exchange for 6 acres (2.4ha) of arable in *Southswansworthe* in the field of Rotherhithe called *Clerkeslonde* (*Cat Anc Deeds*, iv, A7982). This was ratified on 12 November 1370 by Robert Crull, who had succeeded Forester in the property; the farm was £20 yearly for the first two years (from June 1369) and £40 thereafter (*Cal Fine R*, 1369–77, 94).

In 1416, according once more to the Bermondsey annals, Robert Brounesbury alias Rykherst began to enclose the breach of Bermondsey in the parish of Rotherhithe (*coepit includere breccam de Bermundeseye in parochia de Retherhithe*) (*Ann Monast*, iii, 484): whatever was meant by this, the operations plainly did not succeed in permanently safeguarding the abbey site from the Thames tides.

As in the previous period, the fabric of the priory buildings is only infrequently referred to. Some of the buildings were described as in need of repair owing to flooding early in the 14th century, but there are other references to restorations or rebuildings (above, 3.5, 'Documentary evidence'). The 'greater' church of St Saviour of Bermondsey and the high altar (*ecclesia major Sancti Salvatoris de Bermondeseye et maius altare*) were dedicated in honour of the Blessed Virgin and All Saints on 11 January 1332 (Graham 1926, 178; 1937, 145–6). Three altars were subsequently dedicated, to Holy Cross, to 'Drueth' in honour of Blessed Mary and St Thomas the Martyr, and an altar next to the gate of the monks' cemetery, in honour of SS Andrew and James and all the Apostles (*Ann Monast*, iii, 473 under the year 1338). Graham suggests it was the dedication of the three last-mentioned altars in 1338, as recorded by the annals, which marked a further stage in the rebuilding of the conventual church, and that the 'Drueth' altar in a chapel of St Mary and St Thomas the Martyr was endowed from the receipts of *Druettesmarsh* in Rotherhithe, which the priory leased to Thomas de Pykenham, a London merchant, in 1362 (Graham 1926, 178). On 31 December 1346 a faculty was granted to consecrate an altar in the conventual church of Bermondsey in honour of SS Lawrence and Denis (*Reg Edington*, 1346–66, ii, 51). The sacristy of the priory is referred to in a deed of 1334 (and in another undated, ?12th-/13th-century, deed), indicating it lay on the north side of the priory church at this time (Dawson 2002, 6).

As late as 1381, a petition sent to John of Gaunt as the king's regent reported that as a result of the neglect and mismanagement of foreign priors and other burdens the buildings of the priory were in a ruinous condition (TNA: PRO, SC8/93/4628). In 1381 and after a long delay, according to the annals, the cloister and refectory were rebuilt by Richard Dunton, the first English head of the house (*Ann Monast*, iii, 480). The completion of some work on the church seems to be implied by the statement in 1387 that Richard also leaded the nave of the church (*gremium sive navem ecclesie*) and installed nine glass windows in the presbytery, along with gilded 'tables' or reredoses (ornamental screens covering the wall at the back of an altar) for the high altar and morning altar (*Ann Monast*, iii, 481). However, an account roll at the British Library (Graham 1937, 148–9) detailing priory expenditure during the period Easter 1391 to Michaelmas 1392 includes a payment of £53 6s 8d by the prior, perhaps for the completion of his own house, a payment of £64 6s 8d for the roof of the church and other large expenditures of timber and lead for the south aisle. Glass costing £22 was bought for seven windows. From these details it is clear that this phase of work on the conventual church was not finally completed until Michaelmas 1392, after Prior Dunton's resignation as prior in 1390 and death.

By October 1397 St Saviour Bermondsey was regarded as a fit place for the temporary repose of the body of Eleanor, widow of Thomas, Duke of Gloucester, pending her removal to Westminster for burial (*Cal Close R*, 1396–9, 149–50).

Further references to the buildings of the priory of St Saviour include one on 12 January 1385, with regard to alms which had been given to St Saviour to find a lamp before the altar of St Mary in the infirmary of Bermondsey (*Cal Close R*, 1381–5, 501). In her will of May 1349 Matilda de Myms consigned her apprentice William to the care and teaching of Brother Thomas de Alshom at the priory for a period of three years (*Cal Husting Wills*, i, 576). This is of special interest as a rare reference to the school at Bermondsey noted by Stow (1603, i, 73). In 1430, according to the annals (whose reliability at this date, close to their compilation, is much improved), Abbot Thomas had the cloister re-roofed in a stone called slate (*de novo cooperiri fecit claustrum cum petra vocata slad*: *Ann Monast*, iii, 487).

Archaeological evidence

Extensive rebuilding in this period, period M8, involved both the main and second (infirmary) cloisters and the buildings around them, and the chapter house and priory church (Fig 57). Major alterations took place in the south part of the main cloister, to the south end of the east range (B7) and to the refectory (B6), and new structures were erected against the refectory's south wall. The former infirmary cloister (OA2) was rearranged (B14). On the south side, the hall/lodgings (B8) was extended east by the addition of a small room, probably a bedchamber (B8f). On the east side, the infirmary buildings (B10 and B11) were demolished and replaced by a large open courtyard (OA9) on to which a number of separate cells or chambers opened (B13), with alterations in the area immediately to the north (to the yard OA7 and former ? infirmary range extension B12). The water supply and drainage system were enhanced and possibly overhauled. The north side of the second cloister was affected by the remodelling of the chapter house (B4), and the cloister arcade (B5) (on the basis of PCA's excavation) was apparently rebuilt. The east end of the priory church (B3) was also altered. The reredorter (B9) and chapel (B1) remained in use unchanged.

Chapel (B1)

Evidence from the later robbing of the chapel (period P1) indicates that in period M8 the earlier (period M7; above, 3.5) tiled floor was probably repaired, with mid–late 14th-century Penn tiles (designs E1843, E2232 or E2234; <T22>, Fig 146). The glazing of the chapel may also have been completed at this time (above, 3.5, 'Archaeological evidence').

Priory church (B3)

The evidence for the development of the priory (from 1399 abbey) church (B3) in this period consisted largely of segments of robber trench recorded in plan and section by Grimes and which testify to an enhanced, square-ended presbytery and a new north aisle (Fig 57).

The existing north aisle wall was either reduced to its foundations or more probably left *in situ* and pierced with new openings. A new wall was constructed 3.35m to the north, widening the north aisle or (more likely) adding another aisle to the north side of the presbytery. The two apsidal chapels in the north transept were removed and the new aisle so created was *c* 3m wide and *c* 25m long. External buttresses to the new aisle wall may have been added later in the period. There is no direct dating evidence for these developments to the priory church.

This new north aisle wall is labelled '14th century (?) north wall, later (post-monastic) garden wall' on Grimes's published plan (Fig 23). The line of this buttressed wall (labelled 'Wall A' in the Grimes archive) was perpetuated by a (unbuttressed) standing wall and property boundary which can be located on the 1896 Ordnance Survey (OS) map. The superstructure of this wall, which survived to a height of 2.25m and was 0.75m wide, consisted of reused stone from the priory. It is probable that over time the wall had been almost entirely rebuilt from foundation level up.

A short section of north–south robber trench, *c* 9m to the south-east of the new north aisle wall, appears to represent the squaring off of the former apsidal ends to both the original (period M4) north aisle and north side of the presbytery (Fig 23). To the east of this robber trench, Grimes recorded a short section of foundation which had a definite face on its west side but was otherwise not completely revealed. The foundation may be a buttress on the north side of an extended square east end. An alternative explanation for the robber trenches found by Grimes is that they are the remains of a north–south aligned structure appended to the north side of the church.

The hypothesis of an extended square east end is supported to a degree by the evidence for the south wall of the presbytery found in the 1980s on site A. A later robber trench showed that the line of the period M4 apsidal foundation (Fig 21) was extended east and buttressed; this buttress aligns with the north–south section of the 'square end' shown by Grimes. Taken together, these robber trenches and fragmentary foundations can be interpreted as evidence for a symmetrical and extended square-ended presbytery, in contrast to the earlier, asymmetrical, apse echelon scheme (Chapter 4.2, 'The 12th-century priory church'; Fig 69).

Fragments of a large, traceried window, probably from the priory church, were found reused in a later context. The window incorporated large ?trefoliated archlets (A<3112>; CP5.3.4; Chapter 7.2; Fig 139). The sill shows the window was flush with the outer wall face, which implies that it was used in a relatively thin wall. The builders were aware of the deficiencies of ?Reigate stone and used a hard oolitic limestone for the sill and mullion *stoolings*. The internal elevation was whitewashed but bore no evidence of any colouring and shutters. The four-way symmetrical mullion moulding with tapering fillets and hollow chamfers is a widespread form, with published examples occurring in the Lady chapel at Ely ?before 1349 (Morris 1979, 10) and in the north range of Edward III's palace at Rotherhithe in the 1350s where it seems to have been an innovation (Samuel 2009, 27–9). In its essentials the moulding remained in favour until the end of the medieval period, but details of proportioning at Bermondsey are indicative of a 14th-century date.

Burials recorded by Grimes inside the north aisle (Fig 23) are – for lack of any other evidence – included in period M8, when a possibly enhanced presbytery may have become a focus for burial. They comprise a row of apparently three or four, closely packed, with a further burial to the east which is mostly outside Grimes's trench; none are shown as cists.

Chapter house (B4) and cloister (B5)

The east wall of the chapter house (B4) was located at the west limit of excavation of site A, 2.0m from the west end of the chapel nave. The structural evidence for the chapter house consists of the partial remains of one foundation and a robber trench, with no dating for either. The north wall of the chapter house was recorded by Buckler (BL, Add MS 24433, fo 78); no trace of an apse was recorded and the chapter house may have been built rectilinear from the start rather than apsidal (Chapter 4.2, 'The 12th-century priory church'). He also recorded what might have been a projecting jamb of the chapter house entrance; it is also possible that Tudor window embrasures recorded by Buckler originated as a dual entrance, but this is pure supposition.

The wall foundation was constructed of mortared ragstone. It had one offset 120–180mm wide at 2.1m OD and a second offset c 100mm wide at 2.69m OD, on which the wall was set. Where extant, the wall superstructure reached a height of 3.18m OD. A foundation of randomly coursed ragstones in a hard, gravel and sand mortar at the south end of the wall may be a south-east buttress or part of the foundations for the structure built between the east end of the chapter house and the west end of the chapel (B1). This structure was indicated by two foundations 3.0m apart abutting the chapel and chapter house. It may have served as a covered porch for an entrance into either building, or as a covered passage between doorways in both buildings, linking the two. From the standing and robbed remains, it is possible to arrive at a square-ended chapter house c 10m wide, with an east end buttressed at the north and south corners.

Given the lack of dating evidence, it is possible that this rebuilding of the chapter house occurred in the succeeding period (M9), in the mid to later 15th century, or in the preceding period (M7) in the early 14th century. However, it is reasonable to suggest changes to the chapter house were part of a remodelling of the east part of the main cloister at this date, along with the modifications to the east range (B7) and second infirmary cloister (OA2) in this period (below, 'Second cloister (B14) and associated garth (OA2)'). Rebuilding of the cloister arcades probably took place at this time. Preliminary results from excavations by PCA (A Douglas, pers comm) in the north-east corner of the cloister (on the 'Island' site, BYQ98; Fig 3) indicate two phases of foundations for the pentise walls of the north and east cloister walks.

Refectory (B6) and the area to the south-west of the conventual buildings (OA4)

In this period, some refurbishment of the refectory (B6) took place (Fig 57). A new south wall, 1.3m distant from the standing south wall, was built, creating a passage or corridor (presumably covered) along the length of the building on its south side. The original south wall very probably remained to its full height, since the surviving masonry found on site A included superstructure to a height of 3.70m OD (compared to modern street level at c 4.15m OD). In general, on the site of St Saviour Bermondsey, walls that survived to any height into the post-medieval period did so because they were incorporated into the later 16th-century mansion house (period P1; Chapter 5). At the east end of the building a right-angled foundation created a 'lobby' area between the west–east passage and the north–south passage through the ground floor of the east range (B7).

The 14th-century ground-floor passage added to Building 6 would have afforded access from the west cloister range – outside the refectory and cloister – through the east range (B7) (below) into the infirmary cloister, and to the new courtyard (OA9) and buildings (B13) to the east, creating a major west–east access route. There is evidence for a paved walk in a similar position, adjacent to the south side of the refectory,

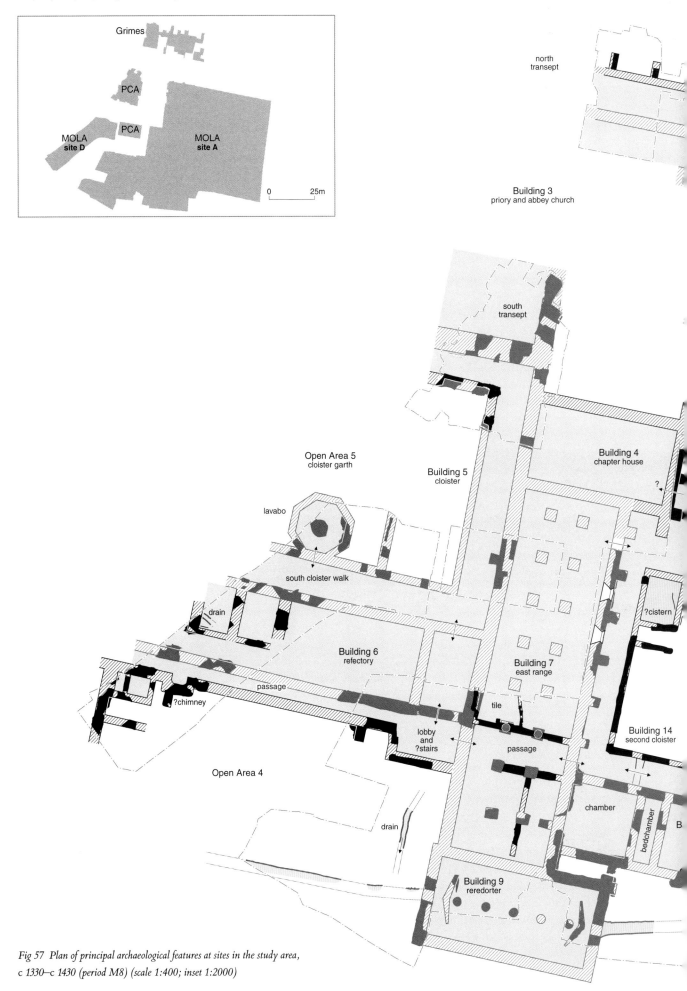

*Fig 57 Plan of principal archaeological features at sites in the study area,
c 1330–c 1430 (period M8) (scale 1:400; inset 1:2000)*

N

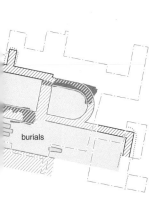

burials

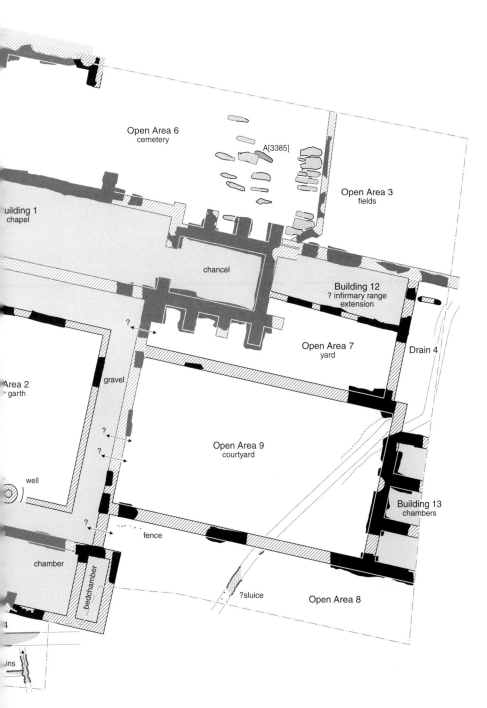

Open Area 6
cemetery

A[3385]

Open Area 3
fields

uilding 1
chapel

chancel

Building 12
? infirmary range
extension

Open Area 7
yard

Drain 4

Area 2
garth

gravel

well

Open Area 9
courtyard

Building 13
chambers

?

?

?

?

fence

chamber

bedchamber

?sluice

Open Area 8

ins

female burial

0   10m

81

from Pontefract Priory (Bellamy 1965, 17, fig 24). There may also have been new, or additional, provision for accessing the upper floors in the south and east ranges. The lobby at the east end of the refectory passage may have housed a stair (these areas of the priory complex were unexcavated). At Castle Acre Priory where the kitchen was adjacent to the refectory, at the west end of the south cloister range, spiral staircases at the west end of the refectory led to passages in the thickness of the north and south refectory walls at approximately the level of the cloister roof (Coad and Coppack 1998, 34).

Fragments of chalk foundations at the west end of the passage (including a chimney) and to the south in Open Area 4 were uncovered on site D (Fig 3; Fig 57, inset), suggesting service buildings. New drains were cut, both south of the lobby (OA4) and within the refectory itself. Internally, towards the west end of the refectory, fragments of sleeper foundations may suggest the addition of internal structures and possibly that the dining hall was shortened, or perhaps that it was embellished by a vault.

East range (B7)

The east range (B7) was altered, it appears, as part of the creation of the new access via the new refectory passage (B6) and the remodelled second cloister (OA2; Fig 57). A wall was built across the ground floor of the east range, dividing off the three south bays of the building. A second wall, joining the piers of the next bay to the south, created an east–west passage linking the main cloister and west ranges with the new second cloister. The two bays at the south end of the east range underwent further division to form at least two individual chambers (Fig 58). The internal walls were coated with a limewash and decorated with red masonry pattern (ie imitation ashlar, outlined in red).

The east range north of the east–west passage may also have been subdivided. The first bay north of the passage had a possible internal partition and the west half had a tile floor. The east wall of the east range (B7) was pierced by a minimum of two openings. At the north limit of excavation, the south jamb of a door was recorded (Fig 59), which would have given ground-floor access from the east range into the north-west corner of the second cloister, again perhaps through a passage. One rectangular Reigate stone block, 470 x 240 x 150mm formed the threshold at 3.44m OD. On its south side and placed at a right angle to it, another large Reigate stone block ran through the thickness of the wall.

Window openings pierced each of the two bays south of the door. The south window had a single splay through the thickness of the wall; its Reigate stone and ragstone fabric had been treated with a render of red, followed by white plaster. The window reveal was 1.10m broadening to 1.40m internally.

Fig 58 View of the ground floor of the east range (B7) in period M8, showing internal divisions, from the east (2.0m scales)

Fig 59 Detail of door opening in the east wall of the east range (B7) in period M8, from the east (0.5m scale)

Fig 60 Detail of north window in the east wall of the east range (B7) in period M8, from the west (1.0m scale)

The splay of the north window was of comparable dimensions and had a wash of white plaster (Fig 60). The architectural fragments evidence (Fig 138) indicated a range of domestic shuttered windows, such as might have been inserted in the east range, but several buildings seem to be indicated (Chapter 7.2, 'Construction phase 5, c 1340–c 1410 (period M8)').

Hall/lodgings (B8)

The hall/lodgings (B8) was extended east by 1.5m (Fig 57). At the same time, the ? service area added in period M6 (Fig 49) was extended south to meet the line of the original south wall of Building 8. The building was now 32m long and a uniform 7m wide. These developments were made possible by the rebuilding (D4, below), slightly to the south, of the eastern section of the west–east aligned stone-built drain (D2). There was no direct dating evidence for the further extension of Building 8; it is based on inference from surrounding developments in Open Area 2 and changes to the drainage system (D2 and D4).

The rooms in Building 8 now resemble very closely the arrangements made in the south cloister range at Cistercian Cleeve Abbey (Somerset) in the 15th century for, it is suggested, senior monks or corrodians. There, two chambers each with adjacent bedchambers formed suites, complete with latrine, for private accommodation (Harrison 2000, 14–15, 36). Building 8 would have provided on either side of a central hall at least two sets of rooms, probably to accommodate senior members of the community.

Demolition of the former infirmary buildings (B10 and B11)

Both north–south aligned infirmary buildings, the infirmary (B10) and former infirmary latrine (B11), were demolished in period M8, with the exception of the former east wall of Building 10, which was retained as the outer wall of the east walk of the new cloister (B14; cf Fig 53 and Fig 57).

Pottery spanning several hundred years (c 1050–c 1500) was recovered from a number of robber cuts, fills and demolition spreads, the latest with a date range of c 1350–c 1500, from A[735]. This date is based on a handle sherd from a large rounded or bunghole jug (cistern) in coarse Surrey-Hampshire border ware (CBW), a form not generally found before c 1350 (Pearce and Vince 1988, 84–5). A diverse range of fabrics and forms was found in the contexts associated with the demolition of the infirmary buildings, all typical of pottery in use on the site throughout the 11th to 14th centuries, with London-type ware (LOND), shelly-sandy ware (SSW) and Kingston-type ware (KING) predominating, principally in jug and cooking pot forms. The upper backfill of the cesspit outside the infirmary (B10) contained 17 sherds of pottery dated c 1350–c 1400, the lower (use) fill pottery dated c 1230–c 1400. The pottery from the upper backfill includes part of a D-shaped dripping dish in coarse Surrey-Hampshire border ware (CBW; cf ibid, fig 117 no. 498), bowls and jugs in Kingston-type ware (KING), part of a London-type ware (LOND) baluster-shaped drinking jug and Mill Green ware (MG) jugs. Although these are all small sherds, none of which come from the same vessel, they demonstrate something of the diversity of forms available by the late 14th century.

A wide range of stone and ceramic building material was also associated with the demolition of the infirmary (period M8) and included a large amount of reused Roman brick and tile, and smaller quantities of medieval flanged and peg roofing tile, Low Countries floor tile, and 15th- to 16th-century red brick (probably intrusive). Some of this material may have formed part of the roofing and/or flooring of the infirmary (B10). One fragment of floor tile is decorated by at least one semicircular line added by a compass, the compass point being clearly visible in the surviving corner (Fig 149, <T30>). The tile has a covering of very worn yellow glaze and is 27mm thick. This is probably of 11th-century date and may originally have been laid in the chapel (B1) to the north (Chapter 7.4).

Second cloister (B14) and associated garth (OA2)

After the demolition of the former infirmary buildings (B10 and B11), a new formal cloister (B14, Fig 57) was created, probably contemporaneously with the construction of the new chambers (B13) and courtyard (OA9) to the east. The new cloister garth (OA2) was 18.35m north–south by 22.5m east–west. The cloister walk itself was *c* 3m wide and had a compacted gravel surface. The pentise walls of the cloister walk rested on narrow foundations between 0.5m and 0.8m wide.

There must have been access points to and from the cloister at each of the four corners. A door in the east wall of the east range (B7) opened on to the north-west corner of the cloister and the passage through the east range (from the refectory passage B6) led to the south-west corner. Entrances are conjectured in the north- and south-east corners of the cloister, because the spatial relationship of the cloister garth (OA2) and the courtyard (OA9) appears designed to accommodate them. Interestingly, there was a north–south partition wall, presumably containing a door or gate, towards the west end of the south walk.

In the pentise wall of the south cloister walk was a well, which occupied a similar position in this cloister, as did the lavabo in the principal monastic cloister (B5). In the north-west corner of the cloister, two parallel west–east wall foundations and a north–south robbing trench may represent the remains of a storage cistern or settling tank (Bond 2001, 96–9).

Former ? infirmary range extension (B12)

Building 12 was altered again in period M8 (Fig 57). The earlier (period M7; Fig 53) south wall was replaced, slightly to the north, with a less substantial one and the building was foreshortened on its east side by the insertion of a north–south wall, making Building 12 13.8m long by 5.5m wide. The north wall of the building, however, was retained. Outside and east of the building and parallel with its north wall a narrow chalk foundation may have been the footing for an external timber stair or for a lean-to. The east wall of Building 12 continued south to adjoin the north-east corner of the new courtyard (OA9). The insubstantial nature of the Building 12 south foundation suggests that it may have supported a timber frame on a masonry plinth, as opposed to a solid wall, and the nature and function of this structure may have changed in this period.

Chambers (B13) and courtyard (OA9)

A large new enclosed walled courtyard (OA9, Fig 57) was created to the south of the chapel chancel (B1) and Building 12, and south of the yard (OA7), following the demolition of the infirmary buildings (B10 and B11). The new courtyard encompassed an area 27.3m east–west by *c* 16m north–south. The retained east wall of the infirmary (B10) served as the courtyard's western enclosing wall.

The courtyard served a series of private chambers (B13) ranged along its east side. Opening on to the east side of the courtyard (OA9) were three separate chambers (Fig 57, B13),

each between 3.5m and 3.7m wide and a minimum 4.3m long. There was no extant evidence for any floors or features within the rooms, which had been heavily truncated by modern concrete footings.

The courtyard (OA9) was presumably reached on the west off the second cloister (B14) – perhaps through an entrance adapted from the earlier (periods M5–M7) infirmary doorways – and presumably there was access to the south and/or north through gates in either or both of its north and south walls. A large stone voussoir (A<3148>; CP5.2.1; not illustrated), recovered during machine clearance, is thought to have come from a gate *c* 2m wide; the massive jamb had a rebate for a door 60mm thick. The Perpendicular moulding can only be roughly dated; examples of this kind of gate or door can be seen at Winchester College (Winchester, Hampshire), where one is dated to *c* 1388 (Harvey 1978, fig 32).

Cemetery (OA6)

Of the 21 graves and grave cuts excavated in this period in the cemetery (Fig 57, OA6), 11 were disposed *c* 1m apart in approximate north–south rows. These 11 grave cuts, which were difficult to distinguish archaeologically owing to later disturbance, were located to the north of the chapel chancel (B1), some 6m from the cemetery wall. The remaining ten, in which no skeletal material was discovered (because of exhumation in period M9), had been placed in a neat row against the cemetery wall.

The skeletal remains available for osteological analysis comprised 12 individuals. These were mainly adult males (eight males/?males: two young adults, four mature adults, one old/ elderly adult, one defined only as adult), with three adults of indeterminate sex and one elderly female (the age and sex breakdown is detailed in Table 20; the female A[3385] is located on Fig 57).

One individual (A[3541]) had a small depressed facture of the skull (left parietal) and one (A[3607]) had three breaks in the right ankle, probably the result of an accident, perhaps a particularly awkward fall (Chapter 7.9, 'Pathology', 'Trauma').

Yard (OA7)

In period M8 the yard (OA7, Fig 57), immediately south of the ? infirmary range extension (B12), remained essentially the same space, but became somewhat longer and narrower owing to the creation of the new courtyard (OA9) to the south and changes to Building 12. Access to the yard (OA7) would have been from the north walk of the second cloister (B14) and there may have been an opening to the east and/or to the courtyard (OA9) to the south.

This yard (OA7) was highly enclosed, surrounded by solid masonry walls on almost all sides. It is questionable whether in fact the space was truly 'open' in this period; it may have had a timber roof or timber lean-tos along the stone walls to the east and south (on the north side, B12 may have had a timber frame on a masonry plinth in this period).

Open ground to the south-east of the conventual buildings (OA8) and stone-built drain (D4)

The ditch here (Fig 53; period M7), perhaps associated with the cesspit attached to now demolished Building 10, fell out of use and was backfilled. Pottery from the ditch backfill is dated *c* 1180–*c* 1230 and so is residual; it is generally fragmented, with no reconstructable vessel profiles, but cooking pots and jugs predominate (discussed in detail in Chapter 7.5). The ditch was then truncated by the new stone drain (D4) which bisected Open Area 8 in this period (Fig 57). Pottery from the construction fill of the new drain is dated *c* 1080–*c* 1350 (LOND). The north-east section of this stone-built drain crossed the new courtyard (OA9), passing beyond the east end of Building 12. A south section of new drain skirted the recently extended hall/lodgings (B8); to the west, this drainage system incorporated the western sections of the earlier drain (D2). The presumed junction between the north-east and south sections lay outside the excavated area.

The drain was traced for some 40+m. The drain base between the stone-lined sides was *c* 1m wide. In the base of the north-east section of the drain, some 4m beyond the south wall of the new courtyard (OA9), were four pairs of opposing postholes, 0.5m apart (Fig 61). At Lewes Priory a two-post structure with two additional posts outside the west wall of the reredorter range has been interpreted as a sluice gate (Lyne 1997, 57–8). Fragments of the oak sluice gate were found within the culvert there. The sluice at Lewes was thought to have engaged the action of the tide to help in flushing out the sewer, with the valve shutting off the water inflow at high tide and reopening at low. Given that the reredorter (B9) at St Saviour does not appear to have operated solely or even mainly on the principle of flushing waste through (above, 3.3, 'Discussion'), it may be that the structure within the drain was intended to control the levels of water in the drain in the eastern area, some distance from the reredorter.

South of the hall/lodgings (B8) a smaller, north–south aligned drain, which emptied into the south section of Drain 4 on its south side, indicates the probable existence of a building beyond the south limit of excavation. Medieval pottery recovered from this north–south drain (A[1865]: 31 sherds from a minimum of six vessels) was dated to *c* 1350–*c* 1400. This includes 26 sherds from a single pipkin in Kingston-type ware (KING) (Fig 62, <P17>; cf Pearce and Vince 1988, fig 95 no. 316). There is also part of a pipkin in late medieval Hertfordshire glazed ware (LMHG; date range *c* 1350–1450), as well as two cooking pots, a possible drinking jug or bottle with a narrow base and part of a crucible, all in Kingston-type ware.

Discussion

An upturn in the fortunes of the house in the mid and later 14th century is indicated by the documentary sources and this is reflected in the archaeological evidence. The scale and extent of both refurbishment and rebuilding, and new construction, in this period is considerable. The priory church and the main (B5)

Fig 61 Detail of postholes (represented by dark stains parallel to the left-hand wall) in the base of the north-east section of stone-built drain (D4) in period M8, from the south (0.5m and 1.0m scales)

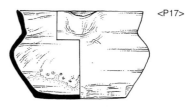

Fig 62 Kingston-type ware pipkin <P17> from the south-east drain complex (D4), period M8 (scale 1:4)

and former infirmary cloisters and adjacent buildings were all affected. The creation of a formal second cloister (B14) and of a new courtyard complex (OA9) to its east is suggestive of planned development on a large scale.

The documentary sources (above, 'Documentary evidence') suggest two (apparently separate) phases of construction related to the priory church (B3). The first is the consecration of various altars in the 1330s and 1340s, beginning with the high altar in 1332. The wholesale reconstruction proposed by Graham (1926) is not supported by the archaeological evidence reported here. One possible alteration around this time concerns the south side of the presbytery. There is evidence from Buckler for a 14th-century south doorway in the presbytery south wall giving access into the cemetery (probably replacing an earlier door), a door which it can be suggested dates *c* 1320–50 (Chapter 7.1, 'Catalogue of maps …', 'Doorway in north elevation, Bermondsey (BL, Add MS 24433, fo 138) …', 7.2, 'Construction phase 5, *c* 1340–*c* 1410 (period M8)'). The altar dedicated in honour of SS Andrew and James and all the Apostles was described as next to the gate of the monks' cemetery (*Ann Monast*, iii, 473 under the year 1338).

The second documented phase of alteration to the church is the 1380s to 1390s: according to the annals, in 1387 Prior Richard Dunton leaded the nave and installed nine glass windows in the presbytery, along with gilded reredoses for the high and morning altars, but other sources show that work on the roof and south aisle, and glazing, was not completed before 1392. Renewal of the roof and reglazing may have followed on from (and been necessitated by) the additions made to the north side of the church and alterations to the east end. This building activity may represent modernisation of the presbytery rather than wholesale reconstruction of the east arm of the church (Chapter 4.2, 'The 14th-century priory church').

Attributable to this phase of renewal of windows is a 14th-century, large traceried window (A<3112>; CP5.3.4; Fig 139), probably from the priory church, and the many traceried window fragments found reused at Harp Lane (Chapter 7.2, 'Construction phase 5, *c* 1340–*c* 1410 (period M8)'). Much of the window glass recovered from Dissolution and demolition contexts is broadly 14th century in date (Chapters 4.2, 'Interior decoration of the monastic buildings: glazing and tiling', 7.6, 'The context and character of the catalogued window glass').

Belonging to this period were two copper-alloy fragments from items of religious significance that were probably used in the church. The fragments were parts of the handles or supports from portable ewers (Fig 63, <S85>, OA6, period M8, <S86>, B9, period M9). These substantial, cast vessels were used in ecclesiastical contexts for ritual cleansing (Theuerkauff-Liederwald 1988, 390–1, 428–9, nos 497–9 and 501).

The reconstruction of the east end of the chapter house in this period would also have involved new fenestration and glazing. Square-ended chapter houses were a standard design in Cluniac houses from the 14th century. The 12th-century apsidal chapter houses at Castle Acre, Thetford and Wenlock were all remodelled in this way (Raby and Reynolds 1979; Coad and Coppack 1998; Pinnell 1999).

The renovations in the 1380s of, it is said in the annals, the cloister and refectory by Prior Richard Dunton (above, 'Documentary evidence') are recognisable in the (largely unexcavated) principal claustral ranges: the additions to the refectory (B6) and a new ?service building on its south side, together with alterations to the east range and perhaps most importantly the remodelled chapter house (B4) and cloister arcade (B5). The elevation of Bermondsey Priory to abbey status in 1399 may be the culmination of this major building and refurbishment programme. The re-roofing of the cloister in

slate recorded in the annals for 1430 would seem to belong to a different programme of repair work (*Ann Monast*, iii, 487).

A new, major west–east access route was created through the south ranges of conventual buildings, linking the main and second cloisters with a third enclosed area to the east. As part of this development considerable changes were made in the layout, number and type of domestic buildings east of the main cloister.

On the south side of the former infirmary cloister the hall/lodgings (B8) was extended east by the addition of a small room, probably a bedchamber (B8f), creating two pairs of rooms on the ground floor, and the building was probably two storeys. It seems that this range was enlarged to accommodate several individuals (rather than the infirmarer as suggested previously) who were provided for differently. No evidence survived for cooking or heating in the form of fireplaces or

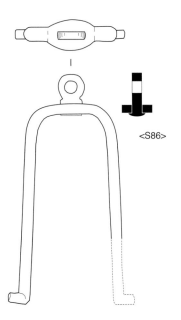

Fig 63 Copper-alloy mount <S85> (from OA6, period M8) and swivelling support <S86> (from B9, period M9), both from portable ewers, similar to the illustrated comparative vessel in the Vleeshuis Museum in Antwerp (after Theuerkauff-Liederwald 1988, no. 557) (scale 1:2; reconstruction not to scale)

hearths inside the suites of rooms in this period, but the central hall may have been retained and this incorporated a fireplace and chimney in the south wall; portable braziers were possibly used elsewhere. Instead of the earlier service area at the east end of this range (period M7), food could now be brought from kitchens in the south-west corner of the main claustral complex, without using the main cloister, via the new passage which ran in a continuous line from the west part of the south range into the south side of the second cloister.

There was no evidence for individual latrines or cesspits for this range or for internal drains, but the reredorter (B9) was only a few metres away, and the new stone drain (D4) ran just to the south. Potable water could have been supplied by the well just outside in the second cloister (OA2). The structure in the north-west corner of this cloister was possibly a storage cistern and may have supplied fresh water; or it may have been a settling tank, and collected the run-off from the cloister roofs, either for reuse or for disposal. The partition in the south cloister walk suggesting a gate or door would have restricted access and ensured privacy for the inhabitants of the chambers and/or for the main cloister.

This range, however, did not approach the level of comfort and privacy provided by, for example, the prior's house at Castle Acre, with its bedchamber, chapel, closet, study and hall, constructed in the west range in the 14th century (Coad and Coppack 1998, 34–40). Nor was it quite as well provided for in terms of latrines and fireplaces as some 15th-century examples of two-room suites. Mention has already been made above of the sets of rooms in the south cloister range at Cleeve Abbey (Harrison 2000, 14–15, 36), while at the modest Cluniac house of Crossraguel (Ayrshire) separate accommodation was provided for (it is thought) some of the monks along the south side of the south court in a row of five small two-room houses, each with its own latrine and fireplace (Raleigh Radford 2006, 13, 23).

On the east side, the infirmary buildings (B10 and B11) were demolished and not replaced, indicating a substantial reorganisation of the house. The former infirmary cloister was remodelled. To the east of this new second cloister a large open courtyard (OA9) was created and on its east side a number of separate cells or chambers (B13) were constructed. Like the hall/lodgings (B8) in the second cloister, these chambers do not appear to have had internal drains or latrines connected to the drain (D4) which ran around the north-west corner of this range, but these chambers were only partially excavated and heavily truncated. These units, no more than 4m across, can be interpreted as further evidence of increasing privatisation and separation in areas of the monastic life. The religious themselves, particularly senior members of the community, and any lay residents or visitors could be accommodated in these ranges. If the Bermondsey suites were occupied by ordinary monks, not just office holders, this would indicate a considerable change in their lifestyle, away from communal living.

A copper-alloy seal stamp (Fig 64, <S48>) recovered from the second cloister garth (OA2) is dated to this period; it could have been used by one of the religious within the community but more likely by a member of the laity. Corrodies for lay

individuals are recorded from the mid 13th century and, while accommodation within the precinct is often clearly implied if not explicitly stated, that described in detail in the 1320s for Nicholas de Tunstal appears to lie to the south and west of the main cloister (Chapter 4.3, 'The inhabitants: lay people'). Outsiders resident in this period included one William, an apprentice, entrusted to the brothers' care and teaching in 1349 for three years (*Cal Husting Wills*, i, 576).

The alterations, in the area immediately to the north of the new courtyard (OA9) and chambers (B13), to the yard (OA7) and former ? infirmary range extension (B12) raise interesting questions about the function of this area. With the infirmary buildings (B10 and B11) demolished and Building 12 apparently 'downgraded' further to a possibly timber-framed, single-storey structure, was Building 12 still part of a functioning infirmary? Or was it perhaps now a service building, associated with the yard (OA7) to its south? The infirmary buildings, Building 10 and Building 11, were not replaced, not on the same site nor in this area, indicating a substantial reorganisation of the house. The record in January 1385 of a lamp having been found before the altar of St Mary in the infirmary of Bermondsey (*Cal Close R*, 1381–5, 501) probably refers to the chancel of the infirmary chapel (B1). The sick and/or infirm could have been cared for together, if not in Building 12 then, perhaps in the chapel nave (B1) (cf above, 3.3, 'Discussion'), or had individual accommodation, for example in the eastern set of chambers (B13).

The demolition of infirmary buildings (B10, B11) and radical remodelling of the second cloister (OA2, B14) and east courtyard (OA7, OA9) combined with the creation of individual accommodation is a development paralleled in other monastic infirmary complexes from the 14th century. The infirmary hall at Waverley was partitioned into rooms, each with a fireplace; the halls at Fountains, Kirkstall (both in Yorkshire West Riding) and Tintern (Monmouthshire) became two-room apartments, each with a fireplace and latrine. At Byland (Yorkshire North Riding), the infirmary was demolished and replaced by a range of two-room sets. When numbers were falling, it was not just senior members of the community who were moving to more comfortable and private lodgings than the communal dormitory (Coppack 2006, 104–5).

The archaeological evidence for the expansion of the domestic conventual buildings, in particular private

Fig 64 Copper-alloy seal matrix <S48> (from OA2, period M8) (scale c 2:1)

accommodation, as witnessed in the chambers (B13) and courtyard (OA9), and the alterations to hall/lodgings (B8), is substantiated by typestones in the architectural fragments assemblage from a range of domestic windows dating after *c* 1350 (Chapter 7.2, 'Construction phase 5, *c* 1340–*c* 1410 (period M8)'). The shuttered windows would have been entirely appropriate in the type of accommodation provided by the hall/lodgings (B8); in the ground-floor chambers the window openings would probably have been in the south elevation, rather than overlooking the second cloister.

This domestic theme is reflected in the ceramics. The total ceramic assemblage from period M8 (discussed in detail in Chapter 7.5, 'Period M8, *c* 1330–*c* 1430') is relatively small (277 sherds) and mostly from small context groups, and a high proportion is residual material. Jugs and cooking pots are still the most common forms (the figures are somewhat biased by the quantity of residual material, especially from the north-east section of D4). The wares in use at Bermondsey were those available throughout the City. Of interest is the material from the area of the second cloister garth (OA2) and associated with the demolition of the infirmary (B10) which relates to the consumption and storage of liquids: drinking jugs and a lobed cup, and a single sherd from a bunghole cistern. Two pipkins recovered from the area to the south-west of the conventual buildings (OA4) would have been used for heating small quantities of food and had a handle and lip for pouring. The only evidence for industrial activity of any sort at this date is one sherd from a crucible in Kingston-type ware (KING) from Open Area 4, burnt from use.

3.7 Change and dissolution: the abbey *c* 1430–1538 (period M9)

Documentary evidence

The 15th century in general saw the continuing steady improvement in the abbey's fortunes that had already been marked in the final decades of the 14th century. A conspicuous feature of the documentary sources, as compared with earlier records, is the almost complete absence of references to the abbey's debts. St Saviour's troubles, however, were not entirely ended. Flooding remained a problem and was still capable of undermining the abbey's finances. A steady decline in the frequency of references to the affairs of Bermondsey in the king's correspondence noticeable from the mid 15th century accelerated in the 16th and was arrested only in the 1530s, on the eve of the Dissolution. The largest single category of topics covered was the abbey estates, usually taking the form of confirmations of leases.

Between September 1443 and August 1483 the abbot of Bermondsey was appointed to a series of commissions of walls and ditches set up to supervise the 'banks of water and marshes of the Thames' in places including Southwark, Bermondsey and

Rotherhithe and, occasionally, Wandsworth, East and West Greenwich and Gravesend (Kent) (*Cal Pat R*, 1441–6, 245; 1446–52, 41; 1452–61, 57, 221; 1467–76, 462, 463; 1476–85, 466). That the abbey was still subject to flooding as late as April 1487 is shown by the exemption of Bermondsey and various other houses from payment of the tenth on that account as well as for 'fires, ruins and accidents' (cf *Cal Fine R*, 1485–1509, no. 140 and *Cal Fine R*, 1471–85, nos 880–2).

Wills of the period occasionally refer to features of the conventual church. The wills of William Kelshall and his wife Alice (1428 and 1433: TNA: PRO, PROB 11/3 quires 16 and 19) refer to the chapel of Holy Cross, where William had been buried under a marble structure. The Lady chapel was mentioned in 1472 as the burial place of Margaret de la Pole (TNA: PRO, PROB 11/6 quire 12) and again in 1497 as the burial place of Ann, Lady Audley, 'in the monastery of St Saviour Bermondsey, under the tower there' (TNA: PRO, PROB 11/11 quire 23); Lady Audley lived at the abbey before her death (Graham 1926, 183–4). The will of Thomas Ashby mentions the chapel of St Thomas (1487: TNA: PRO, PROB 11/11 quire 14).

By this period, recorded benefactions to St Saviour Bermondsey were limited to small sums of money bequeathed to the abbey in return for burial in the conventual church. In the wills noted above, money was also specifically assigned to the abbot and convent for prayers (15–20s), waxes for the high altar in respect of forgotten oblations (3s 4d–6s 8d) and towards the fabric (3s 4d–6s 8d). Wealthier and noble personages often bequeathed vestments and small sums to each individual monk and novice for prayers. The sum of 20s was twice allocated to the abbot, on one occasion in return for attending the burial; the presence of the prior in his place merited a bequest of 6s 8d. In 1513 one testator, Mathew Baker, required to be buried before the image of St Saviour of Bermondsey and left to the abbey his lesser basin of silver (TNA: PRO, PROB 11/17, quire 18 fo 139). Anne Baskerville, whose will was dated 23 January 1513 and proved 17 November 1517, was to be buried in the church as near the body of John Baskerville her late husband as may be conveniently devised and left £6 17s 4d to St Saviour Bermondsey 'to the intent that one of the masters of the said monastery assigned by my lord abbot shall say a Mass at the altar of St Anne within the said monastery "daily and weekly" for a space of two years after her death for praying for souls' (TNA: PRO, PROB 11/18, quire 36 fo 287). John Edgecumbe, in his will of 28 October 1533, left 12d to the high altar and appointed Abbot Robert Wharton as overseer of his will in return for 20s (TNA: PRO, PROB 11/25, quire 7 fo 38).

The major preoccupation of the early years of Abbot John Bromley's tenure (1432–73) was a dispute over the rights of the prior of Lewes as visitor. On 18 February 1433 the king licensed Robert Auncell, Prior of Lewes, to serve as chamberlain of Odo, Abbot of Cluny, for the province of England, Scotland and Ireland, and to visit all houses of the Order, including Bermondsey, which however he was to visit as an abbey and not as a priory (*Cal Pat R*, 1429–36, 263). On 15 July 1434, Prior Robert reported back to Cluny that the abbot of Bermondsey had refused to acknowledge his summons and jurisdiction (Duckett 1888, ii, 37). The situation had as its background a failed attempt by Cluny and La Charité-sur-Loire to reassert their authority over their former English daughter houses (Graham 1926, 160, 161). Again, on the occasion of another visitation almost 20 years later, the king declared on 20 June 1452 that if the prior of Lewes, 'as chamberlain and vicar of Cluny', was to visit Bermondsey he must treat it as an abbey and not as a priory (*Cal Pat R*, 1446–52, 562).

On 12 February 1444 Richard II's letters patent of 1400 giving Bermondsey the status of abbey were inspected and confirmed (*Cal Pat R*, 1441–6, 336). On 4 June 1461, Richard confirmed the agreement between St Mary Graces (Tower Hamlets) and St Saviour Bermondsey concerning the lease of Rotherhithe (ibid, 1461–7, 162). In the years 1465–7 two outlawries were pronounced on persons in Bermondsey and at Birling who had failed to appear in court to answer the abbot's suits for debt (ibid, 1461–7, 451; 1467–77, 10).

On 5 April 1473, the abbey was licensed to elect a successor to John Say, alias Bromley, who had resigned as abbot (*Cal Pat R*, 1467–77, 387) and on 10 April 1473 the king signified to the archbishop of Canterbury his assent to the election of John Marlow (ibid, 388). A mandate for the restitution of temporalities to Abbot John Marlow was issued on 13 April (ibid, 390). In December of the same year a monk of Bermondsey, Thomas Sutbury, was appointed prior of the Cluniac house of St Andrew Northampton (ibid, 415, 418).

Early in 1477 the merchants of the steelyard were freed from their obligation to pay the abbey an annual rent of 18s, in return for which the king undertook to discharge the prior and convent of all manner of corrodies and sustentations granted at the king's prayer, desire, denomination or writing (*Rot Parlt*, vi, 124). This was confirmed at Abbot John's request on 5 May (*Cal Pat R*, 1476–85, 36). On 22 May 1491, sureties of £200 were taken from the abbot of Bermondsey, along with innumerable others, for the loyalty of Thomas Marquis of Dorset (*Cal Close R*, 1485–1500, no. 618).

Despite a rumour in April 1516 that the abbots of Bermondsey and St Albans had succumbed to plague (*L and P Hen VIII*, ii(1), 1831), Abbot Marlow survived until 3 April 1519. On the following day the prior, William Aylesbury, applied to the king for licence to elect a successor (ibid, iii(1), 159), and on 30 April the king assented to the election of Robert Shouldham, a monk of the Benedictine abbey of Bury St Edmunds (Suffolk) (ibid, 205). On 28 April the king forwarded John Rawson as his candidate for the pension which abbots on their election customarily provided for royal clerks (ibid, 206(28)).

On 24 May 1522 the abbot was among those appointed to attend upon the papal legate on his arrival at Dover in connection with the proposed meeting between Henry VIII and the Emperor Charles V (*L and P Hen VIII*, iii(2), 2288(3), appendix 35). A less agreeable aspect of the king's vigorous foreign policy was the annual grant required from the spirituality to cover the expenses incurred in his efforts to recover the French crown: in 1522 Bermondsey (like the priory of St Mary of Bethlehem, outside Bishopsgate, London) was required to pay £100, a figure which compares with the £133 6s 8d paid by Merton Priory, the £333 from Battle Abbey and the £1000 from Winchester Cathedral Priory (ibid, 2483).

On 5 September 1525 the king signified his assent to the election of Robert Wharton to take the place of Robert Shouldham, who had resigned (*L and P Hen VIII*, i, 1621). Wharton, Bermondsey's last abbot, received the abbey's temporalities from the mayor and escheator of London on 1 October (ibid, iv(1), 1680).

The documentary sources list a succession of arrangements in the first decades of the 16th century whereby lands and estates belonging to the abbey were given over under long-term leases, often to well-born tenants. On 19 December 1510, the king confirmed a 51-year lease to Robert Hawkyns of part of the abbey's lordship of the manor of Leigham in Streatham and Clapham (Surrey) at an annual rent of £4 (*L and P Hen VIII*, i(1), 643, 786). On 27 October 1515, he granted to Gerard Danett, squire of the body, and his wife Margaret the manor of Rotherhithe (ibid, ii(2), 1080), but by 26 August 1516 this had been surrendered by Danett, when an inquest at Southwark determined that the Lovell family, who had previously held it, had done so as tenant of Bermondsey Abbey (ibid, 2305). In 1521–2 the abbey released its title in lands in the park of Birling to Lord Abergavenny who proposed to sell it to the king (*L and P Hen VIII*, iii(1), 1290). On 17 June 1527 an indenture was confirmed by which Sir Christopher Garneys and his wife Jane leased to Sir William Blount (Blounte), Lord Mountjoye, all the site and manor place of Charlton (Kent), which they held of the farm of the abbot and convent of Bermondsey, to be held from Michaelmas next for a term of ten years at an annual rent of £3 (TNA: PRO, E326/9080). A damaged document refers to a lease by Abbot Robert Wharton on 21 May 1534 of all that land and grange near the monastery (TNA: PRO, E40/15006). On 8 January 1535, the king requested the abbot and monastery of 'Barnsley' to give him the nomination to the parsonage of Rotherhithe at its next voidance, on the somewhat specious grounds that the vicar of Camberwell's brother, to whom they had given it, had a sufficient living in Suffolk (*L and P Hen VIII*, viii, 25). Finally, on 17 June 1536 Abbot Robert granted to the king all the abbey's manor or hide in Southwark, including advowsons and properties situated in the parishes of St Margaret, St George and in Paris Garden, excepting and reserving an annual pension of 20s from the rectory of St George's (TNA: PRO, E305/6/D2) and this was regranted to the abbey on 20 June (TNA: PRO, E305/5/C61). This catalogue of miscellaneous transactions from 1510 onwards gives the general impression that, voluntarily or otherwise, the abbey's control over its estates was weakening.

As early as 1534 Thomas Cromwell's 'remembrances' showed an interest in the annual values of monastic estates, including Bermondsey's manor of Widford (*L and P Hen VIII*, vii, 923(ii)). In Cromwell's *Valor Ecclesiasticus* in which the annual incomes of all religious houses were comprehensively recorded, Bermondsey's clear annual (ie net) income in 1535 was assessed at more than £474 (£474 14s 4³/₄d) and its gross income (temporal and spiritual) at £548 (£548 2s 5³/₄d); 58% of the gross derived from Surrey and 17% from Kent (*Val Eccl*, ii, 58–60). This can be compared with the *Valor*'s clear net values of other neighbouring religious houses: Merton £957; St Mary Overie Southwark £624; Stratford Langthorne £511; and St Mary Clerkenwell £262 (*Val Eccl*, ii, 51, 63; i, 435, 396). Holy Trinity Aldgate's property in London was worth £355 in 1537 (*VCH* 1909, 472). Among Bermondsey's Cluniac sister houses, Castle Acre's net income was assessed by the *Valor* at £306, Thetford's at £312, Wenlock's at £401 and Lewes's at £920 (*Val Eccl*, iii, 391, 312, 216; i, 332).

A number of Cromwell's agents referred to Bermondsey in their reports. On 1 August 1535 Sir William FitzWilliam explained that he had done nothing with the 'abbeys and priories' because he had heard first that Cromwell had appointed two auditors of his own for the purpose, and then that the auditors would only 'meddle' with Merton, St Mary Overie, Bermondsey and St Thomas's (*L and P Hen VIII*, ix, 4). On 26 September 1535 Richard Layton reported to Cromwell that he had already visited houses in Kent, Sussex and Surrey and was leaving till last St Saviour Bermondsey, St Mary Overy 'and the bawdy hospital of St Thomas in Southwark' (ibid, 444). On 16 June 1536 the king assented to the election of Robert Wharton, Abbot of Bermondsey, as bishop of St Asaph (*L and P Hen VIII*, x, 1256(47)), restoring his episcopal temporalities on 12 July (ibid, xi, 202(42)).

The abbey surrendered to the crown on 1 January 1538 (*VCH* 1967, 74). A list of the larger monasteries dated 1538 (and probably later than 11 February), includes Bermondsey under Winchester diocese (*L and P Hen VIII*, xiii(1), 254). On 22 March it was reported that 'the most part of the saints whereunto pilgrimages and offerings were wont to be made are taken away' – Our Lady of Southwick (ie at the Augustinian priory of Southwick, Sussex), the Blood of Hales (ie at the Cistercian abbey of Hailes, Gloucestershire), St Saviour (ie the rood of St Saviour at Bermondsey) and others (ibid, 564, 580). On 22 April pensions were granted to the late abbot and other religious of the late monastery of 'Barmondsey', numbering 13 in all:

to Robert Wherton [Wharton] bishop of St Asaph £333 6s 8d; Richard Giles late prior £10; Thomas Gaynesborow prior of Derby £7; Thomas Gale BD £6; John Kynder subprior £6; Peter Luke late chaunter £6; John Cutbert £6; Thomas Rokeley, William Paynter, Thomas Stanbak and Stephen Felow 106s 8d each. John Coy 40s and John Marshall 13s 4d. Signed: Thomas Cromwell. (*L and P Hen VIII*, xiii(1), 821; xiii(2), 1196)

Wharton's large pension has led commentators to suggest he lent himself to the surrender (*VCH* 1967, 74).

On 29 May 1538 Richard Long, esquire of the body, was appointed keeper, among other properties, of Bermondsey Abbey and of the parishes of St Margaret and St George Surrey (ie Southwark) and in Parrysgarden (ie Paris Garden, Southwark) (*L and P Hen VIII*, xiii(1), 573).

Archaeological evidence

The major conventual buildings were retained unchanged from the later 14th and early 15th centuries (period M8): the priory church (B3), chapter house (B4) and main cloister (B5 and OA5), refectory (B6) and east range (B7), together with the chapel (B1), hall/lodgings (B8) and second cloister (B14 and OA2) (Fig 65). There was evidence, however, of contraction in the group of buildings to the south-east. Certain buildings or structures suffered partial robbing and parts of the complex appear to have been left in a state of disrepair. The range of chambers (B13) remained but the walls enclosing the courtyard (OA9) are demolished, and the yard (OA7), courtyard (OA9) and land to the south (OA8) become one open space. The stone-built drain (D4) was robbed where it crossed the former courtyard (OA9) and the opening to the drain under the west wall of the reredorter (B9) was blocked, indicating some rearrangement of the drainage systems. Evidence for digging pits in the cemetery (OA6) suggests it went out of use, while Open Area 3 to the east and Open Area 4 to the south-west appear unchanged from the previous period.

Reredorter (B9)

Repairs were carried out in the base of reredorter (B9) in conjunction with alterations to the openings at the east and west ends of the sub-basement (Fig 65). The repairs to the reredorter floor incorporated pieces of Kentish ragstone, peg tiles and the reuse of the original 12th-century floor tiles (period M5; above, 3.3, 'Archaeological evidence'). The western opening was blocked with a chalk rubble foundation faced or surmounted with ragstones. At the east end, the sides of the stone drain (D4) were altered so as to divert it to the south side of the sub-basement, away from the central row of pier bases (Fig 66). The construction materials used to form the new channel were squared Reigate stone blocks and large pieces of chalk and flint cobbles, bonded with a very loose, deep orange, sandy mortar. To the north, the alterations had been crudely tied into the existing drain sides, and the internal face rendered over.

Inside the reredorter (B9) sub-basement, to the north of the drain diversion and overlying the floor repairs was a cess-type fill A[4154], which contained some tile and a large group of pottery (372 sherds) which was fully quantified (discussed in detail in Chapter 7.5, 'Period M9, *c* 1430–1538'). There is a high proportion of joining sherds and complete vessel profiles indicating contemporary dumping on a large scale over a relatively short period. The group can be closely dated to *c* 1430–*c* 1500 and includes a wide range of fabrics and forms made and used during the 14th and 15th centuries, with no residual pottery which definitely pre-dates *c* 1270, and no obviously intrusive material. Surrey whitewares predominate but within that group Kingston-type ware (KING) outnumbers coarse Surrey-Hampshire border ware (CBW) suggesting that the use of KING went on for longer in Southwark than in the City (Chapter 7.5, 'Period M9, *c* 1430–1538'). The KING forms from the cess-type fill are typical of those produced later in the life of the industry, including jugs, a large flared bowl (Fig 67, <P18>) and part of a cup, probably lobed and bearing ?accidental traces of red slip smeared across the base (Fig 67, <P19>). The third most common fabric, Cheam whiteware (CHEA; date range c 1350–c 1500), includes forms which were not introduced until the mid 15th century. As previously, imported pottery is minimal.

Serving vessels make up the bulk of the pottery recovered from the cess-type fill – mainly jugs (eg Fig 67, <P21>) but with a higher proportion of drinking vessels than earlier, and very low numbers of cooking pots – suggesting it derived from service areas, rather than kitchens, and included good quality tableware, which may not have been for everyday use. Related to the function of the reredorter range is the large number of ceramic urinals (used to collect urine) recovered from A[4154] – 59 sherds from a minimum of four purpose-made urinals, two in CBW and two in KING (Fig 67, <P20>). They may have been used in this range or elsewhere, and discarded here or been broken while being emptied.

Deposits of mortar, loam and chalk (and including tile) were dumped over the cess fill, probably as a deliberate seal. A mortar dump A[4156] contained a medium-sized group of pottery (47 sherds; discussed in detail in Chapter 7.5). Dated c 1380–c 1500, this group is essentially similar to the much larger assemblage from A[4154], but with relatively few joining sherds, with the exception of a small rounded jug in KING (Fig 67, <P22>). It includes several long-lived fabrics and forms and could have been deposited at any time while these were still in current use during the 15th century.

Overlying the cess-type deposit A[4154] and mortar sealing layer A[4156] in the north-east corner of the reredorter building (B9) was a large spread of domestic debris A[972]. This extensive spread A[972] measured 4.80m east–west by 3.25m north–south and was c 0.25m thick; it was bounded by the limit of excavation to the west and the period M9 masonry additions to the drain inside the entrance to the reredorter to the south. Debris A[972] was itself overlain by an ash layer A[2483], thickening from 20–50mm in the east to c 100–150mm thick to the west, and a further probable sealing layer of clay and chalk A[2468], with a maximum thickness (to the west) of c 120–150mm. The interpretation of the debris A[972] and ash A[2483] (gp120) is, however, problematic. The debris A[972] produced a major finds assemblage and included a very large pottery group; it was recorded as a single context. However, the site archive makes it clear that A[972] was a dark brown 'organic soil' which included within it lenses of ash and of yellow clay, suggesting that A[972] possibly also had a cess-type content interspersed with 'sealing' material, similar to the period M9 deposits A[4154] and A[4156].

Thus context A[972] may not represent a single event but rather the result of accumulation and deposition on at least several occasions over a period of time, continuing the earlier pattern into the 16th century and up to the Dissolution. Yet the remarkable quantity of ceramic wares, household items and other rubbish in these two contexts, but mainly in A[972], compared, for example, to the earlier period M9 deposits

A[4154] and A[4156], might in itself point to a major clearance rapidly carried out at some time prior to or at the Dissolution.

There are very few objects among the accessioned finds that are intrinsically closely datable, and some of those are residual (eg jetton <S178>, c 1350–c 1400; Chapter 7.7). Only the pottery provides any reasonable dating evidence to inform our interpretation.

The ceramics from the debris A[972] and ash A[2483] deposits were considered together as group 120 and fully quantified, with the pottery categorised as 'medieval', meaning a date range that finishes no later than c 1480 or c 1500, or 'post-medieval', with a date range that begins no earlier than c 1480 or c 1500 (discussed in detail in Chapter 7.5). Context A[972] produced a very large group (1196 medieval sherds/110 post-medieval sherds), A[2483] a much smaller group (10 medieval sherds/27 post-medieval sherds), with the ratio of medieval to post-medieval sherds strongly weighted to the former. The 15th-century material is dominated by Surrey whitewares, the 16th-century material by products of the London-area redware industries. The post-medieval wares date to c 1480–c 1550, with no pottery necessarily any later than the Dissolution. A high proportion of large and joining sherds, and complete vessel profiles, indicates dumping not redeposition.

The pottery could suggest then that the bulk (which dates to the 15th century) was dumped in the reredorter (B9) around the turn of the 15th to 16th century, perhaps between c 1480 and c 1520, with some further, smaller scale, dumping around the time of the Dissolution. This date of c 1520 assumes that the 15th-century wares had a short currency. The wares are overwhelmingly utilitarian – cooking and serving vessels, as well as crucibles, distillation vessels and urinals; the tablewares include bowls, drinking jugs, cups and condiment dishes. There are very few imported wares and little of especial value worth curating. However, these wares may have continued in use longer at Bermondsey than would be expected in a City context. The small number of resident religious in the early 16th century could have contributed to the continued currency of these wares and their presence in the monastery in the 1520s/30s. High proportions of residual material characterise many of the ceramic assemblages from Bermondsey (Chapter 7.5, 'Introduction and methodology') and, interestingly, clearly residual (12th- to early 14th-century) material forms a high proportion of the ceramics from the subsequent robbing and backfill of the reredorter (B9) and drain to the east (D4; Chapter 5.2, 'Monastic buildings completely or largely demolished', 'Reredorter (B9) and Drain 4, and creation of Open Area 12'). There is no such markedly residual element to this group 120 assemblage, although late 14th-century pottery (Kingston-type ware) is present.

Also recovered from A[972] in the reredorter (B9) was a large bone assemblage with a marked diversity of species: it included the major mammalian domesticates in roughly equal proportions, large quantities of domesticate birds, a wide range of game, together with a range of marine, estuarine and freshwater species (Chapter 7.8; Table 18). The presence of sturgeon, deer and swan are very clear indicators of a high-status diet. The

The priory and (later) abbey of Bermondsey

Fig 65 Plan of principal archaeological features at sites in the study area,
c 1430–1538 (period M9) (scale 1:400; inset 1:2000)

N

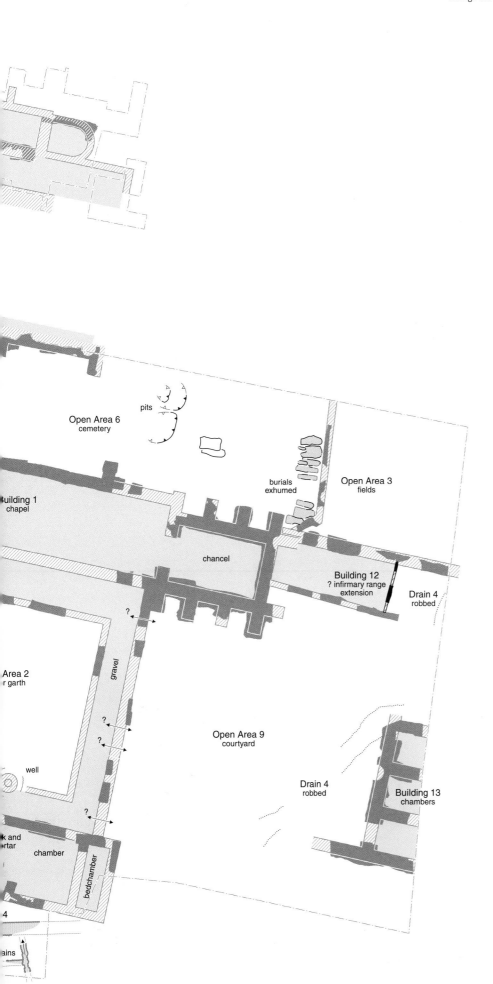

pits

Open Area 6
cemetery

burials
exhumed

Open Area 3
fields

Building 1
chapel

chancel

Building 12
? infirmary range
extension

Drain 4
robbed

?

gravel

Area 2
r garth

?

?

Open Area 9
courtyard

well

Drain 4
robbed

Building 13
chambers

?

k and
rtar

chamber

bedchamber

4

ains

0   10m

Fig 66 Detail of alterations at the east end of Building 9 in period M9, from the north (0.5m scale)

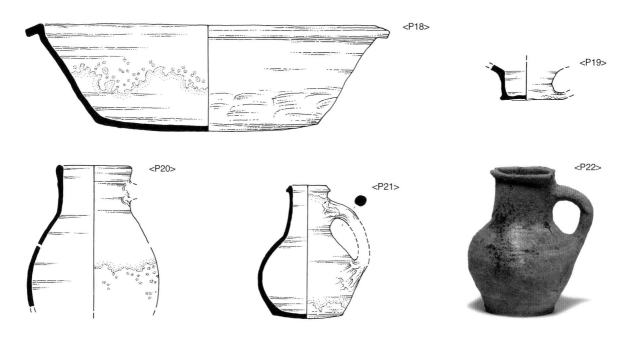

Fig 67 Pottery from the reredorter (B9) in period M9: Kingston-type ware bowl <P18>, cup <P19> and urinal <P20>, and coarse Surrey–Hampshire border ware jug <P21>, from the cess-type fill A[4154]; and Kingston-type ware jug <P22>, from the mortar dump A[4156] (scale 1:4; photo c 1:4)

sieved collections where one sample comprised entirely herring and smelt, and the size of the hand-collected assemblage suggest the bone content of these dumps was highly concentrated. This too might suggest organised rubbish disposal, in this case of kitchen waste, over a period of time perhaps, rather than just clearing out buildings at the Dissolution.

Taking the accessioned finds, the variety is remarkable, including textile, bone styli, book fittings and dress accessories, together with purely domestic items such as five knives, a grater and a cauldron. Glass bottles and beakers, and glass urinals and distillation vessels, mirror the ceramic wares (Chapter 7.7). Urinals and distillation vessels also featured strongly in the pottery from the earlier, period M9, reredorter cess-type fill (A[4154]). There may be some intrusive material present, derived from the overlying demolition deposits (Chapter 5.2), but the quantity of building material recorded from A[972], including floor tiles with a date range of 13th to mid 16th century – mainly 'Westminster' and Low Countries tiles, with small quantities of decorated tiles of Chertsey/Westminster style (Chapter 7.4, 'Medieval ceramic building material', 'Floor tile') – and a small number of window glass fragments from A[972] and A[2483] (Chapter 7.6, 'The context and character of the catalogued window glass') would appear to support the view that there was at least an element of Dissolution waste in A[972] and A[2483], possibly a significant one. Paving tiles and windows were recyclable commodities with a value.

Former ? infirmary range extension/?outbuilding (B12)

The wall at the east end of Building 12 was at least partially robbed. Part of a cooking pot in coarse Surrey-Hampshire border ware (CBW) and a Kingston-type ware (KING) jug from the robber trench fill were dated c 1270–c 1400. The wall was replaced with a far less substantial one 1.0m to the west, further reducing the size of the building.

Chambers (B13)

The chambers that were formerly ranged along the east side of the courtyard (OA9) appear to have been retained in period M9. The large quantity of peg roofing tile found associated with the robbing of this structure suggests it probably had a tiled roof when demolished.

Cemetery (OA6)

There were signs in this period that the cemetery (OA6) was falling out of use. Rubbish pits were dug between the chapel (B1) and the chapter house (B4) and in the central parts of the cemetery (Fig 65). Another indication of the cemetery's contraction is the removal of a row of burials adjacent to the cemetery wall. The graves were backfilled with a mixture of mortar and building materials before the cemetery wall (period M7; Fig 53) was taken down and the foundation robbed of its stone. Two strikingly similar 'pits' c 8m west of the row may also have been the result of grave removal. It is possible that any conspicuous tomb monuments or markers, and more recent and visible burials, were moved, while older burials remained unseen and undisturbed.

The rubbish pit fills included a large quantity of animal bone and oyster shell, pottery and a variety of discarded material including fragments of window glass and lead came,

vessel glass, lead moulds (<S172>–<S174>, Fig 106), a bone stylus (<S34>, Fig 92), iron shears (<S161>) and small copper-alloy items including keys (<S67>, <S68>) and an earpick (<S153>, Fig 99). The ceramic assemblage comprised 223 sherds, with four contexts producing medium-sized groups, three dated to the late 14th and 15th centuries and one dated c 1480–c 1550 (discussed in detail in Chapter 7.5, 'Period M9, c 1430–1538'). With minimal, clearly residual material and a high number of joining sherds, these groups indicate dumping in this area (rather than redeposition) throughout the period and probably up to the Dissolution; early 16th-century pottery was recovered from pit fills A[3101] and A[3068]. In contrast to the groups from the reredorter (B9) and Drain 4 robbing fills in the former courtyard (OA9) where Kingston-type ware (KING) predominates, the most common fabric in the rubbish pits is Cheam whiteware (CHEA). There are small quantities of imported pottery including German stonewares and Spanish vessels. Serving vessels (jugs) predominate with kitchen wares less frequent, but there are a number of bowls and dishes, which could be used in the kitchen and for serving. There are also some unusual forms, including a crucible sherd (in KING) from A[2937], and a trough and a birdpot (both from A[3101]), lending support to the view that the rubbish came from several areas on the site.

Open ground (OA9, combining former courtyard OA9 and yard OA7), and disuse of drain (D4)

The former yard (OA7) was merged into what had previously been a courtyard (OA9) in this period when the boundary walls between the two areas were removed (Fig 65). The stone-built drain (D4) was robbed and backfilled where it crossed the former courtyard (OA9). The north and most of the south walls around the courtyard (OA9) were demolished. Parts of the north wall that had once formed the south-east corner of the former yard (OA7) may have been left standing, and the chambers (B13) on the east side appear to have been retained. The former courtyard (OA9) became open ground with the area to the south (former OA8).

The pottery from the wall robbing trenches all appeared to be residual while the bulk of the pottery associated with the robbing of the north-east section of the stone drain (D4) dates to the mid 14th to 15th centuries (discussed in detail in Chapter 7.5, 'Period M9, c 1430–1538'). The fills of the principal robbing cut all date to this period from the pottery; one medium-sized context (A[597], 50 sherds) can be dated to c 1350–c 1400, with a suggested date for the group nearer c 1350 than c 1400. Towards the south part of the drain, backfill deposits produced medium-sized groups including A[298] (46 sherds), dated to c 1350–c 1400, and A[216] (63 sherds), dated to c 1440–c 1500 by Cheam whiteware (CHEA) forms not introduced until the mid 15th century. Overall, serving vessels especially jugs predominated. This section of drain may have ceased to function during the preceding period (M8, c 1350–c 1430), and may have been robbed and progressively infilled as late as the second half of the 15th century.

Discussion

Signs of change in the structure and routines of domestic life in the monastery are what identify period M9. The denization of the house in 1380 and the subsequent elevation to abbey status in 1399 were probably key points in the refurbishment and rebuilding programme of the late 14th century and this work may have carried through to the early years of the 15th century (period M8; above, 3.6, 'Documentary evidence'). But beyond this, there is no evidence of further remodelling or repair among the conventual buildings within the excavation areas reported here. Instead, there is evidence for contraction. While the second cloister (B14 and OA2) with its south domestic range of suites of paired rooms (B8) continued unaltered in this period, the courtyard complex to the east lost its integrity when the walls enclosing the courtyard (OA9) were demolished. The former yard (OA7) and courtyard (OA9) became one open space with land to the south (OA8). The stone-built drain (D4), where it crossed the former courtyard (OA9), no longer functioned and was robbed and eventually filled in. The former ? infirmary range extension (B12) was reduced in size and may have functioned as a service building or other outbuilding.

The south-east part of the complex apparently continued to be separated from the cemetery area to the north-west by the cemetery wall, but the character of the latter area changed too. No further burials were made here in the period; rather, ten, if not 12, burials were exhumed in the east part of the cemetery. The burials removed were among the most recent (period M8; above, 3.6, 'Archaeological evidence') and were presumably marked and/or their location otherwise recorded. To the west, rubbish pits were dug in the cemetery (OA6); the rubbish apparently came from several areas on the site and the pottery recovered indicates that dumping occurred throughout the period and probably up to the Dissolution. This dating evidence suggests that the careful removal of burials from recognised locations was associated with the pre-Dissolution change of use in this area, or perhaps with the surrender of the house, and very likely performed by people related to the religious institution, as opposed to being disturbance caused by random digging or construction in the post-Dissolution period. The changes and contraction evident in the south-east part of the complex would not support any suggestion that exhumation was prompted by construction work which was planned but not carried out.

The changes made to the drainage system do not indicate that as a whole it ceased to function. The north-east section of the stone drain was disused, but the south section was retained and altered, and must have continued to function, if rather differently. At the east end of the reredorter (B9) the internal cutwater had been rebuilt so that Drain 4 now extended inside the reredorter. With the blocking of the opening at the west end of the reredorter, there was certainly no flow through the body of the reredorter. It is possible that this drain now passed through the south reredorter wall (which lay outside the excavation area) and some more general rearrangement of the drainage system was undertaken. Excess in the reredorter could

still have been drained off or dug out if necessary, much as previously (periods M5 and M6; above, 3.3, 'Discussion' and 3.4, 'Archaeological evidence', 'Reredorter (B9)'). The reredorter appears to have acted as a combined large cess and rubbish pit, for the opportunity was taken to dump rubbish inside the reredorter north of the new drain channel. A large number of serving vessels and some high quality tableware were incorporated into the cess-type fill A[4154] accumulating there and dated *c* 1430–*c* 1500, together with the remains of at least four ceramic urinals, employed, possibly in the reredorter itself, to collect urine for inspection or for use in tanning (Chapter 4.3, 'Specialist craftspeople and industrial activity in the precinct'). The assemblage from this reredorter cess-type fill should be compared with the reredorter group from A[972] and A[2483] (both discussed in detail in Chapter 7.5, 'Period M9, *c* 1430–1538') and the large number of urinals recovered from the reredorter is particularly interesting. Context A[972] produced a major finds assemblage and included a very large pottery group; it was recorded as a single context although it is clear from the site records that the spread, consisting of an 'organic soil', included lenses of ash and of yellow clay, suggesting deposition occurred on several occasions, over a period of time. The dumping of rubbish in the reredorter, therefore, probably continued into the early 16th century, and in the years up to and including the Dissolution (discussed above, 'Archaeological evidence', 'Reredorter (B9)').

The opening up of the former courtyard (OA9) did not necessarily imply a loss of privacy since the south-east conventual buildings were enclosed at least to the north and east by substantial brick walls, whose patterning (including religious symbols) was recorded in detail by Buckler, and which were probably constructed in the late pre-Dissolution period, *c* 1480–1530s (Chapter 7.3). In this area, where the hall/lodgings (B8) and chambers (B13) continued to afford separate accommodation for members of the community, religious or lay, the character of the ceramic assemblage is particularly interesting. Kitchen wares were present in low numbers in the large ceramic group from the reredorter cess-type fill, and also elsewhere, for example in the robbing and infill of the north-east section of Drain 4 (Chapter 7.5, 'Period M9, *c* 1430–1538', 'Reredorter (B9)'). Nevertheless, developments in the forms of cooking vessels available are reflected in the cauldrons, tripod pipkins and frying-pans recovered in this period. But it is serving vessels, especially jugs, which predominate. Continental ceramic imports are limited but do occur in very small numbers in the cemetery rubbish pits between the church (B3) and chapel (B1); these include examples of high-quality decorative containers which had probably been carefully curated for some time. Surrey whitewares (KING, CBW, CHEA) are the most common pottery up to the late 15th century, taking the pottery in the reredorter cess-type fill as typical, although the pattern of sources seen in the Bermondsey material differs from that in the City. Deposits arising from the major post-Dissolution destruction do contain generous amounts of 16th-century ceramics which are noticeably absent from the deposits under discussion in period M9.

The separate lifestyle organised around the second cloister (B14, OA2) with its hall/lodgings (B8) and the courtyard (OA9) with its range of chambers (B13), first seen in period M8, seems to have continued although the courtyard became an open yard. A new and rather untidy pattern of rubbish disposal in this area was possibly accompanied by a contraction of the buildings in use. The monastic community was numerically in decline prior to the Dissolution: there were only 13 religious on the pension list in 1538 (above, 'Documentary evidence'). Some or possibly all of them were probably living in separate suites of rooms or chambers; some of these 'households' were probably located in the second cloister and former courtyard to the east. Lay residents were possibly accommodated to the south and west of the main cloister; here more elaborate accommodation could have been provided for such as the royal widows, Catherine of Valois (d 1437), Henry V's queen, and Elizabeth Woodville (d 1492), widow of Edward IV, both living at the abbey before their deaths – Elizabeth was confined there from 1486 (Kingsford 1905, 142; Graham 1926, 183; *VCH* 1967, 75).

4

Aspects of the medieval priory and abbey

4.1 The foundation and setting of St Saviour Bermondsey

The foundation

The date and circumstances of the foundation of the Cluniac priory at Bermondsey are matters both complex and obscure. The presence of an Anglo-Saxon minster church on the Bermondsey eyot adds to the complexities (Chapters 2.4, 2.5, 3.1, 'Discussion'). The two documents most pertinent to the foundation must be viewed with caution as historical sources: the fallibility of the Bermondsey annals has already been noted and William II's foundation charter survives only as a much later transcript. There would appear to be no solid confirmation of a foundation date other than the references to Alwyn Childe's rents, given in 1082, and in 1089, the arrival of the French monks from La Charité-sur-Loire (annals of Lewes Priory: Graham 1926, 161; see Brett 1992, 297) and the donation of the royal manor. The evident lapse of time between the donation of the city rents to the house and the grant of the royal manor on which to site it presents a further puzzle. The gift of rents might suggest the prior existence of a religious establishment, and this suggestion is reinforced by the oft-quoted Domesday reference to the 'new and beautiful church' at Bermondsey.

The discovery of the chapel (B1) introduces a new element to the consideration of the problems surrounding the foundation. It was constructed on the royal manor in the 11th century. The whole period *c* 1030–*c* 1130, not just immediately post-Conquest, was one of great expansion in the construction of small churches, both rebuilt and new, called the 'great rebuilding' by Richard Gem (Gem 1988, 21; Blair 1991, 110). The date of the chapel and its location seem to replicate in part the pattern of Norman dominance imposed on former Saxon holdings noted at places such as Lewes and Northampton where Saxon small churches or chapels were replaced or rebuilt very soon after the Conquest by new Norman lords, and in addition castle and monastery were juxtaposed. Bermondsey's chapel could well have been built by William I on his new royal manor (the former Saxon royal manor) in the 20 years between the Conquest and the record in Domesday.

The role of Alwyn Childe – the accredited founder according to the priory's own annals and the early 13th-century *Flores historiarum* – remains ambiguous (*Ann Monast*, iii, 425–6; Paris, *Flores*, ii, 21, 26). The commissioning and funding of church building by individuals of means, like Alwyn Childe, or by groups of citizens was in a sense a continuance of the Saxon system, wherein an individual could achieve thegnly status with the ownership of a church (Platt 1981, 3; Blair 1991, 115–19). Perhaps the foundation was the result of a joint partnership to establish a Cluniac house close to London, the land being offered by the royal owner and at least some of the capital being provided by individual interests?

Topography and early landscape

The priory of St Saviour was sited to take advantage of the higher ground provided by the eyot or peninsula of Bermondsey (Fig 6). Its situation to the modern mind appears anything but attractive, set in a marsh landscape which was low-lying and flood-prone, apparently bereft of the appurtenances of civilised living. Comparison with the sites of contemporary establishments, however, indicates that these circumstances were not unusual and indeed were probably sought after. The Cluniac priory of Lewes, founded 1077–82, was located on the Southover ridge, the south edge of which formed the shore of the tidal Ouse estuary (Lyne 1997, 2, 6–7; Fig 1). The Cockshut stream flowed from the ridge through mud flats and salt marsh to disgorge at a point just south of the priory precinct. Archaeological evidence indicates continuing attempts to raise the ground levels in the inner precinct at Lewes in the 13th and 14th centuries.

There was also a spiritual significance to the siting of monasteries on wetlands and peninsulas, where conditions of relative inaccessibility and isolation mimicked the hardships and asceticism which were associated with the desert fathers and the earliest members of the church. Marginal land was also 'cheaper' land to donate. North of the Thames and north of the City of London, the hospital and priory of St Mary Spital was founded in the late 12th century on marginal marshy land on a main road into the City (Thomas et al 1997, 89–90).

Additional factors at Bermondsey could have been its Thames-side minster predecessor and the intentional juxtaposition typical of the Norman period of castle – the White Tower where building work began in the 1070s – and monastery – St Saviour – separated by marsh and the Thames in this case (Fig 2). This situation has topographical precedents, sometimes of a very close proximity indeed, in both Normandy and south-east England. William the Conqueror made Caen (Calvados) his capital in Normandy and commissioned the building of the castle, the monastery (Abbaye-aux-Hommes) and the convent (Abbaye-aux-Dames). The ramparts to the castle, the Bourg le Duc, date from 1060. The Abbaye-aux-Hommes was sited almost in the shadow of the fortress and could be reached from the sea by boat (Duncombe 1989, 5). A tendency can be discerned for Cluniac houses to be found close to the castle of the founder. At Lewes, where the first Cluniac house in England was established, the Late Saxon royal borough was divided between the Norman William de Warenne and William I. William de Warenne constructed a motte and bailey castle in the north-west corner of the Saxon burgh and established Lewes Priory on the opposite bank of the Winterbourne stream (Lyne 1997, 1–2, fig 1). Thetford, Lenton, Pontefract and Northampton priories are further examples of this, while Castle Acre with its priory, castle and walled town has been described as comprising 'one of the best examples of Norman estate planning in the country' (G Coppack, pers comm; Coad and Coppack 1998, 20).

The first requirement of any community was water, and the location of medieval religious houses must have been dictated by the presence of freshwater springs or rivers. However, many of the day-to-day processes carried out at the priory, for example milling, fulling and smithing, need not have required strictly 'clean' water.

The Bermondsey area was formerly criss-crossed by a number of watercourses; these appear to have originated as a combination of both natural braided stream channels and man-made drainage ditches. During the medieval and particularly post-medieval periods, as more land was reclaimed both for agriculture and settlement, a number of natural channels were also canalised. By the 18th century in this area of Bermondsey there was a complex grid of fields bounded by drainage ditches, with various channels supplying water to a number of tanneries (Fig 79; Cowie and Corcoran 2008, 164, 175). Natural streams, some of which had originally been tributaries of the Neckinger, had been channelled into these ditches and sluices, making it difficult to identify the medieval watercourses with certainty (below, 4.2, 'The precinct and home grange'). It appears the Neckinger stream originated as a braided natural channel which flowed eastwards and then northwards to enter the Thames via two separate outlets. The western outlet or channel was latterly known as St Saviour's Dock and the eastern one as Folly Ditch (Besant 1912, 57; Fig 6).

Access by river was no doubt a crucial factor in assembling the materials necessary for the construction of the priory. Building stone, including Caen limestone from France, would have been brought up the Thames to St Saviour's Dock. The recovery from the site of large amounts of Roman building materials led to the suggestion that salvaged tile and stone had been brought in, perhaps by boat along the Neckinger, but recent synthesis of the archaeological evidence for Roman Southwark highlights the proximity of substantial Roman structures (Cowan et al 2009; Chapter 2.3). To what extent the Neckinger channel was affected by tidal flow is uncertain.

The priory was well served by the road link from Canterbury to London (Roman Watling Street); indeed, ease of access to St Saviour Bermondsey and the consequent flow of visitors and guests was something which later was to prove burdensome to the house.

Initially, the outer precinct of the priory was defined by local topographical features, which provided natural boundaries. Thus the west side of the precinct was delimited by the raised causeway later known as Bermondsey Street; the precinct, however, was soon walled down the east side of Bermondsey Street. To the east and south were various ditches and channels – probably a combination of natural and man-made features (above and below, 4.2, 'The precinct and home grange'; see Fig 81). To the north and north-east lay the original main Neckinger channel and the Thames-side marshes such as *Druettesmarsh* (Chapter 3.6, 'Documentary evidence'). (The extent of the area formally enclosed at Bermondsey is discussed below, 4.2, 'The precinct and home grange'.)

In terms of more widespread landholdings, the initial grants of land to the establishment were generous, but would not have been excessive, given St Saviour's connections. The royal manor given to the priory consisted of Bermondsey and the outlying vills of Camberwell, Rotherhithe, Dulwich, Waddon, Leigham (in Streatham) and the hide of Southwark. The Cluniac priory at Castle Acre received a comparable amount in terms of lands and benefices: as well as the churches of Acre, Methwold, Wickmere and Trunch in Norfolk, it was granted the church and advowson of Leaden Roding in Essex (*VCH* 1906, 356; Raby and Reynolds 1983, 3–4). When the priory moved from its original cramped site and was refounded in the valley of the River Nar, further provision was made for it, including '15 acres [6.1ha] of land and two thousand ells in Methwold, five shillings rent of land and one garden; and two acres [0.8ha] of land towards the building of the church' (Raby and Reynolds 1983, 4; the English ell was 45in or 1.15m). Bermondsey can be compared with Thornton Abbey (Lincolnshire), a wealthy house for Augustinian canons, which had a total precinct area of 71.7 acres (29.0ha) (Coppack 1990, 103). The enormously wealthy Cistercian monastery at Rievaulx had in excess of 50 acres (20.2ha) of meadow and pasture alone. In total, St Saviour's assets at its foundation then appear to be on a par with the larger monastic foundations of the 11th and 12th centuries.

4.2 The plan, architecture and development of the monastery

The nature of the evidence

The principal cloister of St Saviour has not been the subject of full archaeological excavation. Much of the cloister south range lies beneath modern Tower Bridge Road. The data that exist for structures or deposits west of the east range have come about as a result of the archaeological evaluation of site D in 1992, but more particularly of Bermondsey Square by PCA from 1998 (BYQ98) (the latter as yet unpublished in detail and not reported here; see Chapter 1.3, 'Archaeological investigations in the study area since the 1950s'; Fig 3). The preliminary results of excavation by PCA of parts of the south transept (BYQ98) and the east range (WBP07) have been included here. Future analysis of these unpublished data may substantially modify both our reconstruction of the 12th-century and later priory church and main cloister and our understanding of the earliest buildings on the site of the priory (Chapter 3.1, 'Archaeological evidence').

The eastern areas of site A (the monastic infirmary and monks' cemetery) were fully excavated before 1990. Subsequent changes in the legislation with regard to development and archaeology (*Planning policy guidance note 16*) meant that full excavation of known archaeological sites became less frequent. *Planning policy guidance note 16* (PPG16; Department of the Environment 1990) changed the emphasis of field archaeology in England by insisting on the preservation *in situ* of the archaeological resource, wherever this was an option. This meant that, unless archaeological remains are under direct threat of destruction, they are to be left unexcavated, on the basis that future generations would have at their disposal improved means to effect their recovery and recording.

In order to attempt a tentative reconstruction of the priory

church and main cloister, this discussion utilises not only the evidence from the modern excavations reported here but also that from Grimes's excavations of 1956 and 1962–3 which revealed part of the north transept and the eastern arm of the priory church (site G, Fig 3). This evidence is compared with the notes and sketches relating to the site compiled between 1808 and 1820 by John Buckler, senior, and his son John Chessell Buckler (Chapter 7.1).

The priory church, however, remains profoundly obscure in many of its details. The reconstructed plan does not purport to be a final or proven reconstruction. The existence of some points in the plan can be firmly established, but the reconstruction as a whole should be seen as an overall impression, drawing on some but by no means all of the comparative evidence. Any attempt to place the church in its architectural context otherwise risks rapidly becoming an exercise in circular arguments.

The 12th-century priory church

The location of Grimes's excavation (Fig 3; Fig 23) in relation to the surveyed structures from site A has allowed us to attempt a reconstruction of the eastern arm of the priory church (Chapter 3.2, 'Archaeological evidence', 'Priory church (B3)', 3.3, 'Archaeological evidence', 'Priory church (B3)'). The east part of the north transept was uncovered by Grimes's work in the 1960s and revealed two diminutive apsidal projections against the transept east wall. The absidioles were no more than 3m across and, therefore, were unlikely to have risen beyond the first stage. They are directly paralleled at St Benoît-sur-Loire in work done between 1070 and 1108. Indeed, the small apsidal chapel is something of a formula in the accomplished Romanesque style and can be seen in numerous French examples, including 11th-century Cluny (II) itself. The small, semicircular chapel was the architectural response to the liturgical requirement for Masses to be performed at different stations on successive days (Conant 1987, 148).

The most ambitious attempt to reconstruct the plan of the east arm was made by Gem (1990, fig 1). His plan was constructed without the benefit of recent excavated evidence or the Grimes archive. An essential element of the plan, the large east–west robber trench of the north aisle sleeper wall, was overlooked. Thus Gem's presbytery width was, at *c* 30ft or just over 9m, very narrow compared to its length. The external width is now thought to be *c* 20.7m based on the best interrelationship of Grimes's excavation with site A. This suggests that the southernmost apse was not, as Gem very naturally assumed, on the central axis of the church. There is room for yet another when Grimes's plan is mirrored on the 'correct' central axis of the church.

This indicates the use of five chapels (including the central apse) at the east end of the presbytery at Bermondsey. In the first, 11th-century, phase of the mother church of La Charité-sur-Loire, six small apsidal chapels were arranged *en échelon*, from the extremes of both north and south transepts, and culminated in the central main presbytery apse, making seven apses in all (Phillipe 1905, plan opp 480; Anfray 1951, 67 figs 5 and 6; Fig

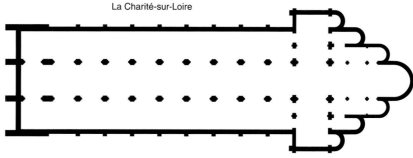

Fig 68 Contemporary (reconstructed) Cluniac churches: La Charité-sur-Loire (east arm 11th century, nave ?pre-dedication in 1107: after Phillipe 1905, plan opp 480 and Evans 1938, 66, fig 11); Castle Acre (east arm late 11th century, nave early to mid 12th century: after Coad and Coppack 1998, 21); Pontefract (early 12th century: after Bellamy 1965, fig 24); Thetford (east arm 1107–c 1120, nave c 1120–40: after Raby and Reynolds 1979, 12–13) (scale 1:1000)

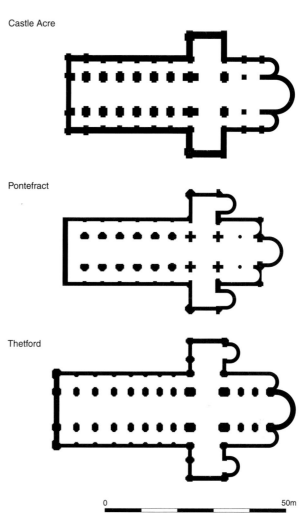

68). A configuration of five presbytery chapels is found at other, lesser churches in the Bourbonnais region of Burgundy and in Burgundy itself (Saint Désiré, Anzy-le-Duc) (Evans 1938, 62).

The contemporary Cluniac churches illustrated on Fig 68, together with the other churches referred to, represent a sample of the type of plan in which traits similar to those at St Saviour can be recognised. A distinctive plan was adopted in some large Cluniac and Benedictine houses combining a large number of chapels with a rectilinear ambulatory. The Benedictine abbey of Chertsey (Surrey) (its 'new minster' commenced 1110: *Anglo-Saxon Chron*, i, 369) employed dimensions very close to those of the reconstructed 12th-century church at Bermondsey. Both Chertsey and St Saviour's Benedictine 'daughter house' of Faversham have evidence of a 'square' or rectangular ambulatory (Philp 1968, fig 4 opp 7, 34, fig 34). The more conventional, three-apse arrangement without an ambulatory, however, was very widespread and can be seen, for example, at the Cluniac churches of Castle Acre, Pontefract and Thetford; at the last two the apsed presbytery is flanked by shorter apsidal aisles (Fig 68). The existence of an ambulatory at Bermondsey would explain the observed non-alignment of the apse and aisle that was recorded on Grimes's excavation.

An excavated foundation on the south side of the east arm of St Saviour Bermondsey hints at an apse that projected beyond the line of the others. The apparent asymmetry may have in any case been intentional; apsidal chapels of different length were used at Chertsey (Poulton 1988, fig 1) to create a markedly asymmetrical plan. The south foundation may alternatively be connected to later alterations on the north side of the east arm. A sixth chapel appears to have been appended to the north side of the arm in period M5 (Chapter 3.3, 'Archaeological evidence', 'Priory church (B3)'; Fig 33), perhaps to create a second minor transept arm as seen at St Benoît-sur-Loire. This plan, if executed (and with the addition of a seventh chapel on the south side), would have created an array of seven chapels like that of La Charité-sur-Loire (Fig 68). However, there is no evidence for a seventh, south, chapel at Bermondsey.

The use of five apsidal chapels across Bermondsey's east end is strongly reminiscent of the parent house of La Charité-sur-Loire. The transept arm was also of similar length and the idiosyncratic rib ornament (Phillipe 1905, illus opp 488) was apparently imitated (cf Chapter 7.2, 'Construction phase 2, c 1190–c 1220 (periods M5 and M6)', 'Unprovenanced arch mouldings'; and Fig 136). The replacement of the east end of La Charité-sur-Loire with a chevet around 1125 (Conant 1987, 217) is the only potential problem with this theory of imitation. This would

place the planning stage, at least, of the Bermondsey great church before 1125 (below). It may be conjectured that the council held by Henry II at St Saviour in the Christmas of 1154 (Gervase, i, 160) is evidence of a functioning presbytery, although the church was not completed for another 52 years to judge from the date (1206) of the translation of the body of the first prior into the choir of the church (Chapter 3.3, 'Discussion'). Such delay was, however, slight by medieval standards.

The conjectural (partly schematic) reconstruction of the priory church and main cloister (Fig 69) shows the 12th-century east arm of the church with the asymmetrical arrangement of five small apsidal chapels proposed here, with a sixth chapel added to the north side; the five apsidal chapels project eastwards from a rectangular ambulatory. The reconstruction of the north side chapel as apsidal internally and externally follows Grimes

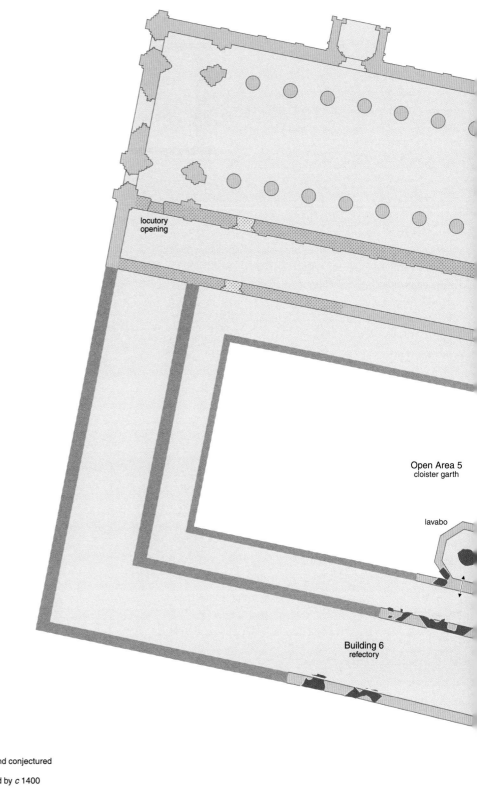

locutory
opening

Open Area 5
cloister garth

lavabo

Building 6
refectory

c 1200 foundation/wall: found and conjectured

c 1200 foundation/wall: removed by *c* 1400

c 1400 foundation/wall: found and conjectured

foundation/wall: schematic

structures recorded by Buckler

Open Area 4

*Fig 69 A conjectural reconstruction of the priory church and main cloister of St Saviour Bermondsey in the late 12th
century (period M5), using detail from St Bartholomew Smithfield, together with a remodelled east arm of the church,
chapter house and north-east cloister arcade of c 1400 (period M8), incorporating the archaeological evidence for the plan of
the eastern parts and Buckler's recorded observations, and using detail from the east arm of Barking Abbey (scale 1:400)*

N

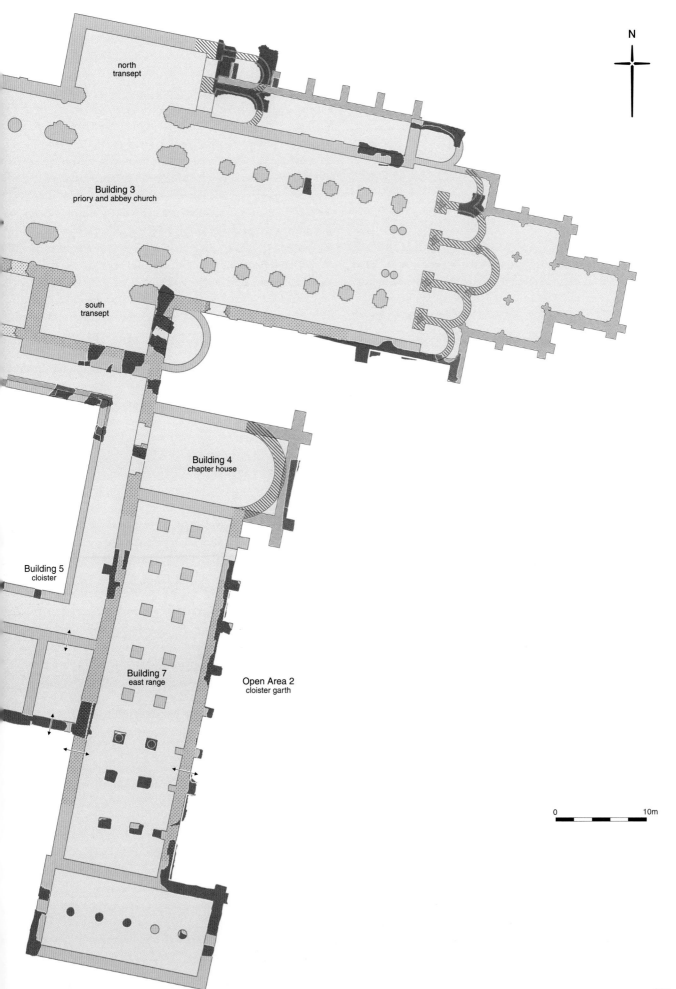

north
transept

Building 3
priory and abbey church

south
transept

Building 4
chapter house

Building 5
cloister

Building 7
east range

Open Area 2
cloister garth

0   10m

(Chapter 3.2, 'Archaeological evidence', 'Priory church (B3)').

The bay interval of the partially excavated east arm was c 3.81m or 12ft 6in (this determination ignores the westernmost buttress, whose spacing was so different to the others as to suggest it was atypical; Fig 69). The reduced bay of the east arm relative to the nave is typical of 12th-century churches. The 12th-century presbytery piers on Fig 69 are based on the nave piers of Rochester Cathedral (Kent), thought to be constructed after 1114 (Cook 1960, 158); they are indicative of the type of pier sometimes used in this location.

Moving west, there was no archaeological evidence for the crossing from the excavations reported here. Furthermore, the crossing had been thoroughly robbed out in Buckler's day:

… it is manifest that the most persevering engines of mischief were busied in the dismemberment and dispersion of the huge basements with the four pillared supports of the tower which we may be sure stood over the intersection of this limb with the longitudinal or main body of the edifice. (BL, Add MS 24432 A, 32v)

The crossing tower would be supported by massive compound piers. The reconstruction (Fig 69) uses detail from St Bartholomew Smithfield (1130s+: West 1993, 29); this building employed columns only in the east arm. An *ex situ*, large round ?respond with a diameter of c 1.78m employed a rectilinear capital with extensions (Fig 71); this may derive from the crossing compound piers but would be too weak to singly support a corner of the tower which probably had external dimensions of c 11.8m (c 39ft).

The archaeological excavations reported here took place to the east and south of the body of the priory church. The analysis of the results of excavation by PCA of the west part of the church and north-west cloister, and areas further to the west (BYQ98), will provide the first extensive archaeological evidence for the form and date of the western part of the priory. For details of the west end of the priory church, we have to rely at this time on limited recovery of *ex situ* architectural mouldings and the observations and drawings made in the early years of the 19th century by the antiquarian, John Chessell Buckler (discussed in detail in Chapter 7.1). As has been said at the beginning of this volume (Chapter 1.3), the quality of this evidence in terms of the techniques of modern archaeology is sadly lacking. Researchers have been misled by a plan produced by Buckler without reference to the accompanying hand-written text, which is hidden away in a companion volume (Chapter 7.1). It is possible that fieldwork and analyses conducted in the future will change entirely the interpretation based on that evidence.

Buckler's chief problem was his failure to locate any evidence for the foundations of the church apart from its south wall and transept and the return of the west front. Structures recorded by Buckler are indicated on Fig 69. Buckler's most important plan (BL, Add MS 24433, fo 70; reproduced here as Fig 123) represents his best effort at reconstruction based on little evidence.

The fit between structures recorded by Buckler and the excavated remains of both the south wall of the presbytery and the monastic east range (the ? service range of Pope's mansion), principally the sub-dorter, is close (Fig 70). (Analysis of recent excavation by PCA of parts of the south nave wall and south-west tower, and south transept, will clarify this.) In other areas matters are much more problematic. Buckler places the north 'garden wall' east of a salient or projection marking the site of the north transept. Replotting of his records with reference to the 1980s archaeological evidence, in particular, the presbytery and east range (as above), shows that the salient marks the probable transept outline but is over 6m too wide west–east (Fig 109). The wall to the east does not move to what should be its alignment as recorded by Grimes (Fig 23), but is rather c 1m to the south (Fig 70); the garden wall was still visible at the time of excavation founded on the north wall of the church, but the location of these excavation trenches is itself a best fit. The position of the 'garden wall' to the west raises questions. The west section of this north wall was logically assumed by Martin (ignoring Buckler's theories) to be founded on the nave wall foundation (Martin 1926, 214). Fig 70 does not show such a correspondence as it conjectures that the nave north wall shares the alignment of the presbytery north wall. Clearly, the details of the north part of the church remain problematic.

The presence of a written measurement of 65ft (19.81m) between the surviving nave south wall and the west garden wall might suggest that the west part of Buckler's reconstruction is reliable. Buckler apparently failed to take the corresponding measurement to the east but then assumed the distance to be the same as its western counterpart. In reality, they may not have been parallel.

When, some years later, Buckler had somehow to reconstruct the plan of the church he was unable to check what had by then been obliterated. He chose to base his reconstruction on his architectural theory that the width of the aisle was always half that of the central vessel (measured from the centre lines of the arcades to the face of the aisle wall) and so assumed that the known width of the south transept represented the width of the central vessel plus that of the aisle. Thus he arrived at 52ft (15.85m) for the internal width of the nave; 158ft (48.16m) for its length from the outside of the west front; 28½ft (8.69m) for the depth of each transept arm and 109ft (33.22m) for the interior width across the nave (including the transepts) (BL, Add MS 24432 A, 33v). From the plotted excavated evidence, it emerges that the external nave width, c 20m, probably falls between the different estimates of Martin and Buckler.

No trace of the later medieval east end was visible to enable Buckler to judge the overall length of the church (BL, Add MS 24432 A, 32v). He was able to trace walls for a length of 83.36m (273½ft) (BL, Add MS 24432 B, drawing on 238). The overall 12th-century length of the church was probably c 98.2m external (c 322ft); the internal length of the nave was probably c 47m (Fig 69). This may be compared with the internal nave length of the motherhouse of La Charité-sur-Loire of c 70.8m.

The nave aisle wall proper was '5/6' or 5ft 6in (c 1.39m) thick (BL, Add MS 24433, fo 70) and was interrupted by a

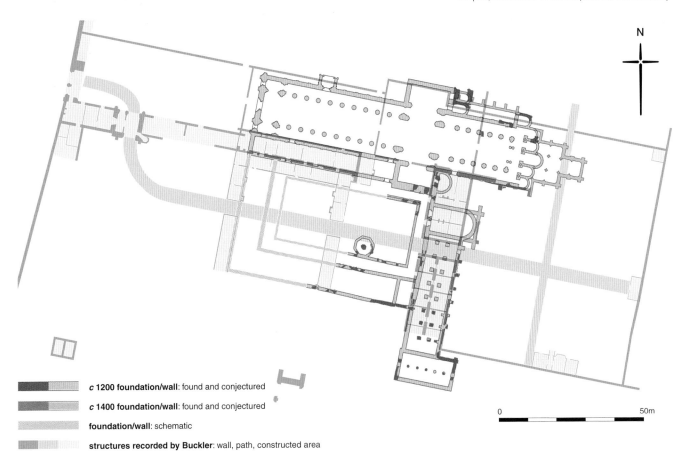

N

c **1200 foundation/wall**: found and conjectured

c **1400 foundation/wall**: found and conjectured

foundation/wall: schematic

structures recorded by Buckler: wall, path, constructed area

0   50m

Fig 70 Detail of the south-west corner of the precinct from the conjectural reconstruction (Fig 81) showing the priory church and main cloister (as shown in Fig 69) with Buckler's ground plan of Sir Thomas Pope's mansion (Fig 109) superimposed (scale 1:1250)

chamfered two-light opening near the west end (Fig 69), with unadorned round heads. This has been identified as a locutory opening (J West, pers comm) and is recorded in greater detail in BL, Add MS 24433, fo 11 (Fig 121). A 'roughened surface' was noted by Buckler in his text as 'full seven ft in thickness' a short distance to the east of the opening, and it ran the height of the wall (BL, Add MS 24432 A, 48). He identified it as the pier supporting the east side of a tower (Fig 69).

The remains (foundations and some superstructure) of this south-west tower were revealed during PCA's recent excavations (BYQ98; A Douglas, pers comm; Gaimster and O'Connor 2006, 316) but cannot be plotted on Fig 69 or Fig 70. Buckler did not see the tower projecting from the south nave wall proven by PCA's excavations. According to Buckler, the south tower of the west front was incorporated in the nave aisle (BL, Add MS 24432 A, 48) and the corner of Pope's mansion was rebuilt in brick after its removal (Martin 1926, 216; Fig 70). The brick wall measured 4.67m from east to west (the width of the tower). The east side was probably once supported by a transverse arch between the aisle wall respond and the vanished nave arcade. It is of interest, in this context, to note the emblems and devices of brick on the north garden court wall that included what appears to be a stylised, twin-towered west front in elevation (Chapter 7.3; Fig 140).

Such a tower would have had a counterpart at the west end of the north aisle and Fig 69 shows in simplified form twin western

towers. The arrangement of a central crossing and twin western towers, although a novelty in the 10th century, was to become a commonplace after Cluny II (11th century) (Conant 1987, 148). Twin western towers were a feature of the Cluniac mother house of Notre-Dame de la Charité (La Charité-sur-Loire) (Fig 68) – and of another church of the Nivernais region, the Cluniac priory of St Etienne of Nevers (Nièvre), built c 1083–97. Examples of towers in the western facade from Romanesque Normandy are found at St Martin de Boscherville (Seine-Maritime) (Benedictine) founded c 1060, the Abbaye-aux-Hommes in Caen founded 1066 by William the Conqueror, the Abbaye-aux-Dames in Caen, founded by William's wife, Matilda, and the great abbey church of Jumièges, which was finally consecrated in the presence of the Conqueror in 1067. Closer to home, the achieved Romanesque western facade found expression at such surviving examples as Castle Acre Priory (Fig 68).

The broad foundation of the west front was also identified by Buckler (Martin 1926, 215) and is recorded as 'six ft six inches wide' (1.98m) (BL, Add MS 24433, fo 58). The reconstruction (Fig 69) uses the extant, largely 12th-century west front of Benedictine Selby Abbey (Yorkshire West Riding), founded in 1069, to conjecture Bermondsey's west end; it also incorporates, like Selby, a north porch on the nave, as the priory's presumed parochial function would have demanded this until the construction of the parish church of St Mary Magdalene (before 1291; below, 'The precinct and home grange').

The nave of St Saviour Bermondsey probably consisted of ten bays, not including the west tower bay (Fig 69). The internal width of 57ft (17.37m) was subdivided by aisles. The worked stone evidence describes a nave arcade of simple round columns with a diameter of 1.47m (1.57m at the chamfered base). PCA's recent excavations show the bay unit width to be 4.07–4.10m (A Douglas, pers comm). The reconstructions here use 4.115m or 13ft 6in (Fig 25; Fig 74). The arcade probably stood on a continuous sleeper wall below floor level; this would have been a minimum of 1.57m wide.

The round, or drum, pier appears in a large group of Romanesque priory and cathedral churches over a period of nearly 150 years. The earliest surviving use of the round pier in England is in the chapel in the Tower of London (1077–87; Gem 1990, 47). They are employed at Tewkesbury Abbey and Gloucester Cathedral, both in Gloucestershire, in c 1100–20 (Service 1982, 116–17), after which, masons at Southwell in Nottinghamshire (c 1120–40), Leominster in Herefordshire (Benedictine, 1121–50) and St Bartholomew Smithfield in the City of London (c 1123–40) all appeared to follow suit. We ought perhaps to look at such Cistercian churches as Buildwas (Shropshire) with its low fat columns (bay interval c 4.3m: Bilson 1909, pl v) to gain an idea of the appearance of the relatively low arcade probably employed at Bermondsey.

The capitals of the ?nave arcade were embellished with two basic forms of scallop ornament – slit and paper-dart – representing at least four columnar piers. The distinctively 'compressed' scallop capitals argue for a construction date for the unlocated arcade in the third quarter of the 12th century (Fig 71). The capitals are similar to the presbytery column capitals at St Bartholomew Smithfield (c 1140) in such details as the profile of the necking but are much lower in relation to the width of the pier; this change may indicate a later date.

The scalloped capital shows a row of semicircles traced on the fascia of the capital, which are prolonged downwards to the necking with truncated cones. One capital had drilled holes at the base of slits in the truncated cones; these recur in the capitals in the nave at Peterborough (Conway Library, Courtauld Institute negative no. 427/67, 15a) which immediately pre-date 1177, when the nave was lengthened by two bays by Abbot Benedict (1177–93: Cook 1960, 178). The distinctive paper-dart motif used in some of the capitals (Fig 71) is an elaboration of the 'v-shaped fillets, diminishing upwards' used in such disparate buildings as Buildwas nave (Bilson 1909, fig 5 iv), as well as St Bartholomew Smithfield and St Lawrence, Ramsgate (Kent) (M Samuel, pers observation). Also illustrated on Fig 71 are two sunk quadrant mouldings probably associated with the ?nave arcade (abacus A<3149> and voussoir A<3082>), together with a conjectural plan of the abacus at the arch springing.

Fig 71 incorporates the scallop ornamented capitals and abaci of the ?nave arcade and other mouldings (shown in detail in the upper portion of the figure) in a conjectural reconstructed elevation of the 12th-century nave arcade, based on the typical bay and pier bases reconstructed in Fig 25.

One part of the church may have employed two chevron sub-arches within each gallery arch (Fig 72). The nave at

Rochester Cathedral points to two types of treatment of the gallery of the arcade elevation. The material displays no unusual traits but is reminiscent of Borg's type 3 (Borg 1967, 135), which he allocates to the second half of the 12th century. The east windows of the Glastonbury Lady chapel, Somerset (Thurlby 1995, fig 24), parallel elaborate late 12th-century chevron arch forms known from Buckler's records (BL, Add MS 24433, fo 93).

There can be little doubt that pointed interlaced arcading marked the triforium level in the ?nave (Fig 73). Intersecting arcading first appears after 1093 at Durham (Clapham 1934, 133). One important technical innovation at Bermondsey was the use of junction blocks at the apices (Fig 73); this element was recovered from both the site Z and site A assemblages (Fig 3; Table 1). Use of these blocks permitted the meshing of arches so that neither takes priority, an innovation seen at the Lady chapel of Glastonbury Abbey (Thurlby 1995, fig 11). At Bermondsey, however, one arch takes priority over the other (Fig 73). It may be conjectured that the absence of meshing indicates an early date but the unusual pointed arch seems 'late'. The moulding is widespread in 'Anglo-Norman' arches, such as those of St Bartholomew Smithfield (c 1140) (Chapter 7.2, 'Construction phase 1, c 1140–90 (periods M4 and M5)', 'Intersecting arcade'). Rounded interlace was also present at Bermondsey according to Buckler (BL, Add MS 24433, fos 122, 123).

The use of hemispherical or half-moon (lunate) stops in parts of the intersecting arcade (Fig 130, Z<109>) is another diagnostic feature also seen in the claustral buildings of Cistercian Fontenay Abbey (Côte-d'Or) and at the Yorkshire abbeys of Fountains, Byland, Roche (West Riding) and Rievaulx (North Riding), and dated to the 1160s (L Grant and G Coppack, pers comm). Cistercian influence as developed in Burgundy and neighbouring regions has been thought to have contributed to the Early English style (eg Conant 1987, 236–7); both pointed arches and hemispherical stops could be seen as examples of these influences.

Fig 74 shows a reconstructed elevation and elevational section of a typical 12th-century nave arcade bay, as constructed in the third quarter of the 12th century, based on the typestones illustrated in Fig 71 and Fig 73. The proportional system which can be seen employed at St Bartholomew Smithfield is here indicated in red (the square root of two) to show the probable height of the arcade to extrados level (ie the upper/exterior curve of the arch). The clerestorey is conjectural, as is the height of the triforium.

The nave and aisles were covered by quadripartite ribbed vaults, but only one rib form from the 12th-century priory church was found at the excavations reported here (A<3125>, Fig 126). This form can be paralleled at Peterborough and was dated by Clapham to the 1120s (1934, fig 42 3). Buckler recorded two variants of 12th-century rib (BL, Add MS 24433, fos 84, 85), which appear to find parallels in the transept chapels at Roche Abbey (c 1165) (Bilson 1909, 200, fig 13, IIIT), but it would be unwise to make much of their very common profile. The nail-head ornament and 'mammiform' projections from the hollow chamfers are probably of greater significance: the recurrence of the latter ornament at the French parent house, La

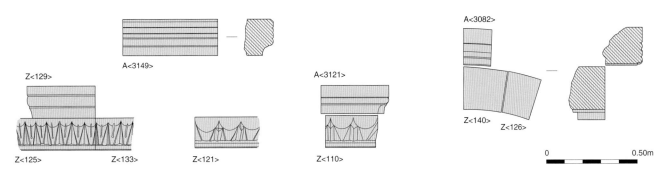

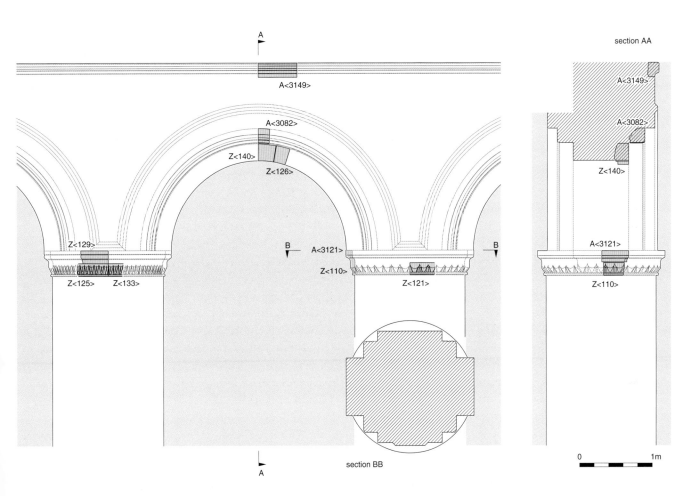

Fig 71 Details of the 12th-century ?nave arcade: upper – arcade pier scallop capitals and arch impost with scallop ornament: capital with slit motif and abacus moulding (Z<125>, Z<133> and Z<129>), round capital (Z<121>) and rectilinear arch impost (Z<110>) with paper dart motif and abacus (A<3121>); sunk quadrant mouldings probably associated with the ?nave arcade: abacus (A<3149>), voussoir (A<3082>), and minor-order arch voussoirs (Z<126>, Z<140>) (scale 1:20); lower left – a conjectural reconstructed elevation showing the possible employment of typestones together with a conjectural plan of the abacus at the arch springing; lower right – sectional elevation of the arcade capital and arch (scale 1:50)

Charité-sur-Loire, is of particular interest. Buckler's two variants are reproduced here in comparison with a rib form found at Harp Lane where a mass of distinctive mouldings can be recognised as originating from Bermondsey Priory (Chapter 7.2, 'Construction phase 2, *c* 1190–*c* 1220 (periods M5 and M6)'; Fig 136). Later rib forms show that vaulting on a large scale continued into the 13th century.

Evidence from the moulding assemblage reveals that the interior of the priory church was brightly painted. Prior to the mid 13th century (ie up to and including period M6), many of the architectural elements were picked out in red, white and black. Twelfth-century capital and pier elements dressed from Caen stone were painted in a succession of coats of bright scarlet, vermilion and white/cream plaster washes and were later coated with successive coats of whitewash. At ?triforium level, the intersecting arcade (Fig 73) was brightly painted with red paint covering the flanking roll and field. The casement hollows were painted white or straw colour and the fillets on

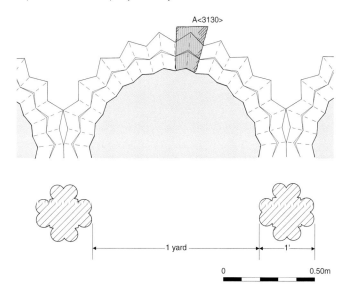

Fig 72 Reconstruction of triforium sub-arch ornamented with chevron A<3130>: upper –elevation; lower – profile of shafting (scale 1:20)

alternating arches red or black. A near-intact arch-moulding (Z<138>; CP1.12.1; Fig 126) was painted white apart from a red-painted roll. An element from a string course A<3147> (CP3.5.2; Fig 135) was picked out in black and white. The label was painted white and the hollow below dark (probably black). This would have caused the string course to stand out from the wall face. Some elements seem never to have been painted, other than with numerous coats of whitewash.

It is not known if the entire decorative scheme inside St Saviour Bermondsey was confined to this somewhat limited palette. There is no evidence for more complex mural scenes such as might have existed on large areas of ashlar wall. It is likely, however, if so much of the church were painted, that some of the interior decoration would have included more specific iconography, such as images of Christ or biblical scenes. Red masonry pattern (ie imitation ashlar) survived on the walls of the east range (period M8), and on wall plaster (from OA12; Fig 154) which would have formed part of the internal plaster decoration of one of the abbey buildings.

The general paucity of decorative details or sculpture in the

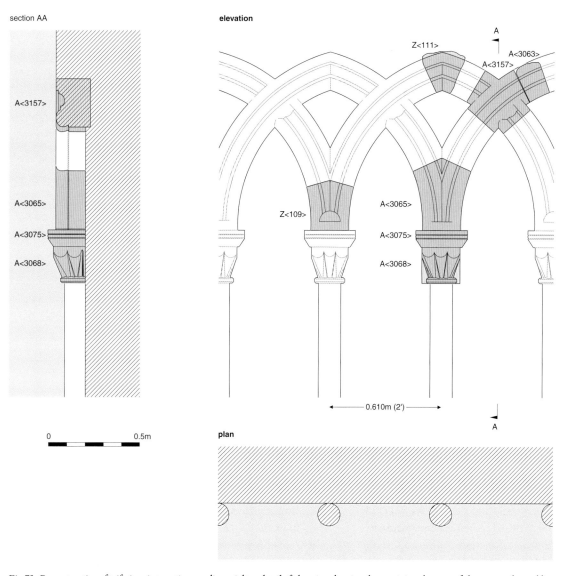

Fig 73 Reconstruction of triforium intersecting arcading: right – detail of elevation showing the surviving elements of the apex arch moulding and shafting (Z<111>, A<3063>, A<3157>, A<3065>, A<3075>, A<3068>, Z<109>) and plan; left – sectional elevation showing surviving elements (scale 1:20)

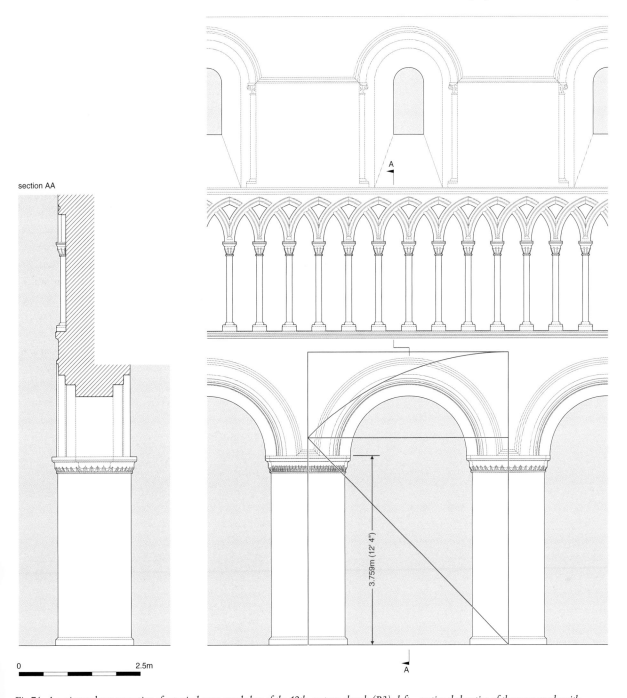

section AA

3.759m (12' 4")

0   2.5m

Fig 74 A conjectural reconstruction of a typical nave arcade bay of the 12th-century church (B3): left – sectional elevation of the nave arcade with intersecting arcading over; and right – elevation (a proportional system to show probable height of the arcade to extrados level is shown in red) (scale 1:75)

architectural fragments assemblage could be explained by the fact that Bermondsey owes more to its Anglo-Norman contemporaries than to its Burgundian Cluniac heritage. There are, however, a handful of features among the architectural fragments which could be said to reflect more widespread influences. The lunate eaves tabling which formed an overhanging ornamental jetty below a roofline (Fig 75) can be paralleled at 11th-century Cluny II. A similar but apparently plainer ornament was used on the tower of the extant south arm of the great transept (Conant 1987, fig 150) and the ornament is also used to mark floor levels in the north-west tower of La Charité-sur-Loire (Graham 1926, pl I). The

hemispherical stops on the intersecting arcades at triforium level (Fig 130, Z<109>) – also seen in the 1160s claustral buildings of Cistercian Fontenay (above) – are perhaps another instance of influence from Burgundy and the kingdom of Arles. A comparatively small cusped arch (<1.24m wide) that formed the outer order of a window or door arch (A<3159>; CP1.17.1; Fig 76) is paralleled in the outer order of the chapter house arcade at the Cluniac house of Wenlock (Evans 1950, fig 57b) and in the tower of St Lawrence, New Romney (Kent) (M Samuel, pers observation). However, it appears to be unusual in Norman architecture and can be defined as an 'exotic' import characteristic of Cluniac architecture. Cusping is 'sufficiently unusual, and its

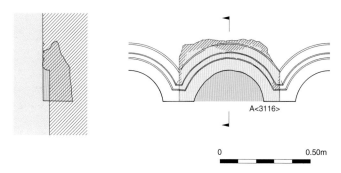

0   0.50m

Fig 75 Reconstruction of lunate eaves table A<3116>: left – section; right – elevation (scale 1:20)

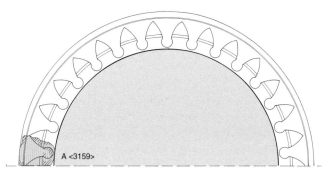

0   0.50m

Fig 76 Reconstruction of cusped arch A<3159>: upper – elevation; lower – plan (scale 1:20)

use sufficiently widely spread within the order, for it to be a recognisable Cluniac characteristic' (ibid, 39). It must never be forgotten, however, that we are looking at an 'Anglo-Norman' building; the English quadrant is a unifying feature of the architecture of the church, occuring in a variety of the most common 'repeat' mouldings such as string courses.

One of the few surviving pieces of figure sculpture, the lion, is an icon associated more particularly with the Lombardic Romanesque and can be paralleled at Moissac (Tarn-et-Garonne), in former Gascony (Fig 31). (The fragment of sculpted relief which may represent the raising of Lazarus is dated to the 11th century: Chapter 3.1, 'Discussion'; Fig 20.)

Part of the explanation for the relative absence of early, pre-*c* 1140, diagnostic sculptural elements from the early church then, could be that the church was indeed a plain, Anglo-Norman, round-pier edifice. The early priory buildings very probably incorporated significant quantities of Roman brick or tile in their construction (Chapters 2.3, 3.3, 'Discussion'). Added to this is the probability that much of the stone was carted away at the Dissolution when most of the priory church was demolished (Chapter 5.1, 'The construction of Pope's mansion', 5.2, 'Monastic buildings completely or largely demolished').

Part of the architectural fragments assemblage comes from another site, Vine Lane in Southwark, near the south bank of the Thames (site Z; Fig 3), where it had been incorporated in a wall round a tin-glazed ware kiln. It is certain that stone, especially the stone from the church, was re-employed locally.

In contrast, the documentary evidence presents a fairly convincing case for a pre-1140 commencement of construction (Chapter 3.2, 3.3). A flood of early endowments would have enabled the monks to embark in the decades immediately after the foundation on an ambitious building programme, which would have included both the priory church and conventual buildings. Henry I is referred to as having enlarged both the priory church and its endowments; Mary, Countess of Boulogne, was buried in the priory in 1115, presumably in the eastern part of the priory church; Henry II held his council at the priory in 1154, possible evidence of a functioning presbytery. But endowments slackened as it appears did the pace of construction, and it took a more drawn-out programme to complete the works. The translation of the body of the first prior into the choir of the church and the dedication of the morning altar in 1206 suggest the church had probably not been completed before that date.

The parallel apses or apse echelon scheme at the building's east end is a conventional one seen in many late 11th-century examples. It may have come directly from La Charité-sur-Loire, which did not develop its east chevet until 1125. This would place the planning stage, at least, of the Bermondsey great church before 1125. Plan alone is not, however, a very reliable indicator of date. The absence of decorative schemes or elaborate figure sculpture argues in favour of a Norman Romanesque style, where the accent is on the interplay of volumes and the management of mass and of space.

The ongoing, major building work after *c* 1140 evidently included substantial work on the priory church to judge from specific elements dated to after that time, such as the scallop capitals dated to the third quarter of the 12th century (above, and Chapter 3.3, 'Discussion'). The architectural fragments evidence suggests the bulk of the construction work occurred in the mid 12th century or later, rather than earlier 12th century. The assemblage does include a few early typestones and, indeed, stone build numbers 1 to 9 all have average early dates of 1080–1100, with large potential date ranges of 80 to 100 years (Chapter 7.2, 'Methodology'; Table 11). The broader, less definitive ranges of the earlier stones in the assemblage inevitably lead to an average mid date around 1150, which may be skewing the picture in favour of a later construction date for the church. Nevertheless, key elements clearly date to the later period, including the wider (presumably nave) round piers, which can be interpreted as evidence for the construction of a 'great church-scale' arcade which could have formed part of the original design but whose execution can be confidently dated to the third quarter of the 12th century. There may have been further delay in completing the building; vaulting on a large scale continued into the 13th century as shown by later rib forms. The available evidence is consistent with a building programme which was conceived in the late 11th century and began at the east end of the church; it spread over the 12th century with the nave finally completed soon after *c* 1200 (Chapter 3.3, 'Discussion').

The priory church of St Saviour and its towers, rising above the surrounding marshes and surrounded by its small metropolis of domestic courts and buildings, would indeed have appeared as an impressive sight to the traveller approaching London up the Thames by boat or along the road from Kent. Beyond lay London bridge and the settlement of Southwark around the south bridgehead, including the pre-Conquest and Domesday 'monasterium' reformed as the Augustinian priory of St Mary Southwark (Blair 1991, 101–2). But dominating the flat marshlands on the south side of the Thames downstream of London bridge was the White Tower on the north bank. St Saviour Priory stood opposite, creating the juxtaposition of castle and monastery so typical of the Norman period. A visit to the abbey of Fleury (Saint-Benôit-sur-Loire) conveys how the church may have looked in the 12th century, visible from many miles around over running water, wheat fields, rushes and fens. The 12th-century priory church of St Saviour was peppered with towers and projecting chapels in the best Cluniac tradition, but the ornament on them reflected the chastened spirit of the Cistercians, who influenced architecture even outside their patronage.

The 14th-century priory church

By *c* 1400 the appearance of the east end of the priory/abbey church (B3) had been radically altered. The documentary and archaeological evidence combine to attest to substantial rebuilding of the priory buildings in the 14th century which included changes to the priory church. Greater economic and administrative stability in the fortunes of the house seems to have been accompanied by refurbishment and expansion of the priory church.

An enhanced presbytery is reconstructed on Fig 69. The wholly conjectural ?Lady/?Rood chapel is based on the extension of the east arm of Barking Abbey and represents an indication of the scale of the lost structure rather than any precise idea of its form. The Barking east arm, for which only fragmentary evidence survives, was extended in the early 13th century by the addition of a 'Saint's chapel' and projecting chapel beyond it (RCHM(E) 1921, 7). It is chiefly of interest in showing how a monastic church comparable in size and age, in the same region, was developed in the 13th century. Another good (surviving) analogy is St Albans where the choir arm was rebuilt *c* 1260–1326 (Cook 1960, fig 13 and 242).

Building work, however, on the chapel of Holy Cross, referred to in 1234, is difficult to place in context or quantify (Chapter 3.4, 'Discussion'). There is evidence for a very elaborate columnar structure of Purbeck marble in the 13th century at Bermondsey in the architectural fragments assemblage (Chapter 7.2, 'Construction phase 3, *c* 1220–60 (periods M6 and beginning of M7)') and in architectural elements recorded by Buckler (BL, Add MS 24433, fos 105–16), and recent work by PCA has recovered further elements of a very fine colonnade of Purbeck marble, perhaps all from the same chapel (material seen by M Samuel, courtesy of PCA). The precise location of 'the chapel of St Mary in the church of the priory of St Saviour' – in

existence by the second decade of the 14th century – is not known (*Cat Anc Deeds*, v, A11652). Nor does the consecration of five altars in the 1330s and 1340s – beginning with the greater church of St Saviour and the high altar in 1332 (*maius altare*), and in 1338 altars to Holy Cross, to 'Drueth' in honour of Blessed Mary and St Thomas the Martyr, to SS Andrew and James, all documented in the annals, and in 1346 an altar to SS Lawrence and Denis – necessarily represent in building terms the wholesale reconstruction proposed by Graham (1926) (Chapter 3.6, 'Discussion'). The annals record under 1206 the earlier dedication of the altar in the choir in honour of the Virgin Mary and All Saints (*Ann Monast*, iii, 450). However, one alteration at the later period is supported by both the documentary and recorded evidence. The altar dedicated in 1338 in honour of SS Andrew and James and all the Apostles was described as next to the gate of the monks' cemetery, while Buckler minutely records in 1818 a south doorway, which it can be suggested dates *c* 1320–50, in the presbytery south wall giving access into the cemetery (probably replacing an earlier door) (Fig 69; Fig 122; Chapter 7.1, 'Catalogue of maps …', 'Doorway in north elevation, Bermondsey (BL, Add MS 24433, fo 138) …', 7.2, 'Construction phase 5, *c* 1340–*c* 1410 (period M8)').

According to the annals, however, a further phase of alteration to the church took place under Prior Richard Dunton. In the 1380s to 1390s Dunton leaded the nave and installed nine glass windows in the presbytery, along with gilded reredoses for the high and morning altars; work on the roof and south aisle, and glazing, was not completed before 1392. A 14th-century, large traceried window (A<3112>; CP5.3.4; Fig 139), probably from the priory church, and the many traceried window fragments found reused at Harp Lane (Chapter 7.2, 'Construction phase 5, *c* 1340–*c* 1410 (period M8)'), can be attributed to this phase. Broadly 14th century in date too is much of the window glass recovered from Dissolution and demolition contexts (below, 'Interior decoration of the monastic buildings: glazing and tiling' and Chapter 7.6, 'The context and character of the catalogued window glass').

This activity may represent the culmination of a phase of modernisation of the presbytery rather than wholesale reconstruction of the east arm of the church. Renewal of the roof and reglazing may have followed on from (and been necessitated by) the additions made to the north side of the church and alterations to the east end (period M8; Chapter 3.6). Evidence recorded by Grimes (Fig 23) testifies to two major changes for which, however, there is no direct dating evidence: the demolition of the two apsidal chapels of the north transept and the addition of a new north aisle; and the creation of an extended and square-ended presbytery. On the south side of the presbytery archaeological evidence from site A showed the south wall was extended east, also suggesting an enlarged east arm (Fig 57). These changes would fit well with the documented work of the 1380s–90s on windows in the presbytery and the roof of the south aisle.

The new north aisle or perhaps more likely the now-reduced north transept may have functioned as the sacristy, which from documentary evidence lay on the north side of the church in

1334 and 1400, and probably earlier (Dawson 2002, 6). This position is paralleled at other Cluniac houses. At Castle Acre Priory, the 12th-century sacristy projected north from the north side of the north transept (Coad and Coppack 1998, 20–1). At Thetford Priory the late 15th-century sacristy was also attached to the north side of the north transept, whereas in the 12th century the sacristy was south of the south transept and only entered from the church (Raby and Reynolds 1979, 8, 11). The later 12th-century sacristy at Pontefract Priory also lay on the north side of the church but occupied the angle between the north transept and the presbytery and was entered from the transept (Bellamy 1965, fig 24).

The cloister

The most striking aspect of the cloister plan is the relation of the east range to the south transept of the church (Fig 69). The east range is clearly not aligned on the same axis as the north and south arms of the crossing. Although the great majority of monastic plans are regular, it is by no means rare for the cloister to exhibit certain deviations from the perfectly square or rectangular plan. The layout of the principal cloister at Wenlock Priory, for example, shows the buildings of the south cloister range to lie at a distinct angle to the other conventual buildings (Morley 1990, 6–7; Pinnell 1999, site plan). For the east range of the main cloister not to share the axis of the church transepts, however, is unusual. A precedent lies in the example of Cluny II itself, which has an entirely offset east cloister range (Conant 1987, 147). Here, the chapter house, parlour and east range lie on a shared north–south axis with the eastern apses of the priory church. The broad north cloister walk houses the scriptorium and the equally broad east walk, the stair to the upper floors of the east range buildings. In the angle between the west wall of the south transept and the south wall of the nave, occupying the dog-leg in the north-east corner of the cloister, the monastic library was located. The plotting of foundations in the north-east corner of the cloister and south transept revealed by PCA's excavations confirms the situation was less complicated at Bermondsey and no such dog-leg existed.

The misalignment of the 12th-century (period M4) priory church and east cloister range suggests different dates for their laying out. Construction in stone of the east cloister range would normally follow construction of the eastern arm of the permanent church, rather than precede it. The full explanation is possibly complex and the existence of earlier buildings has to be a factor. It is possible there was an earlier phase of the priory church (B3; Chapter 3.1, 'Discussion', 3.2, 'Archaeological evidence', 'Priory church (B3)'). An element in the relation of the east range to the south transept at both Cluny II and Bermondsey is the presence on both sites of a small chapel on the north side of the infirmary complex. At Bermondsey the following sequence may be suggested on the basis of the currently available evidence. The first phase 11th-century (period M3) small chapel/church (B1) was free-standing and constructed before the 12th-century priory church to its north-west. The chapel could have been used for the monastic offices

during the construction of at least the east arm of the 'great church' and the masonry east range (B7) begun early to provide living accommodation. The first phase timber latrine (B2) would have been in use during construction and a stone reredorter (B8) replaced the latrine in the first half of the 12th century (Chapter 3.2, 'Archaeological evidence', 'Reredorter (B8)'). The east range would have been one of the first permanent conventual buildings to be finished, enabling the basic material and religious functions of monastic life to take place on a daily basis there and in the closely adjacent chapel.

At Cluny II, the free-standing small chapel on the north side of the infirmary complex is labelled the Lady chapel and has an integral relationship with the chapter house at the north end of the east range. There was direct access from the chapter house to the chapel through an opening in the dividing wall common to both buildings. At Bermondsey, the west end of the first phase chapel (B1) was not recovered on site A; it is probable that it was later obliterated by the rebuilding of the chapter house (B4) (period M8; Chapter 3.6, 'Archaeological evidence', 'Chapter house (B4) and cloister (B5)'; below). The absence of evidence for this crucial area of the monastic complex is frustrating, but it is possible to imagine a close relationship between the chapel and the eastern cloister at Bermondsey in the early years of the 12th century.

The presumed location of the 12th-century chapter house (B4) on the east side of the cloister is indicated on the period plans (eg Fig 21). Its exact relationship, however, to the south transept and to the domestic parts of the east range is not clear from the excavated evidence. One possibility is that it adjoined the north end of the east range and this is the layout conjectured on Fig 69, with a narrow slype or passage between the south transept and the chapter house (although a – small – sacristy is also possible). A second possibility is that the chapter house lay adjacent to the south transept, with the east range extending further north by another bay.

There is no direct evidence for the form of the 12th-century chapter house. The double west entrance is conjectured from features recorded by Buckler (reused in post-Dissolution windows: BL, Add MS 24433, fo 58), who also recorded a south pilaster buttress facing on to the cloister walk (Fig 122; Fig 123). It may have had a semicircular eastern apse, like other 12th-century Cluniac houses such as Castle Acre (founded 1078–81), Lewes (c 1081), Thetford (1103–4) and Wenlock (refounded as a Cluniac priory c 1080) (Raby and Reynolds 1979; Lyne 1997, 12, fig 2; Coad and Coppack 1998; Pinnell 1999). This is the form conjectured on Fig 69. This apsidal layout is also found in 12th-century Benedictine abbeys: an example survives today at Reading Abbey, while the chapter houses at Durham and Norwich (Norfolk) were of this form (Cook 1960, 147). Cook, however, believed that the cathedral priories favoured a rectangular plan (ibid); this plan was certainly as popular as the apse at Benedictine monastic houses. Rectangular examples at Faversham Abbey and Barking Abbey are only known from excavation, but these are apparently primary builds (RCHM(E) 1921, 8; Philp 1968, 23). Given the lack of any positive evidence for an apse at Bermondsey, a rectangular end from the inception seems just as likely, a view reinforced by the institutional links with Faversham.

Archaeological evidence shows the chapter house was subsequently rebuilt as square-ended and the adjacent cloister arcade was also rebuilt. North of the chapter house entrance, Buckler recorded a later medieval, ?sacristy doorway in the north–south wall between the chapter house and the transept (Fig 122; Fig 123). A standard design in Cluniac houses from the 14th century, the 12th-century apsidal chapter houses at Castle Acre, Thetford and Wenlock were all remodelled as square (Raby and Reynolds 1979; Coad and Coppack 1998; Pinnell 1999). At Bermondsey the limited archaeological dating evidence for this rebuilding can only suggest it occurred sometime in the 14th or 15th century. According to the annals, the cloister and refectory were rebuilt by Prior Richard Dunton in 1381, after a long delay (*Ann Monast*, iii, 480). It seems plausible then to see changes to the chapter house as part of the much broader remodelling of the east (B7) and south (B6) ranges of the main cloister, which took place probably in the second half of the 14th century (period M8), along with modifications to the second infirmary cloister (OA2) in this period (Chapter 3.6, 'Archaeological evidence'; below, 'The reredorter, infirmary complex and other domestic buildings').

This discussion has focused so far on the east and south-east parts of the main cloister. Here the enclosed cloister garth (OA5) can be measured and was *c* 21m north–south. Much of the principal cloister, however, remains unexcavated. The greater part of the existing evidence for the main cloister as a whole comes from the antiquarian records made by J C Buckler (Chapter 7.1) and the archaeological work undertaken in the north-west part of the cloister by PCA (BYQ98; above). The results of these recent (unpublished) excavations are not plotted on Fig 69.

The western half of the cloister on the conjectural reconstruction (Fig 69) is a schematic outline only. It follows Buckler, and Martin, in aligning the west wall of the west claustral range with the west front of the priory church (Chapter 7.1; BL, Add MS 24433, fo 70, reproduced here as Fig 123; Martin 1926, fig 1). This alignment, combined with mirroring the width of the 12th-century east cloister walk and south range, results in a rectangular cloister with what seems an excessively long west–east axis.

On the north side of the cloister, a 'gap' between the south wall of the nave and the north cloister walk is shown. Buckler's records can be interpreted to suggest a medieval arcaded structure (indicated by an arcade respond some ?4m in height, indicating a ?arcade against the south nave wall) on the south side towards the west end of the 'gap' and the existence of a set of ?chambers along the north side of the cloister (Chapter 7.1; BL, Add MS 24433, fo 55, here Fig 120; BL, Add MS 24433, fo 70; Fig 123). Buckler recorded remnants of nave aisle windows at a high level. Apparently later medieval in date, the arcade may be part of a late adaptation or conversion of the north side of the cloister (BL, Add MS 24433, fo 25, 'Bermondsey Abbey, relic amongst the ruins of Sir Thomas Pope's mansion'). Subsequently, the north range of the post-Dissolution mansion was sited in the shell between the south wall of the nave and the north cloister arcade, with the masonry southern wall built on the foundation of the cloister arcade; this later range was two chambers deep and overlooked the mansion's courtyard (Chapter 5.1, 'The construction of Pope's mansion').

The actual layout of the western half of the cloister, the existence of such a 'gap' and whether it reflects an earlier arrangement will be clarified by the publication of PCA's excavations in the north-west cloister and south transept. PCA have found simple pilaster buttresses on the external face of the south nave aisle wall here but no trace of cloister-type responds (A Douglas, pers comm). The example of Cluny II with its entirely separate east cloister range may be relevant (Conant 1987, 147).

The reredorter, infirmary complex and other domestic buildings

The expansion of the priory's domestic buildings is a marked feature of the second half of the 12th century (period M5) and suggests a growth in community numbers and new sources of income (Chapter 3.3, 'Documentary evidence' and 'Discussion'; Fig 33). New buildings were constructed and existing ones altered. A second, infirmary, cloister (OA2), was created by the construction of the new east infirmary range (B10 and B11); this courtyard was bounded on the north by an extended chapel (B1) and on the south by the remodelled former reredorter (B8), now a domestic hall cum lodgings. To meet new demands a new reredorter was built and a more elaborate system of water management, which included for the first time a stone-lined principal drain (D2) but reused elements of the earlier ditch system.

The development of the second reredorter (B9) took place early on in the sequential evolution of the monastic plan and was an integral part of the new arrangements. It provided much enlarged latrine provision, integrated with the east range (B7) and possibly the hall/lodgings (B8). The upper floor latrines would have been accessed from the first-floor dorter of the east range, and may have been accessible at first-floor level too from the hall/lodgings (B8), either via the east range (with which this building would have probably connected in the preceding period, M4) or directly. The position of the new reredorter block, across the south end of the east range, was one seen at other Cluniac houses such as Castle Acre, Thetford and Lewes, but the ground-floor design of an open sub-basement is very unusual. The tiled base of the second reredorter (B9) was at the same level (1.55m OD) as the base of the drain (D2), but 1.7m below the ground floor (at 3.25m OD) of the adjacent hall/lodgings (B8). The lack of an internal culvert to channel flowing water through the reredorter must have resulted in inefficient flushing, necessitating cleaning out of the sub-basement periodically while in the interim keeping the water level up to keep down the smell.

The first phase infirmary block was built in the last quarter of the 12th century and comprised a north–south infirmary hall (B10) and a latrine building (B11) of conventional design with an internal stone-built drain (D2). The low floor levels in the infirmary hall (B10) indicate that the entry to the building was down a flight of steps, although there was no archaeological evidence as such. The chalk floor at the north end of the infirmary was at 2.75m OD, whereas the gravel path in the south part of the infirmary cloister, immediately outside the hall/lodgings (B8), was at 3.28m OD. There is little evidence for the internal arrangements of this building. It is not known whether or not the building was aisled and vaulted in stone. The lack of positive evidence suggests that, in its first phase at least, it was a single storey hall with a timber-framed roof. The considerable quantity of Roman ceramic building material found in the robbing debris of the building suggests how the building may have appeared in its final phase (demolished *c* 1330–*c* 1430, period M8; Chapter 3.6, 'Archaeological evidence', 'Demolition of the former infirmary buildings (B10 and B11)'); it is likely that the Roman tile was used chiefly in the quoining and as door and window surrounds.

The lateral partition across the latrine (B11) invites some speculation as to whether there was any sort of segregation being practised in the complex. The hall itself, of course, is laterally divided, the division being centrally placed vis à vis the neighbouring room, so as to suggest the presence of two separate entrances north and south of the dividing wall. The division in the latrine, however, suggests a single entrance south of the line of stakeholes, so that a person wishing to reach the north room of the latrine (B11) would perforce have to pass through the south room. In addition, those people confined to the south half of the infirmary hall had access to the cesspit at its south end. The purpose of this apparent segregation may apply to, for example, the ill and the simply aged, or to monks and (male) laity. It may even apply to the sexes, but this seems less likely; the infirmary at St John's, Canterbury, employed sexual segregation, but with separate entrances *and* latrine blocks at the north and south ends of the building (Tatton-Brown 1984). We do know that females were housed at the priory at various times in its history but records of corrodies before the early 14th century are rare, and male corrodians are recorded far more frequently. The population of the excavated monastic cemetery at Bermondsey north of the infirmary complex contained a high proportion of mature males and very few (eight) females/?females (Chapter 7.9, 'Human variation', 'Sex'; Table 20).

The former reredorter (B8) was considerably altered and now possibly functioned as the infirmarer's lodgings. It was extended east to adjoin the south wall of the new infirmary range (B10) and close off the south-east corner of the new infirmary cloister, but the lodgings itself must have been accessible from the south via the bridge over the stone-built drain (D2). On the north side of the infirmary cloister the chapel (B1) was not only retained but substantially extended. However, the chapel probably continued to function as the priory church at least as late as the 1160s–70s while building work continued on the new 12th-century church to the north-west (above, 'The 12th-century priory church'). It may be that, when no longer required for services, the chapel nave was adapted as a western infirmary hall and that the extended chancel alone served as the infirmary chapel. However, no evidence for latrine provision or cesspits associated with the chapel was found to corroborate such a change of use.

The infirmary's introduction in *c* 1200 appears very much as part of a grand design, albeit one which retained pre-existing buildings (B1 and B8) and elements of the earlier ditch system. Measured surveying of the site for the laying out of new buildings and open spaces is evident. The basic unit of measurement appears to have been the chain, or 22ft (6.71m). The intervals between the buildings and the buildings' parallel alignment were probably arrived at using the basic 3:4:5 triangle, where the units in chains would result in 66ft (20.12m) (length east–west) by 88ft (26.82m) (length north–south) by 110ft (33.53m) (length across the diagonal). The infirmary block (B10) was erected 66ft (20.12m), or three chains, east of the east range (B7), and in a parallel arrangement. This block measured *c* 24.8m internally north–south, making it comparable in size to the infirmary halls excavated at Merton (Augustinian) and at Waverley (Cistercian); this would put Bermondsey in the middle-sized range of infirmary halls (Miller and Saxby 2007, 124–5).

The infirmary complex was an important focus of the house's religious life, symbolising the link between medicine and spiritual healing. The infirmary was both part of the monastery and a completely separate community within it. A chapel was provided, so that the sick could observe the Masses. The 'Observances' or customs of the Augustinian priory of Barnwell (Cambridgeshire) set out the requirements for the master of the farmery:

The Master of the Farmery ought to have Mass celebrated daily for the sick either by himself or some other person, should they in any wise be able to come into the Chapel; but, if not, he ought to take his stole and missal, and reverently, at their bedsides, make the memorials of the day, of the Holy Spirit, and of Our Lady; and, if they cannot sing the canonical Hours for themselves, he ought to sing them for them, and frequently, in the spirit of gentleness, repeat to them words of consolation, of patience, and of hope in God; read to them, for their consolation, the lives of Saints; conceal for them all evil rumours; and in no wise disturb them when they are resting. (Observances 1897, 205)

There can be little doubt that the infirmary was a highly significant area in the monastic complex in the 13th century and into the 14th century. The subsequent demolition of the infirmary block (B10 and B11) in the later 14th to early 15th century highlights a change in the monastic lifestyle – a shift from communal to individual care for the reduced numbers. This then resident change which was part of a major refurbishment and rebuilding programme affecting the church, main cloister and refectory, and subsidiary cloisters or courtyards where individual chambers were created (period M8; Chapter 3.6, 'Discussion'). Elaborate separate accommodation for the prior or abbot was a common feature of monastic houses in the later medieval period, as at Castle Acre in the west range in the later 14th century and early 16th century (Coad and Coppack 1998, 34–40). A payment of £53 6s 8d by Bermondsey's prior, perhaps for the completion of his own house, was recorded in an account roll for 1391–2 (Graham 1937, 148–9).

This reorganisation was followed in the later 15th to 16th

centuries it seems by some contraction, evident in the disuse of the cemetery (OA6), demolition in the eastern courtyard (OA9) and changes to the reredorter (B9) (period M9; Chapter 3.7, 'Archaeological evidence').

Interior decoration of the monastic buildings: glazing and tiling

Glass fragments are by far the most extensive category among the accessioned finds. It was possible to examine only a relatively small part of the whole assemblage retrieved (Chapter 7.6, 'Introduction'). We can be sure that the monastic church and chapter house boasted an array of decorated glass windows and it seems reasonable from the context of the majority of the glass fragments recovered and discussed below that the chapel did too. Other buildings could also have been glazed, but possibly more plainly.

A small proportion of the pieces recovered are from deposits attributed to the period of use of the religious house, and may represent occasional breakage or programmes of replacement (these finds are discussed in detail in Chapter 7.6); potentially these may provide a key, albeit of limited usefulness, to dating for some of the fenestration.

The bulk of the assemblage was recovered from Dissolution and immediately post-Dissolution clearance and demolition contexts, concentrated overwhelmingly in the former monastic cemetery area (OA6) north of the former chapel (B1), with the former chapter house to the west and monastic church to the north (Chapter 7.6, 'The context and character of the catalogued window glass'). Some contexts also included lead window came (Chapter 7.7, 'Monastic house period', 'Items relating to the priory buildings'; Fig 170).

The overall impression of the glass (perhaps inevitably after passing through the devastating filters of the dissolution process and subsequent burial for centuries) is of a chaotic mass of highly decayed fragments. Several of the blue pieces, however (as at other sites), are little decayed with only very superficial deterioration (described as 'durable' in the catalogue). These and a few of the undecayed 'colourless' pieces most readily give an idea of the original quality of some of the monastery's glass as it would have appeared to contemporaries. Many other pieces require strong lighting or interpreted drawings. The great majority of the fragments recovered are so far corroded that even greatly increased resources would perhaps add only a little of significance to the overall picture. Not a single articulation of more than one complete pane in leading has survived (<S53>, Fig 170, comprises the most extensive fragments recovered) let alone any major portion of a light. This rather sombre appraisal of the assemblage is ultimately attributable more than anything else to the efficiency of window lead recycling upwards of four and a half centuries ago, both during the time of the religious house and following its dissolution.

One particularly unusual piece was recovered. This is a flat glass fragment (<G128>, Fig 164) decorated with painted gilt foliate scrolling and may have come from a panel with superficial ornament intended to be seen by direct light, but

which was mainly translucent, so as to allow the viewer to see through to what lay beyond. The 13th-century Westminster retable, for example, features gilding on blue glass in the form of vine and oak foliate patterns (Binski and Massing 2009, 144, figs 1–4). Documentary sources describe 'gilded tables' or windows for the high and morning altars (period M8; Chapter 3.6, 'Documentary evidence'). The fine lines of the foliate design suggest that gold could have been applied in powder form, with a protein-based binder, rather than as leaf (Chapter 7.6, 'Scientific analysis of selected pieces').

Large assemblages were recovered from various pit fills outside the chapel's north wall in the area between the chapel (B1) and church (B3), all with ceramics attributed to the 16th century. The backfill (A[2883], A[2938]) of a large, square pit dug (OA9, period P1) outside the north nave wall of the chapel (B1) yielded the largest number of pieces of window glass from the excavations and is typical. The glass fragments from the pit comprise a wide range of colours as well as colourless pieces, many retaining traces of painted motifs, a relatively small proportion of which are, in their present state, interpretable. Several unused pieces (<G43>, <G45>, <G46>; <G44>, Fig 165) retain their original crown edges and were offcuts apparently never set in lead. Two fragments (<G47>, <G48>) display faulty glass-workmanship and were probably never used. There are several examples of complete or near-complete quarries in pale green/colourless, amber, green and ruby (<G49>–<G52>). Other colours include several relatively undecayed blue and pale green pieces, amethyst and flashed ruby fragments. Painted designs on clear glass include trefoils and other foliate motifs in which three-dimensionality is at times emphasised by median lines, occasionally with subsidiary pellets (eg <G58>; <G73>, Fig 164). Further designs have been identified: a trumpet flower with prominent stamens and silver stain (<G60>); a ?double rose with silver stain (<G62>, Fig 164); complex palmate lobed leaves, thinly painted on unpainted fields (<G63>); an 'axe-blade'-shaped, yellow-brown quarry with a bell-like floral motif (<G65>, Fig 164); and a triangular fragment painted with ashlar masonry (<G82>).

It is hard to interpret this pit fill, and the fills of several other Dissolution date pits in this area, as anything other than Dissolution waste, but the amount and nature of the glass fragments suggest that something slightly more complex than the wholesale destruction of the chapel (B1), and/or other monastic buildings in the vicinity (including the church and chapter house), was taking place. The first stage in the systematic demolition of the building(s) was probably the stripping out and recycling of the lead holding the window glass. This area (OA9, period P1; Fig 111) produced a much more diverse assemblage than the small groups from the other areas, with a much wider range of colours.

The assemblage interestingly included a substantial number of unused, pale green or colourless pieces and offcuts. These were offcuts from the original edges of crown-spun glass, as produced at the glasshouse, which had never been mounted. Some pieces are distorted or otherwise unusable. They may derive from repair work or new glazing of monastic buildings, and they may all simply have been collected together as waste intended for recycling and stockpiled, until cleared out at the Dissolution. However, although the nave of the chapel (B1) was completely demolished at the Dissolution, the chancel seems to have survived until at least the second half of the 16th century. It is possible that these waste pieces derive from immediately post-Dissolution reglazing – in a plainer lighter style – of the chapel chancel on the part of Sir Thomas Pope (Chapter 5.2, 'Elements of the former monastery partly or wholly retained and adapted', 'Chapel (B1)').

The majority of the fragments, which had been mounted, do appear to be 'old' glass as can be seen from the pieces selected for illustration (Fig 164). There are examples of patterns typical of 13th-century grisaille, with stylised leaves and stems, cross-hatching and strapwork (eg <G59>, <G64>, <G66>, <G73>, Fig 164). But the majority are broadly 14th century in date (including probably many of the items catalogued as having 'silver' or yellow stain – a technique first seen in England in the early 14th century and increasingly common in the later 14th century), and extending possibly into the 15th century, as in the case of the 'seaweed' foliage design <G71> (Fig 164; Marks 1993, 154, 166–9, 177). The retention of such 'old' glass, potentially combined with piecemeal repairs, would not, of course, be unusual or unexpected. There is but a single fragment with an inscription <G18> (Fig 164) and none of the painted fragments has been recognised as a human (or angelic etc) figure; this contrasts with finds of decorated window glass at Merton (Egan 2007, 225–6).

Some, or indeed much, of this glass probably came from the windows of the chapel and had been installed (in periods M7 and M8) after the chapel was rebuilt c 1230–c 1330 (period M7). The 14th century was a period that saw considerable renewal of glazing in the conventual buildings in this part of the precinct. The chapter house was remodelled (period M8, c 1330–c 1430), with a new east end, and some of the glass may have come from there or from the documented phase of alteration to the church (including the presbytery and south aisle) in the 1380s to 1390s, when the annals record under 1387 that Prior Richard Dunton installed nine glass windows in the presbytery and accounts for 1391–2 show glass costing £22 was bought for seven windows (Chapter 3.6, 'Documentary evidence'). A 14th-century, large traceried window (A<3112>; CP5.3.4; Fig 139), probably from the priory church, and other traceried window fragments are attributable to this phase of renewal of windows (Chapter 7.2, 'Construction phase 5, c 1340–c 1410 (period M8)').

The rebuilding of the chapel – with the nave widened and chancel rebuilt – also would have required new floors, probably throughout. The very large quantity of demolition material presumed to be from the chapel included substantial numbers of both plain-glazed and decorated 'Westminster'-type tiles, so-called because they were first recognised in the muniment room at Westminster Abbey (for what follows see Betts 2002). Both plain-glazed and decorated tiles are very common in London, occurring on many church and monastic sites. There is little doubt that 'Westminster' tiles were made somewhere in the London area. Some may well have come from the decorated

floor tile kiln found at Farringdon Road (Islington) in the 19th century, although the large scale of production would suggest that other kilns would have been involved in their manufacture. The timespan during which the industry was in operation is still uncertain. The earliest securely dated tiles are those laid in the floor of the muniment room at Westminster Abbey in the late 1250s or early 1260s. Production seems to have continued into the early years of the 14th century. One of the latest 'Westminster' tiled floors may have been that installed in the Guildhall chapel built between 1298 and c 1350 (Betts 2007, 432).

There are 47 different designs (Fig 77) represented among the 334 decorated 'Westminster'-type floor tiles from Bermondsey, the most numerous type in the whole floor tile assemblage. Certain designs such as knights on horseback (W1, W3, W4) could be used singly, whilst others would have been grouped together, such as the tiles with the circle and dot designs (W59, W61, W62, W64). The plain 'Westminster' tiles are mostly glazed green, brown or yellow, with some black tiles and a few with greenish-brown and light green glaze.

Both decorated and square plain tiles are the same size so that they could be used together in the same floors. However, there are so many plain-glazed triangular tiles at Bermondsey that not all could have been used where a pavement laid at a 45° angle met the edge of the wall. This suggests that there were areas which used a large number of these tiles, probably in the form of decorative bands. The 'Westminster' tiled floor found *in situ* at Seal House (106–108 Upper Thames Street, City of London EC4) had two such decorative bands incorporating both square- and triangular-shaped tiles (Schofield 1994, 112, fig 126; Betts 2002, 23, 36, figs 20 and 21, 37). In addition to the chapel, the infirmary range extension (B12) also possibly had a 'Westminster' tiled floor in the 13th century, but this building was subsequently remodelled (in periods M7 and M8) and the floor may have been completely renewed.

The precinct and home grange

Much of our information about the layout of the monastic precinct outside the claustral area, as well as its extent, comes from Dissolution-period and later documentation, including the records made by the antiquarian John Chessell Buckler in the early 19th century (Chapter 7.1). Later commentators, such as Martin (1926) and Grimes (1968), when describing the limits of the precinct in the main closely followed the boundary shown on Buckler's plan of the precinct (BL, Add MS 24433, fo 1, reproduced here as Fig 78), with some adjustments.

Buckler's precinct plan is an accurate record of what he had identified as surviving medieval buildings. However, it also contains elements of artistic licence and reconstruction: he omitted (with the exception of the grange farmhouse) the post-medieval buildings in the area, buildings which are shown on, for example, Rocque's plan of the area in 1746 (reproduced here as Fig 79) and on Horwood's plan compiled in the 1790s (Horwood 1813). Buckler's bird's eye view of Pope's mansion and its setting, looking south (BL, Add MS 24433, fo 53, reproduced in Martin 1926, pl VI/fig 3), adopts a similar approach. We should be wary

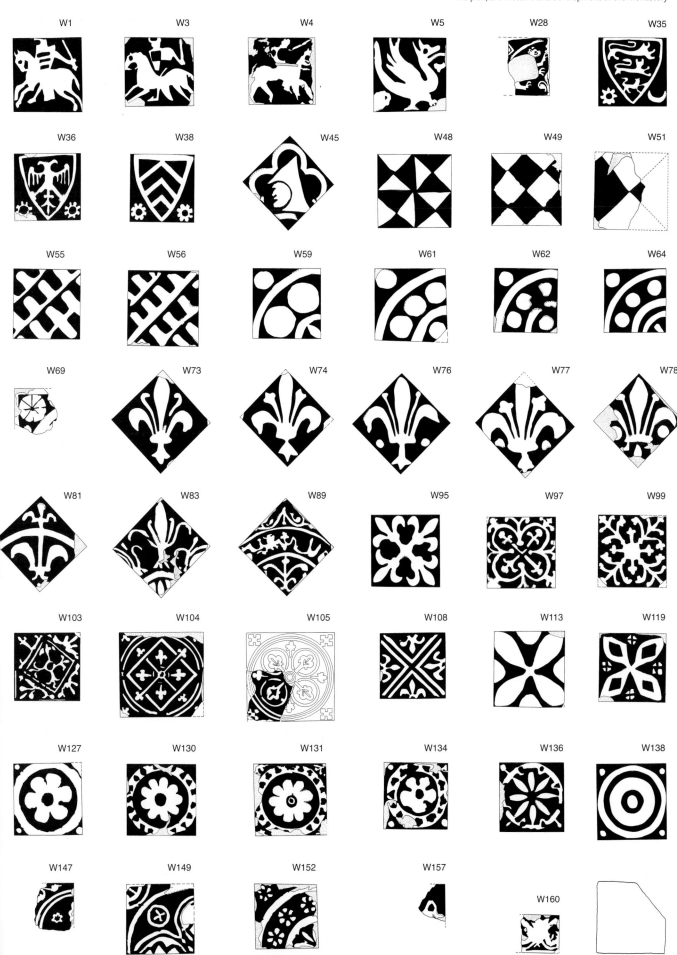

Fig 77 Decorated 'Westminster' floor tile designs and the specially shaped plain tile (unnumbered) from Bermondsey (scale 1:6)

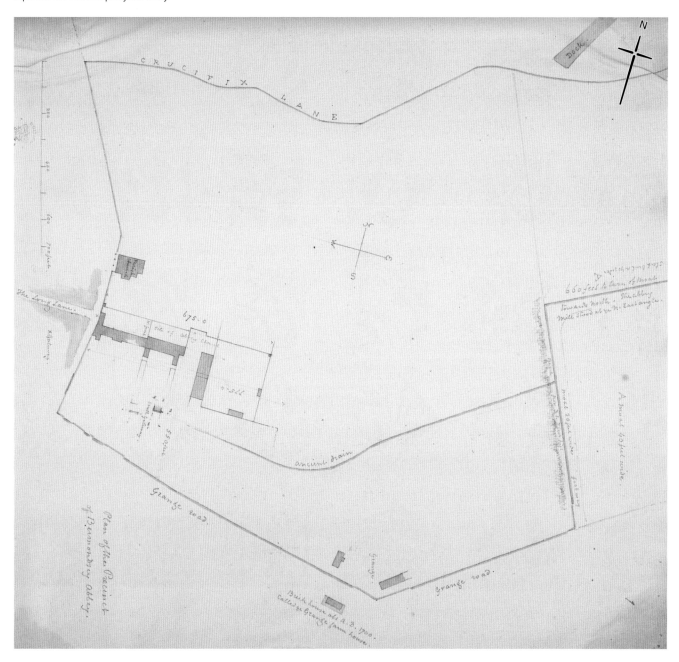

Fig 78 Plan of the precinct of Bermondsey Abbey (?1820) by John Buckler (© The British Library Board, Add MS 24433, fo 1)

of placing too much reliance on the precise details of landscape and other features drawn by Buckler as part of the 'background'.

Buckler showed the western section of the northern boundary as following what he identified as 'Crucifix Lane' (Fig 78) but was actually the line of Five Foot Lane (eg on Rocque 1746, Fig 79), that is modern Tanner Street (cf Fig 3; so-called on the 60 inch OS map of 1893 London sheet VII.96 [edition of 1984–6], but formerly Russell Street, eg on the OS map of 1872). Martin based his 1926 article describing the topography of the priory on Buckler's notes, plans and sketches preserved in the British Library. In what seems to be intended as a correction to Buckler, Martin took the actual Crucifix Lane as the line of the northern precinct boundary, which he considered ran from the junction of Bermondsey Street with Crucifix Lane eastwards and then south, along Church Street (Roper Lane on Rocque 1746, Fig 79), and then east along Tanner Street (Martin

1926, esp 195–6). (Martin did not map the whole precinct, only the north-east corner: Martin 1926, fig 1.) Martin's line follows the parish boundary as shown for example on the OS map surveyed in 1893. However, possibly recognising the 'oddness' of such a north-west area, Martin suggested that it was a later addition, and that the original northern boundary was formed by 'another ancient stream which crossed Bermondsey Street at the point where the latter is joined by Tanner Street', so effectively reverting to Buckler's line (Martin 1926, 196). Martin may be describing a remnant stream from the original main Neckinger channel here. Tanner Street does appear to roughly follow the west–east course of this prehistoric channel (cf Fig 3; Fig 6). Westwards, the meandering route crosses Bermondsey Street and follows modern Morocco Street (not Leathermarket Street) (S Humphrey, pers comm 2008).

The boundaries of the priory precinct at its fullest extent

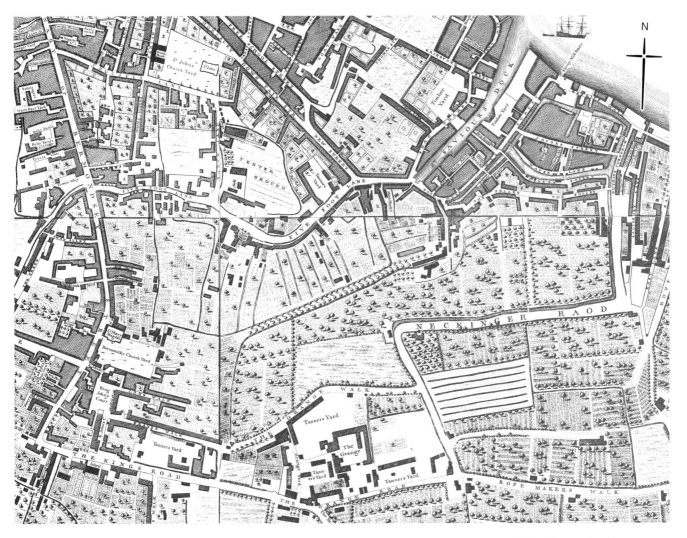

Fig 79 John Rocque's 1746 survey of the area shown in Buckler's early 19th-century plan of the precinct of the former priory and abbey of Bermondsey (shown in Fig 78) (Rocque 1746)

have thus been generally thought to be represented by modern Bermondsey Street to the west, Grange Road and Spa Road to the south and south-east (respectively, The King's Road and The Grange Road on Rocque 1746: Fig 79), and Neckinger Street (also referred to as Neckinger Road on Rocque 1746 and OS 1872) to the east (which Martin thought marked 'the position of the ancient stream of that name': 1926, 195–6). To the north, the precinct boundary has been thought to take a more irregular route, following approximately the line of modern Tanner Street in the east, then of south–north Church Street, and finally Crucifix Lane on the west (*VCH* 1912, 17–24). This is the monastic precinct mapped by Grimes (1968, 212, fig 51) and reproduced here as Fig 80.

The line the north-east section of their proposed precinct boundary took is not clear in the work of Buckler or of Martin and Grimes. It may have followed the course of that part of the moat which lay off Buckler's plan (Fig 78) but which he indicated ran east and then north towards the abbey mill which stood at the north-east angle, that is close to the dock; these sections of the moat can be identified on Rocque (Fig 79). This is apparently the boundary line preferred by Grimes (Fig 80). But Grimes also offers a second choice which follows Buckler's faint straight line

which simply extended the line of the western moat, joining the north-west moat corner to 'Crucifix Lane' and accords with Martin's written description (1926, 196). By this means, Grimes maps an alternative, slightly smaller and perhaps original, precinct that combines this north-east boundary line with a northern boundary running the length of Tanner Street (as per Martin's suggestion that the north-west area was a later addition). This north-east line is that adopted as the precinct boundary in some recent publications (eg Taylor 2008); however, a comparison with for example Rocque (Fig 79) does not suggest any good topographic reason for such a boundary line.

According to Martin, then, the enclosed precinct area at Bermondsey was at its fullest extent approximately 60 acres (*c* 24ha), including 20 acres (8.1ha) of meadow, but excluding the strip of land to the east towards the river where the priory watermill was located (Martin 1926, 198). This would make it comparable in size to the 65-acre (26.3ha) precinct of the rural Augustinian priory of Merton described by John Aubrey (Miller and Saxby 2007, 122), but much larger than for example the *c* 20 acres (8.1ha) of the Cistercian abbey of St Mary Stratford Langthorne (Essex) (Barber et al 2004, 75) and the precincts of monastic houses elsewhere in Southwark and in and on the edge

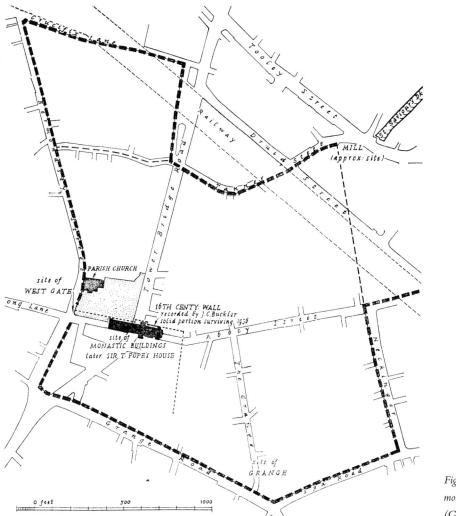

Fig 80 Grimes's 1968 map showing the extent of the monastic precinct and the position of the church (Grimes 1968, 21, fig 51) (scale 1:6220)

of the City of London (Barron and Davies 2007, 26).

The manor of Bermondsey formed part of the priory's initial foundation grant but exactly how much of that property was enclosed to create a formal precinct is not clear. It is very probable that the priory precinct was smaller than has been generally assumed, possibly considerably smaller. Putting to one side the large precinct delineated by Martin and Grimes (Fig 80), Fig 81 shows selected elements of the 18th- to 19th-century street plan, and the boundary of the parish of St Mary Magdalene (as indicated on the 25 inch OS map of 1872, London sheet 77, and the 60 inch OS map of 1893, London sheet VII 96), with the priory (the *c* 1200 and *c* 1400 church and main cloister; Fig 69) added. Superimposed (in red and orange) on Fig 81 are topographical details from Buckler's early 19th-century precinct plan (Fig 78), combined with his ground plan of Sir Thomas Pope's mansion (reproduced here as Fig 109).

The monastic precinct as set out by Buckler and by Martin and Grimes includes within its bounds the home farm of Bermondsey grange to the south-east – which would not normally form part of a monastic precinct – as well as the parish church of St Mary Magdalene on the west; these elements are discussed further below. However, it also includes a large area adjacent to the original main Neckinger channel (ie Five Foot Lane/Tanner Street), between the Bermondsey Street causeway on the west and St Saviour's Dock on the east (Fig 81).

The priory's meadow land was evidently extensive and it is reasonable to assume that much of it lay to the north, to either side of the original Neckinger channel, and to the east, towards St Saviour's Dock and Folly Ditch, on the alluvium and off the gravel island (Fig 6). In 1346 it was alleged that 140 acres (56.7ha) of meadow had been flooded and the prior had lost all his profit, following damage to the prior's close and dikes (*Cal Pat R, 1345–8*, 176–7, 240–1). Much of this land probably lay outside the priory's walls and was enclosed only by ditches. In the 18th century the area immediately south of the original west–east channel was still fields interrupted by numerous drainage channels (Rocque 1746; Fig 79). In the medieval period it was evidently pasture and meadow. Both the 18-acre (7.3ha) pasture called the Convent (*Covent*) pasture and the 12-acre (4.9ha) meadow called the Wyldes to its east, also referred to, for example, in 1541 in Southwell's petition to purchase (TNA: PRO, E318/20/1032; Martin 1926, 206), appear to have lain to the east of the monastic nucleus. Dawson (2008) has argued that they stretched from Tanner Street to Grange Walk, and may not have formed part of the precinct. Thus the formal eastern boundary could have lain further west than that proposed by Buckler, Martin and Grimes. Dovehouse meadow containing 7 acres (2.8ha), Swan meadow of 9 acres (3.6ha), and a pasture of 6 acres (2.4ha) called the Nether gravel pit were all referred to in the 1540s, for example, in 1541 (TNA: PRO, E318/20/1032). A

Fig 81 Reconstruction of the layout of the monastic precinct and home grange showing topographical details from Buckler's 19th-century precinct plan and ground plan of Pope's mansion (Fig 78; Fig 109) and the conjectural reconstruction of the priory (Fig 69), superimposed on selected elements of the 18th- to 19th-century street plan and the parish boundary (scale 1:5000)

meadow of 11 acres (4.5ha) and a piece of arable containing 9 acres (3.6ha) called the Upper gravel pit were described as lying outside the monastery gate next to the grange (TNA: PRO, E318/20/1032).

Dawson (2002, 6) has also recently suggested that the north precinct boundary lay south of modern Tanner Street and much closer to the priory church. He cites deeds dated from the 12th/13th century onwards for property held freehold by private individuals on the south side of Tanner Street, property which is described as stretching from Feffer Street as far south as the wall of the priory or again from Millward Street as far as the wall of the sacristy of the priory. Dawson identifies both Millward Street and Feffer Street – a corruption of Five Foot Lane, he argues – as earlier names for what is now Tanner Street (G Dawson, pers comm).

Taking the latter description to relate to a sacristy on the *north* side of the priory church, this reference at least would imply that this non-priory property lay not far east of Bermondsey Street. Interestingly, excavations to the north of the parish church but south of Tanner Street have recovered evidence for medieval buildings adjacent to the highway: at 163–167 Bermondsey Street, stone (chalk and ragstone) buildings thought to be medieval (possibly 13th or 14th century) in origin were identified, although their function is not clear (Taylor 2008); and slightly further north at 151–153 Bermondsey Street excavation also revealed occupation on the reclaimed land adjacent to the causeway, but here the earliest building was late medieval in date (Wooldridge 2003). Besant's survey of London (1912, 58–9) suggested the highway between the 'Barmsie cross' ('where Bermondsey Lane ran into Tooley Street') and the church of the Holy Rood (St Saviour) was built up early on and inns catered for the many pilgrims. Further research may be able to clarify the history and extent of freehold and leasehold property in this area, and thus what portion of the priory's manor was enclosed within the precinct proper.

A north precinct boundary closer to the north side of the priory church would fit equally well with what various sources tell us about the waterways in this area. The *VCH* suggested in 1912 that the monastery may have been approachable by boat, from the Thames and along the Neckinger (*VCH* 1912, 17). Martin (1926, 195, 218) reported that according to Buckler the Neckinger could still be traced in 1806 to within 80 yards (73.15m) of the abbey gate; Martin added that this stream still flowed beneath the eastern part of Abbey Street (located on Fig 3), so differentiating it from the ancient stream to the north along the line of Tanner Street (and of the original Neckinger channel). Barton also, for example, in his *The lost rivers of London* (1994, 54–5 and map), locates the Neckinger along the north side of modern Abbey Street. Shown as running from the junction of Long Lane and Bermondsey Street eastwards, this puts the (later) Neckinger stream immediately north of the former priory church which underlies Abbey Street. Rocque (1746) shows a watercourse along Five Foot Lane (ie Tanner Street) and another channel further south, but slightly north of modern Abbey Street; both watercourses apparently ran west–east towards Dock Head (modern Dockhead), with a network of drainage channels in-

between suggesting the low-lying nature of this area (Fig 79). To the east the southern channel ran parallel towards Dock Head with a second channel; they are shown either side of a planted 'avenue' on Rocque (perhaps suggesting an embankment?), on the approximate line of what in the 19th century became Park Street and to the east Millstream Road (eg on the OS 1872).

The many ditches and channels (man-made and/or natural) in the vicinity of Bermondsey described by various authors and cartographers do make it difficult to identify with any certainty the medieval watercourses associated with the priory (below, 'Water supply and sanitation'). Martin wrote that Neckinger (Road/Street) marked 'the position of the ancient stream of that name' (Martin 1926, 195–6), but the watercourses identified by Martin as the Neckinger to the south and east of the precinct were originally probably subsidiary channels, which were then possibly partly canalised in the medieval period. The 'ancient drain' shown by Buckler east of the south gate (*le Newe Eastgate*: see below) can be identified with the '... foss; part of it filled up, for a thoroughfare, called Grange Walk', whose line it roughly follows (*Gentleman's Magazine* 1808a, 477; Fig 78; Fig 81). Apparently retained (and reused) by Pope, this drain can be seen to run to a moat 20ft (6.10m) wide, bounded on its west side by a tall bank. On the other (east) side was a footway forming the basis of the existing Neckinger Road (modern south–north Neckinger Street). Buckler shows that the moat turned at right angles eastward and notes that it had a full length of 660ft (201.17m) before turning north in an area off Buckler's plan; Buckler adds that the abbey mill stood at the north-east angle. This moat can be identified with the wide watercourse shown adjacent to and north of 'Neckinger Raod [*sic*]' on Rocque's map of 1746 (Fig 79). A distance of 660ft from the north-west corner of the moat would put the northward turn to the west of the turn of the watercourse shown on Rocque and instead close to the beginning of a south–north planted 'avenue' on Rocque – perhaps suggesting the medieval channel's course (Fig 79). 'Steep bank on ye sides' noted by Buckler against the north side of the moat suggests probably levees connected with flood control. The earthen wall and land of John Yerle in which lies a certain conduit commonly called a sluyce on the east was included in Pope's licence of 1549 to alienate (*Cal Pat R*, 1547–53, i, 368). Many of the channels, natural or canalised, must have been affected by tidal flow, even if only irregularly during episodes of flooding – a serious problem for the priory throughout its history.

The priory watermill lay, according to Martin, just beyond the north-eastern extremity of the precinct, where the western channel of the Neckinger joined the Thames, its position commemorated in the name St Saviour's Dock (Martin 1926, 195–7; Fig 2; Fig 6; Fig 81). Buckler's written note places the abbey mill at the north-east angle of the moat – that is to the east – but Grimes seems to misinterpret this, placing the mill further to the west, on Tanner Street (Grimes 1968, 212, fig 51; Fig 80). Chalk foundations belonging to a medieval mill and associated buildings were found in excavations at Jacob's Island (JAC96; Saxby 1997), located between the confluences of the western and eastern channels of the Neckinger with the Thames

(Fig 6; Fig 81; above, 4.1, 'Topography and early landscape'). This mill has been suggested as being the priory's. It continued in use until the mid 18th century and Jacob's Island was formed through the cutting of mill streams in the post-medieval period (S Humphrey, pers comm 2008). Bermondsey's mill was leased shortly before the Dissolution to John Curlew (Curlewe) for £8 per annum (Martin 1926, 217). There would have been a north-east entrance into the formal precinct but not necessarily as Martin thought in the vicinity of St Saviour's Dock and Bermondsey's mill. The parallel watercourses and planted 'avenue' recorded on Rocque (Fig 79) may be a reflection of an earlier track which led directly to the conventual buildings from the mill and dock.

As we have seen, Martin followed Buckler in placing the south boundary of the precinct along the north side of modern Grange Road and Spa Road (Martin 1926, 195). Buckler's plan showed along this line long sections (in blue) of a watercourse or open ditch which connected with, and presumably drained into, the south end of the moat and shorter sections (in grey) representing presumably culverted lengths of the same watercourse (at the south-west corner, at the junction of Grange Road and Spa Road, and at the junction with the moat) (Fig 78). Nor does Buckler's bird's eye view of the site of Pope's mansion, looking south (BL, Add MS 24433, fo 53, reproduced in Martin 1926, pl VI/fig 3), suggest a southern wall here. In both drawings Buckler has had to reconstruct and extrapolate because he omits post-medieval buildings and properties. Rocque (1746; Fig 79) shows only two lengths of visible watercourse, along the west section of The King's Road (modern Grange Road).

Archaeological investigations at the south-west corner (sites C and F; Fig 81) revealed what is interpreted as the remains of the medieval east–west precinct wall here, confirming Buckler's line (Chapter 3.3, 'Archaeological evidence', 'Open ground to the east and south-west of the conventual buildings (OA3 and OA4) and the precinct wall'; Fig 47). But recent archaeological work further to the east, at 161 Grange Road (GGO06, Fig 81; below, 'Water supply and sanitation'), bears out the interpretation that Buckler's bird's eye view and his plan are showing a ditch – open and covered over – along this southern line. Like the 'ancient drain' to its north, this southern watercourse was very probably part of the water engineering works undertaken by the priory. Its route lay between two buildings labelled 'Grange' (to the north) and a brick house of c 1700 called 'Grange farm house' (to the south) on Buckler's plan (Fig 78). Rocque (1746; Fig 79), for example, also shows a group of buildings, 'The Grange', and associated yards between the eastern section of Grange Walk, which runs north and east, and Grange Road (modern Spa Road). If we take this to indicate the location of the medieval grange or home farm buildings, this suggests Buckler and Martin were wrong: at least the south-east part of the precinct boundary must have lain north of the grange (which would not normally be included within the monastic precinct), and more likely followed the line of modern Grange Walk (Fig 3).

Buckler shows a gate – the 'South Gateway' – to the south of the mansion, adjacent to Grange Walk (Fig 78; Fig 109). A remnant thought to belong to this south gate (sometimes confusingly called the 'east' gate; below) survives on the east side of 7 Grange Walk (Chapter 7.1, 'Catalogue of maps …', 'Ground plan of Sir Thomas Pope's mansion, Bermondsey (BL, Add MS 24433, fo 3) …'). The gateway had evidently been a significant structure: according to Buckler's description, the walls were of flint and stone and stood to a height of 26ft (7.92m) at the beginning of the 19th century (BL, Add MS 24432 A, 176); Buckler shows a double gate opening west and east. The gateway appeared originally to have formed an archway in a continuous range of two-storeyed buildings with a gabled roof (Martin 1926, 206). Just such a range of buildings on the south side of the priory had come to be known by 1541 as the tenement called le Newe Eastgate, which incorporated 'houses, cellars and solars' (TNA: PRO, E318/20/1032; Martin 1926, 206, 'Newe Estgate'; Chapter 5.1, 'Tenants and owners of the site').

The south gate, although relatively new, appears to pre-date the Dissolution. It possibly functioned as a gate between a monastic inner court and part of an outer court to the south and south-east. But its position lends weight to the suggestion that the precinct boundary proper for much of its south-east course followed modern Grange Walk rather than Grange Road, with the south gate serving as an outer gate giving outlet to the south and east. The precinct wall could have run from the south-west corner east for a short distance before turning north to connect with Grange Walk and the south gate; from the south gate eastwards, the precinct boundary may have been formed by a wall or buildings on the north side of Grange Walk (cf Fig 79; Fig 81). Copies (made by Claudina Eastwall-Naijna c 1969) exist in the archives of Southwark Local History Library, London, of two 17th-century plans of the south-west corner of the precinct; the originals, part of the Ram estate, are missing but were photographed in 1949 or 1950 (SL, Maps 174–5, PB 2804 and PB 2806; S Humphrey, pers comm). These show the area south of the mansion house (ie south of Grange Walk), and south-east of a gateway (ie the south gate) (and east of a south–north building range), as a rectangular plot called the 'Cunney-grey' or 'cony green'; this approximates to the area of 'Tanner's Yard' on Rocque (Fig 79). The name suggests that rabbits were originally kept here. The lease of the site of the monastery to Sir Robert Southwell in 1539 refers to an acre of land adjoining called the Coneyyard (below, Chapter 5.1, 'Tenants and owners of the site' citing TNA: PRO, E315 212, fo 136; L and P Hen VIII, xv, 56(7); Martin 1926, 218–19); such a juxtaposition might support the interpretation that the precinct boundary ran east along Grange Walk. At some point the precinct boundary turned north, but this may have occurred much nearer the claustral complex than indicated by Buckler, Martin and Grimes, with the 18-acre (7.3ha) Convent pasture and the 12-acre (4.9ha) meadow called the Wyldes to its east lying outside (above). The boundary on the east and north probably took the form of a bank and ditch rather than a wall. Locating the precinct wall along the east–west axis of Grange Walk presumably owed something to the gradual falling away of the land south of this point towards the south edge of the Bermondsey eyot.

The precinct was walled at the south-west corner as we have seen and also on the west side. The principal entrance to the priory lay on the west, located at the east end of Long Lane (Fig

78; Fig 81). The parish church of St Mary Magdalene stood just to the north of the junction of Long Lane with Bermondsey Street, north of the main outer gate (Martin 1926, 198–9). The relationship is one with a close topographic parallel in the City, between Holy Trinity Priory, Aldgate, and the parish church of St Katherine Cree which lay at the north-west corner of the precinct, just south of the main gate and adjoining Leadenhall Street; it is suggested that the parish church was probably originally a chapel in the churchyard of the Augustinian priory (Schofield and Lea 2005, 5, fig 4, 18, 20, 132–3).

The interpretation followed by Buckler, Martin and Grimes places the parish church of St Mary Magdalene inside the precinct. There is no evidence that St Mary's church was held by anyone before the priory and probably owed its foundation to the priory's wish to accommodate local layfolk other than in the priory church; a presentation to the rectory of the chapel of St Mary Magdalene by the prior and convent is recorded in 1291 (*VCH* 1912, 23). The chapel of the Blessed Sepulchre and St Mary Magdalene of Bermondsey was in the hands of the prior and convent in 1296 (*Ann Monast*, iii, 468). Whether protected by the precinct wall as such, or outside the precinct as suggested by Dawson (2002, 6), there would have been direct access to the parish church from Bermondsey Street to the west, as well as from the priory to the south through what became the parish churchyard. The rectory was worth £17 5s 4d per annum in 1535, of which £10 was the value of the messuage, garden and house annexed to it; the advowson was granted to Robert Southwell in 1541, who alienated it to Sir Thomas Pope, and thereafter it followed the manor (*VCH* 1912, 23). The parish church was almost entirely rebuilt in the early 17th century (ibid, 22).

The only documentary reference to the main outer, west, gate is in a crown grant of 20 July 1576 to John Fareham, which describes land extending from the west gate of the said monastery towards St George's church (ie west-north-west) (TNA: PRO, C66/1144; *Cal Pat R Eliz*, 1575–8, 831). The gatehouse, the front of which was composed of squared flints and dark-red tiles, was nearly entire in 1806, but shortly afterwards it was wholly demolished, together with nearly all the adjacent ancient buildings, and Abbey Street was laid west–east on the site (Brayley 1850, 182–3). The gateway was recorded and described by Buckler (BL, Add MS 24432 A, 176) and often referred to as the 'Great Gateway' or 'Great Gate'. Its position is shown by Buckler on, for example, his plan of the precinct (Fig 78).

Fig 81 illustrates how the core area of the priory may be interpreted as the area above 1.0m OD extending as far south as the south gate and Grange Walk; this area, plus the south-east corner (above), may possibly approximate to that which was formally enclosed in the medieval period. The west gate led from the outside world into an outer court, which was flanked on its east side by the west front of the priory church. The almshouse or hospice was built in 1213, according to the annals, and it probably lay immediately inside, and south of, the outer gate. It was sited on the cellarer's ground against the priory wall and the almoner was to pay the cellarer 10s 4d a year (*Ann Monast*, iii, 452). At the end of the 13th century, a property in Bermondsey was described as lying between the curtilage of Bermondsey

hospital on the east, *Shiteburlane* on the west and the garden called *Beaurepeyr* on the north (*Cat Anc Deeds*, iv, A7979).

Inside the outer west gate and on the south side of the outer court lay the gateway into the inner court. This inner gate was incorporated into the post-Dissolution mansion house and it was to this that it no doubt owed its survival into the 19th century. It was surveyed in great detail by John Buckler (BL, Add MS 24433, fos 1 and 8) and referred to as the 'Abbey Gateway' (Fig 117). The gatehouse originally consisted of three storeys, with access via an octagonal stair-turret at the south-east corner. The gateway consisted of a carriageway and a narrow postern 6ft (2.09m) wide, with a doorway leading into the porter's lodge (Martin 1926, 206–8). The external or north elevation incorporated slender turret buttresses and the wall facing was decorated with a chequerboard pattern of flint and stone, reminiscent of the 16th-century porch of the prior's house at Castle Acre (Coad and Coppack 1998, 34–40). The decoration on the south side suggests a late 15th- or early 16th-century date (Chapter 7.1, 'Catalogue of maps …', 'Abbey gateway, Bermondsey (BL, Add MS 24433, fo 2) …'). This gate in the north-west corner of the lower or inner court (later also known by the name of King John's Court: eg Rocque 1746; Fig 79), is sometimes referred to as the north gate.

The inner court and conventual buildings of St Saviour occupied the south-west corner of the priory's Bermondsey manor. Many of the monastery's domestic buildings have been examined archaeologically and are described in Chapter 3. The priory's watermill, located to the north-east, between the confluences of the western and eastern channels of the Neckinger with the Thames, has also been identified by excavation (discussed above; Fig 6; Fig 81). There were, however, many functional buildings in the inner and outer courts, and beyond, that have not yet been revealed by excavation. A principal source of current knowledge about the service buildings is the documentation regarding the transfer of the property to Robert Southwell, including the crown lease of 1 May 1539 to him of the house and site of the late monastery of Bermondsey, which gives an inventory of the standing structures on the site at that time (TNA: PRO, E315 212, fo 136; *L and P Hen VIII*, xv, 56(7)).

A bakehouse is referred to in three documents: a house called the *Backhouse* is included in Southwell's petition to purchase, dated to 10 March 1541, and is included along with the tenement of New Eastgate (TNA: PRO, E318/20/1032; Martin 1926, 206); our house (*domum*) called the Bakehouse was granted with the abbey site to Southwell on 8 July 1541 (TNA: PRO, C66/702, m 3 (renumbered 44); *L and P Hen VIII*, xvi, 1056(37)); and a house called *le Bachhouse* is referred to in ministers' accounts for 1541–2 (TNA: PRO, SC6/Henry VIII/3465, m 19). Examples of monastic bakehouses have been excavated at Bradwell Abbey (Buckinghamshire), Grove Priory (Bedfordshire) and Thornholme Priory (Lincolnshire) (Coppack 1990, 108). At Thornholme, the bakehouse was a 13th-century conversion of an earlier building: a large sub-circular bread-oven had been inserted, re-employing the flue of a pre-existing chimney. The building was two storeys and on the ground floor had stone floors with an internal drain.

Southwell's petition includes along with the tenement of New Eastgate a house called the *drylarderhouse* (TNA: PRO,

E318/20/1032; Martin 1926, 206) and in his grant of 8 July 1541 this appears as 'our house called (*unam domum nostram vocatam*) le Drye larder house' (TNA: PRO, C66/702, m 3 (renumbered 44); *L and P Hen VIII*, xvi, 1056(37)). Ministers' accounts for 1541–2 mention a house called the *drye lawerhouse* (TNA: PRO, SC6/Henry VIII/3465, m 19). One would expect both the bakehouse and dry larder to be close to the priory's main kitchen.

The brewhouse was evidently located on the south side of the precinct, perhaps some 20ft (6+m) from the kitchen. It was described in 1321 as a boundary, in connection with the grant for life to the priory's corrodian, Nicholas Tunstall (also Nicholas de Tunstal), of a house within the close of Bermondsey, with a place of the court lying near the house; the plot being granted appears to have lain 'between the kitchen and the brewhouse' and its width was 20ft (6.10m) (below, 4.3, 'The inhabitants: lay people', citing *Cal Pat R, 1321–4, 441; Cal Close R, 1327–30, 380–1*). Also granted was a 'stank' (pond) and curtilage between the brewhouse and the monastery's 'new garden' whose boundaries were defined by (south) the road leading to Rotherhithe (ie modern Grange Road) and (north) the 'lane leading to the granges', suggesting the brewhouse lay near the west end of, and adjoining, modern Grange Walk (Martin 1926, 202, 203). The new garden was described in 1322 as containing apple and other trees, vines, hedges and ditches (*Cal Pat R, 1321–4, 441*). The prior's orchard and an orchard called the Vineyard are listed following the bakehouse and the dry larder house in Southwell's 1541 petition (TNA: PRO, E318/20/1032; Martin 1926, 206). The south and south-west parts of the precinct and the outer court area to the west of the church were the most likely locations for the living quarters of permanent lay residents (below, 4.3, 'The inhabitants: lay people'). Buckler's archive also shows that there was a range of buildings between the cloister and the 'east' that is south gate, some of which may have had their origins in the 14th or 15th centuries.

Ministers' accounts for 1539–40 detail a tenement or messuage situated within the close or 'procinct' of the said late monastery, leased to Thomas Debel by conventual lease on 12 January 1538 for 13s 4d per annum (TNA: PRO, SC6/Henry VIII/3464, m 27). The tenement is similarly described in the ministers' accounts for 1541–2 (TNA: PRO, SC6/Henry VIII/3465, m 21d) and again, with the mention of an adjacent garden, in Sir Thomas Pope's petition for purchase in 1544–5 (TNA: PRO, E318/18/880). In a Chancery case of 1606–7, 1¹/₂ acres (0.61ha) of land enclosed within a standing wall and lying on the north side of the mansion house of the late Sir Thomas Pope was described as two separate gardens late in the tenure and occupation of Thomas Devill deceased (TNA: PRO, C2, JAS I/H19/30).

The medieval monastery was supported by a network of agricultural estates centred on farms or granges (Coppack 1990, 121). The principal centre was the home grange, located close to the house. St Saviour's home grange is variously described, usually as lying next, near, or beside the abbey. The modern streets Grange Walk and Grange Road perpetuate the name. The 'lane leading to the granges' evidently ran south of the priory eastwards and Grange Walk is thought to perpetuate the line. Rocque (1746; Fig 79) and Buckler (Fig 78) show the 'Grange'

between Grange Walk and Grange Road, to the east (above). Martin (1926, 216–17) concluded that the grange buildings lay to the south-east of the main cloister but *within* the precinct which would be extremely unusual and, it is argued, unlikely. The distinction between the monastic precinct and the grange may have been somewhat blurred because of their proximity.

On 21 May 1534, the abbey leased the grange with 'all lands, meadows and pastures' to one Ralph Wryn, gentleman, to be held for 60 years at a farm of £48 (TNA: PRO, SC6/Henry VIII/3464, m 25d). The grange is referred to (but not included) in Southwell's purchase of the abbey site on 8 July 1541, where it is described as being next to the Upper gravel pit outside the gates of the monastery (TNA: PRO, C66/702, m 3 (renumbered 44); *L and P Hen VIII*, xvi, 1056(37)). A deed of 1576 seems to imply that the (or a) grange lay not far from the (outer) west gate (the only medieval or 16th-century reference found to the west gate: TNA: PRO, C66/1144; *Cal Pat R Eliz, 1575–8, no. 831*), but the home grange's location east of the south or 'New Eastgate' is clear from the earlier 16th-century documentation.

An action in Chancery in June 1548 between David Cornwall and the heirs of William Gardiner concerned a leasehold interest in the farm or grange called Bermondsey grange, with appurtenances (TNA: PRO, C78, 13, enrolment no. 17); the property in question was specified as:

> The hall, kitchen and all other houses and partitions, jointures and buildings of the dwelling house of William Gardiner the elder and all manner of houses, barns, stables, edifices and buildings set and being in and upon the east part of the said dwelling house except the parlour and loft over the same parlour and adjoining to the hall of the said dwelling house and the courtyard of the same, the great thatched barn being over the west side of the same courtyard and also the close of the west and backside of the said great barn, The one half of the said courtyard and one close called the Bull hill and the two marsh grounds thereunto adjoining containing by estimation 17 acres [6.9ha], and one other close called the Upper Bull hill containing by estimation 49 acres [19.8ha] ...

The 13th- to 15th-century home grange at Waltham Abbey in Essex included, ranged around the grange yard, an aisled barn of 12 bays some 64m long, a hay barn, plough-house, ox-house and stable. The smaller hay barn at Waltham was *c* 30m long and capable of storing the produce of 198 acres (80.1ha) of meadow land (Coppack 1990, 122–5). A barn or 'great hayhouse' at Bermondsey is mentioned in Southwell's petition for purchase (1541). It is not described in any detail, merely as the boundary of a parcel of land extending from the gate called New Eastgate (ie the south gate). It presumably formed the eastern boundary; there was a garden adjacent, next to the dormitory of the said late monastery. Another barn is described as situated at the end of the 18-acre (7.3ha) pasture called Convent pasture, which was included in the 1541 petition along with the tenement of New Eastgate, as was the 12-acre (4.9ha) meadow called the Wyldes to its east (TNA: PRO, E318/20/1032; Martin 1926, 206). In the 1548 description (above), 'the great thatched barn' lay on the west side of the grange courtyard.

The priory's home grange played a crucial role in the economic effectiveness of the establishment while it was directly managed. The sparse recovery of foetal/neonate and infant poultry, rabbits, cattle, sheep and pigs from all periods suggests that some or all of these species may have been kept close to the monastery, although there is no reason to suppose that they provided the sole source of supply (below, 4.3, 'Diet and food preparation', and Chapter 7.8). It must be remembered that the level of recovery is small and may reflect the occasional purchase and inclusion of very young animals in the diet. Bream, carp, roach and pike are all able to thrive in even small ponds and could have been kept in the monastic fishponds. Excavations on the north side of Tanner Street (VIY97; Heard 1998) recorded a large artificial pond between the north bank of the Neckinger and a north–south aligned ditch (Fig 81). The pond was associated with a series of ditches, the fills of which contained 12th- to 14th-century pottery, and may have been created as part of a complex of fishponds.

Water supply and sanitation

The priory was located on higher ground in a watery environment precisely so that the huge demands of the establishment for water could be met. Water was needed for ritual purposes, for cooking, for flushing away waste, for horticulture, for fishponds, for industry and for all the daily functions such as brewing, baking, laundering and milling (Bond 2001, 100–5). Potable water would have been kept separate from drainage, requiring a fairly complex and extensive system of water management at the priory. Identifying the medieval watercourses, however, is problematic (above, 'The precinct and home grange').

The use of either of the two nearest large watercourses – the Neckinger to the north (which may have been tidal) and the more distant but freshwater Earl's Sluice to the south (Fig 6) – to supply water would have involved large-scale engineering works. However, such works were standard at monastic sites: the 'ancient drain' and 'moat' recorded by Buckler (above, 'The precinct and home grange'; Fig 78) give some, limited, indication of the watercourses and earthworks which would have been associated with the priory. The excavations themselves yielded little evidence for the water supply. No lead pipes were found but would have existed. Fresh water would have been needed in the 12th-century lavabo outside the refectory in the main cloister garth (OA5) for washing, but would also have been a requirement for the cistern outside the bathhouse in the second, infirmary, cloister. It is probable that such a supply came from a natural spring or springs, somewhere on the Bermondsey eyot (Fig 6). More limited supplies of fresh water may have come from wells; a well and a ?cistern in the second cloister were part of the changes made later, in the 14th century (period M8; below).

The 12th-century plan of the waterworks at the cathedral priory of Christchurch, Canterbury, indicates that fresh water was piped first to the two great priory lavers: to the one in the infirmary cloister and then to the one outside the refectory in

the great cloister (Coppack 2006, 144–5). The lavabo was invested with a high degree of spiritual significance, related to the rites of Christian baptism. Although the lavabo at Bermondsey had been extensively robbed of its masonry (and pipework) and was not fully excavated, its plan indicates linear channels from the centre on both its east and west sides (discussed in detail in Chapter 3.2, 'Archaeological evidence', 'Cloister walk (B5) and cloister garth (OA5)' and 'Discussion'). These channels probably contained the lead pipes, which supplied the water to the laver and then carried it on to the next station.

Although the form of the Bermondsey lavabo is ambiguous, it appears to have had similar dimensions to and probably broadly resembled that at the Cluniac priory of Wenlock (Morley 1990, 8; Coppack 1999; Pinnell 1999, 10; Coppack 2006, 152–3). The Wenlock structure of *c* 1220 reused parts of an earlier lavabo of the 1170s to 1180s (Fig 82). Water was fed into a circular central fountain or cistern on deep foundations and encircled by a basin; water then flowed out of the basin through the mouths of 16 carved heads into a circular shallow trough (Coppack 2006, 153).

The Bermondsey lavabo building is shown reconstructed in plan as octagonal (Fig 21), like the Wenlock example. There, the 1220s building was octagonal and interpreted as having open arcades which supported a roof (Fig 83). Battle's laver house was also octagonal (built after 1172), St Augustine's Canterbury was hexagonal and Exeter's and Lewes's (the laver dated to the 1160s) were circular (Coppack 2006, 152).

The Christchurch Canterbury plan indicates that the water, having passed through the laver, was then piped around the buildings of the priory, via the refectory to the kitchen, bakehouse and brewhouse; a branch from the main pipe fed a building labelled 'bathhouse and chamber' (Coppack 2006, 144–5). The possible bathhouse at St Saviour Bermondsey (B8, period M4) has been discussed in some detail (Chapter 3.2, 'Archaeological evidence', 'Reredorter (B8)' and 'Discussion'; Fig 21). It is perhaps sufficient testament in itself to the standards of hygiene encountered in monastic institutions, standards which were no doubt very much higher than those pertaining in the medieval community at large. There was no evidence of a piped water supply to or from the cistern outside Building 8. The mortar-lined channel in the foundation on the east side of the room may have carried a pipe which disgorged into the adjacent ditch (D1). Unfortunately, the degree of truncation and disturbance caused by modern footings in this area limited the recovery of information.

The Christchurch Canterbury sequence and the infirmary's need for clean water might suggest that at Bermondsey there was a source on the east side of the precinct. Unfortunately, there was no evidence of a supply to the 12th-century or later infirmary buildings (B10 and B12). Clean water may also have come in from the south-west and flowed out around the conventual buildings to the east. South-west of the eyot flowed the freshwater stream which fed the watercourse to the south and east later known as 'Earl's Sluice' (Cowie and Corcoran 2008; Fig 6). The small square structure over Drain 3 in the south-west corner of the precinct (sites C and F; Fig 47) may

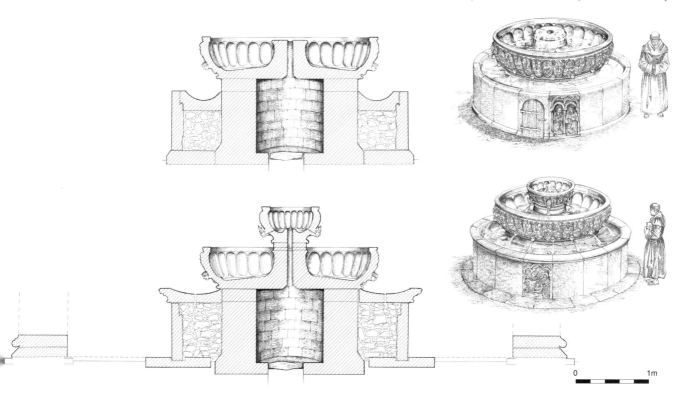

Fig 82 A reconstruction of the Wenlock lavabo: upper – as originally built in the 1170s or 80s; lower – as rebuilt in the 1220s (reconstruction by Glyn Coppack, drawn by Brian Byron; reproduced courtesy of Glyn Coppack) (cross sections scale 1:50; reconstructions not to scale)

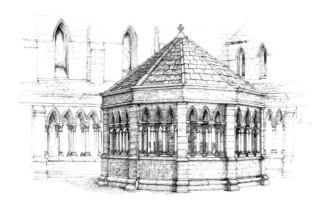

Fig 83 A reconstruction of the Wenlock lavabo building as rebuilt in the 1220s (reconstruction by Glyn Coppack, drawn by Brian Byron; reproduced courtesy of Glyn Coppack) (not to scale)

have been a latrine or wash house, or perhaps a conduit house or water tower, with the stone-lined drain (D3) the channel for the pipework, creating a closed conduit (Bond 2001, 94–5).

South of the priory cloister, two man-made channels flowed eastwards, along the line of what became Grange Walk and (further south) along Grange Road. Both apparently drained into a larger south–north channel or 'moat' parallel to modern Neckinger Road (or Street); this turned east and then north-east to join the Folly Brook outlet (discussed in detail above, 'The precinct and home grange'; Fig 81). The moat was evidently an integral part of the priory's water engineering works and may have provided a head of water to drive machinery.

The 'ancient drain' shown by Buckler (above 'The precinct

and home grange'; Fig 78) is roughly 20m south of the later (periods M5–M9) reredorter and runs from east of the south gate (*le Newe Eastgate*; also discussed above) in a generally eastwards direction. The stone-built drain (D3, site F) identified in the south-west corner of the precinct could have connected with it, south of the reredorter; the priory's service buildings seem to have been compressed into this area (above, 'The reredorter, infirmary complex and other domestic buildings'). This drain may have supplied fresh water for domestic use and finally linked up with the 'ancient drain'. The drains identified in the excavation running along the south side of the cloister (D1, D2) would also have connected with this feature, as would those to the east of the conventual buildings. The exact relationship is not known but the 'ancient drain' probably functioned as the priory's 'main' drain.

Recent archaeological work has provided some information about the southern watercourse shown by Buckler which served the home grange complex (above, 'The precinct and home grange'; Fig 78). Excavation in 2006 on the corner of modern Grange Road and Spa Road, at 161 Grange Road (GGO06, Fig 81), revealed a sequence of west–east drainage channels here: an open ditch replaced by a timber-lined drain (made of vertical planking with base plates, and no evidence for a lid), replaced in turn by a well-built stone drain which had at one time an arched roof (*c* 3m wide and up to 1.10m high, built of mainly ragstone and chalk and incorporating some architectural mouldings including one of the 12th century). The construction of the stone culvert was dated by pottery to *c* 1270–*c* 1350; it may have gone out of use in the medieval period. Although there was insufficient evidence to demonstrate the direction of flow, it presumably emptied into the moat to its east (Mackinder in prep). This sequence has some parallels in the priory where the earliest latrine ditch (D1, periods M3 and M4; Fig 14; Fig 21) on the south side of the priory was replaced in the later 12th century (further to the south) by a new stone-built drain (c 1.3m wide and of very similar construction) which passed along the south side of the cloister and under the reredorter (D2, periods M5–M7; Fig 33; Fig 49; Fig 53); this drain was considerably modified in the 14th century (D4, periods M8 and M9; Fig 57; Fig 65).

The water systems at Bermondsey were, it seems, a fairly complex network. The late 11th- to 12th-century (periods M3 and M4) drainage system followed the earlier, pre-priory (period M2), drainage system on the east. In the second half of the 12th and first half of the 13th centuries (periods M5 and M6) the sewerage system (D2) had to serve both the main latrine (the reredorter, B9) to the south and the infirmary latrine (B11) to the east. The only evidence for direction of water flow comes from the channel on the east side where it seems to be north to south. Was it affected by or dependent on tidal flow? When the eastern section of the drain was then disused and robbed (period M7), the infirmary building (B10) was provided with an adjacent (external) cesspit. The 14th-century (period M8) remodelling of the second cloister and creation of a third courtyard (OA9) with separate chambers (B13) on its east side required considerable changes to both the supply of fresh water and the removal of waste water, and a new drain (D4) with a southern sluice was built running across the courtyard further to the east.

While the infirmary latrine was constructed to be a flushing system, the later 12th-century reredorter (B9) was designed rather differently. The earlier timber latrine (B2) and first stone reredorter (B8) could have been cleaned out by a west–east or east–west waterflow in the drain (D1). In contrast, the sub-basement of the second stone reredorter (B9) seems to have functioned primarily as a large cesspit, and the new drain (D2) presumably combined with sluices to keep standing water in the building and to drain it prior to cleaning out. There was some flow of water, to judge from the early–mid 13th-century insertion of cutwaters (period M6), but whether this was west to east, coming from the direction of the kitchens, or vice versa is not known. When, in the later 15th to 16th centuries (period M9), contraction occurred and the eastern section of ditch was robbed, the reredorter was blocked at the west end and the drain altered to channel any water to the south. With reduced numbers of monks and a change to more individual accommodation, use of the reredorter latrines could have declined considerably.

4.3 The people and life of the monastery

The inhabitants: lay people

The documentary sources (and occasionally finds evidence) demonstrate something of the variety of people – other than its own religious personnel and servants, and craftsmen and

labourers, for example, as necessary – housed permanently or temporarily by a medieval monastery. As we have seen, Bermondsey hosted large assemblies – for example, the king's court in 1154, crusaders in 1250 – and regularly housed visitors, ranging from pilgrims to eminent religious officials from the Continent and assorted individuals plus possibly their entourages, wanting lodgings, hospitality or succour.

St Benedict had lain on his monks an obligation and a duty to provide hospitality and the Cluniac emphasis on prayer and attendance at services left little room for manual labour. The presence of some *conversi* or lay 'converts' among the inhabitants is likely, in addition to servants (Burton 1994, 178–80). On 7 October 1253, Mabel the convert received from the prior of Bermondsey one mark for two years for her maintenance at the house (*pro exhibucione sua in domo predicta*) (*Cal Close R*, 1251–3, 509). If a lay member under vows, as her name suggests, she would have been segregated from both professed monks and male *conversi*, and possibly restricted to the monastery's outer court. References to a school at St Saviour Bermondsey by Stow (1603, i, 73) and in a 14th-century will indicate that boys (and teachers) probably dwelt at the priory (below, 'Material culture and the religious life').

The early periods saw the monastery involved with a large number of influential Anglo-Norman families. William, Count of Mortain, released from the Tower of London in 1140 then took the habit at St Saviour and was buried there. From the mid 13th century the documentary sources attest to a large number of corrodies at Bermondsey. The earliest reference dates to 1247–8, and details a fine between Ernald Geraudon and Prior Imbert concerning the grant of a corrody (*Pedes finium*, 1159–1509, 32). In 1310–11, Adam Russel released to John de la Bare of London his right in a curtilage in the parish of St Mary Magdalene, Bermondsey 'next the curtilage of the chapel of St Mary in the church of the priory of St Saviour' (*Cat Anc Deeds*, v, A11652). Both references clearly imply accommodation within the precinct, although there is no specific mention of a corrody in the second example. In these, and in later cases, private persons of means had come to an arrangement with the house by which, in their old age, they would be accommodated, clothed, fed and given a fixed pension there in exchange for the down payment of a sum of money.

A detailed description of what was involved is provided by the text of a priory charter of 11 March 1321, preserved in a royal inspeximus and confirmation of 28 June 1324:

Peter prior of St Saviour Bermondsey and the convent of that house grant to Nicholas de Tunstal a corrody there to be received in their house for life in the following form: viz each day of his life a white monastery loaf of the price of $1/2$d, a brown loaf (*bissum*) of price $1/2$d; a gallon of monastery ale of price 1d, a half gallon of the second ale price $1/2$d from their cellar at Bermondsey; two dishes of meat (*fercula*) on each one of the four flesh days every week and of the price of $11/2$d a day from their kitchen, and for the other three days fish or other things in the same way as one of the monks, of the price of $11/2$d; and every day two dishes of pottage of the price of

¹/₄d from the kitchen; and every year one robe of fur of the
suit of their clerks or esquires, as he pleases, of the price of
20s, to be received yearly from their chamber at Christmas;
also a house within their close of Bermondsey to dwell in,
with a plot of the court lying near the said house and
adjoining the wall of John le Mazeliner, between the priory
kitchen and brewhouse and 66ft [20.12m] long by 20ft
[6.10m] wide at each end, and a pond and curtilage between
the brewhouse and the new garden of the prior and convent
one end of which abuts on the lane leading to the granges and
the other on the highway leading to Rotherhithe, with free
ingress and egress whenever he chooses; also every year four
cart loads of wood, and two of straw to be carried at their
expense to his house at Bermondsey; and also two acres
[0.8ha] of meadow in their meadow under *Danieleswalle* for
the maintenance of his horses, as it is enclosed with ditches; to
hold to him for life, and to carry, take away, or assign,
wherever, whenever and to whomsoever he will, as well
without the said house of Bermondsey as within it. And they
or their successors may pay the said corrody and the above
price as they prefer. (*Cal Pat R*, 1321–24, 441; *Cal Close R*,
1327–30, 380–1)

This was supplemented by a charter of 11 June 1322 in
which Nicholas was additionally granted for life part of the new
garden which adjoined his existing plot:

part of the new garden with the apple trees and other trees in
it lying between the court of the said Nicholas on one side
and the said new garden on the other, of the length of 26¹/₂
perches [133.30m], whereof one end abuts on the lane leading
from their court to their granges and is of the width of 2¹/₂
perches [12.58m] and the other end abuts on the highway
leading to Rotherhithe of the width of 3¹/₂ perches [17.61m],
with its vines, hedges and ditches, free ingress and egress and
all other appertinances. (*Cal Close R*, 1327–30, 380–1)

There are examples of another category of corrody, in
which no accommodation appears to have been provided, rather
an annual cash payment and the presentation of goods in kind.
One such was that of John de Besevile, tailor of London, who
was to receive 7 marks per annum from the prior and convent
of Bermondsey (*Rot Parlt*, i, 372 no. 16). On 16 October 1355
the priory's grant for life was confirmed to William Turk
fishmonger of London of a yearly pension of £20 in their
house, a robe of the suit of their esquires or 20s every
Christmas, and two cartloads of good hay in their meadow of
Bermondsey (*Cal Pat R*, 1353–8, 288).

From the later 14th century a more elevated class of
corrodian becomes evident. The earls of Gloucester claimed
right of maintenance when at Bermondsey (*VCH* 1967, 75),
perhaps because they were former owners of some of the priory's
estates. Earl Ralph died seized of a lodging within the priory in
1372 (ibid). Between 1386 and 1399 John of Gaunt, as king of
Castile and Leon, was in correspondence with the prior and
'chaplains' of Bermondsey about the granting of corrodies by

alien houses for a life term in exchange for a sum of money
(TNA: PRO, SC8/93/4628). In November 1497 the will of Ann,
Lady Audley described her as being 'of the close of the monastery
of St Saviour Bermondsey' (TNA: PRO, PROB 11/11 quire 23).

From the beginning of the 14th century, there are records of
another sort of arrangement, whereby the king sent his
superannuated retainers to the priory to be fed, clothed and
housed. On 4 May 1313, he sent William de Topclyve, who had
served him 'long and usefully' to Bermondsey to receive the
necessaries of life in food and clothing in place of the former
incumbent Thomas le Long (*Cal Close R*, 1307–13, 579).
Topclyve was replaced in March 1323 by William Bale, who was
to receive the same maintenance for life (*Cal Close R*, 1318–23,
699). If the king ever made any payment towards the maintenance
of his former servants, his communications on the subject only
rarely mention the fact. On 9 March 1400 the king instructed
the abbey to admit a clerk of his chapel, Peryn de Archemont,
issuing him with letters patent under the common seal of the
house specifying 'what he shall take and what the priory will do',
and himself undertaking to provide for Peryn's maintenance
'for which no provision is yet made' (*Cal Close R*, 1399–1402,
125). On 21 October 1403 Thomas Fermour was sent to the
abbot and convent to replace Peryn, who had since died (*Cal
Close R*, 1402–5, 279). Fermour survived Bermondsey's
hospitality much longer than most of his colleagues, volunteering
as late as June 1415 to make way for Reynold Pope, the king's
serjeant (*Cal Close R*, 1413–19, 290). Eighteen months later, after
Pope's death, Thomas Tunbrigge, yeoman of the king's kitchen,
was sent to receive his maintenance on 28 January 1417 (ibid,
380). In the last of the series of royal preferments, on 12
December 1461, William Philpot, groom of the king's cellar,
was sent 'to take such corrody as any other person had therein'
(*Cal Close R*, 1461–8, 99). On 26 June 1462 John Kendall, the
king's servant and Margaret his wife were sent to take such
corrody or maintenance as William Philpot groom of the cellar
or any other person had (ibid, 165). A final reference to a
corrody occurs in February 1519 when John Treis, yeoman of
the jewelhouse, was granted for life the corrody in the
monastery of Bermondsey, in place of William Redde and Alice
his wife, deceased (*L and P Hen VIII*, iii(1), 102(18)).

It is notable that in almost all these cases the latest royal
corrodian was clearly the replacement of another who had
either died or given up his place there, and whose own earlier
'appointment' is also recorded. In the years 1400–39 a long
succession of occupants of the same corrody can be traced in this
way. All this might suggest that the number of royal corrodies
in existence at one time was quite limited, and it is possible that
there was only one. On the other hand, the king must have had
innumerable servants to provide for in this way, and even if
fairly shared out among other religious houses in the London area
the number at any one house could well have been somewhat
larger than one or two. A couple of cases (Peryn de Archemont
in 1400 and William Philpot in 1461) do not appear to have been
replacements, and so may have been additions to the existing
complement. There were also lengthy periods (as in the years
1361 to 1400) when the Close Rolls make no mention of

corrodies at Bermondsey, and which are difficult to interpret: it seems unlikely, however, that they had ceased to operate at these dates. At three points in the priory's history corrodies, apparently both private and royal, were prohibited because they were so onerous: in 1327, 1401 and 1475 (*Cal Pat R*, 1327–30, 136; 1401–5, 23; *Rot Parlt*, vi, 124; *Cal Pat R*, 1467–77, 509–10).

In Bermondsey's final years, there is some documentary evidence for a different type of residence arrangement. Thomas Debel is named as lessee for his life and his wife's from 12 January 1538 of a tenement or messuage with garden within the close, previously held by William Strake (TNA: PRO, SC6/Henry VIII/ 3464, m 27); they presumably occupied this property in person.

Identifying objects with specifically lay connotations is difficult. A small lead trough (Fig 84, <S190>) which was recovered from backfills in the drain west of the reredorter range (B9; OA12, period P1) and so probably of monastic-period date illustrates the problem. It is thought to be a feeding trough for a caged bird; several are known from London, including one from the latest phase of the religious house of St John, Clerkenwell (Sloane and Malcolm 2004, 360 <S107>). Were the religious prior to the Dissolution as or less likely than lay members of the community to have kept domestic pets? A seal matrix (Fig 64, <S48>) recovered from the second (infirmary) cloister garth (OA2, period M8) has a variant of the hunter's cry 'soho' as its legend (common on 14th-century seals), accompanied by a motif of the hunting hound in the forest. This may be thought of as more likely to have been used by a member of the laity, but that secular may have been a visitor rather than a resident.

Demography and health of the burial population

Analysis of the population of the cemetery (OA6, Chapter 7.9) has enabled comparison between the inhabitants of St Saviour and those of other London monastic houses. Bermondsey appears typical of monastic sites in demonstrating a sex bias among the articulated burials. When the individuals of indeterminate sex (48) were omitted, there were 137 men (male and ?male) but only 8 female (female and ?female) burials, giving a male:female ratio of 17.1:1 (Table 4). This is of the same order of magnitude as in the eastern cemetery of the Gilbertine priory of St Andrew Fishergate, York (15.7:1: Stroud and Kemp 1993, 254, table 55), and at two houses close to London with large excavated populations, the Cistercian abbey of St Mary Stratford Langthorne and Augustinian Merton Priory. At both Stratford Langthorne and Merton the burial population is thought, like Bermondsey, to represent principally the monastic community: at Stratford Langthorne, the burials were from the church and external areas, with the vast majority from the north-east cemetery (an overall male:female ratio of 19.0:1: Barber et al 2004, 86); at Merton, clear areas of more mixed age and sex burials (the church and north burial area), distinct from almost exclusively male areas with very few children (the chapter house and south burial area), lower the overall male:female ratio (11.2:1: Conheeney 2007, 266–8). The overwhelming majority of the excavated Bermondsey burials, and of the analysed individuals, were located in the external cemetery area south of the church, between the church (B3) and the chapel (B1), later the infirmary chapel; only seven burials were excavated inside

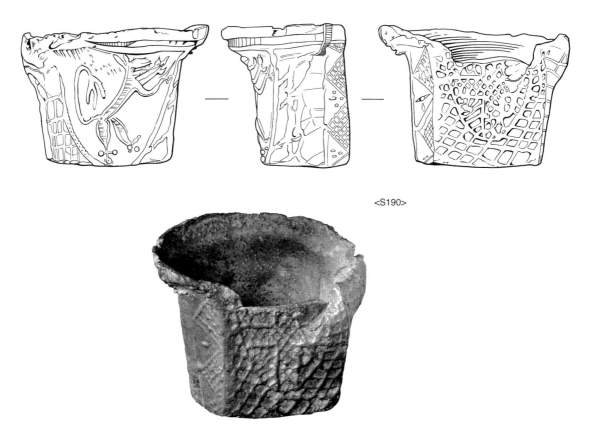

<S190>

Fig 84 Lead feeding trough for a caged bird <S190> (from OA12, period P1) (scale 1:1; photo c 1:1)

Table 4 The burial population: summary of age and sex

Age (years)	Male	?Male	Female	?Female	Indeterminate	Total no.
Adolescent (11–15)	0	0	0	0	1	1
Young adult (16–25)	19	2	1	0	1	23
Mature adult (26–45)	55	6	2	1	1	65
Old/elderly adult (≥46)	29	2	1	1	2	35
Adult (16+)	15	9	1	1	43	69
Total	118	19	5	3	48	193

the chapel. (None was excavated within the main claustral area, that is within the monastic church, cloister or chapter house.) This south-east cemetery clearly catered for the male religious community.

Five of the seven burials excavated within the chapel were analysed; all were adult, three males, one female and one of indeterminate sex (two males aged 26–45 years in period M4; one male, one female and one of indeterminate sex in period M6).

The low proportion of women (8:137, or 4.2% of the 192 adults) buried in the priory is in accordance with a monastic house, but it is unfortunate that most of the female skeletons were too damaged for much to be revealed about them. The sole female skeleton that was sufficiently complete for stature estimation was that of a very tall woman A[3262] (OA6, period M7).

The largest group of ageable men among the burials was that in the age range 26 to 45 years, that is mature but not elderly (54.0% of ageable adults). The next most populous category was that demonstrably over the age of 45 (27.4% of ageable adults). Other comparable populations show similar frequencies, for example St Mary Stratford Langthorne 22.7% (White 2004, 173) and Merton Priory 27.9% (Conheeney 2007, 266), suggesting that, overall, roughly a quarter of deaths occur in this age group. At St Saviour Bermondsey, the occurrence of a skull A[1579] showing Paget's disease, a disease of ageing, showed that the prolific disarticulated bone also included very old individuals.

Another disease associated with ageing (in particular male ageing) is DISH (diffuse idiopathic skeletal hyperostosis: Chapter 7.9) and this was recognised in 7.8% of individuals (15/193) at Bermondsey (Fig 85). This prevalence is relatively high compared to modern populations where it is usually about 3%. It is, however, comparable with the 8.6% seen at Merton Priory (Conheney 2007, 273) and the prevalence of 6.9% in the burials from the church of St Mary Graces, London (Grainger and Phillpotts in prep). Stratford Langthorne has a very similar frequency of 8.7% (White 2004, 176) which points to a very close similarity across monastic cemetery sites in the London area. If we consider the disease as one of male ageing and the incidence at Bermondsey as 15 cases out of the total number of known males, then the prevalence is 15/137, which is 10.9%. At the priory and hospital of St Mary Spital, London, the prevalence was 20% (three cases) within the church (B1), where

the burials were predominanrtly male and well into their 30s, and some much older, consistent with an area assigned to clerical and/or wealthy burials (Thomas et al 1997, 112). When the more mixed age and sex populations from the hospital's external cemeteries are brought into the total, the overall percentage is much lower, at 3.8%. The high prevalence of DISH at monastic sites is thought to be related to a calorie-rich diet and obesity (with attendant late-onset diabetes). Indeed, it has been suggested that DISH was something of an 'occupational hazard' of monastic life (Waldron 1985; Gilchrist and Sloane 2005, 212).

The population at the priory of St Saviour Bermondsey was typical of medieval monastic sites: as a religious house for men the burial population was (not surprisingly) predominantly male. It was also a mature population. The absence of adolescents (a single 11 to 15-year-old was identified) and children from the site has implications for palaeopathology as well as for demography. Thus, there were no indications of the common diseases of childhood or of developmental deficiency in the skeleton (such as rickets or scurvy), with the sole exception of cribra orbitalia. This was present in 5.2% of possible cases, indicating that there were problems of metabolism, possibly iron-deficiency anaemia but almost certainly aggravated by internal parasites. On the other hand, the high proportion of DISH (consistent with what has been

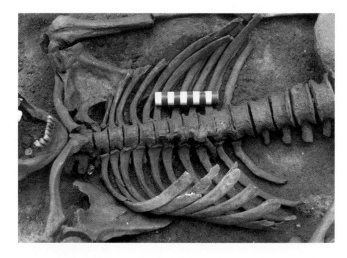

Fig 85 Detail of a skeleton A[2871] in the external cemetery (OA6, period M7) with fused vertebrae, evidence for DISH (fusion occurs via new bone growth between vertebrae), from the north (0.1m scale)

shown for the higher clergy at other sites) suggested that certain of the monastic community or the nobility choosing burial in the priory were enjoying a diet far richer than was available to the lay poor.

Tuberculosis, present in skeleton A[3231] (OA6, period M7) and possibly two other men, is now considered to be a disease of poverty. Although on admission to the Order the Cluniac monks swore a vow of poverty, it is obvious that their standard of living (as measured by diet, hygiene, shelter, sanitation and medical care) was better than that of the majority of the population. Therefore, the conditions for the transmission of tuberculosis probably depended on the close proximity in which the community lived, prayed and worked. Sinusitis, present in a minimum of four men, was a disease of neither rich nor poor but of air pollution, obviously difficult to escape in a monastery. It is known that Benedictine novices in the 15th century had to submit to a medical examination before admission to the Order and to swear that they were free of infection (Hatcher 1986). Cluniac houses may have had a different procedure but the three potential tuberculosis sufferers presumably developed their symptoms only after their late teens, although there is always the possibility that the infection itself had been contracted earlier in life.

Cases of tuberculosis have been identified at several urban monastic sites (Gilchrist and Sloane 2005, 211; Chapter 7.9, 'Infectious disease', 'Specific infections') and in the cemetery populations at the suburban London monastic houses of Stratford Langthorne (White 2004, 177) and Merton Priory, where the large infirmary may have contributed to the presence (and transmission) of this disease (Conheeney 2007, 275). It has been suggested that periosteal rib lesions have strong links with tuberculosis (Chapter 7.9, 'Infectious disease', 'Non-specific infections'); these were seen in two individuals at Bermondsey (in OA6, periods M6 and M7) and at Merton Priory (Conheeney 2007, 275).

Periostitis, particularly tibial periostitis, is commonly seen in archaeological populations (Gilchrist and Sloane 2005, 212) and may be the result of infection by common bacteria, systemic disease or minor trauma (everyday knocks and blows) (Chapter 7.9, 'Infectious disease', 'Non-specific infections'). The occurrence of periostitis in the Bermondsey population invites comparison with the prevalence of periostitis in the medieval population of St Mary Spital. At the medieval hospital of St Mary it was found that individuals buried in the church were taller and enjoyed better health than those buried in the cemetery areas (Conheeney 1997, 229). They also suffered from a far lower prevalence of periostitis. In percentage terms, 28.6% of the St Mary Spital church interments had periosteal lesions compared to 27.6% (right leg) and 34.6% (left leg) out of the entire Bermondsey population. The percentages for burials in the cemetery areas at St Mary Spital were 55.5% (OA2) and 46.7% (OA5), far greater than both the church burials on the same site and the numbers from Bermondsey. If the burials in St Mary Spital church can be presumed to have some sort of rank or status on the grounds of their burial place, height and general health, then it is interesting to note a similar percentage of the

same pathology in the entire cemetery population at St Saviour Bermondsey.

Monasteries are usually regarded as the repositories of medical knowledge and this was important at a time when there were few physicians and they tended to live and work in towns. The expertise accumulated in the infirmary over the centuries would be invaluable in treating simple disorders and in dealing with trauma, notably the splinting, setting and reduction of limb and other fractures (Greene 1992). This appears to have been the case at Bermondsey (except for the extreme complications of the Pott's fracture), where the overall fracture frequency rate is 6.7% (13/193). The situation at Bermondsey thus contrasts with that at Stratford Langthorne where White (2004, 178) points to a low number of fractures, varying from 0.5% to 3.2% of individual bones, but most of those fractures healed very badly.

There were no injuries suggestive of interpersonal violence. This is in contrast to other monastic sites where lesions on the skull, principally, but also elsewhere in the skeleton, were indicative of assault: St Andrew Fishergate, York (Stroud and Kemp 1993, 231), and Stratford Langthorne (White 2004, 178). At Merton Priory, Conheeney (2007, 270) reports severe cases of skull trauma, all of which were the result of interpersonal violence. The absence of evidence for deliberately inflicted injury may be surprising in view of documented instances at St Saviour Bermondsey, such as the incident involving the monk Arnulf in 1261 (below, 4.4, 'St Saviour as a London monastery').

Burial practice and burial location

Archaeological evidence for a range of burial practices survived, but in keeping with the burial areas investigated – mainly the external monastic cemetery – there was little evidence for elaborate or costly forms of burial. Some burials were placed in graves variously lined with stone or with chalk or plaster and some were in wooden coffins, but these were a minority. There were no stone or lead coffins in the cemetery or chapel, and there was no evidence for markers or other visible above-ground structures.

Some 204 or so burials made at the priory in the chapel (B1) and external cemetery (OA6) were excavated, together with four (empty) graves dug in the second half of the 11th century or first half of the 12th century (period M3/M4) in the quarry area (OA2) south of the chapel. The majority have been phased and are dated to the 12th to mid 15th centuries (periods M4–M8). Burial in the external cemetery took place in more or less orderly rows; it began in the western part north of the chapel and south of the priory church, and continued to develop eastwards through time, until burial ceased altogether in this area after the mid 15th century. No burials were assigned to the final period of the monastic house.

Of this number, some 22 were buried in lined graves – 16 in stone-lined graves or 'cists' and a further six where the evidence suggested a grave lined wholly or partially with mortar, plaster and/or crushed chalk – from the 12th to mid 14th century (Table 5). Three were in the chapel (B1), the rest in the

Table 5 The occurrence of wall and base linings in graves at Bermondsey, by period and land use (excludes examples excavated by Grimes)

Period	Land use	Context no. of skeleton (of grave if none)	Sex	Age at death (years)	Wall lining	Base lining	Description/comments
M4	B1	A[3804]	-	-	✓	✓	grave cut lined with chalk and plaster; no skeleton survived
	OA6	A[2762]	male	26–45	✓	-	mortared stone cist (chalk; some ragstone and greenstone)*
	OA6	A[2765]	indeterminate	adult	✓	-	mortared stone cist (chalk), with head niche (including 'pillow'); mortar skin to lining
	OA6	A[2801]	male	26–45	✓	-	mortared stone cist (chalk), with head niche; mortar skin to lining
	OA6	A[3897]	male	≥46	-	✓	some crushed chalk at base of cut
	OA6	A[4006]	?male	adult	✓	-	mortared stone cist (chalk)
M5	OA6	A[2701]	male	≥46	✓	-	mortared stone cist (chalk and tile), with head niche
	OA6	A[2837]	indeterminate	adult	✓	-	mortared stone cist (chalk) with west end of lining stepped to form head niche
	OA6	A[2910]	indeterminate	adult	✓	-	a partial, mainly mortar lining, but uncertain
	OA6	A[3005]	male	16–25	✓	-	mortared stone cist (chalk); head niche only survived (horseshoe-shaped, two courses each side)
	OA6	A[3986]	male	26–45	✓	-	mortared stone cist (chalk; some ragstone)
	OA6	A[4056]	male	≥46	-	✓	crushed chalk lining at base of grave
M6	B1	A[3522]	male	adult	✓	-	mortared stone cist (chalk)
	B1	A[3596]	female	adult	✓	-	unmortared stone cist (chalk); head niche only survived (three blocks, one either side of head, one in base as 'pillow')
M7	OA6	A[3294]	male	26–45	-	✓	plaster lining around body (no evidence of coffin), anthropomorphic grave cut
	OA6	A[3312]	male	16–25	✓	-	mortared stone cist (chalk) with head niche (niche has three chalk blocks with inscribed 'X's)
	OA6	A[3374]	indeterminate	adult	-	✓	large grave cut with plaster lining (evidence of wooden coffin)
	OA6	A[3531]	male	26–45	✓	-	unmortared stone cist (chalk); blocks round head
	OA6	A[3534]	male	≥46	✓	-	mortared stone cist (chalk); north side only survived
	OA6	A[3546]	-	-	✓	-	mortared stone cist (chalk); no skeleton survived
	OA6	A[3619]	indeterminate	adult	✓	-	mortared stone cist (chalk; some ragstone and greensand); north part only survived
	OA6	A[3823]	male	≥46	✓	✓	mortared stone cist (chalk)

* 'ragstone' and 'greensand'/'greenstone' (ie Reigate stone): as described by the excavator

cemetery (OA6); of these 22, 12 were assigned to the 12th century (periods M4 and M5). Outside the north wall of the church (B3), Grimes excavated six graves with stone cists which also appear to date to the 12th century (periods M4 and M5). Of the 28 burials made in the infirmary chapel ('Lady chapel') at the Cluniac priory of St Pancras, Lewes, 14 were buried in full cists (Lyne 1997, 71–4, 78–80); these cist burials are thought to belong to the late 11th to 13th centuries. The practice of lining graves with stone was widespread in England in the 12th century and is known from a number of monastic houses including Augustinian Holy Trinity Aldgate and Merton priories (Schofield and Lea 2005, 152–4; Miller and Saxby 2007, 152–4). Cist burials increased at Merton in the 13th century, and there and elsewhere continued to be used until the Dissolution (Gichrist and Sloane 2005, 134–7). At Merton, however, the latest cist burials were concentrated within the chapter house and immediately outside it, rather than in the external cemetery areas. The practice was a minority one: less than *c* 5% of the graves excavated at Merton (36/721), and *c* 8% at Bermondsey (16/204; 11%, 22/204), while no stone linings were found at Cistercian St Mary Stratford Langthorne (out of 667: Barber et al 2004, 100–4).

There were two broad shapes of cist found: rectangular (or tapering) and, equally common at Bermondsey, rectangular with a head niche ('anthropomorphic'). There was a good deal of variety as illustrated by the four tapering rectangular cists immediately south of the south wall of the church in Fig 86:

the row of three (period M4) comprise cists with a head niche composed of 'ear muff' or head support stones A[2801], with a head niche with a 'pillow' stone A[2765], and with no niche A[2762], while the head niche of the single (period M5) cist to the west A[2837] is formed by stepping in the wall lining. Some cists had thin skims of plaster or mortar over the interior of the wall linings (eg A[2765] and A[2801], Fig 86) and occasionally over the base of the grave. One cist A[3312] had three 'X's or crosses incised on the blocks of the head niche. The head niche for burial A[3005] (period M5) was a curved horseshoe-shape, made of four blocks, two blocks in two courses on each side of the head (Fig 87). Both shapes, with a head niche or without, may have been covered with grave slabs such as the ones found at Lewes Priory (Lyne 1997, 139–41). One 12th-century cist (A[2765], illustrated on Fig 30 and Fig 86) was constructed with slots in the top course of the wall which could take cross supports for a stone slab or other (eg wooden) cover which would have been below ground. A few graves had no stone linings but only chalk or plaster on the base of the grave cut (Table 5). The earliest burials (period M4) in the chapel included A[3804] where unusually both the sides and base were lined.

A few graves (10 or *c* 5%, from OA6, periods M5–M8) were unlined but incorporated a head niche (ie anthropomorphic grave cuts). The possible symbolism of this grave shape, with its emphasis on the head, its currency from the late 11th or early 12th centuries and its disappearance apparently by the 14th century are discussed by Gilchrist and Sloane (2005, 132–3). In

Fig 86 View of cist graves in the cemetery (OA6) adjacent to the south wall of the church (B3), from the north: left, from top, A[2762], A[2765], A[2801], period M4; right, A[2837], period M5 (2.0m scales)

Fig 87 Horseshoe-shaped head niche for burial A[3005] (OA6), period M5, from the east (0.2m scale)

one such anthropomorphic grave (elderly adult male A[3883], OA6, period M5) a pillow of sand may originally have been contained within an organic 'bag'.

There was limited evidence for wooden coffins: coffin nails or other ferrous objects were recorded in 21 burials (c 10%), in the fill or in the case of a few possibly in situ (OA6, periods M4–M8). The majority of interments were probably made in shrouds (or possibly habits) but there was very little evidence to substantiate this.

The majority of burials were supine, heads to the west and arms extended. Three burials had their arms in a praying position (elderly adult male A[3268], adult male A[2967], adult female A[3262], all OA6, period M7); one cist burial (A[2765]; Table 5) had the arms touching each shoulder. Two males, one adult and one elderly adult, were buried prone (A[2640], A[2669], both OA6, period M7). Such burials are unusual, but in this monastic context may be symbolic of penitence (Gilchrist and Sloane 2005, 153–4). The three 13th- to 14th-century examples from Merton Priory, it has been suggested, may have been accidentally rather than deliberately positioned (Saxby and Miller 2007, 151).

Grave location and burial practice may allow some conclusions to be drawn about the profile of the women buried at St Saviour Bermondsey. Of the eight females and possible females identified, seven were buried in the external cemetery area (OA6), beginning in the 12th century (one in period M4, one in M5, four in M7 and one in M8: Table 20); their chronological and spatial distribution neatly illustrates the conclusion that the cemetery filled from west to east through time (Fig 21; Fig 33; Fig 53; Fig 57). Of the four females/?females interred between the mid 13th and the early–mid 14th century (period M7), one was probably buried in a wooden coffin (19 ferrous objects, ?nails, were recorded on site) and one burial was made in an anthropomorphic grave cut. There is no evidence for any other grave elaboration, personal items or religious objects, but this is not unusual seen against the cemetery population as a whole. The presence of this small number of females in the monastic cemetery suggests that they held a particular relationship to the community, through patronage, religious role (for example as servants), or family ties (for example to members of the community).

The female members of wealthy families, described by documentary sources as being buried at the priory, such as Mary, Countess of Boulogne, in 1115 (Chapter 3.2, 'Documentary evidence'), were more likely to have been buried within the main claustral area, and in particular inside the monastic church, where no burials were excavated. The only female identified within the chapel (A[3596], B1) was buried between *c* 1200 and *c* 1250 (period M6), one of a group of three burials at this location in this period. She was buried with a stone head niche including a pillow, and one of the others – a (headless) adult male A[3522] – was buried in a stone cist. Of the seven burials excavated within the chapel, five were analysed; all were adult, three males, one female and one of indeterminate sex (Table 20). The two males buried in the chapel earlier, *c* 1100–50 (period M4), were identified as mature adults, aged 26–45 years. This age and sex profile, and the use of cists or masonry linings, is comparable with the external cemetery. It is difficult to see any compelling evidence in this very small number of burials that the chapel was a more exclusive area of burial than the external cemetery. However, there is in addition some suggestion that the exterior cist burials were focused on the chapel and on the church for they did tend to be located either adjacent to the south wall of the church (three in M4; three in M5) or close to the north wall of the chapel (one in M4; two in M5; a group of six north of the chancel in M7).

While there is no archaeological evidence for burial slabs or memorials, the cast copper-alloy letters <S26>–<S28> (Fig 88) found in post-Dissolution contexts have obvious reference to monastic-period burials. Of Lombardic form, as produced from *c* 1280 to *c* 1350, letters of this type were likely to have been used on slabs or grand tomb monuments, such as might have

been found in the priory church (B3) or in the chapel (B1). The mosaic shale inlay was also possibly part of a grave cover (Chapter 7.4, 'Stone building material'; Fig 141).

Documentary evidence for burial is mostly concerned with the location of important individuals within the priory church. In 1206, the body of the first prior, Peter, was moved into the choir of the church (*Ann Monast*, iii, 450). Fifteenth-century wills mention, for example, the Lady chapel as the burial place of Margaret de la Pole (1472) and of Ann Lady Audley (1497), and the chapel of Holy Cross as the burial place of William Kelshall (1428) and his wife Alice (1433) (TNA: PRO, PROB 11/6, quire 12; TNA: PRO, PROB 11/11, quire 23; TNA: PRO, PROB 11/3, quires 16 and 19). The burial of noble individuals brought prestige to a house, so much so that it was at times the cause of dispute (Golding 1981, 67). A striking example of this is the case of Roger Bigod, Earl of Norfolk, who founded the Cluniac priory of Thetford. According to a 15th-century chronicle and a charter of Henry I, when Roger died at an episcopal manor not far from Norwich, his body was conveyed to Norwich Cathedral in defiance of his wish to be buried at Thetford. During the subsequent lawsuit, the priory initially claimed that Roger had given his own, his wife's and his son's body to Thetford, but then gave way to the bishop of Norwich (Golding 1981, 67–8).

Diet and food preparation

Analysis of the hand-collected and wet-sieved bone has provided a detailed insight into the nature and range of the monastic diet (Chapter 7.8). The remains derive from a wide range of fish, bird and mammal species; Table 18 shows the recovery of hand-collected and wet-sieved bone in terms of period, species and fragment count. It must be remembered, however, that the relative lack of sampling effort (or loss of samples in the decades since the excavation) has skewed the recovery of species in favour of the larger and more robust forms. It can be assumed that a greater sampling coverage would have added to the species diversity of the assemblage and effectively increased the spatial and chronological spread of many of the smaller species. The bone recovered came from the area to the east, and also south-east, of where the main monastic kitchens would have been located. There was considerable variation in sample size: for example, between a minimum of

<S26> <S27> <S28>

Fig 88 Copper-alloy letters <S26>–<S28> from 13th- to 14th-century funerary inscriptions (scale c 1:1)

128 hand-collected fragments (period M7) and a maximum of 4429 (period M9) to which the reredorter dumping A[972] contributed 4203 fragments or *c* 95% (Table 18).

The bulk of the meat diet was derived from beef, mutton and pork from animals with an age range of foetal/neonate to fully adult but consisting mainly of young adult and fully adult. Only a few fragments were definitely identified as goat. There was considerable recovery of domestic poultry, particularly chicken and goose, with a much smaller representation of domestic duck/mallard and possibly domestic dove.

There was a diverse, though not abundant, group of fish and wild 'game' birds and mammals, including species associated with agricultural land (eg wood pigeon, grey partridge, rabbit and hare); the Thames margin and marshes (eg teal, swan, snipe and woodcock); the river and other freshwaters (bream, carp, cyprinids (probably including roach) and pike); and the estuary and coastal waters (plaice/flounder, mackerel, sole, gadids (cod and related species), gurnard, herring, and smelt, conger eel and porpoise). The migratory species, sturgeon, salmonids, and eel, could have been obtained from riverine or estuarine fisheries.

The great diversity of the faunal remains, particularly in the light of the small size of the assemblage, implies that the monastery was provisioned from a wide range of sources. Although the diversity and composition vary between periods, this may be, at least partially, a reflection of the inter-period variation in sample size (above and Table 18). Throughout the hand-collected group the predominance of beef, mutton and pork from subadult and adult animals suggests that meat arrived on site either 'on the hoof' or as complete carcasses and was then processed *in situ*. This was probably also true of domestic poultry. The recovery of neonate/young infant chickens, geese, lambs and piglets does suggest that animal husbandry was carried out on at least a limited scale.

The diverse group of wild 'game' bird and mammal species recovered, although limited in terms of quantity, has considerable implications in terms of the manner in which the abbey was provisioned. These species derive from a variety of habitats some or all of which would have been sufficiently close to the site to be feasible as a provisioning source.

The diet of the community at St Saviour Bermondsey was of a consistently good quality and periods M6 and M9 show definite indications of high-status consumption. Period M6 yielded three fragments each of red deer and fallow deer, two species that were very strictly controlled throughout the medieval period and beyond. Hunting and consumption of deer were well outside the scope of all but the wealthiest and most powerful in society. A large, relatively heavy arrowhead (<S188>) found in a post-Dissolution context in Open Area 9 would have been a suitable weapon for the hunting of large mammals. The much larger bone group from period M9 (A[972], dumping in the reredorter B9) shows a similar incidence of fallow deer (one hand-collected and three wet-sieved fragments: Table 18). The same group yields considerable evidence throughout all the faunal groups – fish, birds and mammals – for higher status consumers. The fish species include sturgeon, for centuries a royal fish, together with highly

esteemed and expensive food species such as gurnard, carp and pike. The occurrence of carp is particularly interesting. This central Asiatic species was introduced into the British Isles, perhaps in the first half of the 16th century (Lever 1977, 443), and would have been an unusual and expensive delicacy before its wider distribution throughout suitable waters. The bird group includes a diverse range of game species (eg partridge, snipe and woodcock), as well as examples of high-status consumption and rarity such as mute swan. Mute swan, although a species indigenous to Britain, was brought into semi-domestication immediately after the Norman Conquest and appropriated as 'birds royal', the property of the crown, between the 13th and 18th centuries (Stamp 1969, 217). Swans, especially cygnets, thus became a highly valued species for the table, with their consumption effectively restricted to those at the top of the social scale.

The game mammal species are confined to hare, rabbit, roe deer, red deer and fallow deer. Hare is found in only a few instances in periods M6, M7 and M9. Rabbit appears in periods M4–M6, M9 and P1, and was particularly abundant in period M9 reredorter group A[972]. This species was introduced early in the Middle Ages and was probably still rare on mainland Britain until the late 12th century (Lever 1977, 65). They were initially kept in warrens and probably did not become established as feral populations until the mid 13th century (ibid, 33). Many monastic houses kept and ran such warrens. Bermondsey's warren was probably located on the one acre (0.4ha) of land called the 'Coneyyard' referred to in 1539; it lay south-east of the south gate (above, 4.2, 'The precinct and home grange'). The kitchener's account of 1416–17 for Selby Abbey not only quantifies the numbers in the rabbit warren, but also mentions the keeping of dogs specifically to hunt them (White 1993, 23–4). As a result of this very controlled distribution, particularly in the early part of the medieval period, the consumption of rabbit implies a certain degree of status. They appear regularly on the menu at feasts and banquets in the late 14th and early 15th centuries (Lever 1977, 68). Their skins were also regarded as of high value.

Overall, the diet of the community at St Saviour Bermondsey can be considered of consistently high quality in terms of staple species (cod, herring, plaice/flounder, chicken, goose, beef, mutton and pork), with evidence from all the principal faunal groups for additional very high-status consumption. When the species composition of the diet is compared with that quoted for the funeral feast for the bishop of Bath and Wells in 1424 (White 1993, 38), the similarities are striking for all faunal groups. The funeral menu is particularly useful in that it lists fish species as an option for the religious men at table. Apart from the main domesticates, the bird and mammal species common to the two groups are swan, woodcock, partridge, snipe and deer. The common fish species are herring, eel, salmon, pike, plaice, cod, sole, gurnard and roach. Such a close correlation between the two faunal assemblages suggests that some at least of the inhabitants of St Saviour enjoyed a significantly protein-rich and varied diet. The species present in the assemblages from two contemporary medieval sites south of the river – from the Southwark palace of the bishops of Winchester and from Augustinian Merton Priory – suggest similar conclusions; like Bermondsey, these included red, fallow and roe deer, hare and rabbit, swan, and pike and sturgeon (Reilly 2006; Miller and Saxby 2007, 140–1).

The faunal characteristics of the Bermondsey animal bone groups then have considerable implications in terms of the status of the house and its occupants and their general lifestyle. A comparison of the overall assemblage with that from the priory and hospital of St Mary Spital (Locker 1997; Pipe 1997) highlights several differences. Although equally diverse, the total pre-Dissolution assemblage from St Mary Spital is dominated in terms of fish by herring, plaice/flounder and cyprinids with no strong representation of the 'white fishery', that is cod and related species (gadids), and little real evidence for high status apart from one fragment of sturgeon dermal scute (Locker 1997). The fish diet at Bermondsey is based on gadids but with significant components of herring, smelt, plaice/flounder and comparatively fewer cyprinids. There are also significant numbers of highly esteemed species such as conger eel, gurnard and pike. In general, there is more emphasis on estuarine/marine species at Bermondsey, with true freshwater species much less preferred; the fish assemblage from nearby Winchester Palace (Southwark) was again very similar in this respect (K Reilly in Seeley et al 2006, 240–1). With respect to birds and mammals the assemblages at Bermondsey and St Mary Spital are very similar in terms of species composition, age distribution, carcass-part representation and butchery evidence. Bermondsey does differ in that although the meat diet is dominated by beef, there are significantly greater components of poultry, mutton and pork than are seen at St Mary Spital and also significantly greater abundance and diversity of game and high-status species. These differences are particularly striking if the groups from the last pre-Dissolution period from each site are compared (Bermondsey, period M9: Chapters 3.7, 'Archaeological evidence', 'Reredorter (B9)', 7.8; Table 18; St Mary Spital, period M7: Pipe 1997, 233–4).

Although it is not possible to specify the location of processing sites within the monastic complex, the very clear butchery evidence seen allows some comment to be made on the pattern of carcass preparation. For the three major domesticates, cattle, sheep and pig, a very uniform procedure is apparent. The animals were decapitated and then split sagittally (down the midline) to produce 'sides' and to allow removal of the spinal cord. The heads were also split in this way to allow removal of the brain, and the cheek-meat and tongue were removed. The lower jaws were disarticulated from the skull to facilitate this process. The carcasses were then subdivided by disarticulation at the shoulder and hip, the shoulder often being removed as a 'joint'. There was evidence for further disarticulation at the 'elbow' and 'knee' and removal of the feet. Splitting was done using a heavy blade such as a cleaver, the finer work was done using a range of blades, some very fine. There was some evidence for splitting of the larger limb bones of cattle, in particular the metapodials, to allow removal of the marrow.

Butchery marks were also seen on chicken, goose, partridge and woodcock. These suggest that the legs had been removed at the articulation with the pelvis and then also disarticulated at the 'knee'. The feet were severed at the tibia/tarsal articulation and the wing removed at the base of the humerus and severed again at the 'elbow'. In each case, the work was skilfully done with a range of fine, sharp knife blades.

There was also definite evidence for butchery of horse. This was seen in period M4 (c 1100–50), and mainly consisted of heavy chops across the major limb bones which would have resulted in disarticulation at the major joints, removal of meat from the major limb bones and removal of the feet. This may be interpreted as preparation of food for kept animals rather than for human consumption. While cat is present in periods M5 and M6, the greatest prevalence of cat and dog bones occurs in period M9, in the reredorter dumping A[972] (Table 18). Whether or not these animals were being kept as pets within the monastery is difficult to ascertain. Pet birds do appear to have been kept (above, 'The inhabitants: lay people'; Fig 84, <S190>). The high number of domestic cat and dog bones in the late 15th to early 16th centuries may suggest that these animals may have belonged to laity – visitors or residents – housed within the precinct. But on a large rural estate, be it secular or religious, cats and dogs would have earned their keep as working animals, and their presence could be explained in this way. The kitchener's account of 1416–17 for Selby Abbey mentions the keeping of dogs for the purpose of hunting rabbits raised in the monastic warren (White 1993, 23–4).

Considerable butchery evidence was recovered from the fish remains. Again this mainly involved the use of knives. The larger fish, particularly pike and the gadids, showed evidence that the head was removed and the body then filleted to remove the vertebral column. The smaller species such as the cyprinids either showed little obvious butchery evidence or appeared to have been transversely chopped.

The wide carcass-part representation and butchery marks observed on virtually all the wild and domestic species recovered from the site suggest that the majority of carcass preparation was done on site with the animals arriving intact. Probable exceptions to this are the sturgeon and porpoise where only a few fragments, respectively four and one, were found. This may imply that these species were brought to the site as prepared cuts. The large quantity of smelt from the dump A[972] in period M9 provides a definite indication of off-site preparation (Table 18). In this case, the species was represented by the vertebral column only; there was no recovery of cranial or caudal elements. This strongly suggests that preliminary removal of the head, tail and possibly also fins was done elsewhere and the fish brought to site in much the same anatomical condition as modern tinned small fish such as pilchards and sardines.

An important find linked to food preparation is a near-complete object which appears to be a spit-support in shelly-sandy ware (SSW) (Fig 89, <P23>). It is in the form of a solid column of clay with a slightly flared base and a circular hole drilled through its thickness 50mm from one end, which is no

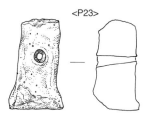

Fig 89 *Spit-support in shelly-sandy ware <P23> from the robbing fill of Drain 4, period P1 (scale 1:4)*

great height for a joint of meat, other than a small bird. The hole is 12mm in diameter on one side and tapers to 7mm on the other side. The other end is incomplete, although very little appears to be missing. No other medieval or later spit-supports have yet been identified in London in any fabric. Spit-supports are known in a brick fabric in late medieval contexts in the Netherlands (Heidinga and Smink 1982). Closely comparable examples have also been recognised recently in Hull (Evans and Verhaeghe 1998–9). Spit-roasting was one of the chief methods of cooking meat used throughout the Middle Ages, the function of the spit being to keep the meat at the right distance from the fire to prevent burning, and to allow it to be turned so that it was evenly cooked. Most of the brickware spit-supports identified in the Netherlands, as well as the Hull examples, are wedge-shaped and decorated with chip-carving and stamps, and have one or more hollows or holes, sometimes at different levels (Heidinga and Smink 1982, 64–73, figs 4–12). They range in date from the late 13th to the 16th century (ibid, 73). The Bermondsey example is, therefore, much earlier, dating from a time when cooking would take place over a central hearth, rather than in a fireplace against the wall. The absence of any trace of sooting or abrasion around the hole is surprising if the interpretation as a spit-support is correct. Although the use of fired clay instead of an iron support or forked branch seems an unlikely choice, examples are known from the Bronze Age into the Roman period from across Europe (ibid, 78, figs 14, 20).

Another unusual item associated with cooking from the artefact-rich A[972] is a copper-alloy grater (Fig 90, <S117>). This was made out of sheet copper alloy that was pierced with many holes, which have sharp, upstanding perimeters. This rather rough-and-ready (and so far unparalleled) object appears to combine the grating and shredding functions of the modern kitchen tool; it would perhaps have been suitable for cutting some vegetables finely and grating garlic, but it is unlikely to have been robust enough for most spices such as nutmeg or pepper. Of 19 knives recovered from the site, 13 of them were from A[972] in Building 9.

A fragment survives from a ceramic mould (Fig 91, <S119>) that is thought to have been used for the production of pastries at a benefactor's feast or other festival. The London-type ware (LOND) mould is circular, *c* 92mm in diameter, and depicts a man's face in low relief, with rough drapery at the neck. The jaw and mouth on one side survive along with a flanking curl of hair, all within a linear circle. A channel at the base is for the introduction or escape of excess of the material to be moulded.

There is no sign of heating after the initial firing, so the mould was probably broken without ever having been used.

Material culture and the religious life

The medieval monastic artefactual assemblage is the most varied from all the sites of religious houses excavated in the London area so far, with a series of individual items that can be seen as directly relevant to the main functions of this rich and important foundation. There are several unusual individual objects of considerable intrinsic interest, but it is the exceptional diversity and size of the assemblage as a whole that is so remarkable and hints at the richness of the house at Bermondsey, with its continuing royal patronage and connections. That diversity and size is due to the very large numbers of accessioned finds (and window glass and building materials) from Dissolution and immediately post-Dissolution clearance and demolition contexts (detailed in Chapter 7.7), and in large part to one particular such material assemblage, that from the dumps inside the reredorter building (A[972] and A[2483], B9, period M9). Although the original provenance of this portable material is generally unknown, as often is its specific date, it is reasonable to assume that these items are from

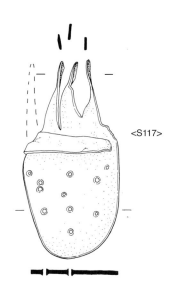

Fig 90 *Copper-alloy grater <S117> from the reredorter (B9, period M9) (scale 1:1)*

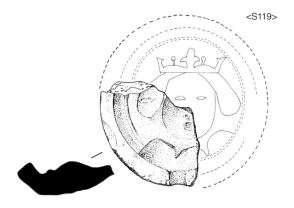

Fig 91 *London-type ware ceramic mould <S119> from garden area (OA11, period P1) (scale 1:2)*

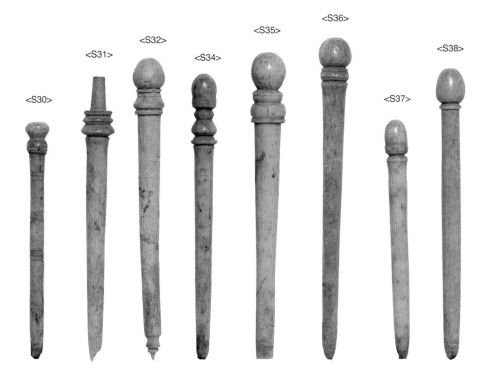

Fig 92 *Bone styli <S30>–<S32> (from B9, period M9), <S34> (OA6, period M9), <S35>, <S36> (OA9, period P1), <S37> and <S38> (OA12, period P1) (scale c 1:1)*

the lifetime of the monastic house, or (in the case of some) at least current during its Dissolution phase.

Writing, for example, is evidenced by finds of bone styli (Fig 92; <S30>–<S32>, <S34>–<S38>). Three seal matrices (<S47>, Fig 38; Fig 169; <S48>, Fig 64; <S49>, Fig 93) are further evidence for the production of written documents at the priory. A stone pestle (<S120>, Fig 178) with traces of red ?vermilion may have been used to prepare colour for manuscript illumination or mural painting. The production of vellum for manuscripts is suggested by vessels for the collection of urine which could have been used in tanning (below, 'Specialist craftspeople and industrial activity in the precinct').

The priory (not surprisingly) was certainly in possession of, if not producing, books as indicated by fragments of book mounts. A fragment of a hinged clasp (<S45>, Fig 94) from a demolition deposit in Open Area 9 was found in association with ceramics dated *c* 1350–*c* 1500. This, and another example (<S46> from A[972], Fig 94) may have belonged to the early 15th century (cf Egan 1998a, 277–80, nos 921–5 fig 214).

Stow's reference to a school at Bermondsey is supported to an extent by the mid 14th-century reference to Matilda de Myms's apprentice William who was to be given into the care and teaching of one Brother Thomas de Alshom for three years (*Cal Husting Wills*, i, 576; Stow 1603, i, 73). The practice of receiving boys (or girls, in a nunnery) as oblates was one of two ways of recruiting novices into a religious institution (Burton 1994, 174). Children were usually offered to a monastery as oblates by their parents or guardians. There, they received their education alongside aristocratic children until, at the age of 17, they made their vows of conversion to the religious life. The other class of novice consisted of literate adults; when the class

of oblates was abolished at the Lateran Council of 1215, adult novices came to be the more usual recruit (ibid). Much later, in the 18th century, the presence of a school in the porch over the

Fig 93 *Copper-alloy seal matrix <S49> from the reredorter (B9, period M9) (scale c 2:1)*

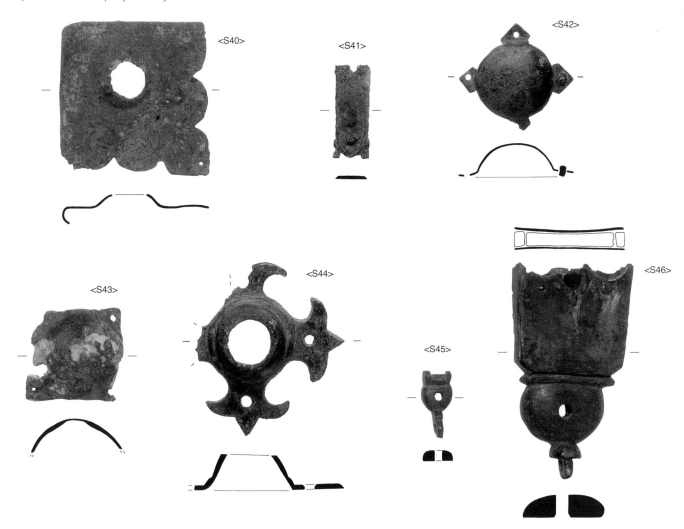

Fig 94 Copper-alloy book mounts <S40>–<S44> and book clasps <S45> and <S46> (scale c 1:1)

west door of the parish church of St Mary Magdalene may testify to the continuance of a schooling and teaching tradition centred on the priory.

A limited number of dress accessories was recovered, all of them from later contexts (Fig 95). These include a purse hanger (<S139>) and frame (<S137>), two buckles (<S124>, <S125>), two strapends (<S128>, <S130>), a dress hook (<S148>) and a lacechape (<S147>). Strapend <S130> is a form commonly found in the 14th century. Objects of personal adornment (Fig 96) include a brooch (<S143>) and a plain finger ring (<S144>). The smaller of the two brooches was engraved with a zigzag pattern round the frame and probably belonged to the 14th century since the fashion for copper-alloy circular brooches seems to have come to an end by c 1400 in London. The finger ring (Fig 96, <S144>) is also of copper alloy, but with the gilding intact it would have looked like a far more expensive accessory. A fragment of textile (<S50>) incorporated fine silver thread and was presumably from a rich ecclesiastical dress or a furnishing fabric. Of the three pendants found (Fig 96, <S149>, <S151>, <S152>), the sheet leaf, an apparently secular decoration, would have been highly fashionable before the late 15th century. The number and form of the dress accessories find a fairly close parallel with those at St Mary Spital (Egan 1997), apart, perhaps,

from the textile fragment, which signifies the presence of costly apparel or furnishings at the priory.

The importance of music and the sung liturgy in contemporary Benedictine houses is well attested. The act of making music suggests a high level of cultural attainment and presupposes certain skills which some, at least, of the community would have needed to possess. The robbing backfill (OA12, period P1) of Drain 4 in the former courtyard (OA9) yielded a square-headed peg (Fig 97, <S29>) which has been interpreted as a peg from a stringed instrument (cf A Wardle in Egan 1998a, nos 939–43), presumably in this case used as an accompaniment in religious services. Tuning pegs are recurrent finds at the sites of religious houses and have been found at Battle Abbey and at St Augustine's Abbey, Canterbury (G Egan in Thomas et al 1997, 109, table 14 category U).

A number of other items can be closely associated with the institution's religious life. The most notable is the copper-alloy figure of Christ crucified (Fig 98, <S25>; described in detail in Chapter 7.7, 'Monastic house period') and again found in the robbing debris in Drain 4 (period M9). This figure, decorated with champlevé enamel, was probably made at Limoges in France. It dates from the early 13th century, and is likely to have been attached to an altar or processional cross.

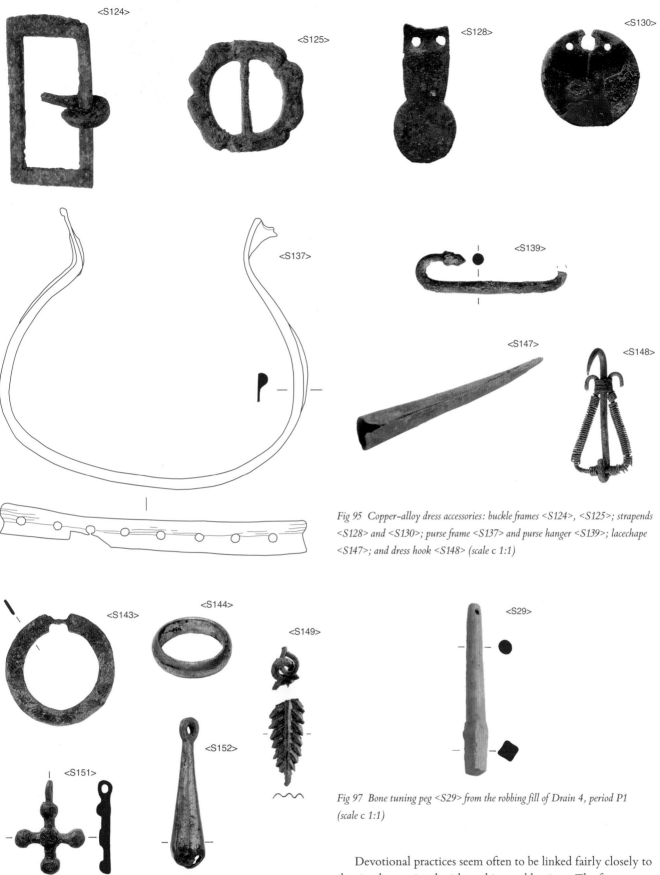

Fig 95 *Copper-alloy dress accessories: buckle frames <S124>, <S125>; strapends <S128> and <S130>; purse frame <S137> and purse hanger <S139>; lacechape <S147>; and dress hook <S148> (scale c 1:1)*

Fig 96 *Copper-alloy items of personal adornment: brooch <S143>; gilded finger ring <S144>; leaf pendant <S149>; cross pendant <S151>; and bell pendant <S152> (scale c 1:1)*

Fig 97 *Bone tuning peg <S29> from the robbing fill of Drain 4, period P1 (scale c 1:1)*

Devotional practices seem often to be linked fairly closely to the rituals associated with washing and hygiene. The free-standing lavabo outside the refectory (B6) and the recovery of fragments from two two-spouted water holders are evidence of both a practical concern with hygiene and washing and of the ritual and spiritual importance that the act of cleansing represented (Fig 63, <S85>, <S86>). These items would have had

141

<S25>

Fig 98 Copper-alloy figure of Christ crucified <S25> from the robbing fill of Drain 4 (OA9, period M9) (scale 1:1)

obvious domestic uses, but in the monastic context could have been used for ritual cleansing. One fragment was recovered from the cemetery (OA6) in period M8; the other was from the cess-type fill of the reredorter (B9) in period M9, suggesting that the latter at least was, like the urinals from this context, associated with the use of the reredorter (Chapters 3.7, 'Archaeological evidence', 'Reredorter (B9)', 7.5, 'Period M9, c 1430–1538').

The handle from a large basin in post-medieval slipped redware with green and clear glaze (PMSRG) (now lost) with a grotesque face-mask was found in the former cemetery (garden OA9, period P1); the basin may originally have had liturgical associations. A number of comparable examples are known in the Museum of London reserve collection, forming part of an important group of highly decorated basins with grotesque face-masks made in London and the Low Countries (Gaimster and Verhaeghe 1992, cf figs 2–3). The elaborate decoration

suggests that they were made for the luxury pottery market, which may account for their scarcity in the archaeological record (ibid, 312). The Bermondsey find, therefore, is especially important since it is the only example to have been recovered in London from an archaeological context. It has been suggested that these highly decorated and unusual bowls or basins were used as wine-coolers or that they were connected with aquamaniles, lavabos and ewers in function, and were thus made for 'the liturgical and social ritual of washing the hands' (ibid, 314). This practice was well established in the upper levels of society in the late Middle Ages, from where it percolated down the social scale, fuelled by the ever-present power of social emulation. It is likely that the vessels represent an attempt by potters to imitate in their own medium forms made in metalware, thus making them available to a wider socio-economic group or 'middle class' (ibid, 317). Since none of the other London finds has a clear provenance, it is difficult to see whether, as a group, they had particular religious associations. It is quite possible that there were also metalware toilet vessels in use in the abbey at the same date, but, in the absence of other evidence, the presence of this extraordinary ceramic form stands alone to represent a function which must once have been a normal feature of monastic life.

Certain accessories associated with personal hygiene and commonly found in medieval contexts include three earpicks (<S153>–<S155>, Fig 99) and two toothpicks (<S156>, <S192>, Fig 99), all from pre-Dissolution or Dissolution and later contexts. An incomplete pair of shears <S161>, probably dating to the late 14th century and discarded in a pit in the former cemetery (OA6, period M9), was probably employed for cutting hair.

An enigmatic find amongst the robbing debris in the southern, west–east stretch of Drain 4 (OA12, period P1) was a rectangular brick structure 0.63m by 0.53m and 0.31m high (Fig 100). The structure was lined inside and out with plaster, which on the outside was decorated with incised circles and whorls. Given its location, it is probable that the object came from the hall/lodgings (B8) or reredorter (B9) or from an unknown building south of the drain. It could be a font or cistern, except that the internal plaster lining makes an association with water unlikely. It is possible that, as a small altar table, it could have been housed in the hall/lodgings (B8), implying that one of the rooms in that building was in use as a chapel, an idea which, though possible, is unsubstantiated by other evidence. Brick was in use in the precinct in pre-Dissolution buildings and other structures (Chapter 7.4, 'Brick').

In support of an increasing privatisation and separation in areas of the monastic life is the presence of a large number of keys, mostly recovered from the reredorter (B9, period M9) and from the former cemetery (OA6, period P1) and the area south of the former reredorter (OA12, period P1), with examples occurring from the 13th century onwards (period M6). At least 12 rotary keys <S71>–<S76>, presumably a bunch, were recovered along with a slide key <S58> for a padlock from the same context in Open Area 12 (cf the bunch found at St Mary Spital: Egan 1997, 202–3 and 36, fig 26). A substantial key <S63> was presumably for a major door and another key <S64> may have been some kind of master or skeleton key that could operate a number of locks of similar size.

There are almost no luxury items of a domestic nature in the accessioned finds assemblage. A fragment of rare medieval white glass (Fig 101, <S100>) from the dump inside the reredorter building (B9, period M9) was from a rounded drinking vessel decorated with trails. Fragments of nine vessels in white glass are known from various, mainly secular, contexts in London. One other piece has been found on the site of a religious institution – the nunnery in Clerkenwell (cf Egan 1998a, nos 691–4, and Egan 1998b, in which the present item is no. 9).

The ceramic assemblage also presents a picture of apparent ordinariness, in contrast to, for example, the fish, bird and mammal evidence for high-staus consumption (above, 'Diet and

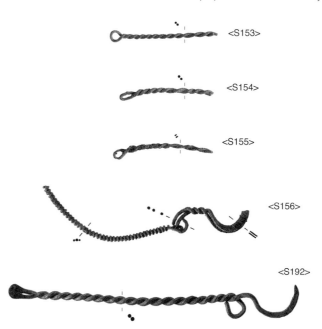

Fig 99 Copper-alloy earpicks <S153>–<S155> and toothpicks <S156> and <S192> (scale c 1:1)

Fig 100 Brick and plaster ?altar, from Drain 4 (OA12, period P1) (0.63 x 0.53 x 0.31m)

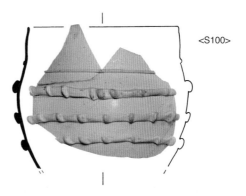

Fig 101 Fragment of white glass drinking vessel <S100> from the reredorter (B9, period M9) (scale c 1:2)

food preparation'). This is very likely the result of the limited nature of the excavations, wherein the areas that were fully excavated were the cemetery, chapel, infirmary and reredorter, not areas where high quality ceramics would be expected. At Carthusian Mount Grace Priory (Yorkshire North Riding), for example, individual monks' cells contained high levels of imports, whereas the kitchen area did not (G Coppack, pers comm; Coppack 1991). The suggestion is that the communal life may be conducted using more utilitarian items. Where notions of individualism come into play, along with the creation of spaces that are private, high quality personal items become invested with greater value. Ceramics are usually dumped close to where they were in use. The Bermondsey ceramics appear to derive in the main from buildings in the immediate vicinity and to reflect the use of these areas.

At Bermondsey, for each period, the ceramic groups are almost entirely of a mundane and domestic character, with few imports. For the 11th to 12th centuries (periods M3–M5) the rarity of imported wares such as red-painted ware (REDP) from the Rhineland and Andenne-type ware (ANDE) from the Meuse valley is in striking contrast to other London (City) sites of the period. A single sherd of a jug in early Rouen ware (ROUE) from Building 10 in period M5 is a high quality rarity. The priory's ceramic needs were in general met by what was available in the London area and to the south-east.

However, there are exceptions such as the Mill Green ware (MG) found in period M7 (c 1250–c 1330) that may well have represented a more expensive and perhaps even fashionable choice, used to grace the tables of the wealthier members of society. Also the occurrence in the late abbey period (M9) of small quantities of relatively exotic imports – such as the jar or *albarello* in Andalusian lustreware (ANDA), other Spanish vessels and jugs in Saintonge ware both with polychrome decoration (SAIP) and with green glaze (SAIG) jugs – show not only contacts with the Continent but pots that were used to decorative advantage in a limited sense, including at the table. It should be remembered too that high value items that are not broken are more likely to be removed, as may have happened at the Dissolution.

There are, however, also a number of ceramics with possible religious connections from Bermondsey Abbey. There are 14 sherds from a minimum of six vases or jugs in south Netherlands maiolica (SNTG; eg Fig 161, <P54>), dated to the late 15th to early 16th century, which may represent not so much conspicuous display, but which could have come from vessels with specific connotations. In the context of the abbey this could be highly significant. These come from the post-Dissolution robbing backfill of the drain to the east of the former reredorter (D4/OA12, period P1; Chapters 5.2, 'Monastic buildings completely or largely demolished', 'Reredorter (B9) and Drain 4, and creation of Open Area 12', 7.5, 'Period P1, 1538–c 1650', 'Former reredorter (B9) and Drain 4') as does another ceramic find with religious connections. This concentration of a small group of related artefacts with very specific and uncommon associations and functions is certainly suggestive.

Ring-handled vases in south Netherlands maiolica (SNTG) are often known as altar vases, a term derived in large part from the frequent occurrence of the IHS monogram and religious symbols in the decoration. This interpretation, however, is challenged by the frequency of secular motifs and the discovery of many examples in domestic contexts, where they may well have served as flower vases (Hurst et al 1986, 117, fig 54). Unfortunately, it is not possible to reconstruct the decoration on the Bermondsey examples, and it is also difficult to be certain of the original form for most of the surviving vessels – at least one jug is represented by a handle sherd, although these and other forms were rarely traded. It is certainly tempting to view the SNTG from the drain as part of the religious furnishings of the abbey at the end of the 15th and early 16th centuries, pre-dating the Dissolution, especially since there is a small cluster of related vessels in one area.

Another highly significant find from the drain (D4/OA12, period P1; Chapters 5.2, 'Monastic buildings completely or largely demolished', 'Reredorter (B9) and Drain 4, and creation of Open Area 12', 7.5, 'Period P1, 1538–c 1650', 'Former reredorter (B9) and Drain 4') is part of a miniature standing costrel or oil pot in Raeren stoneware (RAER) (Fig 102, <P24>). Only the rim and one lug at the neck survive (Hurst et al 1986, fig 94 no. 308). There is a marked concentration of these vessels on sites in Norway, in contexts dated to the last quarter of the 15th century (Reed 1992, 72). The form is clearly multifunctional, and may have been used, among other things, to hold oil in connection with, for example, spinning or for ointment. There is, however, evidence that they could also be used for religious purposes, since a number have been found in Norway in the vicinity of medieval churches, as well as in the bishop's residence in Oslo and the graveyard of St Olav's church in Trondheim. One was found under the altar tablet in Logtu church, north Trondelag, and another in a side altar in Trondenes church (ibid). The Logtu find contained fragments of bone and wood in a small silk bag, with a wax seal of Archbishop Gaute (1475–1510), while the Trondenes example held a splinter of bone wrapped in linen, sealed with wax; a piece of parchment attached to the costrel with an inscription in Latin clearly showed that the vessel had been deposited as a

<P24>

Fig 102 Miniature Raeren stoneware costrel or oil pot <P24> from the robbing fill of Drain 4 (OA12, period P1) (scale c 1:1)

reliquary at the time of the dedication of the altar. There is also speculation that the form could have been used to hold holy water, or perhaps oil for liturgical purposes, so its significance at Bermondsey Abbey is obvious. While it is possible that both the south Netherlands maiolica (SNTG) vases and the Raeren stoneware (RAER) costrel were used for non-religious purposes, their occurrence together is also suggestive. It seems highly probable that the SNTG vases or jugs were used in the abbey itself, rather than later, post-Dissolution, and that the drain backfill material came from a wider area of the abbey than most of the ceramic assemblages and was part of a phase of clearance and demolition prior to the construction of the post-Dissolution mansion.

A third ceramic find with religious connections was found in the latest dumps in the reredorter (B9, period M9). This was part of a beaker in Siegburg stoneware (SIEG; date range *c* 1300–1500), with an applied stamped medallion depicting the Madonna and Child (Fig 158, <P46>). While this imagery may have been common in its day, the beaker's occurrence in the reredorter perhaps adds weight to the suggestion that some of this very large deposit of debris was the result of clearance immediately prior to or at the Dissolution.

Many of the larger ceramic groups appear to contain significant amounts of residual pottery. This is true throughout the life of the monastery, and is also clearly seen, for example, in the post-Dissolution robbing backfill of the drain to the east of the former reredorter (D4/OA12, period P1; Chapters 5.2, 'Monastic buildings completely or largely demolished', 7.5, 'Period P1, 1538–*c* 1650', 'Former reredorter (B9) and Drain 4'). The issue of the date of the large dumps in the reredorter (B9, period M9) is the principal example of the potential curation in the priory of collections of ceramic articles (Chapters 3.7, 7.5). It may be that the products of kilns were ordered in large numbers and simply stored until used, if they ever were. Whatever the answer, the disposal of large amounts of consistently old ceramics appears to be a characteristic feature of St Saviour Bermondsey.

Specialist craftspeople and industrial activity in the precinct

The extensive accessioned finds assemblage indicates the presence of a number of specialist workers at the monastery. The requirement for masons and master masons on the site must have been fairly constant. Evidence for the measured survey of open areas and new buildings is reinforced by the recovery of a pair of copper-alloy dividers (Fig 103, <S164>) among the material dumped in the former reredorter (B9, period M9). This well-made instrument would have had a number of potential precision uses, such as the measuring of architectural plans or setting out ornate windows.

There is evidence for a range of manufacturing activities within the monastic precinct, mostly in the later periods (M7–M9, *c* 1250+). The significant number of urinals, both ceramic and glass vessels, found mainly in the reredorter (B9) in period M9, from the cess-type fill (A[4154]) and the overlying

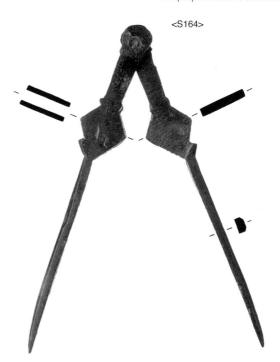

<S164>

Fig 103 Copper-alloy dividers <S164> from the reredorter (B9, period M9) (scale c 1:1)

dumps (A[972], A[2483]), and in Dissolution-period robbing (D4/OA12, period P1), along with other vessels such as jugs which had evidently been reused as urinals, points towards the collection of urine for tanning (Chapters 3.7, 'Archaeological evidence', 'Reredorter (B9)', 7.5, 'Period M9, *c* 1430–1538', 'Reredorter (B9)', 7.7, 'Monastic house period', 'Items used in the priory', 'Glass bottles'). At the Benedictine (Tironian) Humberstone Abbey (also Humberston; Lincolnshire) a substantial group of pre-Dissolution-date (early 16th-century) ceramics dumped in the reredorter drain included urinals, together with jugs with white salts on their inner surfaces suggesting they were used as urinals (Hayfield 1984), while a number of glass urinals were recovered from Merton Priory (Miller and Saxby 2007, 137). Tanning could take place on high-status sites, where the production of vellum for books was an important activity.

Another noteworthy collection of pottery relates to industrial functions, including distillation (Table 6). All the vessels are in 14th- and 15th-century fabrics. Parts of two cucurbits were found. One is in coarse Surrey-Hampshire border ware (CBW), and is represented by a narrow, rounded, almost pointed base, unglazed and with thick red haematite deposits internally (Fig 104, <P25>). The other is more complete; it is in late London-type ware (LLON) and of conical form with a deep upturned flange below the rim (Fig 104, <P26>). There is a small patch of glaze inside the base and a lightly inscribed six-pointed star is marked below the flange. Its purpose is now unclear, although it may have some alchemical associations. Four glass distilling vessels were also recovered, including at least one cucurbit – possibly, because of its size, a collecting vessel (Fig 104, <S110>; OA11). The distilling vessels,

Table 6 Industrial ceramics from the priory and abbey of St Saviour Bermondsey ordered by period and land use

Period of deposition	Land use	Context	Context type	Pottery fabric	Pottery form
M3	OA2	A[985]	(?flood) deposit	early Surrey ware (ESUR)	crucible
M8	D4	A[1865]	drain	Kingston-type ware (KING)	crucible
M9	OA6	A[2937]	pit fill	Kingston-type ware (KING)	crucible
	B9	A[972]	dump	coarse Surrey-Hampshire border ware (CBW); Kingston-type ware (KING)	crucible
	B9	A[972]	dump	coarse Surrey-Hampshire border ware (CBW); late London-type ware (LLON)	cucurbit
P1	OA9	A[3069]	pit fill	Spanish mercury jar (MERC)	mercury jar
	OA10	A[2184]	pit fill	-	crucible
	D4/OA12	A[515]	robbing fill	coarse Surrey-Hampshire border ware (CBW)	crucible
	D4/OA12	A[569]	robbing fill	London-area early post-medieval redware unglazed (PMRE)	alembic
	D4/OA12	A[2349]	robbing fill	Spanish mercury jar (MERC)	mercury jar

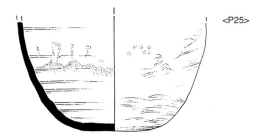

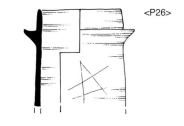

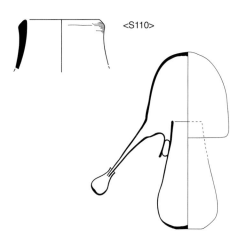

Fig 104 Ceramic and glass cucurbits, from period M9: in coarse Surrey-Hampshire border ware <P25> and late London-type ware <P26> (both from A[972], B9), and in glass <S110> (from OA11) (scale 1:4; reconstruction of cucurbit and alembic not to scale)

both ceramic and glass, came mostly from the reredorter dump (A[972], period M9), or the robbing fill of the adjacent drain (D4/OA12, period P1).

Cucurbits were used as an integral part of a distillation unit in the late medieval period and later (Moorhouse 1972; Haynes et al 1998). The liquid to be distilled was heated in the cucurbit and another vessel, the alembic, with a domed top leading to a folded shoulder, rested on top. The evaporated liquid condensed on the alembic dome and ran down the sides to the lower folded collecting channel, before being directed down the spout (Fig 104). When associated with evidence for metalworking, they may indicate that the production of sulphuric acid for use in parting precious metals and assaying was taking place in the vicinity. Evidence for this process has been found in 16th-century contexts in the Cripplegate area and at the Tower of London (City of London) (Sewart 1996; Pearce 2001). More recently, sherds from probable cucurbits in coarse Surrey-Hampshire border ware (CBW), identical in form to the Bermondsey example, have been found in 15th-century contexts at Baltic Exchange (City of London) clearly associated with metalworking (Pearce 2002, table 22). These important sherds show that the process was known in London at this date, rather earlier than previously thought. It appears that some form of metalworking was being carried out at St John Clerkenwell and at St Mary Clerkenwell at the same date (ie pre-Dissolution), although on a very small scale (Blackmore 2004, 354; Sloane and Malcolm 2004, 221; St Mary Clerkenwell: L Blackmore, pers comm). Alternatively, the use of distilling apparatus in the preparation of herbal remedies should also be considered. This activity is known to have been carried out on monastic sites for several hundred years, the principal aim being to prepare the distilled juices of healing plants grown in the physic garden by releasing their essential oils (Wilson 1973). Alchemical processes were commonly practised in religious houses and their use involved both glass and ceramic vessels (Moorhouse 1993, 142). Moorhouse quotes a number of late 15th-century 'recipes' for the production of *aqua vita* or alcohol, for producing pigments and for medicines (ibid,

145–6). The absence of definite metalworking residues on the sherds makes this a distinct possibility for these Bermondsey ceramics.

The industrial ceramics include five sherds from two crucibles in Kingston-type ware (KING) and coarse Surrey-Hampshire border ware (CBW), one of which has a deep red, powdery deposit inside the base. In total, there are ten sherds from a minimum of seven crucibles recorded on site A (Table 6). This is a low figure and shows that, although some form of industrial activity making use of such vessels took place on site, it was never an important feature of the life of the monastery. With the exception of one sherd which may have come from a glass-working crucible, all crucibles are in Surrey whiteware fabrics, whose refractory clay was ideal for the strong temperatures required to melt metals. They may have been used for copper alloys, although no residues survive. Alternatively, they may have had some use in the preparation of medicines. Most examples are burnt and sooted to some extent.

Two other ceramic finds may have associations with medicinal preparations or with metalworking: sherds from two Spanish mercury jars (MERC), one of which was found in the (period P1) robbing backfill of the drain (D4) west of the reredorter (Fig 162, <P60>). These small, glazed, thick-walled jars were used to transport and store mercury. Mercury readily forms alloys or amalgams with various metals, including gold, silver and copper. When the amalgam is heated, the low boiling point of the mercury causes it to evaporate, leaving behind the metal with which it was amalgamated. The mercury can then be recovered by allowing the vapourised metal to condense on a cold surface (Hodges 1964, 92). Mercury can also be used in gilding and silvering, when an amalgam of the metal with gold or silver is applied to the surface of the object to be treated, and then heated to expel the mercury. Alternatively, a copper or bronze object can be treated with mercury to form a copper amalgam on the surface, and gold leaf applied. Heating once again dispels the mercury (ibid, 96–7). Given the other evidence for metalworking from the site, it is quite likely that one or more of these processes were taking place.

Waste from metalworking in the form of scraps of copper-alloy sheeting and casting waste or slag, together with the unfinished products of the manufacturing process, indicate that metal objects were indeed being produced on site. A two-part ceramic mould (Fig 105, <S166>) with external luting would have produced four rings probably of copper alloy, with diameters of 15mm, 16mm, 18mm and 23mm. As there is no connecting groove between the rings, the flow of metal through the mould must have been along channels in the corresponding, missing part of the mould. The products, if they were plain rings, seem more likely to have been buckle frames than for curtains (Egan and Pritchard 1991, 57–9, nos 211–15). The additional find of an incomplete copper-alloy rectangular buckle frame (Fig 95, <S124>), which has excess metal from the casting blocking some of the loop, adds weight to the suggestion that buckles were being manufactured on site. Some confirmation for the production of everyday dress accessories within a religious complex in the medieval period is given by finds from the

Fig 105 Ceramic metalworking mould <S166> (unphased) (scale c 1:2)

Bedern site at York (Richards 1993; Egan 1996), while Merton Priory, unusually for a London monastic site, produced a small ironworking assemblage (Miller and Saxby 2007, 137).

Two shells or bones of common cuttlefish (*Sepia officinalis*) were recovered from the reredorter dumping in period M9 (A[972], B9). This species is common around all British coasts at depths of up to 250m and is particularly abundant in inshore waters during the summer spawning period (Hayward et al 1996, 262). These 'bones' are known to be useful as easily worked blocks suitable for manufacture into 'once-only' disposable moulds for casting small metal items (Pipe 1990). Cuttlefish 'bone' may also be ground into a fine powder called 'pounce', which was used for drying the ink on newly scribed documents.

The manufacture of specialist items at St Saviour Bermondsey is also attested by the recovery of three lead hands (<S172>–<S174>, Fig 106; Fig 187; Chapter 7.7, 'Monastic house period') which appear to have been for the manufacture of figurines either on site or at another centre. The lead hands would be used to make a clay mould which could then be used to reproduce the hands in a metal such as silver or copper alloy. These master forms were apparently not completely finished when discarded in rubbish pits in the cemetery (OA6, period M9), but the end products may well have been intended to be devotional figures of saints given the attitude of the hands. These finds demonstrate the presence of skilled medieval craftworkers in metal, producing items either for the monastery itself or for sale to a wider public (see below, 4.4 and Fig 108, for pilgrims' badges).

Bead making also took place within the precinct in the later monastic periods. A bone bead, with flat ends (one with a concentric groove) and a bifacially bevelled edge, was recovered from the dumping in the reredorter (B9, period M9; <S39>, Fig 107). The bead was turned and smoothed from wear and had presumably been worn as part of a cheap rosary. Two parts of a broken waste panel from bead making (<S175>, Fig 107) were found in a demolition spread (OA10, period P1) over the former cemetery and fields (OA6, OA3). The panel is a cattle or horse metapodial, trimmed flat, from which eight circular pieces of bone, with diameters up to 12mm, had been cut by turning

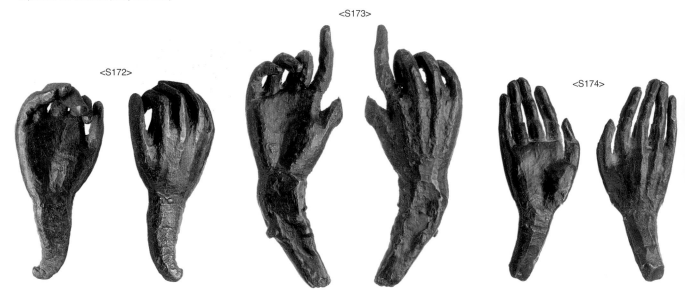

Fig 106 *Lead master forms <S172>–<S174> from the former cemetery (OA6, period M9) (scale c 1:1)*

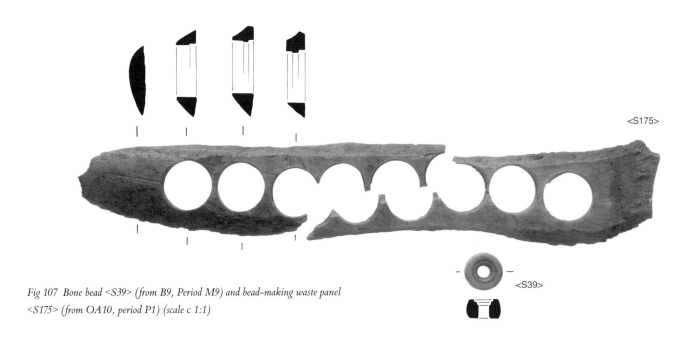

Fig 107 *Bone bead <S39> (from B9, Period M9) and bead-making waste panel <S175> (from OA10, period P1) (scale c 1:1)*

from both sides. It is likely that bone beads were manufactured on site for cheap rosaries, although similar waste has been found on secular London sites (Egan and Pritchard 1991, nos 1557–81).

4.4 The monastery in its wider context

The monastic economy

The priory's income came principally from its properties. It received tithes from the churches under its ownership (spiritualities) and money in the form of rents and the payment of leases from tenants occupying secular monastic properties (temporalities). The success of the priory therefore depended initially on how much it could attract in the way of gifts and endowments. Shortly after 1100, Henry I confirmed by charter grants of land made to St Saviour Bermondsey since the time of its foundation. As well as the manor of Bermondsey and Rotherhithe, the grants included lands in Essex, Hertfordshire, Surrey, Kent and Somerset.

In the papal Taxatio of 1291 (the assessment made in that year for the tenth collected for Pope Nicholas IV) Bermondsey's annual total income amounted to £208, of which £160 derived from temporalities and £48 from spiritualities. Of the total, 92% (£192) was made up of items worth £2 or more (Table 7).

In the *Valor Ecclesiasticus* of 1535 Bermondsey's annual total gross income amounted to £548, of which £412 derived from temporalities and £135 from spiritualities (*Val Eccl*, ii, 58–60). Of the total, 88% (£483) was made up of items worth £10 or more (Table 8).

The only feature that these two sets of data, from 1291 and 1535, have in common is the 4:1 ratio of income from

Table 7 Sources of income listed in the Taxatio *for 1291 valued at more than £2, by county and parish*

County	Parish	Value of spiritualities	Value of temporalities	Total value
Surrey	Camberwell	-	£6	£6
	Croydon	-	£11	£11
	Bermondsey	£7	-	£7
Middlesex	London*	-	£50	£50
Kent	Birling	-	£11	£11
	Charlton	-	£11	£11
	Sutton	-	£11	£11
Essex	Hallingbury	-	£9	£9
	Sheering	-	£11	£11
	Harlow	£2	-	£2
	Fifield	£3	-	£3
	Doddinghurst	-	£2	£2
Buckinghamshire	Burnham	-	£3	£3
Hertfordshire	Bengeo	-	£4	£4
Bedfordshire	Bedford	-	£3	£3
Huntingdonshire	Ellington	£4	-	£4
Berkshire	Upton	£7	£4	£11
Dorset	Melcombe	£7	-	£7
Somerset	Kingweston	-	£7	£7
	Preston	-	£8	£8
Kent	Stone	-	£3	£3
	Genele	£2	£3	£5
Wiltshire	Inglesham	-	£3	£3
Total		£32	£160	£192

* Income from all the priory's London parishes, see Table 9

Table 8 Sources of income listed in the Valor Ecclesiasticus *for 1535 valued at more than £10, by county and parish*

County	Parish	Value of spiritualities	Value of temporalities	Total value
Surrey	Bermondsey and Rotherhithe	-	£187	£187
	Warlingham	-	£20	£20
	Croydon	£24	-	£24
	Southwark	-	£15	£15
	Dulwich	-	£13	£13
	Leigham	-	£13	£13
	Camberwell	£10	-	£10
Middlesex	London	-	£25	£25
Kent	Chalk	-	£20	£20
	Charlton	-	£20	£20
	Shorne	£20	-	£20
	Cobham	£12	-	£12
	Kemsing	£12	-	£12
Essex	Cowick	-	£15	£15
	Hallingbury	-	£10	£10
Hertfordshire	Widford	-	£28	£28
	Bengeo	£9	-	£9
Berkshire	Upton	-	£14	£14
Somerset	Preston	-	£16	£16
Total		£87	£396	£483

periods in the priory's history demonstrate (eg the tenure of Adam de Stratton: Chapter 3.5, 'Documentary evidence'). The impetus for the alienation of many of its landholdings from the end of the 12th century may have come about as a desire to raise capital to fund building programmes. Whatever the reason, it appears to have had a detrimental effect on the overall financial health of the monastery in later years. The financial soundness of St Saviour was also greatly damaged by the natural disasters which affected its estates close to home on the south bank of the Thames. The priory's local properties seem to have grown more numerous from the end of the 13th century.

St Saviour Bermondsey as a London monastery

St Saviour's property interests in the City of London are of special interest in that they constituted its earliest endowments, given by Alwyn Childe in 1082. In the papal Taxatio of 1291 the priory was credited with temporalities in 60 London parishes, totalling £49 7s 3d and accounting for 25% of its total income in that year (Table 9). These were supplemented by a further £7 10s 8d from St Andrew Holborn, St Magnus, St George (Eastcheap) and the abbot of Westminster, though no spiritualities from the City appear to be listed in 1291. No direct comparison is possible with the circumstances on the eve of the Dissolution since the *Valor Ecclesiasticus* fails to itemise the abbey's City interests and simply totals them at £17 6s 1d. From temporalities alone, however, it is very clear that the value of

temporalities and from spiritualities. Of the discrepancies the most notable is Surrey, which in 1291 could only muster an income of £25, but in 1535 one of £262 from temporalities (plus £53 from spiritualities), well over half the total income for the period. Since Bermondsey's holdings in Surrey must always have represented a large proportion of its entire estates, and the data for 1291 were obviously incomplete, the likeliest explanation is the severe flooding of that year, which would have affected most of the manors in question. Another concern is the 66% fall in the value of London properties and rents between 1291 (£50) and 1535 (£17).

Table 7 and Table 8 indicate that the greater source of the priory's income was the rents and lease payments arising from its wide property interests in the surrounding counties. In effect, the priory was a landlord on a large scale and a major administrative centre (Chapter 1.2). It appeared to have been able to act independently in its financial and property dealings. Certainly St Saviour was free of the requirement to solicit papal permission; whether the house had to refer to the vicar-general at Lewes Priory or to La Charité-sur-Loire, its mother house in France, is not known. The priory's success was also very much a matter of management, as various disastrous

the priory's London assets decreased by almost exactly two-thirds between the two dates (*Val Eccl*, ii, 58–60).

Most of the priory's interests took the form of rents or quitrents. The ownership of land in the City was mentioned in only six cases: land in All Hallows Gracechurch Street in the reign of King John (*Cat Anc Deeds*, ii, A2215); land to the east of the steelyard in All Hallows the Great sold for a rent soon after 1297 (*Ann Monast*, iii, 481; *Cal Inq Misc*, iv, 275; *Cal Close R*, 1381–5, 501); land in All Hallows Lombard Street mentioned in 1212–13 (*Cart Holy Trinity*, no. 335); land in St John Walbrook granted to Bermondsey before 1249 and sold for a rent in 1249–53 (*Cart Holy Trinity*, nos 460, 462); tenements in St Martin Vintry and St Nicholas Cole Abbey held in 1235–6 (*London Possessory Assizes*, 170); and tenements in St Mary le Bow and St Mary Magdalen Milk Street exchanged with Lewes Priory for property in St Olave Southwark in 1292 (*Ann Monast*, iii, 467). A further case, which may be identified with any of the six listed, concerned City land held by the prior in 1244 (Chew and Weinbaum 1970, no. 216).

A common feature of the references to priory lands in the City is that they all date from the 13th century or (in a single case) the early years of the 14th. Several of them are expressly noted as having been sold off in exchange for an annual rent by named priors. The prior who sold what must have been an extremely valuable waterfront tenement next to the

steelyard was William, who was in office from 1293 to 1297, his tenure coinciding with the major inundations of 1294 when the priory's plight was probably severe. Limited as the evidence is, it seems likely that Bermondsey's straitened circumstances throughout the second half of the 13th century and the first half of the 14th, and its constant need for ready cash in the face of repeated flooding on the one hand and unrelenting financial exactions from popes and kings on the other, was the principal explanation for the loss of its freehold property and consequent sharp diminution of revenue from the City that had once been much the largest single source of its income.

This lies in sharp contrast to the situation described at St Mary Clerkenwell, where there is no evidence for a great change in property distribution and where the value of the nunnery's properties in London in 1535 are recorded as £172 19s 4d (*Val Eccl*, i, 395). A comparison of the figures from each house indicates that St Saviour Bermondsey owed much less to London than those religious houses outside London on its northern purlieus. Perhaps the same conditions pertained for the monastery's income and holdings as for its ceramic trade network, in that it looked south of the Thames to its own immediate hinterland, the river being in fact a boundary, if not a barrier?

The record made at the London eyre of 1276 of the death of a Londoner at the hands of a monk of Bermondsey following a Sunday wrestling match between the prior's men – in other words, presumably, his servants – and those of the town reveals a different aspect of relations between the monastery and its neighbours. On Sunday 4 September 1261, Richard de Borham, a Londoner, and many other people from town, attended a wrestling match (*luctus*) at 'Bermundeseye outside the City'. There they wrestled with the men of the prior of Bermondsey. A quarrel arose among them and when Richard and his companions chased the prior's men into the priory, a monk called Arnulf and other monks from the priory entered a solar above the gate and pelted Richard and his companions with stones. A stone thrown by Arnulf crushed Richard and he was killed. From the records of the court (15 years after the alleged event) it emerged that Arnulf was still alive and living in the priory. He was arrested and the prior of Bermondsey was ordered to be distrained on all his lands; the mayor and alderman were instructed to trace persons present at the fight and death. Arnulf, asked at length how he wished to clear himself of the death, declared that he was a clerk and not bound to answer. The mayor and aldermen declared that he was guilty of the killing, and it was testified that he had previously been arrested and released on bail to William de Kent, mercer, William de Laufar, spicer, and others, who had failed to present him. Consequently they were all in mercy, and because Arnulf had been harboured in the priory from the time of the murder until the present, and it was adjudged the prior and convent knew his crime, judgement should be on the prior for harbouring him (Weinbaum 1976, no. 116; cf also ibid, 613, 615 and *Cal Close R*, 1261–4, 10–11).

Table 9 *The value of Bermondsey's temporalities in the City of London in 1291, in descending order of value (*Taxatio)

London parish	Value (£ s d)	London parish	Value (£ s d)
St Mary le Bow	£3 0 0	St John Walbrook	£0 10 0
St Dionis	£2 11 4	St Mary Magdalen Fish Market	£0 10 0
St Botolph Billingsgate	£2 7 0	St Matthew Friday Street	£0 10 0
St Leonard Eastcheap	£2 6 9	St Michael Cornhill	£0 10 0
St Martin Cannon Street	£2 4 7	St Thomas Apostle	£0 10 0
St Michael Cannon Street	£2 3 7	St Olave Monkwell Street	£0 9 0
St Dunstan in the East	£2 3 0	All Hallows Barking	£0 8 9
St Peter Wood Street	£2 0 3	St Andrew Cornhill	£0 8 4
St Martin Vintry	£1 16 0	St Michael Paternoster	£0 8 0
St Pancras	£1 15 0	All Hallows Gracechurch	£0 7 0
St Andrew Hubbard	£1 13 0	Holy Trinity the Less	£0 7 0
St Nicholas Cole Abbey	£1 10 0	St Botolph Aldersgate	£0 6 8
St Mary Bothaw	£1 8 4	St Nicholas Shambles	£0 6 8
St James Garlickhithe	£1 7 8	St Christopher	£0 6 0
St Lawrence Cannon Street	£1 6 10	St Stephen Walbrook	£0 6 0
St Michael le Quern	£1 2 10	St Michael Queenhithe	£0 5 6
All Hallows the Great	£1 1 4	All Hallows Coleman church	£0 5 0
St Margaret at the Bridge	£0 17 0	St Benet	£0 5 0
St John Zachary	£0 16 0	St George	£0 5 0
St Benet Sherehog	£0 14 8	St Michael Wood Street	£0 5 0
St Mary Woolchurch	£0 14 0	All Hallows Fenchurch Street	£0 4 8
St Sepulchre	£0 14 0	St Mary at Hill	£0 4 6
St Edmund Gracechurch Street	£0 13 4	St Swithun	£0 4 6
St Margaret Pattens	£0 13 4	St Margaret Moyses	£0 4 0
St Clement Cannon Street	£0 12 8	St Martin Outwich	£0 3 0
St Nicholas Olaf	£0 12 0	St Vedast	£0 3 0
St Agnes	£0 11 0	St Duncan in the West	£0 2 8
St Mary Abchurch	£0 10 3	St Nicholas Hakun	£0 2 2
All Hallows the Less	£0 10 0	St Michael Bassishaw	£0 2 1
All Hallows Staining	£0 10 0	St Mary Monthaut	£0 2 0

St Saviour Bermondsey as pilgrimage centre

Bermondsey was a focus of pilgrimage due to the discovery (according to the annals) of a Holy Rood on the banks of the Thames near the priory in 1117. Evidence for St Saviour Bermondsey as a pilgrim attraction was recovered in 1992 from a waterfront site opposite the Tower of London, west of Tower Bridge Road and immediately west of Vine Lane (VIN88; site Z on Fig 3). This excavation site (ABO92; Abbots Lane) lay to the north of the Bermondsey precinct and was the location of the medieval moated residence known as Fastolf Place (Blatherwick and Bluer 2009). A pilgrim badge recovered from the late 16th-century fill of the moat is identifiable as a souvenir of Bermondsey (ABO92 <90>, [4]; ibid, 138, 200; described and illustrated in Egan 2005, 204–5; Fig 108).

This pilgrim souvenir is a lead badge that features Christ crowned and bearded, nailed (? or tied) by the hands to a cross and wearing a long tunic, standing on a column capital (for what follows see Egan 1999; 2005, 204–5, no. 1133). Flanking scrolls carry in blackletter (? mixing some capital letters with lower case) the Latin legend, *ecce (?)signum // berm·(?ondsi)y*, with the last word particularly difficult to make out in its entirety; this can be read and translated as 'the sign of Bermondsey'. The image is in the style of the 11th century or earlier, but the use of blackletter is characteristic of pilgrim badges of the late 15th or early 16th century.

The defining features are the crown and the garment, which is probably the seamless robe worn by Christ on the way to Calvary, as described in the Gospels. The architectural support means that the image was proably based on a specific piece of sculpture or metalwork at the shrine of origin and the legend on this more recent find seems to confirm a Bermondsey origin. This is the latest of a small number of similar objects found in London, and beyond, which Spencer (1998, 169–70, no. 190d and variants 190e–g) had earlier suggested were images of the rood at Bermondsey Abbey. Spencer further suggested that the similarities between Christ crucified on the (probable) Bermondsey souvenirs and Christ crucified on badges from Lucca, Italy, derived from the rood at Bermondsey being a copy of that at Lucca (ibid, 254–5).

These badges are physical testimony to the enduring popularity of the Bermondsey rood to pilgrims. Popular

Fig 108 Pilgrim souvenir badge depicting St Saviour's rood from Abbots Lane (ABO92 <90> [4]) (scale c 1:1; detail 2:1)

devotion to the Bermondsey rood in the 15th and early 16th centuries is documented for example in a few wills. William Kelshall was buried in the chapel of Holy Cross in 1432 and was to be joined by his wife Alice (TNA: PRO, PROB 11/3 quires 16 and 19); John Wippill clerk asked in 1504 to be buried at (*coram*) the image of St Saviour (TNA: PRO, PROB 11/14 quire 18 fo 138); Matthew Baker in 1513 asked to be buried before the image of St Saviour if he died at Bermondsey (TNA: PRO, PROB 11/17 quire 18 fo 139). Pilgrimages to the rood are occasionally documented in other sources: John Paston wrote on Holy Rood day, 14 September 1465, to his wife Margaret, 'I pray you visit the Rood of North Door [in St Paul's], and St Saviour at bermondsey, while you abide in London ...' (Graham 1926, 182–3). By the 1530s, however, offerings to Holy Cross (ad crucem Sancti Salvator') were said to be worth only 66s 8d per annum (*Val Eccl*, ii, 58). The image of St Saviour is recorded as being taken down along with those of other pilgrimage saints early in 1538 (*VCH* 1967, 74).

The role of St Saviour Bermondsey within the Cluniac Order and relations with other religious

There are numerous instances of priors visiting Cluny, one of the main ways in which the Order ensured its discipline and coherence. Non-attendance had to be explained (eg 1238: Duckett 1888, ii, 201, item 441). When priors attended the chapter general they were armed with royal letters of protection for specified periods varying between six months and two years. Though frequent these were not regular and, as recorded in for example the 13th century, hardly met the expectation that heads should attend chapters general every two years. The more usual arrangement was for six to eight months, as in 1273 and 1286 (*Cal Pat R*, 1272–81, 7; 1281–92, 225). Lengthier periods (eg in 1259: *Cal Pat R*, 1258–66, 14; 1292: *Cal Pat R*, 1281–92, 506; 1298: *Cal Pat R*, 1292–1301, 53, 328) are perhaps to be explained (as in 1292) by visits to both Cluny and the mother house of La Charité-sur-Loire. On these occasions the priors would appoint others to act for them in their absence, and for similarly specified periods, and the appointments would be ratified by letters patent or, occasionally, letters close, along with the grants of protection. Numerous royal protections and passports continued to be issued in favour of the abbots of Bermondsey on their visits abroad in the 14th century, seven of them in the period up to 1325, though only five in the long period 1325–60. Most of those will have been to the chapter general at Cluny, mother house of the Order, or to La Charité-sur-Loire, Bermondsey's own mother house.

Relations with the priory's diocesan, the bishop of Winchester, were not always cordial, particularly in the first two decades of the 14th century when the priory's finances were at their worst (Chapter 3.5, 'Documentary evidence'). Of frequent concern to the compilers of the Bermondsey annals were settlements of diputes with other clergy and houses concerning tithes and pensions (eg in the 13th century: *Ann Monast*, iii, 456–65; and 14th century: *Ann Monast*, iii, 481); the sums involved varied considerably, both major and minor amounts being recorded.

Symptomatic of Bermondsey's restored stability and good reputation in the final third of the 14th century was the appointment of two successive priors, Peter de Tenolio and Richard Dunton, as vicar-generals in England of the prior of La Charité-sur-Loire (*Cal Pat R*, 1367–70, 362; 1374–7, 354). On 26 November 1390 the king licensed Bermondsey's prior, along with the archbishop of Canterbury, as legate of the Holy See, and the prior of Thetford to exercise the jurisdiction granted to them by the pope over places and persons of the Cluniac Order

(*Cal Pat R*, 1388–92, 334). On 18 January 1397, Archbishop Thomas restored the temporalities of Wenlock to its prior and to John, Prior of Bermondsey, who had been deputed by the pope during the schism to take the places of the abbot of Cluny and prior of La Charité-sur-Loire, and whose fealty the king had taken (*Cal Pat R*, 1396–9, 61). On 17 November 1399 Abbot John of Bermondsey and Thomas Styward received from the king the custody of the manors of Cluniac houses in England, to be held for the duration of the wars with France (*Cal Fine R*, 1399–1405, 19).

5

After the Dissolution: the development of Bermondsey House, 1538–c 1650 (period P1)

5.1 Documentary and graphic evidence

Tenants and owners of the site

On 1 May 1539 the house and site of the late monastery of Bermondsey were leased to Robert Southwell, gentleman. Included in the terms of the lease was an acre of adjacent land called the Coneyyard and the liberty of fishing and hawking in the marshes of Bermondsey and Rotherhithe, all for a term of 21 years at a rent of 53s 4d (TNA: PRO, E315/212, fo 136; *L and P Hen VIII*, xv, 56(7)). The lease excluded all manner of buildings within the monastic site which the king ordered to be demolished and removed. Southwell, who was solicitor of Augmentations and Receiver of Requests, paid £498 on 8 July 1541 for the purchase of the site, including in particular the church, bell tower and churchyard (a common descriptive phrase in Augmentations documents), and all buildings within the precinct, together with the New Eastgate, the garden next to the dormitory, the bakehouse, the dry larder house and various pieces of land (TNA: PRO, C66/702, m 3 (renumbered 44); *L and P Hen VIII*, xvi, 1056(37)).

Southwell's earlier petition of ?10 March 1541 (TNA: PRO, E318/20/1032) and the subsequent lease and sale detail the property that Southwell obtained. It included all that messuage, mansion and tenement called the New Eastgate situated next to the site of the said late monastery (*totum illud mesuagium mansionem et tenementum vocat le Newe Eastgate situat' iuxta scitum dicti nuper monasterii*) and all houses, cellars, solars pertaining to the same messuage and tenement (*ac omnia domas celaria et solaria eidem mesuagio et tenemento*) (TNA: PRO, C66/702, m 3 (renumbered 44)); the lands extended from the New Eastgate to the end of the house called *le greate heyhouse* in Bermondsey (TNA: PRO, E318/20/1032).

On 28 August, Southwell and his wife Margaret received a licence to alienate his newly acquired property to Sir Thomas Pope, treasurer of the Court of Augmentations, and his wife Elizabeth (TNA: PRO, C66/755, m 35 (renumbered 19); *L and P Hen VIII*, xvi, 1135(15)). Since October 1539 Sir Thomas Pope had received annuities from the estates of numerous monasteries including Bermondsey (*L and P Hen VIII*, xvi, 745; xvii, 184). On 30 April 1544 he paid £387 19½d for the purchase of property in St Mary Magdalene Bermondsey and Rotherhithe formerly belonging to the abbey (ibid, xix(1), 10(9)). He had also been petitioning for the lease of other parcels of abbey property in and around the precinct as early as 1543, including *le Whytyngplace*, a garden outside the wall of the abbey, the New Eastgate, *Utterwildes* and *le Covent*. According to Stow 'the Abbey church was then pulled downe by sir Thomas Pope knight, and in place thereof, a goodly house builded of stone and timber' (1603, ii, 67). Manning and Bray add that Pope was said to have taken down the church and adjacent buildings, and to have erected a dwelling-house on his manor from the materials, and that the property, thenceforth called Bermondsey House, contained some 20 acres (8.1ha) (1804–14, i, 203), representing a third of the area of the precinct as reconstructed by Martin (1926, 198; cf Chapter 4.2, 'The precinct and home grange').

In 1544 John Erle was in dispute with Sir Thomas Pope and his wife Elizabeth concerning, it was recorded, a watermill, wharf, orchard, 20 acres (8.1ha) of meadow, 2 [?w—] and verge of one of two walls and of a herbage extending from the mill to the Stewse called Rotherhithe Stewse, in St Mary Magdalene, Bermondsey and Rotherhithe; also the eastern part of a dock called Seynt Savyours Dock in Bermondsey; excepting all fisheries and increase of swans with the said dock and all goods and chattels of felons and fugitives in Bermondsey (*Surrey feet of fines*, 1509–58, no. 448). On 26 September 1544 John Pope and Antony Foster of London were granted property including a rent of 3s 4d and service as the common fine of Bermondsey manor, a watermill called *Sainte Savyars Myll* in the parishes of St Mary Magdalene, Bermondsey and Rotherhithe, late in the tenure of John Curlew and now of John Erle, with the fishery and fee of swans within the dock called *Savyars Doke* in St Saviour Bermondsey (*L and P Hen VIII*, xix(1), 340(45)). Pope's licence of 16 January 1549 to alienate to Alderman William Garrarde included the earthen wall and land of John Yerle in which lies a certain conduit commonly called a sluyce on the east (*Cal Pat R*, 1547–53, i, 368).

The property was reconveyed to Southwell by Pope on 4 March 1555, the remainder of the estate originally purchased from Sir Robert being sold on 10 November 1556 to Robert Trappes, goldsmith of London (Manning and Bray 1804–14, i, 203). By 6 July 1557, Sir Robert Southwell was once more in possession of the 'site and capital messuage, mansion house of the dissolved monastery of Bermondsey nigh unto Southwark', which had been sold to him by Sir Thomas Pope. On the same day he leased it to Sir Henry Sydney for £20 a year for the first two years and £30 subsequently, with the option of purchase if Sir Henry or his heirs paid £600 in a single payment (TNA: PRO, C78, 20/13). In the accounts for 1557–8 of John Bagott, servant to Sir William and Sir Henry Sydney, are references to 'necessaries laid into the place at Barmesey, 28s' and to the 'carriage of stuff from Westminster to other places and Barmeseye, 7s 6d' (HMC 1925, 254). On 14 March 1561, Sir Robert's son, Thomas 'of London, gentleman', was licensed to alienate the 'site, capital messuage or mansion of the lately dissolved monastery of Bermondsey, otherwise called Barmondsey place' to Thomas, Earl of Sussex, and Henry Sydney Kt, president of the council in the marches of Wales, and their heirs and assigns (TNA: PRO, C66/964, m 4; *Cal Pat R*, 1560–3, 20). Thomas, Earl of Sussex, died there in 1583 (Manning and Bray 1804–14, i, 203). A letter dated 9 January 1590 from his brother and heir, Earl Henry, to Lord Willoughby is signed from his 'howse of Barmondsey' (HMC 1907, 303).

On 19 June 1601 Earl Henry's son, Earl Robert, who was indebted for £3260, sold to James Anton his:

capital messuage mansion house and site of the dissolved monastery of St Saviour of Barmondsey otherwise called Barmondsey place and all orchards gardens stables houses

buildings and grounds whatsoever situate lying and being within the walls inclosing the said capital messuage mansion house, and all his part of a stable without the walls of the said capital messuage and mansion house; [and] also his estate and interest and term of years of and in a convenient place in the stable yard in Bermondsey, in which yard the late stables of Sir Thomas Pope did then stand, and of and in the land enclosed with a standing wall containing by estimation one and a half acres [0.6ha] lying on the north side of the late mansion house of the said Sir Thomas Pope in Bermondsey being then divided into two separate gardens late in the tenure and occupation of Thomas Devill deceased. (TNA: PRO, C2, JAS I/H19/30)

In the first half of the 17th century the site changed hands several times and on the death of the holder in 1631 it was to be divided among three heirs, signifying the end of the property as such (*VCH* 1912, 21).

The construction of Pope's mansion

The church had probably already suffered much damage from the king's commissioners and stone-hungry locals between 1538 and the time when Thomas Pope acquired the site shortly after 8 July 1541 (Martin 1926, 213). The destruction of the abbey buildings was so advanced when Pope commenced his mansion that the ruins of the nave had to be repaired first, before they could be reutilised (BL, Add MS 24432 A, 32, 156). Pope died in 1559 by which time the construction of the house was presumably complete, but very little information survives (Martin 1926, 213).

Destruction in the early 19th century of Bermondsey House would have left us ignorant of the form of Pope's mansion had not two generations of the talented Buckler family lived nearby and earned their living as artists. The Bucklers painted watercolours but are chiefly valued for their pencil and ink drawings and preparatory pencil drawings. The notable detail and accuracy can mislead the viewer into assuming they are looking at the equivalent of a photograph, but the Bucklers sometimes exercised artistic licence (Doggett 2002, 13). The Bermondsey views show they were indeed capable of restoring details, shifting buildings and sightlines or omitting what in their view was irrelevant. The records of surviving buildings in Hertfordshire, however, are testimony to their general precision and accuracy (ibid). The state of preservation recorded by Buckler indicates that parts of the building must have been occupied not long before his recording. The treatment here concentrates on the main features of the house, but scope exists for a more detailed reconstruction (a fuller history and details of the Buckler records are given in Chapter 7.1).

The quadrangle

The house consisted of a single quadrangle, with a separate range running parallel some distance to the east (Fig 109). This was divided into two houses (the 'north and south house'). It is likely

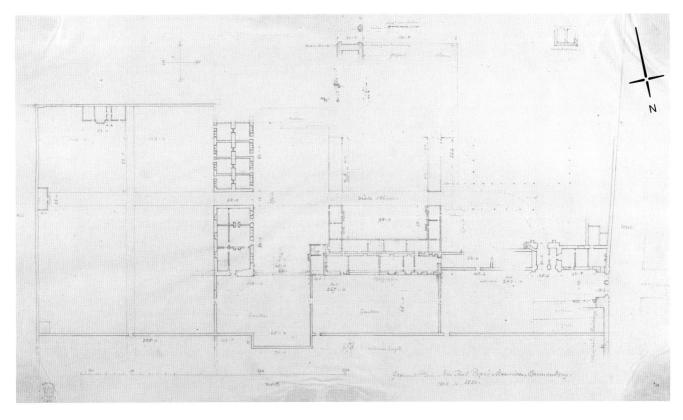

Fig 109 Ground plan of Sir Thomas Pope's mansion, Bermondsey, by J C Buckler, 1808 to 1820 (north is to the bottom) (© The British Library Board, Add MS 24433, fo 3)

that another range connected the south house to the quadrangle to the west. The church and its ancillary buildings were for the most part levelled and only the gatehouses and the great eastern brick circuit of walls were retained in a recognisable form. Some monastic foundations and even stretches of wall were re-employed, but most were removed for their stone. In some cases, the original converter of a monastic house would later remodel their own work (Doggett 2002, 57) and something like this may have happened at Bermondsey; certainly a number of alterations were made by subsequent owners.

The first known phase of the mansion inhabited the shell between the south wall of the nave of the abbey church (B3) and the cloister arcade (B5), with the masonry southern wall built on the foundation of the cloister arcade (cf Fig 70). The masonry wall was thickened when the quadrangle was built, so as to contain additional fireplaces for a range of chambers overlooking the courtyard. The north range was thus two chambers deep.

Dimensions recorded by Buckler show that the courtyard was 29.87m wide west–east and extended at least 35.05m to the south (BL, Add MS 24433, fo 3; Fig 109). The full extent of the quadrangle is not known because it had been robbed of its south range, probably in the early 18th century (BL, Add MS 24432 B, 5v). The complete quadrangle is shown, as if viewed from the south, in W Faithorne and R Newcourt's map of 1658; the north range bears little resemblance to that recorded by Buckler.

In contrast to the north range, the west and east side ranges were only one room deep. The west side range appears from

Buckler to have reused at least the foundation of the west wall of the west range for its own west wall (cf Fig 70). If the east wall re-employed an existing foundation then the west monastic range may have been substantially modified (and possibly narrowed) in the last years of the abbey. The abbot's lodgings may formerly have occupied part of the west range. At the time of the Dissolution, abbots' houses could be very comfortable and up-to-date (Doggett 2002, 50). No attempt, in contrast, seems to have been made to re-employ existing foundations for the east side range; this was constructed on what had been the main cloister garth (OA5, period M9) and west of the monastic east range which became a ?service range (below).

A view in the former Guildhall Library's Print Room Collection (now part of the London Metropolitan Archives) (Fig 110; previously published in Schofield and Lea 2005, 183, fig 160) of the north range and part of the west range shows the ground floors built of brick and, at least in the case of the north range, masonry, suggesting adaptation of the monastic buildings. The first floors are timber-framed, with very large timbers which it has been suggested may have been taken from the monastic buildings (Schofield and Lea 2005, 184). The constructional details of the quadrangle as recorded by Buckler are discussed in Chapter 7.1 ('Catalogue of maps…', 'The north half of the west courtyard of Sir Thomas Pope's mansion, ground floor (BL, Add MS 24433, fo 4) …' and 'No caption, no main caption, north point or scale bar [west courtyard of Bermondsey mansion, first floor] (BL, Add MS 24433, fo 5) …').

Fig 110 View of the north range and quadrangle of Bermondsey House as recorded by J C Buckler in 1827 (LMA, Pennant's London Collection 37, cat no. p5369402) (Guildhall Library, City of London)

?Service range (the former east range, B7)

Two houses, 'north' and 'south', on a common north–south alignment stood to the east of the quadrangle (Fig 109; Fig 112). They were separated by the Long Walk (possibly in the form of a ground-floor passage with rooms above) and were two storeys high, so forming a continuous range at the upper level. Parts of the former monastic east range (B7) had been retained and modified to fit the scheme for the new mansion house; the Buckler survey drawings show the entire range on the east side of the monastic cloister (including the apsidal chapel to the south transept) as having been divided into two blocks, possibly part of a service range.

Both houses were 14.3m (48ft) wide with substantial external masonry walls, but contrasted in internal arrangment. The south house was the only structure recorded by Buckler which was also excavated in the 1980s. Much of the fabric of the east range (B7) was apparently retained. The undercroft, however, was removed and replaced by a series of apartments or lodgings. The south house was divided by a north–south central wall containing fireplaces, with ?brick partition walls subdividing it into eight chambers; these were lit by three-light mullioned windows. Thus on the ground floor there were eight equal-sized rooms, each with a door and window opening, and perhaps provided accommodation for servants. No internal record of the upper floor seems to exist, but the external appearance suggests that the whole building was split into four individual houses, the great medieval pitched roof of the east range being replaced by four small roofs running crosswise. The roofing of the former east range was recorded in an aerial view of the remains of the abbey by Buckler (BL, Add MS 24433, fo 53, 'Bird's eye view of the abbey, & of Sir Thos Pope's mansion,

Bermondsey'; also 'General view of site from north-west in 1805' engraved by Robert Wilkinson, originally published in Wilkinson 1819, pl 49, reproduced in Graham 1926, fig 12).

The north house was divided by a ?half-timbered party wall into three large and three small chambers; the windows here were smaller and more irregularly distributed. The north block is shown as having three major fireplaces and may have been a kitchen or bakehouse. Other views and plans show that the north and west walls contained much monastic fabric and that only the east and ?south walls of the north house were post-Dissolution in their entirety. It was, however, an entirely new building positioned to exploit as many of the old walls of the south transept and chapter house as possible (Fig 112). The roofs were more complex than those of the south house. A single roof ran north–south on the east (narrow) compartment abutted by narrow pitched roofs running crosswise across the house to cover the large chambers.

5.2 Archaeological evidence

The abbey church (B3) and the majority of the conventual buildings were demolished (Fig 111). The late 13th-/early 14th-century (period M7) chancel of the former infirmary chapel (B1) appears to have been left standing, at least in the early post-Dissolution period, as was the adjacent building to the east (the former ? infirmary range extension/?outbuilding, B12; period M8). The ?14th-century (period M8) wall of the north aisle to the church also survived and became a boundary to a post-medieval walled garden. Parts of the refectory (B6) and five bays of the east range (B7) were retained. The south wall of the former hall/lodgings (B8) was incorporated as part of the post-medieval south garden wall. Numerous pits were dug in the former cemetery (OA9 and OA10, formerly OA6) and in the second cloister (OA11 formerly OA2).

Monastic buildings completely or largely demolished

Abbey church (B3)

The abbey church (B3) was reduced to its foundations. There is no dating evidence for the robber trench found at the north limit of site A. The careful dismantling of the structure is implied by the absence of building rubble on the south side of the church. The records from the Grimes work in 1956 chiefly describe the overwhelming amount of modern debris from demolished air-raid shelters. The ?14th-century north aisle wall (period M8) of the church was retained by Sir Thomas Pope for incorporation into the garden of his mansion (Fig 112). Subsequently, it was mentioned in an early 17th-century Chancery bill (the 'standing wall' in TNA: PRO, C2, JAS I/H19/30, quoted above, 5.1, 'Tenants and owners of the site'), mapped by Buckler between 1808 and 1820, and then again by the Ordnance Survey in 1894, by which time it had become a property boundary between two rows of tenements. When Corbett recorded the wall in 1956, it stood to a height of 2.25m and incorporated many reused medieval architectural fragments.

Former hall/lodgings (B8)

Building 8 was demolished, apart from the south wall, which was left upstanding and survived to a height of 3.58m OD in 1988 (Fig 111). Buckler recorded it (in 1808–20) as the south garden wall of the mansion (Fig 112). Pottery from demolition debris and burnt deposits gave a date range of c 1480–c 1600 (Raeren stoneware, RAER; London-area early post-medieval redware, PMRE; London-area post-medieval bichrome redware, PMBR).

Reredorter (B9) and Drain 4, and creation of Open Area 12

The former reredorter (B9) and the west–east section of Drain 4 were finally robbed of their building stone and effectively erased from the landscape, creating an open area (OA12) in the southern perimeter of the mansion house. The robbing cut (subgp355) to the stone-lined drain extended from the east opening of the reredorter eastwards for c 20m, continuing into the east limit of excavation. Robbing of the east end of the reredorter included some demolition material within the body of the building.

The backfills of the robbing of the east end of the reredorter and Drain 4 east of Building 9 produced 545 sherds classed as medieval (meaning a date range that finishes no later than c 1480 or c 1500) and 245 post-medieval sherds (with a date range that begins no earlier than c 1480 or c 1500). The pottery

from the robbing of Drain 4 was fully quantified (discussed in detail in Chapter 7.5, 'Period P1, 1538–c 1650'); there were three large contexts (more than 100 sherds each) – A[515] (D4), A[518] (D4) and A[1764] (B9) – and one of medium size A[539] (D4). With their mix of late 15th-century and early 16th-century fabrics and forms, these groups are broadly similar to the stratigraphically earlier reredorter groups from debris A[972] and ash A[2483] (A[1764] overlay the clay sealing layer A[2468] within the north-east corner of the reredorter). Serving vessels, mainly jugs and drinking vessels, together with pottery used in the kitchen for cooking and food preparation, predominate. However, there are significant differences in composition between the two assemblages – the reredorter dumping and the robbing backfills.

The proportions of medieval to post-medieval pottery have changed, with the post-medieval now dominant. Significantly, there is also a far higher proportion of residual 12th- to early 14th-century pottery present in the robbing of both the reredorter (B9) and Drain 4, and even 11th- to 12th-century wares, especially in the reredorter. With relatively few joining sherds or reconstructable profiles, much of the pottery in the reredorter robbing backfills is undoubtedly redeposited. The backfills of Drain 4 also have a mix of fabrics, dating from the 12th to 15th centuries, but, in contrast to the reredorter robbing backfills, in each of the two large contexts A[515] and A[518], Surrey whitewares are the predominant medieval fabric group.

Imports also feature in contrast to earlier assemblages, for example, a medieval baluster jug in late Rouen ware (ROUL) (Fig 161, <P50>), although medieval imports are still relatively scarce. Imports are much more marked among the early 16th-century pottery. Rhenish and Low Countries wares predominate, including for example south Netherlands maiolica (SNTG) or tin-glazed ware with polychrome decoration. There are some unusual vessels present such as a miniature standing costrel or oil pot in Raeren stoneware (RAER), a possible reliquary (Fig 102, <P24>; discussed in Chapter 4.3, 'Material culture and the religious life'). The 16th-century local wares also include a variety of forms such as a sprinkler watering pot. Taking all the evidence together it appears that the pottery was coming from a wider area of the monastery than earlier.

The pottery from the drain west of the reredorter presents a very similar pattern to the groups from the backfills of the robbing of the east end of the reredorter and Drain 4 east of Building 9. The west drain backfills produced in all 103 medieval sherds and 318 post-medieval sherds; the largest context A[2349] was fully quantified (91 medieval/277 post-medieval). While the pottery might suggest the west section of drain may have been backfilled slightly later than the eastern, when the west entrance to the reredorter was blocked in period M9 (Chapter 3.7, 'Archaeological evidence', 'Reredorter (B9)'), the west section of drain was very likely disused. However, like all these groups, there are no common pottery types present definitely introduced after c 1550. The reredorter and drain were robbed and backfilled, therefore, in the Dissolution/immediately post-Dissolution period.

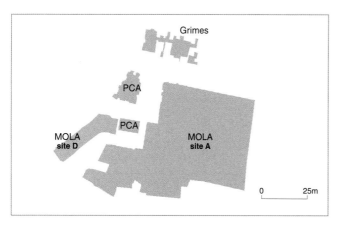

Fig 111 Plan of principal archaeological features at sites in the study area, 1538–c 1650 (period P1), superimposed on the pre-Dissolution archaeological evidence (period M9) (scale 1:400; inset 1:2000)

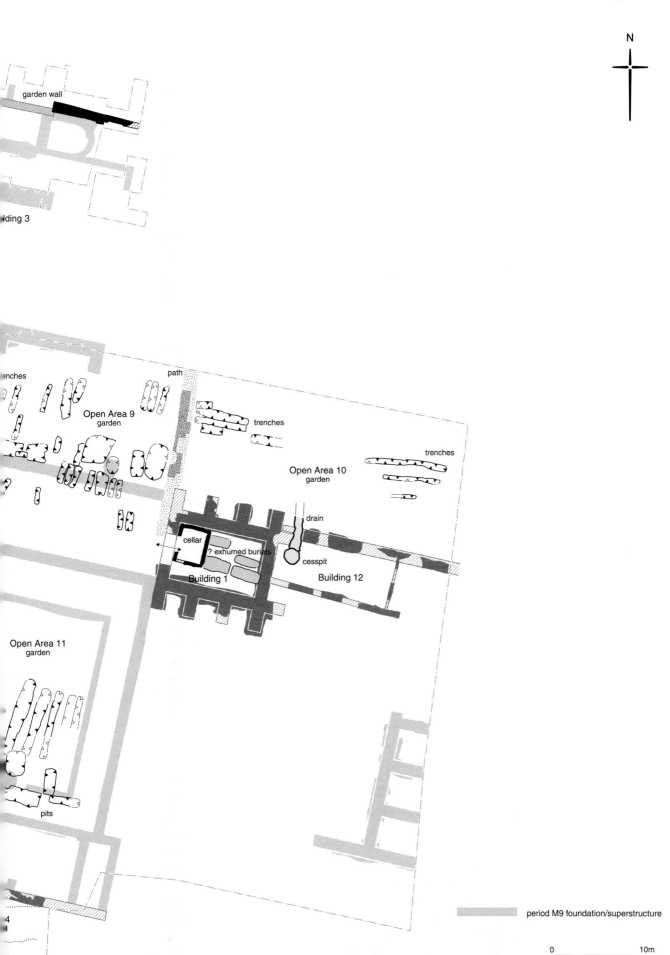

N

garden wall

lding 3

enches

Open Area 9
garden

path

trenches

trenches

Open Area 10
garden

cellar

? exhumed burials

Building 1

drain

cesspit

Building 12

Open Area 11
garden

pits

4

Area 12

period M9 foundation/superstructure

0   10m

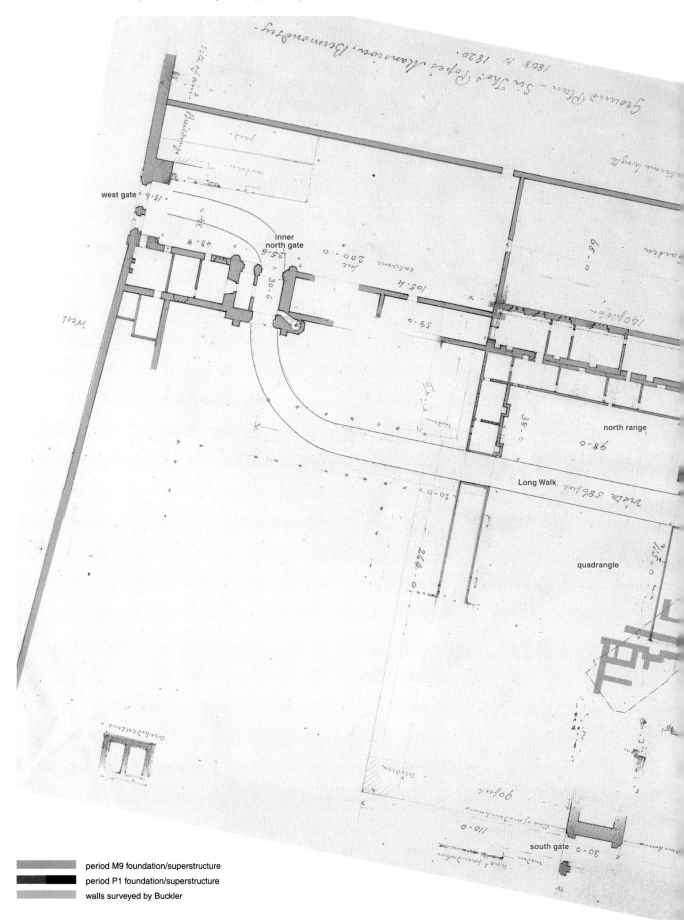

period M9 foundation/superstructure
period P1 foundation/superstructure
walls surveyed by Buckler

Fig 112 Buckler's 19th-century survey of the mansion house (Fig 109)
superimposed on the 1538–c 1650 (period P1) structural evidence reported here
(cf Fig 111) (scale 1:600)

N

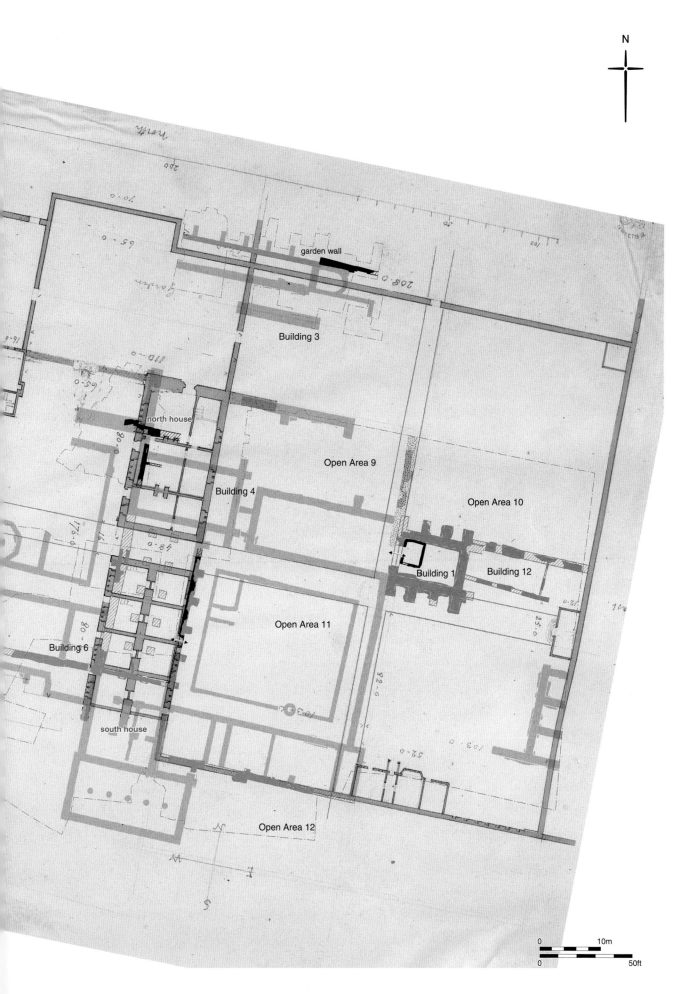

garden wall

Building 3

north house

Open Area 9

Building 4

Open Area 10

Building 1

Building 12

Open Area 11

Building 6

south house

Open Area 12

0   10m

0   50ft

Elements of the former monastery partly or wholly retained and adapted

Chapel (B1)

The nave of the chapel (B1) was completely demolished. The buttressed chancel seems to have survived until at least the second half of the 16th century. Certainly, a cellar was dug in the north-west corner of the ground floor (Fig 111), disturbing earlier, medieval burials (four large grave-shaped cuts suggest some exhumation took place). The cellar was 2.85m east–west by 3.52m north–south and its walls were constructed of reused medieval building materials. The chapel chancel may have been reglazed in the immediate post-Dissolution phase: pit fills in the area north of the chapel (B1; OA9, period P1) produced a number of pale green or colourless glass fragments that had apparently never been mounted, including offcuts retaining their original bevelled edges (eg from A[2976], <G96>, <G97>, Fig 113; Chapters 4.2, 'Interior decoration of the monastic buildings: glazing and tiling', 7.6, 'The context and character of the catalogued window glass'; though see painted fragment <G69>, Fig 164).

The paths recorded by Buckler in the ?formal garden (BL, Add MS 24433, fo 3; Fig 109; Fig 112) seem to be influenced by the west wall of the chapel chancel, supporting the excavation evidence that this survived the Dissolution for some time, and by the north walk of the second cloister.

Former chapter house (B4)

It is unclear exactly in what way the chapter house (B4) became part of the post-medieval great house (Fig 112). Most of the building lay beyond (west of) the limit of excavation and is only known through the records of the antiquarian J C Buckler, who recorded features for example on the west side of the chapter house (Chapter 4.2, 'The 12th-century priory church'; Fig 69;

Fig 70). The north-east corner of the structure was robbed away, but this may have happened later in the post-medieval period. The survival of some of the east wall of the chapter house to a height of 3.18m OD indicates that the building was probably retained, if only partially.

Former cloister (B5)

The south and east walks of the cloister (B5) were demolished. There is no dating evidence for the demolition as it lay largely within unexcavated parts of site D (Fig 3). The north walk of the cloister was retained as part of the north range of the mansion house (above, 5.1, 'The construction of Pope's mansion'; Fig 112).

Former refectory (B6)

The height (3.70m OD) at which parts of the south refectory wall survived into the modern age is enough to suggest that it was spared destruction and somehow incorporated into the manor house after the Dissolution. The wall appears to coincide with the south end of a building shown by Buckler on the east side of the mansion house court (Fig 111; Fig 112). It may have formed the south side of the main court of the house.

Against the inner face of the wall, a rectangular, brick-lined pit or cistern was constructed against the chalk foundations. The pit was 1.6m north–south by 1.0m east–west and 0.63m deep. Its base was lined with bricks laid on bed. The top of the pit coincided with the foundation offset.

This building (B6) was largely unexcavated and it is likely that the pottery collected from the upper parts of robbing deposits while cleaning is contaminated with unstratified material or sherds from other deposits; indeed, the pottery may reflect this to some degree. A near-complete Spanish starred costrel (STAR) (Fig 160, <P49>; Chapter 7.5, 'Period P1, 1538–c 1650') was recovered from a partially excavated backfill

<G96>

<G97>

Fig 113 Fragments of crown window glass retaining original rounded edges <G96>, <G97> from pit fills in the area north of the chapel (B1; OA9, period P1) (scale c 1:1)

in the robber trench of the west wall of the passage. These vessels have been found on a number of sites across England in early 17th-century contexts and a large pottery assemblage dating to the first half of the 17th century was recovered from the cesspit in Building 12 (below).

Former east range (B7)

The ?service range, comprising a north house and a south house, was founded on the former monastic east range (B7). The archaeological evidence shows changes made to the northern bays of Building 7. The windows and north door in the east wall of Building 7 were stripped of their facings and blocked (Fig 114). A section of the east wall, from floor level at *c* 3.3m OD up to a height of 3.8m OD, was cut back and refaced with rough brickwork. A new door was inserted in the east wall, in what was now the second bay ground-floor room from the south.

?Outbuilding (B12)

Building 12 (the former ? infirmary range extension/?outbuilding) was retained and, at the west end of the building, a cesspit and a drainage gully were inserted. The cesspit was backfilled at the end of period P1, with waste deposits which contained a large and very interesting pottery group (A[3376], 166 sherds) which was fully quantified and dated *c* 1640–70 (discussed in detail in Chapter 7.5, 'Period P1, 1538–*c* 1650'). Border wares (BORD) are the most common wares in this group, with an unusually large proportion of tin-glazed ware making this the second most common ware. A wide range of imported pottery from a variety of sources – including Germany, the Low Countries, Italy, Portugal and China – not only contrasts with the paucity of imports from the medieval abbey but suggests the occupants of Bermondsey House in the first half of the 17th century enjoyed a high standard of living (Fig 163).

South-west precinct (OA4)

The precinct wall was retained as the west and part of the south boundary to the new private estate. Against the inner face of the wall, near the south-west corner of the precinct, was a brick cellar, entered by a short flight of steps (site F, not illustrated). Rubbish and gravel pits 13m north of the wall contained pottery dated *c* 1550–*c* 1700.

Gardens (OA9–OA11)

Much of the land to the east of the new post-medieval mansion in the area of the former east end of the abbey church (B3) and land to the south became a number of separate gardens or garden areas (OA9–OA11) once many of the conventual buildings had been demolished.

The cemetery (OA6) was now no longer in use and the land became part of a larger garden (OA9; Fig 111; Fig 112), defined to the north by the surviving north aisle wall of the former

Fig 114 Detail of blocked door in the east wall of the east range (B7) in period P1, from the west (0.5m scale)

abbey church (B3) and its 16th-century continuation east. To the west, the garden was delimited by the post-medieval mansion house, and to the east, by the north–south foundation of a path dividing it from another garden to the east (OA10).

This garden (OA9) was characterised by horticultural trenches, a series of 25 north–south aligned linear pits; many of these had a layer of silt in the base, suggesting they had lain open after they had been dug. The slots were all *c* 2.0–2.5m long, with rounded ends, and between 0.5m and 1.0m wide. They had then been backfilled with demolition debris, dated *c* 1480–*c* 1600. A large square pit dug against the remaining foundations of the chapel nave (B1) and two large linear slots to the north of it, contained pin-making waste.

Another large square pit near the former chapel, which extended 2.9m north–south by 2.8m east–west, yielded sherds of 15th-century date and earlier, together with London-area early post-medieval redware (PMRE; date range *c* 1480–*c* 1600) and early Surrey-Hampshire border whiteware (EBORD; date range *c* 1480–*c* 1550). The complete top of a sprinkler watering pot was found in pit fill A[2938]. A most unusual sherd in fill A[2883] (probably in London-area post-medieval slipped redware with a green glaze (PMSRG); date range *c* 1480–*c* 1650) resembles a large, heavy tubular handle, blocked at one end with a plug of white-firing clay (Fig 115, <P28>). The upper surface is incised with shallow diagonal cuts at regular intervals. The vessel from which this handle originally came would need to have been quite substantial in construction to support its weight. As yet no satisfactory identification has been made. This pit produced the largest number of fragments of window glass from the excavation (Chapters 4.2, 'Interior decoration of the monastic buildings: glazing and tiling', 7.6, 'The context and character of of the catalogued window glass') together with lead window came (<S53>; Chapter 7.7, 'Monastic house period').

A deposit full of demolition material, A[3460], abutting parts of the former chapel chancel (B1) foundations, included 123 sherds of post-medieval (ie post-*c* 1480) pottery (51 ENV)

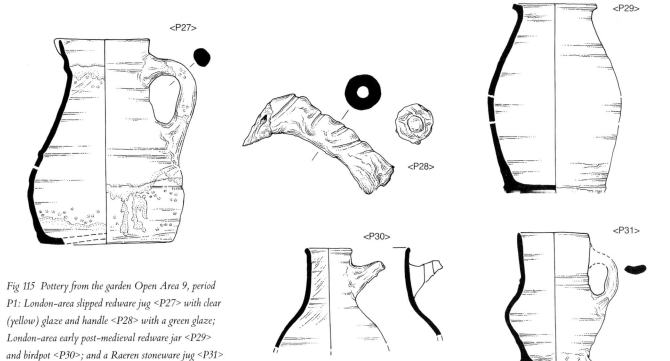

Fig 115 Pottery from the garden Open Area 9, period P1: London-area slipped redware jug <P27> with clear (yellow) glaze and handle <P28> with a green glaze; London-area early post-medieval redware jar <P29> and birdpot <P30>; and a Raeren stoneware jug <P31> (scale 1:4)

with numerous joining sherds and a number of complete vessel profiles, together with a jetton dated *c* 1500–25 (<S179>; Chapter 7.7, 'Monastic house period'). The assemblage consists largely of local redwares in the usual range of forms, in particular cauldrons, pipkins, bowls and jugs, among which are several sherds each from two pear-shaped jugs with rilled necks in slipped redware with clear (yellow) glaze (PMSRY) (Fig 115, <P27>). In addition, there are sherds from a chafing dish and a 'goblet' or vase in PMSRY, an unglazed, rounded jar in London-area early post-medieval redware (PMRE) (Fig 115, <P29>) and a sprinkler watering pot, together with a Raeren stoneware jug (RAER) (Fig 115, <P31>). Much more unusual is part of an anthropomorphic face-mask handle from a large basin in post-medieval slipped redware with green and clear glaze (PMSRG) (not illustrated). The face has eyes formed of applied strips of white clay or slip, with additional details in white- and red-firing clay, such as a moustache or beard, each closely stabbed (to represent ?hair). These are highlighted in copper-stained green glaze, while the overall glaze appears a dull olive colour.

To the east of this garden, separated by a path, was another garden area (OA10; Fig 111; Fig 112) bounded to the south in part by the surviving medieval walls (former B1, B12). In the centre of the area were seven east–west aligned linear gullies, the remains of horticultural trenches. Context A[3035] produced pottery dated *c* 1550–*c* 1600: part of an unidentified vessel in Surrey-Hampshire border whiteware with a green glaze (BORDG) and six sherds from a sprinkler-type watering pot in London-area early post-medieval redware (PMRE). From three east–west aligned slots near the south-west corner of Open Area 10, and a pit fill in adjacent Open Area 9, came sherds from a cup, a mammiform costrel and two drinking jugs in early Surrey-Hampshire border whiteware (EBORD),

Raeren stoneware (RAER) jugs and a drinking jug and 14 sherds from a birdpot in PMRE, including the perch support (Fig 115, <P30>; cf Stephenson 1991).

To the south of Open Area 9 and Open Area 10 was a further garden area (OA11; Fig 111; Fig 112) defined on its south side by the south wall of former Building 8, and to the west, by the former Building 7 now part of the mansion house. North–south aligned horticultural trenches were dug in the centre of the area. The latest pottery recovered from pit fills was dated *c* 1550–*c* 1600.

5.3 Discussion

The key aspect of the immediate post-Dissolution period is the location and development within the former monastic precinct of the Tudor mansion, Bermondsey House. Thanks to its rural situation, the mansion at Bermondsey was preserved intact into the early 19th century (Schofield 1984, 142; Schofield and Lea 2005, 184). This meant that the initial 'conversion' of the monastic buildings survived. Nearer the City, such adaptations were usually swept away by more magnificent buildings that took the place of earlier conversions (Schofield and Lea 2005, 181–5). The alterations at Bermondsey were swift, practical and not particularly innovative in terms of layout and organisation of space. Attention to this process has become a focus of study in other counties (Howard 2003) and the opportunity is taken to place the mansion in context.

The archaeological evidence demonstrates the destruction of much of the monastic building in the east part of the precinct.

It also accords with the Buckler plan of the house and grounds drawn in the early 19th century (Fig 112). The siting of the mansion on the principal monastic cloister is paralleled in several examples where monastic establishments were given over to individuals as private estates, as for example in the case of the precinct of Holy Trinity Priory Aldgate where Sir Thomas Audley probably rebuilt and lived in the west range of the cloister (Schofield and Lea 2005, 18). At St Mary Clerkenwell, where the cloister was located on the north side of the church, the west range, formerly the prioress's apartments, and the north range, formerly the refectory, became the capital messuage of the post-Dissolution estate of the duke of Norfolk (Sloane in prep).

Although the new mansion at Bermondsey was sited on the principal monastic cloister, and some foundations (and some superstructure) of the former north and west ranges were reused, substantial work was undertaken to create a new modish building. Elsewhere, post-Dissolution houses, such as Ashridge (Hertfordshire), could re-employ cloisters with little alteration (Doggett 2002, fig 20). But cloisters were often of several different periods on different levels and alignments, making reuse impractical (ibid, 51). The main Bermondsey cloister had been rebuilt in the 1380s (period M8; Chapter 3.6, 'Archaeological evidence', 'Chapter house (B4) and cloister (B5)'; Graham 1937, 148) and was probably glazed and in good order. The relatively small size of the cloister was a problem in many post-Dissolution conversions (Doggett 2002, 51, 62), but this was not the case it seems at Bermondsey where the east side range of the quadrangle lay within the former cloister garth. At Bermondsey it was the area to the east of the mansion – the site of the former infirmary complex and subsidiary cloisters, which had already seen some contraction and disuse prior to the Dissolution (period M9; Chapter 3.7, 'Archaeological evidence') – which became a walled and regularly laid out garden.

It is probable that the Bermondsey mansion was arranged round three courtyards, maintaining the sequential passage from public to private already established in the architecture of the monastery. The outer and inner monastic courts seem to have remained essentially the same with the monastic gateways in place and the main cloister taking the form of the central inner space, surrounded by the ranges of the new mansion house (Fig 112). Henry VII's (Richmond) palace at Richmond on Thames was arranged on this plan, with the principal apartments arranged around a small inner courtyard (Dixon and Lott 1993, 98).

The quadrangle that eventually straddled the cloister resembled the plan of the directly contemporary inner quadrangle at Nonsuch Palace (Surrey). The east range of the palace was divided by an internal service wall (Summerson 1991, fig 9). Thurley reconstructs the first floor of the palace (1993, fig 85) on the basis of excavated and documentary evidence. He believes the exterior of the east range was occupied by the king's privy chambers, while a privy gallery overlooked the courtyard; the resemblance to the recorded first-floor plan of the north range at Bermondsey becomes noteworthy. Nonsuch was a rare greenfield development for the ageing king and an inner group of courtiers, comprising his privy court and favourites (Thurley 1993, 63). The court visited Nonsuch in June 1545 when Henry showed it to them for the first time (ibid). As a relatively small-scale 'hunting box' it was not inconceivable that it should be imitated.

In general, new buildings after the beginning of the 16th century took the form of courtyard houses, with occasional emphasis on the gateway, such as at the Cambridge colleges of Trinity and St John's (Dixon and Lott 1993, 98). A reason for the persistence of these 'rambling courtyard structures' may have been the sheer speed with which many of the monastic conversions were made (Howard 1997, 106). Courtier houses, in common with the royal palaces of the time, were manifestly vehicles of display and ceremony. In the absence of the monarch, royal palaces were left with a skeleton staff, who, in anticipation of the next royal visit, would begin a frantic campaign of necessary repairs. The approach was one in which, when extra facilities were required for lavish entertainments, whole ranges of temporary lodgings were built, such as the temporary palace constructed for the Field of the Cloth of Gold in 1520 (ibid). The rapid conversion, therefore, of previously existing monastic structures and the retention of their essential forms betrays an attitude to buildings in which their permanence and durability is of lesser importance than their immediate symbolism as icons of power, ceremony and ostentation. The retention of gatehouses in particular confirms the early Tudor concern with the facade, often without regard to an integrated architectural scheme. In the 1540s and early 1550s the courtyard house was still very much in vogue (Doggett 2002, 63) and the mansion was, therefore, one of the relatively rare complete conversions to occur in that period.

There is no proof Sir Thomas Pope visited Nonsuch with the court, but as the treasurer of the Court of Augmentations, he could observe and imitate the architectural preferences of his master, Henry VIII. More importantly, his position allowed him the resources to build afresh in the newest style. If this is the case, Bermondsey can be seen as a clever and economical adaptation of existing walls and foundations to create an up-to-date effect. It followed the standard pattern for houses without halls, and the missing south range of the quadrangle, therefore, may have held a gatehouse.

The south wall of the former monastic hall/private lodgings (B8) and the north aisle wall of the church (B3) each survived to significant heights and are shown, in correspondence with the Buckler records (Chapter 7.1), to have formed parts of an encircling wall. The red brick walls which formed the north-east corner of the garden are known from the detailed Buckler records of their unusual patterning. Stylistically these wall sections can be dated c 1480 to 1530s and the religious nature of some of the decoration is consistent with a late pre-Dissolution date. However, it is possible that these walls were the work of Pope in the 1540s (Chapter 7.3; Fig 140).

This perimeter wall may have incorporated the three main gates of the former south-west precinct: the outer west gate (the Great Gate, on Bermondsey Street) in alignment with the former nave; the inner north gate; and the south gate (Fig 112).

The north gate would have been the access to the new mansion's outer court or forecourt.

Bermondsey Abbey was on the road to Kent and Sussex; this was by far the busiest route for Henry VIII (Thurley 1993, 56). It had long been an important hostel for travellers of all classes since Norman times, including kings and queens, although no certain mention of a 'dedicated' royal lodging exists (Martin 1926, 204–5). The only drawback for the king when he suppressed the monasteries was the loss of free lodging they were obliged to provide for him and all travellers as part of their Christian duty. Henry's palaces in the area, such as Eltham (Kent), allowed him to relinquish Bermondsey rather than adapt it for his own needs, as he did with several abbeys between London and the Channel ports (eg Chertsey, Reading, St Augustine's Canterbury; Thurley 1993, 56).

The possibility of furthering himself by supplying hospitality to the king cannot have been absent from Pope's mind; but any such ambition was frustrated by the king's death in 1547. The house passed to another family on Pope's death in 1559. If this building was indeed built with royal entertainment in mind, it would have set a pattern that was to be widely imitated in the reign of Elizabeth.

The archaeological and ceramic findings together demonstrate the new land uses in the immediate post-Dissolution period. The reredorter and drain were robbed and backfilled in the Dissolution/immediately post-Dissolution period. The redeposited character of the ceramic assemblages from these backfills suggests the material came not from clearing out items from the monastic buildings but from demolition of those buildings, which probably began in or after 1544 when Sir Thomas Pope acquired the site. Gardens were laid out (OA9–OA11) east of the new mansion house. Horticultural trenches were identified in Open Areas 9 and 10,

and in Open Area 11. A total of 34 sherds from a minimum of 15 sprinkler watering pots in London-area early post-medieval redware (PMRE; date range c 1480–c 1600) were recovered from site A (Table 10). With the exception of the birdpot from the cemetery (OA6) in period M9, all fall within the post-Dissolution period, with a particular concentration in Open Area 9 (22 sherds/4 ENV). There is also an interesting group of redwares in Open Area 11, confirming that at least part of this area was given over to horticultural and related activities during the 16th century. There are sherds from a watering pot, an unglazed deep bowl with a single hole through the rim, which was probably used as a flowerpot, and from two birdpots. Sprinkler watering pots were used during the first half of the 16th century, in particular, and took the form of a bottle-shaped vessel with a broad, perforated base, a very narrow neck and single hole at the top. The vessel worked by being immersed in water which would fill it through the perforations in the base; holding the thumb over the hole at the rim, would retain the water until the thumb was released, allowing a fine sprinkling to be directed from the base.

Evidence for purpose-made ceramic flowerpots is scant at this date. The deep bowl form described above, with its typical rim perforation, may well have been used to hold plants; quite how the perforation worked is unclear – it may have been used to hold a cane or stick to form a support frame or for tying down branches which needed training (MPRG 1998, 10.14). Unless examples with rim perforations survive, it is difficult to determine from sherd collections how many deep bowls might have been used as flowerpots, since the form is multifunctional and could just as easily have been used in the kitchen. There are no recorded examples on the site of any of the more elaborate and decorative ceramic flowerpots and urns known to have been made at this period.

Table 10 Distribution of sprinkler watering pots and birdpots, all in London-area early post-medieval redware, from Bermondsey, ordered by period and land use

Period	Land use	Context	Context type	Form
M9	OA6	A[3101]	pit fill	birdpot
P1	B8	A[2066]	robbing fill	sprinkler-type watering pot
	OA9	A[2938]	pit fill	sprinkler-type watering pot
	OA9	A[3035]	trench fill	sprinkler-type watering pot
	OA9	A[3301]	pit fill	birdpot
	OA9	A[3303]	trench fill	birdpot
	OA9	A[3460]	demolition deposit	sprinkler-type watering pot
	OA9	A[3974]	robbing fill	sprinkler-type watering pot
	OA11	A[189]	pit fill	sprinkler-type watering pot
	OA11	A[549]	pit fill	sprinkler-type watering pot
	OA11	A[569]	robbing fill	sprinkler-type watering pot
	OA11	A[569]	robbing fill	birdpot × 2
	OA11	A[808]	pit fill	sprinkler-type watering pot
	OA12	A[235]	demolition debris	sprinkler-type watering pot
	OA12	A[368]	pit fill	birdpot
	D4/OA12	A[518]	robbing fill	sprinkler-type watering pot × 2
	B9/OA12	A[1764]	robbing fill	sprinkler-type watering pot
	OA12	A[2309]	pit fill	sprinkler-type watering pot
-	-	A[504]	-	sprinkler-type watering pot

There are 29 sherds from a minimum of six birdpots, found in areas of the site that also yielded watering pots (Table 10). Birdpots are bottle-shaped vessels which could be attached to a wall to provide nesting for small birds whose eggs could then be collected through a cut-out opening in the base. A built-in support on the shoulder for a wooden perch encouraged birds to enter through the narrow neck (Stephenson 1991). Although not strictly horticultural, these vessels have a related function in providing for the collection of eggs from species other than poultry. The form dates to the 16th century and later in the London area. Seventeenth-century Dutch genre paintings show them in use and it is possible that the original inspiration for the form came from the Low Countries (ibid, fig 2).

There was some evidence for craftworking post-Dissolution. A group of 29 copper-alloy pins (<S198>, A[3873] OA9) represents a a manufacturing assemblage, and includes uncompleted components, discarded misworkings and lost finished pins. In all, five post-Dissolution contexts (A[295] and A[339] OA11; A[2613], A[3033] and A[3059] OA9) produced extensively modified pinner's bones (eg <S195>–<S197>, Fig 116). Two cattle metapodials (<S196>, <S197>) were found in association with both copper wire and pins (Chapter 7.7, 'Dissolution and later period'). A horse metatarsal had also been shaped into a pinner's bone. This involved sawing off one end of the bone and grinding flat each 'face' of the remaining mid-shaft to produce a hollow, square-sectioned rod. Each face of the bone was then sawn with a series of sloping cuts. The end of the bone was held in a clamp, and wires laid into the sawn cuts. The ends of the wires were then filed, rotated and filed again to produce long sharp points. Drilled holes in the proximal articulations of these modified bones are often interpreted as a means to facilitate clamping during the process.

The earls of Sussex owned the mansion house and site for most of the second half of the 16th century, but – in debt – sold the site in 1601 (above, 5.1, 'Tenants and owners of the site'). The relative lack of alteration to Pope's original work, apart from the possible renewing of ceilings in the early 17th century, shows that the house went into slow decline indicated by the study of the engravings (Chapter 7.1). The fall in the popularity of the courtyard house towards the end of the 16th century (Doggett 2002, 61) was no doubt a related factor. 'Foggy noysomenesse, from Fenns or Marshes …' was considered a serious drawback in the site of any house of pretension (ibid, 70) and the house was increasingly surrounded by impoverished industrial and maritime development. Nonetheless the large ceramic assemblage recovered from the cesspit in the ?outbuilding (B12) and dated to the first half of the 17th century indicates that Bermondsey's occupants enjoyed a relatively high standard of living and exactly mirrors the greater diversity in both function and form of the ceramics of this period (Chapter 7.5, 'Period P1, 1538–c 1650'). The unusually high proportion of tin-glazed wares has been commented upon. It reflects with great immediacy the specific cultural emphasis of Southwark. Imported wares in the cesspit group are extremely wide-ranging and perhaps reflect London's role as a port.

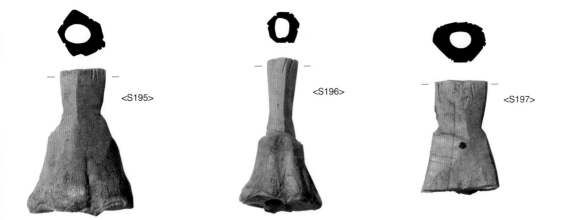

Fig 116 Pinner's bones <S195>–<S197> (from OA9, period P1) (scale c 1:2)

6

Conclusions

6.1 Attainment of research aims and conclusions

The site of the Cluniac priory of St Saviour in Bermondsey is one of the very few of the Order in England that has been investigated on a reasonably large scale and using modern archaeological techniques. The others include Pontefract in Yorkshire West Riding, Thetford and Castle Acre in Norfolk and Lewes in Sussex (Bellamy 1965; Raby and Reynolds 1979; Wilcox 1989; Lyne 1997; Coad and Coppack 1998; Fig 1). The study of the priory and later abbey of Bermondsey has chiefly focused on the results from the fully excavated areas of site A (Fig 3), the monastic eastern ranges: the east range of the main cloister, the chapel, the second infirmary cloister, the cemetery and further ranges and areas to the east. A second, key element of the project was to incorporate the records resulting from the work on the priory church done by W F Grimes between 1956 and 1962–3. The results from three 'rescue' evaluations/ excavations and a watching brief also contributed towards the available data on the priory site. Incorporated in the final stage of publication (2008) was recent structural evidence recorded by PCA in the area of the south transept (BYQ98) and east range (WBP07; Fig 3, inset).

A fundamental requirement of the research aims set out in the post-excavation assessment report of 1997 (Steele and Sloane 1997) was to construct a common chronology for all the constituent sites in the project and this forms Chapters 2, 3 and 5, with accompanying period plans (Fig 10; Fig 14; Fig 21; Fig 33; Fig 47; Fig 49; Fig 53; Fig 57; Fig 65; Fig 111). The chronological progression through the periods is described in Chapters 2, 3 and 5. The period plans, together with antiquarian evidence, form the basis of a partly schematic reconstruction of the layout of the church and main cloister (Fig 69; Fig 81). These plans will inform subsequent work or development in the vicinity of the Scheduled Ancient Monument as well as providing a starting point for future research programmes, in particular the analysis and publication by PCA of their excavations of the western parts of the priory church and main cloister (BYQ98, in 1998, 2002, 2004–8).

An important aim of the project was to determine the nature and extent of Saxon activity within the study area given, in particular, documentary evidence for an Anglo-Saxon minster at Bermondsey. The recovery of a significant finds group for the 8th and 9th centuries AD, but no associated features, indicates the presence of a permanent and important Middle Saxon settlement in the vicinity of site A.

Analysis of the priory buildings has led to significant results. The earliest buildings on the site are the free-standing masonry chapel and the timber latrine within a ditched enclosure. Both of these have been identified as part of the foundation period monastery. The latrine is an example of a temporary building not previously identified on a Cluniac site, although temporary buildings have been recognised at Benedictine (eg Sandwell Priory, Staffordshire) and Cistercian houses (eg Sawley Abbey, Yorkshire West Riding, and Bordesley Abbey, Worcestershire)

(Astill et al 2004, 126; Coppack 2006, 91–2). The chapel, however, may have been built before the arrival of the first monks in 1089 and before the foundation of the priory in the 1080s; the entry in Domesday in 1086 regarding the 'new and beautiful church' on the manor of Bermondsey may be referring to this chapel. The Anglo-Norman oligarchy regarded the Cluniac congregation as distinct and rendered it more so by choosing it for almost all its first wave foundations in the newly conquered country. Cluny presented a golden opportunity to build new religious foundations which were certainly not English, but neither were they Norman (Golding 1981, 77). However, Bermondsey could be another example of the siting of a Cluniac monastic church over or adjacent to an earlier one. Lewes – the first and senior English Cluniac house – was possibly sited over a pre-Conquest church (Lyne 1997, 18); at Wenlock, the Cluniac priory initially reused Leofric's minster church constructed c 1040 on the site of St Milburge's abandoned Saxon double monastery and a new priory church on the same site was constructed after 1200 (Pinnell 1999, 15–18). The chapel is also an important structure, not only as an addition to the small number of known Late Saxon or Saxo-Norman churches but in terms of its retention – for, like the free-standing chapels at Cluny and at Lewes, it was retained – and subsequent development.

The rebuilding of the Frankish church and monastery at Cluny in the 10th to 11th centuries involved a significant departure from the St Gall plan. Cluny II incorporated a chapter house with a free-standing chapel beyond, a design innovation which came to be translated via the overwhelming influence of Cluny into the tradition of the Burgundian and subsequently the Anglo-Norman Romanesque (Conant 1987, 55–7). It hardly seems possible to unravel the architectural threads that have contributed towards the mature Romanesque plan and style evident at St Saviour Bermondsey. Whether the built monastery owed more to its immediate position inside the Cluniac hierarchy or to the Cluniac tradition filtered through the lens of the Anglo-Norman state builders, is a question which is hard to answer.

We are led inevitably on to the question of the distinctiveness of the Cluniacs as an Order. To begin with, the presence of certain key structures on the site can be said to have a specifically Cluniac resonance. These structures are the free-standing chapel (above, and Chapter 3.1), the detached laver standing in its own building in the cloister (Chapter 3.2), and the possible bathhouse (Chapter 3.2). Twelfth-century lavers are known from other Cluniac houses, such as Lewes and Wenlock, and from older Benedictine houses, but are relatively rare in Britian compared to the Continent; Cluny and its daughter house La Charité-sur-Loire both possessed free-standing lavabos of this type. The 12th-century Bermondsey bathhouse/reredorter range is of exceptional importance as the only excavated example in England of a possible early monastic bathhouse. The practical and ritual significance of bathing and the obvious interrelationship of the religious, medical and healing aspects in the monastic life are highlighted by the possible presence of this key building. That bathhouses were a

recognised feature of Cluniac establishments is unsurprising. As an Order, the Cluniacs were keen to emphasise the ritual aspects of the Benedictine Rule: symbolic bathing/baptising/cleansing would no doubt have fitted with their observance of an elaborate liturgy.

All monks of the Order were, in principle, professed at Cluny itself and so must have seen its layout and architecture. The cultural unity of the Order and the way in which that was manifested in the medieval built environment, however, became inevitably diluted: first by time, since by c 1100 the architecture had developed over some 200 years, and secondly by geography, as the predominant force in each region seems to have been the local architecture. Where the demands of the liturgy were catered for in the buildings, these elements are often as attributable to the Benedictine as to the reformed rule. Such elements might include, for example, numerous apsidal chapels for the saying of Masses on successive days; the employment of a stone vault to enhance the sung Mass; and the provision of a free-standing lavabo in the main cloister. The elaborate sculpture often thought of as the signature of the Cluniac style is a regional and temporal development of the Romanesque, witnessed in buildings in the 12th century as far apart as Kilpeck in Herefordshire and Moissac in France. There are surviving elements from the early phase of Cluniac architecture in England which suggest a lavishness of design consistent with the practices of the Burgundian house: for example, some impressive sculpture from Lewes and the ornate chapter house, and the lavabo at Wenlock (Burton 1994, 42). There were unfortunately only two pieces of 12th-century figure sculpture among the architectural fragments from Bermondsey.

Cluniac 'distinctiveness' was possibly reflected then to some degree in the layout and function of the early monastic buildings. In highlighting these aspects, the present volume has an important contribution to make to Cluniac scholarship. Bermondsey's plan has a complexity which is seen at other English Cluniac houses, such as Lewes and Wenlock: founded in the 11th century and well endowed, these houses were able to retain and adapt early or pre-existing buildings, and (in Bermondsey's case) to spread over a wide area.

By way of contrast, the planning and development of the priory in the following centuries has been shown to have elements that are paralleled in the houses of other orders, in London and beyond (Wright 2008). The great priory church, built to the north-west of the chapel, was evidently begun in the early 12th century, but like other religious houses work progressed over several decades as funding allowed: major portions – to the west – were still under construction in the second half of the 12th century.

The architectural style of the church cannot be assessed from the nature of the surviving evidence, other than to point to regional English motifs taking priority over any observed 'Cluniac' influence. The widely used quadrant, for example, seems to originate in England. The east end is best seen as the adaptation of a northern triple-apse plan with a rectangular ambulatory to the liturgical demands of a Cluniac church; the best extant examples of the triple-apse plan are in Belgium at

St-Feuillen (Fosses) and St Bavo. Clapham recognised a distinctive type of plan with a rectangular ambulatory ('type B1') and believed it to be characteristically Anglo-Norman (1934, 18–50). This type of plan has been suggested as an influence on such London projects as Holy Trinity Priory (before 1147–8: Schofield and Lea 2005, 76–7). A strong Cistercian influence seems to have made itself felt towards the end of building, which may connect with the dearth of sculptural elements. Subsequent alteration follows a typical pattern for English great churches.

A thriving community and growing numbers brought expansion, seen in the priory's domestic buildings in the second half of the 12th century – a new reredorter block (across the south end of the east range as at other Cluniac houses such as Castle Acre, Thetford and Lewes, but elsewhere too) and a second, infirmary, cloister and complex. Bermondsey's building work was taking place alongside that at the second wave of monastic foundations in or close to the City of London or Southwark: the Augustinian priories of Holy Trinity Aldgate, St Mary Overie and St Bartholomew Smithfield, the Augustinian nunnery of St Mary Clerkenwell and the Knights Hospitallers' priory of St John Clerkenwell were all founded in the first half of the 12th century.

At Bermondsey in the 14th century, the recovery of economic stability and sound management were accompanied by a remodelling of the church and cloister, the demolition of the communal infirmary buildings allowing an updating to more individual accommodation and the expansion of the ranges and courtyards eastwards; all this culminated in the change from priory to abbey status in 1399. Elsewhere at London's monastic houses and hospitals there was building work, some of it substantial. The eastern extension of the priory church and rebuilding of the chapter house in the 14th century is paralleled at Augustinian Merton Priory, for example (Miller and Saxby 2007, 119–21).

After this high point at Bermondsey, falling numbers – and perhaps a shift of focus – seem to be reflected in the contraction of domestic buildings and disuse of the cemetery on the priory's eastern side. While there is evidence for late building work on Bermondsey's gatehouses, for example, the 16th-century church of St Saviour was fundamentally a 12th-century church, though with a heavily altered east end, and the 12th-century east range was the basis for the east (service) range of Pope's later 16th-century mansion. Changes were taking place, including to the reredorter, which were not entirely consistent with former functions. Here we approach a very interesting period, or periods, of 'transition'.

The archaeological evidence for the immediate pre-Dissolution and Dissolution period is fascinating, but ambiguous in that it relies on dates for ceramic groups which are not ambiguous in themselves but that can be interpreted in different ways. In the case of the reredorter, they can be interpreted as a clearing out in the 1520s or/and continued dumping up to (and including) the closure. This raised the question, was Bermondsey Abbey perhaps consciously preparing for the Dissolution? The king signified his assent to the election of Robert Wharton, Bermondsey Abbey's last abbot, on 5 September 1525. Throughout the ensuing ten years, the value of monastic estates, including at least one manor belonging to Bermondsey Abbey, was under assessment by Thomas Cromwell. In June 1536, the king assented to the election of Wharton as bishop of St Asaph; if not in the nature of a direct reward or compensation, this indicates that relations between the king and the abbot had been maintained over the preceding decade. The amount of Wharton's pension, at £333 6s 8d, is staggering when placed alongside the assessed annual incomes of the religious houses of Holy Trinity Aldgate at £355 and St Mary Clerkenwell at £262. It suggests a large degree of cooperation on Wharton's part at least. Bermondsey's monks may have felt differently and indeed did not fare so well.

The communal latrine, however, may not have been used as it had earlier, if separate accommodation had become standard, and also community numbers were low. If, based on ceramics, the bulk of the reredorter dumping took place perhaps between c 1480 and c 1520, with some further, smaller scale, dumping around the time of the Dissolution, this assumes that the 15th-century wares had a short currency. In any case, dumped material typically would consist of items previously stored and forgotten or unused or damaged, whereas current, undamaged or valuable items were presumably kept and removed from the site. A second transitional period is that after the surrender of the abbey at the beginning of 1538. The period between 1538 and 1541, when Robert Southwell finally purchased the estate, may have been the occasion for the clearance of any remaining items associated with monastic life; after Sir Thomas Pope began his demolition works in 1544, large quantities of debris might be expected. Analysis showed significant differences in composition between two main assemblages – the reredorter dumping and the later robbing backfills of the reredorter.

The artefactual and environmental assemblages from the immediate pre-Dissolution and Dissolution period, particularly from the reredorter and drain, are certainly exceptional in their diversity and richness. They illuminate activities and aspects of the house hardly evident in earlier material. The subsequent conversion of the religious house to courtier's mansion – a transformation seen at many of London's religious houses north of the river – is illustrated here primarily through the records made by Buckler in the early 19th century.

Despite the fact then that the priory lands and buildings have suffered greatly from the impact of urbanisation and that almost no standing remains are left, it has nevertheless proved possible to reconstruct its physical and institutional history and the research aims of the project have largely been attained.

6.2 Further research questions

Although most of the research questions at the centre of the project have been answered within the limitations of the evidence, there remain a number of issues that are either unresolved or have been newly brought to light as a result of the project.

There remains a question concerning the exact location of the Middle to Late Saxon settlement on the Bermondsey eyot. Finds (and Late Saxon features) found on site A suggest a settlement of some status and durability, but indicate that the nucleus of Saxon activity was elsewhere, possibly to the north-west, on the higher ground. The research issue for further work in the local area, therefore, centres on the location of the Anglo-Saxon minster and location, nature and extent of Saxon settlement in Earl Harold's royal manor of Bermondsey.

There is uncertainty regarding the sequence either side of the foundation period of the priory. There was no close dating evidence for the construction of the Saxo-Norman chapel excavated on site A. Is this the 'new and beautiful church' of 1086? Was there any element of continuity between the Anglo-Saxon minster and the Saxo-Norman chapel? or between the location of the Anglo-Saxon minster and the later, 12th-century, priory church?

The layout, form and development of much of the west cloister and precinct and of the nave of St Saviour's church itself are in the main (with the notable exception of Buckler's evidence) matters of conjecture in this volume. These are key research questions which can only be resolved by archaeological work in and around Bermondsey Square, analysis and publication. If the priory church took several decades to complete, as argued here, how far do PCA's recent excavations to the west elucidate this process?

Taken together, Buckler's records and the recent discoveries by PCA will significantly increase our knowledge of the architectural styles employed in the priory church. The Harp Lane (HL74) assemblage has been shown belatedly to be another major group from Bermondsey; full analysis of this archival material would not only enhance our understanding of the later architectural period, but also throw light on the widespread trade in reused stone following the Dissolution (Chapter 7.2, 'Introduction: the assemblage'). There is also considerable potential for the use of remote sensing techniques in the analysis of the great church plan, both to confirm the position of the 1950s–60s Corbett and Grimes excavations and to trace the north wall of the nave and its putative tower and porch.

There are other gaps in our knowledge of particular areas of the precinct. The true extent of the monks' cemetery has yet to be established and the route of the precinct boundary has yet to be definitively proven. Further work tracing medieval properties through deeds and the use of map regression techniques could provide insights here.

A future detailed comparison of pottery assemblages across religious sites in London might clarify and explain a number of issues to do with the equipping and maintenance in ceramic wares of large communal establishments. The types and functions of vessels from different sites, as well as the source of the ceramics, would add to the body of current knowledge about the relative economic health of individual houses, as well as supply further detail regarding catering practice, diet and status. Further research might usefully address the issue of separate trade networks in ceramic vessels operating on each side of the Thames.

The large assemblage of window glass from site A represents a vast, untapped source of information not only about the priory buildings and their fenestration, but also about the manufacture, use and reuse of medieval glass in general. It would surely also provide a record, albeit of a fragmented nature, of the iconography and cultural references current in the medieval monastic community and by inference in the wider medieval population.

The process of suppression has proved to be a particularly interesting aspect of the project and one which could be expanded and enhanced by a detailed comparison of the same period at other monastic houses. Although it was possible to identify the location on site A of the post-medieval mansion, the full extent of the building remains to be established, as does much of the detail one might hope to recover from archaeological investigation, such as the building's development, status, the function of rooms within it and when it fell out of use. PCA's recent excavations should throw light on many of these questions regarding the history and development of the mansion house. Of considerable interest, too, is the form and extent of the formal gardens indicated by the antiquarian drawings of John Chessell Buckler; the relationship between former monastic houses and 16th-/17th-century formal gardens is one worthy of fuller examination.

7

Specialist appendices

Textual conventions, including the style of catalogue entries and abbreviations used in the catalogues, are explained in Chapter 1.5.

7.1 Buckler plans

Mark Samuel

John Chessell Buckler (1793–1894) was a gifted painter and draughtsman known mainly for his prints of architectural subjects, such as the series of cathedrals produced in 1822 (Russell 1979, 151). His father John (d 1851) was his senior by more than 30 years (below) but their work was very similar (ibid, 196). The family lived in Bermondsey at the turn of the 18th century (Oxford DNB). Although John Chessell went on to publish a seminal work on Eltham Palace (1828), his archaeological ability, in the modern sense of interpreting 'below-ground' evidence, has received less attention; in some ways, he deserves to be recognised as a pioneer in monastic archaeology.

Before 1800, the taste for Gothic architecture would have been confined to a small rich elite had it not been for the *Gentleman's Magazine*, which forms 'an inexhaustible treasury' for the modern researcher (Clark 1995, 72). This genteel quarterly allowed almost anyone to publish notices about matters of general interest; this they did not hesitate to do in heated correspondences, usually anonymously. Incredibly, the subject of Gothic was of popular interest (ibid) and the *Gentleman's Magazine* regularly published articles on its origin, as well as descriptions of local antiquities and discoveries. The magazine forms a record of the general destruction of what remained of medieval London and its environs in the early modern period and rarely fails to provide some important snippets of information on individual sites.

The *Gentleman's Magazine* reveals that the recording of Bermondsey Abbey was a family affair. The best-preserved monument of Bermondsey in about 1800 was a subsidiary gatehouse immediately east of the partially demolished Great Gatehouse (the outer west gate). 'J.C.' (almost certainly the father) took a view of the south side of the Inner Gatehouse (the inner north gate) as far back as 1779 (*Gentleman's Magazine* 1808a, 477) before John Chessell was born. He recorded the north side in 1785 (ibid). It was demolished in 1805 (Martin 1926, fig 9) when his son was only 12. These views are apparently lost.

The 'J.C.' signing the *Gentleman's Magazine* article is presumably John Buckler, senior; he was clearly very precocious in 1779 and 1785 when he 'took a view'. The reference to two 'very young Artists' (*Gentleman's Magazine* 1810, 513, pl II) in later correspondence is to his sons, John Chessell and George H, who signed their work reproduced opposite in the article. C J M Whichelo was also attracted to Bermondsey at about this time and produced an aerial view, much the same stone details and a view of the interior (1811) of Pope's house. Engravings based on these were reproduced in Robert Wilkinson's *Londina Illustrata* (1819, pls 48, 49).

In 1808 'the mad rage with the major part of the Bermondseans to get rid of every particle of those documents which proved their district once had a page in history' led to the construction of Abbey Street across the site of the abbey church (*Gentleman's Magazine* 1808a, 477). 'I have then, before the last devastating arm is raised, taken a survey of the whole site, and thus report accordingly' (ibid). Buckler's report is, however, brief and impressionistic, the chief points of interest being the dating of the east garden quadrangle to the reign of Edward IV (cf below, 7.3) and the existence of a 'foss', partially filled up to form Grange Walk (*Gentleman's Magazine* 1808a, 477). It is likely, however, that he provided the groundwork for the general plan of the mansion (BL, Add MS 24433, fo 3; Fig 109), the single most important drawing in the Buckler collection. The disparity between the Bucklers' visual and verbal powers is a continual problem in interpreting these records. They presumably made field records which were subsequently discarded; all the drawings were 'worked up' off site.

Buckler, senior, provided an update in August 1808, when he published a plate of architectural fragments which had 'been taken out from the rubble of the walls now pulling down …' (*Gentleman's Magazine* 1808b, 681 and pl II). He identified that several periods were represented and that stone had been reused, but he called 'Saxon' what we now call Anglo-Norman or Romanesque: this was a typical error of the time (Clark 1995, 38) that reflected the general assumption that Gothic architecture originated from before the Danish invasions. In November, he published a further series of architectural details (*Gentleman's Magazine* 1808c, 977 and pl II).

The construction of Abbey Street required the clearance of frontages to the north and south. The creation of a new south frontage required the removal of the Inner Gatehouse and the ancient buildings flanking it in 1805. Buckler was incensed that utilitarian buildings immediately to the south were left undisturbed (*Gentleman's Magazine* 1808a, 477). The north range of the west quadrangle of the mansion was also removed slightly later. This proved to incorporate the south wall of the church nave, much of which survived as superstructure. It was destroyed in 1809 (*Gentleman's Magazine* 1810, 513).

Buckler, senior, recruited his young sons in the recording of the north range of the mansion and their efforts are celebrated in a subsequent article published in December 1810 (*Gentleman's Magazine* 1810, 513). Two plates were published '… being the joint efforts of two very young artists' (ibid). One showed the north-west corner of the mansion, while the other was a plate of architectural fragments, two of which had already been illustrated in 1808. The caption indicates they were drawn by John Chessell and engraved by his brother George; no doubt Buckler, senior, saw this as a useful exercise. Whatever his intention, a lasting interest was established in the mind of the 17-year-old. The process of demolition was apparently complete by this stage (ibid). The continued existence of some of the 16th-century work is implied by the

work of C J M Whichelo, who recorded the 'Inside of a room adjoining those under the Hall, Bermondsey Abby', the drawing dated 1811 (Wilkinson 1819, pl 1), but it is not clear what is shown.

From this stage on, there were no more notices in the magazine, and it is necessary to use John Chessell Buckler's unpublished account (BL, Add MS 24432) to try and piece together events. Very few of the drawings themselves are dated and there is little or no cross-reference to his manuscript text. One detail (BL, Add MS 24433, fo 138) is dated 1818. The general plan (BL, Add MS 24433, fo 3; Fig 109) is dated 1808–20 which presumably was the main period of 'rescue recording'. The dated drawings indicate that the easternmost structures survived for several more years. The recording was not completed until 1823 and John Chessell Buckler's account was not to be compiled for many years. His apparent intent was to write a book like his later work on Eltham Palace, but he instead donated the records to the British Museum (now the British Library) in 1859. Embarrassment at their relative disorder may have been the cause of a strange condition that the public could not consult them for 30 years. He relented three years later (BL, Add MS 24432 A, i). His continued fascination for monastic archaeology can be seen in his superb records of Reading Abbey made in 1824 or soon after (Slade 1976, 47). These too were deposited in the British Museum (now the British Library) in an unpublished state (BL, Add MS 36400A).

Why did Buckler go to such trouble? Records of ancient buildings were a saleable commodity in the architectural community, which would explain his exquisitely detailed records of the Inner Gatehouse (BL, Add MS 24433, fo 2; Fig 117). Thomas Rickman's *An attempt to discriminate the styles of English architecture* had appeared in 1817, and the subject was in vogue amongst the educated elite. Access to good illustrations and engravings was all-important for would-be publishers and something of this competition can be seen between Rickman and John Britton (Aldrich 1985).

A purer spirit of archaeological research is also apparent; John Chessell's careful tracing and reconstruction of the priory church suggests that a publication was intended. His 'ready for engraving' church plan (BL, Add MS 24433, fo 70; Fig 123) was never to appear in published form and Buckler was to be remembered as a draughtsman rather than an antiquary in his own right.

Buckler was not the first person to restore near-destroyed monastic plans in England; Lewes Priory was surveyed for the artist Francis Grose in 1772 (Poole 2000, 36) and Sir Henry Englefield published plans and sections of Reading Abbey in 1782 in the sixth volume of *Archaeologia*. However, Buckler's methodical progression from observed remains to interpreted reconstruction and his careful demarcation between surviving and conjectural evidence was novel.

Buckler engraved some of his views, which eventually appeared in various topographical volumes such as Pennant's *London* (1790) and Wilkinson's *Londina Illustrata* (1819). The picturesque 'Inner Gatehouse' was also recorded by draughtsmen and engravers such as Henry de Cort, F Nash and C J M Whichelo (Martin 1926, figs 6–8). A small selection were published or mentioned by A R Martin, including several important non-Buckler records. The lack of archaeological information prevented a proper understanding of Buckler's records, notwithstanding Martin's valiant efforts (1926, fig 2). Martin succeeded in accurately predicting the position of the north side of the east arm, and it was this information that presumably alerted Grimes to the significance of this bomb-damaged area.

Grimes and Corbett's discoveries (Grimes 1968, 210–17) did not, in themselves, provide a key to understanding Buckler's records, nor was the attempt made. It was only when the south wall of the church was identified in the 1980s excavations that the width of the church could be broadly determined for the first time. This provided for the first time the approximate position of the church's long axis.

Returning to the British Library, the key source is a bound calf volume containing 161 drawings, of which folios 1–71 and folios 135–61 are topographical, ranging from large-scale maps to precise records of *in situ* architectural detail. Folios 72–134 record architectural fragments from the priory. About 30 of the topographic records are intended to illustrate the monastic remains, while another 60 concentrate on the post-Dissolution mansion of Sir Thomas Pope. An accompanying text (BL, Add MS 24432 A and B) runs to two volumes; this is disorderly and contains much that is irrelevant for our purposes (Martin 1926, 192), but certain sections throw light on the thinking behind some of his most important and otherwise enigmatic drawings. Some direct description stands out that must have been made on the spot; the text also confirms that Buckler sought out and dug out foundations to answer questions posed by the surviving superstructure.

No field notes survive and all his extant drawings are drawn to scale, with measurements carefully jotted down. He transferred the more important measurements to his finished drawings; a very useful habit. He assumed that buildings were orthogonal (squared) in plan unless this was obviously not the case. This worked well where a building was orthogonal, but created difficulty when dealing with large areas and irregular plans, as witnessed by BL, Add MS 24433, folio 3 (Fig 109) where several adjustments are needed to fit the plan to the modern Ordnance Survey.

Very long overall measurements were taken, probably with a chain. Using his chain, he would take several long overlapping measurements from several independent points along the same alignment. This led to a certain amount of cumulative error. His large-scale plans of independent structures had to be laboriously reduced with dividers and fitted on to his smaller scale plans. Some of his large-scale plans are lost, being only known through the reduced versions. It has been possible to reproduce this reduction process, using graphics programmes, to allow a greater degree of precision than achieved by Buckler.

The distinction between superstructure and foundations in plan was sometimes uncertain (Martin 1926, 193), but the views clear up most points. The advanced use of colour conventions marks his work out (degrees of survival and conjecture as well as materials are indicated).

Catalogue of maps, plans and measured drawings of monastic structures

The catalogue gives the published records in their probable order of creation. His plans of the priory and abbey and the mansion that was draped over its remains are described here, but minute details of the woodwork and fittings of the mansion are outside the scope of this report.

Abbey gateway, Bermondsey (BL, Add MS 24433, fo 2), before August 1805 (scale 1:24)

Scaled monochrome plan of the Inner Gatehouse that separated the approach quadrangle from the mansion outer court or forecourt at ground-floor level; drawn in pencil with most dimensions written in (Fig 117). The ornate mouldings of the north front gate plinths are enlarged in both plan and elevation. The high finish suggests this is a final state drawing for engraving. Henry de Cort's watercolour (Martin 1926, fig 9) shows the gatehouse mostly demolished by August 1805. The early date suggests the involvement of Buckler's father, John.

DESCRIPTION

The gatehouse was described by Martin (1926, 206–7) on the basis of this plan (not cited). The ground floor was divided into wide and narrow passages for vehicles/riders and pedestrians. The north pedestrian entrance is omitted, although Whichelo's view (Martin 1926, fig 7) shows a door here, also observed '… stopped up and nearly obliterated …' by Buckler, senior (*Gentleman's Magazine* 1808a, 477). The north side was adorned with a chequer-work of ashlar and flint (BL, Add MS 24433, fo 6) with flanking polygonal turrets for ?chimneys. The north gate jambs and arches were elaborately moulded but the south openings had simple chamfers (Fig 117). A turret on the south-east angle contained a spiral stair and the complete building would have been embattled, with the turrets rising above the crenellations. The building was truncated and turned into a dwelling at an unknown date, but originally stood three floors high, perhaps with a chapel in the upper floor (Martin 1926, 200).

INTERPRETATION

The mouldings and the brick diaperwork on the south side are all consonant with a late 15th- or early 16th-century date and can be compared to parts of the West Front at Hampton Quadrangle Palace (*c* 1514; Wight 1972, l 35). The Bermondsey gate was flanked by ranges of ?contemporary buildings. The jettied half-timbered building between this and the Great Gate, that is the west outer gate (BL, Add MS 24433, fo 6) was thought by Martin to be a guesthouse for the poor. The almonry was probably immediately inside the Great Gate (west gate) (Martin 1926, 201). Partly demolished walls shown abutting the east side of the gatehouse may mark its site.

The north half of the west courtyard of Sir Thomas Pope's mansion, ground floor (BL, Add MS 24433, fo 4), undated (scale 1:144)

Unfinished pencil, ink and washes, no captioning/date; dark wash distinguishes monastic superstructure from the mansion masonry walls and monastic foundations (Fig 118). The

position, orientation and scale of this structure are known from BL, Add MS 24433, folio 3 (Fig 109).

DESCRIPTION

The north range or wing is shown at ground-floor level with adjoining portions of the west and east sides of the quadrangle. It still existed in 1820 (Martin 1926, fig 10), a date at variance

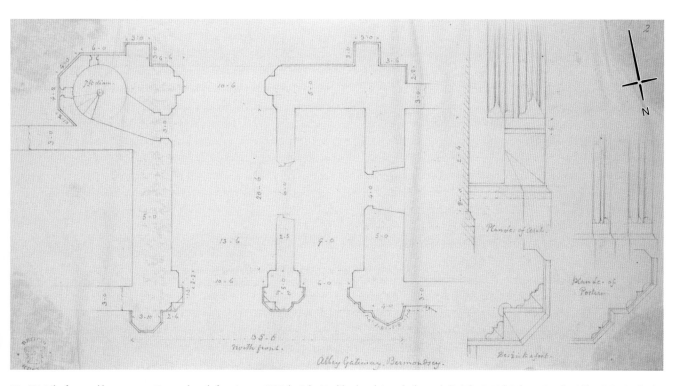

Fig 117 The former abbey gateway, Bermondsey, before August 1805, by John Buckler (north is to the bottom) (© The British Library Board, Add MS 24433, fo 2)

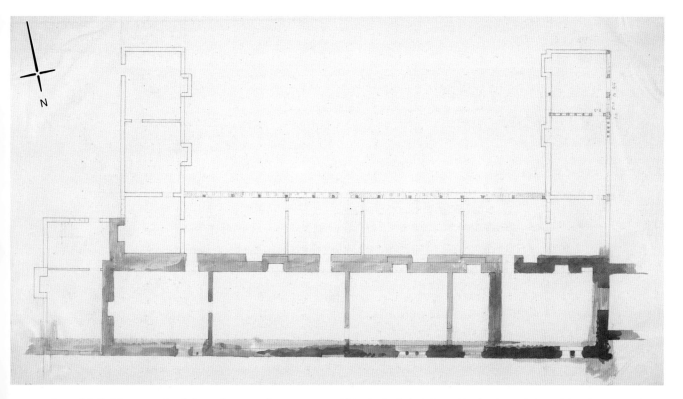

Fig 118 The north half of the west courtyard of Sir Thomas Pope's mansion, ground floor (undated), by John Buckler (north is to the bottom) (© The British Library Board, Add MS 24433, fo 4)

with Buckler, senior's assertion that all had been levelled by 1810. Other records were made during and after the removal of the timber parts of Pope's house (BL, Add MS 24433, fo 25) but are undated. A ?composite view of the north side of the mansion showing the ashlared nave aisle wall is dated '1815 and 1818' (BL, Add MS 24433, fo 9). The southern range of the courtyard was thought by Buckler to be the site of the hall, but had been replaced by brick houses by the early 18th century (BL, Add MS 24432 B, 5v).

A masonry wall divided the north wing of the quadrangle into two parts along its length; the chambers on the north side of the masonry wall being rather larger. The quadrangle was of close-studded half-timbered construction. There was a continuous gallery around the courtyard on the upper floor, with walls of timber and presumably wattle infill; this had a considerable effect in diminishing the bulk of the building (BL, Add MS 24432 B, 5v). The side ranges were one room thick, with chimney stacks of brick and timber-studded construction projecting into the courtyard at intervals of 18ft (5.49m). A small staircase wing at the east end provided access to upper floors via a dog-leg stair. The chambers were entered from each other through off-centre doors near the courtyard wall.

INTERPRETATION

The first phase of the mansion used the south wall of the nave as its north wall and its solid southern wall was built on what was probably the foundation of the cloister arcade.

The quadrangle appears to have been built in two stages. The first act was the building of a masonry house on the site of the north cloister walk. A timber quadrangle was later added to the south. The southern masonry wall was thickened so as to contain

additional fireplaces for the chambers overlooking the courtyard.

A view in the London Metropolitan Archives (Fig 110) shows the ground floor of the quadrangle on the north and west as masonry dressed with brick. The north side of the courtyard is clearly shown as studded half-timber construction at ground-floor level in the (more reliable) plan. Views such as Fig 110 indicate the first floor was extensively half-timbered. Only the north side of the quadrangle bore any relationship to the underlying monastic cloister. Dimensions recorded by Buckler show that the courtyard was 29.87m wide and extended at least 35.05m to the south (BL, Add MS 24433, fo 3; Fig 109).

The plan of the quadrangle resembled that of the inner quadrangle at Nonsuch Palace, where the 'double-thickness' east range was similarly divided by an internal service wall (Summerson 1991, fig 9). While this may be entirely coincidental, it is worth bearing in mind that the two buildings were directly contemporary, and the treasurer of the Court of Augmentations would have been well placed to observe and imitate the architectural preferences of his master, Henry VIII.

No caption, no main caption, north point or scale bar [west courtyard of Bermondsey mansion, first floor] (BL, Add MS 24433, fo 5), undated (scale 1:144)

West courtyard of the mansion, north wing and adjoining parts of west and east wings at first-floor level; wash conventions distinguish construction materials (Fig 119). This plan differs in some details from the various surviving views of this range and is presumably more reliable. It can be scaled through comparison with BL, Add MS 24433, folio 3 (Fig 109). The plan tallies closely with Buckler's description (BL, Add MS 24432 A, 13v).

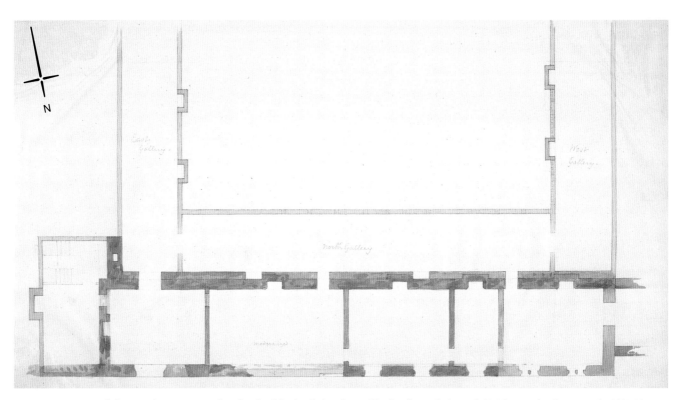

Fig 119 West courtyard of Bermondsey mansion, at first-floor level (undated), by John Buckler (north is to the bottom) (© The British Library Board, Add MS 24433, fo 5)

DESCRIPTION

The north component of the north wing shared partitions and fireplaces with the ground floor, but the south component formed a continuous gallery 29.87m (98ft) in length. Access was gained by the dog-leg staircase at the east end. This stair annex rested on two medieval wall foundations running southwards and 3.65m apart.

The constructional details of the quadrangle are recorded in a near-continuous series of 40 drawings (BL, Add MS 24433, fos 16–69). Buckler recorded the building in an advanced state of decay but commented that the upper floor was better preserved, being less accessible to vagrants (BL, Add MS 24432 A, 13v).

The first floor of the half-timbered quadrangle formed four galleries about 4.57m (15ft) wide, partitioned only at their ends. The galleries were, as in the ground floor, heated at regular intervals by brick fireplaces dressed with stone: the many records show standard fireplaces ornamented by pseudo-elliptical or angular arches; the spandrels with shields or devices. Such fireplaces were probably mass-produced in the North Downs (Samuel 1997, 193) and good examples can be seen at Sutton House (Hackney). All walls were wainscotted and of studded construction. Integral frames for paintings were provided (BL, Add MS 24432 A, 13v). The exterior of the upper floor on the side ranges was jettied out on a continuous coving. The studs and rails were connected by serpentine braces, a 'common feature of the second quarter of the 16th century' (Schofield 1984; Fig 110). The roof trusses were of simple braced construction and not intended to be seen.

The coved plaster ceilings of the galleries were, at least in part, timber-ribbed on a perspective cuboid pattern very similar to that of the Brown Gallery, Knole House, Sevenoaks (Kent). The latter is considered typically Jacobean (Jackson-Stops 1978, 17); an indication of Bermondsey's long history of alteration prior to its decline.

INTERPRETATION

This plan shows the mansion, but an inconspicuous detail of the monastic church deserves to be highlighted. A length of the aisle wall 12.41m long survived at first-floor level and was punctuated at regular intervals by mansion windows (Fig 119). The reuse of the surround of a monastic aisle window as the site of a new window was described by Buckler further east (BL, Add MS 24432 A, 13v). It seems likely that the three mansion windows occupy the position of old windows and therefore 'fossilise' the bay interval of the church. They have been used therefore as a guide in the reconstruction of the church plan.

Thurley (1993, fig 85) reconstructs the first floor of Nonsuch Palace on the basis of excavated and documentary evidence. The exterior of the east range was occupied by the king's privy chambers, while a privy gallery overlooked the courtyard; the arrangement being reminiscent of Bermondsey's north range. Henry showed Nonsuch to his court for the first time in June 1545 (ibid, 63) and it may be conjectured that Pope was amongst the visiting courtiers. Pope may have remodelled his house to copy this 'ideal' design. Bermondsey would in that case have followed the standard pattern for houses without halls. The missing south range, therefore, may have held a gatehouse. The complete quadrangle is shown in W Faithorne and R Newcourt's map of 1658 (Faithorne and Newcourt 1658; Martin 1926, 194).

Ancient walls and foundations at the north [sic] west angle of the abbey church, Bermondsey (BL, Add MS 24433, fo 55), undated (scale 2/12 [1:72])

This pencil drawn plan is twice the scale of the mansion plans and was intended to highlight monastic masonry at the south-west corner of the priory church exposed after the removal of the superstructure of the north range of Pope's quadrangle in ?1818 (Fig 120). Only the west end of the mansion north range is shown. Reductions to wall thickness made during the construction of the mansion are carefully indicated. Areas of surviving superstructure are hatched and extant wall faces are highlighted as solid line. The rubble foundation is shown naturalistically. Like most of his plans, the normal orientation is reversed.

DESCRIPTION

This plan agrees with BL, Add MS 24433, folio 4 (Fig 118) in all details of the plan, but shows several important details in higher resolution. Comparison with BL, Add MS 24433, folio 58 (Fig 122) allows the plan to be correctly oriented; it shows three chambers or spaces of monastic date. The north wall is called the 'Inside of Church wall – North elevation of mansion' and walls to the west can be identified with the range of buildings flanking the Inner Gatehouse. To the east, the medieval wall faces are cut back to enlarge the 'modern room' at the north-west corner of the mansion quadrangle. The north-west corner of the mansion descends into a roughened mass of foundation running northwards. Another wall 5.47m long runs parallel to the south on a thick foundation and terminates with a three-sided chamfered respond facing east. This is depicted in a view as a massive feature standing to a height of at least 4.0m (BL, Add MS 24433, fo 25).

The north wall (the south nave aisle wall) was c 1.39m thick and was interrupted by a chamfered two-light opening near the west end, with unadorned round heads. This is recorded in greater detail in BL, Add MS 24433, folio 11 (Fig 121). A 'roughened surface' was noted by Buckler in his text as 'full seven feet in thickness' a short distance to the east; it ran the height of the wall (BL, Add MS 24432 A, 48). He identified it as the pier supporting the east side of a tower. Again, the normal orientation is reversed.

INTERPRETATION

Buckler interprets the grey foundation running northwards as the 'west front' in his finished plan of the 'Abbey Church' (BL, Add MS 24433, fo 70; Fig 123). The outer wall of the west claustral range can be identified with the southern continuation of this foundation (Martin 1926, fig 1), making, that is, the west wall of the west range aligned with the west front.

The identity of the opening in the south wall of the aisle is

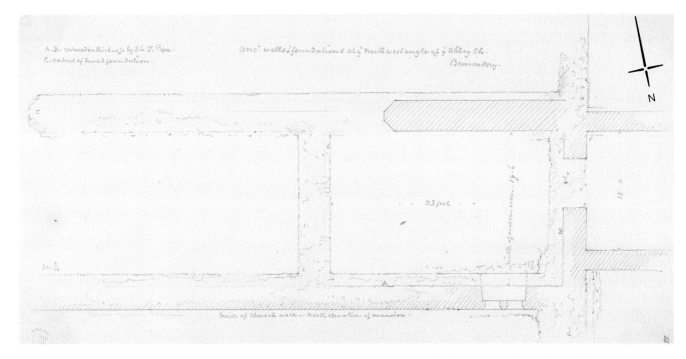

Fig 120 Ancient walls and foundations at the north [sic] west angle of the abbey church, Bermondsey (undated), by John Buckler (north is to the bottom) (© The British Library Board, Add MS 24433, fo 55)

less clear: it is too low and faces 'the wrong way'. It has been suggested that it was a locutory opening (J West, pers comm) and that the space to the south was a locutory as at Norwich. In this case the locutory was enclosed within the bulk of the west range of the cloister.

An ashlared wall terminating in a mysterious chamfered respond was embedded in the south wall (Fig 120) and loomed some 4.0m or so above the demolished ruins of the mansion (BL, Add MS 24433, fo 25). An inverted chamfer stop at the summit (ibid) marks where an arcade arch sprang to the east, and it follows that one or more correspondingly massive arcade piers rested on the recorded foundation. This arcade arch is unconnected to the church, but seems to indicate a series of arched openings separating the ?locutory from the north cloister walk. Several features show this was not a cloister arcade: scale, the position *within* the north cloister range and the absence of an abutting west cloister arcade (the south side is shown as smooth ashlar). It appears to be late medieval in date.

A cloister arcade would normally be expected in such a position, but it appears that what we are seeing is an internal arcade that formed the division between a ?locutory and other chambers that lay between the nave and the cloister walk to the south. In that case, the cloister walk may have lain in the position later occupied by the southern component of the mansion north range. While it seems likely that the cloister arcade foundation would be re-employed to support the north courtyard wall, Buckler makes no mention of it.

It can be speculated that the cloister was moved south from the wall of the nave when the arcaded structure was built. There are advantages to such an interpretation. The ashlared respond wall then acts as the north side of a ?slype running between the locutory and the cellarer's range to the outer court.

The obstructing part of the east wall of the 12th-century west claustral range would have been demolished when the arcaded structure was built, but its foundation was recorded alongside the respond by Buckler. He mentions the great difficulty of distinguishing between foundations of different periods in this area (BL, Add MS 24432 A, 15–16). Alterations in this area on this scale might have included adaptation of the west range, into for example prior's/abbot's lodgings (Chapter 4.2, 'The cloister').

It was suggested by Buckler that the south tower of the west front was incorporated in the nave aisle (BL, Add MS 24432 A, 48) and the corner of the building was rebuilt in brick after its removal (Martin 1926, 216). The brick wall was 4.67m from east to west, which may represent the width of the tower.

The tower was probably supported on its east side by a transverse arch between the aisle wall respond (whose traces were observed by Buckler) and the vanished nave arcade. Part of the brick north wall of the east garden court was decorated with what appears to be a twin-towered west front in elevation (below, 7.3).

The broad foundation of the west front was identified by Buckler (Martin 1926, 215) and is recorded as 6ft 6in (1.98m) wide (BL, Add MS 24433, fo 58; Fig 122). The unbroken ashlared aisle wall surface (Add MS 24433, fo 9) implies that vaulting, if any, was supported on corbels. This practice was extremely common in Burgundian architecture and spread through Cistercian influence (Bilson 1909, 259). A relatively thin church foundation was permissible by the absence of vault responds and Buckler records it as 5ft 6in (1.68m) wide at several points in his records. This diminishes to 1.39m in the superstructure of the base of the tower (at the locutory opening) which was presumably the same as the nave wall thickness. While no nave buttresses were recorded by Buckler, they have since been recorded by PCA (A Douglas, pers comm; Chapter 4.2, 'The 12th-century priory church').

On north side, near west angle, Bermondsey Abbey (BL, Add MS 24433, fo 11), undated (scale c 1:19)

Sketch elevation of twin-light chamfered opening in pencil, annotated with dimensions (Fig 121).

DESCRIPTION

This important drawing shows an opening with paired lights with round heads. The lights were about 5ft (1.526m) high with a proportion of 1:3. The central mullion was 1ft (0.305m) wide. Comparison with BL, Add MS 24433, folio 55 (Fig 120) shows the opening had plain reveals and a pronounced chamfer. The embrasure was slightly splayed. The window is set into an ashlared wall face that appears contemporary. The ashlar lifts average 10in (0.254m). The sill of this opening was about waist height (BL, Add MS 24433, fo 45: reprinted in Martin 1926, fig 11). (See also Buckler's view of 1808: LMA, Wakefield Collection, cat no. p5367969; cf *Gentleman's Magazine* 1810, 513.)

INTERPRETATION

The opening was contemporary with the ashlared south wall of the nave. It would have allowed monks in the locutory to talk with layfolk in the nave (J West, pers comm). It could probably be closed from the south side with shutters and would permit surveillance of the interior of the west portal of the nave if required.

The pairing of simple chamfered lights in the chapels of the south transept of Fountains Abbey, Yorkshire West Riding (Bilson 1909, pl 6), is reminiscent of the Bermondsey openings. This is in accord with the general mid–late 12th-century nature of the architectural fragments (below, 7.2, 'Construction phase 1, c 1140–90 (periods M4 and M5): important stone groups from the 12th-century priory church (B3)').

Doorway in north elevation, Bermondsey (BL, Add MS 24433, fo 138), 1818 (scale 1:16 and 1:4)

Finished version in pencil with scaled elevation and careful details of the moulding. This was a monastic door through the south wall of the east arm of church and was retained as the north entrance to the east block of Sir Thomas Pope's mansion. Another view shows damaged areas of the base of the door jambs (BL, Add MS 24433, fo 22). The lower part of the elevation is therefore not reliable as a record. The door survived until 1820.

DESCRIPTION

The door opened southward and had a two-centred arched head. The embrasure was sharply splayed (BL, Add MS 24433, fo 58; Fig 122). The two-order moulding incorporated hollow chamfers, a roll and a diagnostic wave mould. The arch was not keyed into the surrounding ashlar and seems to have stood slightly proud of the wall, 5ft (1.524m) thick to the east (BL,

Fig 121 On north side, near west angle, Bermondsey Abbey (undated), by John Buckler (© The British Library Board, Add MS 24433, fo 11)

Add MS 24433, fo 70; Fig 123). The wall increased further in thickness to the west, the reveal being clearly indicated. The 1818 ground surface apparently corresponded more or less with the monastic external (cemetery) ground surface.

Buckler mentions that the surrounding wall was retained to a height of 12ft (3.66m) '… to take a useful position on the north side of the mansion …' (BL, Add MS 24432 A, 32v) and that '… in 1820, its masonry was solidly and beautifully perfect …' (ibid, 36; see also Buckler's 1827 view: LMA, Pennant's London Collection 33, cat no. p5369520).

INTERPRETATION

Martin makes no mention of this door, even though Buckler makes its monastic date plain, even marking it as being in the south wall of the 'Sanctuary' (BL, Add MS 24433, fo 58; Fig 122).

The mid to late 14th century probably marks the modernisation of the Romanesque east arm rather than its complete rebuilding (Graham 1937; Chapter 4.2, 'The 14th-century priory church'). Parts of the 12th-century arcades survived to the end but Romanesque doors were more easily cut out and replaced (below, 7.2, 'Construction phase 5, c 1340–c 1410 (period M8)'). This door is from that period; Grimes stated that the door 'has a fourteenth-century look' (1968, 216) and Morris's first variety of wave moulding (1978, 23) becomes common after about 1320. This door may have been newly inserted rather than a direct replacement. 'The door of the monks' cemetery' is mentioned next to a new altar dedicated to St Andrew, St James and all the Apostles in 1338 (Graham 1937, 146). Corpses were taken from the infirmary to the choir where the Office of the Dead would be chanted and the body was taken out for burial by the same door. The door may also have led to the chapter house through a half-timbered pentise.

Ground plan of Sir Thomas Pope's mansion, Bermondsey (BL, Add MS 24433, fo 3), 1808–20 (scale 1:503)

Pencil, orientation reversed (north to the bottom; Fig 109). The site of the church is indicated, as are the outer, inner and south gatehouses and associated houses, part of the precinct wall, the west courtyard building and east range of Sir Thomas Pope's mansion, as well as the east garden with paths and gazebos. A survey was made by Buckler, senior (*Gentleman's Magazine* 1808a, 477), and the plan by his son certainly draws on this and other records to show the form of the mansion as completely as possible in about 1800.

DESCRIPTION

This map shows the mansion of Sir Thomas Pope, and also forms an important record of the priory buildings on which it was based. Almost all the major dimensions of the drawing are noted down. The complex was subdivided by a 'vista' of 586ft (178.6m); this later formed a street called Long Walk, subsequently mostly obliterated by Tower Bridge Road. 'Modern' buildings are only shown in outline where adjacent to historical remains. Some details seem to have been roughly added.

The map is the only surviving dimensional record of the east garden, two houses to the east of the quadrangle separated by Long Walk and the full circuit of garden walls to the north. The mansion formal garden is also recorded. All were derived presumably from discarded field records. The exterior of the two houses is well known from views such as BL, Add MS 24433, folio 22. They were two floors high and ran north–south on a common alignment. The full extent of the south house was not known because it had already been robbed of its south wall.

Both houses were 48ft (14.63m) wide and had substantial masonry walls. Their interiors were completely different; the south house being divided by a central wall containing fireplaces, while partition walls of ?brick subdivide it into eight chambers illuminated by three-light mullioned windows. Founded on the east range, this was the only structure recorded by Buckler which was also excavated in the 1980s (Chapter 5.1, 'The construction of Pope's mansion').

The north house was divided into three large and three small chambers by a ?half-timbered party wall. The windows were smaller and less regularly distributed. From other views and plans it appears the north and west walls contained much monastic fabric (eg LMA, Pennant's London Collection 33, cat no. p5369520) and that only the east and ?south walls were entirely post-Dissolution. It did take as much advantage as possible of the foundations of the south transept and chapter house. The roofs were more complex than the south house: here a single roof ran north–south on the east (narrow) compartment abutted by narrow pitched roofs running crosswise across the house to cover the large chambers.

Parts of the Great Gatehouse and a third gatehouse on Grange Walk are also shown. Both are shown in a partially demolished state. The former was already partially demolished before 1772 (Martin 1926, 198). All other buildings on the plan are derived from records described elsewhere in this catalogue.

INTERPRETATION

The Great Gatehouse (the outer west gate) was described by Martin (1926, 198 and figs 4, 5). Little survived of it apart from the outer main arch and flanking passageway, but it was apparently little more than a facade even when complete, being only 4.72m deep (BL, Add MS 24433, fo 3; Fig 109). This permitted little space for chambers above, but a chamber over the side passageway was reached through a door in the south. The Great Gatehouse seems to have been a more restrained structure than the Inner Gatehouse, lacking ornate turrets. It was flanked by a massive precinct wall.

The Great Gatehouse seems to have had a larger counterpart of similar late medieval date to the south of the claustral complex. Buckler describes it as 'a conspicuous relic of a gateway whose front faced the west. The ponderous side wall, 30ft [9.14m] in length and about 26ft [7.92m] in height, retains the piers of the broad arches which carried the superstructure over the road which traversed this part of the monastic enclosure: these piers are 3ft 6 inches [1.07m] in thickness and 10ft [3.05m] in height and retain the sturdy iron hooks on which the oaken gates formerly moved' (BL, Add MS 24432 A, 176). Martin believed a two-storey range fronted a mass of service buildings to the east. He identifies the gatehouse with the 'Newe Estgate' which led to 'the grange', 'the great hay house' 'dry larder house' and 'back house' at the time of the Dissolution (Martin 1926, 206, n 50; Chapter 5.1, 'Tenants and owners of the site'). The gatehouse was not, it seems, very old in 1538.

A remnant of the 'Estgate' can still be identified (2009) on the east side of 7 Grange Walk, embedded in a 17th-century terrace of small houses. If Buckler's thumbnail plan on BL, Add MS 24433, folio 3 is to be believed, it seems there was a double gate with gates opening inwards from both the west and east facades. The remnant incorporates the south Reigate stone jamb of the east-facing opening, including two surviving pintles and the stump of a third, as well as other ?reinforcing ironwork. Buckler's plan also hints at a side passage on the south (?within the extant 17th-century buildings).

Buckler, senior, asserted that the east formal garden wall was built during the reign of Edward IV (1461–83) (*Gentleman's Magazine* 1808a, 477). The west end of the south wall met Building 8 (Fig 112). Several lamp niches were built into the south wall (ibid; BL, Add MS 24433, fos 3, 140) to provide illumination for stabling or other ephemeral lean-to buildings on that side.

Other views and details (BL, Add MS 24433, fos 7, 54, 140, 141) show the garden wall stood 11ft and 1in high (3.38m) (BL, Add MS 24433, fo 141). It had a steep coping of brick and a series of plinths and enclosed almost all the built-up area to the south and east of the church, being presumably culverted over the drains. Fig 140 shows the monumental scale of the wall and and its picturesque appearance created by an assortment of emblems such as crossed keys interspersed with areas of diaperwork, described in detail below (7.3).

The north elevation as recorded by Buckler shows three builds. The coped wall terminated 48ft (14.63m) west of the north-east angle, where it met a different and taller wall that ran another 65ft (19.81m) to the west (BL, Add MS 24433, fo 7), at which point it was demolished (below). Before that, it presumably met the church presbytery (below). A door with a four-centred head allowed passage to the north. The 'tall wall' was adorned with a series of brick emblems such as a 'church west front' (below, 7.3). The wall's appearance suggests it once stood taller. Could this even be the north side of an otherwise unknown brick building connected to the church east end?

After the Dissolution, a garden wall was built over the foundations of the demolished north side of the east arm and north transept (Grimes 1968, fig 52; Fig 23) and, it was assumed, the north foundation of the nave. Without excavation in the churchyard, the relationship of the nave to the garden wall can only be conjectured but the distance of the wall from the south nave wall was marked as 65ft (19.81m) (BL, Add MS 24433, fo 3).

The garden wall joined the tall wall at a ragged break presumably caused by the demolition of the church (BL, Add MS 24433, fo 7). At face value, the plotting of Corbett and Grimes's excavation presents problems when Buckler's plan is directly overlaid on it as the corresponding part of Buckler's plan falls *c* 1m to the south (Fig 70). For this exercise, the plotting of Grimes (discussed above, Chapters 3.2, 'Archaeological evidence', 'Priory church (B3)', 4.2, 'The 12th-century priory church') is treated as the most reliable evidence for the width of the presbytery, but Buckler's plan may in fact be correct in its measure of that dimension. Without re-excavation of Grimes's area (left as lawn, where the structural evidence could still survive) there is no certainty on this point. The eastern *c* 15m of the north garden wall (running from the north-east corner) may be earlier than the heavily patterned brick wall further west; the eastern section – if pre-Dissolution and earlier than the western section – may originally have extended west and abutted the east arm of the church (cf below, 7.3). This eastern section of the north wall could have, together with the south and east walls, served as a monastic flood defence.

Plan of the precinct of Bermondsey Abbey (BL, Add MS 24433, fo 1), ?1820 (scale 1:2540)

East to top; buildings, watercourses and earthworks connected with the priory and mansion are shown (Fig 78). The eastern

limit of the precinct is not shown.

DESCRIPTION
It is not always clear from the plan whether a topographical feature was used as evidence or if documentary evidence was being employed. Crucifix Lane is confused with a street further south ('Five Foot Lane' on eg Rocque 1746, ie modern Tanner Street) and the eastern limits of the precinct are not shown. It shows several watercourses and earthworks not otherwise recorded.

INTERPRETATION
The plan of the mansion is reduced from the 1:503 plan (BL, Add MS 24433, fo 3; Fig 109). The map was used as the basis for a reconstruction of the precinct by Grimes (1968, 211 and fig 51), and earlier by Martin (1926), but neither credit it. Grimes refers to it as a 'tracing of the 25-inch plan', apparently assuming that Buckler used the 25-inch Ordnance Survey as a basis (Grimes 1968, 211) although this series was not commenced in London until the 1860s.

It may be assumed that an 'ancient drain' shown sweeping eastwards from immediately south of the general area now identified as the priory reredorter was retained by Sir Thomas Pope for much the same purpose. The plan is discussed in detail above (Chapter 4.2, 'The precinct and home grange').

Plan of the remains of the abbey of St Saviour, Bermondsey, Surrey (BL, Add MS 24433, fo 58), after 1823 (scale 1:312)

A working drawing in pencil that draws together all records of monastic structures traced by Buckler. These comprise the gatehouse complex, the south wall of the nave and east arm, the foundations of the south transept/east claustral range, including two chapter house burials, while subtracting post-Dissolution features (Fig 122). No conjectural features are shown. The peculiar scale is presumably dictated by the format size.

DESCRIPTION
The drawing is an amalgam of earlier large-scale plans; the detailed Inner Gatehouse plan made before 1805 (BL, Add MS 24433, fo 2; Fig 117) and the substructures of the quadrangle

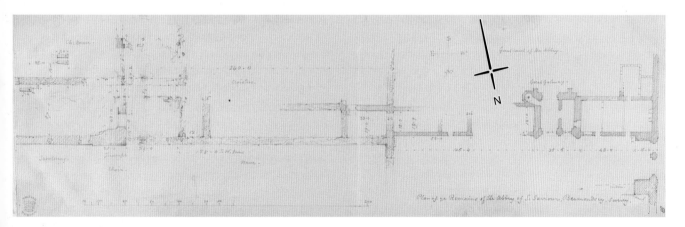

Fig 122 Plan of the remains of the abbey of St Saviour, Bermondsey, Surrey, after 1823, by John Buckler (north is to the bottom) (© The British Library Board, Add MS 24433, fo 58)

north range (BL, Add MS 24433, fo 55; Fig 120). Corresponding records of the south transept/east claustral range, the Great Gatehouse and the ?contemporary jettied structure next to it are lost. The composite elevation of the Inner and Great Gatehouse (BL, Add MS 24433, fo 8) reproduced by Martin (1926, fig 5) was presumably based by Buckler on BL, Add MS 24433, folio 58 and a variety of other records.

INTERPRETATION

The transept/east claustral range foundations were apparently poorly preserved, but Buckler writes 'there can be no doubt as to the general measurements of the south transept, not of course taking into account the chapels on the eastern side, of the former existence, as will be presently shown, no reasonable doubt can be entertained' (BL, Add MS 24432 A, 33v).

The east transept wall survived because it had been incorporated into the west side of the post-Dissolution north house on the site of the former east range. Buckler believed the chapel entrance was an original 12th-century arrangement.

The profile wall of the transept … presented a very picturesque appearance, new and ancient masonry – the symmetrical kind of the Norman builder, and the promiscuous gatherings of the more modern artisan, ingeniously commingled, and usefully associated. … The (*probably apsidal*) [Buckler's words] chapel opened only to the transept and seemingly has left without disguise a rough and irregular mass of masonry [visible near the left end of the plan], attached to the side wall, and seemingly as lofty as the room. … [It] seems confirmed in this instance, by the existence in perfect preservation, to the height of the chamber, of the piers of the aperture, once overarched, forming the communication between the apse and the chapel [*sic*, he means transept]. The opening is 11 feet [3.35m] in width with finished masonry in regular courses, both in the reveal and in the transept to the angle, a length of 14 feet 4 inches [4.37m]. The mullioned and transomed window has been easily inserted, and was easily removed, to the interesting appearance of the Norman workmanship (BL, Add MS 24432 A, 34–34v)

The north transept recorded by Grimes (1968, fig 2) gave on to twin absidioles, entirely removed in the ?14th century. Buckler confesses (BL, Add MS 24432 A, 34) that he never saw the single apse shown in his reconstruction (BL, Add MS 24433, fo 70; Fig 123). However, the preliminary results of recent archaeological excavations at Bermondsey Square, Southwark (BYQ98; Fig 3; A Douglas, pers comm) tend to support the view that the 12th-century south transept had a single apse (Chapter 3.2, 'Archaeological evidence', 'Priory church (B3)'; Fig 69). The asymmetry of the transept arms seems beyond doubt.

Buckler describes the chapter house remains:

which though slight, afford certain signs of its position. In this instance, as with other monastic churches, it stood parallel with the front of the transept, and was separated

therefrom by a passage for communication between the cloisters and the buildings beyond toward the east. This arrangement is clearly denoted, and the graves and coffins which have been discovered, and which were once under the protection of [the chapter house] roof, suggest ample dimensions for its length and breadth. The basement of the north wall was 5 feet 8 inches [1.73m] in thickness. Several of the stone built coffins with their remains were found in a state which renders it certain that they had never before been disturbed. The area of this room and the shape of its upper end must remain uncertain. It appears to have had a vestibule from the cloister, 39 feet [11.89m] in length, a measure equal to the interior breadth of the transept, whose walls may have been said to give the scale for this antechamber (BL, Add MS 24432 A, 33)

Deep uncertainty about the chapter house persists. Architectural probability suggests the south wall would align with the south wall of the chapel (B1). Alternatively, its south wall line may have been marked by a strip buttress recorded by Buckler (BL, Add MS 24433, fo 58; Fig 122). This would suggest an internal width of 7.56m. The south wall of the northern of the two houses probably rested on the chapter house (cf Fig 70). Martin's (1926, 202) suggestion that the distribution of the burials gave a clue to the chamber's internal width (*c* 9.19m) makes sense. It is puzzling, therefore, that Buckler does not mention it. Fig 69 reconstructs a chapter house with an internal width of *c* 8m.

An elevation of the west side of the north house (BL, Add MS 24433, fo 26) shows a massively built and studded door with a Tudor pseudo-elliptical arched head (see also LMA, Pennant's London Collection 33, cat no. p5369520). Measurements written on the drawing plot the door on the east end of the 'passage for communication' (slype). It was re-employed in the north house without alteration and, therefore, was not distinguished by Buckler as a monastic feature.

The same elevation gives the lie to Buckler's claim that fair ashlar work ran continuously from the transept chapel opening to the body of the church (BL, Add MS 24432 A, 34v). The ashlar wall north of the chapel opening is noted as being 5ft (1.524m) wide. It meets a vertical joint, beyond which a rougher face is shown running to the north-west angle of the house. This was implicitly 2.84m wide and may mark the site of a massive respond in the crossing area. Such a respond would be expected at the opening of the transept and would have been cut away and replaced with a regular wall face after the Dissolution.

An ancient spur wall 12ft (3.66m) west of the transept was recorded by Buckler as surviving to first-floor level (BL, Add MS 24432 A, 13v). This rules out the presence of an unbroken cloister walk against the nave wall, at least in its final form. Comparison with other Cluniac abbeys such as Castle Acre shows that the processional door from the east cloister walk was positioned next to the transept. It may be conjectured that the spur is not an original feature; it may have been built to one side of the processional door after the north cloister walk was possibly shifted south (above, 'Doorway in north elevation, Bermondsey (BL, Add MS 24433, fo 138) …').

Ground plan of the abbey church, Bermondsey (BL, Add MS 24433, fo 70) after 1823 (scale 1:215)

Highly finished ink and wash plan purporting to show the plan of the priory church (Fig 123), showing superstructure, foundations and conjectured foundations, together with the brick (garden) wall.

DESCRIPTION

The high finish of this ink and wash plan may indicate the intention of engraving what was the culmination of all Buckler's efforts. It is, in intent, an interpreted reconstruction plan of the priory church. Superstructure is shown in black, foundations in various tones of mid-grey according to preservation while conjectured foundations are shown either in light grey or broken line. Brick is shown in red.

The plan sets out the dimensional information from all other plans, but BL, Add MS 24433, folio 58 is the chief source. The finished plan sets out the physical evidence with a degree of certainty that may be misleading. For example, he omits the door to the monks' cemetery and conflates the width of the nave wall foundation with that of the superstructure (which was narrower). The positions of the north garden walls derive from BL, Add MS 24433, folio 3 (Fig 109) with their inherent inaccuracies. The locutory and chapel openings are clearly shown, however.

The indication of the north side of the priory church and the centre lines of arcades are the most beguiling features of the plan. One arcade apparently subdivides the transept arm. These are based wholly on Buckler's beliefs about the proportions of

church plans and no evidence was ever found by him for them. Buckler did his best to try and trace walls within the body of the church but was defeated by the thoroughness of Pope's robbing.

Of St Saviour's church, the longitudinal measure of the nave can be accurately ascertained but the breadth cannot be exactly defined. The south wall in its original length and thickness having been spared, has proved an unerring index to the rest of the remains, but the opposite or north wall was completely demolished, and with it the pillars and every other portion of the superstructure … every other wall, the interior and the exterior, with the arcades and all the pillars of this eastern portion, were clean swept away; the ground upon which they stood having been completely upturned, and the graves, with which but few exceptions, torn open and their contents dispersed. … It is manifest that the most persevering engines of mischief were busied in the dismemberment and dispersion of the huge basements with the four pillared supports of the tower which we may be sure stood over the intersection of this limb with the longitudinal or main body of the edifice. (BL, Add MS 24432 A, 32v)

It is probably significant that he makes no mention of the north garden wall, suggesting an unsuccessful search for a nave wall below it.

INTERPRETATION

This plan represents Buckler's best effort to advance on the basis of very little evidence. It may be asked why he did not use the

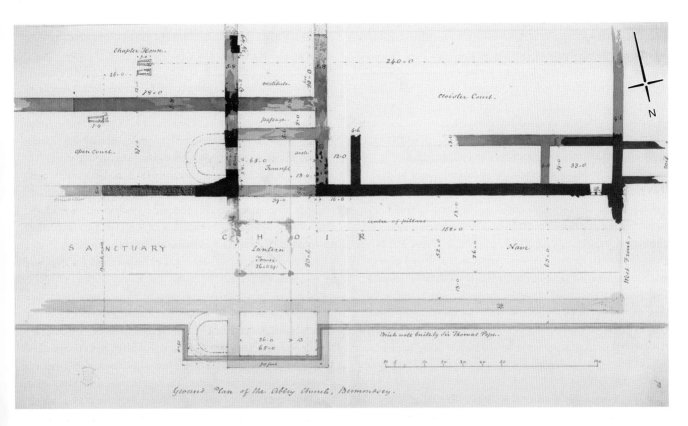

Fig 123 Ground plan of the abbey church, Bermondsey, after 1823, by John Buckler (north is to the bottom) (© The British Library Board, Add MS 24433, fo 70)

position of the brick wall north of the nave as a guide to the probable width of the nave. Martin ignored Buckler's theories and plausibly assumed that this wall was founded on the nave wall foundation (1926, 214). (This wall does not, however, plot on the north nave wall in the 'best fit' reconstruction (Fig 70) here.)

It must be assumed, therefore, that Buckler checked the brick wall and found nothing below it. He instead operated, years later, on an assumption that the known width of the south transept represented the width of the central division plus that of the aisle. This was based on an architectural theory that the width of the aisle was always half that of the nave (measured from the centre lines of the arcades to the face of the aisle wall).

The clear width of the transept, 39 feet [11.89m], supplies the measure for the nave and south aisle, 26 feet [7.92m] and 13 feet [3.96m]. The latter of these two dimensions being doubled, the interior width of the nave, 52 feet [15.85m], is obtained; its length from the outside of the west front being 158 feet [48.16m]. The depth of each wing of the transept proving to be 28 feet and a half [8.69m], it follows that its interior width across the nave was 109 feet [33.22m] … (BL, Add MS 24432 A, 35v)

In the light of accurately plotted excavated evidence, it emerges that neither Buckler nor Martin were right and that the nave width fell between their two very different estimates. This does at least have the advantage of producing a series of plan dimensions that are plausible for a mid-sized British Cluniac or Benedictine church of this period.

7.2   Architectural fragments

Mark Samuel

Introduction: the assemblage

Of the architectural fragments found in excavations at Bermondsey Priory (abbey from 1399) carried out from 1956 to 1989 the vast majority were found in the 1980s. The 'sculpted stone index' made during the principal excavation (1984–9, site A, BA84; Fig 3; Table 1) records 796 stones, but the total number of fragments was greater owing to the system of at times listing two or more stones under one number. This assemblage was 'scanned' by the author in 1991 and recording requirements quantified as part of the project assessment. The final total was 848 architectural fragments, the majority being moulded. There were only two pieces of figural sculpture in this assemblage, both dated to the 12th century – a lion and a human head (Fig 31; Fig 32) (excluding the 11th-century panel: see Chapter 3.1; Fig 20).

An additional 227 fragments were recovered from an excavation on the Southwark waterfront at Vine Lane (VIN88; site Z; Fig 3; Table 1). Despite severe damage and hard adhering

mortar, it gradually became clear that they too came from Bermondsey Priory and it was decided to integrate the Vine Lane assemblage into the analysis of St Saviour Bermondsey. It was not possible to include the medieval architectural fragments from Harp Lane, across the river (HL74; Schofield 1998, 133). These were suggested as coming from the nearby City church of St Dunstan in the East, but they are more likely to have derived from Bermondsey Priory (a small selection are illustrated in Schofield 1984, 75, fig 58). For example, identical and highly idiosyncratic pointed interlaced arcading springer blocks were recovered from both sites A and Z (BA84 and VIN88); voussoir fragments of this sort were found on the Harp Lane site; a distinctive quadrant abacus moulding occurred on all three sites, as well as being recorded by Buckler at Bermondsey (below, 'Construction phase 1, c 1140–90 (periods M4 and M5): important stone groups from the 12th-century priory church (B3)', 'Unprovenanced abaci'). Richard Lea's records (1981) showed Harp Lane to have many later mouldings of a sort not found at the other sites, but on a truly monastic scale.

Fragments recently excavated by PCA are not considered here, other than to observe that the majority appear to compare to typestones already recognised (material seen by this author MS, courtesy of PCA). A minority, however, compare to the more ornate typestones of the sort recorded by Buckler. It is hoped that more will be understood of the 13th-century developments at the church once these have been analysed. Further examples of fragments of types recorded at Harp Lane (HL74) have also been recovered, confirming the identification of the Harp Lane material beyond reasonable doubt.

On excavation, the condition of the Bermondsey assemblage was excellent with well-preserved tooling below easily removed reused mortar. The treatment of the entire assemblage has followed the flow chart recommended by the Council for British Archaeology (CBA 1987, 6–7) except as regards 'making the archive record'. The project did not allow for curatorial activities such as the creation of a comprehensive inventory for all retained architectural fragments, including duplicates; instead the project aimed to maximise the amount of interpretation with the minimum of recording (below). At a conservative estimate only 501 of the 848 fragments from site A needed individual records (60%) while 114 of the 227 from site Z needed recording (50%). This comprehensive 'curator' approach was impractical on several counts and the final report relies on 103 recorded site A stones (21% of the 1991 recommendation) and 35 site Z stones (31%), while two stones recovered by Grimes and Corbett in the 1950s were also recorded.

Many of the stones were reused by Sir Thomas Pope as part of his new house on the site of the cloister. Between 1808 and 1820, John Chessell Buckler recorded 65 monastic stones from the demolished mansion that can now be directly compared to the recent assemblage. He also made a detailed record of the mansion and its monastic substructure (above, 7.1). His stone records demonstrate that the architecture of the priory was more sophisticated than is apparent from the surviving stones and reference is made to the most important of these drawings.

Methodology

Classification

Interpretable isolated stones and the best examples of duplicated stones were categorised as 'typestones'. The final 138 typestones were selected, based on the 1991 scan, according to the following criteria:

a representative sample from each of the principal construction/architectural periods;

a concentration on the well-represented earlier work;

a concentration on stones addressing issues regarding the plan/architecture of the early church (in comparison to La Charité-sur-Loire, St Benoît-sur-Loire etc); and

a concentration on multi-stone groups that give visual impressions of the vanished buildings.

Typestones were grouped according to demonstrable relationships into stone groups (see the archive catalogue) and these were then placed in build and construction phases. The construction phase is a subjective method of combining the many builds into manageable blocks that reflect an apparent building history. ORACLE uses each typestone's date span to order the builds chronologically. The construction phase is centred on the builds or concentration of builds that contain the most stone groups (the 'peaks'). The limits of the phase are defined by apparent breaks in construction and/or the smallest and most poorly dated builds (the 'troughs'). The results of this initial statistical analysis are summarised in Table 11. The dating of each construction phase was then further refined.

Each typestone is referred to by its construction phase, its build and its stone group (eg CP2.9.4). This system allows each stone to be related to the archive catalogue and fully exploit the ORACLE database used by MOLA (below).

Dating

The previous section explains how the construction phases were arrived at; this section outlines the basis of the dating for the individual typestones. During analysis, apparent inconsistencies emerged between the architectural fragments and stratigraphic dating; these are discussed further in Chapter 4.2 ('The 12th-century priory church' and 'The 14th-century priory church'). Perhaps the most problematic – the date of construction of the great priory church – is explicable if major building work was ongoing after *c* 1140 and included substantial work on the priory church (Chapter 3.3, 'Discussion'). With so little of the church itself within the excavation area, there is effectively no *in situ* material to relate the *ex situ* stone assemblage to, other than structures recorded by Buckler and the east range undercroft.

The architectural fragments were dated by three methods which are, in order of accuracy, moulding pattern, tooling techniques and petrology. Each typestone has been researched to identify parallels and to understand its stylistic affinities. This has been done primarily to deal with site-specific questions such as date and possible function, but a stated project aim has been the reconstruction of the building history of the priory, particularly in its earlier periods.

Certain assumptions have had to be made about the stylistic context of the Romanesque phase of Bermondsey Priory owing to limitations on research time. Lindy Grant (pers comm), on inspection of the best typestones which were set aside for photography, set the earliest architecture firmly in the context of the 12th century. The author has, after consulting with Jeffrey West, used a relatively well-dated and documented 12th-century church as a 'control' (St Bartholomew Smithfield). The closeness of the two churches may be of significance because London-based masons could have worked on both. Large round piers were employed at both churches (many round pier elements were found on site Z). If Bermondsey Priory proved to be technically similar, it could help demonstrate the probable function of many of the stones from the destroyed church. The similarity of key mouldings, or the lack of it, would be assessed through moulding records of St Bartholomew Smithfield. This would have important implications for the dating of Bermondsey Priory. West's preliminary inspection of the assemblages indicated that the architecture was best studied in the context of major Romanesque or Anglo-Norman monuments in south-east England; European Romanesque affinities could be studied through secondary sources.

A corpus of major 12th-century London monastic assemblages exists, on paper and on the MOLA ORACLE database, in the Museum of London archive; these include Merton Priory and the hospitals of St John Clerkenwell and St Mary Spital (Thomas et al 1997; Sloane and Malcolm 2004; Saxby and Miller 2007). Research in the Conway Library was made of surviving 12th-century monastic architecture and lapidary collections in south-east England; this threw some light on the affinities of the style of architecture at Bermondsey Priory.

Table 11 Summary of builds and construction phases (CP1–5)

Construction phase and build no.	Earliest build average early date	Latest build average late date	Range in years*	No. of stone groups
CP1.1–1.20	1080	1250	20–150	38
CP2.1–2.9	1160	1300	50–140	14
CP3.1–3.5	1200	1300	43–100	15
CP4.1–4.3	1200	1350	40–150	3
CP5.1–5.3	1325	1466	63–125	10

* the difference between average early date and average late date for each build

MOULDING PATTERN AS A MEANS OF DATING

The pattern-based system of relating developed by Richard K Morris was used: each moulding is 'broken up' into its constituent elements (here called patterns) and these elements, rather than the entire moulding, form the basis of comparison. Moulding elements are compared with surviving published parallels to provide approximate dates using Morris's catalogue (1978); these can be more accurate than medieval pottery dates (Stocker 1993, 19) when associated with documented monuments, but the author does not attempt to identify mouldings with a known master mason.

The initial period after 1066 was stylistically heterogeneous and moulding development in any regular sense only really started in the 12th century. The inference-ridden world of 12th-century dating is well described by Rigold (1977, 102). In contrast, the period 1250–1400 'encompasses the most inventive phase in the development of medieval mouldings' (Morris 1978, 19). The Perpendicular and Tudor styles are notoriously hard to date on the basis of moulding development (ibid). Some moulding patterns were used for long periods and could even be revived, while for example many types of base moulding can occur simultaneously in the same pier base. Despite these unknowns, each typestone was given a date span for statistical purposes (above).

TOOLING AND MASONS' MARKS AS A MEANS OF DATING

Surface finish did change throughout the Middle Ages (Stocker 1993, 23) and tooling marks form a rough means of dating. In a 'typical' assemblage, the architectural fragments would be outnumbered by plain ashlar blocks and other plain structural elements. Rubbing records enable the recognition of the particular 'fists' of individual banker masons within an assemblage. This can allow plain elements (ie ashlars, quoins and scoinsons) to be related to mouldings. This technique has played an important role in distinguishing builds at Bermondsey Priory, and was also used extensively at Merton Priory (Samuel 2007, 176). The criteria are summarised elsewhere in a report on St Gregory's Canterbury (Samuel 2001, 153–4). Masons' marks are little use as a means of dating or plotting relationships except within a single building or assemblage (Alexander 1996, 219) and were rare at Bermondsey; the few important examples are discussed below.

PETROLOGY: STONE USED FOR FREESTONE DRESSINGS, AND RUBBLE, AT ST SAVIOUR BERMONDSEY

No systematic scientific geological study of the St Saviour assemblage has been carried out, but David F Williams identified some samples and confirmed other identifications. Parsons has pointed out how geologically unqualified researchers can perpetuate errors of identification in the archaeological literature (1990, xi). Despite this reservation, some conclusions can be made about the building stone used at Bermondsey Priory. The 1991 scan of the whole assemblage took into account all dressed building stone and was a more accurate guide to the overall proportions of dressed stone of all periods than the selected typestones.

The great majority (93%) of the (848, ie excluding site Z) architectural fragments from St Saviour Bermondsey were dressed from one building stone. This was glauconitic sand/limestone with no oolitic structure; this composition is usually described as 'greensand' (Sherlock 1960, 18) which can derive from anywhere in the extensive Gault and Greensand deposits (for example Eastbourne, Sussex: Lyne 1997, 133). It is here termed 'Reigate' stone because the North Downs in the area of Mertsham and Reigate are the most well-documented and probable source for the London basin. Although scientific tests can distinguish variation in the composition of Reigate-type stone, it can only be provenanced to a general area (Domingo 1994, 243). Reigate stone was used almost exclusively after *c* 1200 in the priory. A note of caution must be sounded here, however; 'Packstone' from the Calvados area of Normandy, for example, is superficially similar to greensand. Recent analysis of building stone from, for example, the Whitefriars, Canterbury, and Holywell Priory, Shoreditch, Hackney (Middlesex), has shown that many published visual identifications of 'Reigate stone' made in the past must be called into doubt because some types of Caen stone bear a strong superficial resemblance to Reigate stone.

Twenty-two occurrences of a light creamy-yellow fine-grained limestone were noted. This has been identified as Caen stone from Normandy. The properties of this stone make it rather better for external use than Reigate stone (Caen is very variable in its weathering qualities). Several otherwise identical 12th-century typestones have been found cut from both types, but the Caen stone seems to have been favoured for piers and mouldings in the 12th-century church.

Seventeen occurrences of oolitic limestones were limited to dressings dated to the 12th century. Most of these are spar prominent hard, orange, oolitic limestone with sorted lenses of shell fragments. Paler examples with small ooliths can also be seen, although it is notoriously difficult to pinpoint the exact sources of oolitic limestones transported for use elsewhere (Parsons 1990, 41). The lion (A<3118>, Fig 31) and blind arcade (A<3070>, Fig 133) were identified as probably Taynton stone of the Middle Jurassic of Oxfordshire (D F Williams, pers comm). The oolitic limestone was resistant to weathering and abrasion, and so selected for external decorative use and also for bases in the 12th-century church. After 1200, it seems to have fallen out of favour, occurring only once as a sill in an otherwise ?Reigate stone 14th-century window (below, 'Construction phase 5, *c* 1340–*c* 1410 (period M8)', 'Traceried window'; A<3112>; CP5.3.4).

Ten fragments of polished shaft dressed from Purbeck marble have been identified. Large elaborate arcade capitals and ?cloister bases were identified as Purbeck marble in the early 19th century (BL, Add MS 24433, fos 105 and 116). Two instances of imported marble veneers were seen but these have not been examined in detail (below, 7.4, 'Stone building material', 'Imported marble'). A single instance of what may have been Tournai marble was observed in 1991 but was subsequently lost.

It is instructive to see how the proportions of freestone

petrology in typestones differ at Bermondsey Priory, Merton Priory (Samuel 2007) and St Gregory's Canterbury (Blows 2001), and to compare Bermondsey with the partially extant remains of the Cluniac priory at Lewes and Benedictine Faversham Abbey (founded 1148). The dominance of a particular type of stone is marked at all three of the first group of monasteries – Bermondsey, Merton and St Gregory's Canterbury. 'Reigate stone' (from the Upper Greensand of Surrey) also played a very important role at the Augustinian Merton Priory, but Taynton stone (Oxfordshire) was extensively employed in the mid 12th-century phase (Samuel 2007, 177). In contrast, the 12th-century Augustinian priory of St Gregory at Canterbury (1145+) was faced with Caen stone (Blows 2001, 184). The Cluniac priory of Lewes was faced with Upper Greensand or Malmstone in its earliest 11th-century phase; Quarr limestone was also heavily employed between 1077 and *c* 1140 (Lyne 1997, 133) after which Caen stone was very extensively employed as a facing stone. At Faversham, the architectural fragments assemblage shows that Caen stone, as at Bermondsey, was the favoured facing material for the interior of the 'period I' church, constituting about 15% of the total building stone used on the site (Philp 1968, 39). Greensand (here denoting a wide range of glauconitic sandy limestones found in the Upper Greensand) is more limited to 13th-century work than at Bermondsey. Scientific examination showed that some of this may have derived from Betchworth (Surrey), but some may have derived from much further east near Sevenoaks (Kent) (ibid, 40) and it is possible that some of the 'Reigate stone' used at Bermondsey in fact derived from Kent, or may be in fact from Normandy (above). Although there is evidence that Reigate stone was quarried from the start to be used at Bermondsey, it has been suggested that the loss of Normandy in the reign of John may have intensified the exploitation of the North Downs quarries at Reigate and elsewhere (Tatton-Brown 1990, 76).

Convenience of quarries meant that the freestone of choice varied considerably from monastery to monastery, while the foundation date also seems to have affected the choice of stone. The peculiar situation at Lewes reflects its early foundation date. Could date have played a role in determining the type of stone used at Bermondsey? The complete absence of the distinctive Quarr stone could indicate a lack of building work prior to *c* 1140. Quarr limestone was the chief building stone at Lewes Priory in its first phase, from 1077 until *c* 1140 (Lyne 1997, 133). Similarly, the trade in Tournai marble tailed off during the third quarter of the 12th century (ibid, 134) and apart from one possible occurrence, it is absent at Bermondsey. Is this negative evidence that the construction of the great church of Bermondsey Priory commenced in earnest after *c* 1150?

A survey of the Romanesque buildings of east Kent by Tatton-Brown (1980, 213–14) indicates that the hiatus in supply of Quarr limestone there appears to occur *c* 1100–20. This is based on evidence from the royal keep, Christchurch Cathedral Priory and St Augustine's Abbey (all in Canterbury), all of which employ Quarr stone in initial Norman work within the period 1070–1120. Although Tatton-Brown notes the use of

Quarr stone in the chapel of the White Tower (London), no comprehensive survey of that significant Norman building had taken place at that time. Work on the White Tower by Roland Harris (2008, 30–8; pers comm 1998) has since identified a hiatus in the construction technology of the building, whereby the use of Quarr limestone ashlar ceases at around first-floor level. The construction break is assigned by Harris to *c* 1083. The apparent hiatus in supply of Quarr stone in London some 20 years before that of east Kent may be attributable to distance. Quarr is used in the much more distant first phase Romanesque north transept and east arm of Norwich Cathedral (*c* 1096–1119) but its occurrence is sporadic, and the principal first phase building stone is Caen (Gilchrist 1998, 129–30). The post-1083 recommencement of work at the White Tower identified by Harris sees the employment of Caen stone, visible in the chapel arcade capitals and two complete piers. If the early date for the hiatus in the supply to London is accepted, the absence of Quarr at Bermondsey and the use of Caen stone in the mouldings of the first phase priory church does not necessarily indicate a post-*c* 1140 construction date. The preponderance of Caen at Norwich Cathedral is similarly not regarded as a late 12th-century phenomenon (Gilchrist 1998).

Quarr was most often found as simple ashlar in the Romanesque buildings of east Kent and in Norwich Cathedral, a factor which may have contributed towards its absence from the St Saviour Bermondsey assemblage. Indeed, the merits of petrological analysis on an archaeological assemblage as opposed to a standing building may be called into question.

Stone rubble was used in various walls and foundations (identified by Ian M Betts). The vast majority is Kentish Rag limestone and Hassock sandstone from the Maidstone area of Kent, referred to as 'ragstone' in the text. A small quantity of Caen stone from northern France is also present, probably dressing waste. One fragment of Caen stone was found associated with the tile hearth in the hall/lodgings (B8) in *c* 1150–*c* 1200 (period M5; Chapter 3.3, 'Archaeological evidence', 'Hall/lodgings (B8)'); the other pieces came from dumping in the (second) reredorter range (B9) in period P1. Chalk rubble was found associated with the robbed out remains of the chapel (B1) and in the area (OA9) to the north of the former chapel (period P1).

Construction phase 1, *c* 1140–90 (periods M4 and M5): masons' marks

Masons' marks are usually absent from the exposed surfaces of the typestones, but the bed surfaces are frequently scored with a large 'X' (Fig 124). This may be a completion mark used by the banker mason. Only one stone group from this phase (CP1.14.1) was regularly marked (below, 'Blind and open chevron arches'). Straight scribe lines probably were placed on stones to assist the setters. One string course block has two parallel scribe lines on the upper bed, which may have been used to control the accurate setting of the string course under stretched strings. On capitals, compass points describe the shaft profile below the necking and were also used to set out the

Fig 124 An example of 'X' – a possible completion mark – on the bed surface (A<3130>-type) (Conway Library, Courtauld Institute of Art, London. © Courtauld Institute of Art) (scale c 1:5)

scallops. The beds of one chevron springer block show the uncut reverse portion of the moulding as a scribe line, showing that a template was used in this period.

Construction phase 1, c 1140–90 (periods M4 and M5): important stone groups from the 12th-century priory church (B3)

Basal elements

A badly abraded, oolitic limestone (?Taynton stone), cabled respond (A<3156>; CP1.1.1; Fig 125) was apparently encountered during excavations in the 1950s and 60s and two stones of this type are held at The Cuming Museum (Southwark). One of these forms half a respond base which projected 0.306m (one statute foot) from the wall plane while the other incorporates a re-entrant (Conway Library, Courtauld Institute negative no. A79/1674). The former may well be the stone recorded lying loose as a 'Saxon Capital' by Whichelo in 1811 (Wilkinson 1819, pl 1). Buckler also recorded a cabled base for triple round shafts (BL, Add MS 24433, fo 78). The style of the cabled base is unusual enough to warrant some discussion. Rigold picks out an

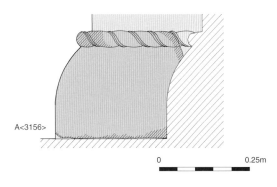

Fig 125 Cabled respond base A<3156> (scale 1:10)

example of the weighted double-convex form (used in a round base) as pre-dating 1072 (1977, 113). The English or statute foot suggests a 12th-century date and Clapham does not date twisted or cable ornament earlier than c 1120 (Clapham 1934, 130).

The base moulding A<3155> (CP1.10.1; Fig 126) is ambiguous in its application and could have served as either a single course plinth or as the sub-plinth to a base moulding. It could derive from a compound pier base or a wall respond. It was probably recovered during the 1950s excavation. The oblate form fits large supports in great churches (Rigold 1977, 111).

The narrow nave pier and aisle responds

The form of the ?nave arcade piers must have been decided at an early stage. The great majority of the piers were, if survival is a guide, of simple round form (also, Fig 25; Chapters 3.2 and 4.2). There is no unambiguous evidence for the more elaborate compound piers that would have been required at such points as the crossing and the western towers; these must be conjectured (Fig 69). The pier width (c 1.52m) is not a round number in feet; this suggests that the pier width has been indirectly calculated from other unknown proportional formulae.

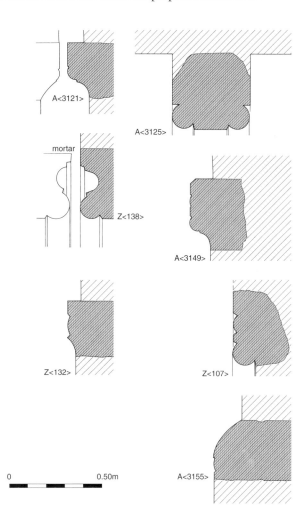

Fig 126 Moulding details from the 12th-century church (B3): rectilinear capital abacus A<3121> and arcade moulding Z<138> compared with (left) examples from St Bartholomew Smithfield; rib A<3125>; abaci A<3149> and Z<132>; window rearch Z<107>; and base moulding A<3155> (scale 1:20)

The capital and pier elements are all dressed from Caen stone and are rather roughly executed. These tool marks were removed by polishing in only one instance. The capitals were painted in a succession of coats of bright scarlet, vermilion and white/cream plaster washes, and later with successive coats of whitewash, perhaps indicating reduced income or changes in taste.

The standard abacus moulding (Z<129>; CP1.11.3; employed in Fig 71) of the ?nave piers was finished and independently reconstructs as a circular abacus c 1.67m wide; this is of course wider than the pier width. Another typestone was probably associated with aisle wall responds (A<3094>; CP1.11.1); it may indicate a complex respond profile with re-entrants as at St Bartholomew Smithfield. The two abaci were perhaps used in close conjunction. Variants of this type of abacus were very widespread. For example, at St Bartholomew Smithfield the abaci are taller and less undercut (see A<3149> and Z<132>, Fig 126; author's observation) which may have a chronological significance. Significantly, the best known parallel was excavated in the north transept of Faversham Abbey (Philp 1968, 42 and fig 12, 19). The abacus on the wide round piers differs in several respects.

The wide pier

Unlike the narrow pier, the scanty evidence for this form allows a wide degree of uncertainty in the width, and in the relationship of the parts. The only evidence for the width of the pier is a segment of necking on Z<130> only 0.18m long, which indicates a total width of c 1.78m.

The two scalloped capital elements are the same height and their position in relation to the circumference of the pier can be determined (Fig 71). The weakly projecting element Z<110> may have supported a rectilinear transverse rib (as at St Bartholomew Smithfield) whilst the strongly projecting element Z<130> may have supported an arcade arch. The width of this impost and its extreme degree of projection are conjectured.

The abacus A<3121> differs from that used in the ?nave, possessing a taller impost and a smaller roll or bead. The north chancel responds at Noron L'Abbaye, Calvados (Hoey 1997, fig 9) and the Transitional period church at Polebrook, Northamptonshire (Howard 1936, pl 71), used abaci of similar appearance. The abacus is more similar to those in the presbytery and ambulatory capitals of St Bartholomew Smithfield (Fig 126) than the ?nave abaci (eg Z<129>, Fig 71) which may have a chronological significance.

The capitals

The paper-dart capital as used on the narrow pier (Chapters 3.3, 'Archaeological evidence', 'Priory church (B3)', 4.2, 'The 12th-century priory church') is varied only by the width of the scallop-unit which is c 1.07m or c 1.27m wide. The paper-darts are syncopated in their arrangement, being omitted from the joins between elements of the capital, perhaps due to the difficulty of carving this ornament in two separate halves. The circumference of the narrow paper-dart capital would fit 48 scallops or 12 per

quadrant (Z<116>), rather than the 40 or 10 per quadrant of the wide paper-dart capital (Z<121>; CP1.11.5; Fig 71). Although these may seem minor details, they give some insight on the level of planning needed to create a scalloped capital. The angle occupied by each scallop had to be carefully calculated and each block was cut to occupy a known segment of the capital's circumference. Both capitals were variants of the normal nave columnar pier. A paper-dart 'Saxon Capital' was recorded lying loose by Whichelo in *Londina Illustrata* (Wilkinson 1819, pl 1).

The second type of capital was embellished with distinctive slits (A<3071>, Z<125>; CP1.11.6). The two variants differ in their height and the width of the scallop unit. There were 74 scallops in one (Z<125>; Fig 71) and c 52 (?50) in the other which was higher to accommodate the wider, taller scallops. The 'slits' appear to be an afterthought because they are quite irregular. The paper-dart capital appears in buildings such as the Holy Sepulcure, Cambridge (c 1130) (author's observation).

Windows

These are only scrappily represented by three fragments that do not permit a full reconstruction (Fig 127). Only one typestone (A<3126>; CP1.3.1) derives from a window, the other two (Z<107>; CP1.10.3; Fig 126; A<3128>; CP1.10.3; Fig 127) deriving from an embrasure that may have served another purpose.

A simple window light is represented by A<3126> (Fig 127) which could have derived from a window in the church. The

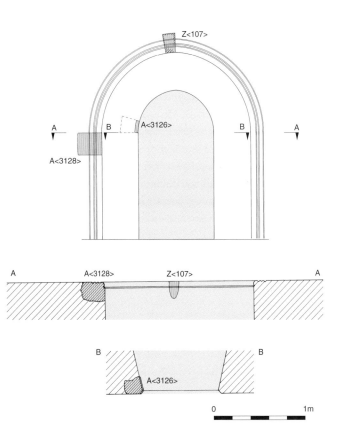

Fig 127 Reconstructed window (A<3126>) and embrasure (Z<107>, A<3128>) elements: upper – exterior elevation; lower – mouldings at the springing line (scale 1:40)

form is widespread and is recorded, for example, at Waltham Abbey (Fletcher 1943, 454:D) where the nave was completed *c* 1150 (Fernie 1985, 73) and St Gregory's Priory, Canterbury (author's observation). The ?window embrasure was widely splayed and has no evidence for glazing. The external opening may associate with a rerearch moulding with a plain reveal such as A<3126>. The quadrant firmly links the structure to the priory church. The association of these three fragments, however, is uncertain.

Unprovenanced abaci

These display the conscious introduction of the quadrant into an existing moulding. This is illustrated where the straightforward abacus form associated with the ?nave incorporates an additional 'tier' of quadrant (A<3149>; CP.10.6; Fig 126). Another example sketched by John Chessell Buckler was apparently very long although the length is unrecorded (BL, Add MS 24433, fo 127). This and another example recorded at Harp Lane (Lea 1981: HL74 <231>) were slightly lower (178mm) than A<3149> (190mm) but were otherwise identical to it. The careful dressing of the beds indicates that the string course was set in an ashlared wall.

The quadrant is associated with the later 12th century and is considered to be an English innovation (Morris 1992, 14). Another form of abacus was dressed from Reigate stone rather than the ubiquitous ?Caen stone (Z<132>; CP.1.10.5; Fig 126). The abacus displays substitution of a quadrant in place of the normal roll. Paint traces suggest that both abaci served as internal string courses. One role may have been to define the horizontal divisions of the arcade elevation (Fig 74), as at St Bartholomew Smithfield.

Doors

As with windows, these are represented rather than reconstructed by the ?Caen stone fragments that survive. One plain voussoir (A<3076>; CP1.4.1) allows the width of the opening to be measured as *c* 1.19m (slightly less than 4ft) with rebates to take a timber door 1.36m wide and 45mm thick. The execution is of a very high standard. The size too argues that this was rather more than a domestic door. The voussoir may have been framed by two chevron outer orders (A<3069>; CP1.15.1; Fig 128; Fig 131) (A<3144>; CP1.15.2; Fig 128; Fig 129) that were also found reused in the walls of Sir Thomas Pope's house. The typestones were probably employed in the ornamented jambs of a portal (L Grant, pers comm). The complete door(s) would have had a recessed surround, perhaps with several orders of chevron and other ornament. Both elements were securely fastened when setting by ?timber dowels (Fig 128; Fig 129). The overall effect was similar to the north door on the west front at Lincoln (Lincolnshire) but less ornate. Two different sizes of door, perhaps the central west door and aisle door seem to be represented, but other claustral locations are just as possible.

Paint surviving on the larger of the two blocks A<3144> shows that the main face and roll were painted vermilion, while the fillets and hollow were painted white. Scribelines cut into

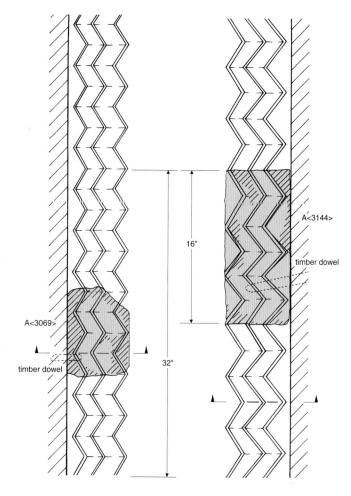

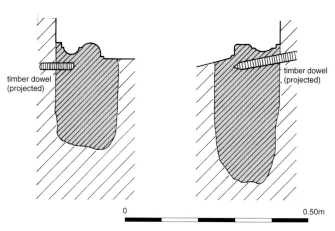

Fig 128 Portal surround chevrons A<3069> and A<3144>: upper – elevation; and lower – mouldings in plan (scale 1:10)

the main faces of the chevron jambstones witness careful measurement prior to cutting; despite this, an error can be detected on the larger of the two (Fig 129).

Blind and dual arcade

An engaged pilaster capital and abacus (A<3068>, A<3075>; CP1.10.8) are of high quality with fine carving carried out with a very sharp boaster. The abacus has a simple profile with the ubiquitous quadrant and only the front is ornamented; it is

A<3144>

Fig 129 Chevron portal surround A<3144> with dowel hole in bed for attachment (Conway Library, Courtauld Institute of Art, London. © Courtauld Institute of Art) (scale c 1:5)

possible that the capital was used with blind arcading (Fig 73).

A fragmentary ?Reigate stone capital (A<3074>; CP1.10.10) was supported by paired columns and was significantly wider than the engaged capital A<3068> (Fig 73). It had a reconstructed length (including the abacus) of 2ft (0.61m) and possibly was associated with a cloister. The dual scalloped capital resembles *ex situ* ?cloister capitals at Bristol Cathedral (Gloucestershire) which was founded in 1142 (Paul 1912, fig 3, 233). Two fine Caen stone capitals with trefoil motifs surviving in the parish church may derive from a columnar cloister arcade (Lockett 1971, pl 12 nos 3 and 4, n 5).

Lunate eaves tabling

These roughly finished blocks (A<3116>; CP1.10.11) formed an overhanging ornamental jetty below a roofline (Fig 75). There is no evidence to suggest that they were supported on projecting sculpted heads or other ornaments. This may reflect links with the Cluniac Order (Chapter 4.2, 'The 12th-century priory church').

Intersecting arcade

A wide variety of elements (CP1.12.1) were found in post-medieval walls. It is implicit that they derive from structures that existed at the time of the Dissolution.

Surviving parts included springer junctions (Fig 130, A<3065> and Z<109>), intersections (Fig 130, A<3157>) and a pointed apex block (Z<111>, Fig 73). Several of the blocks had carefully tooled and painted soffits but no definite evidence of an open arcade was seen. At least two junction springers were terminated with half-moon (lunate) stops (eg Fig 130, Z<109>), but two others lacked this (eg Fig 130, A<3065>).

The variation in moulding seems to be unconnected to any specialisation of function; the radius in both types falls between 0.7m and 0.8m. The most reliable measurements average at 0.751m. An arch reconstructed on this basis has a bay 2ft (0.61m) wide (Fig 73), strong circumstantial evidence for the correct value. The overlapping nature of the arches meant that the columns were spaced at intervals of 1ft.

The small areas of nave and presbytery wall recorded by Buckler were of plain ashlar (BL, Add MS 24433, fos 9, 138) ruling out the use of blind arcading along these walls. The intimate association in reuse of the intersecting arcade with the round piers in the Vine Lane assemblage (site Z) suggests that the arcade derives from the triforium. The carefully flattened reverses of the intersection elements (A<3157>, Fig 73; Fig 130) show that they could be fitted back to back to form an open arcade, but evidence in the form of a coupled capital is missing. The blind arcade is therefore illustrated (Fig 73). The arcade was brightly painted with red paint covering the flanking roll and field. The casement hollows between them were painted white; variety was introduced by painting the fillets on alternating arches red or black. Fig 74 reconstructs the elevation of nave arcade and triforium or gallery arcade.

Intersecting arcades first appear after 1093 at Durham (Clapham 1934, 133). Comparison with photographs of intersecting arcade at the Conway Library reveal no satisfactory parallel, but a similar moulding is used in the arcade arch major order at St Bartholomew Smithfield (Z<138>, Fig 126). Although the differences in proportioning argue against a direct link, a date after *c* 1140 is indicated.

One important technical distinction was the use or absence of intersecting junction blocks. Where such components were used, it was possible to make the mouldings mesh without one taking priority over the other (rather like intersecting railway tracks). This treatment seems to have been a later development

used, for example, in the Glastonbury Lady chapel after 1184 (Thurlby 1995, 107). The Bermondsey example is unusual in that it uses this motif, while one moulding continued to take priority over the other. This could indicate an intermediate date between *c* 1093 and *c* 1190. Pointed arches are a 'later' feature; it may reflect Cistercian influence which is thought to have contributed so much to the Early English style (Conant 1987, 237). The arcade is unlikely to pre-date *c* 1150. Hemispherical or half-moon stops may also be an exotic feature supporting this connection (Chapter 4.2, 'The 12th-century priory church').

Blind and open chevron arches

Elaborate, late 12th-century chevron arch and rib forms were carefully recorded by Buckler (BL, Add MS 24433, fos 93, 94), but no examples of these were found in the recent excavations. Little evidence for other chevron arches was found apart from a 'standard mould' chevron employed throughout the priory church (CP1.13.1; Fig 131). Similar typestones of this sort were found in diverse contexts. At least one derived from an arch demolished during the existence of the monastery. This stone (A<3070>) had been recut with another moulding (A<3147>), but the majority were reused in Sir Thomas Pope's house, indicating that they came from features extant at the Dissolution. The chevron of the outer roll projects in only one dimension towards the soffit, but the inner roll projects towards the soffit and outwards towards the viewer. Lozenge-shaped projections fill the gaps thus created on the soffit. The wall depth was 1ft (0.30m).

The common moulding was laid out on geometric

Fig 130 Intersecting arcade elements: upper – plain springer A<3065>; middle – springer with lunate stop Z<109>; lower – intersecting element A<3157> (Conway Library, Courtauld Institute of Art, London. © Courtauld Institute of Art) (scale c 1:5)

Fig 131 Oblique view of chevron arcade voussoir (A<3069>/A<3130>-type) (Conway Library, Courtauld Institute of Art, London. © Courtauld Institute of Art) (scale c 1:5)

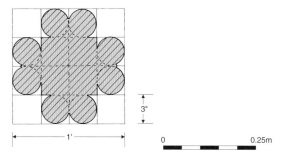

Fig 132 The geometric basis of the 'standard mould' chevron (scale 1:10)

principles (Fig 132) where 1ft was divided into quarters and then sixteenths. Five types of arch were created through subtle variations in the angle of the chevron unit. There is no published parallel for this precise form of chevron but its three-dimension complexity and the complete occupation of the main face and soffit by chevron ornament is reminiscent of Borg's 'type 3', 'which seems to belong to the second half of the [12th] century alone' (Borg 1967, 135). There was fragmentary evidence for a smaller version (A<3146>; CP1.13.3) of the moulding in an unknown structure whose destruction can be quite closely dated to between *c* 1220 and *c* 1300 by the recut moulding A<3147> (CP3.5.2; Fig 135).

The recut blind arcade springer (A<3070>, Fig 133; A<3147>, Fig 135) in oolitic limestone (probably Taynton stone: D F Williams, pers comm) is abraded and severely weathered; this feature was demolished long before the Dissolution. The sub-arch is similar to A<3130> (below, and Fig 72) except that ten rather than 12 chevron units were used. This blind arcade was probably on the exterior of the church, as at Tewkesbury Abbey, and shows signs of having been repeatedly whitewashed.

Open arcades were represented by a number of fragments. The most elaborate of this stone group was an open arcade (probably internal), dressed from ?Reigate stone (A<3086>, A<3093>), with 14 chevrons. Such an arcade was perhaps employed in a gallery sub-arch but its reconstructed width is

uncertain. The survival of three examples including a duplicate makes this the most well represented and perhaps the commonest form of arcade.

Typestone A<3130> was also an open arcade (Fig 72; Fig 131) but the hard oolitic limestone (?Taynton stone) implies that it was for external use. It was one of a pair forming the apex of the arch. The arch would have been well suited for a cloister arcade, but the absence of weathering argues that it was used internally. Rochester Cathedral nave employs two chevroned sub-arches in each gallery arch (Clapham 1934, pl 22). The arch was *c* 1 yard wide (0.919m) and the centre to spacing of the supporting pillars was 4ft (1.22m). An intact typestone A<3085> is a conundrum because it has a change in angle on one bed; however, in other respects, the same type of arch as A<3130> is represented, but due to some error the setter had to trim one of the joint surfaces for the voussoir to fit. This voussoir retained minute traces of white paint.

A fragmentary and oolitic limestone (?external) typestone A<3153> derived from an open arch destroyed before the Dissolution and recut as a ?jamb mould. The arcade shared the same radius as A<3093> but with only nine chevron units in the arch. The oolitic limestone arch was 'stopped' with cream-coloured paint. This could derive from the predecessor of the cloister referred to as rebuilt in 1381 (Graham 1937, 148) and was perhaps reused in its 1381 successor.

?Arcade minor order

Parts of this type of arch were found at site A (BA84) and site Z (VIN88), and it is improbable that only one example of this arch form existed. They were distinguished by bastard joints and masons' marks scored into the main face. ?Caen stone and ?Reigate stone were used indifferently and the arch(es) were subsequently whitewashed many times. The uniformity of the voussoir allows the radius to be confidently reconstructed (Fig 74). There are two masons' marks, otherwise very rare in this phase: the axe form (Fig 134) occurs twice and is primarily interesting in that it represents a mason's tool. The other is a V with what appears to be two added qualifying marks. These

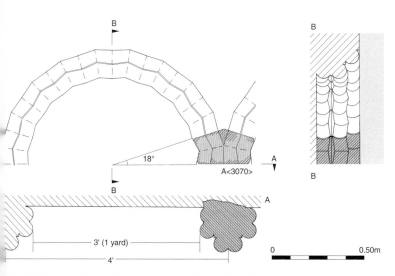

Fig 133 External chevron blind arcading A<3070> (scale 1:20)

Fig 134 Voussoir with masons' axe mark (A<3143>) (Conway Library, Courtauld Institute of Art, London. © Courtauld Institute of Art) (scale c 1:5)

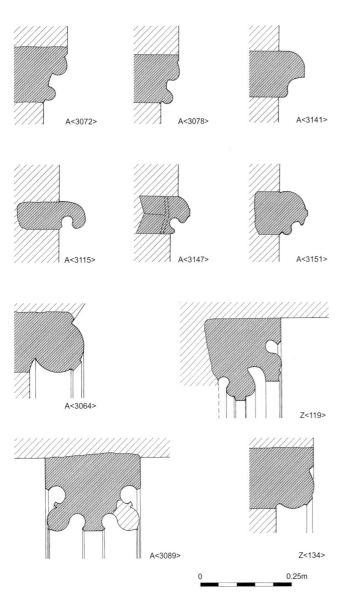

qualifying marks, seen in a much later context at Whitehall Palace (Westminster), may have a chronological significance (Samuel 1999, 166); neither is paralleled in Davis's 1954 catalogue.

Transitional abaci

Several elements indicate that construction continued on a small scale between the period of *c* 1170 and 1200, before the next major waves of building. Technically, these roll-adorned mouldings are Norman although stylistically they are very different to the quirk and chamfer derived abaci that are characteristic of that phase. The ?Caen stone abacus (A<3072>; CP1.18.1; Fig 135) fitted an engaged capital 9in (0.23m) square and a decorative blind arcade is indicated. A cut-out was later made for a timber upright (a ?stall). All or part of the capital was painted vermilion, but only traces survived. This sort of

Fig 135 Moulding details from construction phases 1–4: abaci A<3072> and A<3078> (CP1); string course A<3141> (CP2); string courses A<3115>, A<3147>, A<3151> and arch voussoirs A<3064> and Z<119> (CP3); rib A<3089> and vertical moulding Z<134> (CP4) (scale 1:10)

abacus was popular in the Transitional or Early English period and can be seen at Slimbridge church, Gloucestershire (Howard 1936, pl 94). A variant of the same moulding (A<3078>; CP1.19.1; Fig 135) was executed in ?Reigate stone but its architectural role is uncertain. The mould, particularly of the former, is closely paralleled at the Cistercian house of Dore (Herefordshire) where the nave was probably built shortly before 1175 (Bilson 1909, 200, fig 5:VIII). It may be concluded that styles favoured by the Cistercian Order had some affect on the Cluniac church of St Saviour, if only that the Cistercian Order was the chief patron of masons at that time.

Construction phase 2, *c* 1190–*c* 1220 (periods M5 and M6)

The late 12th to early 13th century seems to have seen the building of a 'great church-scale' arcade incorporating round piers that surpassed the width of the 12th-century ?nave piers represented by a very few drum fragments (Z<130>). The building of wide piers formed part of the original design of the church and a delay on the completion of the parts of the building that used these piers is the most likely interpretation of the evidence. Work on additional chapels and claustral buildings may have followed on from the completion of the church. There is no observable break in construction, but this phase deals with those elements that derive from structures other than the church, as well as the church.

The east range (B7) undercroft vaulting

Machine clearance over the area of the east range (B7) revealed simple chamfered ribstones (A<3131>; CP2.1.1) as well as base and pier fragments (Chapter 3.3, 'Archaeological evidence', 'East range (B7)'; Fig 34; Fig 35). The span of the complete rib (assumed to be semicircular) was *c* 4.12m across. This is compatible with the apparent north–south dimension of the undercroft bay (*c* 4.6m), of which this may well be a transverse rib. The rib resembles those used in the vaulted cellar at Boothby Pagnell, which Wood dates to *c* 1200 (Wood 1965, pl xvi:a) and it could have belonged to the east range. It is not clear from the archaeological evidence whether the east range was extended south in period M5 or existed in this form in period M4 (Chapter 3.2, 'Archaeological evidence', 'East range (B7)', and 'Discussion'); the east range is interpreted as receiving a new vault in period M5, or possibly early in period M6.

Unprovenanced arch mouldings

These are placed in this phase by the presence of such features as the *ogee keel* which is dated from *c* 1175 in piers and arch profiles (Morris 1992, 8). It is probable that several fine vault ribs found in the excavations of Harp Lane (Lea 1981: HL74 [122] <213> and <205>; Fig 136) derive from the same phase. A small fragment was found at Bermondsey (A<3113>; CP2.3.1). Buckler also recorded a variety of 12th-century ribs (BL, Add MS, 24433, fos 72, 84, 85, 93; Fig 136). The near-intact

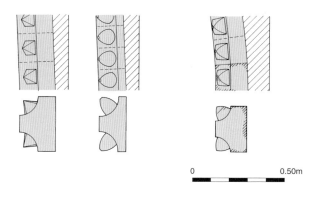

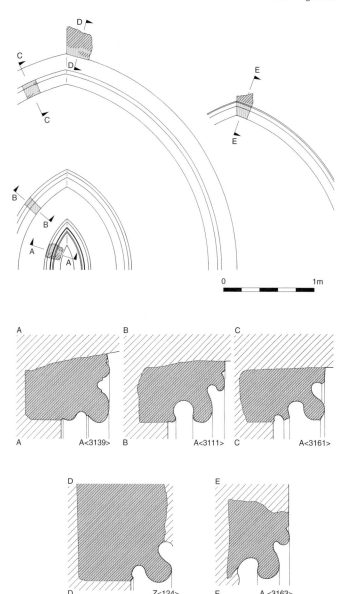

Fig 136 Vault ribstones from the 12th-century priory church (B3): right – found at Harp Lane (after Lea 1981: HL74 <205>); left – two examples recorded by Buckler (after BL, Add MS 24433, (from the left) fo 84, fo 85) (scale 1:20)

moulding (A<3161>, A[2059]; CP2.2.1; Fig 137) was reused in a wall and retained much paint. It was painted white apart from a red-painted roll. It may have formed part of a large two-centred arch (Fig 137). The similarity of the arch geometry indicates a possible association with Z<124> (CP3.1.5; Fig 137).

String course

The bold form of this string course is unparalleled (A<3141>; CP2.5.3; Fig 135). It is related to this build by petrology and tooling.

Round pier possibly from the priory church

The element Z<141> (CP2.6.1) represents about a sixth of the entire circumference of a column shaft 1.61m (5ft 3^1/$_3$in) wide. Differences in diameter and various technical features are all indicative of a different construction phase to the heavy round pier (CP1.11.4, c 1.78m wide). The pier elements bore masons' marks. The mark is a widespread 'W' form which can be seen in a Decorated/Perpendicular context at Patrington, Yorkshire East Riding (Davis 1954, 52), and it once existed in the late Norman crypt at St John Clerkenwell (Fincham 1933, 65, VII), but this mason's mark is very widespread and no link is suggested.

Simple window form

A window with external glazing rebates was ornamented by no more than a chamfer (A<3142>; CP2.8.1). The saddlebars were spaced at intervals of 0.195m.

Construction phase 3, *c* 1220–60 (periods M6 and beginning of M7)

This phase of construction follows on after an apparent diminution of activity. It incorporates mouldings such as the undulating pendant roll (author's term) and the roll-and-fillet; the former feature may indicate the presence of a mason from the contemporary Winchester/Salisbury workshops (Morris

Fig 137 Stone arch mouldings from construction phase 2 (A<3161>) and construction phase 3 (A<3139>, A<3111>, Z<124>, A<3163>), and reconstructed arches (mouldings scale 1:10; reconstructions 1:40)

1990, 169). The undulating form of the roll can be compared to soffit and rib moulds in St Frideswide's, Oxford, and was a motif quite frequently seen in the south of England especially from the 1220s (ibid, 171). The axial roll-and-fillet was popular across England for soffit terminations in the Early English style (Fletcher 1943, 454, G, J, L). Statistical analysis of the dating suggests that construction peaked in the 1240s. The stone used was exclusively Reigate stone apart from Purbeck marble for decorative shafting and some spectacular architecture only known from Buckler's records; this has not been researched in detail but probably belongs to this period (below).

The observation of arcade pier elements and capitals by Buckler indicates that an entirely new building or building element of the highest quality was constructed at this time (BL,

Add MS 24433, fos 108, 109, 113). Its pier moulding was a round shaft with four engaged round colonnettes. This was closely paralleled in the south transept of Westminster Abbey (1245–60) and the nave (restored) of St Mary Overie, Southwark (c 1213–35). The capital form (ibid, fo 108) as recorded by Buckler, is similar to that of the vestibule to the chapter house at Westminster Abbey (RCHM(E) 1924, 95). He unfortunately gives no scale but a large size is implicit. The vault rib A<3059>, Z<113> (CP3.1.7; Fig 50), whatever its location, shows similarities with nave aisle vaults at Westminster (ibid, 1260–9) but may be significantly earlier. One possibility is that part of the church was timber-ceiled until the mid 13th century; Buckler's records of a variety of 12th-century ribs argue against this (BL, Add MS 24433, fos 72, 84, 85, 93; Fig 136). Another possibility is the chapel of St Cross, which was under construction in 1234 (*Cal Close R*, 1231–4, 409). It may also be noted that a new chancel was constructed for the chapel (B1) in period M7 (c 1250–c 1330).

Other typestones from this construction phase point to the construction of buildings connected with the day-to-day running of the priory. These include a small lancet window, with provision for removable glazing. Archaeological evidence indicates changes to the domestic buildings around the infirmary courtyard in period M6 and in period M7 (Chapter 3.4, 3.5).

Arch voussoirs

These cannot be related to any architectural feature but all seem to be internal and several retain paint. They probably derived from arcade arches or the rerearches of windows and display similarities that suggest the same parent structure.

The typestone A<3139> (CP3.1.1; Fig 137) seems to have derived from a comparatively small arch and is difficult to date accurately. A much heavier moulding derived from an intermediate-sized internal arch with a multiple-order moulding (A<3064>; CP3.1.2; Fig 135). It was originally painted a buff tint but was later whitewashed. The moulding was also observed at Harp Lane (Lea 1981: HL74 <245>). The roll-and-fillet is stylistically similar to the vault rib A<3059> (CP3.1.7; Fig 50). So too is a busily moulded white-painted voussoir Z<119> (CP3.1.8; Fig 135).

The undulating pendant roll also occurs in the apex voussoir A<3163> (CP3.1.4; Fig 137). The arch was intermediate in scale and shows traces of white paint. Its position in the complete arch profile cannot now be determined due to recutting, but the moulding is very similar to A<3111> (CP3.1.6; Fig 137) and the two perhaps formed part of the same building. The second arch was comparatively small and was perhaps two-centred. The two seem to have been parts of related arches, rather than the same arch. The second voussoir was painted white and the hollow was then painted red. The quirk at the main face was picked out in black.

A large multiple-order two-centred arch Z<124> (CP3.1.5; Fig 137) was not less than 3m across at the soffit. The incomplete moulding incorporates an undulating roll and angle-fillet and is cut to fit the apex of the arch. A hole drilled in the bed shows that the apex of the arch was reinforced by a timber dowel while the mortar set. The moulding is similar (without a fillet) to the second order of an arcade arch in the Lady chapel at St Frideswide, Oxford (Morris 1990, fig 69:316). The Lady chapel is dated c 1230 (ibid, 169).

Lancet window

The window (CP3.2.1) was only c 0.4m wide with a two-centred opening. It had a simple chamfered moulding (Z<135>, Z<136>, Z<142>) with an external rebate. The embrasure was sharply splayed. A central glazing bar ran into the apex of the reveal and the glass was fixed in front of it. The widespread and functional window profile is well paralleled in the parish church of West Walton (Norfolk), an archetypal *Early English* structure (c 1180–c 1275: Fletcher 1943, 454:K) and a loose jamb of this type was recorded at Faversham Abbey (Philp 1968, fig 12:25).

Purbeck marble shafting

The fragmentary shafting base A<3088> (CP3.3.1) derives from a part of the priory ornamented with shafts. Nine plain fragments of shaft were observed in 1990. The scale of Purbeck marble used in the priory was much greater than the surviving evidence. Buckler recorded a fine three-unit round pilaster capital (BL, Add MS 24433, fo 105) and a coupled colonnette base (ibid, fo 116); the presence of a cloister built of this stone, therefore, cannot be ruled out. Further elements in this stone have recently been excavated by PCA (material seen by M Samuel, courtesy of PCA).

Labels and string courses

A label or hood moulding (Z<123>; CP3.4.2) falls into Morris's fourth variety of wave (1978, 28). The stone is of a type rare in England and is thought to show French influence (ibid). It formed the major order of a larger arch moulding, but the overall size of the feature was small.

The string course A<3115> (CP3.1.3; Fig 135) could have many applications, but was probably internal. The heavy drip moulding is stylistically similar to the ?arcade voussoir A<3111> (CP3.1.6; Fig 137).

Its fresh condition confirms that A<3151> (CP3.5.1; Fig 135) was internal. The execution is of an exceptionally high standard and the moulding is polished. The bearing surfaces were also polished to permit a tight fit. The smaller string course A<3147> (CP3.5.2; Fig 135) was recut from a chevron. The label was painted white and the hollow below dark (?black); this made the string course stand out from the wall face.

Construction phase 4, *c* 1260–*c* 1300 (period M7)

The Decorated period is barely witnessed by the extant fragments, but Buckler meticulously recorded two types of moulding of apparent 13th-century date. An excellent clustered pier capital (BL, Add MS 24433, fo 104) was represented by 'many ... fragments with slight variations'. A polygonal double respond base manifested itself in 'many specimens of this pattern, nearly alike' (ibid, fo 115). Buckler observed these at the same time as a rib form subsequently excavated in the 1980s. Which building formed the source of the fragments seen by Buckler is unknown.

The presence of the three-quarter hollow-and-fillet is stylistically distinct from construction phase 3 and marks the last period which can be associated with major vault construction. The date of the construction phase is also reflected in the tooling technique: the striated finish reaches the practical limits that can be attained with a chisel. The extremely fine reeding on ?Reigate stone was carried out with a sharp chisel blade c 40mm wide. Each band of tooling was carefully aligned to prevent breaks between chisel marks.

The priory's fabric fund was mentioned in 1287 (Graham 1926, 177) and Martin suggested this might indicate contemporary building activity (Martin 1926, 210). The chapel of St Mary in the church of the priory of St Saviour was in existence by 1310–11 (*Cat Anc Deeds*, v, A11652). The archaeological evidence puts the extension of the east end of the priory church – the usual position for a Lady chapel (another possibility as new work at this date) – later, in period M8 (Chapter 3.6, 'Archaeological evidence', 'Priory church (B3)'). In 1497 Ann Lady Audley asked to be buried in the chapel of Our Lady in the monastery of St Saviour Bermondsey under the tower there (TNA: PRO, PROB 11/11, quire 23), suggesting that there may have been subsidiary towers over the chapels.

Major vault

There were at least three occurrences of an elaborate rib form (A<3089>; CP4.3.1; Fig 135) in A[1572], but no related mouldings survive. The broad, flat, chamfered mitre soffit is level with the flanking rolls, an unusual feature. The apparent centre respected by the rib varies greatly from 11.86m to 1.97m (average 4.9m). The contrast between the high values obtained from the former rib and much smaller values from the duplicate suggest two different radii may be represented. There is no indication if the form was a diagonal or transverse rib. The form was also recorded by Buckler (BL, Add MS 24433, fo 85a). No parallel is known, but patterns approximating to three-quarter hollow with fillets indicate a date after c 1250. The absence of a keying spine on the back of the block is a clue that the rib pre-dates the 14th century (author's observation).

Miscellaneous

Part of a vertical moulding (Z<134>; CP4.2.1; Fig 135), could have been used in many applications. This angle roll seems to be influenced by an earlier angle roll A<3064> (CP3.1.2; Fig 135). 'In later Gothic the junction between the fillet and roll is curved and closer to the profile of an ogee' (Morris 1992, 14). This can be viewed as a later version of the moulding.

Construction phase 5, c 1340–c 1410 (period M8)

The emphasis on the earlier architectural history of the priory allows only a summary study of the period after c 1300, a period in which, if the extant stonework is a guide, the core of the priory saw little change. This construction phase is based on a sample of the most datable mouldings from this period, associated with windows and a gate. Generally, later medieval mouldings become progressively harder to date accurately after c 1360 and architectural context is absent here. Major alterations in this period were apparently restricted to gateways and domestic buildings.

The mouldings, however, permit only the most general idea of when construction work occurred, but we are assisted by the increasing detail of the documentary record, although it is still very sparse compared with other sites. Similarities can also be observed between the excavated assemblage and assemblages from the relatively well-documented, 'greenfield' 14th-century developments of Edward III's moated manor house at Rotherhithe and of St Mary Graces north of the river (Blatherwick and Bluer 2009; Grainger and Phillpotts in prep).

A large amount of building occurred in the 50-year period following the Black Death, a period which ended with the priory becoming an abbey in 1399. This involved the construction of new domestic buildings, indicated by several types of large windows. This is borne out by the archaeological evidence for substantial work in period M8 in the south (refectory) range (B6), the second cloister (B14) and to its east the courtyard (OA9) and chambers (B13) (Chapter 3.6). Only a handful of complex tracery elements survive. This rarity may reflect accidents of survival. Buckler repeatedly asserted that the nave wall had been semi-obliterated before Pope chose to make it the north wall of his house (BL, Add MS 24432 A, 156) and Buckler was disappointed that 'none of the abbey masonry seems to have strayed beyond the precinct. Not a house or wall having ancient masonry in their composition' (ibid, 147). It might be argued that the scarcity of these tracery fragments is because the higher parts of the church incorporating them had already been sold for reuse far afield before Sir Thomas Pope decided to build his house (Chapter 5.1, 'Tenants and owners of the site'). A large quantity of complex tracery was recorded in an excavation at Harp Lane (Lea 1981), but time and resources meant it was not possible to include this tracery in this project, and its source could not be proven beyond reasonable doubt in the 1990s. It is discussed here in conjunction with typestones also found at Bermondsey Priory. The documentary record (below), however, does strongly indicate a general replacement of the Romanesque windows in the late 14th century.

Edward III's moated manor house was being built in the 1350s and the standard window moulding used there (Samuel 2009, 27–31, 160–4, esp figs 127, 130) resembles that used in some of the unprovenanced windows in the priory buildings. Movement between projects by some of the masons involved in the royal works may have occurred (Schofield 2009, 155).

Documentary evidence was in the past interpreted as indicating complete rebuilding of the presbytery in the first quarter or so of the 14th century (Graham 1937, 145), but no extant architectural fragments can be attributed firmly to this period; the rededication of altars may have sometimes occurred for less drastic reasons (Chapter 4.2, 'The 14th-century priory church'). Many traceried window fragments reused at Harp Lane are attributable to the renewal of windows in the presbytery by Prior Richard Dunton in 1387 (Martin 1926, 212) or to reglazing in the 1390s, according to Graham (1937, 148), of the nave. This raises the question of what was done that demanded the (?re)consecration of the high altar in 1332 (ibid, 146). Some work occurred in this period; Buckler's records of the intact doorway to the monks' graveyard in the south aisle of the presbytery (BL, Add MS 24433, fo 138; Fig 122) show that, according to Morris's criteria (1978, 23), it dates after c 1320 and would be unusual after c 1350. As one of the alterations implied by the high altar dedication, the door was probably an insertion in the 12th-century wall rather than a direct replacement.

The presbytery windows renewed in 1387 were probably of 12th-century date. The documented glazing of both the presbytery and the nave south aisle (implied by its rebuilding) in this period may well have involved the replacement of outmoded and decaying windows and renewal of the roof rather than the wholesale reconstruction proposed by Graham (1937, 148–9). New, 14th-century glazing is evidenced by surviving glass fragments, but rebuilding of the main cloister, chapter house and refectory in period M8 are also indicated (Chapter 4.2, 'The 14th-century priory church'). After the 1390s, the abbey church apparently stood largely unaltered until its destruction.

Alterations in this late period typically involved improvements to the abbot or prior's house. There is no way of distinguishing the latest of the mouldings from those that may derive from Sir Thomas Pope's house. The records of Buckler and others imply that the two gateways of the abbey were built or rebuilt in the latter half of the 15th century or in the early years of the 16th century (above, 7.1, 'Catalogue of maps …', 'Abbey gateway, Bermondsey (BL, Add MS 24433, fo 2) …' and 'Doorway in north elevation, Bermondsey (BL, Add MS 24433, fo 138) …'), and the outer wall was probably altered (below, 7.3).

Casemented doors and windows

Several large window jambstones were found during clearance of site A. Coatings of mortar indicate that they owe their survival to reuse. The width and number of lights of these windows is conjectural. Their plain splayed embrasures and the rebates for shutters indicate domestic or 'secular' use. Four typestones have similarities that indicate the guiding hand of the same master mason (A<3057> and A<3058>, A<3066>, A<3079>, A<3138>, Fig 138). The size of the windows varied, so several buildings seem to be indicated and the same moulding was adapted to suit them. By this period, all windows had glazing grooves. The mouldings were dressed on all surfaces with a wide-toothed claw tool, a sign characteristic of the period, but these marks were almost entirely removed on the

moulding with a comb.

A multiple-light window with glazing and shutters was represented by two stones (A<3057>, A<3058>; CP5.1.2; Fig 138). The very robust moulding probably occurred in major and minor forms. An alternative reconstruction would provide a four-light opening with a central *strong* mullion and two minor-order mullions. The internal wall face was not parallel to the outer wall face. Saddlebars, if present, have left no sockets on either typestone. Several coats of whitewash were applied internally during the existence of the window. The window moulding is typical but the proportioning closely resembles the robust window moulding used in the inner court of Edward III's great house at Rotherhithe (Samuel 2009, 160–4, esp figs 127, 130) which was being constructed mainly between 1353 and 1356 (Colvin 1963, 993; Blatherwick and Bluer 2009, 15–17). It differs in having an external hollow casement as well as being more massive.

The jambstone (A<3060>; CP5.1.1) derived from a wall >0.58m thick but the glazing reveal and the adjacent mouldings are gone. The window was sunk in a deep external hollow

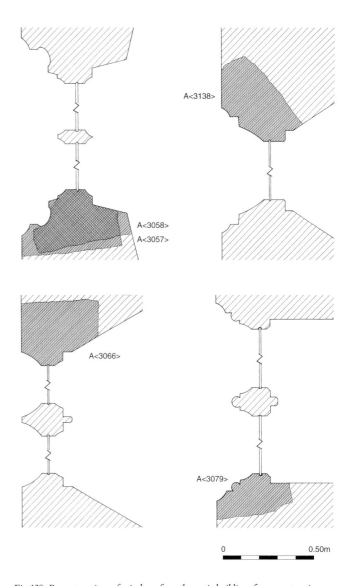

Fig 138 Reconstructions of windows from domestic buildings from construction phase 5 (A<3057> and A<3058>, A<3138>, A<3066>, A<3079>) (scale 1:20)

casement. This pattern is reminiscent of buildings in the south-east of England in the last quarter of the 14th century, such as Winchester College (cloister) and Canterbury Cathedral (west gate) (Harvey 1978, fig 30).

An incomplete moulding (A<3148>; CP5.2.1) evidently derived from the arch of a great gate, *c* 2m wide, although the arch centre could not be accurately measured. The very widespread moulding is typical of the Perpendicular style, occurring in collegiate buildings such as Winchester College (Harvey 1978, fig 32). On this basis a late 14th- or early 15th-century date can be suggested. The gate moulding includes a deep rebate for the timber gate and was set in a casement hollow, mostly unrepresented.

Traceried window

The complete element A<3112> (CP5.3.4; Fig 139) derived from a traceried window. The setting-out was straightforward, using the foot, divided by thirds into units of 4in; the minor-order moulding being, for example, 4in (0.10m) across. The lost strong mullion (major order) was probably 6in (0.15m) wide and repeated the geometry at a larger scale. The style of tracery can be identified as alternate tracery or straight reticulated. The small scale of the accompanying lights shows that this fragment formed the junction between two cinquefoiled sub-archlets in a reticulation (Harvey 1978, fig 9). The fragment was high above the springing line and close to the eyelet. There is no evidence to suggest any finish other than whitewash. The moulding is unremarkable, falling into a broad category of narrow hollow-chamfered mullion forms that enjoyed widespread favour throughout the Perpendicular period in south-east England (Morris 1979, 10). The rounded ogee keel axial termination is a feature of the Decorated period; the unusual manner the fillet is used to form a raised arrow pattern at the spandrel suggests a

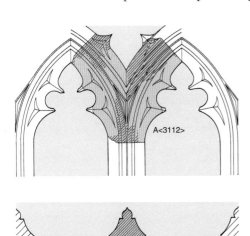

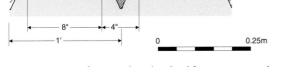

Fig 139 A reconstruction of a traceried window detail from construction phase 5 (A<3112>) (scale 1:10)

date at the beginning of the Perpendicular period (*c* 1350). This traceried window could have been in the priory church or elsewhere, for example in the chapter house.

7.3 The patterning in the brick garden walls

Terence Paul Smith

The north and east garden walls of Bermondsey Abbey were of red brick decorated on their external (respectively north and east) faces with various patterns in darker bricks. The north wall is the bottommost horizontal wall at the left of Fig 109, where north is to the bottom; the east wall runs vertically from it at far left. The walls are no longer extant but are known from early 19th-century pencil drawings and watercolours by John Chessell Buckler (1793–1894) (above, 7.1). Many of them are pasted, sometimes more than one to a page, on the recto of (some of) the leaves of a large bound volume which was, as an inscription at the front notes, 'Presented [to what was then the British Museum Library] by G. J. C. Buckler Esq / 22ᵈ April 1862' (BL, Add MS 24433); each drawing or painting is given a separate 'folio' number. Others are pasted, again sometimes more than one to a page, on the recto of the leaves of a large bound volume in the former Guildhall Library's Print Room Collection (Pennant's London Collection, now part of the London Metropolitan Archives), with each illustration given a separate catalogue number with the prefix p.

That both walls were of *red* brick, as one would expect, is confirmed by a watercolour (BL, Add MS 24433, fo 46) showing their inner (south and west) faces: this shows no decoration, although curiously a monochrome wash drawing (LMA, Pennant's London Collection 30, p5369046) shows regular all-over diaper on the east wall, though none on the north wall. The outer face of the north wall is shown in a pencil drawing (BL, Add MS 24433, fo 7) and in a monochrome wash drawing (LMA, Pennant's London Collection 36, p5368325), the latter showing dark patterning against a light background (Fig 140; previously published in Schofield 1993, 139, fig 115). To the east is a stretch of regular all-over diaper, the individual lozenges of the uppermost row topped by small Greek (equal-armed) crosses. The higher section of wall to the west of this had a cross *pommé* (that is, with arms ending in roundels) on a stepped base; a saltire (St Andrew's) cross; overlapping triangles forming a Shield (or Star) of David; a stylised picture of a building with a semicircular arch topped by a gable and flanked by towers with gabled or conical heads with finials in the form of crosses; an arrangement of four lozenges; a circle topped by a small cross – probably a representation of an orb – an elaborate design resembling a merchant's mark; and a lozenge with a V descending from its lower angle. The east wall is shown in a small scale and rather sketchy pencil drawing dated 1809 (BL, Add MS 24433, fo 54). It had discrete stretches of all-over diaper interspersed with various individual designs: a Greek

Fig 140 View of parts of the north wall of the garden of Sir Thomas Pope's mansion in Bermondsey by J C Buckler (LMA, Pennant's London Collection 36, cat no. p5368325) (Guildhall Library, City of London)

cross, saltire crosses, a circle with a vertical line across the top of its circumference, a single lozenge, a double lozenge, a single isosceles triangle, double isosceles triangles, and several X shapes that appear to be crossed keys (*keys in saltire*). By 1819 most of this wall had been demolished, the small remaining and ruinous northernmost section being shown in a larger and more detailed pencil drawing of that date (BL, Add MS 24433, fo 15): this shows a single and a double lozenge and confirms that two at least of the X shapes were indeed crossed keys, one set shown with wards upwards and inwards, the other with wards upwards and outwards.

These decorative schemes are of some interest. Brickwork patterning began, in England, in the early 15th century, under influence from the Baltic region of northern Europe, in parts of which it was already well established (Smith 1985, 10–15; and see eg Herrmann 2005, 107–9). The earliest English example seems to be that at Stonor Park, Oxfordshire (1416–17) – although the (internal) diagonal mesh there is constructed in a manner different from that which superseded it. Sometimes the patterns were created as a means of using accidentally overfired bricks, as in the late 15th-century brickwork of London Wall at St Alphage Garden, City of London (Smith 2004b, 260–1), though at other times the darker bricks appear to have been deliberately manufactured (Firman and Firman 1967, 309; P Minter, pers comm). The bricks are normally black or blue-black (and sometimes but not always glazed) against a red background, as on part of Sir Thomas Pope's post-Dissolution

mansion at Bermondsey, shown in a watercolour (BL, Add MS 24433, fo 45); occasionally, yellow examples occur (Jesus College, Cambridge: gatehouse, *c* 1500–10) as do green examples (Wainfleet School, now public library, Lincolnshire, *c* 1484) and red examples against a yellow background (Fisher Gate, Sandwich, Kent, 1571); but none of these are at all common. (A rare variant is the red brick diaper against a black background of knapped flint at the 15th-century Tonford Manor, Thanington, Kent.) Sometimes, diaper patterns might be created, or incomplete runs finished, using paint (Mercer 1962, 92–4; Easton 1986, 15–17), as in a section preserved at Hampton Court Palace, Richmond upon Thames (Thurley 2003, 35, fig 36). The designs were created using mostly contrasting headers, although stretchers might be introduced as necessary. Surrounding bricks sometimes required cutting to shape. The roundels of the cross *pommé* at Bermondsey appear to have been formed of obliquely laid headers and would have involved cutting of the surrounding red bricks.

Such patterning began as individual designs, mostly simple lozenges, somewhat inconsequentially placed, as at Tattershall Castle, Lincolnshire (probably *c* 1439 onwards) and Queens' College, Cambridge (1448: Smith 1992), although an all-over diagonal mesh had been achieved at Eton College, Berkshire, in the 1440s (Goodall 2002, 254) and on the gatehouse at Rye House, Hertfordshire, by *c* 1443 (Smith 1975, 121–2). All-over diaper became dominant in the later 15th and throughout the 16th centuries, with a few examples persisting into the 17th century, as at Sudbury Hall, Derbyshire, as late as the 1660s (Cornforth and Wall 1975, 6); but simple individual designs continued in use, as at Smallhythe church, Kent (1516–17), Goltho chapel, Lincolnshire (probably c 1530: Smith 1997, 8, 10), and as late as c 1700 on the Black Lion, Fishpool Street, St Albans. The south front of the gatehouse at Bermondsey Abbey itself combined both forms (BL, Add MS 24433, fo 60): the lower storey had all-over diaper but the upper storey and the adjacent south-east stair-turret had various individual designs of linked lozenges. Sometimes the patterns were restricted to the more important 'show' faces of a building, as on the Goltho chapel and the 15th-century chancel of Bardney church, Lincolnshire (Smith 1990, 176).

The most elaborate forms, involving pictorial or heraldic designs and/or owners' initials, belong to a much more restricted period, beginning c 1480 and lasting down to the 1530s (Moore 1991, 216–18), although innovative designs had been introduced at Eton College from some time in the 1440s (Goodall 2002, 254 with 262, n 45). The more complex forms occur on monastic buildings (London Charterhouse: Washhouse Court, which includes the initials IH for John Houghton, the last prior, 1531–5: Barber and Thomas 2002, 38), episcopal palaces (Croydon), and – in the appropriate form of crosses – on churches, notably in Essex (eg Sandon: Lloyd 1983, 129). But some of the most elaborate occur on a secular building: the gatehouse of Kirby Muxloe Castle, Leicestershire (1480–4, unfinished) has the owner's initials WH (for William Lord Hastings), the *maunch* or sleeve from the arms of Hastings (*Or a maunch gules*), a ship, and 'what seems to be the lower half of the figure of a man' (Peers 1957, 16).

As has been observed, it 'is difficult to interpret diaper [and related] patterns: in some buildings they were evidently executed by specialist craftsmen, … but in others they look more like the products of ingenious but bored foremen or labourers' (Goodall 2002, 254). Put otherwise, the problem is that of deciding whether the designs were independent, and almost casual, contributions of the bricklayers or whether they were an element of the overall conception of the master (brick)mason and/or a requirement of the patron. It seems virtually certain, however, that some of the more pictorial or heraldic designs and owners' initials were in the latter class (Smith 1990, 176). Such examples demonstrate that 'this form of decoration could be adapted to have some meaning and significance on an appropriate building' (Howard 1987, 175, writing specifically of Croydon Palace).

Some of the Bermondsey designs have obviously Christian resonances: the various crosses, large and small, the crossed keys, the Shield of David and possibly the orb. The crossed keys (emblem of St Peter and hence of all subsequent popes, based on Matthew 16:19) occur also at Croydon Palace in the late 15th century, where they are shown wards upwards and outwards, as in one of the Bermondsey depictions; a cross on a small pedestal also occurs at Croydon (Wight 1972, 381 and 45, fig 2; Moore 1991, 217, fig 99). The stylised building on the west section of the north wall may also have religious significance since it appears, from the cross-finials atop the towers, to be the west

front of a church. The meaning, if any, of the other designs is difficult to gauge. The design resembling a merchant's mark is, so far as this author is aware, without parallel in English brickwork: assuming that the wall was monastic (below), could it perhaps be the mark of a lay benefactor? The several lozenges and triangles are common enough motifs and no iconic significance should be attached to them.

J C Buckler's father, also named John (1770–1851), stated that the east wall was built during the reign of Edward IV (1461–83, interrupted 1470–1: *Gentleman's Magazine* 1808a, 477). The elaborate designs suggest that it was not built before the very end of that reign, and may in fact be later. On stylistic grounds, the most that can be said is that the wall probably belonged to the period beginning c 1480 and ending some time in the 1530s.

The higher western portion of the north wall would have been more or less contemporary. The eastern section, with its simpler patterning, was probably of a different – earlier *or* later – date, for there was a clear straight joint between the two sections of brickwork; the face of the western section of the north wall appears to project slightly north of the eastern (Fig 140; and BL, Add MS 24433, fo 7). Grimes's excavation plan (Fig 23) shows the west part of a foundation for the 'post-monastic (garden wall)', east of the reused medieval wall (above, 7.1, 'Catalogue of maps …', 'Ground plan of Sir Thomas Pope's mansion, Bermondsey (BL, Add MS 24433, fo 3) …').

The religious nature of the more pictorial forms is consistent with a date in the late pre-Dissolution period. But although this has been thought the most likely dating for the walls (and see Schofield 1993, 139, caption to fig 115, where the brickwork decoration is described as 'a monastic fashion'), it would be rash to dismiss altogether the possibility that this mode of building may have persisted, in this instance, for just a further decade and that the walls were therefore the work of Sir Thomas Pope. The religious symbols would not be inappropriate, even in this secular context, since he was one of those men who, though benefiting from the Dissolution, were staunch Henrician Catholics 'who hated Luther and Cranmer' (Dickens 1967, 204). If such a date were to be accepted, then one might even be tempted to see in the papal *keys in saltire* a rebus or visual pun on Sir Thomas's surname. His house, it is worth remembering, did include some diaper patterning, albeit of a simpler form (BL, Add MS 24433, fos 9, 45, 53; LMA, Pennant's London Collection 6, p5359533).

7.4   The building materials

Ian M Betts

Methodology

A very large stone and ceramic building material assemblage was recovered from excavations at Bermondsey (priory and abbey), comprising 195 large boxes of roofing tile, brick, plain floor tile and stone, and 32 smaller boxes of decorated floor tile, together with some fragments of painted wall plaster. Only the most important items were fully recorded, these being all the decorated floor tile and the majority, but not all, of the plain-glazed tiles. As for the other material, mainly roof tile, brick, stone rubble and Roman ceramic tile, material from selected contexts has been examined. Unfortunately, there was insufficient time to fully record the building material from all the key selected contexts. Despite these limitations, it is still possible to identify the main types of ceramic and stone building material used in the construction of the priory.

All the material examined has been recorded using standard Museum of London recording sheets and ceramic fabric codes. This comprises fully recorded material, as outlined above, and other material which has only been briefly scanned. In the case of scanned building material, normally only the form has been recorded and size measurements, where available. Other details such as fabric, the number of fragments and weight have not been added to the record sheets. Where ceramic fabric numbers are given in the text these refer to type samples held at the Museum of London; detailed fabric descriptions are available from the LAARC as part of the research archive and are also posted on the LAARC and MOLA pages of the MOL website: www.museumoflondonarchaeology.org.uk. The full ceramic building material report is available in the relevant research archive (Betts 1998).

Stone building material

Sandstone roofing

Fine-grained sandstone roofing is believed to have roofed the chapel (B1) at the time of the Dissolution, and probably dates from the widening of the nave and rebuilding of the chancel in *c* 1250–*c* 1330 (period M7; discussed in detail in Chapter 3.5, 'Archaeological evidence', 'Chapel (B1)').

Slate roofing

Small quantities of grey roofing slate occur at Bermondsey from the 12th century. It was found in the foundations of the east range (B7) in *c* 1100–50 (period M4) and in wall construction and as part of a tiled surface in the hall/lodgings (B8) in *c* 1150–*c* 1200 (period M5; discussed in detail in Chapter 3.3, 'Archaeological evidence', 'Hall/lodgings (B8)' and 'Discussion'). Roofing slates were found associated with various other buildings in later periods (M7 and M8), but there is no evidence to say that it actually came from the roof of any particular building. However, the annals record that Abbot Thomas in 1430 had the cloister re-roofed in a stone called slate (*slad*) (*Ann Monast*, iii, 487; Chapter 3.6, 'Documentary evidence').

No roofing slates have any complete dimensions; although one has two neatly cut edges at right angles. A few tiles have round- or oval-shaped nail holes between 10mm and 12mm in diameter.

Rubble and reused ?Roman building stone

Stone rubble – mainly ragstone, with some Caen stone and chalk – used mainly in various walls and foundations, is described together with the stone used for freestone dressings above (7.2).

Two other stone types, ferruginous sandstone and oolitic limestone, are restricted to Open Area 1 (period M2) and Open Area 2 (period M3), that is to the period *c* AD 850–*c* 1150. These are almost certainly Roman in date as is the chalk rubble in Open Area 1 (period M2). These stones may have been brought to the site along with the Roman ceramic tile for reuse.

Paving

Some thick fragments of fine laminated sandstone could have been used as paving rather than as roofing. The earliest fragments of possible sandstone paving are from period M3, but these were found associated with Roman ceramic tile so may well be Roman in date. The earliest probable medieval example was found reused in Drain 2 (D2, period M7). Two fragments of light grey limestone, which could also have been used for paving, were recovered from the area (OA9) to the north of the former chapel (period P1).

Imported marble

A number of marble fragments were recovered, mainly from post-Dissolution contexts. Certain marble types such as the green porphery wall veneer from southern Greece, the Campian vert from the Pyrenees (period M9, and A[3438] unphased, respectively) and the white marble from Drain 2 (period M5) are almost certainly Roman in date (Pritchard 1986, 174–5). Whether Roman marble was deliberately brought in for reuse in the medieval abbey is far from certain. Other marble fragments, which could be either Roman or medieval, include various small fragments which may have been used as flooring or come from tombs or inscriptions.

Shale inlay

From dumping in the reredorter (A[972] B9, period M9) came a dark grey to black, roughly L-shaped, mosaic inlay made from Kimmeridge cementstone from Dorset (Fig 141). The purpose

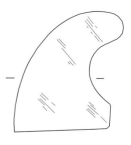

Fig 141 Mosaic inlay (A[972] from B9, period M9) made from Kimmeridge cementstone (scale 1:2)

of this inlay is unclear, though the bevelled edge and smooth top surface suggests that it was set into a floor, possibly as part of a grave cover (cf eg Stopford and Wright 1998, 317–19).

Medieval ceramic building material

Floor tile

The second reredorter (B9) built in the second half of the 12th century was paved with large unglazed floor tiles, subsequently reused (Chapter 3.3, 'Archaeological evidence', 3.7, 'Archaeological evidence'). The most likely areas to have been paved with plain-glazed and decorated floor tiles would have been the main priory church (B3), the chapter house (B4) and the chapel (B1). From the demolition rubble overlying the chapel (B1) came numerous 13th- and 14th-century floor tiles which undoubtedly formed part of the floor of the building. These are of plain and decorated 'Westminster' type, plain Low Countries and Penn type, plus a few decorated tiles belonging to the fine clay group (periods M7 and M8; Chapter 3.5, 'Archaeological evidence', 3.6, 'Archaeological evidence'). The ? infirmary range extension (B12) also apparently had a tiled floor of plain and decorated 'Westminster' tiles, laid in period M6 or M7 (Chapter 3.4, 'Archaeological evidence', 3.5, 'Archaeological evidence'). One of the ground-floor rooms in the east range (B7) in period M8 had a tiled floor of uncertain type (Chapter 3.6, 'Archaeological evidence').

The cess-type fill and mortar sealing layer (A[4154], A[4156]) in the second reredorter (B9, period M9; Chapter 3.7, 'Archaeological evidence') included four types of floor tile: 'Westminster' (design W77), Penn, Low Countries and what can be described as Chertsey/Westminster style (<2191> and <1606>). The floor tiles present among the building material subsequently dumped in the reredorter (A[972] B9, period M9; Chapter 3.7, 'Archaeological evidence') are mainly 'Westminster' (designs W56, ?W73, W77, W78, Fig 77) and Low Countries tiles, with small quantities of decorated tiles of Chertsey/Westminster style (<2121>).

Early unglazed tile

Fabric type: 2273
Large square unglazed floor tiles (284–293mm square) dating to the 12th century were used to pave (and reused to repair) the reredorter (B9, periods M5 and M9). A decorated fragment of floor tile in the same sandy fabric was recovered from A[235] (OA12, period P1). This tile, which measures 25–28mm in thickness, has part of a semicircular line in one corner and is covered by a light brown glaze (Fig 142, <T1>). The presence of glaze, together with knife-trimmed sides, suggests this tile may be slightly later in date, possibly late 12th or early 13th century. It could be contemporary with peg tile in fabric 2273. A more complete floor tile in the same fabric, which may have a similar pattern, is known from the Cistercian abbey of St Mary Stratford Langthorne (Smith 2004a, 138).

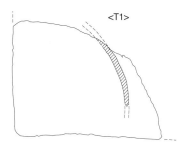

Fig 142 Early glazed floor tile <T1> (scale 1:3)

'Westminster' tile

Fabric types: 2195, 2199, 2892
'Westminster' floor tiles are the most numerous among the assemblage of floor tiles at St Saviour Bermondsey. Tiles of 'Westminster' type are so-called because they were first recognised in the muniment room at Westminster Abbey. Production began *c* 1250 and probably continued into the early years of the 14th century (Chapter 4.2, 'Interior decoration of the monastic buildings: glazing and tiling'; Betts 2002).

DECORATED TILE
The 334 decorated 'Westminster' floor tiles from the abbey comprise 47 different design types (Fig 77; previously published in Betts 2002 at a scale of 1:3). Table 12 lists the designs from Bermondsey by W number (ie 'Westminster' no. as set out in Betts 2002) and cross-references designs previously illustrated in Eames (1980) and Degnan and Seeley (1988), these being the numbers prefixed by the letters E and LP respectively (the letters LP referring to Lambeth Palace chapel where tiles with this design were first recognised; Degnan and Seeley 1988).

The majority of 'Westminster' tiles found in London measure between 100mm and 115mm square. Similar tiles were used at Bermondsey, although the size range is slightly larger: 100–124mm square. Evidence from elsewhere (Betts 2002, 21) suggests the smaller examples (100–106mm square) may be of slightly different date to the remainder. A larger size of 'Westminster' tiles, again probably slightly different in date, were also made in London. Only two Bermondsey tiles belong to this larger group (these measure 134mm square), both decorated with design W104 (Fig 77).

A solitary rectangular-shaped border tile measures ? x 56mm by 1 x 22–23mm (Fig 77, W160). Very few such tiles seem to have been made by the 'Westminster' tilers; the only other example currently known is from the abbey of St Mary Stratford Langthorne (Betts 2002, 62, fig 48 W159; Barber et al 2004, 139, 141, fig 93). A very worn tile from the reredorter dump A[972] (B9, period M9) showing what appears to be a lion beneath a semicircular border (Fig 77, W28), is also of unusual size (? x 91 x 26mm).

Bermondsey Abbey designs W104 and W105 are illustrated in Eames (1980) as E2504 and E2505 respectively. The Eames tiles, which have been examined at the British Museum, are not of 'Westminster' type, but were made with much better quality

Table 12 Frequency of decorated 'Westminster' (W) floor tile designs

Design no./E or LP design no. (Fig 77)	No. of tiles
W1/E1366	6
W3	2
W4	1
W5/E1941	9 (includes 1 uncertain example)
W28	1
W35	3
W36	3 (includes 1 uncertain example)
W38	2
W45	1
?W46/?E2015 (not illus)	1
W48/E2034	22
W49	8
W51	8
W55/E2049	3
W56	27
W59	6 (includes 1 uncertain example)
W61/E2109	16
W62	7
W64/LP16	1
W69	1
W73/E2143	1
W74/E2144	3
W76/E2147	2
W77	27
W78	3
W81	3
W83	5
W89	4
W95/E2185	3 (includes 1 uncertain example)
W97/E2488	7
W99/E2478	16
W103/E2471	18 (includes 1 uncertain example)
W104	2
W105	1 (similar to E2505)
W108/E2209	7
W113/E2287	9
W119	2
W127/E2324	16 (includes 1 uncertain example)
W130	11
W131/E2364	2
W134	2
W136	2
W138/E2068	20 (includes 1 uncertain example)
W147	1
W149/E2775	4
W152/E2798	3
W157	1
W160	1
Uncertain	30
Total	334

wooden stamps and a deeper white slip. The 'Westminster' tilemakers seem to have copied the designs on to their own stamps.

Four decorated tiles from the abbey are decorated with typical 'Westminster' designs (W74 and W136, Fig 77), but were not made using normal 'Westminster' clay types. Instead, they were made with a fine clay characterised by the presence of various dark red and black iron oxide and clay inclusions (fabric 2851). These tiles are also distinctly thinner than most other 'Westminster' tiles, measuring only 18–23mm. Certain tiles also have finer moulding sand on their base. It would seem unlikely that these tiles came in with the other 'Westminster' tiles used at Bermondsey. Perhaps, they represent a separate later period of 'Westminster' floor tile production. If so, the small number of such tiles would suggest they were made to patch existing areas of flooring. Unfortunately, none were found in medieval contexts so their full significance is uncertain.

PLAIN-GLAZED TILE

The majority of plain-glazed 'Westminster' tiles have either a green-, brown- or yellow-coloured glaze. There are also a number of black tiles and a few with greenish-brown and light green glaze. The latter, together with those of yellow colour, are the result of the application of a white slip layer prior to the addition of the lead glaze. Certain tiles are very poorly made with warped and uneven upper surfaces (such as the greenish-brown-glazed tile from A[4147] OA2, period M8). Despite this, these tiles show signs of wear, so they must still have been used, although presumably not in a prominent position.

Tiles of all colours were frequently scored diagonally and broken into two triangular shapes after firing, although in one case (A[3019] OA6, period M9) the tile, though scored, was never broken. A few tiles were scored diagonally in two directions, to produce four small triangular tiles. For some reason, however, these tiles were still only split into two larger triangular-shaped tiles. Triangular tiles were needed where pavements were laid at a 45° angle, the tiles being set where the pavement met the edge of the wall. At Bermondsey, there are so many triangular tiles that this could not have been their sole, or even primary purpose and there must have been areas, probably decorative bands, which incorporated a large number of these tiles.

The size of square plain-glazed 'Westminster' tiles is, not surprisingly, the same as their decorated counterparts to allow both to be used together in the same floors. Plain tiles in size groups 1 and 2 are present in large numbers although, interestingly, there are no plain tiles in the larger size (group 3). The thickness of both plain and decorated examples is normally between 20mm and 30mm, although the tile with design W64 (LP16) is only 17–18mm thick. One plain tile, which measures 110 x 109 x 25mm and has a brownish-green glaze, is very unusual in having one corner cut off prior to firing (A[3498] OA9, period P1; Fig 77; previously published in Betts 2002, 7, fig 1 no. 4). Presumably this specially shaped tile was needed for a specific area of floor. It is significant that tile was cut to shape at the tilery, not on site, which suggests that it may well have been made specifically for the priory. Odd-shaped tiles are also known from Merton Priory (Betts 2007, 200, fig 200 <T70>) and the nunnery of St Mary Clerkenwell (Betts 2002, 7–8).

One further tile which may belong to the 'Westminster' tile group has a yellow-coloured glaze, A[584]. The fabric is finer than other 'Westminster' tiles from the priory (fabric 3081) and is further distinguished by having its base partly scraped smooth.

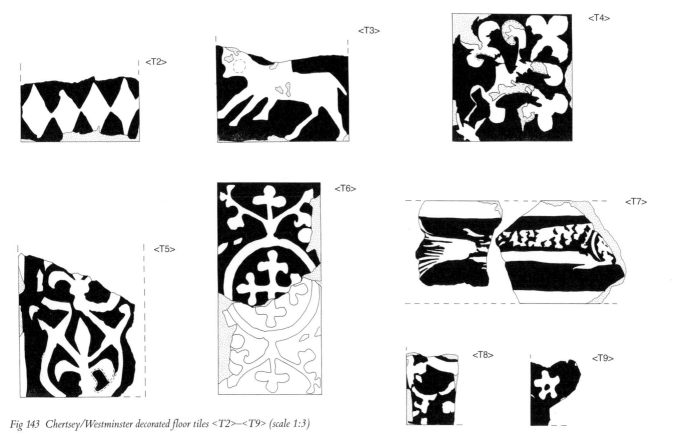

Fig 143 Chertsey/Westminster decorated floor tiles <T2>–<T9> (scale 1:3)

Chertsey-/Westminster-style tile

Fabric types: 1811, 2320, 2894

This is an unusual group of decorative square and border tiles comprising geometric designs and tiles with a knight on horseback and a fish (Fig 143, <T2>–<T9>). The fish design (Fig 143, <T7>) is strongly reminiscent of that found on tiles in the chapter house at Westminster Abbey dating to the 1250s. The Westminster Abbey tiles may originate from the Chertsey area of Surrey which made similar tiles. The Bermondsey tiles, although showing certain similarities of style, are of much poorer quality that those of Chertsey/Westminster type. On certain designs the slip is so thin that the underlying clay body is clearly visible. This may have been why many of the tiles were apparently never used.

There are 15 tiles in this group with a total of eight designs, of which at least three are rectangular border tiles (Fig 143, <T5>–<T7>). These measure 81–84mm and c 100mm in width with a thickness of 16–23mm. None are complete but the length of <T6> can be estimated at 168mm. The square tiles, which are decorated with at least three designs, are 98–109mm square. Both rectangular and square tiles are between 16mm and 23mm in thickness.

The tileries supplying Penn and 'Westminster' tiles to London seem to have produced very few rectangular border tiles, although mention has already been made of the extremely rare 'Westminster' example from Bermondsey (Fig 77, W160). The need for border tiles, perhaps to frame tiles of other types, may have been the reason such tiles were brought to the priory.

It is not certain where these tiles were made, although the knight on horseback (Fig 143, <T3>) is markedly similar to one of the London area 'Westminster' designs (Betts 2002, W1; cf Fig 77). Presumably, they were made somewhere in the London area, or close by. The dating of these tiles is also uncertain, but the parallels with both 'Westminster' tile and the Chertsey/Westminster group would point to a date in the second half of the 13th century.

Fine clay group

Fabric types: 3081, with small amount of 2317

A number of decorated tiles have a fleur-de-lis design set within two circular bands (Fig 144, <T10>). They are similar in appearance to those of Chertsey/Westminster style, although the clay used for their manufacture is very different. None of the decorated tiles of the fine clay group have the frequent

Fig 144 Fine clay group decorated floor tile <T10> (scale 1:3)

quartz sand of the Chertsey-/Westminster-style tiles. There are a total of 17 tiles in the fine clay group which measure 106–111mm square by 17–26mm in thickness (most are only 19–23mm). They would have been set into the floor in groups of four to produce circular patterns. The date and origin of these tiles is uncertain, but they may have come from the same source as the Chertsey-/Westminster-style tiles, although perhaps representing a different phase of production.

Eltham Palace group

Fabric types: 2316, 2320, 2324

Tiles of this type were found *in situ* in the hall built for Bishop Antony Bek at Eltham Palace (Eames 1982, 238). The tiled pavement is believed to have been laid around 1305. Similar tiles, almost certainly from the same tilery, were used at nearby Lesnes Abbey (ibid, 244). The actual location of the kiln making these tiles has not been found, although it presumably lay somewhere to the south-west of London.

Tiles of Eltham Palace type are occasionally found in London, although their numbers are modest compared to earlier 'Westminster' and later Penn tiles. There are a total of 17 Eltham Palace-type decorated tiles from Bermondsey, with five different designs (Fig 145, <T11>–<T15>). Two (<T12>, <T15>) have been found at Eltham Palace itself (Eames 1982, 240, fig 12 nos 2 and 7), whilst a third <T11> is illustrated in Eames (1980) as design E1779. Design E1779 was identified by Eames as a possible Wessex area design, but it is now certain that it belongs to the Eltham Palace group. A further decorated tile <T16> with the bottom part of a fleur-de-lis design probably belongs to the Eltham Palace group, although it is in a slightly more sandy fabric (type 1813).

Plain-glazed tiles were used at Eltham Palace although at

Bermondsey only a plain light green tile (A[189] OA11, period P1) has been identified which may belong to the Eltham Palace group. None of the Bermondsey Abbey tiles, which measure 18–23mm in thickness, are complete but elsewhere such tiles measure around 135mm square. All are probably of late 13th- or early 14th-century date.

Penn tile

Fabric types: 1810, 2894, 3076, 3246

Penn in Buckinghamshire was the location of one of the most successful commercial medieval floor tileries known in Britain. The main period of Penn floor tile production occurred after the Black Death when large quantities of predominantly decorated tiles arrived in London from *c* 1350 until *c* 1390.

There are 76 decorated examples from the priory, comprising 24 different design types. The designs are illustrated in Fig 146 and the Bermondsey examples are listed in Table 13. The designs previously published by Eames (1980) are denoted by the letter E and those by Hohler (1942) by the letter P. Most of the other design types are currently unpublished (<T17>–<T24>). In the case of design <T22>, the Bermondsey example shows more of the design than in Hohler's illustration (Hohler type P157). Three other tiles (<T23>) partially correct Eames design type E1831 (Hohler type P110). Of particular interest at Bermondsey is an example of a tile with a design which has also been found at the abbey of St Mary Graces (Grainger and Phillpotts in prep) but is very rare in London (Fig 146, E1407); the inscription reads 'SIGNUMSC'E CRUCIS:' (sign of the blessed Cross).

Many decorated Penn tiles from the priory are fragmentary. Relatively few have surviving length/breadth measurements and those that do measure between 105mm and 120mm square by

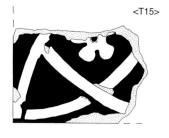

Fig 145 Eltham Palace-type decorated floor tiles <T11>–<T15> and probable example <T16> (scale 1:3)

Fig 146 Penn decorated floor tile designs from
Bermondsey Priory: designs previously published
by Eames (1980; courtesy of the Trustees of the
British Museum) and Hohler (1942) (scale 1:6;
<T17>–<T24> 1:3)

*Table 13 Frequency of decorated Penn floor tile designs and
other designs from Bermondsey Priory previously unpublished*

Design no. (Fig 146)	No. of tiles
E1407/P2	1
E1843	2
E1952	3
E2227	1
E2231/P54	4
E2232/P44	6
E2232/P44 or E2234	2
?E2234	1
E2264	6
E2340/P67	2
E2392	3
?E2409/P66	3
E2467/P99	2
E2791	1
E2835	1
E2837	2
P124	2
Other designs (Fig 146)	
<T17>	1
<T18>	1
<T19>	6
<T20>	3
<T21>	1
<T22> (corrects P157)	1
<T23> (corrects E1831/P110)	3
uncertain including <T24>	18
Total	**76**

16–24mm in thickness. The only exceptions are two unusually thick Penn tiles which measure 26–27mm (design E2264/P99, Fig 146) and 25–26mm (<T22>, Fig 146) respectively.

Very few plain-glazed Penn tiles seem to have been brought into London. By the mid 14th century, plain glaze Low Countries floor tiles seem to have been preferred. Presumably such tiles were cheaper. This is certainly the case at Bermondsey, which has vast numbers of Low Countries tiles but hardly any plain Penn examples. The examples that do exist have greenish-brown, brown and green and yellow glazes and measure 102–110mm square by 20–24mm in thickness. Example <T24> (Fig 146) illustrates a possible Penn tile with an unusual cream-coloured slip. Normally Penn tiles found in London have the decorative design in a more yellowish glazed slip.

Low Countries tile

Fabric types: 1678, 2323, 2504, 2497 (calcium carbonate types); 3063, 3064 near 2850 (silty types); 2324

Plain-glazed Low Countries floor tiles (often called 'Flemish' tiles) can normally be identified by nail holes in their top surface and their distinctive fabric types. The fabric of the Bermondsey tiles is almost entirely clays rich in calcium carbonate. The date when Low Countries floor tiles were imported into London is uncertain, but it is unlikely to be much earlier than *c* 1300, a time

when English plain-glazed 'Westminster' tiles seem to have been readily available. Plain-glazed Low Countries tiles continued to be imported until the mid–late 16th century, later imported tiles normally being distinguished by their larger size.

The majority of plain-glazed floor tiles used at Bermondsey Abbey, at least from the 14th century, seem to have been of plain-glazed Low Countries type; certainly large numbers were found during the excavation. These tiles are normally coloured yellow, brown or various shades of green, whilst others are mottled dark and light brown or have brown and yellow streaks. One tile has a light green glaze above a white slip. These tiles were normally laid in the chequerboard pattern, with those of yellow glaze alternating with tiles of other, darker, colours.

Most Low Countries floor tiles from Bermondsey have between two and five round nail holes, which are between 1mm and 2mm in diameter (most have a diameter of 1.5mm). The different nail hole arrangements are shown in Fig 147. Those with four holes, but with one missing from the corner (type 5) were probably made with a damaged five-nail cutting board. As with tiles of 'Westminster' type, there are a number of plain triangular examples, although they are not common.

A variety of differently sized tiles are present: these are listed in Table 14. Most are of the smaller size, but the proportion of these larger tiles may be underestimated, as they are more easily broken. There are certainly a number of thick Low Countries tile fragments which must belong to tiles of larger size.

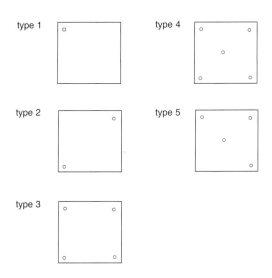

Fig 147 Nail hole arrangements in Low Countries floor tiles, types 1–5 (scale 1:6)

Table 14 Low Countries floor tile groups by size and nail hole type

Group	Length/breadth (mm)	Thickness (mm)	Nail hole arrangement (as per Fig 147)	No. of tiles
1	110–119	20–26	2, 3 and 4	49
2	121–130	24–30	3	8
3	176–181	23–24	1	1
4	244–249	28–33	5	3

Table 14 shows four size groupings based on length/breadth measurements. All have round nail holes with the exception of the tile in group 3 which has a single hole 2.5mm square. Tiles in all four groups are made using calcium carbonate-rich clays. There are a few tiles made with silty fabric types, but none of these are complete.

Plain-glazed Low Countries floor tiles are notoriously difficult to date with any accuracy. The smaller sized tiles (groups 1, 2) are probably 14th or 15th century, whilst the larger tiles (groups 3, 4) are probably late 15th to late 16th century. The earliest reliably dated Low Countries floor tiles came from a robber infill associated with Building 12 (B12, period M7; Chapter 3.5, 'Archaeological evidence'), although there is no certainty that they actually came from the building itself. The few silty fabric plain-glazed Low Countries tiles from Bermondsey are almost certainly either late 15th century or early post-medieval in date. There is also a solitary unglazed tile, probably from the Low Countries, from A[2673]. This is post-Dissolution in date, and may well have come from Bermondsey House.

Dieppe group

Fabric group: 3241

Late 14th-century decorated floor tiles from northern France are only known from seven sites in London. Work by Norton in 1993 has shown that these tiles were probably manufactured in the Dieppe area (Seine-Maritime) in the last quarter of the 14th century, although production may have extended into the early years of the 15th century.

Four examples were recovered from Bermondsey Abbey, three of which are decorated. All the decorated tiles (from A[1], A[2406] OA11, period P1; A[3008] OA6, period M9) are Norton design 25 (Fig 148, <T25>; Norton 1993, fig 4). The other tile has a plain yellow glaze with a diagonal knife cut. Although the tile was intended to be split into two triangular shapes this was not carried out. The Dieppe group tiles are 104mm square with a thickness of 18–22mm.

Dutch tile

Fabric type: 2320

The latest decorated floor tiles found at Bermondsey are from the Netherlands and date to the 16th century. They were probably laid down shortly before the Dissolution, or alternatively they may have been brought in to pave part of Bermondsey House. Only three tiles are present, none of which are complete. The tiles are 18–23mm thick and two have an unpublished design (Fig 148, <T26>) whilst the third is too small to identify (Fig 148, <T27>); all are from A[4213]. Similar tiles do occur on other London sites, but are uncommon.

?English floor tile

Fabric types: 1811, 2894

There are two floor tiles with nail holes in their surface which are significantly smaller than any of the Low Countries tiles discussed above. These tiles, which measure 102–106mm square by 20–23mm in thickness, have two holes set in diagonally opposite corners (Fig 147, Low Countries type 2). One hole is oval in shape (2 x 3mm) whilst the other is 2.5mm square. Although nail holes are normally a feature of imported Low Countries tiles, certain English tilemakers did occasionally use nailed wooden blocks to help cut the clay to a square shape before firing. Neither of the Bermondsey Abbey tiles is made using characteristic Low Countries type clays, so they may well be of English manufacture. They are similar in both size and fabric to Penn tiles, although they have slightly finer moulding sand on their base. It is not certain that they were actually made at Penn. The tiles have a plain brown and a yellow and green glaze. One is from a post-Dissolution layer, whilst the other was reused in alterations to the reredorter (B9, period M9; Chapter 3.7, 'Archaeological evidence').

Straight-sided scored tile

Fabric type: 2586

Under this heading are four heavily worn floor tiles which are characterised by having sanded rather than knife-cut sides, which is the normal practice. The clay used (fabric 2586) would suggest manufacture somewhere close to London.

Three tiles are characterised by knife-scored decoration (Fig 149, <T28>, <T29>). These scored lines are far too shallow to have been made with the view to splitting the tiles after firing. One tile has the remains of a plain brown glaze, the other two tiles are so worn that glaze only now survives on the tile sides. These tiles, none of which is complete, have a thickness of 27–29mm. The earliest fragment was found in the fill of a

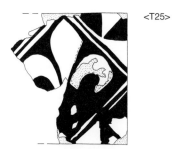

Fig 148 Decorated floor tiles from Dieppe <T25> and the Netherlands <T26>, <T27> (scale 1:3)

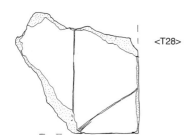 <T28> 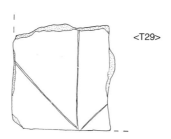 <T29> 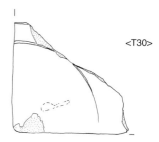 <T30>

Fig 149 Straight-sided scored tiles <T28>–<T30> (scale 1:3)

robber cut associated with the disuse and robbing of part of Drain 2 (period M6; Chapter 3.4, 'Archaeological evidence').

The fourth tile was found in a robber fill associated with the demolition of the infirmary hall (B10, period M8; Chapter 3.6, 'Archaeological evidence'). It is decorated by at least one semicircular line added by compass, the compass point clearly visible in the surviving corner (Fig 149, <T30>). The tile, which has a covering of very worn yellow glaze, measures 27mm in thickness.

These scored floor tiles bear a striking similarity to a set of incised tiles in the Pyx chamber in Westminster Abbey, recently studied by Warwick Rodwell after being revealed by cleaning of the chamber's tiled floor. Two in particular (<T28> and <T29>) have a pattern closely matching one of the 11 designs found reused in the Westminster Abbey floor. A further tile, with another decorative pattern, was found during excavation in the adjacent undercroft museum in 1986 (WST86; Betts 1996, 21–2, fig 2 b). Both the Pyx chamber and museum were originally one, and formed the undercroft of the dormitory of *c* 1066–75 (Bradley and Pevsner 2003, 193).

Both the Pyx chamber and museum tiles have been dated to the 11th century (W Rodwell, pers comm; Betts 1996, 22). If the Bermondsey tiles date from/to the same period, which would seem likely, then they were probably used as flooring in the chapel (B1; Chapter 3.1); alternatively, they may come perhaps from another, Saxo-Norman, building on the site (Chapter 2.5).

Sandy clay tiles

Fabric type: 3084

There are two fragmentary tiles (A[520], A[647]), 32–34mm thick, made using a distinctive fine sandy clay (fabric 3084). Both are unusual in having a pink-coloured slip under their green glaze. Similar tiles were found in a post-Dissolution floor at St Mary Spital (Crowley 1997, 199) and during more recent excavations on the site of the former Spitalfields Market, Tower Hamlets (SQU94; Keily et al 1998). The St Mary Spital tiles are complete and measure 240–250mm square. A number of these tiles were incorporated into a floor of post-medieval date at 274–306 Bishopsgate, City of London (BOS87 [44]; Schofield 1998, 243). The Bishopsgate floor, however, seems to have consisted primarily of reused medieval floor tiles (Keily 1990). If the sandy fabric tiles from Bermondsey are post-Dissolution

rather than monastic, then they may have been used to floor part of Bermondsey House. The origin of these tiles is not known.

Tin-glazed tiles

There are a number of tin-glazed wall and floor tiles from the site of the former abbey. The earlier tiles were used as paving, probably in post-Dissolution Bermondsey House, whilst later tiles were set on walls.

Floor tiles

Fabric types: 2196, 3067 and pink version of 3078
There are five tin-glazed floor tiles from the site of the abbey: four are polychrome (A[242] contained two tiles, A[1126], A[1138]), whilst the other is blue on white (A[1]). These tiles probably all date to the early to mid 17th century. Three designs are present. The first is a ?pomegranate fruit with fleur-de-lis border decoration in yellow, brown, blue and green on white (Fig 150, <T31>; A<3746>, A[242]). Tiles of this design were made at the Pickleherring pothouse, off Vine Lane in Southwark, London (Tyler et al 2008, 54–5, Pickleherring design 9, fig 75 <T12>). A complete tile with a similar design is in the Museum of London (MOL no. P624). The second design is floral in brown and blue on white (Fig 150, <T32>; A<772>, A[1138]) and may be English or Dutch. A complete tile with the same design, but with green replacing brown, is in the Museum of London (MOL no. 6930). The third design shows part of a floral and geometric design (Fig 150, <T33>; A[1]) and is English. Tiles of very similar design were made at the Pickleherring pothouse and one such was found on site at Vine Lane (VIN88, <21> [+]; Tyler et al 2008, 53–4, Pickleherring design 5, fig 74 <T7>).

Wall tiles

There are a total of 28 decorated tin-glazed tiles which range in date from the mid 17th to the 18th century. Most of these are later than *c* 1650 and therefore outside the scope of the current volume. The remaining, earlier tiles form a very rare group of five mid 17th-century blue on white wall tiles (fabric 1819; A[1], A[242], A[375]). They are probably London products from either the Pickleherring or Rotherhithe pothouse (Tyler

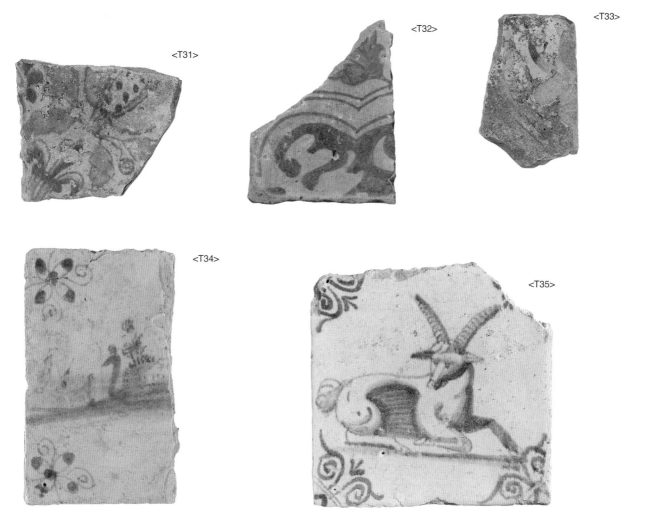

Fig 150 Tin-glazed floor tiles <T31>–<T33> and wall tiles <T34>, <T35> (scale c 1:2)

et al 2008, 40–59, 72–92). Three tiles show landscape scenes with 'spider head'-style corner motifs (Fig 150, <T34>; A<3745>, A[242]), whilst the other two tiles have so-called 'barred ox-head' corners. One has a horned animal, possibly a ram, in the tile centre (Fig 150, <T35>; A<773>, A[242]). These tiles seem to represent an attempt by English tilemakers to imitate Dutch wall tiles, which were arriving in London in increasing quantities by the mid 17th century. This would explain the appearance on these English tiles of the spider head corner decoration, normally a distinguishing feature of Dutch wall tiles.

Roofing tile

Shouldered peg, flanged and curved tile

Fabric type: 2273

Tiles of this type, particularly shouldered peg and curved tile, occur on many City of London sites. Flanged tiles, which were used with curved tiles in the same manner as Roman imbrex and tegula, are somewhat less common. They were introduced around the mid 12th century and continued in use into the early 13th century when they were superseded by lighter,

smaller and undoubtedly cheaper peg tile (Betts 1990, 221–3).

Only a few fragments of flanged, shouldered peg and curved tile have been found at Bermondsey Priory, the earliest fragment being a reused curved tile from the hall/lodgings (B8, period M5; Chapter 3.3, 'Archaeological evidence'). What they do show is that at least certain monastic buildings had tiled roofs as early as the second half of the 12th century.

Peg tile

Fabric types: mainly 2271, 2273, 2276, 2586, 2816 with small amount of 2274, 2278, 3090, 3097

In London, peg tiles first appeared in the late 12th century and continued to be the principal form of ceramic roof covering until the widespread use of pantiles after the Great Fire of 1666. The vast majority of peg tiles, including the majority of Bermondsey examples, were almost certainly made at tile kilns close to London. Most of these seem to have been east of London where tilemaking is recorded in Stepney (Tower Hamlets) from 1366 (McDonnell 1978, 114). In the later 14th and 15th centuries Woolwich (Greenwich) was a principal centre for the manufacture of roof tile, supplying both the City and Westminster (Cherry 1991, 194). Roof tile manufacture was also undertaken at St Mary Clerkenwell in the 14th to 15th centuries (Betts 1995b) but few if any of its products, based on fabric evidence, seem to have been used at St Saviour Bermondsey.

Only two tiles are not of local manufacture. They both originate from tileries in north Kent. The first, which came from backfill in the reredorter (B9, period M9; Chapter 3.7, 'Archaeological evidence'), is made from a white-coloured clay (fabric 2278). The second, from the infirmary courtyard (OA2, period M5; Chapter 3.3, 'Archaeological evidence'), is characterised by creamy-white silty inclusions (fabric 3097). These may represent a one-off batch brought in for minor repair work.

It is extremely difficult to date peg tiles with any precision. At Bermondsey, as at other sites in London, tiles made before the late 15th century tend to be thinner and are frequently characterised by the presence of glaze. Post 15th-century Bermondsey peg tiles tend to be slightly thicker and the glaze is no longer present. The types of nail holes found in these later peg tiles are more diverse: not only are they round, but they can be square, triangular or even hexagonal in shape (Table 15). Earlier and later types have two nail holes per tile. One of the latter has what appears to be the impression of the tool head used to make the holes (Fig 151, <T36>). Diamond holes are made with a square hole punch deliberately put in at a 45° angle to the tile sides.

The principle use of peg tile was as roofing, but these tiles were employed in a variety of other ways. They were used in wall foundations, in flooring and set vertically in hearths. The large quantity of peg tiles found at Bermondsey suggest many of the monastic buildings were tiled, although it is very difficult to be certain exactly which. Only the infirmary (B10) can be stated with reasonable certainty to have had a tiled roof by the time it was demolished (period M8; Chapter 3.6, 'Archaeological evidence', 'Demolition of the former infirmary buildings (B10 and B11)').

A number of tiles have surviving size measurements (Table 15) and three approximate size groups are present, based on both fabric and date. The majority of tiles with complete breadth measurements found at Bermondsey are probably of late 15th- to 16th-century date. These form the majority of tiles

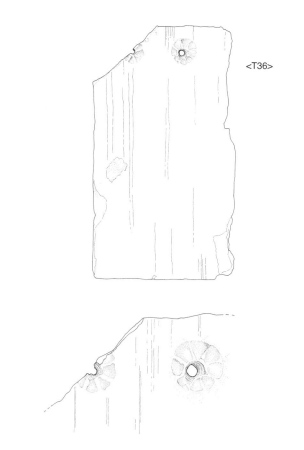

<T36>

Fig 151 Peg tile <T36> with impression of tool head used to make the hole (scale 1:4; detail 1:2)

in group 2, which are remarkably similar despite differences in fabric type. The slightly smaller tiles in group 1 are associated with other tiles with a splash glaze and are almost certainly medieval. For some reason, some of these have only the right hole punched all the way through. The tiles with the greatest breadth (group 3) have a more uniform glaze covering and again are medieval.

One very unusual feature at Bermondsey is the large number of peg tiles made in sandy fabric type 2273; such tiles are extremely rare elsewhere in London. Why the priory should have so many of these tiles is uncertain, unless they were especially made for it. The tiles were probably introduced after the earlier forms of roofing tile (discussed above) ceased to be made around the beginning of the 13th century. Many tiles have a uniform covering of lead-glaze on the top of the lower third of the tile, which seems to have been a feature of late 12th- and 13th-century peg tiles.

Curved ridge tile

Fabric type: 2273, 2276, 2586, 2816

Covering the ridge of most buildings with tile and stone roofs would have been curved ridge tiles. In the 12th century, the curved tiles used with flanged tiles probably served this purpose on many buildings. Only with the switch to peg tile roofs were purpose-made ridge tiles needed. Ridge tiles were made using the same clays as that used for peg tiles, so there is

Table 15 Peg roof tile size (mm)

Group	MOL fabric type	Length (mm)	Breadth (mm)	Thickness (mm)	Nail hole type
I	2271	–	138–144	10–12	round
2	2271	–	149–163	10–14	round, hexagonal, triangular
	2276	266	141–152	11–14	round, square
	2586	–	143–161	11–15	round, diamond
	2816	–	147–163	11–13	diamond
3	2273	–	173	11–13	round
	2586	–	173	13–14	?

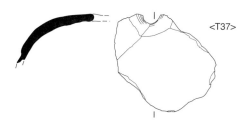

little doubt that both were made together at the same tileries. Certain tiles were held in place by a nail driven through a hole located along the top edge near the tile edge. One Bermondsey tile still has a round nail hole, 10mm in diameter, surviving in this position. Curved ridge tiles are easily broken; no complete, or even partially complete, examples have survived from the priory.

Roof finials

Situated on the crest of the roof on certain buildings would have been decorative finials. Two fragments were found in post-Dissolution contexts associated with the former ? infirmary range extension (B12): both were circular in shape with green glaze, one in coarse London-type ware (LCOAR) (Fig 152, <T37>) and one in Kingston-type ware (KING) (Fig 152, <T38>; Chapter 3.5, 'Archaeological evidence', '? Infirmary range extension (B12)').

Fig 152 Fragment of ceramic roof finial <T37> in coarse London-type ware and roof finial <T38> in Kingston-type ware (scale 1:4)

Brick

Red brick

Fabric types: 3032, 3046, 3065

All the red bricks found at Bermondsey (priory and abbey) are probably made using local London brickearth deposits. Bricks were being produced at Deptford (Lewisham), for use in London, as early as 1404 (Schofield 1984, 129) although it was not until the second half of the 15th century that building in brick became widespread.

Fragments of red brick were intrusive in robbing infill of the ? infirmary range extension (B12, period M7; Chapter 3.5, 'Archaeological evidence'), as probably were further fragments found associated with the robbing of the infirmary (B10, period M8; Chapter 3.6, 'Archaeological evidence'). Fragments were found dumped in a pit associated with the chapel (B1, period M9; Chapter 3.7, 'Archaeological evidence').

Red brick was being used in building construction at Bermondsey before the Dissolution as shown by the walls recorded by Buckler and discussed above (7.3). Red brick was certainly used (perhaps reused) in Thomas Pope's mansion, Bermondsey House, where monastic walls were cut back and refaced in brick. One of these bricks, used for the blocking and refacing of a window (A[3315]) measures 244mm in length, which is more typical of medieval rather than later 'Tudor' brickwork. At Billingsgate Market Lorry Park (BIG82; Betts 1991) in the City of London, bricks of similar size (although made from a less sandy local clay) were used in the construction of an undercroft, which later became part of the church of St Botolph. They probably date from either the late 14th or the second half of the 15th century. The Bermondsey example may be of similar date.

Other bricks found at Bermondsey are smaller and probably date from the late 15th or 16th century. The sizes of these so-called 'Tudor' bricks, many of which have sunken margins, are listed in Table 16.

Table 16 'Tudor' brick size (mm)

Period found	Fabric	Length (mm)	Breadth (mm)	Thickness (mm)
M3*	3046	-	105	48
M7*	3033	-	95	50–52
M7*	3046	-	98–101	-
M8*	3033	209	100–102	51–52
M8*†	3065	244	115–117	5–57

* later contamination; † sunken margin

Yellow brick

Fabric type: 3031

From post-Dissolution contexts A[483] and A[549] are two fragments of moulded brick (Fig 153, <T39>, <T40>). These probably originally formed part of a decorative string course in the walls of one of the priory buildings. Part of one moulding has what appears to be either white paint or slip on its underside. The white material on the upper side was presumably removed by weathering. These bricks are relatively small, one measuring 37mm in thickness, the other 51–57mm. Similar bricks have been found on a number of London sites where they are dated from around the mid 14th to the mid 15th century. Ryan (1996, 31–3), who has noted similar bricks at various sites in Essex, believes that they are probably Low Countries imports.

Uncertain tile type

Fabric types: 2271, 2816

There are six fragments of tile, made from local London area clays, which are of a type so far unique to Bermondsey. All are characterised by a uniform covering of spotted yellow glaze and have moulding sand on their sides. They may have been

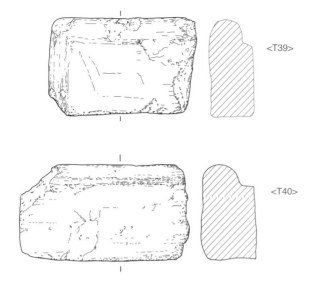

Fig 153 Two fragments of mid 14th- to mid 15th-century moulded brick <T39> and <T40> (scale 1:4)

fragments of roofing tile, although they would be unusually thick, or they may have been set into walls as decoration. They measure 18–26mm in thickness and one has a complete breadth of 115mm which is considerably smaller than peg or other types of ceramic roof tile.

Fig 154 Medieval painted wall plaster (upper from A[515]; lower from A[518]) (scale c 1:1)

There is little indication as to where in the priory or abbey these tiles were used. The earliest fragment came from the fill of a robbing cut associated with the hall/lodgings (B8), while other tiles were found in the garden (OA9, period P1; Chapter 5.2, 'Monastic buildings completely or largely demolished' and 'Elements of the former monastery partly or wholly retained and adapted').

Medieval painted wall plaster

Small amounts of medieval wall plaster were found associated with the robbing of the infirmary (B10, period M8), although these are not necessarily from the building itself, and in the mansion house southern perimeter (OA12) and reused in the mansion house (period P1). The plaster found associated with Building 10 is plain white, whilst that from the mansion house is plain red. The red plaster was found attached to a fragment of Kentish Rag limestone which was used as infill to block a window.

The plaster from Open Area 12 consists of a number of decorated fragments which would have formed part of the internal plaster decoration of one of the monastic buildings. Two fragments have red masonry pattern (ie imitating ashlar), using double red lines (one from A[515] is illustrated on Fig 154); another has the trace of a decorative scheme in red and black (A[518]; Fig 154). Internal painted imitation ashlar decoration was an extremely common device in Britain.

7.5 The pottery

Jacqui Pearce

Introduction and methodology

A total of 185 boxes of post-Roman pottery from site A (BA84) was spot-dated, mostly during 1995, in accordance with standard MOLA practice, with additional spot-dating of remaining contexts carried out in 1997. The data were entered in the first place on to the Unix system which has now been superseded by the ORACLE database. This allowed for a record of fabrics, forms, approximate context size and date range, but did not include any form of quantification. This information, in the form of a sherd count and rough estimate of the number of vessels, based on featured sherds such as rims, was, however, noted as standard on the paper record. The data were subsequently transferred from Unix to the ORACLE database and now exist in this form. This report is limited to contexts which lie within the area of study and the chronological parameters defined by the research aims for the project, that is, from the Late Saxon period up to the mid 17th century; all pottery from contexts dated later than *c* 1650 was excluded, although the original spot dates are recorded in the database.

Once the spot dates had been transferred to ORACLE, the data were revisited to add in records of sherd count (SC) and estimated number of vessels (ENV); only those contexts within the area of study were amended in this way. This means that all contexts which fall outside these parameters do not have this information recorded and are not included in any of the statistics given in this report. In addition, all pottery, including small contexts with fewer than 30 sherds, in groups which included medium and large contexts (ie 30–100 sherds and more than 100 sherds respectively) was quantified by weight (in g) and estimated vessel equivalents (EVEs), a method which totals the proportion of rims present by fabric and form. Changes in a number of spot dates necessitated by subsequent examination, and the consequent amendment of the original organisation of groups which had been fully quantified meant that several groups which included medium and large contexts are no longer fully quantified by weight and EVEs as well as sherd count and ENVs. Unfortunately, there was insufficient time either to quantify fully all pottery from the study area, or to rectify the omissions brought about by these changes. Consequently a full record of sherd counts and ENV exists for all pottery, but only a partial record of weight and EVEs for some of the larger groups; the fully quantified data are quoted here whenever appropriate.

Complete lists of the pottery codes employed are available from the LAARC as part of the research archive and are also posted on the LAARC and MOLA pages of the MOL website: www.museumoflondonarchaeology.org.uk.

A total of 261 contexts yielded medieval pottery (dating between *c* AD 900 and *c* 1480), including residual material in post-medieval contexts. The great majority of these are small in size (226 contexts). There are 23 medieval contexts of medium size, ten classed as large, and one as very large (multiple boxes). In all, 5563 sherds of medieval pottery from a minimum of 2995 vessels were recorded in the main area of study. Post-medieval pottery ranging in date from *c* 1480 to the mid 17th century, but including some later, intrusive sherds, was found in 60 contexts, of which 39 are small, six are of medium size and five are large. A total of 1822 sherds from a minimum of 834 vessels was recorded, including pottery intrusive in medieval contexts.

A high level of chronological mixing is evident in a sizeable proportion of the contexts examined, with abraded sherds, residual and intrusive material common. This is not unexpected, given the demolition, robbing and rebuilding which took place in the area of the excavation.

In discussing functional groupings and trends, forms have been organised into broad categories according to their principal function. This provides a guide only, since many common forms were multifunctional: while the principal function of jugs, for example, is to serve liquid, jars may be used for storage or cooking (in fact, most vessels of jar form recorded as cooking pots show evidence for having been heated, so the term 'jar' is reserved for vessels thought not to have been used in this way). Bowls and dishes could be used in food preparation, dairying, cooking and serving; to allow for such ambiguities, a number of dual codes have been created, such as 'kitchen/storage', for use where either or both functions are suspected. Single function

categories, such as 'kitchen' and 'serving' are used when describing the principal function of a form. Post-medieval functional groupings are more complex than earlier, owing to a great proliferation of specialised vessel forms in all industries from the 16th century onwards. There is always the danger that our interpretation of any particular vessel's function may be coloured by modern usage of similar forms or by misleading terminology. The functional categories used here, therefore, should be regarded as convenient guides only, giving a broad overview of the range of common uses to which pottery was put and their relationships within the context of the whole, and allowing comparison to be made between groups within the site.

The pottery was considered according to chronological periods, tracing the main trends apparent in source and supply, and relating this to patterns observed throughout the London area. This was followed by a consideration of function in relation to spatial analysis, comparing the finds from Bermondsey with assemblages from other excavated religious houses in London. General conclusions for each chronological period from the 12th century to 1538 (periods M4–M9) will be found below, and briefly summarised in the 'Discussion' section of that period in Chapter 3. Detailed descriptions of significant groups also appear below, by period (M7–P1, *c* 1250–*c* 1650) and land use. The small groups of pottery from periods up to *c* 1100 are discussed in Chapter 2.5 (Late Saxon, *c* AD 850–1050, period M2) and Chapter 3.1 (*c* 1050–*c* 1100, period M3), based on analysis by Lyn Blackmore. Illustrated vessels are catalogued in Table 17.

Period M4, *c* 1100–50

All the fabrics recovered as part of the ceramic assemblage for period M4 are those commonly found throughout the London area. Handmade coarsewares of the second half of the 11th to first half of the 12th century from a variety of sources predominate (50.8% SC/40.3% ENV) and of these early medieval shell-tempered ware (EMSH; date range *c* 1050–*c* 1150) is by far the most common. On petrological grounds EMSH is closely related to pottery of similar date from north-west Kent. It may have been made from clay of the Woolwich Beds, which underlie north Kent and extend into Southwark (Vince and Jenner 1991, 63–4). In the City, where early medieval sand- and shell-tempered ware (EMSS) and early Surrey ware (ESUR) dominate, early medieval shell-tempered ware (EMSH) is less frequent than in contemporary deposits at Bermondsey Priory (Vince 1991b, fig 3). Both EMSS and ESUR are present at Bermondsey but in relatively small quantities compared with early medieval shell-tempered ware (EMSH). Other sites show a similar preference for EMSH, for example Hibernia Wharf, Southwark (HIB79; Pearce 1997b, 2), and Merton Priory, Surrey (Stephenson 2007, 214–18). This is an interesting pattern which appears to be related to sources supplying pottery north and south of the river, suggesting that during the 11th century Southwark may have had well-established trade networks south-east of London and that these tended to dominate supply

Table 17 Catalogue of illustrated medieval and post-medieval pottery

Catalogue no.	Context	Fabric	Form	Period of deposition	Land use	Fig no.
<P1>	A[2121]	CHAF	jar/bowl	P1	OA11	8
<P2>	A[2752]	IPSF	storage jar	M4	OA6	8
<P3>	A[1046]	EMGR	spouted pitcher	M3	OA2	18
<P4>	A[4134]	LCOAR SHEL	cooking pot	M5	B8	37
<P5>	A[4134]	LCOAR EAS	jug	M5	B8	37
<P6>	A[4393]	LCOAR GRIT	bowl	M5	B8	37
<P7>	A[4393]	LCOAR GRIT	cooking pot	M5	B8	37
<P8>	A[4308]	SHER	cooking pot	M5	D1/B8	37
<P9>	A[1125]	BLGR	handled cooking pot	M5	D2	46
<P10>	A[1125]	LOND	jug	M5	D2	46
<P11>	A[1125]	LCOAR GRIT	cooking pot	M5	D2	46
<P12>	A[1125]	SSW	cooking pot	M5	D2	46
<P13>	A[1122]	SSW	cooking pot	M6	B8	52
<P14>	A[1122]	SSW	cooking pot	M6	B8	52
<P15>	A[1122]	SSW	cooking pot	M6	B8	52
<P16>	A[1122]	SSW	bowl	M6	B8	52
<P17>	A[1865]	KING	pipkin	M8	D4	62
<P18>	A[4154]	KING	bowl	M9	B9	67
<P19>	A[4154]	KING	cup	M9	B9	67
<P20>	A[4154]	KING	urinal	M9	B9	67
<P21>	A[4154]	CBW	jug	M9	B9	67
<P22>	A[4156]	KING	jug	M9	B9	67
<P23>	A[515]	SSW	? spit support	P1	D4/OA12	89
<P24>	A[518]	RAER	costrel	P1	D4/OA12	102
<P25>	A[972]	CBW	cucurbit	M9	B9	104
<P26>	A[972]	LLON	cucurbit	M9	B9	104
<P27>	A[3460]	PMSRY	jug	P1	OA9	115
<P28>	A[2883]	PMSRG	handle	P1	OA9	115
<P29>	A[3460]	PMRE	jar	P1	OA9	115
<P30>	A[3303]	PMRE	birdpot	P1	OA9	115
<P31>	A[3460]	RAER	jug	P1	OA9	115
<P32>	A[2752]	LSS	lamp	M4	OA6	155
<P33>	A[1339]	LCOAR	jar	M7	B10	156
<P34>	A[3626]	LOND EAS	jug	M7	B12	156
<P35>	A[967]	EMSH	jar	M7	D2	156
<P36>	A[548]	EMSH	bowl	M7	D2	156
<P37>	A[693]	EMSH	bowl	M8	OA8	157
<P38>	A[972]	CHEA	biconical jug	M9	B9	158
<P39>	A[972]	CHEA	saucer	M9	B9	158
<P40>	A[972]	KING	jug	M9	B9	158
<P41>	A[972]	KING	condiment dish	M9	B9	158
<P42>	A[972]	KING	urinal	M9	B9	158
<P43>	A[972]	LLON	pipkin	M9	B9	158
<P44>	A[972]	LLSL	cooking pot	M9	B9	158
<P45>	A[972]	RAER	jug	M9	B9	158
<P46>	A[972]	SIEG	beaker	M9	B9	158
<P47>	A[96]	KING	jug	M9	D4/OA9	159
<P48>	A[597]	LCOAR	curfew	M9	D4/OA9	159
<P49>	A[2096]	STAR	costrel	P1	B6	160
<P50>	A[1764]	ROUL	jug	P1	B9/OA12	161
<P51>	A[518]	CHEA	lid	P1	D4/OA12	161
<P52>	A[518]	PMSRY	jug	P1	D4/OA12	161
<P53>	A[518]	LCWW	cauldron	P1	D4/OA12	161
<P54>	A[515], A[518]	SNTG	vase	P1	D4/OA12	161
<P55>	A[518]	? RAER/LANG	jug	P1	D4/OA12	161
<P56>	A[539]	PMSRY	bowl	P1	D4/OA12	161
<P57>	A[2349]	PMSRY	carinated bowl	P1	D4/OA12	162
<P58>	A[2349]	PMSRY	jug	P1	D4/OA12	162
<P59>	A[2349]	PMSRY	goblet	P1	D4/OA12	162
<P60>	A[2349]	MERC	jar	P1	D4/OA12	162
<P61>	A[3376]	BORDY	tripod pipkin	P1	B12	163
<P62>	A[3376]	SNTG	bottle	P1	B12	163
<P63>	A[3376]	TGW	charger	P1	B12	163
<P64>	A[3376]	NISG	bowl	P1	B12	163
<P65>	A[3376]	POTG	bowl	P1	B12	163

at the expense of the more varied range of wares found on City sites, such as early medieval sandy ware (EMS), early medieval sand- and shell-tempered ware (EMSS) and early Surrey ware (ESUR) (Vince and Jenner 1991, 59–62, 73–5).

Non-local wares are limited to one sherd of St Neots ware (NEOT), the source of which appears to lie within the Bedfordshire, Huntingdonshire and Cambridgeshire regions (Vince and Jenner 1991, 55). Surprisingly there are no East Anglian imports, notably Ipswich-/Thetford-type ware (THET), which appears regularly on City sites from the 10th to the 12th centuries (Vince 1991b, 271, fig 7; Pearce in prep). This may suggest that the Thames acted as something of a southern boundary to regular trade with East Anglia.

Imported wares are strikingly rare on the site in the 11th to 12th centuries, represented by three sherds alone: from a blue-grey ware (BLGR) *kugeltöpfe* or handled cooking pot, a pitcher in red-painted ware (REDP), both from the Rhineland, and a jug in north French unglazed ware (NFRE). Red-painted ware is the most common imported pottery found in the City at this date, continuing in use up to *c* 1200 (Vince 1991b, 271, fig 7; Pearce in prep). Andenne-type ware (ANDE), from the Meuse valley, is also relatively frequent on City sites but is very poorly represented at St Saviour Bermondsey at any date; it is not present in period M4 at all. Pottery and goods from the Rhine and Meuse valleys came into London regularly during the 10th to 12th centuries and were largely landed at Queenhithe (City of London; Blackmore 1994, 30). Red-painted ware and blue-grey ware in particular are quite common in waterfront assemblages from Bull Wharf (City of London; BUF90, UPT90; Pearce in prep). These imported wares were circulated within the City but appear not to have reached Southwark in the same quantities.

In common with 10th- to 12th-century assemblages throughout the London area, cooking pots or jars are overwhelmingly the predominant form present in period M4. During the 10th and 11th centuries these were the principal forms of vessel used for cooking as well as for storage, and pots or jars provided the mainstay of all the local handmade coarseware industries and of the wheel-thrown Late Saxon ware. Whether or not jar-shaped vessels were used for storage or cooking can generally be determined by the presence or otherwise of external sooting and heat-blackening, especially around the base of the pot, as well as the presence of food residues inside. A fair number of the period M4 cooking pots are sooted to some extent, although sherds near the rim may be free of soot and so give a misleading impression of how many vessels were used for this purpose. Four sherds from three bowls, two in early medieval shell-tempered ware (EMSH) and one in shelly-sandy ware (SSW) were all sooted externally, showing that they had been used to heat foods. A similar function is suggested by the handled, round-bottomed cooking pot or *kugeltöpfe* in blue-grey ware (BLGR) (one sherd). All of these cooking and food preparation vessels are typical of the very limited and largely non-specialist range in use at all levels of society, both in the City and elsewhere in Southwark at the same date.

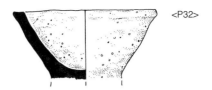

Fig 155 *Pedestal lamp in Late Saxon shelly ware <P32> (from OA6, period M4) (scale 1:4)*

Serving vessels are represented by jugs and pitchers and are much less frequent in period M4 than are kitchen wares. Spouted pitchers are found in Late Saxon shelly ware (LSS; date range *c* AD 900–1050) and possibly in clear-glazed London-type ware (A[2752]), although the similarity with cooking pots may inevitably have led to the misidentification of non-distinctive body sherds. Spouted pitchers are the main form imported in red-painted ware (REDP) (one sherd in period M4 from A[2752]) and are generally associated with the wine trade. Otherwise, jugs are the chief form of serving vessel found from the early 12th century onwards. In period M4 these are almost all made in London-type wares as is the case throughout the London area.

The only other form represented amongst late 11th- to early 12th-century pottery from period M4 is a pedestal lamp in Late Saxon shelly ware (LSS) (<P32>, Fig 155) from the cemetery soil (OA6). This form of portable lighting is relatively uncommon in the archaeological record, and functioned by means of a wick floating in oil held in a shallow bowl standing on a solid pedestal (Pearce 1998). Apart from this one vessel, all other pottery of this period can be related to cooking, food preparation, serving beverages and possibly storage. The assemblage is entirely mundane and domestic in character, with nothing which can be identified as industrial. Moreover, there is no pottery which can be equated with households or establishments of higher social standing, such as fine-quality glazed Andenne-type ware (ANDE) or Stamford-type ware (STAM), nor any significant concentration of imported wares.

Period M5, *c* 1150–*c* 1200

Glazed wheel-thrown pottery (coarse London-type wares) is the most common source represented in late 12th- to early 13th-century contexts, as elsewhere in London: by *c* 1180 London-type wares and shelly-sandy ware (SSW) together dominated ceramic supply to the City, as shown by the large assemblages from Billingsgate Market Lorry Park and Seal House, both in the City of London (BIG82, SH74; Vince 1985, fig 12b–c). By the early 13th century, coarse London-type ware (LCOAR) and related shell- and grit-tempered fabrics were no longer being made and London-type ware (LOND) alone was produced, remaining one of the chief sources of pottery used in London until the mid 14th century when it ceased production (Pearce et al 1985, 19–21). At Bermondsey, coarse London-type fabrics together account for 20.5% SC/15.7% ENV of all pottery in period M5, although LCOAR alone constitutes less than half of this. The LCOAR variants had not been recognised when the London type-series was published (ibid), and coarse London-type ware with gritty inclusions (LCOAR GRIT) remains relatively uncommon in the City. Neither variant continued into the 13th century. London-type ware (LOND) is found in similar overall proportions to LCOAR (19.6% SC/16.3% ENV), and occurs mainly as jugs decorated in styles common during the second half of the 12th and early 13th century: early style decoration, based on the application of thick lines of white slip; the north French and Rouen styles, which were introduced during the last quarter of the 12th century, with their applied decoration and coloured slips imitating French prototypes; and three sherds from a highly decorated (LOND HD) vessel, probably of mid 13th-century date. The number of LOND jugs with recognisable decoration is quite small (1.8% SC/3.3% ENV of all pottery in period M5), leaving a considerable number of sherds with no surviving decorative elements except perhaps an overall white slip, and clear or green glaze (103 sherds/28 ENV). Since most of these come from jugs, it appears that the array of serving vessels in use at this date were quite plain and functional, rather than decorative.

Wheel-thrown coarsewares constitute the other main source of pottery at this period, and by far the greatest number of these consist of cooking pots in shelly-sandy ware (SSW). South Hertfordshire-type greyware (SHER) is of minimal importance, and this remains so until SSW ceased production in the early 13th century (Vince 1985, fig 12c–d). It may be that SHER was more common north of the river during the late 12th century than on sites in Southwark, suggesting the possibility of different trade networks, and that its main market did not extend much further south before c 1200 since this area was well provided with local coarsewares (SSW, LOND/LCOAR). It may even be suggested that there were centres producing these local wares south of the river and easily accessible to the priory (no kilns have yet been discovered anywhere in the London area). The analysis of pottery from City sites suggests, however, that there was an increase in the frequency of SHER during the early 13th century throughout the London area, as SSW fell out of production after c 1220 (Vince 1985, fig 12). It remains possible that there was, nevertheless, a greater bias towards SSW south of the river during the late 12th century, as shown by comparison of material from periods M5 and M6 with data derived from the massive waterfront dumps along the north bank of the Thames (for example, at Seal House and Billingsgate Market Lorry Park; ibid).

Eleventh- to 12th-century handmade coarsewares are present in some quantity: together they account for 18.6% SC/30.2% ENV of all pottery from period M5, the third most common source.

The imported ceramics from period M5 include a near-complete blue-grey ware (BLGR) kugeltöpfe, discarded in Drain 2 and a single sherd of early Rouen ware (ROUE) from deposits beneath Building 10. The latter is a high quality rarity on the site and the precursor of the London French-inspired styles. Early Rouen ware would have been a relatively expensive commodity, associated with the wine trade. It is not a common find in London assemblages although it was very influential in the development of London-type wares, with far-reaching consequences for other English ceramic industries (Pearce et al 1985, 131–2). It was of superior quality to the London copies it inspired and was probably used at table as a sign of higher status, although it is unlikely that it reached the priory through regular trade. Rhenish wares (blue-grey or Paffrath ware (BLGR)) and red-painted or Pingsdorf-type ware (REDP) are among the most common imported pottery found in the City at this date (for example at Bull Wharf; Pearce in prep). There are no other French or Rhenish imports, nothing from the Low Countries (such as Andenne-type ware (ANDE), which is regularly found in City assemblages) and nothing from East Anglia, thus continuing the trend observed in period M4 whereby potteries in the London area and the South East supplied the bulk of the priory's ceramic needs.

Cooking pots are the main ceramic form found in period M5. There are particularly high concentrations in Building 10 and Building 8 (81.2% SC/82.4% ENV and 96.9% SC/90.9% ENV respectively). In Building 8, kitchen wares and kitchen/serving wares together (ie cooking pots and bowls, which are multifunctional forms) account for 77% SC/54.3% ENV of all pottery. In all other contexts cooking pots outnumber jugs, the only other form of consequence, although not to the same degree as in Building 8 and Building 10. These figures are in keeping with the typical functional breakdown on domestic sites throughout London during the late 12th to early 13th century, a time when greater diversification of ceramic forms was taking place to meet developing household requirements.

In part, the balance of forms is a function of the prevailing ceramic trends during the late 12th and early 13th centuries. These trends were dictated by the relatively simple requirements of the consumers. The jar-shaped cooking pot, used to slow-cook or stew meals in bulk, remained the principal form of ceramic cooking vessel throughout the country until the late Middle Ages. It therefore formed the mainstay of all coarseware industries supplying London although some degree of specialisation is apparent with the growth of industries whose products were based largely on the use of glaze. London-type ware potters, therefore, showed a marked tendency to concentrate on jug production, which owes its development largely to the introduction into the region of glazing technology at the end of the 11th century. From the mid 12th century onwards, jugs constituted an increasingly large proportion of the potter's output. Although the range of jug forms found in period M5 is relatively limited, this is simply a reflection of what was available at the time. Jugs were used primarily for bulk serving and their appearance could be enhanced by decoration. They became ever more elaborate during the 13th century. At St Saviour Bermondsey there are relatively few decorated jugs suitable for making a show at the table in period M5 and the early Rouen ware (ROUE) jug constitutes the only example of a 'special' imported vessel. During this period the London-type ware potters took advantage of every opportunity for adornment using coloured slips and glazes, incised and applied decoration. Their fashionable decorated jugs could be used at table, both for everyday meals and for grander entertainment and not simply as containers for the storage and serving of liquid. The late 12th- and early 13th-century jugs from Bermondsey give the impression of a thoroughly utilitarian array, not overly impressive in appearance, but more than sufficient to serve the needs of the community and any visitors.

Period M6, *c* 1200–50

The large 12th-century pottery group from the chimney construction trench outside the (?infirmarer's) hall/lodgings (B8; Chapter 3.4, 'Archaeological evidence') seems most likely to represent a clear-out of kitchen wares from inside the building. The pattern of fabric breakdown is much the same as in period M5, with a high proportion of wheel-thrown coarsewares (437 sherds of shelly-sandy ware (SSW) as opposed to one of south Hertfordshire-type greyware (SHER)). Shelly-sandy ware is overall the most common fabric. There is also a relatively high proportion of 11th- to 12th-century handmade wares, the second most common source. These are once again derived almost entirely from the kitchen, although the presence of two near-complete, smashed cooking pots in early Surrey ware (ESUR) in A[1122] has grossly distorted the proportion calculated by sherd count, weight and EVEs, making the fabric appear more common than it may originally have been.

London-type wares are the third most common source, and are mostly typical of 12th-century assemblages, with similar quantities of both coarse London-type ware (LCOAR) and London-type ware (LOND). Identifiable styles of decoration date to the late 12th century, but no later. The absence of 13th-

century Surrey whitewares, as well as of contemporary London-type wares, suggests that the bulk of the pottery discarded from Building 8 derived from an earlier period of use. Neither apparently was it considered worth keeping, or moving to another location. In terms of form, cooking pots account for the bulk of pottery recovered from Building 8 in period M6 (92.9% SC/82.1% ENV).

Period M7, *c* 1250–*c* 1330

Infirmary (B10)

A deposit A[1339] beneath the floor at the south end of the infirmary (B10) was dated *c* 1080–*c* 1200 by the pottery present and probably either disturbed the underlying cesspit fill (A[1389], also dated *c* 1080–*c* 1200, period M5; Chapter 3.3, 'Archaeological evidence') or was itself part of the cesspit. Context A[1339] yielded a medium-sized group of 37 sherds from five ENV, including the complete profile of a cooking pot or jar in unglazed coarse London-type ware (LCOAR) (Fig 156, <P33>; cf Pearce et al 1985, fig 67 nos 339–40) and 23 sherds from a cooking pot in early Surrey ware (ESUR).

? Infirmary range extension (B12)

A section of the south wall robbing trench A[3626] produced 16 sherds of medieval pottery dated *c* 1140–*c* 1200. These include sherds of shelly-sandy ware (SSW) and parts of two jugs in London-type ware with early style decoration (LOND EAS) in a trellis pattern in red and white slip. One of these is of large squat form (cf Pearce et al 1985, fig 20), and has a small, neat, circular post-firing hole in the shoulder, the purpose of which is unclear (Fig 156, <P34>).

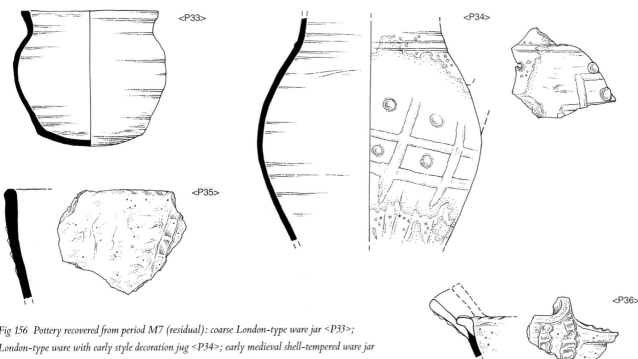

Fig 156 Pottery recovered from period M7 (residual): coarse London-type ware jar <P33>; London-type ware with early style decoration jug <P34>; early medieval shell-tempered ware jar <P35> and socketed bowl <P36> (scale 1:4)

Drain 2

The pottery from contexts in the stratigraphic group describing the disuse and robbing of the north-east section of Drain 2 (gp23) numbered a total of 246 sherds from a minimum of 137 vessels (4249g/4.05 EVEs). This includes one large context A[548] (167 sherds/76 ENV/2645g/2.98 EVEs) and one context of medium size, A[270], dated *c* 1180–*c* 1230. All pottery from the group was fully quantified. There are very few complete vessel profiles and a relatively small proportion of joining sherds (collections of miscellaneous body sherds are counted as one ENV and this statistic on its own may give a distorted perspective on the relation between sherd numbers and vessel completeness). Assemblages of this kind are entirely consistent with what would be expected in a sequence of robbing backfills, derived from generalised dumping perhaps over several years, as opposed to the often more specific concentration of domestic rubbish in, for example, a cesspit.

Apart from 14 sherds of intrusive 16th- to 17th-century pottery in contexts A[499], A[578] and A[967] the bulk of the pottery recovered from the various backfills of Drain 2 consists of fabrics and forms in contemporary use during the 12th century, especially the second half. One sherd from a cooking pot in Kingston-type ware (KING), dated broadly to *c* 1230–*c* 1400, was found in context A[583] (robbing backfill of D2), but this is the latest readily identifiable medieval pottery in any of the period M7 backfills. Otherwise the latest distinctive fabric introduced into London is London-type ware, decorated in the Rouen style (LOND ROU; date range *c* 1180–*c* 1270) together with several sherds which may have come from jugs decorated in related French-inspired styles of similar date. There is, however, a reasonable quantity of 11th- to 12th-century handmade coarsewares which were in current use largely between *c* 1050 and 1150 (11.4% SC/14.6% ENV/16.9% Wt/10.6% EVEs). Although these would have continued in use into the second half of the 12th century, some time after production had finally ceased, this figure will include a proportion of residual material. Early medieval shell-tempered ware (EMSH) is by far the most common of these fabrics, occurring mostly as cooking pots, some of which have applied, thumbed strips. From A[967] were sherds from a large straight-sided storage jar with applied strips (Fig 156, <P35>); a very large rounded bowl (rim Diam 440mm) with a thumbed rim and applied strips in diagonal (probably V-shaped) patterns and part of a spouted pitcher with incised, wavy decoration (cf Vince and Jenner 1991, fig 2.48 no. 124). Context A[548] yielded part of a rounded, socketed bowl with heavy, applied, thumbed strips along the top of the rim and down the length of the socket (Fig 156, <P36>). The frequency of early medieval shell-tempered ware (EMSH) relative to other contemporary fabrics, such as early Surrey ware (ESUR) and early medieval sand- and shell-tempered ware (EMSS), has already been commented on (above, 'Period M5, *c* 1150–*c* 1200').

Wheel-thrown coarsewares are the predominant fabric group in the drain backfills. As in other late 12th-century groups on the site, shelly-sandy ware (SSW) is the major component (49.2% SC/46.7 ENV/54.1% Wt/66.7 EVEs) with only six sherds of the contemporary south Hertfordshire-type greyware (SHER), whose main period of use post-dates the end of the shelly-sandy ware industry (from *c* 1220 onwards). Apart from one bowl sherd in A[548], cooking pots are the only form recognised in SSW, including vessels with grouped thumbing at the rim and applied thumbed strips in horizontal, vertical and diagonal or V-shaped schemes.

After shelly-sandy ware (SSW), London-type wares are the next most common fabric in this group (33.7% SC/29.9% ENV/23.1% Wt/13.8% EVEs). The finer London-type ware (LOND) is far more frequent than coarse London-type ware (LCOAR) and coarse London-type ware with shell inclusions (LCOAR SHEL) combined (23.6% SC/13.1% ENV/15.1% Wt/7.4% EVEs of all gp23 pottery), suggesting a deposition date nearer the end of the 12th century, rather than the middle, coinciding with the phasing out of the coarser fabrics at the turn of the century. This is a pattern observed on City sites where London-type ware is more than twice as common as coarse London-type ware after *c* 1170/80 (Vince 1991b, 268). In both fabrics jugs are the main form, including both early rounded and baluster jugs, with early style decoration in white and red slip. No north French-style jugs were positively identified and only one Rouen-style jug, again suggesting a latest date in the last quarter of the 12th century.

As in all other groups of similar date from the site, imports are minimal, limited to one sherd of blue-grey ware (BLGR) and one of red-painted ware (REDP). The relative scarcity of pottery imported from the Continent is noteworthy and a similar downturn in imports is apparent in the City during the late 12th to mid 13th centuries (Vince 1985, 47), although imports tend to be more abundant on sites along the waterfront, such as Bull Wharf (Pearce in prep). Kitchen wares, chiefly cooking pots, are by far the most common forms represented in the drain backfills (77.8% SC/67.1% ENV/76.8% Wt/91.1% EVEs), with serving vessels (jugs and pitchers) as the other principal form.

Yard (OA7)

The backfill in the robbing trench of the wall on the south side of the yard abutting the north-east corner of Building 11 produced a total of 147 sherds from a minimum of 42 vessels. Two contexts A[1281] and A[937] from the robbing group (gp29) were fully quantified (125 sherds/31 ENV/1859g/0.85 EVE) and included several joining sherds. The pottery from A[1281] was dated *c* 1270–*c* 1350. This is based on the presence of 51 sherds from at least six jugs in Mill Green ware (MG) together with a further three sherds from one MG jug in the small backfill context A[937]. Together these account for 41.5% of all pottery from the robbing group by sherd count (20.6% ENV/27.6% Wt/94.1% EVEs). This is an unusually high total for MG, second only to London-type ware (LOND) in this group (50.7% SC/55.9% ENV/64.8% Wt/5.9% EVEs). It can in part be accounted for by the fragile nature of the fabric, which causes it to become very fragmented when broken. Both squat and conical forms are represented, with the typical *sgraffito* decoration in regularly spaced vertical stripes (cf Pearce et al 1982, figs 3–4, 11).

A variety of London-type ware jugs, in both the highly decorated style (LOND HD) and white slip-decorated (LOND WSD) styles, are represented: a baluster jug in the highly decorated style with polychrome glazing and ring-and-dot stamps arranged in V-shaped panels (cf Pearce et al 1985, fig 52 no. 185); a baluster jug with clear glaze over a white slip and an incised oval handle with thumb stops or 'ears'; sherds from at least five tulip-necked baluster jugs with white slip and clear glaze (cf ibid, fig 37); two white slip-decorated jugs and a Rouen-style jug. Both the highly decorated and the Rouen-style jugs represent a taste for more elaborate decoration prevalent during the first half of the 13th century. By the last quarter of the century, plainer, simpler styles and undecorated vessels predominated, including flared and tulip-necked balusters, and white slip decoration. There are, in addition, sherds from two unglazed drinking jugs, one conical and one baluster-shaped (cf ibid, figs 65–6). These forms are generally associated with drinking by their terminology, although some at least may have been made to given specifications for use as measures (ibid, 41).

The paucity of Surrey whitewares present in this group is notable. Kingston-type ware (KING) and coarse Surrey-Hampshire border ware (CBW) together account for only 2.4% by sherd count (6.5% ENV/1.3% Wt). By the late 13th century, Kingston-type ware (KING) was one of the most common fabrics used in London (Pearce and Vince 1988, fig 9b–c) and a higher proportion would normally be expected in a large assemblage of this date. Since CBW is limited to four sherds from a cooking pot this strongly argues for a date of deposition before the mid 14th century, by which date, CBW was by far the most common kind of pottery used in London (ibid, fig 9e–f). The pottery from the robber trench displays a marked emphasis on serving vessels (80% SC/64.5% ENV/83% Wt/100% EVEs). Although jugs would also be used for storing liquids, the decorative nature of most of those recovered suggests that they were intended equally for the table.

Period M7 discussion

Pottery from contexts allocated to period M7 (notably D2) include a very high proportion of 11th- to 12th-century pottery, as well as earlier material. The high level of chronological mixing apparent in the pottery recovered from period M7 and from other periods seriously inhibits analysis and the recognition of trends and patterns of use. Wheel-thrown coarsewares, are the second most common fabric group present in period M7, principally shelly-sandy ware (SSW), with minimal south Hertfordshire-type greyware (SHER). Although London-type wares are the most common single source of pottery at this period, this includes a relatively high proportion of types datable to the 12th and early 13th centuries (35% SC/51% ENV of all London-type

wares). This figure may well be higher, since 136 body sherds of London-type ware (LOND) cannot be assigned to any one decorative style through lack of diagnostic features. Even the few imports recovered probably date mostly to the 12th century or earlier. In total, therefore, at least 62.8% of all pottery from period M7 by sherd count (72.2% ENV) can be considered residual.

The breakdown of fabrics found in the fully quantified large context A[1281], in the yard (OA7), is more typical of the late 13th to early 14th centuries. This shows an interesting pattern in which London-type ware (LOND) is by far the most common fabric present, and includes one sherd only which could date as early as c 1180 (LOND ROU), and nothing else definitely attributable to the 12th century. Recognisable decorative styles in LOND include jugs in the highly decorated (LOND HD) and white slip-decorated (LOND WSD) styles, both of which date to the mid to late 13th century, while forms typical of this period include tulip-necked baluster jugs and drinking jugs (both baluster-shaped and conical). At this date, London-type (LOND) and Kingston-type wares (KING) are the most common sources of pottery found in the massive waterfront dumps at Trig Lane and Swan Lane (TL74, SWA84) along the Thames foreshore in the City, a pattern which seems to be general throughout the London area (Vince 1985, fig 18). It is noticeable that by the 13th century, after the demise of shelly-sandy ware (SSW), south Hertfordshire-type greyware (SHER) forms one of the most common coarsewares used in the City (ibid), but remains scarce at Bermondsey (there are only 15 sherds altogether in period M7, and none in A[1281]). Although the rarity of this fabric in 12th-century contexts can probably be explained by the popularity of SSW, which appears to have marginalised the products of the Hertfordshire kilns, the continuation of this pattern into the 13th century may show that the Thames acted as an approximate southern boundary for distribution of the ware. The picture is further complicated by the contemporaneous production, in the Limpsfield area of Surrey, of visually similar unglazed greywares, made in a similar range of forms and using closely comparable decorative techniques. These fabrics can be difficult to distinguish by normal means (x20 magnification and macroscopic examination). No Limpsfield wares have definitely been identified at Bermondsey and quantities of SHER remain low, even as residual sherds in later periods. It may be that the priory was not buying much pottery from either source, or that SHER was less important in Southwark than in the City.

The large quantity of Mill Green ware (MG) recovered from the yard (OA7) is noteworthy (51 sherds in A[1281]). Figures derived from the massive waterfront groups at Seal House and Trig Lane show that at the height of its popularity Mill Green ware supplied between 10% and 20% of the City's pottery, and this at a time when jugs were the most common form in use (Pearce et al 1982, 270). Mill Green ware (MG) was made in kilns at Ingatestone (Essex) and, although it had a relatively short period of use in London, it was exceptionally well made, thinly potted to a remarkable degree, attractively glazed and of superior quality. Modern ceramicists' notions of status as implied by quality, are often influenced primarily by the presence of good quality or unusual imported wares, especially in abundance. Consequently, the significance of pottery produced much closer to home may all too easily be overlooked. Compared with contemporaneous local London-type wares, Mill Green ware (MG) may well have represented a more expensive and perhaps even fashionable choice, used to grace the tables of the wealthier members of society as a demonstration of quality and taste. Whether this applies to the pottery used at Bermondsey Priory, or whether the material discarded in this area came from the immediate vicinity or further afield, is not altogether certain, but it is clear that good quality jugs did form part of the stock of pottery in the possession of the priory.

Normally at this date, Kingston-type ware (KING) forms a sizeable proportion of large assemblages of London pottery, both from City sites and south of the river (Vince 1985, fig 18). A wide variety of jug forms in different decorative styles were made in the Kingston-type industry during the late 13th-century, as well as various kinds of cooking vessels and other forms (Pearce and Vince 1988, 82–3). There are, however, no more than 20 sherds (19 ENV) of KING in period M7 contexts at Bermondsey, and only three of these come from the large context A[1281] (2.4% SC/2 ENV or 6.5%/1.3% Wt). This is unusual, although the quantity of KING rises dramatically in later periods. It may be that glazed whitewares took longer to establish a hold on the market in Southwark than in the City, or that the figures are biased by the high proportion of 12th-century and earlier pottery in the period M7 sample. It is also noticeable that there is very little coarse Surrey-Hampshire border ware (CBW) present in this period. This coarse whiteware from the potteries of the Surrey-Hampshire borders is first found in small quantities in the City in contexts dated to the last quarter of the 13th century (ibid, 16–17, fig 9c), increasing its hold on the market until, by the mid 14th century, it was by far the most common source of pottery used in the City (ibid, fig 9e–f). There is no CBW in context A[1281] and it does not appear subsequently to have occupied such an important place in the supply of pottery to the priory as it did to the City.

Imported pottery in period M7 is, once again, of minimal importance, accounting for only 1% by sherd count (1.8% ENV), all of it residual.

As in period M6, cooking pots and jugs of various forms predominate, although the figures are biased by the large quantity of 12th-century pottery present. Apart from cooking pots, other forms used for cooking recovered from period M7 features dated to the late 13th to early 14th century include bowls, which were adaptable to many uses, and part of a D-shaped dripping dish in coarse Surrey-Hampshire border ware (CBW). This is an uncommon form, semicircular in plan and slab-built, with a tubular handle opposite the straight side of the vessel. Surviving examples are generally sooted externally, especially opposite the handle (cf Pearce and Vince 1988, 63–5, fig 117 no. 498). They were most likely used to catch the juices

from a spit-roast joint, and would have been pushed into the embers beneath, thus accounting for uneven blackening. This is the first evidence for the use of this form on the site, although the presence of a probable spit-support in shelly-sandy ware (SSW; Fig 89, <P23>) shows that this common method of preparing meat was, unsurprisingly, in use from at least the 12th century.

Period M8, c 1330–c 1430

Open ground to the south-east of the conventual buildings (OA8)

The pottery from the backfill of the ditch in this area (OA8, Fig 53) is dated c 1180–c 1230 and is generally quite fragmented, with no reconstructable vessel profiles. A total of 177 sherds from a minimum of 73 vessels was recovered; this group was fully quantified (2492g/1.37 EVEs). Wheel-thrown coarsewares are the most common fabrics found (49.7% SC/37% ENV/45% Wt/42.3% EVEs), and the bulk of these are cooking pots in shelly-sandy ware (SSW) (82 sherds/21 ENV/1064g/0.48 EVE). As in comparable groups from St Saviour Bermondsey, south Hertfordshire-type greyware (SHER) is much less frequent (6 sherds/6 ENV/57g/0.10 EVE). London-type wares are the next most common source of pottery (37.3% SC/47.9% ENV/40% Wt/42.3% EVEs). These are mainly jugs decorated in the early style with various schemes in white, and occasionally also red slip. There is also one sherd from a green-glazed jug decorated with overall, closely spaced, fingertip-impressed dimples, again typical of the late 12th century (cf Pearce et al 1985, fig 18 nos 31, 32). Sherds from two green-glazed baluster jugs in the north French style and one in the Rouen style date the context to after c 1180 when these influential styles were introduced from the Continent.

Eleventh- to 12th-century handmade coarsewares are much less frequent and may be residual, restricted to early Surrey ware (ESUR) and early medieval shell-tempered ware (EMSH) (9% SC/8.2% ENV/13.4% Wt/15.3% EVEs). There is a flared bowl in the latter (Fig 157, <P37>; cf Vince and Jenner 1991, fig 2.47 nos 116–18). Imports are restricted to two sherds of red-painted ware (REDP) from the Rhineland, two sherds of Andenne-type ware (ANDE) from the Meuse valley and one sherd from a jug in north French monochrome (NFM); a high quality, fine, glazed whiteware which is rare on the site. There is little variety in form, with cooking pots and jugs predominating, as in most other contemporary assemblages throughout the London area.

<P37>

Fig 157 Early medieval shell-tempered ware bowl <P37> from ditch backfill in Open Area 8, period M8 (scale 1:4)

Period M8 discussion

A large number of contexts allocated to period M8 date on their pottery to the 12th to 13th centuries, or earlier. There are also several contexts dated to the period *c* 1270–*c* 1350, and these no doubt include vessels still in use after *c* 1350, even if they were out of date and no longer made (for example, Mill Green ware (MG) jugs). In all 23.1% of all pottery from period M8 by sherd count (13.3% ENV) can be considered residual and very unlikely to have been in contemporary use during the late 14th century or later. As in earlier periods, this degree of contamination can largely be accounted for by robbing activity that has the additional drawback of creating uncertainty about the location on site of the discarded pottery when in use. This must be borne in mind when interpreting the spatial distribution of pottery at all periods. In addition, all but one of the 29 contexts were small, a factor which has implications for chronological refinement. The single medium-sized group came from context A[1865], the small north–south drain associated with Drain 4 (Chapter 3.6, 'Archaeological evidence', 'Open ground to the south-east of the conventual buildings (OA8) and stone-built drain (D4)').

Surrey whitewares are the most common source of pottery at this date, a trend observed throughout the London area. The breakdown of whitewares, however, differs from that usual for City sites with Kingston-type ware (KING) marginally more abundant than coarse Surrey-Hampshire border ware (CBW) (19.9% SC/15.1% ENV and 16.3% SC/12.1% ENV respectively; cf Pearce and Vince 1988, fig 9e–h). Since these figures are based on a relatively small sample (277 sherds), derived largely from small and frequently contaminated contexts, they cannot be considered truly representative. A much larger sample including large and closely datable contexts would be required to give a more accurate picture of ceramic supply to the abbey during the late 14th and early 15th centuries. The relationship on the site between KING and CBW is perhaps better illustrated by pottery from period M9, and will be discussed further (below, 'Period M9, *c* 1430–1538', 'Period M9 discussion'). There is very little Cheam whiteware (CHEA), a late whiteware first used in the City in the mid 14th century (Pearce and Vince 1988, 17).

London-type wares are the second most common source of pottery (16.2% SC/23% ENV, excluding 12th- to late 13th-century types), although 36 jug sherds cannot be ascribed to any particular datable style. There are also several sherds of Mill Green ware (MG) and the coarse variant Mill Green coarseware (MG COAR), which were largely in use in London *c* 1270–*c* 1350, together accounting for 6.1% of all pottery by sherd count (7.9% ENV) and continuing an interesting trend which shows that fine quality tablewares were reaching the priory from Essex during the first half of the 14th century, presumably via the City. Small quantities of late medieval Hertfordshire glazed ware (LMHG) were present (6 sherds/4 ENV) from production centres in the St Albans region, which are as yet unlocated (Jenner and Vince 1983, 152; Turner-Rugg 1995, 52). This fine, glazed pottery was used in London *c* 1350–*c* 1450 in a

limited range of forms and seldom constitutes more than a small proportion of large assemblages (cf Pearce and Vince 1988, fig 9e–h). The same pattern of occurrence is found at Bermondsey and confirms that most, if not all, of the fabrics in use in the City were also available in Southwark.

There are no residual imports. All those recovered could have been in contemporary use during period M8. The total is again very small (four sherds) including one vessel in French Saintonge ware with a mottled green glaze (SAIM), one in Siegburg stoneware (SIEG) from Germany and two in Dutch red earthenware (DUTR) from the Low Countries. These show simply that widely available imported wares were in use at the priory and abbey at this period, as they were throughout the London area.

As in earlier periods, jugs and cooking pots remain the most common forms in period M8, although the figures are somewhat biased by the relatively large number of residual sherds present. Cooking pots are the major form recovered from the demolition of the infirmary building (B11) and from the chambers (B13) and courtyard (OA9; which do include residual material). In the second cloister garth (OA2) they occur in similar proportions to jugs of various forms. Sherds from two pipkins come from the area to the south-west of the conventual buildings (OA4) (one in late medieval Hertfordshire glazed ware (LMHG) and one in Kingston-type ware (KING)), but there are no other forms of cooking vessel in period M8. Pipkins were used for heating smaller quantities of food than could generally be accommodated in the average cooking pot, and were adapted by the addition of a handle and lip to allow pouring. They may be seen as successors to the blue-grey ware (BLGR) *kugeltöpfe* of the 11th and 12th centuries and imply a greater range of cooking procedures than could be catered for by the large, jar-shaped cooking pot alone; that is, more stages to the cooking of a single meal than would be needed to make a simple stew or pottage where all the ingredients were heated in one pot, and hence probably more dishes served at one meal.

There are relatively few decorated jugs, although by the early 14th century the various ceramic industries of the London area were concentrating largely on the production of plain forms or very simple decoration, probably in order to maximise production totals by speeding up the manufacturing process. By the end of the 14th century, locally made jugs can no longer be seen as objects for display, but rather as utilitarian forms alone, although fine quality vessels from the Saintonge in south-west France may have remained something of an indicator of status (there is one sherd of French Saintonge ware with a mottled green glaze (SAIM) in this period, and further sherds in period M9). One form introduced around the middle of the 14th century is represented by a single sherd from the demolition of the infirmary (B10): it comes from a large rounded or bunghole jug (cistern) in coarse Surrey-Hampshire border ware (CBW). This substantial form, with its heavy strap handle, thumbed base and applied bunghole near the base to take a wooden spigot, was used in brewing ale which could be drawn off through the spigot as required (Pearce and Vince 1988, 55–6).

Further examples in period M9 show that alcoholic beverages were kept in quantity in the abbey. Drinking vessels present in the same area (the area of the second cloister garth OA2 and the demolished former infirmary B10) are related in function, although a variety of other materials would also have been used for this purpose, not all of which have survived (such as wooden drinking bowls). Sherds from two drinking jugs and part of a Siegburg stoneware (SIEG) *Jakobakanne* are the only evidence for this form in pottery in period M8. There is also part of a lobed cup in 'Tudor green' ware (TUDG), a form which was first made in the London area in the early 14th century, in Kingston-type ware (KING) (examples have been found in excavated kiln material from Eden Street, Kingston upon Thames (Surrey): Stephenson and Miller 1996, 72–3). They were produced in TUDG, the distinctive glazed fineware element of the Surrey whiteware industries, from *c* 1380 and throughout the 15th century (Pearce and Vince 1988, 88). It is possible that the larger forms were intended for communal drinking, although smaller vessels were probably for individual use, as here. The quality and extreme fragility of the thin-walled TUDG, which was principally reserved for tablewares, especially drinking vessels, is such that it was unlikely to have been used for everyday dining, but reserved for special occasions.

There is one sherd from a crucible in KING from the area south-west of the conventual buildings Open Area 4, burnt from use. This is, however, the only evidence for industrial activity of any sort at this date.

Period M9, *c* 1430–1538

Reredorter (B9)

A[4154] and A[4156] (B9)

A cess-type fill A[4154] in the north-east interior of the reredorter (B9) produced a large assemblage which was fully quantified (372 sherds/106 ENV/5964g/2.92 EVEs). The high proportion of joining sherds and complete vessel profiles in A[4154] indicates contemporary dumping on a large scale over a relatively short period. Closely dated to *c* 1430–*c* 1500, the group includes a wide range of fabrics and forms made and used during the 14th and 15th centuries; there is no residual pottery which definitely pre-dates *c* 1270, and no obviously intrusive material. Surrey whitewares (KING, CBW, CHEA, TUDG) are the major fabric group (82% SC/76.4% ENV/78.8% Wt/74% EVEs), although Kingston-type ware (KING) unexpectedly outnumbers coarse Surrey-Hampshire border ware (CBW). Since the group clearly dates to the mid to late 15th century, this may lend support to the suggestion (below, 'Period M9 discussion') that use of KING went on for longer in Southwark than in the City and that as a consequence CBW had a smaller share of the market. Cheam whiteware (CHEA) is the third most common fabric after KING and CBW, which is more in keeping with the pattern recorded on City waterfront sites at the end of the 14th century (Pearce and Vince 1988, fig 9g), although by the mid 15th century CBW accounts for more than half the City's pottery while KING is of minimal importance and probably residual (ibid, fig 9h).

The forms which are found in Kingston-type ware (KING) from the cess-type fill are typical of those produced later in the life of the industry and many can be paralleled in the recently excavated early 14th-century kiln waste from Eden Street in Kingston upon Thames (cf Stephenson and Miller 1996, 72, pl 2). They include a tulip-necked baluster jug, small rounded jugs, rilled baluster jugs, bowls (including 21 sherds from a large flared form (Fig 67, <P18>) and part of a cup, probably lobed and bearing ?accidental traces of red slip smeared across the base (Fig 67, <P19>). Forms in coarse Surrey-Hampshire border ware (CBW) are typical of those found in mid 14th-century contexts in the City: large rounded and bunghole jugs or cisterns, including one with red slip-painted decoration, cooking pots and flared bowls. There are no cooking pots with bifid rims, a common type introduced *c* 1380 (Pearce and Vince 1988, 85). There are, however, forms present in Cheam whiteware (CHEA) which were not introduced until the mid 15th century (11 sherds from three barrel-shaped drinking jugs, three sherds from barrel-shaped jugs and part of a rounded jug; ibid, 86, fig 47).

An extremely interesting feature of the pottery from A[4154] is the relatively large number of ceramic urinals which were recovered. A total of 59 sherds from a minimum of four purpose-made urinals accounts for 15.9% of all A[4154] pottery by sherd count (3.8% ENV/8.6% Wt/15.4% EVEs). Two of the urinals are made in coarse Surrey-Hampshire border ware (CBW) and two in Kingston-type ware (KING). There are two principal forms of urinal in medieval pottery: one has a basket handle over the closed, domed top and an opening with a shallow neck set to one side (cf Pearce and Vince 1988, fig 101 no. 390). The other form has a handle set to the side at an angle, with an opening cut in the side (MPRG 1998, 10.28, 1–2). The Bermondsey examples are very fragmentary, so it is difficult to reconstruct the original form with confidence, although one vessel in CBW has part of the cut-out opening surviving (cf Pearce and Vince 1988, fig 119 no. 529) and the other in the same fabric has a reconstructable profile, showing a jug form with vertical handle (Fig 67, <P21>). These forms used for the collection of urine are distinguished from ordinary jugs by the tell-tale presence of thick flaky deposits covering the interior of the vessel, which is usually completely glazed. The overall glazing of vessels is never found on jugs used for the normal purposes of holding beverages. A third urinal, in KING, is also of jug form, glazed inside and out (Fig 67, <P20>). In addition, there are sherds from at least two jugs, unglazed internally, which appear to have been reused as urinals. They display the characteristic flaky deposit which is not associated with normal liquid storage and serving. One is in CBW and one in late medieval Hertfordshire glazed ware (LMHG).

There are two sherds from a jug in Earlswood-type ware (EARL; date range *c* 1200–*c* 1400), made in Surrey. This pottery is rarely found on sites north of the river and generally has a more southerly distribution. The only other glazed jugs recovered in the cess fill come from Mill Green in Essex and include several sherds each from a conical and from a baluster jug. The high quality of Mill Green ware (MG) has already been noted (above) and its presence together with the slightly later 'Tudor Green' (TUDG) drinking vessels show that good, if not exceptional tablewares were available for use in this part of the abbey. Sherds of late London-type ware (LLON) and late London-type slipware (LLSL), both of which were first made c 1400 (Vince 1985, 58), confirm that deposition was taking place in the 15th century. Jugs, a cauldron and a pipkin are the main forms identified. Another contemporary introduction is 'Tudor Green' (TUDG), a very fine, glazed whiteware made from c 1380 in the various Surrey whiteware industries and used almost exclusively for good quality tablewares, mostly drinking vessels (Pearce and Vince 1988, 79–81). Sherds from two cups, probably lobed, and three drinking jugs were found.

Imported pottery is once again of limited importance. Nothing unusual or exotic was found to suggest the use of high quality or status ceramics, although the 'Tudor Green' (TUDG) drinking vessels might have fulfilled this function. All imports recovered at this date are those widely available throughout the London area and these were strictly utilitarian. They include sherds from jugs in Langerwehe stoneware (LANG) and one in Siegburg stoneware (SIEG), both of which were introduced into London from the Rhineland c 1350 (Blackmore 1994, 35–7) and sherds from a cauldron and a frying-pan in Dutch red earthenware (DUTR), first used in London at the same date (ibid, 37).

The bulk of the pottery recovered from the reredorter cess fill was used for serving and as is usual at this date, jugs predominate. There is also a higher proportion of drinking vessels than in earlier contexts, while the quantity of kitchen wares is noticeably low, with no more than 12 sherds from cooking pots. This suggests that most of the pottery discarded in the cesspit was derived from service areas, rather than the kitchens. It also included good quality jugs and drinking vessels, which may not have been for everyday use. The number of urinals is exceptional and clearly relates to the function of the reredorter range.

A mortar dump A[4156] over the cess fill contained a medium-sized group of pottery (47 sherds/26 ENV) dated c 1380–c 1500. There are relatively few joining sherds, although one small rounded jug in Kingston-type ware (KING) could be completely reconstructed (Fig 67, <P22>). The composition of this group is essentially similar to the large context A[4154], with various late forms of jug in KING and London-type ware (LOND), as well as in coarse Surrey-Hampshire border ware (CBW) and Cheam whiteware (CHEA). There are, however, no 15th-century introductions, such as late London-type ware (LLON) or CHEA barrel-shaped jugs. The latest pottery is a sherd from a jug in 'Tudor Green' (TUDG). There is also part of a drinking jug in Langerwehe stoneware (LANG) and of a jug in Saintonge ware (SAIN). The group includes several long-lived fabrics and forms and its deposition could have taken place during the 15th century at any time while these were still in current use.

A[972] and A[2483] (B9)

Context A[972] yielded a very large pottery group (1196 sherds/361 ENV medieval and 110 sherds/58 ENV post-medieval pottery – where 'medieval' means a date range that finishes no later than c 1480 or c 1500, and 'post-medieval' a date range that begins no earlier than c 1480 or c 1500). Context A[2483] was much smaller (10 sherds/7 ENV medieval pottery and 27 sherds/14 ENV post-medieval pottery). The two contexts together yielded 24.55kg/19.34 EVEs medieval and 11.86kg/8.43 EVEs post-medieval pottery and are considered as a whole in group 120. There is a high proportion of large and joining sherds, as well as complete vessel profiles. The material represents dumping on a massive scale in the reredorter (B9). The bulk of the medieval pottery consists of common fabrics and forms in use throughout the late 14th and 15th centuries; the overall composition of the assemblage and the presence of a reasonable quantity of mid to late 15th-century types indicates that the main period of deposition took place right at the end of the medieval period (c 1450–c 1500). The ratio of medieval to post-medieval pottery is overwhelmingly in favour of the former, and the post-medieval material can be dated comfortably to c 1480–c 1550, and includes no pottery necessarily any later than the Dissolution. In other words, the group probably dates to the period at the turn of the 15th and 16th centuries and could have been deposited before the Dissolution. The proportion of 15th-century pottery is very much higher than would be expected for a large early 16th-century assemblage (for example, from Cripplegate Buildings, Wood Street (WFG18) in the City: Pearce 2001; and from Baynard's Castle also in the City: J Pearce, pers observation). Utilitarian forms such as cooking pots and other kitchen wares, as well as serving vessels such as jugs, which were in everyday use, would not normally be expected to endure for several decades. Neither do they have any intrinsic aesthetic value which might ensure an exceptionally long survival. This group of ceramics, however, is one part of a very large quantity of domestic debris recovered from the reredorter, and the dating and interpretation of this group, and of contexts A[972] and A[2483], is discussed in detail in Chapter 3.7 ('Archaeological evidence', 'Reredorter (B9)').

Surrey whitewares are the predominant fabric group (76.3% SC/70.1% ENV/69.9% Wt/70.6% EVEs of all medieval pottery), as expected for 15th-century London-area assemblages. Coarse Surrey-Hampshire border ware (CBW) and Cheam whiteware (CHEA) are the most common fabrics, although there is little difference in frequency between the two. There is also a quantity of 'Tudor Green' (TUDG) (55 sherds from 22 ENV) which was produced at various kilns during the 15th century, as for example at Farnborough Hill (Hampshire) where it was made alongside CHEA at the turn of the 15th/16th century, developing into the slightly more robust early border ware during the early 16th century (Pearce 1997a). Both fabrics are represented in group 120, reinforcing the transitional dating suggested.

Jugs and cooking pots of various types are the main forms found in coarse Surrey-Hampshire border ware (CBW), Cheam whiteware (CHEA) and Kingston-type ware (KING). Large rounded and bunghole jugs predominate in CBW, with heavy thumbed bases and broad strap handles, stabbed and incised. Cooking pots include forms with everted and bifid rims, as well as cauldrons (two complete profiles) and a pipkin. There is also part of a domed lid, a form probably made for use with a cooking pot. Other forms in CBW include bowls, a crucible, a cucurbit from a distillation unit and sherds from a minimum of nine possible urinals. Jugs are again the main form found in CHEA, including numerous mid to late 15th-century barrel-shaped vessels, both jugs and drinking jugs (at least 31 vessels are represented). There are also sherds from numerous biconical jugs, as well as conical and rounded forms (totalling 217 sherds from 55 ENV). A total of 57 sherds (24 ENV) come from drinking jugs, both barrel-shaped and biconical, including one complete biconical vessel (Fig 158, <P38>). There are relatively few cooking pots in CHEA (7 sherds from 4 ENV) but there are parts of at least three lids, the two forms probably being related.

The only other forms in this fabric are a number of measures and small dishes or saucers, one of which is complete (Fig 158, <P39>). A similar bias towards jugs is shown by the KING, which includes several sherds from a pear-shaped form (Fig 158, <P40>), as well as rounded, conical and baluster jugs, few of which are decorated. There are also cooking pots, at least five crucibles, three urinals (eg Fig 158, <P42>) and a condiment dish, which may originally have had a basket handle (Fig 158, <P41>; cf Pearce and Vince 1988, fig 99 no. 372). There are several sherds of 'Tudor Green' (TUDG), the 15th-century fine tableware element of the Surrey whiteware industry (55 sherds/22 ENV). These include lobed and necked cups, globular and rounded drinking jugs, a conical and a rounded jug, one of which has a urine-like internal deposit. Related to these vessels in fabric and form are a number of vessels, mostly drinking jugs, in early Surrey-Hampshire border whiteware (EBORD) (10 sherds/5 ENV).

There is a much lower proportion of 15th-century

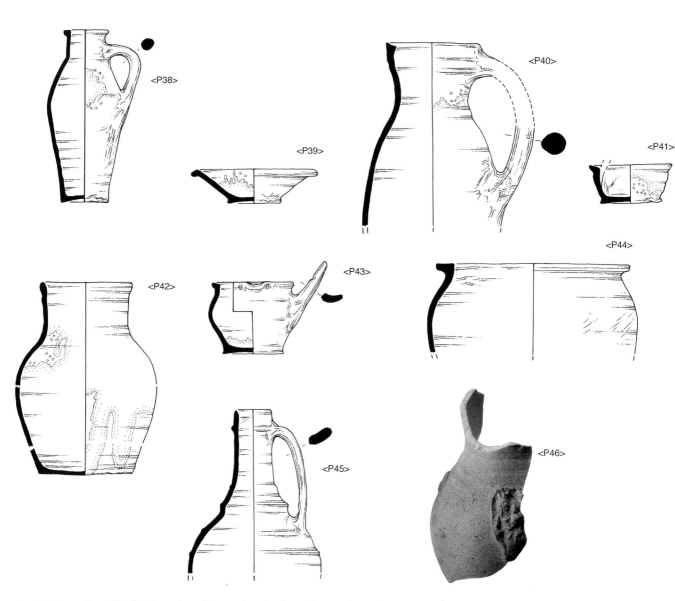

Fig 158 Pottery from A[972] in the reredorter (B9, period M9): Cheam whiteware biconical jug <P38> and saucer <P39>; Kingston-type ware jug <P40>, condiment dish <P41> and urinal <P42>; late London-type ware pipkin <P43>; late London-type slipware cooking pot <P44>; Raeren stoneware jug <P45>; and a fragment of a Siegburg stoneware beaker <P46> (scale 1:4; photo c 1:2)

London-type wares such as late London-type ware (LLON) and late London-type slipware (LLSL) (11.3% SC/9.5% ENV/15.3% Wt/11.4% EVEs). These include rounded, unglazed jugs and a near-complete pipkin in late London-type ware (Fig 158, <P43>; cf Vince 1985, fig 31 nos 1, 5) and similar forms in late London-type slipware, as well as a cooking pot (Fig 158, <P44>) and a rim support or knob from a chafing dish. The London-type wares represent the revival of the local redware industries after an apparent hiatus in production when London-type ware (LOND) came to an end c 1350. Developments in technology and an increased scale of production during the course of the 15th century gave rise to the strong London-area redware industries of the 16th century and later. London-area early post-medieval redware (PMRE) and London-area post-medieval redware (PMR) developed directly from LLON. London-area post-medieval slipped redware (PMSR) was a development from LLSL and London-area post-medieval bichrome redware (PMBR). Together these redwares account for 73% by sherd count of all pottery from the reredorter dated to c 1480–c 1550 (69.4% ENV/74.4% Wt/69.5% EVEs) demonstrating their predominance in London at this date. This includes cauldrons and pipkins in both the bichrome redware and the early post-medieval redware (PMRE); part of a rectangular dripping dish and a colander in PMRE; jugs in PMRE and in slipped redware with a clear (yellow) glaze (PMSRY) and bowls and dishes in PMSRY and in slipped redware with green glaze.

Imports form a very low proportion of pottery recovered from the reredorter (1.4% SC/3% ENV/1.1% Wt/5% EVEs of the medieval pottery, ie up to c 1480). This is quite in keeping with the pattern observed throughout the life of the establishment. The elevation of the house to abbatial status at the end of the 14th century does not appear to coincide with any noticeable increase in the ceramics recovered in the quantities or kinds of pottery normally associated with higher status sites (such as exotic imports). The Continental wares found are those widely available throughout the London area, and come mostly from the Rhineland and the Low Countries. There are sherds from jugs in Langerwehe stoneware (LANG) and drinking jugs in Siegburg stoneware (SIEG), including a tall-necked *Jakobakanne* and a *trichterhalsbecher* with flared neck, as well as a beaker with an applied moulded medallion depicting the Madonna and Child (Fig 158, <P46>). The latter is a most interesting find in view of the religious context. There are also drinking jugs in Raeren stoneware (RAER), dating to c 1480–c 1550, and part of a narrow-necked jug (Fig 158, <P45>; Gaimster 1997, fig 74l, probably from Aachen). Low Countries imports span the 15th and early 16th centuries and include Dutch red earthenware (DUTR) cauldrons and pipkins, frying-pans and a bowl and sherds of Dutch slipped red earthenware (DUTSL) and Dutch slip-decorated red earthenware (DUTSD). French wares are represented by one sherd of Saintonge ware with polychrome decoration (SAIP) and there are two Spanish imports: part of a jar or *albarello* in Paterna blue ware (PATB) and two small sherds of mature Valencian lustreware (VALM) with degraded glaze.

Cemetery (OA6)

A total of 223 sherds from a minimum of 112 vessels was found in the rubbish pit fills. Four contexts produced pottery groups of medium size. One of these, A[3068] was dated to c 1480–c 1550; the other three spanned the period of the late 14th and 15th centuries. There are numerous joining sherds, especially in the larger contexts, suggesting contemporary dumping rather than redeposition, coinciding with the disuse or contraction of the cemetery. The bulk of the pottery dates to the late 14th to 15th centuries, with very little obviously residual material: this is limited mainly to a few sherds of 11th- to 12th-century coarse London-type ware (LCOAR), shelly-sandy ware (SSW) and London-area greyware (LOGR), and some 13th- to early 14th-century Mill Green ware (MG) and Kingston-type wares (KING). The latest pottery recovered from these features dates to the early 16th century and was probably in use up to the time of the Dissolution (from pit fills A[3101] and A[3068]).

Cheam whiteware (CHEA) is the most common fabric present in the cemetery pits (50.2% SC/38.4% ENV). In a series of six intercutting pits south of church (B3), Cheam whiteware (CHEA) is between two and four times as numerous as coarse Surrey-Hampshire border ware (CBW) in all but one case. By comparison, Kingston-type ware (KING) is rare in the cemetery pits (three sherds only), which presents a different pattern from that recorded for other contemporary groups on the site. In period M9, for example, KING is the most common fabric present in the reredorter (B9) and Drain 4 robbing fills in the former courtyard (OA9). Jugs are the main form represented in CHEA, including rounded, barrel-shaped and biconical forms, although body sherds are not always easy to attribute. There are also sherds from cooking pots, bowls, drinking jugs, small dishes or saucers (used to hold sauces and possibly condiments at the table), lids and part of a ?cup, glazed internally, from A[2890]. More unusually, there is the rim sherd from a vessel or jar of cooking pot shape, with red slip-painted decoration, as found in the kiln material from Parkside, Cheam (Marshall 1924, 89–92, figs 12–14; Pearce and Vince 1988, 75). This kind of decoration is usually reserved for jugs, so its occurrence on a different form is of interest.

The imported pottery includes some noteworthy sherds. In addition to Siegburg stoneware (SIEG) and Dutch red earthenware (DUTR) (one and four sherds respectively), there are four sherds from a jar or *albarello* in Andalusian lustreware (ANDA) in A[2890]. Early Andalusian lustreware is found only rarely in late 13th- and 14th-century contexts in the City (Blackmore 1994, 38). Late lustreware from Andalusia is found in late 15th- and early 16th-century assemblages from London and elsewhere (ibid, 39). The glaze on the Bermondsey find is too badly degraded for the decoration to be reconstructed, so it is difficult to date the piece. It is more likely, however, to be of 15th-century date than earlier, given the context. There are also three sherds from a second vessel of Spanish origin, possibly a jar or jug, in A[3068]. The glaze on these too is so badly degraded that confident attribution is difficult. There do appear to be traces of manganese or blue decoration and the piece was found alongside early 16th-century pottery. It could be, therefore, Isabela polychrome ware (ISAB) of the early 16th century (Hurst et al 1986, 54–7) or perhaps, mature Valencian lustreware (VALM), datable to the 15th century (ibid, 42–8). The presence of these two vessels, however, does show that Spanish pottery found its way to the late medieval abbey in very small quantities, probably as souvenirs of pilgrimage or gifts, rather than as regular trade goods.

Early 16th-century pottery is limited to jugs, cauldrons and pipkins in London-area early post-medieval redware (PMRE), part of the base of a birdpot (also PMRE, from A[3101]), Raeren stoneware (RAER) drinking jugs and, also from A[3101], a cauldron and trough or sub-rectangular dish in London-area post-medieval slipped redware with clear (yellow) glaze (PMSRY). The purpose of these troughs remains an enigma. Many have two compartments, the front one being smaller and perforated with holes in the base. They are made in London-area post-medieval slipped redware (PMSR) and in Surrey-Hampshire border ware during the 16th century but in no other industries supplying the London area. Some of the redware examples have *sgraffito* decoration and it is possible that they were used to hold plants or flowers. Whether the sherd in question came from a single- or a double-compartmented vessel is uncertain.

Jugs are the main form present in the cemetery rubbish pits (OA6), especially in the 15th-century contexts (50.3% SC/46.4% ENV of all medieval pottery). Kitchen wares are less frequent, although there are a number of multifunctional vessels, such as bowls and dishes, which could be used in cooking, food preparation and serving. The presence of more unusual forms, such as the trough in London-area post-medieval slipped redware (PMSR) and the birdpot, shows that a range of functions was represented in the material discarded in this area and that the waste came from more than one location on the site. There is one burnt sherd from a crucible in Kingston-type ware, in context A[2937], but no other evidence for industrial activity.

Open ground (OA9, combining former courtyard OA9 and yard OA7), and disuse of drain (D4)

The bulk of the pottery associated with the partial robbing of the second stone drain (D4) dates to the mid 14th to 15th centuries. The fills of the principal robbing cut all date to this period and include one medium-sized context A[597] with 50 sherds (44 ENV), which can be more closely dated to c 1350–c 1400. Jugs are by far the most common form present in a variety of fabrics (67.1% of all pottery in principal robbing fills by SC/65.7% ENV). Jug forms include large rounded or bunghole jugs or cisterns, with heavy, thumbed bases, in coarse Surrey-Hampshire border ware (CBW), introduced c 1350 (Pearce and Vince 1988, 55–6). There is also a wide variety of jug forms in Kingston-type ware (KING): highly decorated polychrome (KING HD) and pellet-decorated (KING PELL) jugs; baluster jugs and small rounded jugs (a late form introduced c 1310; ibid, fig 41). Part of a jug has

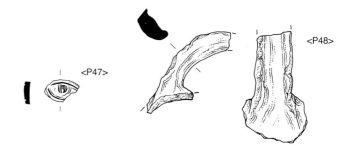

Fig 159 Pottery from the partial robbing of Drain 4 in period M9: Kingston-type ware jug with anthropomorphic decoration <P47> and a coarse London-type ware curfew or fire-cover <P48> (scale 1·4)

anthropomorphic decoration, surviving as a single, applied, oval eye from a face modelled below the pouring lip (Fig 159, <P47>; cf Pearce and Vince 1988, fig 86 no. 236). A number of jug forms are embellished with combed wavy decoration and incised horizontal bands, with stamped boss decoration and with the mid to late 14th-century 'wheatear' pattern (Pearce and Vince 1988, 43, fig 27f). Other forms in Kingston-type ware (KING) are far less common, consisting of one sherd each from a cooking pot and dish. Overall, KING is more numerous in the Drain 4 robbing fills than coarse Surrey-Hampshire border ware (CBW), which numbers only 14 sherds/10 ENV. The date of deposition, therefore, appears to be nearer the middle of the 14th century than the end, when border ware would normally be expected to predominate. This is borne out by the number of late forms present in KING, which finally went out of production (or at least, was no longer exported to London) around 1400, as well as by the absence of Cheam whiteware (CHEA), first used in the capital c 1350 (Pearce and Vince 1988, 17). Apart from KING, the main fabric in the principal robbing fills is London-type ware (LOND), which was going out of production in the mid 14th century (Pearce et al 1985, 135). Late forms again are present, including drinking jugs, tulip-necked or flared baluster jugs with overall white slip and clear or green glaze. Other contemporary fabrics include sherds from two jugs in Mill Green ware (MG) and two in late medieval Hertfordshire glazed ware (LMHG). In A[597], there is also a sherd from one of the very few imports found on the site, part of a jug in green-glazed Saintonge ware (SAIG) from south-west France. A more unusual form is represented by a residual sherd in the same context from a curfew or fire-cover in coarse London-type ware (LCOAR) (Fig 159, <P48>).

Backfill deposits towards the south part of the drain yielded pottery groups of medium size that are closely datable. The latest pottery comes from context A[216] (63 sherds/50 ENV, together with three sherds of post-medieval pottery dating to the 16th/17th and 19th centuries) which is dated to c 1440–c 1500 by the presence of Cheam whiteware (CHEA). This includes part of a barrel-shaped drinking jug, a type not introduced until the mid 15th century (Pearce and Vince 1988, 17–18, fig 47). Overall there is not a high proportion of CHEA in this or any other robbing backfill (a total of nine sherds: 4.2% SC/4.7% ENV of all pottery from D4, OA9). Coarse Surrey-Hampshire border ware (CBW) is more frequent, both in

A[216] and in other contexts (19.4% SC/20.6% ENV of all pottery in OA9) but is outnumbered by Kingston-type ware (KING) (30.7% SC/30.6% ENV). This is noteworthy, since from the mid 14th century CBW was the dominant source of pottery found in the City, almost twice as common as KING which declined noticeably between c 1350 and c 1400 (ibid, 17, fig 9e–g). Forms in CBW and CHEA known from City sites to have been first used in the mid 14th century, are all represented in sufficient quantities not to be considered intrusive. The dominant whiteware, however, is KING, including late forms and styles of decoration such as 'wheatear' stamped bosses and small rounded jugs. There are also 16 sherds (ten ENV) from jugs in late medieval Hertfordshire glazed ware (LMHG) which again was not introduced into London until c 1340 (Jenner and Vince 1983, 152).

The other medium-sized context in subgroup 924 is A[298] (46 sherds/32 ENV), dated to c 1350–c 1400. This again includes a similar balance of fabrics as A[216], with Kingston-type ware (KING) and London-type ware (LOND) predominating. Coarse Surrey-Hampshire border ware (CBW) and late medieval Hertfordshire glazed ware (LMHG) are present in forms datable to the mid 14th century. One sherd from a jug in Saintonge ware with even green glaze (SAIG) (A[298]) brings the total imported pottery in the disuse of Drain 4 (OA9), period M9, to two sherds, both from the same fabric and form, and possibly even the same vessel; a very low figure indeed.

Jugs are the most common form represented in the Drain 4 robbing backfills. Serving vessels account for 63% of all pottery in the backfills by sherd count (58% ENV). This pattern is normal for the 14th and 15th centuries and is repeated on sites throughout the London area. Although a greater variety of ceramic cooking vessels was being made at this date in many of the industries which served London, cooking pots only were found in this area of the site. There were also sherds from eight drinking jugs in London-type ware (LOND) and Cheam whiteware (CHEA) and relatively few bowls and dishes which could be used for both cooking and serving food (no more than 10 sherds/7 ENV). The variety of forms, therefore, is quite limited in view of what was available, although a wide range of common jug forms was found.

Period M9 discussion

Surrey whitewares are by far the most common source of pottery in late 15th-century contexts (that is, up to c 1480, when major changes in the ceramic industries which supplied London were taking place, completely altering the balance of pottery sources). Pottery from the cess-type deposit A[4154] in the reredorter (B9) was quantified and taken as representative of ceramic supply during the later 15th century. The ratio of Kingston-type ware (KING; date range c 1230–c 1400) to coarse Surrey-Hampshire border ware (CBW; date range c 1270–c 1500), however, is not typical of the pattern observed in large assemblages from the City where CBW is almost twice as common as KING by the mid 14th century and continues to dominate the market until the end of the 15th century (Pearce

and Vince 1988, 17, fig 9e–h). At Bermondsey, KING accounts for 26.8% of all pottery by sherd count (24.2% ENV) and CBW for 28.2% SC/24.9% ENV. There are especially large quantities of KING in relation to CBW in the reredorter (B9) and in Drain 4 (OA9). Cheam whiteware (CHEA; date range c 1350–c 1500) occupies third place in terms of frequency, although it would normally be more abundant in relation to CBW by the early 15th century, a time when KING was no longer in contemporary use in the City.

Two main possibilities are suggested by this pattern. One is that the supply of Kingston-type ware (KING) to locations south of the river continued when the supply to the City had dwindled. The City quickly became saturated by whitewares made in the potteries of the Surrey-Hampshire borders. The discovery at Bankside in Southwark of a large dump of whiteware wasters which are indistinguishable in fabric and form from Kingston products (Dennis and Hinton 1983; Pearce and Vince 1988, 7), may suggest that they were made there, although no kilns have yet been located. If the Kingston-type industry did indeed extend as far north as Southwark, then it is not impossible that it should have continued to supply this area after Kingston-type whitewares had ceased to be used in the City. A comparison with the range of ceramics from St Mary Spital for the period 1400–1538 shows that at the medieval hospital site Cheam whiteware (CHEA) did predominate over other ceramic types (Thomas et al 1997, 87).

Conversely, the balance of fabrics in robbing cut fill A[597] in Drain 4 at Bermondsey could suggest the robbing took place around the middle of the 14th century (period M8), before Cheam whiteware (CHEA) had come to full prominence, and not in the late 14th or 15th century. The discarded material, therefore, would have been made and used during the previous half century or more. This possibility may be reinforced by the quantity of London-type ware (LOND; date range c 1080–c 1350) recovered, particularly in this area (for example, 10.2% SC/14.7% ENV of all medieval pottery in period M9; 23.7% SC/23.6% ENV of all pottery in OA9), including late forms, since this industry seems to have ceased production in the mid 14th century (Pearce et al 1985, 135).

However, the likelihood is that London-type ware (LOND) is residual by the late 14th century, and there appears to have been a hiatus of some 50 years during which no local redwares were produced is potentially significant in the Bermondsey context (Pearce et al 1985, 135). Around 1400 a revival of redware production in the London area saw the start of an industry which eventually came to dominate the capital's supply from the end of the 15th century onwards. Late London-type ware (LLON) and late London-type slipware (LLSL) are both found at Bermondsey but not in large quantities. This pattern is typical of early 15th-century assemblages from the City (Vince 1985, 58) and appears to continue into the second half of the century, with local redwares only coming to the fore as production of coarse Surrey-Hampshire border ware (CBW) ceased at the beginning of the 16th century.

The 16th century saw the development of London-area early post-medieval redware (PMRE) and the related London-area post-medieval bichrome redware (PMBR) and London-area post-medieval slipped redware with clear (yellow) glaze (PMSRY): these are the local redwares which formed the mainstay of London's domestic pottery during this period. Further advances in glazing and manufacturing techniques at the turn of the 16th/17th century gave rise to London-area post-medieval redware (PMR), the main coarseware fabric used in the capital during the 17th century and beyond (Orton 1988, 297). During the 16th century, slip-coated and bichrome-glazed redwares (PMSRY and PMBR) were made alongside PMRE at two of the known production centres, at Kingston upon Thames (Nelson 1981) and Woolwich (Pryor and Blockley 1978). The relatively small quantities and types of 16th-century redwares in period M9 are consistent with a pre-Dissolution date.

As in earlier periods, the number of imported vessels remains low. France, Germany and the Low Countries are still the main suppliers: Saintonge ware (SAIN), Saintonge ware with even green glaze (SAIG), Siegburg stoneware (SIEG), Langerwehe stoneware (LANG), Raeren stoneware (RAER), Dutch red earthenware (DUTR) and Dutch slipped red earthenware (DUTSL) were all widely distributed throughout the London area at this date. In all, 24 sherds from a minimum of 13 jugs from the Saintonge were recovered from the main study area and at least seven more examples are recorded from outside this area. Most (ten vessels) are Saintonge ware with even green glaze, which was largely imported *c* 1280–*c* 1350 and is widely regarded as a high quality tableware. Its lustrous glaze, fine fabric and fragile construction make this pottery ideally suited for display and serving at special occasions, rather than for everyday use. Saintonge ware with a mottled green glaze (SAIM) remained in contemporary use for longer, while examples of the highly decorative Saintonge ware with polychrome decoration (SAIP) in late 14th-century (and later) contexts are either residual or, more likely, carefully curated (Blackmore 1994, 35). The Rhenish stonewares and Dutch red earthenware are strictly utilitarian, the former used largely for serving or liquid storage vessels and drinking jugs and the latter for kitchen wares. The exception is the Siegburg stoneware (SIEG) beaker with a medallion depicting the Madonna and Child (Fig 158, <P46>).

There are also four sherds from a jar or *albarello* in Andalusian lustreware (ANDA), and part of a jar or *albarello* possibly in Isabela polychrome (ISAB), both from the material cleared out into pits in the cemetery (OA6), so it is difficult to determine where they were originally used. These would originally have been exotic and decorative items: probably imported as containers, they were also displayable. Part of another jar or *albarello* in Paterna blue ware (PATB) was recovered from the reredorter, together with sherds of mature Valencian lustreware. The quantity of Spanish pottery recovered from the site is extremely small, and probably came into the possession of the abbey as gifts or souvenirs of pilgrimage.

The occurrence in the late abbey of all these relatively exotic imports (the Saintonge ware with polychrome decoration (SAIP) and Saintonge ware with even green glaze (SAIG) jugs and the Spanish vessels), albeit in very small numbers, most of

which were quite likely to have been carefully looked after and kept for some time, suggests a range of contacts with the Continent, some perhaps casual. They also show clearly that pots were used to decorative advantage in a limited sense, including at the table.

The 14th and 15th centuries saw a great increase in the range of forms produced in the various ceramic industries that supplied London, and some of these developments are reflected at Bermondsey in the late medieval abbey. Many of these changes relate to kitchen wares, with new forms of cooking vessels made by several of the major industries. Cauldrons and tripod pipkins were first made in the London area in London-type ware (LOND) in the late 13th century (Pearce et al 1985, 20, fig 8), and were also produced in the contemporaneous Kingston-type industry. The advantage of these forms with their three short feet or longer legs is that they can be used as free-standing cooking vessels, rather than needing to be suspended over the hearth, or placed in a metal trivet (cf Egan 1998a, 153, fig 121). This has the effect of elevating them above the embers without the need for additional equipment, thus avoiding the danger of burning the contents which would always have existed with cooking pots placed directly on the hearth. The idea was probably inspired by metal cooking vessels. There are no examples associated with the abbey of contemporary tripod cooking vessels before period M9, either cauldrons with their two opposed loop handles or tripod pipkins with their single, straight or ladle-type handle which allowed them to be used like a saucepan, and the contents poured out. In period M9, there are sherds from cauldrons in the pottery from the reredorter (B9), in Dutch red earthenware (DUTR) and one in late London-type ware (LLON), as well as examples in London-area early post-medieval redware (PMRE), in which they are far more common. By the 16th century, cauldrons and pipkins had largely replaced the simple jar-shaped cooking pot as the principal means of heating food.

Other specialised forms include three Dutch red earthenware (DUTR) frying-pans and three pipkins in late London-type ware (LLON), late London-type slipware (LLSL) and London-area early post-medieval redware (PMRE), in the cess-type fill in the reredorter (B9), in the pits in the cemetery (OA6) and in Drain 4. The latest reredorter group (contexts A[972], A[2483]) also produced frying-pans and pipkins in DUTR and pipkins in London-type wares (in LLON, eg Fig 158, <P43>; and in LLSL). Pipkins have been found in various fabrics in earlier pottery from the site, right back to the round-bottomed, handled blue-grey ware (BLGR) *kugeltöpfe* in 12th-century contexts (periods M4 and M5). Frying-pans, however, are a new form at Bermondsey. Made in the form of a shallow dish with a single straight handle at the rim, either solid or socketed, these vessels are known in both Kingston-type ware (KING) from the mid 14th century and in coarse Surrey-Hampshire border ware (CBW) (Pearce and Vince 1988, fig 42, fig 97 no. 334, fig 117 nos 492–7). The form is better known in London in Dutch red earthenware from the mid 14th century (Blackmore 1994, 37). Its presence clearly implies the adoption of cooking methods other than stewing or slow-cooking in a large cooking pot. The shallow, open form and provision of a handle suggest frying or rapid heating of foodstuffs, and the form is frequently illustrated in 16th- and 17th-century Dutch genre paintings as a utensil for cooking pancakes, as, for example, in 'De Pannekoeckebackerij' of 1560 by Pieter Aertsen (reproduced in Ruempol and Dongen 1991, 281). Whether this use was made of them in England, or at Bermondsey Abbey in particular in the late Middle Ages, is unclear. It is quite likely that, with developments in cuisine at this date, especially in better-appointed households, several related uses could be made of this form to cook different components of a meal.

A large number of ceramic urinals was recovered from the reredorter (B9) in period M9, from the cess-type fill A[4154] and the overlying dumps, A[972] and A[2483], together with one from the period P1 robbing fill of Drain 4, A[515] (D4/OA12, in KING). These all had the characteristic flaky, off-white deposit on the inside. The dumps produced 66 sherds from at least 13 vessels identified as urinals, including 42 sherds from a single purpose-made urinal in KING (Fig 158, <P42>); of the 66 sherds, 13 sherds/9 ENV in CBW could come from reused jugs. In addition, there are 39 sherds/9 ENV from jugs which all appear to have been reused to collect urine. Most of the purpose-made vessels are in Surrey whiteware fabrics, KING and CBW but not Cheam whiteware (CHEA). The urinals are of jug form, glazed inside and out (which ordinary jugs are not). Most are of rounded form, which is probably the most suitable shape, and fabrics include CHEA, London-type ware (LOND), late London-type ware (LLON), late medieval Hertfordshire glazed ware (LMHG), 'Tudor Green' (TUDG) and one sherd of London-area early post-medieval redware (PMRE). Among the purpose-made forms is part of a basket-handled vessel in Kingston-type ware.

The concentration of ceramic urinals in the reredorter (B9) is highly significant and its significance reinforced by the glass urinal and six glass bottles, which could have been used as urinals, also from the reredorter dumps (below, 7.7, 'Monastic house period', 'Items used in the priory', 'Glass bottles'). These vessels may have been dropped while being emptied, or been discarded in the reredorter having been broken in the east range (B7) or elsewhere. Urine was used in tanning and it may be that these vessels were used for its deliberate collection, rather than solely for night-time relief.

The reredorter dumps also produced the largest group of vessels associated with industrial processes from any period: two crucibles and two cucurbits from distillation units as well as a number of glass distilling vessels (Chapters 4.3, 'Specialist craftspeople and industrial activity in the precinct', 7.7, 'Monastic house period', 'Items used in the priory', 'Glass distilling vessels'; Table 6).

To summarise, the amount and diversity of the post-medieval ceramics from the site reflect the trends observed in similar ceramic groups on both monastic and secular sites nationwide. From the mid 14th to mid 15th centuries, a contraction had taken place in the native ceramic industries that reflected a wider economic and demographic decline (Gaimster and Nenk 1997, 173). The ceramics for this period were

functional, plain and with limited forms and were dominated in London by Surrey whitewares, coarse border wares and wares from the Cheam industry. High quality tablewares, where they existed, consisted of Rhenish stonewares, French earthenwares and Iberian lustrewares (ibid). Imported wares recovered from Bermondsey (priory and abbey) total four sherds for the period 1330–1430 (period M6) and these are from France (Saintonge ware with mottled green glaze, SAIM), Germany (Siegburg stoneware, SIEG) and two sherds from the Low Countries (Dutch red earthenware, DUTR).

After c 1450, a significant expansion in cross-Channel trade meant the arrival of new commodities on a far greater scale. The increased commercial contact had far-reaching consequences in cultural and social spheres, especially since communities of immigrant workers, merchants and tradespeople also came to settle and work in the ports and manufactories of south-east England. Dutch traders from Utrecht, Haarlem and Middelburg, Flemings from Bruges and Germans from Cologne and Aachen settled in the East-Anglian cloth-manufacturing centres of Norwich and Colchester and in the City of London and Southwark (ibid, 172). At the beginning of the 1441 tax year around 1500 alien names were reported in the City. Between 1440 and 1540 the Southwark parish of St Olave supported around 350 *Doche* immigrants alone.

Period P1, 1538–c 1650

Former refectory (B6)

Eleven sherds from a near-complete Spanish starred costrel (STAR) (Fig 160, <P49>) were recovered from a partially excavated backfill in the robber trench of the west wall of the passage of the former refectory. These distinctive vessels are thought to have been made in Seville, and have been found on a number of sites across England in early 17th-century contexts, although it is not known whether they were traded full or empty (Hurst et al 1986, 63). The decoration of this example is unusual, but not unknown in London, consisting of a blue-painted spiral on the shoulder, rather than the typical eight-pointed eponymous star (cf the large and very interesting group, dated c 1640–70, from the cesspit backfill in Building 12, the former ? infirmary range extension/?outbuilding, below).

Former reredorter (B9) and Drain 4

The robbing backfills excavated from the east end of the reredorter and from Drain 4 east of Building 9 produced 545 sherds from a minimum of 348 vessels with a medieval date, and 245 sherds/136 ENV of post-medieval date. Included were three large contexts with more than 100 sherds each: A[515] (D4), A[518] (D4) and A[1764] (B9), and one of medium size A[539] (D4). All pottery from the robbing of Drain 4 was fully quantified (5975g). All the groups have a mixture of late 15th-century and early 16th-century fabrics and forms as did the stratigraphically earlier reredorter groups from A[972] and A[2483]. There are significant differences in composition,

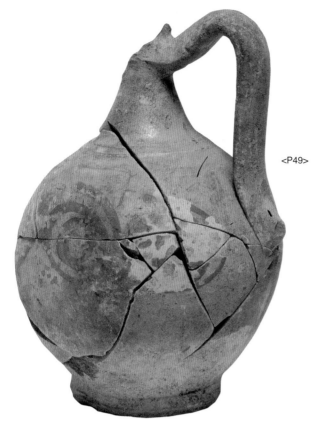

<P49>

Fig 160 Spanish starred costrel <P49> (from B6, period P1) (scale c 1:2)

however. Post-medieval pottery is now dominant. Context A[518], for example, yielded 142 sherds/91 ENV of medieval pottery dated to *c* 1430–*c* 1500, and 169 sherds/88 ENV of post-medieval pottery, dated to *c* 1480–*c* 1550.

Furthermore, there is a far higher proportion of residual 12th- to early 14th-century pottery present in the robbing of both Building 9 and Drain 4. For example, 19.5% SC/19.5% ENV/32.3% Wt/49% EVEs of all medieval pottery in the robbing cut (subgp355) to the drain consists of 12th- to 13th-century shelly-sandy ware (SSW) and south Hertfordshire-type greyware (SHER); while these fabrics constitute an even higher proportion in the Building 9 robber fills: 37.8% SC/22.6% ENV (weight and EVEs not calculated for all pottery in these backfills). There are also a number of sherds of 11th- to 12th-century handmade wares, especially in the Building 9 robbing backfills (11.2% SC/12.9% ENV), including early medieval shell-tempered ware (EMSH), early medieval flint-tempered ware (EMFL), early medieval sand- and shell-tempered ware (EMSS), early medieval sandy ware (EMS), London-area greyware (LOGR) and blue-grey ware (BLGR). Twelfth-century fabrics are also relatively frequent, particularly coarse London-type ware (LCOAR), London-type ware jugs in the early style (LOND EAS) and calcareous London-type ware (LCALC).

The Building 9 robbing backfills, having the highest proportion of 12th- to early 14th-century pottery, with relatively few joining sherds or reconstructable profiles, include a large quantity of redeposited material, although the latest pottery found in the large context A[1764] dates at the earliest to the late 14th century (including as it does coarse Surrey-Hampshire

border ware (CBW), Cheam whiteware (CHEA) and 'Tudor Green' (TUDG). One noteworthy and unusual vessel for Bermondsey Abbey is represented by 18 sherds from a baluster jug in late Rouen ware (ROUL), with applied vertical red strips and a hollow, thrown handle, stabbed at intervals along its length (Fig 161, <P50>). Since medieval imports are so scarce at the abbey, this find, indicating the presence of high quality tablewares, is of some interest, being the only vessel of its kind recovered.

A similar mix of medieval fabrics dating from the 12th to 15th centuries is found in the backfills of Drain 4, which include the two large contexts A[515] and A[518]. In each of these, however, Surrey whitewares are the predominant fabric group (in contrast to the reredorter robbing backfills). Both contexts include a relatively high proportion of Cheam whiteware (CHEA): conical, large rounded and bunghole jugs, bowls, cooking pots (including the late 14th-century lid-seated form with bifid rim) and a domed lid, probably made for this kind of vessel (Fig 161, <P51>). Cheam whiteware also takes the form of barrel-shaped jugs, biconical drinking jugs, small dishes and a measure. As in other large groups from the site, especially those dating to the late 14th and early 15th centuries, Kingston-type ware (KING) outnumbers both coarse Surrey-Hampshire border ware (CBW) and Cheam whiteware (CHEA) in each of the large contexts A[515] and A[518].

In both drain contexts A[515] and A[518], medieval imports are relatively scarce. Apart from residual red-painted ware (REDP) and blue-grey ware (BLGR), however, there is one sherd from a baluster jug in late Rouen ware (ROUL) in A[515], which can be compared with the more numerous (18) fragments found in the robbing backfill A[1764] in the reredorter (B9). Whether or not it originally came from the same vessel is hard to tell, but if so the sherds are significantly dispersed. There are also 11 sherds with polychrome decoration from a jug in Saintonge ware (SAIP) in A[518] – sherds from part of the rim and neck, with a parrot-beak bridge spout. There was a sherd of clear-glazed Saintonge ware with *sgraffito* decoration (SAIC) in the same context, as well as part of a Siegburg stoneware (SIEG) *Jakobakanne* and two jugs in Langerwehe stoneware (LANG). France and the Rhineland are the main sources of all imported pottery used in the abbey at this date, as is the case elsewhere in London. The range of other imports is very narrow on the site before the 16th century.

The early 16th-century pottery is typical of that found elsewhere (eg in the reredorter dumping A[972] and A[2483]) and includes a high proportion of local redwares (54.2% SC/53.3% ENV/72.5% Wt/77% EVEs). Cauldrons and pipkins are the main forms in post-medieval redware, post-medieval bichrome redware (PMBR) and post-medieval slipped redware with clear (yellow) glaze (PMSRY), as well as bowls of various types, including the complete profile of a carinated vessel with pinched thumbing at intervals around the base (Fig 161, <P56>). Jugs are also relatively common, including sherds from two rounded forms and two conical jugs, one in London-area early post-medieval redware (PMRE) and one in London-area post-medieval slipped redware with clear (yellow) glaze (PMSRY) (Fig 161, <P52>; cf Dawson 1979, fig 9 nos 133–4). There are

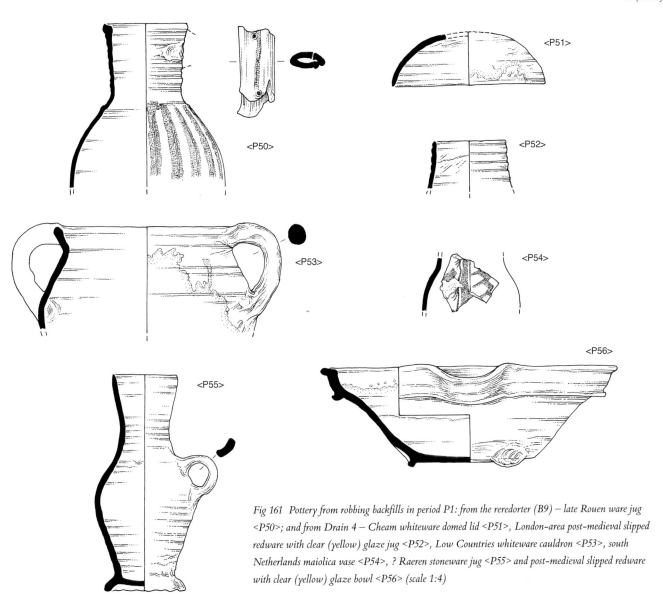

Fig 161 *Pottery from robbing backfills in period P1: from the reredorter (B9) – late Rouen ware jug <P50>; and from Drain 4 – Cheam whiteware domed lid <P51>, London-area post-medieval slipped redware with clear (yellow) glaze jug <P52>, Low Countries whiteware cauldron <P53>, south Netherlands maiolica vase <P54>, ? Raeren stoneware jug <P55> and post-medieval slipped redware with clear (yellow) glaze bowl <P56> (scale 1:4)*

also sherds from sprinkler watering pots, a possible bottle and two bucket-handled pots in A[539] and A[518].

Early Surrey-Hampshire border whiteware (EBORD) drinking jugs and cups are also relatively common (16.6% SC/12.5% ENV) but imports account for a higher proportion of all early 16th-century pottery (33.7% SC/36.4% ENV). This represents a marked change from the balance of sources noted throughout the medieval period when imports were very much in the minority. Rhenish and Low Countries wares predominate and include Dutch red earthenware (DUTR) pipkins and a frying-pan, a bowl in Dutch slipped red earthenware (DUTSL) and a pipkin in Dutch slip-decorated red earthenware (DUTSD), as well as sherds from two cauldrons in Low Countries whiteware (LCWW) (from A[518] and A[515]), a relatively uncommon fabric in London (Fig 161, <P53>). There are also 12 sherds from at least four vessels in south Netherlands maiolica (SNTG) or tin-glazed ware with polychrome decoration in A[518] and A[539], datable to c 1475–c 1550 (Hurst et al 1986, 117). Sherd-links are present between contexts in at least one instance: part of a probable ring-handled vase (Fig 161, <P54>). A much larger jug in

Raeren stoneware (RAER) or Langerwehe stoneware (LANG) (Fig 161, <P55>) would most likely be used for serving wine. Other transitional Rhenish stonewares include RAER drinking jugs. Possible religious connections can be seen in the presence of part of a miniature standing costrel or oil pot in RAER in A[518] (Fig 102, <P24>). There is some evidence that such vessels may have been used as reliquaries (Reed 1992). The only other Continental import in this group is part of a type 1 flask in Martincamp-type ware (MART1) from Normandy (Hurst et al 1986, 102–4, fig 47 nos 142–3).

Backfills in the drain (gp308, D4) west of the reredorter (B9) produced a total of 103 sherds/88 ENV of medieval pottery and 318 sherds/127 ENV of post-medieval pottery, including one large context, A[2349] in subgroup 745, which was fully quantified: 277 sherds/108 ENV/7043g/5.07 EVEs post-medieval pot; 91 sherds/78 ENV/1192g/0.68 EVEs medieval pot. All other contexts in this group are small (fewer than 30 sherds), dating to the 16th century, with minimal quantities of residual 13th- to 15th-century pottery.

Context A[2349] is dated to c 1480–c 1550, with a proportion of 15th-century fabrics and forms which suggests that it was deposited at the same time as the other large groups in this area of the site (namely robbing fills of B9). Surrey whitewares, especially coarse Surrey-Hampshire border ware (CBW) and Cheam whiteware (CHEA) predominate in the 15th-century material (57.3% SC/53.1% ENV/46.6% Wt/63.2% EVEs of all medieval pottery), with London-type ware (LOND) the second most common source, a few sherds of residual 12th-century pottery and no imports. There is about three times as much early 16th-century pottery in numbers of sherds, suggesting that the main period of deposition may have taken place somewhat later than in other parts of the drain, although there are no common types definitely introduced after c 1550 (eg Surrey-Hampshire border ware and Frechen stoneware, FREC). Redwares are by far the most common source (82.4% SC/79.3% ENV/77.4% Wt/57.4% EVEs of all post-medieval pot). There are numerous cauldrons, pipkins, jugs, bowls and dishes of various types in London-area early post-medieval redware (PMRE) and a similar range of forms in slipped redware with a clear (yellow) glaze (PMSRY). In the latter fabric is a large carinated bowl with pinched thumbing around the base (Fig 162, <P57>) and several rounded jugs of similar form (56 sherds from a minimum of nine vessels; Fig 162, <P58>). A near-complete 'goblet' or vase in PMSRY is elaborately decorated with thumbing around the rim and two horizontal zones of regularly spaced, diagonal impressions around the body (Fig 162, <P59>).

There are four sherds of early Surrey-Hampshire border whiteware (EBORD) in subgroup 745, and imports are the second most common source (16.3% SC/18.1% ENV/22.3% Wt/41% EVEs of all post-medieval pottery). This fits in with the pattern recorded in other early 16th-century groups from this area of the site (above). Raeren stoneware (RAER) is the main fabric, including 27 sherds from at least ten drinking jugs and 13 sherds from a minimum of seven jugs, one of which has rouletted decoration. Rather more unusual is a near-complete Spanish mercury jar (MERC), with overall green glaze (Fig 162, <P60>). This small form is very thick-walled and was probably used to transport and store mercury, which was both of great value and of high density (Brown 1995, 321, fig 24.2 no. 16). Mercury is known to have been mined in Spain and the Near East, and fragments of similar ceramic containers have been found in Southampton (Hampshire) in 15th-century deposits, while importation of mercury into Southampton is attested in contemporary port books (ibid).

The breakdown of forms (both medieval and later) shows a marked bias towards serving, with jugs and drinking vessels predominating (43.1% SC/25.4% ENV/44.7% Wt/50.1% EVEs of all post-medieval forms are jugs; 9.1% SC/7.6% ENV/19.4% Wt/15% EVEs are drinking vessels). The remaining pottery was largely used in the kitchen for cooking and food preparation.

Outbuilding (B12)

The backfill of the cesspit in Building 12 (the former ? infirmary range extension/?outbuilding) produced a large and very interesting group (A[3376]: 166 sherds/84 ENV/4852g/5.04

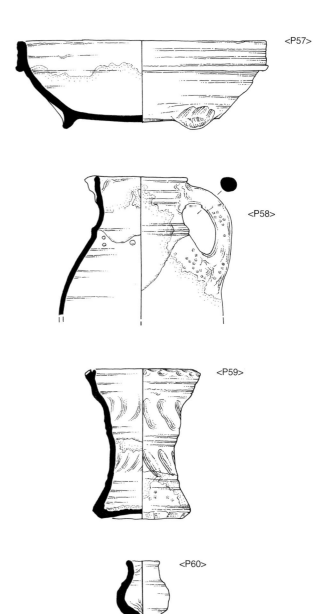

Fig 162 Pottery from backfill context A[2349] (D4, period P1): London-area early post-medieval slipped redware carinated bowl <P57>, jug <P58> and goblet <P59>; Spanish mercury jar <P60> (scale 1:4)

EVEs) which was dated c 1640–70.

Analysis of the pottery shows some significant trends. Surrey-Hampshire border whitewares (BORD) are the most common source, mostly clear- or yellow-glazed forms (BORDY), with a small quantity of green-glazed vessels (BORDG) and two sherds with brown glaze (BORDB), one of them from a rounded mug. The introduction of brown glaze and of the mug form are both dated to the second quarter of the 17th century (Pearce 1992, 96) and are associated particularly with the potteries at Cove, Hampshire (ibid, 27). A wide range of forms is represented in border wares from this group: flanged dishes, wide and deep rounded bowls, a chamber pot, the complete profile of a porringer, a butter pot or jar and 27 sherds from a tripod pipkin with ribbed body and external lid-seating (Fig 163, <P61>; BORDY; ibid, 18–20, cf

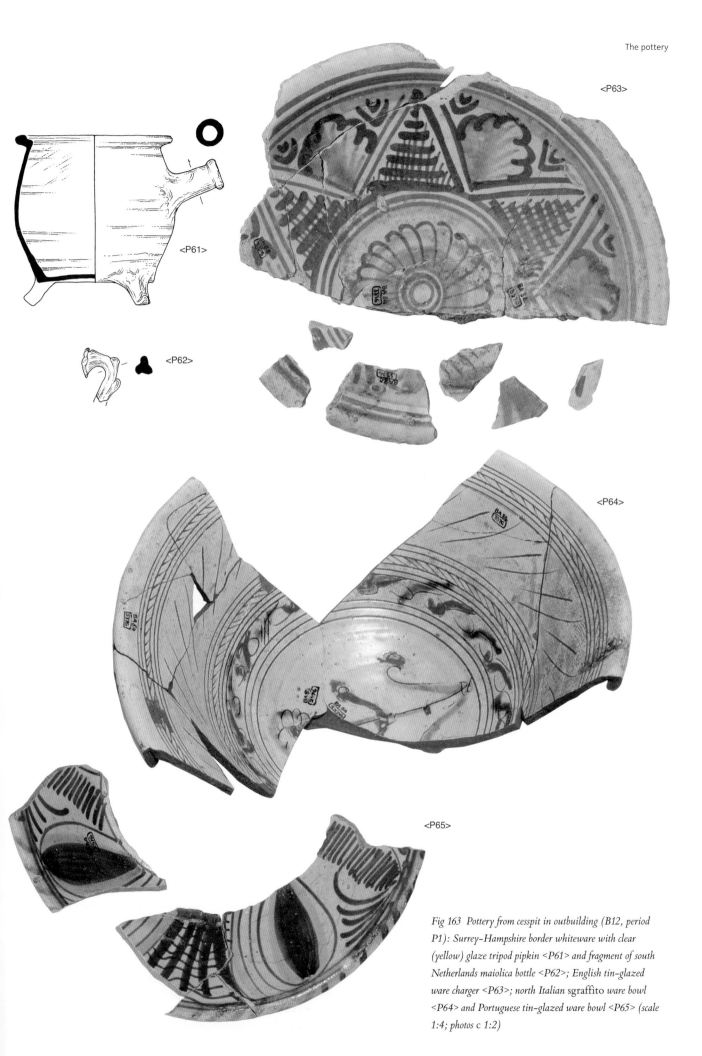

Fig 163 Pottery from cesspit in outbuilding (B12, period P1): Surrey-Hampshire border whiteware with clear (yellow) glaze tripod pipkin <P61> and fragment of south Netherlands maiolica bottle <P62>; English tin-glazed ware charger <P63>; north Italian sgraffito ware bowl <P64> and Portuguese tin-glazed ware bowl <P65> (scale 1:4; photos c 1:2)

fig 28 nos 149–54). There are also sherds from a chamber pot, bowl, flanged dish, porringer and two tripod pipkins in Surrey-Hampshire border redware (RBOR), made at the same kilns as the more common whitewares. This diversity of functions reflects the great versatility of the border ware industry which catered for a far wider range of domestic needs than any other ceramic industry supplying London during the late 16th and 17th centuries. By the mid 17th century border wares were among the most common pottery used in London, as shown by the analysis of large excavated assemblages from the City (ibid, 97), so its predominance in the backfill of the cesspit is unsurprising. What is unexpected, however, is the frequency of tin-glazed ware or delftware, which is the second most common source of pottery in the group (37 sherds from a minimum of 20 vessels).

Normally tin-glazed ware constitutes a much smaller proportion of large domestic assemblages in the mid 17th century (Orton and Pearce 1984, fig 30). It is less common than border wares, local or 'coarse' redwares and fine Essex redwares, so the relative frequency of this decorative fineware, much of which was used for display as a statement of status, is highly suggestive. There are several vessels decorated in Orton's group D (TGW D; Orton 1988, 327), broadly datable to c 1640–70: dishes and a bowl with blue and white decoration, a polychrome cylindrical jar and two blue and white porringers of Orton's type B (TGW B; ibid, 311). In addition, there are sherds from a jar, two chamber pots and a ?bottle with plain white glaze (Orton group C (TGW C); ibid, 321–7); and part of a mug with manganese-speckled glaze (Orton group B; ibid, 321). Rather more magnificent and certainly intended for display are two chargers, one of which (Fig 163, <P63>) has polychrome decoration with oak leaves and a splayed footring, typical of the Wapping factory (Tower Hamlets) (R Stephenson, pers comm); the other has the common pinwheel decoration in the centre of the base. The presence of biscuit-fired tin-glazed ware (BISC) (sherds from a bowl, dish and jar), and part of the base of a saggar used to contain vessels during firing, may be explained by the strength of the delftware industry in Southwark at this date, and the common practice of dumping industrial waste away from the factories, often for use as hardcore (Tyler et al 2008).

There is a wide range of imported pottery from a variety of sources, including Germany, the Low Countries, Italy, Portugal and China. The contrast with the paucity of imports from the medieval abbey is striking. Some are fabrics which were widely available throughout the London area, such as Frechen stoneware (FREC) and Westerwald stoneware (WEST) Bartmänner and jugs from the Rhineland. Others, however, are more unusual and less frequently found. These include part of a jug or bottle in south Netherlands maiolica (SNTG) with a very elaborate, decorative handle, embellished with a series of shallow scrolls along its outer edge (Fig 163, <P62>). In its manufacture, this may have been influenced by late 16th-century Venetian glass. There are also eight sherds from a rounded bowl with a hooked rim in north Italian sgraffito ware

(NISG) or Pisa graffita tarda. The bowl is decorated internally with a central vertical flower stem, inside a series of concentric circles with sgraffito details incised through an overall white slip under a clear glaze, all highlighted in green and orange-brown (Fig 163, <P64>; cf Hurst et al 1986, 30–3, fig 13 see also pl 5). The vessel also has a series of diagonally sloping inverted Vs running around the outside, highlighted alternately in green and orange-brown. The glaze stops short of the base, although the white slip covers the whole vessel, inside and out, including the base. The flowering stem was the most typical design used at Pisa between 1575 and 1625 and large numbers have been found in Plymouth (Devon), dated to c 1550–1650 (ibid, 32). Although not elaborately decorated, this is still an unusual find in London and an object which would have been used for display.

Another decorative and relatively uncommon import is a small flared bowl in Portuguese faience (POTG), with a beaded rim and shallow footring base. It is tin-glazed inside and out and has loosely painted internal decoration in a dark, greyish blue and paler blue, based on a series of vertical lenses and alternating horizontal steps (Fig 163, <P65>). A few random diagonal blue lines have been casually painted on the outside. The painting is very free and bold, and is typical of styles current in the Portuguese repertoire during the first half of the 17th century, prior to the introduction of manganese outlining on blue and white faience in the so-called 'second cycle' of decoration c 1637–51 (cf Pinto de Matos and Monteiro 1994, fig 56). The decoration of Portuguese faience during the late 16th and early to mid 17th centuries was inspired by Chinese blue and white porcelain of the Ming dynasty, in particular the Wanli period (1573–1622), and fuelled by the large-scale importation of this so-called Kraakporselein to Portugal and the Low Countries during the early 17th century. Portugal was pre-eminent in the distribution of Chinese wares in Europe and started production of its own, less expensive version of blue and white porcelain at the end of the 16th century. It is interesting, therefore, to find two sherds of Chinese blue and white export porcelain (CHPO BW) in the same context. One comes from a teabowl, possibly of 18th-century date. The other is part of a dish, made during the last part of the Ming dynasty, which came to an end in 1644, and possibly of the form known as a klapmuts, after the woollen Dutch hat it resembled. It is decorated in panels with ogival moulded contours and alternating narrow, straight panels, which correspond with Rinaldi's group II, dated c 1595–1610 (Rinaldi 1989, 124, pl 132). This is the genuine Kraakporselein and is not at all common in London. At this date it would have been available in limited quantities only to the wealthier members of society. Its presence on the site in a mid 17th-century context, together with a selection of other relatively uncommon imports, and a large quantity of decorative unsourced English tin-glazed ware (TGW) suggests that during the first half of the 17th century at least, the occupants of Bermondsey House were enjoying a high standard of living.

7.6   The window glass

Geoff Egan

Introduction

The glass assemblage from Bermondsey (priory and abbey) is by far the most extensive category among the accessioned finds. Only a small subsample of the total body of material could be looked at in any detail. In addition, the condition of the surviving material was poor and it was clear that a rigorous recycling programme had taken place, even at the time of the Dissolution. This has made it impossible, with the limited resources available in the current project and within the parameters of this volume, to achieve reconstructions of window designs or to recognise series of designs or motifs in the glazing of individual buildings.

A substantial portion of the surviving glass fragments remain unstudied in the research archive; in some cases simple cleaning may in future readily reveal items at least of equal interest to those published here. The majority of the glass was relatively stable. Only a small selection of the painted fragments (*c* 15) were surface cleaned to assess their appropriateness for publication illustration, leaving *c* 500+ pieces of glass unassessed in this way. The very brief catalogue descriptions and comments, therefore, are by no means the final word on what is available for study on Bermondsey's clearly extremely impressive decorative glazing schemes.

In the archive catalogue of selected window glass (<G1>–<G128>), and in the select catalogue of illustrated items published here, the following terms to describe the glass are used:

   colour – by transmitted light as currently apparent (apart from opaque green etc which is specified);
   colourless – without qualification, is translucent where well preserved but even the undecayed pieces are stained yellowish and have patches of deeper brown dirt;
   painted – with pigment that is now reddish brown (unless otherwise indicated), this is iron-oxide based;
   silver stain – a late medieval development, gives a translucent yellow wash;
   edge fragment – retaining original, rounded edge (bevel) as produced in the manufacture of crown-spun glass;
   original outline shapes were produced by grozing unless otherwise indicated.

A single <G> number frequently includes more than one fragment, possibly tens or even hundreds of fragments; only the illustrated pieces are individually catalogued below.

The context and character of the catalogued window glass

Only a small proportion of the catalogued glass comes from pre-Dissolution contexts, and even less from contexts earlier than the mid 15th century; this probably does reflect biases in survival and recovery.

A few fragments of window glass were catalogued from period M2, Open Area 1 contexts, including <G126> (A<1655>, A[4229]), decayed (original shape and colour uncertain). Apparently from before the accepted date for the foundation of the religious house (and before the construction of the chapel (B1) in the second half of the 11th century, Chapter 3.1), this would imply the existence of an unrecorded, earlier, high-status building in the area if the stratigraphic dating is correct. Two fragments catalogued from period M2, Open Area 1, <G4> (A<1319>, A[1063]; decayed) and <G6> (A<1532>, A[2356]; superficially decayed but originally colourless) were from contexts where 12th-century pottery suggests there is at least some intrusive material.

A few decayed fragments were recorded from the earliest monastic periods: from contexts dated to the second half of the 11th century (period M3: <G1>, <G2> x 3 fragments, OA3) and to the first half of the 12th century (period M4: <G7> x 2 fragments, B7; <G94> green, OA6). Demolition deposits *c* 1330–*c* 1450 (period M8) from the former infirmary building (B10) included a decayed fragment with a painted design <G22> and a blue fragment <G23>.

Slightly more, and better preserved, fragments were catalogued from the final period of monastic occupation, *c* 1430–1538 (period M9), from pit fills in the external cemetery (OA6): decayed fragments with painted designs (<G10>, <G12>, <G20>, <G24>, <G34>), green fragments with and without painted designs (<G19>, <G25>, <G33>), and blue fragments (<G13>) including a sub-rectangular quarry (<G11>). Fragment <G24> (Fig 164) has a feather- or grass-like design. Other motifs include foliate designs, beading and parallel lines. Lead window came, some articulated (<S52>, Fig 170) was also recovered from this area (OA6, period M9).

The bulk of the catalogued items come from Dissolution and immediately post-Dissolution clearance and demolition contexts (Chapter 5.2); some contexts also included lead window came. The dumping inside the reredorter (B9, period M9) produced a major finds assemblage which included a small number of window glass fragments (<G26>–<G31> from A[972], and <G93> from A[2483]) – blue and pale green glass with painted designs including lines, cross-hatching and a border pattern with pellets – and four possibly unused window leads (<S51>, Fig 170). Further fragments of blue (G89>, <G90>, Fig 164, <G92>) and pale green (<G91>) glass were recorded from the backfill (A[2349] OA12, period P1; Chapter 5.2, 'Monastic buildings completely or largely demolished', 'Reredorter (B9) and Drain 4, and creation of Open Area 12') of the drain (D4) in the area west of the former reredorter (B9), and other decayed fragments from this general area (<G5>, <G35>). A few pale green and decayed fragments (some painted) also survived in the area of the former courtyard (OA2) (<G3>, <G8>, <G14>, <G36>–<G39>, OA11, period P1).

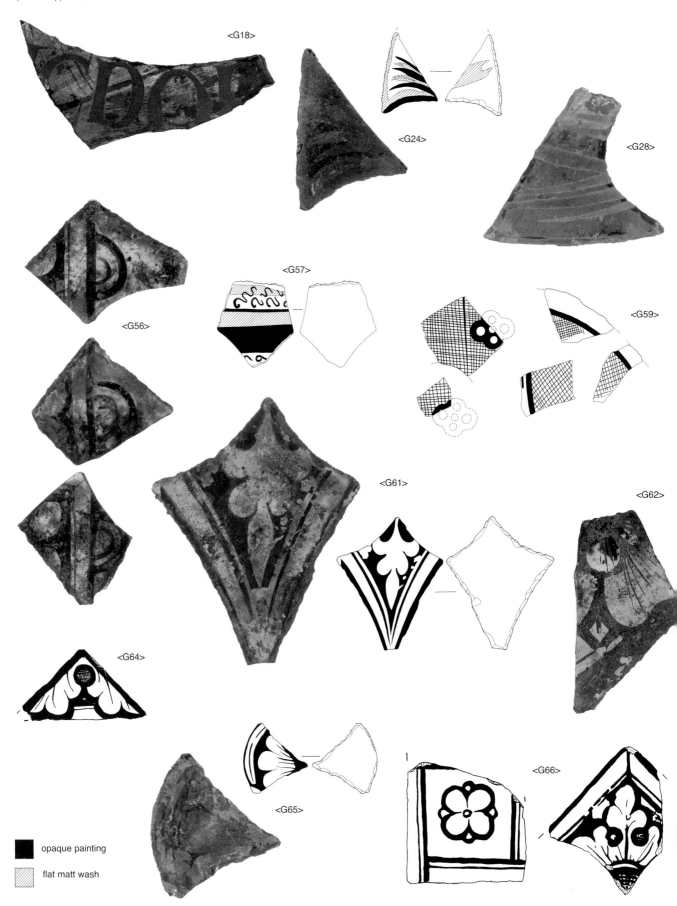

opaque painting

flat matt wash

Fig 164 (also facing and overleaf) Medieval window glass: <G24> from Open Area 6, period M9; <G28> from Building 9, period M9; <G18>, <G56>, <G57>, <G59>, <G61>, <G62>, <G64>, <G65>, <G66>, <G69>, <G71>–<G74>, <G81>, <G86>, <G118>, <G119>, <G121>, <G127> from Open Area 9, period P1; <G90> from Open Area 12, period P1; and <G122> unstratified, <G128> unphased (scale 1:2; photos c 1:1; except <G121> 1:2, reconstruction not to scale and <G127> 1:2)

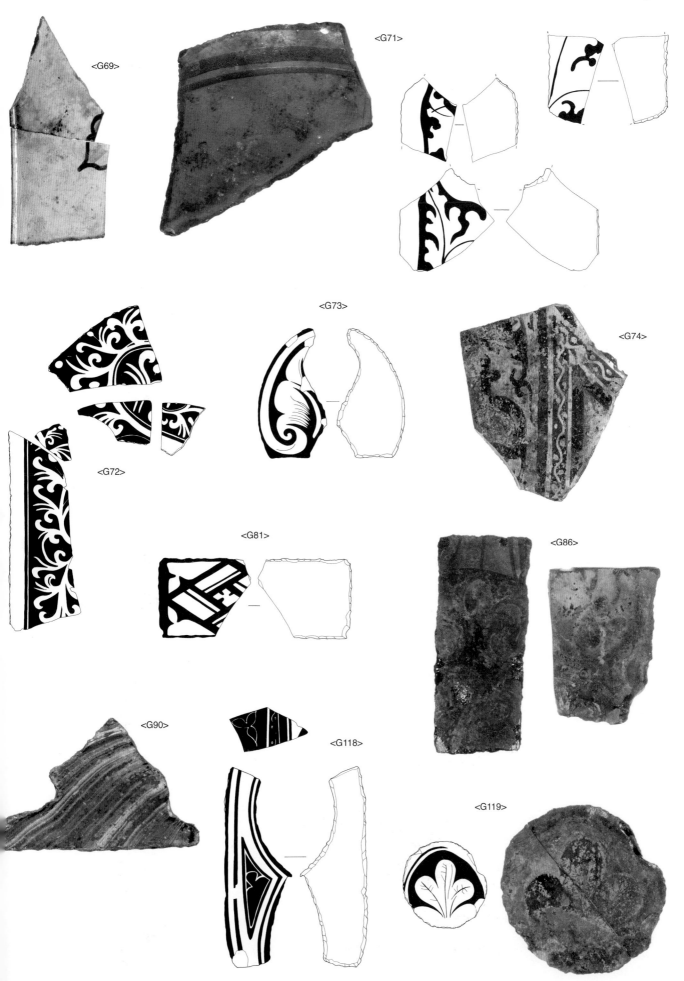

<G69>

<G71>

<G72>

<G73>

<G74>

<G81>

<G86>

<G90>

<G118>

<G119>

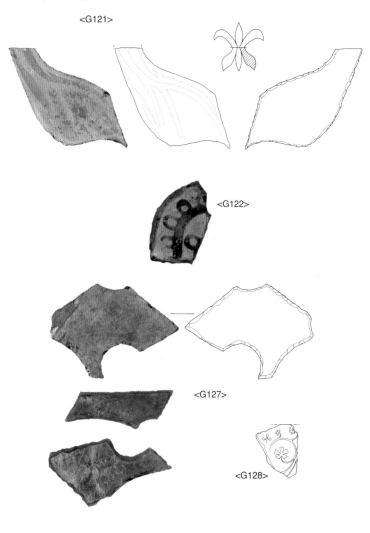

<G121>

<G122>

<G127>

<G128>

Fig 164 (cont)

Most of the catalogued material, however, comes from various pit fills in the former monastic cemetery area (OA6) north of the former chapel (B1), to the west of the former chapter house (B4) and to the north of the former monastic church (B3). This area (OA9, period P1) produced a much more diverse assemblage than the small groups from the other areas discussed above, with a much wider range of colours and included a substantial number of unused pieces and offcuts.

A large pit near the north chapel wall produced the largest number of recorded fragments from the excavation: <G41> from fill A[2938] and <G43>–<G87> from A[2883] (OA9, period P1), together with window came <S53> and pottery dated *c* 1480–*c* 1550 (Chapter 5.2, 'Elements of the former monastery partly or wholly retained and adapted', 'Gardens (OA9–OA11)'). One semicircular section of leading with its decorated glass survived intact (<S53>, Fig 170). Painted motifs survive on many pieces, but most are not interpretable in their present condition. This group includes fragments of flashed ruby <G45>, <G47>, <G50>, <G55>, <G85>, amethyst <G46> <G54>, <G83>, amber <G52>, <G86> (Fig 164), blue <G53>, <G71> (Fig 164), <G72> and <G73> (Fig 164), green <G84>, yellowish-brown <G65> (Fig 164), yellow <G80>, <G81> (Fig

164) and flesh-coloured <G82> glass, together with many colourless, pale green and decayed fragments. Quarry shapes include lozenges, triangles, rectangles and a tear-shaped quarry <G73> (Fig 164). Some designs employ silver stain <G57> (Fig 164), <G60>, <G62> (Fig 164), <G69> (Fig 164), <G76>, <G77> and back painting <G70>, <G87>. The back painting on one piece was scientifically analysed (below, 'Scientific analysis of selected pieces'). In addition, interestingly, there are a number of pieces which retain their original bevelled edges and show no sign of having been set in lead <G43>–<G48>; these include pieces of amethyst, flashed ruby and pale green glass, apparently offcuts, some of which are very narrow, being little more than the bevel itself, while others are up to *c* 45mm broad. Example <G44> (Fig 165) shows four somewhat distorted offcuts. Two of these fragments (<G47> and <G48>) display faulty glass-workmanship.

A second large group <G106>–<G120> and <G125> from pit fill A[3303] is very similar in character; it includes offcuts of pale green and flashed ruby glass with the original bevel <G107>–<G109>, a variety of quarry shapes including roundels <G111>, and a range of colours – amethyst, flashed ruby, amber, blue, green – and pale green/colourless glass, as well as hundreds of fragments of decayed and/or uncleaned fragments. A few pieces had readily identifiable motifs, for example <G118>, <G119> (Fig 164), and <G125> with rosettes. The silver colour on the back of one example <G117> was analysed (below, 'Scientific analysis of selected pieces'). Hundreds of fragments <G124>, with a small range of colours (mainly colourless, with green, amethyst and superficially decayed blue) and painted motifs also survived from the uppermost fill of A[3007].

The range of material in these very large groups is typical of that of the other smaller groups and occasional fragments derived from pit fills in this area (OA9, period P1; Chapter 5.2, 'Elements of the former monastery partly or wholly retained and adapted', 'Chapel (B1)'): <G15>–<G18> from A[2706] which include a fragment of inscription (<G18>, Fig 164); <G95>–<G104>, <G127> from A[2976] which include offcuts retaining their original rounded edges (<G96>, <G97>, Fig 113); <G32> from A[3059]; <G40> A[2797]; <G105> A[3301]; <G121> (Fig 164) A[3498]; <G123> A[2987]).

One fragment (<G128>, Fig 164) was most unusually identified as gilded glass: it is clearly decorated with painted gilt scrolling and was scientifically analysed (below, 'Scientific analysis of selected pieces'); it may have come from a panel (Chapter 4.2, 'Interior decoration of the monastic buildings: glazing and tiling').

Fig 164 illustrates a selection of the more complete pieces and clearest designs. These, and what they and the rest of the assemblage, can tell us about the glazing of the monastic buildings and the stripping of the lead and glass at the Dissolution are discussed further in Chapter 4.2 ('Interior decoration of the monastic buildings: glazing and tiling').

Catalogue of the illustrated window glass

<G1>–<G17> not illustrated (see archive catalogue)

<G18> (Fig 164)
A<2208>, A[2706]; period P1, OA9
Durable-blue fragment painted with … (I)CDO(B,P or R)… in neat, Lombardic lettering.

<G19>–<G23> not illustrated (see archive catalogue)

<G24> (Fig 164)
A<1639>, A[2863]; period M9, OA6
Decayed fragment grozed on two sides; painted (?grass) in two colours.

<G25>–<G27> not illustrated (see archive catalogue)

<G28> (Fig 164)
A<1633>, A[972]; period M9, B9
Durable-blue, sub-triangular fragment with arc cut-out 51 x 41mm, with painted lines.

<G29>–<G43> not illustrated (see archive catalogue)

<G44> (Fig 165)
A<3648>, A[2883]; period P1, OA9
Four somewhat distorted pale green pieces, retaining original rounded edges; these are apparently offcuts never set in lead. Cf <G96>, <G97> (Fig 113).

<G45>–<G55> not illustrated (see archive catalogue)

<G56> (Fig 164)
A<3601>, A[2883]; period P1, OA9
Three fragments of ?lozenge-shaped quarries from a border, each with concentric double arcs and lobed/?foliate motifs to either side of a running ?linear frame.

<G57> (Fig 164)
A<3581>, A[2883]; period P1, OA9
Fragment painted with multiple-band motif with two areas of sinuous lines; silver stain.

<G58> not illustrated (see archive catalogue)

<G59> (Fig 164)
A<3660>, A[2883]; period P1,OA9
Five fragments with motifs on fields of cross-hatching.

<G60> not illustrated (see archive catalogue)

<G61> (Fig 164)
A<3583>, A[2883]; period P1, OA9
Concave quadrilateral quarry, with cinquefoil reserved against solid field and flanked by two-line border.

<G62> (Fig 164)
A<3566>, A[2883]; period P1, OA9
?Double rose, with silver stain.

<G63> not illustrated (see archive catalogue)

<G64> (Fig 164)
A<3605>, A[2883]; period P1, OA9
Colourless, triangular quarry, 68 x 38mm, with foliate motif flanking cross-hatched roundel.

<G65> (Fig 164)
A<3651>, A[2883]; period P1, OA9
'Axe-blade'-shaped, yellowish-brown quarry, 36 x 36mm, with bell-like floral motif.

<G66> (Fig 164)
A<3585>, A[2883]; period P1, OA9
Two more-complex foliate motifs (both illustrated); one a ?diamond-shaped quarry, one ?rectangular.

<G67>, <G68> not illustrated (see archive catalogue)

<G69> (Fig 164)
A<3656>, A[2883]; period P1, OA9
Fragment with part of a painted floral motif and silver stain, which retains the original crown-spun edge. There is no sign of it having been mounted so this piece may have been discarded because of breakage at an early stage after painting; it is nevertheless notable in both retaining the edge and being painted.

<G70> not illustrated (see archive catalogue and below, 'Scientific analysis of selected pieces')

<G71> (Fig 164)
A<3659>, A[2883]; period P1, OA9
Four pieces painted on blue: motifs comprise foliation ('seaweed') and parallel lines.

<G72> (Fig 164)
A<3589>, A[2883]; period P1, OA9
Five blue fragments very well painted with trailing foliate motifs in reserve.

<G73> (Fig 164)
A<3593>, A[2883]; period P1, OA9
Tear-shaped blue piece painted in reserve with an accomplished trefoil tendril with three-dimensionality emphasised by wiped/scraped lines.

<G74> (Fig 164)
A<3608>, A[2883]; period P1, OA9
Colourless fragment painted with crocketed ?canopy, detailing in silver stain.

<G75>–<G80> not illustrated (see archive catalogue)

<G81> (Fig 164)
A<3592>, A[2883]; period P1, OA9
Incomplete, yellow ?rectangular piece, c 50 x 42mm, painted with fret-like motif around ? angular quatrefoil in reserve and flanked by reserved (architectural) daggers.

<G82>–<G85> not illustrated (see archive catalogue)

<G86> (Fig 164)
A<3636>, A[2883]; period P1, OA9
Two amber pieces painted with foliate motifs; one a complete rectangular quarry 25 x 59mm, with the motif in reserve.

<G87>–<G89> not illustrated (see archive catalogue)

<G90> (Fig 164)
A<1530>, A[2349]; period P1, OA12
Durable-blue triangle 56 x 34mm with arc cut-outs.

<G91>–<G95> not illustrated (see archive catalogue)

<G96> (Fig 113)
A<3617>, A[2976]; period P1, OA9
Pieces retaining original bevelled edges (c 30 in total, 12 illustrated), colourless/pale green, up to c 80 x 65mm.

<G97> (Fig 113)
A<3615>, A[2976]; period P1, OA9
Sub-triangular fragment, 33 x 21mm, partly grozed along the original bevelled edge. ?Discarded because of breakage.

<G98>–<G117> not illustrated (see archive catalogue; <G117> scientifically analysed, see below, 'Scientific analysis of selected pieces')

<G118> (Fig 164)
A<3595>, A[3303]; period P1, OA9
?Border pane with one long edge biconcave, 105 x 37mm, painted with outlines around triangular field with asymmetrical dagger

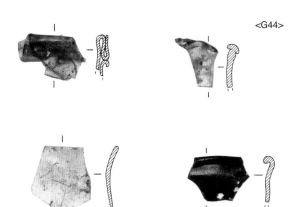

<G44>

Fig 165 Fragments of pale green window glass <G44> retaining original rounded edges and distorted, from A[2883] (OA9, period P1) (scale c 1:2)

(architectural) motif; also a second, similar fragment.

<G119> (Fig 164)
A<3620>, A[3303]; period P1, OA9
Durable-blue roundel, Diam 46mm, painted with trefoil in reserve.

<G120> not illustrated (see archive catalogue)

<G121> (Fig 164)
A<1577>, A[3498]; period P1, OA9
Incomplete, pale blue quarry, surviving 82 x 41mm, neatly grozed to shape of ? fleur-de-lis or fleuron petal, broken off at base.

<G122> (Fig 164)
A<1336>, A[1]; -, - (1984 site clearance)

Fragment of blue ?half roundel, surviving 23 x 16mm, painted with series of loops in a border defined by lines and with a further loop etc in the centre.

<G123>–<G126> not illustrated (see archive catalogue)

<G127> (Fig 164)
A<3007>, A[2976]; period P1, OA9
Three plain blue, complete or near-complete quarries with arc cut-outs; 70 x 50mm, 58 x 20mm, 68 x 36mm.

<G128> (Fig 164)
A<1637>, A[2923]; -, -
Fragment of gilded glass painted with a floral scroll (below, 'Scientific analysis of selected pieces').

Scientific analysis of selected pieces

Elizabeth Barham

X-ray fluorescence (XRF) analysis was carried out on the surface 'gilded' area and on the 'ungilded' side of one fragment of gilded glass painted with an accomplished floral scroll (A[2923] unphased; <G128>, Fig 164). Only the presence of gold distinguishes the spectra of the gilded from the ungilded area. Other elements detected are consistent with the colourant ions, residues of lead cames and constituent modifiers of medieval window glass. Lighter elements such as potassium and sodium were not sought during the analysis. An organic, protein-binding medium may have been used to affix the gold to the glass but this could not be confirmed because of the deteriorated nature of the gilding. XRF analysis suggested the presence of small quantities of mercury which may indicate the gold was applied as an amalgam.

An example of apparent back painting was also studied. One piece of glass <G70> (A<3631>, A[2883], OA9, period P1) which was apparently painted on both sides (the stripes of paint on the outer surface mirroring those on the inner surface) was examined and analysed by XRF. The results suggested the presence of back-matched corrosion. Medieval stained glass artists sometimes applied smeared or stippled paint to the outer side of a glass piece to supplement and match the paintwork on the inside. Since this paint was porous and could retain water, it encouraged corrosion to take place whilst *in situ*, with the resulting 'back-matched' effect (Newton 1976).

A piece <G117> (A<3594>, A[3303], OA9, period P1) with outline foliate motif in the usual red paint on one face, the design echoed in a silver colour on the other, was analysed. The silver colouration was examined by XRF analysis to attempt to determine whether paint had been applied there. The resulting spectrum does not give any reading for silver or higher readings

for iron than those obtained from visually plain areas of the glass, but there are significantly larger readings for calcium in the 'silvery' parts. This would be consistent with gypsum and syngenite (calcium-sulphate based) corrosion products occasionally found on medieval window glass. These results are consistent with the phenomenon known as back-matched corrosion (Newton 1976).

7.7   The accessioned finds

Geoff Egan

The finds from the site of the Cluniac monastery of St Saviour Bermondsey are not only the fullest from any of London's religious houses, they also include significant Saxon material that seems to require a reassessment to be undertaken of evidence for the area at that period.

The finds listed below are grouped into three basic series, based largely on their suggested date of origin as interpreted from current artefact research: pre-religious house (Saxo-Norman), the period of the religious house (c 1080–1538) and post-Dissolution to c 1650.

There are dispersed hints, by no means all from primary contexts, of a significant and prosperous Mid and Late Saxon settlement (discussed in Chapter 2.4, 2.5). From the archaeological evidence currently available, during the earlier part of this period Bermondsey was second only in the central London area to Lundenwic, albeit a very much smaller second.

The medieval assemblage is exceptional (discussed in Chapter 4.3, 'Material culture and the religious life' and 'Specialist craftspeople and industrial activity in the precinct'). It is perhaps possible, quite apart from the individual objects which are the high points of this present catalogue, to see in the diversity and size of the medieval assemblage as a whole (particularly when set alongside the often paltry finds groups from some of the other London religious houses) hints of the richness of the foundation at Bermondsey. Many of these finds come from the reredorter dump (A[972] B9, period M9) whose context and dating are discussed in detail in Chapter 3.7 ('Archaeological evidence').

The post-Dissolution assemblages (of which only those from the first century of that era feature in this publication) partly reflect the new residential and industrial usage of the former precinct and they largely correspond with the range of finds from other inland sites on the south side of the River Thames.

All items considered to belong to the Saxo-Norman period have been listed below (a total of 24), with a view to presenting the evidence for this difficult epoch as fully as possible. A total of c 300 items were catalogued for the main medieval period, from which a third or so have been selected for this volume. These were chosen on the basis of their intrinsic interest, or because they have something particular to impart about life in the religious house. The full catalogue can be consulted as part of the research archive. A more rigorous selection has been made from the catalogue entries for the Dissolution and later period(s).

Pre-monastic house period

Objects from periods M1 and M2, and objects of pre-monastic date residual in later contexts.

DRESS ACCESSORIES

Four strapends where the decoration is reasonably distinct all belong to recognised later Anglo-Saxon types. Gabor Thomas comments as follows:

Examples <S5> and <S7> are versions of the commonest variety of later Anglo-Saxon strapend with a tapering profile, split attachment end and zoomorphic terminal in the form of an *en face* animal mask (Thomas 2003, class A). Both carry decoration on their main panel, that appearing on <S7> taking the form of a crouching Trewhiddle-style beast with its head facing the attachment end which is adorned in the standard way with a palmette motif. The decoration on <S5>, obscured by corrosion, is also likely to have been Trewhiddle-style in inspiration. Both are broadly datable to the 9th century AD. Strapends <S2> and <S6> are representative of another very widespread Late Saxon form distinguished by a wedge-shaped split-end and parallel-sided shaft terminating in a stylised animal head (ibid, class B). Typical for the class, the decoration is very restrained, in both cases being confined to incised borders at the split-end and at the waist. This class was current for a longer duration than its more highly decorated counterpart, extending from the 9th through until the 11th centuries.

<S1> Stone finger ring (Fig 13)
A<454>, A[2969]; period M2, OA1
An incomplete shale ring; plain, with sub-triangular-section hoop, Diam 20mm.
Cf Pritchard 1991, 154 and 156, fig 3.38, in association with waste from a manufacturing assemblage found in the City, provisionally dated to the late 11th/early 12th century and using stone either from Kimmeridge in Dorset or Whitby in Yorkshire North Riding.

<S2> Copper-alloy strapend (Fig 9)
A<391>, A[3211]; period M2, OA1
Bent and not quite complete; bifurcate, bilobed inside edge tapers to solid, animal-head terminal of perfunctory style (the ears are voided); 41 x 10mm; two rivets; sub-rectangular iron fragment adhering on underside near end.
9th–11th century AD.

<S3> Copper-alloy strapend
A<604>, A[3211]; period M2, OA1
Slightly corroded; sheet plate with round end, 22 x 8mm.

<S4> Copper-alloy strapend
A<536>, A[1124]; period M4, B7
Main, bifurcated-triangular part continues as solid strip; 42 x 11mm; engraved outline at inside end, transverse line defining vestigial modelling (? cf animal head) at terminal; two rivets survive.
?Late Saxon or very early Norman.

<S5> Copper-alloy strapend (Fig 9)
A<917>, A[1060]; period M5, B8
Incomplete and corroded; tapering, *c* 35 x 9mm; ?single forked casting, most of interlace on main panel is obscured by corrosion; part of animal-headed terminal (with round ears) survives; two prominent rivets survive.
c 9th century AD.

<S6> Copper-alloy strapend (Fig 9)
A<434>, A[3513]; period M7, OA6
Worn, tapering, forked casting; L 43mm, W 11mm at triangular attachment tab, which has the engraved outline of a debased animal head at the terminal. The two rivets survive.
9th–11th century AD.

<S7> Copper-alloy strapend (Fig 9)
A<701>, A[2464]; period M8, B12
Not quite complete, elongated sub-oval, slightly bilobed on inside edge; 49 x 11mm. Sub-circular motif with central crouching, large-eared animal in curvilinear style with sub-spiral fillers in field, all with traces of ?niello; animal-headed terminal (with round ears). One of original two rivets survives; a fragment is broken off where the second one was inserted.
An accomplished accessory.
c 9th century AD.

<S8> Copper-alloy brooch (Fig 13)
A<556>, A[1586]; period M2, OA1
Circular, Diam 43mm; triangular section; uneven inner edge; constriction and notch for missing pin; worn.
This is a large brooch for this relatively early date.

COMBS

<S9> Antler comb (Fig 9)
A<949>, A[739]; period M4, B8
Fragment of end plate; W 35mm, surviving L 25mm. A few graded teeth on both surviving sides; broken off at central hole for strip.

<S10> Antler comb (Fig 9)
A<952>, A[937]; period M7, OA7
Fragment of side strip; surviving L 33mm, W 10mm; incised quadruple chevrons and transverse bands; tooth-cutting marks along both sides (11//8 per 10mm); three holes for rivets.

<S11> Antler comb (Fig 9)
A<950>, A[775]; period M8, OA2
Fragment of plate; W 41mm, surviving L 14mm; six teeth per 10mm on both sides, broken off at central hole for strip.

VESSELS AND FOOD PREPARATION/CONSUMPTION EQUIPMENT

<S12> Glass vessel (Fig 166)
A<1306>, A[974]; period M7, B11
Pale green with frequent tiny bubbles, fragment of flaring rim, Diam *c* 120mm. Multiple concentric, pale, opaque yellow trails marvered in; folded edge.
This undecayed piece from a prestigious drinking vessel, probably a beaker, is an unusual find in the heart of London of one of the early varieties of medieval glass (identified by John Shepherd). Yellow trailing in a spiral on green seems to be well known on vessels from the period of the 8th to 11th centuries AD in England (see Harden 1956, 152–3; 1978, 10–11) but publication at the level of detail that might define very close parallels for the present fragment is so far lacking.

<S13> Iron ?knife
A<157>, A[2969]; period M2, OA1
Very corroded blade; surviving L 98mm.

<S14> Lead plug
A<310>, A[4229]; period M2, OA1
Relatively compact repair, 32 x 25mm, fairly flat externally with a tiny fragment of reduced ware vessel still adhering; total Wt 51g.
A repair plug for holed ceramic vessel.

<S12>

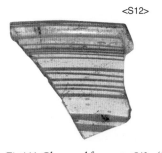

Fig 166 Glass vessel fragment <S12> (from B11, period M7) (scale c 2:1)

LOOM WEIGHTS AND OTHER PRODUCTION ITEMS

<S15> Loom weight
A<1258>, A[3941]; period M2, OA1
Smallish fragment, neatly formed; Diam c 115mm, H 72mm, Diam of hole c 20mm; burned at top prior to present breaks. This example, <S16> and <S17> are loom weights for warp-weighted looms. All are of baked red (oxidised), sandy, slightly micaceous clay with sparse but occasionally sizeable flint and grog inclusions. They are fragmentary and of the 'bun'-shaped form (cf Pritchard 1991, 167–8 and 259–60, nos 176–80; Walton Rogers 1997, 1752–3, nos 6585–9; Goffin 2003, 218).

To put the present three finds into perspective, some 1024 fragments, representing c 200+ loom weights, were recovered from the Lundenwic excavation at the Royal Opera House site, Westminster (Goffin 2003, 216).

<S16> Loom weight (Fig 9)
A<1257>, A[3871]; period P1, OA9
Almost a half, uneven; Diam c 120mm, H 43mm, Diam of hole c 25mm; flat base. An object of triple-roundel form (possibly a metal mount) has been impressed unevenly into the top at one point; partly burned after breakage.

<S17> Loom weight
A<1256>, A[1759]; -, -
Just under a half, uneven; Diam c 130mm, H 47mm, Diam of hole c 30mm.

<S18> Iron slag
A<107>, A[3211]; period M2, OA1
Small lump of slag, encrusted with sand; no response when touched with magnet.

<S19> Lead runnel
A<420>, A[3211]; period M2, OA1

<S20> Lead ingot (Fig 167)
A<554>, A[575]; -, - (from 19th-century cesspit)
?Ingot; rough and uneven, cast equal-armed cross; 44 x 41mm, Wt 28.4g. A slight protrusion at the end of one arm could reflect the provision for attachment found on pendants. Too crude and heavy to be a pendant, this could be either some kind of mortuary cross for burial with a body, or, more likely, simply a cruciform ingot, rather than a poor-quality souvenir of the 'rood of grace', which became one of the abbey's most popular visitor attractions (Chapter 4.4, 'St Saviour Bermondsey as pilgrimage centre'). Cruciform ingots could have been produced in a mould, like an incomplete London one from the late 11th century or later (Pritchard 1991, 166–7 and 259, no. 175, from Milk Street and suggested to have been for a Thor's hammer, though a cross of the same shape as the present one is a possible alternative).

<S21> Bone tool (Fig 9)
A<1618>, A[1865]; period M8, D4
Incomplete; long bone of cattle or horse carved into round/oval-section pin; broken off at transverse hole at wide end; surviving L 144mm, max Diam 8mm.
Presumably residual from the Saxo-Norman period, function uncertain. MacGregor discusses 'expanded-headed' pins (generally with a hole at right angles to that in the present find), which he dates to the Viking period in England, and also draws attention to similarities in form with earlier Saxon styli of copper alloy, though he feels unable on the evidence available to define their use (MacGregor 1985, 120 and 114–15, fig 64 nos 36–8; cf Pritchard 1991, 203–4 and 264, nos 228 etc for similar London finds; and Walton Rogers 1997, 1783 for 'needle-like' tools found at York).

Fig 167 Lead ingot <S20> (unphased) (scale c 1:1)

SCEATTA COINS

This small group of coins remains the sole focus (in the area that is the present heart of London) of these issues from ? the later part of the period c AD 600–c AD 750 (most probably the early 8th century AD). The recent discovery of two potentially contemporary Northumbrian stycas at Bull Wharf (BUF90), just across the Thames on the City waterfront gives a further complexity to the nature and significance of specie in this part of the region at this time.

Two of these finds have already been published by Stott (1991) with comments from Michael Metcalf, from which some of the details below are taken (the accession numbers have been changed in the interim) and some of the further details were furnished by Michael Hammerson. Sceattas were first assigned type numbers in *A Catalogue of English Coins in the British Museum* (BMC) (Keary 1887) and the alphabetical seriation is that devised by Rigold (1977) and further refined by Stewart (1984).

<S22> Silver (probably alloyed with copper alloy) sceatta (Fig 168)
A<2647>, A[3456]; period M2, OA1
Wt 0.92g. 'Jewel' head on shield // bird and branch. 'South Wessex/London' issue; BMC 39/49; North 1975, i, no. 103; (not published by Stott).

<S23> Silver (probably alloyed with copper alloy) sceatta (Fig 168)
A<1652>, A[1652]; period M4, B7
Wt 0.86g. Stewart series K, imitative (?bust with cross) // 'wolf's' head. The first side may have a very stylised version of North 1975, i, no. 89. Previously published as Stott 1991, 306, no. 20 figs 20a and b (former acc no. 559).

<S24> Silver (probably alloyed with copper alloy) sceatta (Fig 168)
A<2648>, A[2752]; period M4, OA6
Wt 1.10g. Diademed, draped bust right, the hand with cross // 'standard' with three crosses and ∴. Stewart series G; cf North 1975, i, no. 43 (which omits the hand). Previously published as Stott 1991, 305, no. 17 figs 17a and b (former acc no. 1362).

Fig 168 'Sceatta' coins <S22>–<S24> (scale c 2:1)

Monastic house period

Objects from periods M3–M9, and ones of monastic date from period P1 presumed residual. Included here are finds from Dissolution/pre-Dissolution contexts, in particular the dumping, A[972] and A[2483] (B9, period M9), inside the reredorter building (B9; Chapter 3.7, 'Archaeological evidence'). Material also included comes from Dissolution/immediately post-Dissolution clearance and demolition contexts, from the area west of the (former) reredorter (B9), in backfills, for example A[2349] (OA12, period P1), of the drain (D4), and to the north from a pit fill A[2276] (OA11, period P1) in the former courtyard (OA2). Some objects from the former monastic cemetery area north of the chapel (B1) are also included (OA9, period P1): from the demolition deposit, A[3460], abutting parts of the former chapel chancel (B1) foundations, from robbing fills A[3503] and A[3519] sealed by A[3460], and from the fills A[2938], A[2883] of a large pit near the former chapel (B1) (Chapter 5.2, 'Elements of the former monstery partly or wholly retained and adapted'). These objects are presumed to be from the lifetime of the monastic house, or at least current during its Dissolution phase.

Items relating to the institution's religious functions

FIGURE OF CHRIST CRUCIFIED

<S25> Copper-alloy figurine (Fig 98)
A<1640>, A[96]; period M9, D4/OA9
Cast, hollow-backed appliqué (ie originally mounted on a cross) figure of Christ crucified, decorated with champlevé enamel; H 157mm, surviving W 91mm (extant width; both hands are broken off). There are two holes for attachment in the splayed base, the head is inclined to the left and the eyes appear closed. The flat band of the crown, which has been added separately and is incomplete at the top, has triangular panels picked out with paired, discontinuous engraved lines. Details of the facial hair, body, legs and feet are also added by engraving. Folds in the loincloth are rendered by a series of triangular, enamelled areas (now green). The girdle is picked out in enamel that is now brown. Traces of gilding survive in low areas but the majority has worn off; there is a tear in the left side of the loincloth.

The figure, presumably manufactured at Limoges in France, is likely to have been attached to an altar or processional cross. It is a stock product, with some perfunctory detailing: the legs, for example, are not three-dimensionally separated, there has been no attempt to represent a realistic ribcage and there seem never to have been glass eyes, as in a figure of c 1195–1210 in the Louvre, Paris (O'Neill 1996, 186–7, no. 50; cf Thoby 1953, passim). Other enamelled figures from London are published by Ward Perkins (1940, 288 and pl 81). A similar but better-preserved figure of Christ, attached to the enamelled cross, was found in the cathedral close in Salisbury, Wiltshire (Cherry 2001, 39–41 with details of further English finds) and another crucifixion figure attributed to the late 12th century came from West Stow in Suffolk (Campbell 1998, 73 and fig 26b). Although it is difficult to identify any Christ-figure of directly comparable quality, this is, nevertheless, the most impressive and perhaps the most immediately significant of the finds from the religious house (despite its residuality as excavated). It probably dates from the early 13th century.

TOMB LETTERS

All are cast and of Lombardic form, as produced from around the 1280s to the 1350s, and have worn surfaces. Two of the three standard sizes are represented (Blair 1987, 140 and fig 148). (Thanks to John Blair for advice on these objects.)

<S26> Copper-alloy letter (Fig 88)
A<972>, A[3460]; period P1, OA9
'L': H 38mm, W 30mm, Th 2.05mm. Size II.

<S27> Copper-alloy letter (Fig 88)
A<973>, A[1]; -, - (1984 site clearance)
'G': H 41mm, W 31mm, Th 2.10mm; edges only roughly finished. Size III.

<S28> Copper-alloy letter (Fig 88)
A<971>, A[1]; -, - (1984 site clearance)
'L': H 46mm, W 33mm, Th 1.65mm; taller riser serif than in preceding item. Size III. John Blair observes that the tall serif may indicate a relatively late date, possibly post-1335.

TUNING PEG

<S29> Bone tuning peg (Fig 97)
A<953>, A[518]; period P1, OA12
Square-headed peg, L 43mm, with string hole near other end; no clear sign of use.

For a stringed instrument (cf A Wardle in Egan 1998a, nos 939–43), presumably in this case used as an accompaniment in religious services. Tuning pegs are recurrent finds at the sites of religious houses as well as appearing in secular contexts (see G Egan in Thomas et al 1997, 109, table 14, category U; present at Battle Abbey; St Augustine's Abbey Canterbury; Chester, Cheshire).

STYLI

These are almost universal among finds assemblages from religious houses (Egan in Thomas et al 1997, 109, table 14 category H; Egan 1998a, nos 899–911). There are nine in all from the site, compared with 15 from Battle Abbey (Geddes 1985, 151–2, nos 6–20, fig 45). For use with waxed tablets. All are turned and (except <S31>) with terminal knops for erasure.

<S30> Bone stylus (Fig 92)
A<550>, A[972]; period M9, B9
L 63mm; turned, with worn terminal knop and moulded collar; three sets of triple grooves along the shaft; trace of iron pin survives.

<S31> Bone stylus (Fig 92)
A<548>, A[972]; period M9, B9
L 75mm; turned, with triple-reel collar; the top is a tapered rod with a central hole; the base has been adapted by carving to an off-centred, nib-like point, which is worn. Besides the unusual form of moulding, this stylus lacks the knop of the great majority of the others at this site and elsewhere, having instead possible provision for holding a second pin at the top end (?never present); presumably adapted with the quill-like end following breakage and loss of an original iron pin (a hint of the hole for which survives).

<S32> Bone stylus (Fig 92)
A<551>, A[972]; period M9, B9
L 80mm; turned, with worn terminal knop on moulded collar; rougher moulding at other end with its carved point. The integral point is almost certainly an adaptation to replace an original metal pin.

<S33> Bone stylus
A<3650>, A[2937]; period M9, OA6
Incomplete; surviving L 54mm, broken off at knop; rusted iron pin.

<S34> Bone stylus (Fig 92)
A<549>, A[3008]; period M9, OA6
L 76mm; worn knop on moulded collar; rust from missing iron pin.

<S35> Bone stylus (Fig 92)
A<542>, A[2706]; period P1, OA9
L 85mm; worn knop on moulded collar; pin missing from large hole at end.

<S36> Bone stylus (Fig 92)
A<552>, A[2987]; period P1, OA9
Turned bone stylus, L 87mm; worn terminal knop with moulded collar; the copper-alloy pin has broken off in the shaft.

The use of copper alloy for the point is unusual but not unknown in styli of this sort and may well represent a replacement for an original one of iron.

<S37> Bone stylus (Fig 92)
A<538>, A[4159]; period P1, OA12
L 63mm; worn, acorn-shaped knop on reel; discolouration from missing iron pin.

<S38> Bone stylus (Fig 92)
A<547>, A[4159]; period P1, OA12
L 78mm; worn, oval knop on reel; remains of iron pin, facetting around which suggests it was replaced, necessitating retrimming of the shaft, after breakage of the original end.

retaining pivot rod and broken off at loop of the sheet part originally attached to the cover; 18 x 8mm. Boss with central hole, and holed tab with moulded terminal; traces of gilding.

The central hole was to accommodate a corresponding pin set on the book cover and the hole in the terminal is thought to have held a cord etc (probably used to help keep the volume closed) – cf <S46>, and Egan 1998a, 277–80, nos 921–5 fig 214, from deposits dated to the early 15th century.

<S46> Copper-alloy book clasp (Fig 94)

A<911>, A[972]; period M9, B9
Composite, with forked spacer; 57 x 31mm; slightly tapering sheets have engrailed edge (broken off on one side). The front sheet, with a round, grooved aperture and two rivets, is bent inwards. A rebated, transverse bar connects the boss, which has a central hole for the corresponding pin and a flared terminal with a notched loop for a tie (missing); leather from strap survives.

From a very large book (cf Egan 1998a, nos 919–25 fig 214, of which this is a non-hinged variant, and nos 38 and 542–4).

BEAD

<S39> Bone bead (Fig 107)
A<956>, A[972]; period M9, B9
Bead has flat ends (one with a concentric groove) and bifacially bevelled edge; Diam 10mm, L 5mm; turned; smoothed from

wear.

Presumably from a cheap rosary (and monastic period date). See bead-making waste panel <S175>, below.

BOOK MOUNTS AND CLASPS

<S40> Copper-alloy book mount (Fig 94)
A<999>, A[253]; period M8, B10
Sheet corner mount 41 x 41mm, folded over along external sides, triply scalloped along internal ones. Two small holes for rivets and a larger one with bevelled perimeter, which, like the straight edges, is flanked by a stamped border of beading between lines; stamped, foliate scrolling in tooled field.

The Renaissance-style decoration shows this must have been fairly new (c 1520+) when discarded. Intrusive in this context.

<S41> Copper-alloy book mount (Fig 94)
A<879>, A[2483]; period M9, B9
Incomplete, sub-rectangular sheet plate, surviving 25 x 10mm; bevelled edges and doubly notched surviving end; broken off at one of three holes for rivets, the other two retaining rusted traces.

The use of iron rivets on copper alloy suggests re-attachment.

<S42> Copper-alloy book mount (Fig 94)
A<802>, A[2276]; period P1, OA11
?Cast; domed circle, with three surviving (of original four) flat,

angled tabs around edge, each with a hole for a rivet (all except one of which are missing); 22 x 21mm (cf Egan 1998a, no. 926).

The shortness of the rivet remaining in the present item (with only 2.5mm of 3.5mm for purchase) may have been unsuitable for the suggested use on a book cover.

<S43> Copper-alloy book mount (Fig 94)
A<561>, A[2818]; period P1, OA9
Corroded; sub-square sheet with central dome, 24 x 24mm; holes at surviving corners for attachment.

<S44> Copper-alloy book mount (Fig 94)
A<360>, A[3519]; period P1, OA9
Cast; incomplete; ornate cruciform (estimated 50 x 50mm) with tripartite arms (two survive complete); central hole in bevelled, rebated surround.

The raised central area may have been to hold a gem, though the base metal suggests it would have been of a non-precious material such as glass.

<S45> Copper-alloy book clasp (Fig 94)
A<861>, A[2706]; period P1, OA9
Cast end piece from hinged clasp,

SEAL MATRICES

<S47> Lead/tin and stone seal matrix (Fig 38; Fig 169)
A<544>, A[4134]; period M5, B8
Metal corroded in part; round, plano-convex main part of lead/tin, pointed at base and with animal-headed, looped terminal at top; Diam 26mm, Th 8mm, max L 40mm, with centrally set gem of ?jet (now cracked); the device is a lion passant with LEO above (engraved the right way round) and ?'Lov' below (roughly scratched on the surface, again the right way round) all cut on the gem, and on the metal the surrounding legend +SECRETVM+RESERO (all lettering is Lombardic and the Ss are reversed). The metal is particularly corroded on the plain back and around the animal-head terminal.

The gemstone may be reused as set (cf Spencer 1984, no. 6 fig 3) but it was probably less than a century old when discarded in the present combined form. The Latin legend ? 'I retain the secret',

drawing attention to the security of the contents of any document sealed with this stamp, is a variation of a fairly common reference in official medieval seal legends (the lion may refer to the fierceness of retribution for any tampering). Here it probably identifies the 'secret' stamp produced as subsidiary to a main one of dignity for the priory (cf *sigillum secreti* etc, Harvey and McGuiness 1996, 70–1, noting that bishops used engraved gems as counterseals particularly in the 12th century, and 118 listing). The added observation on the gem in the same language that the main device is a lion (seemingly repeated half-heartedly by a less confident hand, in a ?Scandinavian/Germanic language) would have come out in reverse, but it perhaps makes sense, if several matrices that were potentially confusable were available in the institution, as a quick – if rather drastic – reference to identify the main device among

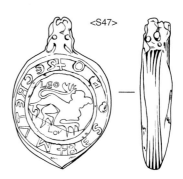

Fig 169 *Lead/tin seal with gemstone (?jet) setting <S47> (from B8, period M5) (scale 1:1)*

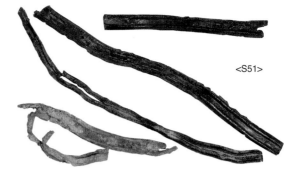

somewhat similar designs (it can be very difficult for the unaccustomed eye to read complicated, incuse figurative images). The accomplished rendition of the animal and the relative heaviness of this object confirm that this was an important security aid, presumably held by one of senior members of the monastery. (Thanks to John Cherry for advice on this item.)

<S48> Copper-alloy seal matrix (Fig 64)
A<2775>, A[4147]; period M8, OA2
Disc, Diam 20mm, with pierced, radial tab for attachment and grip during use (cf Ward Perkins 1940, 295, fig 90 no. 4): a dog under a tree with a cross-hatched oval of foliage, *SOHOVTALEBOT around (Lombardic lettering). The variant of the hunter's cry 'soho' is common on 14th-century seal legends, but the accompanying motif of the hunting hound (a talbot, to which this call would be

directed) in the forest, has apparently not been noted previously (Harvey and McGuiness 1996, 118 listing under *sohou*).

This off-the-peg stamp (from the second cloister garth, OA2) could have been used by almost anyone within the religious community or perhaps more likely from the laity.

<S49> Copper-alloy seal matrix (Fig 93)
A<543>, A[4154]; period M9, B9
Slightly corroded: circular, with facetted handle tapering to suspension loop; Diam 22mm, H 24mm. The engraving does not appear to be of a particularly high standard: two standing human figures, under adjacent canopies, one wearing a ?mitre and with a ?crozier, the other seemingly holding a rod-like object. [? I or T]EAT VS·A· around (rough Lombardic lettering).

The significance of both figures (?ecclesiastic and saint) and the legend is obscure.

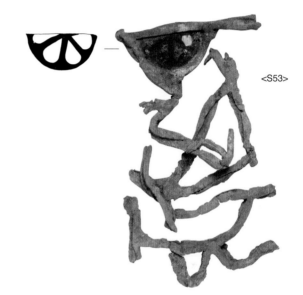

TEXTILE

<S50> Textile
A<2783>, A[972]; period M9, B9
Fragments/scraps of patterned textile with fine silver thread.

Presumably from rich ecclesiastical dress or a furnishing fabric.

Items relating to the priory buildings

WINDOW CAME AND OPENWORK GRILLE

<S51> Lead window came (Fig 170)
A<2789>, A[972]; period M9, B9
Four ? unused window leads, total Wt 86g.

<S52> Lead window came (Fig 170)
A<303>, A[2906]; period M9, OA6
Several pieces, including some articulated (one, illustrated, folded into a tight ball), total Wt 74g.

<S53> Lead window came (Fig 170)
A<1079>, A[2883]; period P1, OA9
Four fragments, including ones with triangular and semicircular tracery, the latter retaining now-opaque glass (36 x 19mm visible), which is painted in red with a half wheel-like motif.

<S54> Lead grille (Fig 170)
A<1017>, A[611]; period M9, OA9
Fragments from three sides of a lozenge-shaped grille, estimated *c* 100 x 85mm. Little remains of the openwork tracery apart from corner trefoils of two different patterns. The surviving scraps had the greater part of the grille roughly cut from them with a bladed implement and were subsequently folded together.

These remains look like the result of a determined removal operation, presumably to extract recyclable metal from a tenacious frame. Lead grilles are among the most characteristic finds from religious houses (G Egan in Thomas et al 1997, 109, table 14G).

Fig 170 Lead window cames <S51>–<S53> and grill <S54> (scale c 1:2)

FIXTURES AND FITTINGS

<S55> Copper-alloy bracket (Fig 171)
A<337>, A[972]; period M9, B9
Robust, cast copper-alloy cylinder

with constriction towards basal knop, H 74mm, Diam 21mm (16mm internally); spike at side for fixture, L 60mm; main part roughly file-finished.

The lack of parallels suggests this was not a standard item; perhaps to hold a banner or flag rather than a candle (for which it would seem to be unnecessarily heavy and relatively elaborate; cf <S78>, Fig 173).

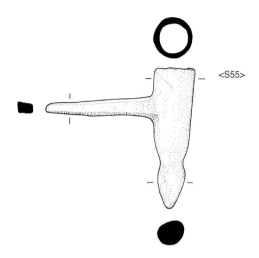

Fig 171 Copper-alloy bracket <S55> (from B9, period M9) (scale 1:2)

SECURITY EQUIPMENT

A group, presumably a bunch, of at least 12 rotary keys with bows of at least three different shapes was recovered from A[4151] to the south of the claustral complex in the area of the mansion house southern perimeter (OA12) (see <S71>–<S76>), along with slide key <S58> for a padlock (compare the bunch found at St Mary Spital: Egan 1997, 202–3 and 36, fig 26). Only three locks are identified, compared with ?29 keys (including the apparent bunch of ?13 keys).

<S56> Copper-alloy padlock
A<536>, A[1124]; period M4, B7
Cylindrical, octagonal case, L 46 x max Diam 13mm, with series of engraved lines transversely at both ends, and pierced tab holding tapered, animal-headed bar, together 27mm; pierced tab and loop of mechanism (most of which is missing) are in locked position.

Several of these small, copper-alloy padlocks are known from religious house sites and elsewhere, both in London (eg Egan 1998a, no. 244) and more widely.

<S57> Iron padlock key
A<1855>, A[3460]; period P1, OA9
L 71mm overall; kidney-shaped bow 32 x 20mm; shank L 32mm protrudes into bow; and has slot which continues into shield-shaped bit 21 x 35mm.

<S58> Iron padlock key
A<1885>, A[4151]; period P1, OA12
L c 73mm; oval, angular-topped bow 29 x 25mm, shank L 22mm with slot continuing into shield-shaped bit, W c 13mm, L c 27mm, with ?double-armed cross warding-aperture configuration.

Found with 12 rotary keys (<S71>–<S76>).

<S59> Iron padlock key
A<176>, A[3284]; -, -
Incomplete (? broken in excavation): oval bow 26 x 19mm; shank L 22mm narrows to distorted bit, the end of which is missing.

Both aspects of the damage seem unrelated to any strain from trying to operate any lock.

<S60> Copper-alloy slide key
(Fig 172)
A<569>, A[1]; -, - (1984 site clearance)
L 46mm; H-shaped bit at right angle to tapering-strip shank, which becomes oval in section and has looped, circular bow, Diam 6mm.

Perhaps for a lock on a casket. See Egan 1998a, nos 258–9, which are from deposits attributed to c 1150–c 1350. Although others of this form are gilded, no obvious trace remains in the present instance.

<S61> Iron mounted lock
A<1811>, A[2937]; period M9, OA6
Part of rectangular, robust sheet plate 80 x 77mm, with key aperture L 17mm and having two concentric, arched wards (the larger apparently displaced), part of riveted key guard, bar held by ?two hasps, and aperture for main securing hasp; a further, ?bifurcate feature parallel to and surrounding the hasp aperture was (presuming it lies on the outer side of the plate) perhaps to help locate the main hasp.

<S62> Iron rotary key
A<1873>, A[4134]; period M5, B8
Overall L 86mm: round bow Diam 30mm; shank L 59mm has moulded knop at top; bit 20 x 32mm is asymmetrical; traces of coating.

A well-made key, particularly at this relatively early date.

<S63> Iron rotary key
A<138>, A[4156]; period M9, B9
Incomplete, ?kidney-shaped bow, shank L c 155mm, bit 36 x 58mm has asymmetrical warding; traces of coating.

A substantial key presumably for a major door.

<S64> Iron rotary key
A<1812>, A[4156]; period M9, B9
L 145mm: kidney-shaped bow 48 x 30mm; shank L 115mm has narrowed pin; bit 19 x 32mm is possibly slightly bent from protracted use.

The minimal warding may mean this was some kind of master (skeleton) key that could operate a number of locks of similar size.

<S65> Iron rotary key
A<1876>, A[4154]; period M9, B9

Incomplete; ?oval bow W 25mm, shank L 64mm, bit 15 x ?20mm has asymmetrical warding; possible hint of coating.

<S66> Iron rotary key
A<1801>, A[2937]; period M9, OA6
L c 75mm: kidney-shaped bow 26 x 18mm; hollow shank L 54mm; bit 19 x 22mm is asymmetrical.

<S67> Iron rotary key
A<2246>, A[3008]; period M9, OA6
L 40mm: oval bow 21 x 14mm; shank L 24mm; bit 13 x 13mm is asymmetrical.

This well-made key has relatively complex warding for its small size.

<S68> Iron rotary key
A<1828>, A[3008]; period M9, OA6
Most of bow missing, surviving L 144mm: shank L 132mm; bit 26 x 45mm is symmetrical; traces of coating.

<S69> Iron rotary key
A<162>, A[2706]; period P1, OA9
L 141mm: kidney-shaped bow 50 x 28mm; shank L 113mm; bit 37 x 47mm has symmetrical warding which seems to include smith-added end tines (presumably as a repair).

<S70> Iron rotary key
A<2157b>, A[3460]; period P1, OA9
L 92mm: tripartite bow 25 x 25mm has offset, thickened top; hollow shank L 62mm; bit 18 x 26mm has asymmetrical warding including one circular cleft; traces of coating.

<S71> Iron rotary key
A<1879>, A[4151]; period P1, OA12
L c 50mm: lozenge-shaped bow 23 x 22mm with round hole; shank L c 28mm; bit 12 x 18mm appears asymmetrical. Part of a group, presumably a bunch, of at least 12

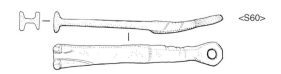

Fig 172 Copper-alloy slide key <S60> (unstratified) (scale 1:1)

rotary keys (<S71>–<S76>), along with a slide key (<S58>) for a padlock, from A[4151].

<S72> Iron rotary key
A<2883>, A[4151]; period P1, OA12
L 56mm: kidney-shaped bow 18 x 26mm; shank L 44mm protrudes into the bow; bit 14 x 23mm is asymmetrical.

<S73> Iron rotary key
A<1891>, A[4151]; period P1, OA12
Rusted mass of at least three keys with bows clustered to suggest this was a single, joined bunch: one with ?oval bow, L c 83mm; another with oval- or kidney-shaped bow of similar dimension; the third is obscured even on X-ray plates.

<S74> Iron rotary key
A<2012>, A[4151]; period P1, OA12
Very corroded; two keys with oval bows, both c 30 x 22mm, L 68mm, bit (only one measurable) c 14 x

20mm; traces of copper corrosion within hollow shank and on bits; the adjacent bows suggest these may originally have been on a string together.

<S75> Iron rotary key
A<155>, A[4151]; period P1, OA12
Two keys with bows together: bows c ?25 x 20mm, L c 65 and 57mm, bits ?18 x 17mm and ? 15 x 17mm.

<S76> Iron rotary key
A<1884>, A[4151]; period P1, OA12
L 58mm: oval bow 25 x 15mm has offset, thickened top, collared shank L 42mm, bit 18 x 30mm has internal aperture and nine tines in symmetrical ward configuration.

<S77> Iron rotary key
A<1820>, A[504]; -, -
L 170mm: round bow Diam 41mm; shank L 130mm tapers at end; bit 30 x 36mm is asymmetrical with simple S/Z-shaped warding.

LAMPS

<S78> Copper-alloy candle holder (Fig 173)
A<369>, A[4159]; period P1, OA12
Distorted sheeting: ?cup H 24mm, with two tab feet 16 x 10mm (presumably originally at a right angle) each with a hole for a rivet, one of which, cut from wire, survives. Presumably from a holder that would have been attached to a sheet dish with a long, horizontal handle, ie a chamber stick (cf Bangs 1995, 177–8, nos 173ff, no. 179 is a plain version). Bangs notes that the

notion that chamber sticks existed only from the late 17th century is erroneous, as the present find demonstrates, and while attributing all those he catalogues to the Low Countries, admits the likelihood of other places of manufacture. Cf a similar cup from Guildford Priory (Poulton and Woods 1984, fig 45 no. 34).

<S79> Stone lamp
A<1772>, A[4159]; period P1, OA12

Buff, fine, micaceous sandstone: squared block, 114 x 113mm and H 111mm, with rounded, central well. Chamfered along one side at the base, angled at the shoulders to give an octagonal profile at the top and with angled rebates to the mid point. Blackened by burning within the well and externally at the break in one of lower corners; also broken at the rim on one side. The basal chamfer suggests this was adapted from a building stone.

Stone (cresset) lamps are not common in London outside institutions (Ward Perkins 1940, 174–6, fig 54), none having been recognised from the period c 1150–c 1450 (for a recent survey based on finds from lay sites, Egan 1998a, 126–7).

<S80> Glass lamp (Fig 173)
A<2180>, A[518]; period P1, OA12
Pale green, partly decayed; central basal well, surviving H 30mm.

Items used in the priory

CASKETS/BOXES

<S81> Copper-alloy casket mount
A<1013>, A[1274]; period M6, B8
Distorted and incomplete D-section length (now in two parts), surviving 188mm, W 3mm; traces of gilding; broken off at expansions for attachment holes.

Biddle (1990, 762–89) classifies all similar items as coming from religious caskets. Given the ecclesiastical character of the present site this is probably true of <S81> and <S82>, though the crudity of some examples calls such an interpretation into question. Gilded mounts of this kind tend to be from the earlier end of the period represented by the accompanying ceramics (in the context of a religious house they may have continued in use somewhat later).

<S82> Copper-alloy ?finial (Fig 174)
A<598>, A[375]; -, -
Decorative ?finial: L 48mm, max W 9mm; tube tapering towards

boss defined by a double collar to each side and a flat, spear-shaped terminal with Romanesque-style, leaf-vein ?engraving on one side and an end boss defined by a double collar. Some gilding survives. A fragment of what this

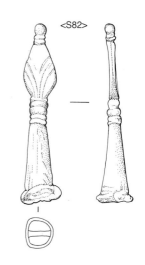

Fig 174 Decorative ?finial <S82> (unphased) (scale 1:1)

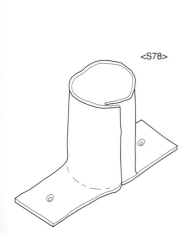

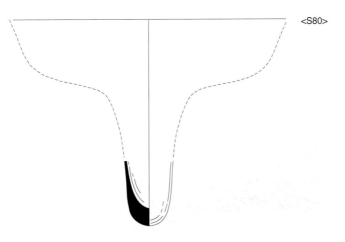

Fig 173 Copper-alloy candle holder <S78> and glass lamp <S80> (both from OA12, period P1) (<S78> oblique view, scale c 1:1; <S80> 1:2)

was originally attached to survives in a corroded state.

Presumably from a prestigious display item, such as a chasse (a small building-shaped container, often of richly enamelled copper alloy, used in a religious context for storing relics, for example), from the religious house.

<S83> Copper-alloy lid (Fig 56)
A<806>, A[967]; period M7, D2
Domed sheet octagon, 65 x 62mm, with turned-down edge flange; part of cast strip survives, bevelled along sides and with angled end

(broken off at the other), held by two rivets; fragments broken off main sheet at this point and from opposite side.

Lid, probably not from a vessel but a shallow box of the kind used to hold folding scales for weighing (more familiar from round versions – cf Egan 1998a, nos 484–6, and fig 142 for a complete example with its contents from Roche Abbey). These seem, as in the present instance, to have been vulnerable to breakage around the hinge and closure (here of a different form from the hook in the parallel cited).

METAL VESSELS

<S84> Copper-alloy cauldron (Fig 175)
A<470>, A[2937]; period M9, OA6
Distorted fragment, L 270mm and H 95mm (in present, flattened state), of sheet wall and thicker, slightly offset, plain rim with remains of two iron rivets; there are also several small, undiagnostic fragments.

Probably from a cauldron, originally with an iron reinforcing band around the rim (cf Egan 1998a, fig 139 for a complete example).

<S85> Copper-alloy ewer mount (Fig 63)
A<193>, A[3463]; period M8, OA6
Incomplete, cast finial: flat ornate-cruciform appendage, surviving 25 x 24mm, with arms having angled terminals, damaged at end; broken off at top above bulbous moulding. This decoration is broken from one of the cusps of a triple-arched handle on a similar vessel to that of which <S86> was part, or from the

base of a more ornate version of its swivel. Although these two-spouted water-holders had alternative domestic uses, an ecclesiastical connection seems more likely in the present instance. Cf Theuerkauff-Liederwald 1988, 390–1 and 428–9, nos 497–9 and 501, two of which are (or were until relatively recently) still in churches in the Netherlands and Germany (no. 499, formerly at St Vitus Church at Olfen in the Odenwald, is a particularly close parallel); these all have bearded-man mounts to hold the handles on to the vessels.

<S86> Copper-alloy ewer mount (Fig 63)
A<2740>, A[4154]; period M9, B9
Incomplete, cast, stirrup-form swivelling support: H 115 x (originally) 60mm. Separate, swivelling loop on pin at top; bifurcated, inverted U-shaped frame (one arm of which is broken off) with horizontal,

outward-facing, integral support rod.

Presumably originally symmetrical, this would have supported a substantial, cast vessel, such as a two-spouted hanging laver for washing ('lavabo'), as specifically used in ecclesiastical contexts for ritual cleansing (Theuerkauff-Liederwald 1988,

361–475) most of those illustrated have moulding on the handles but no. 557 in the Vleeshuis Museum in Antwerp (Fig 63) is plain (much the same form of swivel in iron is known on well buckets). One of the human-bust mounts that attached these handles to the vessels was recently found in London (MOL acc no. 94.171/1).

GLASS BOTTLES

A glass urinal and ten glass bottles, some of which could have been reused as urinals, are listed below; most are from monastic period contexts, notably A[972]; the two from period P1 are probably also of monastic date. Most of the fragments identified were base pieces from pale green vessels with flared rims and diameters of c 45–70mm. Urinals are typically globular, round-based and with thin walls.

<S87> Bottle (Fig 176)
A<978>, A[4154]; period M9, B9
Decayed, originally opaque-red fragments of plain glass. Flaring rim, Diam 90mm, with upper part of flared wall, surviving H 55mm.

The unusual, very striking, original 'sealing-wax' colour can be paralleled in a small number of medieval glass vessels in England and on the Continent (Noël Hume 1957, 104, fig 1, a London find attributed to the 13th century; cf Egan 1998a, 218). No synthesis of the varied forms for which it is known has so far been attempted. The discovery of the present fragments at Bermondsey Priory raises the question of whether there might have been some particular significance for a vessel apparently of unremarkable form in this colour in a religious context (cf <S100> another glass vessel of unusual colour).

<S88> Bottle (Fig 176)
A<1399>, A[972]; period M9, B9
Decayed neck and flaring rim, Diam 35mm.

<S89> Bottle
A<2381>, A[972]; period M9, B9
Decayed, slightly flaring rim with angled taper at edge, Diam 45mm.

<S90> ?Bottle
A<1521>, A[972]; period M9, B9
Angled rim of bottle (?or drinking-vessel base) with folded edge, Diam c 70mm.

<S91> Bottle
A<1514>, A[972]; period M9, B9
Decayed, relatively thick, convex base (flat internally), surviving Diam c 85mm.

<S92> Bottle
A<1561>, A[972]; period M9, B9
Decayed fragment of relatively

<S84>

Fig 175 Copper-alloy cauldron fragment <S84> (from OA6, period M9) (scale c 1:2)

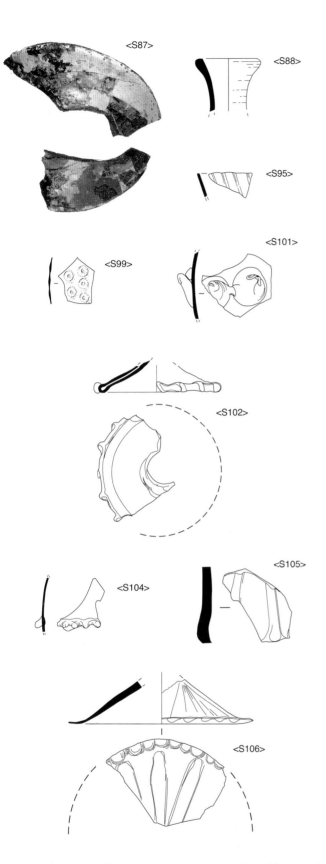

Fig 176 *Glass items: bottle fragments <S87>, <S88>, <S95>; and fragments of drinking vessels <S99>, <S101>, <S102>, <S104>–<S106> (scale 1:2)*

Decayed, flaring ?rim with angled edge, Diam c 70mm.

<S95> Bottle (Fig 176)
A<1337>, A[2863]; period M9, OA6
Superficially decayed, colourless fragment from rim of wry, ribbed vessel. Many small bubbles. Diam at top c 50mm.

Probably from a long-necked, globular-bodied flask or bottle, fragments from several of which have been found in London (L Keys in Egan 1998a, no. 647) in contexts dated to the late 14th/early 15th centuries (with reference to another from Southampton attributed to the 15th/16th century).

<S96> Bottle
A<2163>, A[2308]; period P1, B8
Pale green (originally evenly translucent), superficially decayed, curving base fragments, thickening towards centre; Diam 140mm+ (J Shepherd, pers comm).

<S97> Bottle
A<2377>, A[518]; period P1, OA12
Decayed neck fragment with slightly flared, fire-rounded rim, Diam 34mm, originally pale green, blocked with chalky mortar (traces on the outside too).

The blocking may relate to some kind of chemical process or distillation.

GLASS DRINKING VESSELS

Fragments of glass drinking vessels; two from period P1 are probably also of monastic date.

<S98> Beaker
A<1503> and A<1564>, A[972]; period M9, B9
Decayed fragments, including slightly flaring rim, Diam c 60mm; ?spiral moulding.

<S99> Beaker (Fig 176)
A<1676>, A[972]; period M9, B9
Two corroded, originally colourless, thin wall fragments, Diam c 60mm, moulded with rows of roundels. From one or two vessels (Cf L Keys in Egan 1998a, nos 669 and 671, beakers attributed to the early 15th century).

<S100> Drinking vessel (Fig 101)
A<1910>, A[972]; period M9, B9
Opaque, matt white glass. Rounded wall fragment of vertical-sided vessel with plain rim Diam 85mm, expanding to 96mm, surviving H 75mm; one plain, fairly narrow, applied horizontal trail and three thicker pinched, ones; the glass appears slightly greenish by transmitted light. Presumably a drinking vessel.

Medieval white glass is very unusual across Europe, though fragments of nine vessels are known from various, mainly secular, contexts in London. The present fragment and one from the site of the nunnery of St Mary in Clerkenwell, appear to be from religious institutions (cf Egan 1998a, nos 691–4; Egan 1998b, in which the present item is no. 9). See fragment <S87> for another vessel of unusual colour.

<S101> Drinking vessel (Fig 176)
A<1677>, A[972]; period M9, B9
Fragment of almost colourless glass. Folded, flaring base with self-coloured, applied trail.

<S102> Drinking vessel (Fig 176)
A<1331>, A[2938]; period P1, OA9
A fragment of a similar glass to <S101>, almost colourless with an applied and pinched trail, Diam c 70mm.

<S103> Vessel
A<1338>, A[2863]; period M9, OA6
Decayed fragment of vertical rim with slight wry ribbing, Diam c 60mm. ?Beaker.

<S104> Vessel (Fig 176)
A<1383>, A[2863]; period M9, OA6
Slight superficial decay in wall fragment of colourless, flared vessel, having pinched, applied trail (?part-way up rather than at base). Many small bubbles; Diam at trail c 50mm.

<S105> Vessel (Fig 176)
A<2181>, A[518]; period P1, OA12
Colourless fragment of flaring wall with moulded, vertical ribs, max Diam c 100mm.

thick, pushed-in base, originally green, surviving Diam 105mm.

<S93> Bottle
A<1562>, A[972]; period M9, B9

Decayed, pushed-in base fragment.

<S94> Glass urinal
A<1501>, A[972]; period M9, B9

<S106> ?Vessel (Fig 176)
A<1391>, A[518]; period P1, OA12
Pale green, incomplete, pushed-in base, Diam c 100mm. Facetted

moulding, continuing more densely on side. Possible ?bottle (J Shepherd, pers comm).

GLASS DISTILLING VESSELS

<S107> Distilling vessel
A<1520>, A[972]; period M9, B9
Decayed, tapering rim, Diam at top c 30mm. ?Cucurbit.

Corroded fragment: max surviving Diam c 70mm; alembic base (identified by J Shepherd).

<S108> Distilling vessel
A<1513>, A[972]; period M9, B9
Decayed, originally pale green, vertical-sided neck (flares slightly towards one end), surviving L 86mm. ?Alembic head.

<S110> Distilling vessel (Fig 104)
A<1304>, A[1244]; period M9, OA11
Colourless, superficially decayed: thickish fragment narrowing towards plain rim, Diam at top c 80mm. Cucurbit (collecting vessel, J Shepherd, pers comm). See also <S97>.

<S109> Distilling vessel
A<1512>, A[972]; period M9, B9

FOOD PREPARATION AND CONSUMPTION EQUIPMENT

A total of 19 knives were recovered from the site, 13 of them from A[972], period M9, in the reredorter. Of these, two were rusted together and five had makers' marks; four illustrated (<S112>–<S115>, Fig 177), two of which were versions of demi fleur-de-lis.

<S111> Iron knife
A<158>, A[972]; period M9, B9
Whittle-tang knife, broken off at both ends, surviving L 80mm; surviving L of blade 63mm, W 20mm+; with inlaid copper-alloy maker's mark: demi fleur-de-lis.

maker's mark: voided triangle with tabs on two of the sides. One rivet survives; traces of wooden scale.

<S114> Iron knife (maker's mark Fig 177)
A<1837>, A[972]; period M9, B9
Incomplete, scale-tang knife, surviving L 133mm; blade survives L 45mm; four tubular, copper-alloy rivets; hints of wooden scales; inlaid maker's mark: ?plume with scroll.

<S112> Iron knife (maker's mark Fig 177)
A<1824>, A[972]; period M9, B9
Incomplete blade, surviving L 115mm, W 21mm, and trace of whittle tang; inlaid maker's mark: ? crown over I.

<S115> Iron knife (maker's mark Fig 177)
A<1834>, A[972]; period M9, B9
Incomplete, whittle-tang knife; broken off at both ends, surviving L 136mm, tapering blade surviving L 16mm, W 21mm; with inlaid copper-alloy maker's mark: demi fleur-de-lis over saltire.

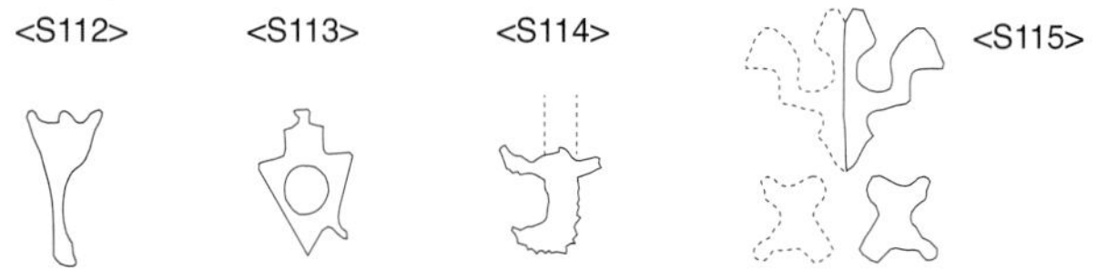

<S113> Iron knife (maker's mark Fig 177)
A<1833>, A[972]; period M9, B9
Handle incomplete: scale-tang knife, surviving L 126mm; pointed blade L 107mm, W 18mm. Has curved back, non-ferrous shoulder strip; with inlaid copper-alloy

<S116> Bone handle (Fig 56)
A<947>, A[583]; period M7, D2
Incomplete scale, surviving L 82mm, W 21mm; holes for two rivets with rust traces around; series of single and paired, compass-engraved circle-and-dot motifs.

<S117> Grater (Fig 90)
A<526>, A[972]; period M9, B9
Sheet copper alloy, 52 x 26mm; flat, approximately D shaped part, roughly multiply pierced (leaving sharp, upstanding perimeters to most of the holes), and four strips (? of original five), one of the

survivors is displaced, bent at right angles to the former; apparently complete, except for one strip.

This rather rough-and-ready, and so far unparalleled, object appears to combine the grating and shredding functions of the modern kitchen tool.

<S118> ?Cauldron
A<3052>, A[972]; period M9, B9
Copper alloy, cast fragment. everted rim, estimated Diam c 400mm; possibly burnt. Probably from a tripod cauldon for cooking (cf Egan 1998a, no. 446 fig 131).

MOULD

<S119> Ceramic mould (Fig 91)
A<1629>, A[569]; period P1, OA11
Fragment of ?circular, London-type ware (LOND; approximate date range 1080–1350) mould with round edge, surviving portion 50 x 50mm (projected diameter if a full roundel, c 92mm). A ?man's face, a curl of hair and drapery at the neck, all within a linear circle (cf conventional representations of the king on medieval English coins: the circle, which is broken by the neck, might perhaps have been intended as a halo but it may simply be a border), with a channel at the base. Apparently unused.

Possibly for making pastries (? for a founder's or benefactor's feast or other festivals, see Nenk 1992 for ceramic ?waffle moulds of comparable date to that indicated for the present item). The production of lasting devotional images seems a less likely purpose, though see the head portion from a mould-made, full-length ceramic figurine of the Virgin from the Austin Friary at Leicester, Leicestershire (Clay 1981, 139–40, no. 75) and cf Ward Perkins for a ceramic mould for similar figurines, there described as a 'cake mould' (1940, 293, pl 93).

A PESTLE AND A SCOURER

<S120> Stone pestle (Fig 178)
A<1777>, A[500]; period P1, OA11
Rubbing stone (pestle). A natural ovoid, reddish, very fine-grained ? quartzitic sandstone pebble (identified by Ian M Betts), 70 x 32 x 27mm, with one end rubbed flat and traces of bright red material around edge.

Presumably used as a crusher/mixer for the pigment ?vermilion (cinnabar or red mercuric sulphide, not analysed) for manuscript decoration or mural painting (see Pritchard 1991, 170–1, fig 3.53 for two 12th-century oyster shells found in the City in domestic contexts and containing vermilion; and eg the palettes from Merton Priory: Egan 2007, 223, <S33>–<S35>).

<S120>

<S112>   <S113>   <S114>   <S115>

Fig 177 Maker's marks <S112>–<S115> on iron knives (scale 2:1)

Fig 178 Stone pestle <S120> (from OA11, period P1) (scale c 1:2)

<S121> Copper-alloy scourer
(Fig 27)
A<895>, A[1124]; period M4, B7
Brush, a group of wires, L 56mm, gauge 0.42mm, U-bent at top (some at bottom too) and bound together near top by multiply looped and twisted strand of similar gauge; strands at the scouring end are bent over from use. The bundle would presumably have been mounted into a (?wooden) handle.

This robust brush could have had a number of potential uses in everyday cleaning, perhaps for cooking vessels or in manufacture; it may have been specifically for use on metals.

Personal items

DRESS ACCESSORIES

<S122> Copper-alloy pin
A<1093>, A[2863]; period M9, OA6
L 73mm, visible part of head appears to be a cap hammered for attachment.

<S123> Copper-alloy buckle
A<2154>, A[253]; period M8, B10
Presumably a buckle frame: expands with rebates to outside edge 25 x 44mm; the bar seems to be separate.

Apparently a small version of the T-shaped frames usually of a large size appropriate for horse harness (cf Egan 1995a, 59–61, nos 40 and 47 fig 45, the former from a deposit attributed to the late 13th/early 14th century).

<S124> Copper-alloy buckle
(Fig 95)
A<2802>, A[972]; period M9, B9
Rectangular buckle frame 35 x 22mm, with slightly convex outer edge; cast pin, which is incomplete and fixed on what appears to be one of the sides, has excess metal from the casting still blocking some of the loop.
?Unused.

<S125> Copper-alloy buckle
(Fig 95)
A<374>, A[+]; -, -
Sub-circular buckle frame in the form of a five-petalled rose, Diam 33mm, with central bar; pin missing.
Presumably 16th century (cf Margeson 1993, 28–9, no. 157 fig 15; Egan and Forsyth 1997, 217).

<S126> Copper-alloy buckle
A<880>, A[1]; -, - (1984 site clearance)
Double-loop frame, the smaller, internal loop being rectangular and the outer one oval, 21 x 32mm, pin missing (a simpler version of Egan and Pritchard 1991, 102–3, no. 472, fig 65, with references to others).

The form has been found on several religious house sites in London and elsewhere (Merton Priory, St Augustine's Abbey, Sandwell Priory), as well as in secular contexts (Egan 2007, 228–9, <S226>).

<S127> Copper-alloy buckle
A<522>, A[2923]; -, -
Circular, Diam 43mm; cast pin has notched grip near loop (see Egan and Pritchard 1991, 57–8, fig 36 no. 32).

<S128> Copper-alloy strapend
(Fig 95)
A<524>, A[972]; period M9, B9
Sheet front or back plate from composite strapend, 37 x 17mm; concave inner edge, curving sides and terminal circle; holes for two rivets (cf Egan and Pritchard 1991, 140–1, no. 652 fig 92; this unstratified accessory has a forked spacer).

<S129> Copper-alloy strapend
A<516>, A[972]; period M9, B9
Composite strapend, 17 x 16mm; slightly tapering sheet front and back plates with moulded inner edges; the front one has decoratively bevelled sides; both plates are centrally roughly pierced and have crudely engraved pairs of lines at the top and diagonally. Both have a central terminal broken off; three rivets; traces of leather strap survive.

The central piercing (possibly an indication this is from a book) is paralleled on several rectangular clasp/strap mounts. Cf <S131> and <S132>. The decoration on some examples of both categories of mounts, found together, seems to form a continuing combined motif, emphasising the connection.

<S130> Copper-alloy strapend
(Fig 95)
A<533>, A[972]; period M9, B9
Front sheet from composite, circular strapend, Diam 26mm; circular aperture at top, with angled groove; holes for two rivets; dented from a hard knock in the middle (cf Egan and Pritchard 1991, 140–1, nos 648–9 fig 92, from contexts assigned to c 1270–c 1400).

The grooved aperture in the present one (which these parallels lack) seems to have been common in the late 14th century but may go into the 16th century.

<S131> Copper-alloy strapend
A<562>, A[3008]; period M9, OA6
Sheet (?front) plate with round end and concave top edge, 31 x 15mm; hole for rivet; now-black coating on one face. Cf <S129>.

The coating suggests this is from the late 15th century.

<S132> Copper-alloy strapend
A<404>, A[4159]; period P1, OA12
Sheet front and back plates with cast forked spacer, 43 x 18mm. Both plates have concave attachment edges with central leaf-like cut-outs and taper towards a terminal roundel. The two rivets survive. Cf <S129>.

An elegant variant on a common form.

<S133> Copper-alloy strapend
A<994>, A[1]; -, - (1984 site clearance)
Rectangular, 21 x 8mm; front and back plates and one tapered side piece survive, along with the separate rivet.

A simpler version of Egan and Pritchard 1991, 136–7, nos 623–9 fig 89 (all of which have parallel-edged strips at the sides).

<S134> Copper-alloy girdle mount
A<393>, A[972]; period M9, B9
Cast, robust circular mount, Diam 39mm, with single, integral rivet; sexfoil in three-dimensionally rendered hexagram, foliate motifs in the angles. Plain border; traces of gilding.

A well-made accessory, presumably for a girdle, and with a motif considered apotropaic in the Middle Ages (cf Egan and Pritchard 1991, 203, no. 1094 pl 4f for the motif, and 181–4, nos 933 pl 2 for a somewhat more

Fig 179 Copper-alloy mount <S135> (from OA9, period P1) (scale c 1:1)

expensive, armorial version of this category of mount). Alternatively, it is possible that this mount was from the centre of a mazer bowl.

<S135> Copper-alloy mount
(Fig 179)
A<567>, A[3974]; period P1, OA9
Sheet squared quatrefoil 18 x 18mm; bevelled edges; hole for attachment.
Possibly a book mount.

<S136> Copper-alloy strap loop
A<820>, A[1134]; period P1, OA11
Rectangular frame 21 x 14mm (strap W up to 17mm); central ridge along top; off-centred hole for missing separate (?internal) rivet.

See Egan and Pritchard 1991, 231–2, nos 1248–9 fig 147, both from deposits assigned to the late 14th century.

<S137> Copper-alloy purse frame
(Fig 95)
A<839>, A[972]; period M9, B9
Incomplete purse/pouch frame (in two pieces), c 85 x 65mm: strip with pipe edge along one side and suspension hole at present ends (broken off at both); series of holes along the whole length (for attachment of the pouch); all bent into appropriately baggy shape. Not a high-quality item; perhaps discarded when the second of the end loops became broken as a result of sustained use.

<S138> Copper-alloy purse frame
A<618>, A[3460]; period P1, OA9
Fragment of rod-like, curving frame, surviving L 47mm; off-centred, pierced hole for attachment; oblique grooves along opposite side; traces possibly of now-black coating; ?cut partly through at one end.

<S139> Copper-alloy purse hanger
(Fig 95)
A<386>, A[4151]; period P1, OA12

Incomplete pendent bar, L 42mm, retaining one of original pair of bent ends with expanded terminals.

Cf Egan and Pritchard 1991, 223–4, fig 140, with references to other London finds.

<S140> Copper-alloy clasp or strap plate (Fig 180)
A<394>, A[2219]; -, -
Sub-rectangular front plate 36 x 28mm; doubly concave ends with central V notches; sides each have paired transverse notches flanking a longer bevel; the plain back plate is slightly larger.

<S141> Copper-alloy clasp or strap plate (Fig 180)
A<1550>, A[4197]; -, -
Sub-rectangular front plate 35 x 20mm; ends asymmetrically engrailed and with central round apertures having angled grooves; the similar back plate lacks the grooves and shows marked abrasion on one side of the hole.

<S142> Copper-alloy clasp or strap plate (Fig 180)

A<866>, A[1]; -, - (1984 site clearance)
Sub-rectangular front plate 33 x 22mm; triply engrailed ends with angled grooves in central concavities; engraved border lines at sides with transverse hatching. The incomplete, plain back plate is slightly smaller.

Presumably later medieval.

<S143> Copper-alloy brooch (Fig 96)
A<312>, A[2349]; period P1, OA12
Corroded, circular, Diam 31mm. Engraved zigzag breaks the frame into a running series of triangles, the outer ones being hatched. Constriction for missing pin.

Probably residual from the 14th century since the fashion for circular brooches of this metal seems to have been coming to an end by c 1400 in London.

<S144> Copper-alloy finger ring (Fig 96)
A<517>, A[972]; period M9, B9

D-section finger ring, Diam 21mm; retains most of gilding.

With the gilding intact this thick ring would have looked like an expensive accessory.

<S145> Gold finger ring
A<811>, A[2064]; -, -
Plain, wire-like ring, Diam 21mm, Wt 0.7g, slight thickening at point of joining of the two original ends.

This very small ring, not weighing even one gram and about as thin as it is possible to get with one intended for wear, is in the medieval tradition which seems to have been superseded by a more substantial style as the precious metal became significantly more widely affordable in the post-medieval period (cf Egan and Forsyth 1997, 229). There is a parallel from a burial assigned to c 1220–c 1350 in the north transept of the abbey of St Mary Stratford Langthorne (Essex), to the north-east of London (Barber et al 2004, 152, <R80>).

<S146> Copper-alloy button
A<831>, A[131]; period M9,

D4/OA9
Biconvex head (probably solid to judge from the X-ray plate), Diam 12mm. Separate wire loop, traces of tin coating which in parts retains a mirror-like surface.

Cf Egan and Pritchard 1991, 276–7, nos 1384–95, fig 178, which are attributed to the mid 13th/early15th centuries.

<S147> Copper-alloy lacechape (Fig 95)
A<2451>, A[2937]; period M9, OA6
L 51mm, Diam c 6.5–c 2mm, edge-to-edge join.

Larger and more acutely angled than the great majority of these finds.

<S148> Copper-alloy dress hook (Fig 95)
A<902>, A[1]; -, - (1984 site clearance)
Copper-alloy composite, wire accessory; L 35 x 18mm. Central, slightly offset hook, looped around bent triangular frame with recurved ends and lengths of thinner wire spiralled around (cf <S150> from A[972] and Egan and Forsyth 1997, 234, fig 15.10).

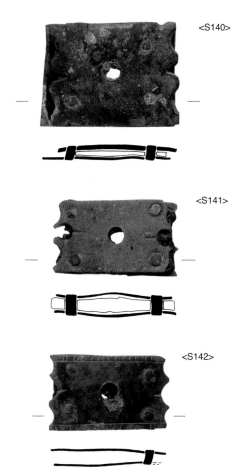

<S140>

<S141>

<S142>

Fig 180 Clasp or strap plates <S140> and <S141> (unphased), <S142> (unstratified) (scale c 1:1)

PENDANTS

<S149> Copper-alloy pendant (Fig 96)
A<521>, A[972]; period M9, B9
Stamped-sheet pinnate leaf, 29 x 10mm, with loop attached to looped-wire fragment.

An apparently secular decoration; the high point of the medieval fashion for wearing leaf pendants came before the late 15th century, according to Scott (1980, 36; cf Egan and Pritchard 1991, 217–20, no. 1188, figs 136–7 and pl 3 for ones from the early part of that century).

<S150> Copper-alloy wire pendant (Fig 181)
A<472>, A[972]; period M9, B9
Elaborate, composite wire pendant, overall 35 x 12mm: S-link holds three loops bound together with a separate, densely spiralled coil. Each of the loops continues into two strands (one of the six is incomplete), each sleeved into dense coils to either side of three larger spirals (which are themselves made up of more-open

coils) – the six strands expand outwards to the middle and all come together again at the bottom, into a further densely

<S150>

Fig 181 Copper-alloy wire pendant <S150> (from B9, period M9) (scale c 2:1)

spiralled coil, to emerge as recurved loops; four of these (presumably all of them originally) each hold a freely swinging wire loop, which terminates in a flattened sub-lozenge pendant.

This complicated, delicate object, actually very simply made from a minimum of 16 components and probably cheap to purchase, would have caught the light with every movement of the wearer. It seems a rather unlikely trinket to be found in a religious establishment; it was perhaps intended for a young child. (Cf Egan and Forsyth 1997, 234, fig 15.10.)

GROOMING TOOLS

<S153> Copper-alloy earpick (Fig 99)
A<852>, A[2863]; period M9, OA6
Twisted wire with end loop, L 29mm.

<S154> Copper-alloy wire earpick (Fig 99)
A<1089>, A[972]; period M9, B9
Earpick: spiralled, copper-alloy wire with end loop, L 25mm (the identification seems probable, even though this could be one part of an object similar to <S156> and <S192>. Cf <S153> and <S155> and Egan and Pritchard 1991, 380 nos 1764–9.

<S155> Copper-alloy wire earpick (Fig 99)

<S151> Copper-alloy cross (Fig 96)
A<913>, A[4154]; period M9, B9
Equal-armed cross with lobed terminals and suspension loop, 25 x 19mm; traces of gilding.
Cf Griffiths 1995, nos 67–9.

<S152> Copper-alloy pendent bell (Fig 96)
A<406>, A[2706]; period P1, OA9
Pendent bell, rumbler form: elongated and tapering to loop at top; L 40mm, max Diam 9mm. Made from single, hammered and folded piece of ?copper; most of surface gilding survives; pea present (?stone).
Probably from a multi-part pendant.

A<1090>, A[3519]; period P1, OA9
Copper alloy. Twisted wire with end loop, L 27mm. (Cf <S153> and <S154>).

<S156> Copper-alloy wire toothpick (Fig 99)
A<804>, A[972]; period M9, B9
Toothpick of copper-alloy wire, two parts: incomplete, hammered curved hook continuing with spirals and loop total L 21mm linked to incomplete part consisting of curving spirals, L 39mm.
Cf Egan and Pritchard 1991, 378, fig 251 bottom left for a somewhat similar item of sheeting. Cf <S192>.

Tools and production items

TOOLS

<S157> Quernstone
A<2075>, A[3405]; period M4, OA2
Pinkish, coarse millstone grit, probably originating in northern England (identified by David Williams). Edge fragment, of lower stone, Diam c ?220mm, Th 28mm; tooling on upper face, both surfaces worn.
The stone is an uncommon one for this use in London, but it is known both from the Roman and medieval periods.

<S158> Quernstone
A<2563>, A[520]; period P1, OA11
As <S157> (including reuse), but

plano-concave. Diam c 280mm, part of hole for central spindle survives. There is an extended, rounded pit on one face, possibly for a manual handle. Worn on both faces (it was presumably turned over during the period of use) and also on the outside rim, which has areas of an almost mirror-like surface on the high points (to either side of a less finely smoothed band along the centre) from rotary abrasion, which has removed all but faint traces of earlier tooling.
This fragment is of a rather small diameter and the wear on the rim (quite uncharacteristic of the normal use of this kind of stone) is not readily paralleled either in its

location or the extreme smoothness. Polishing to the sides of a less markedly smoothed area is perhaps consistent with a secondary (or even tertiary) use ? as a flywheel, with a broad (?leather) band here to transfer the rotary motion, the main tension being at the centre but with enough play at the sides to produce, over a sustained period, the pattern of wear now evident. The time at which this object saw the usage that produced this effect is uncertain. (Thanks to Richenda Goffin for discussion of this object.)

<S159> Stone hone (Fig 29)
A<1774>, A[1045]; period M4, OA2
An incomplete hone made out of a very fine-grained, slightly micaceous, brownish limestone. One surviving end, 82+ x 25 x 17mm, neatly bevelled and evenly tapering.

<S160> Stone hone
A<778>, A[270]; period M7, D2
Hone made out of a fine-grained, whitish-brown schist. Incomplete, rectangular, with one original end surviving, 59 x 17 x 12mm.

<S161> Iron shears
A<1106>, A[3008]; period M9, OA6
Incomplete, loop missing. Surviving L 120mm; blades taper from W 8mm and their inner ends are shaped so that together they make a trefoil-headed void; angled tips.
Cf Cowgill et al 1987, no. 335 fig 72, attributed to the late 14th century, for a similar shaping of the blades. This relatively delicate tool was presumably for cutting human hair, possibly but by no means certainly tonsures in the religious establishment.

<S162> Copper-alloy needle (Fig 182)
A<504>, A[1573]; period M2, OA1
L 91mm, punched eye is split open; filed triangular-section point. The form is familiar from the late 13th century onwards (Egan 1998a, nos 838ff).
Presumed to be intrusive in this context.

<S163> Copper-alloy needle (Fig 183)
A<506>, A[972]; period M9, B9
Needle; L 37mm; blunter point than is usual. Presumably resharpened after more than half the original length was broken off (cf <S162>).
No parallel for the adaptation of this inexpensive category of implement has been traced.

<S164> Copper-alloy dividers (Fig 103)
A<555>, A[972]; period M9, B9
Dividers; L 92mm. The arms differ in that one forks to accommodate the other, single, one when folded away. Both have lozenge-shaped grips flanked at each end by knops and taper, offset-hexagonal in section, to the points; the iron rivet

<S162>

<S163>

Fig 182 Copper-alloy needle <S162> (from OA1, period M2) (scale c 1:1)

Fig 183 Copper-alloy needle <S163> (from B9, period M9) (scale c 1:1)

has rusted.

Cf Henig 1988, 179–80, no. 6 for a similar pair with grips of a different shape from St Augustine's, Canterbury. This well-made tool would have had a number of possible precision uses: measuring architectural plans or setting out ornate windows, for example.

EVIDENCE FOR METALWORKING

<S165> Stone lead-working mould A<3042>, A[1]; -, - (1984 site clearance)
Part of one element of a ?two-part mould, in fairly soft, fine-grained mudstone/siltstone (identified by Ian M Betts). 228 x (surviving) 150mm; flat inner surface with ingate forking into three channels (the outer pair give an ogival outline, maximum surviving dimensions c 130 x 127mm); roughly shaped outer side, the top 50mm of which has been smoothed. Presumably for casting lead (Egan 1998a, on nos 49–53).

This kind of stone is widely available in lowland England. The darkening of the surface is not restricted to the casting area and so there is no clear indication of whether or not the mould was used. The smoothed area on the outer side was presumably for ease of handling or to facilitate wiring together with the other part for casting. The products remain unidentified: it is tempting to see this as some kind of proforma frame into which glass and leading details could be set, the complete unit then being placed into a window space, as a means of mass production for installing glass into repeated, ogival-headed window-light apertures. The practicalities of this, however, are extremely doubtful and no corresponding frame of leading has been recognised among the recovered assemblages from the site, or apparently elsewhere.

<S166> Ceramic metalworking mould (Fig 105)
A<2056>, A[3746]; -, -
Fragment of one slab element of a ?two-part mould, with external luting, surviving 82 x 45mm. Tapered ingate at top, for producing four ?rings, Diam successively 16mm, 15mm, 18mm and 23mm, where it is broken off; the inner surface of the slab part is blackened (reduced) from firing, in contrast with the light pinkish (oxidised) remainder. As there is no connecting groove between the rings, the flow of metal through the mould must have been along channels in the corresponding, missing part of the mould. The products, if they were plain rings, seem more likely to have been buckle frames than for curtains (see Egan and Pritchard 1991, 57–9 for the latter).

This isolated piece of evidence for the specific products presumably of a local copper-alloy foundry (clay moulds being preferentially used for this metal, Egan 1996, 87–8) is not in itself immediately suggestive of manufacture at a religious institution. The religious context, nevertheless, seems definitive (see buckle <S124> which appears possibly unfinished, from A[972], period M9). Some confirmation for the production of everyday metal items within a religious complex in the medieval period is given by the metalworking watermills and workshops excavated at Bordesley Abbey (Astill 1993).

<S167> Scrap copper-alloy sheeting (Fig 184)
A<867>, A[3503]; period P1, OA9
Three pieces of scrap copper-alloy sheeting: a bent strip in two parts, L 100mm, W 4mm. A sub-rectangular sheet, 14 x 9mm, pierced near one end. One irregular, symmetrical cut-out with faint parallel ?guidelines on one face; perhaps diagnostic of a particular component or product.

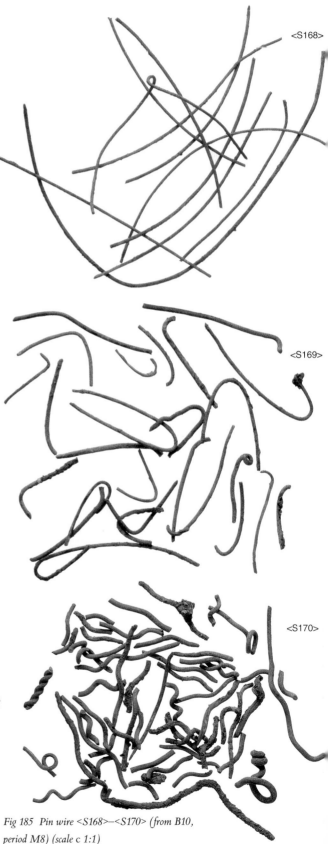

<S167>

Fig 184 Scrap copper-alloy sheeting <S167> (from OA9, period P1) (scale c 1:1)

The following lengths of copper-alloy wire <S168>–<S171> are all from a single context and may, like <S40> also from this context (above), be intrusive.

<S168> Copper-alloy pin wire (Fig 185)
A<857>, A[253]; period M8, B10

Hundreds of (fairly) straight and evenly curved lengths, gauges c 0.75–c 1.50mm, one

<S168>

<S169>

<S170>

Fig 185 Pin wire <S168>–<S170> (from B10, period M8) (scale c 1:1)

c 200mm (see <S169>), L up to
150mm.

<S169> Copper-alloy pin wire
(Fig 185)
A<3563>, A[253]; period M8, B10
Tens of pieces of wire with U
bends: gauges c 0.75–1.10mm;
(some or all probably more fully
surviving versions <S168>).

<S170> Copper-alloy wire (Fig 185)
A<1000>, A[253]; period M8, B10
Tens of short lengths of wire,
gauges c 1.05–1.75mm, all loosely
spiralled (some tighter than the
majority, one of two-ply);
surviving L up to 50mm.

<S171> Copper-alloy wire
(Fig 186)
A<3564>, A[253]; period M8, B10
Wire L 12mm, longitudinally
grooved and twisted at one end,
gauge c 0.75mm.
    Possibly waste from adapting
wire for precious metal inlay
(? for inferior quality cloth-of-gold
or -silver).

<S171>

Fig 186 Copper-alloy wire <S171>
(from B10, period M8) (scale c 2:1)

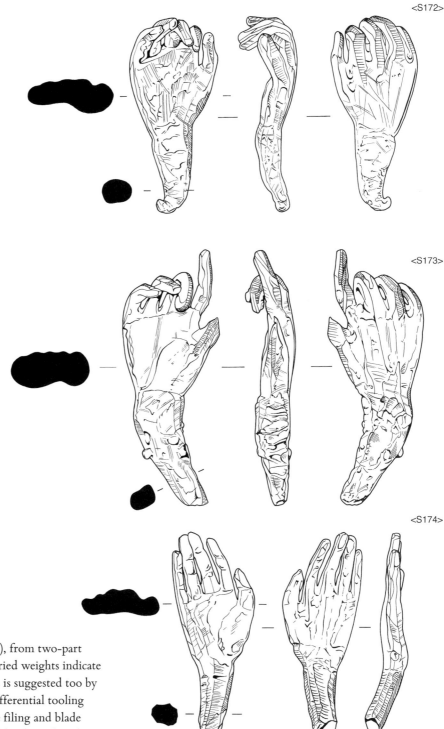

<S172>

<S173>

<S174>

Fig 187 Lead master forms <S172>–<S174> (from OA6, period M9) (scale 1:1)

The following three hands (<S172>–<S174>), from two-part
moulds, are clearly related, though their varied weights indicate
they are probably from different moulds (as is suggested too by
their slightly diverse dimensions, though differential tooling
accounts for some of the variation). Surface filing and blade
marks show there has been some individual finishing, but this
need not have been anything more than the usual touching up
needed for most fine metalwork following casting. <S174> is
less-fully finished than the other two, though the mould seam is
still present on <S172> and all of them could have benefited
from further attention. It seems more likely that the different
positions of the fingers are the result of bending the soft metal
cast in one basic form, than that these variations came directly
from moulds for different poses. This would allow wide scope
for artistic variation in the final product(s) for a relatively little
initial outlay of precision work.
    Accomplished pieces (Fig 106; Fig 187), these are probably
master forms or *patrons* (see Egan 1996, 92, fig 6) made for the
serial manufacture of final products from moulds of clay, into

which the lead hands would be pressed in order to be able in
turn to reproduce their shape in a metal with a higher melting
point than lead, such as copper alloy or, perhaps more likely in
the present case, silver. It looks as if these particular items were
discarded without having been finished to the point at which
they would have been used. Satisfactory products would
presumably have been incorporated into high-quality figurines
which would have been assembled from several component
parts, of a single metal or a variety of materials (eg a wooden

body). These end products may well, in the religious house, have been devotional figures of saints etc (the attitudes of <S172> and <S173> may perhaps be seen respectively as holding an object/beckoning and pointing).

These remarkably detailed and unusual finds vividly illustrate something of the possible working methods of skilled medieval craftsmen in metal, whether the final products were for the abbey itself or for sale to a wider public.

<S172> Lead mould (Fig 106; Fig 187)
A<540>, A[2863]; period M9, OA6
Human right hand, held cupped: L 51mm, W of palm 23mm, Th 7mm and Wt 48g. Casting seam removed and stem trimmed.

<S173>Lead mould (Fig 106; Fig 187)
A<539>, A[2937]; period M9, OA6
Similar to preceding item but fingers in pointing gesture and some dimensions are larger: L 68mm, width of palm 22mm, Th 9mm, and Wt 64g. Stem untrimmed, casting seam removed, thumb cut off with a blade. The last piece of damage may have occasioned the discarding of this item. (Two lead offcuts <1704>, possibly from one or two irregular ingots, were

found in the same deposit).

<S174> Lead mould (Fig 106; Fig 187)
A<541>, A[3165]; period M9, OA6
Similar to preceding items, but hand held flat: L 54mm (including tool-tapered arm/stem), W of palm 22mm, Th 6mm, Wt 30g. Casting seam partly removed.

<S175> Bead-making waste panel (Fig 107)
A<939>, A<2392>, A[234]; period P1, OA10
Joining parts of a broken waste panel, together 155 x 25mm, trimmed flat from a cattle or horse metapodial and from which eight circular objects Diam c 13mm have been cut by turning from both sides. (May be post-Dissolution in date.)

Numismatic items

COIN

<S176> Silver coin (Fig 54)
A<2651>, A[1249]; period M7, B8
Base silver, irregular flan, Diam 18mm, Wt 0.85g; Flemish 'pollard' (imitation with bare-headed potentate of sterling penny of Edward I): uncrowned head, saltire cross to sides of drapery, [+M]ARCH(IO)[N](A)[MVRC] around // long cross with pellets in

three quarters, star in fourth, G(C)[O] [MES] (F)LA D(RE) around.
Denier of Gui of Dampierre (1279–1305), for Flanders and Namur (cf Mayhew 1983, 33, type 17, 17a and b on pl 4, the former in a London collection; ibid, 255 notes several of these found in Britain).

JETTONS

<S177> Copper-alloy jetton
A<438>, A[277]; period M8, OA9
Diam 21mm, multiply stabbed and three holes around perimeter. Shield with star over three fleurs-de-lis (quatrefoil) AVE MATIA [sic] (star) PL...A (star) B around // central quatrefoil, (cross) fleurdelisée, letters over stars in angles A, T, A, .., all in quatrefoil.
?Probably late 14th-/early 15th-century French, or could be Tournai; no parallel traced. It

is just possible that this was reused as a balance pan, the holes being for strings and the stabbing being to give a dished profile.

<S178> Copper-alloy jetton
A<2660>, A[972]; period M9, B9
Copper-alloy jetton, Diam 22mm, rough: king standing in canopy, saltires and pellets to sides // triply-stranded cross fleurdelisée, fleurs-de-lis in angles, all in

squared quatrefoil tressure, series of Us around.
English, c 1350–c 1400. Cf Mitchiner 1988, 123, no. 277 (not a precise parallel).

<S179> Copper-alloy jetton
A<2667>, A[3460]; period P1, OA9
Diam 26mm. Shield with arms of France modern, trefoil with annulet above and below to sides, crown BOLE:HVVEOL:BEOLE:BOB: around // orb with cross in ornate border, BONOR:BOVVNOE: VREE: around.
Nuremberg, nonsense-legend issue, c 1500–25. Cf Mitchiner 1988, 357, no. 1082.

<S180> Copper-alloy jetton
A<2652>, A[569]; period P1, OA11
Incomplete flan, Diam 23mm: shield with six fleurs-de-lis, grouped pellets around // (crude) cross fleurdelisée with circle, pellets inside and outside.
French, king's administration, c 1285–1325. Cf Mitchiner 1988, 155, nos 356–7.

<S181> Copper-alloy jetton
A<2656>, A[1108]; period P1, OA11
Incomplete, bent flan, corroded, Diam 19mm: round human/simian or leonine face, pellets in border // triply-stranded cross fleurdelisée and (pellets) with (?saltires) around, saltires (etc) in border.
English, c 1302–50. ? Cf Mitchiner 1988, 175ff (no precise parallel).

<S182> Copper-alloy jetton
A<2658>, A[2406]; period P1, OA11
Diam 25mm. King standing in canopy holding sceptre with fleur-de-lis, AVE M+ +ARIA around, line of trefoils in exergue // central quatrefoil, triply-stranded cross fleurdelisée, flower-in-vase motifs in angles, all in quatrefoil, +A+ +V+ +E+ +M+ around.
French, c 1326–50. Cf Mitchiner 1988, 164, no. 403.

<S183> Copper-alloy jetton
A<2663>, A[2406]; period P1, OA11
Diam 27.5mm, centrally holed by square-sectioned object, crude: shield with arms of France modern, pellets around, X AVE

MARIAoGRACIAo around // central quatrefoil, triply-stranded cross fleurdelisée, .V. in angles, all in quatrefoil, ·Os around.
Tournai stock issue, c 1415–1500. Cf Mitchiner 1988, 227, no. 684.

<S184> Copper-alloy jetton
A<2662>, A[4159]; period P1, OA12
Diam 26mm. Shield with three fleurs-de-lis and base of a fourth, flower-and-leaves motif above and to sides, +AVE MARIAxGRACIAxDN around // central quatrefoil, triply-stranded cross fleurdelisée, ornate ?plant motif in angles, all in quatrefoil, .(A). .V. .E. .M. around.
French, Charles VI, c 1385–c 1422. Cf Mitchiner 1988, 178, no. 457a (not a precise parallel).

<S185> Copper-alloy jetton
A<396>, A[1]; -, - (1984 site clearance)
Corrosion holes, Diam 19mm. Shield with lion rampant, annulets above and to sides, border of saltires alternate with sexfoils // cross moline with annulets and pellets, border of annulets alternate with sexfoils.
English, c 1302–50. Cf Mitchiner 1988, 112 nos 201ff (no precise parallel).

<S186> Copper-alloy jetton
A<2665>, A[1]; -, - (1984 site clearance)
Diam 25.5mm. IHS (horizontal cross on H) on field of cinquefoils, three fleurs-de-lis above and one below // similar device to that on first side, but two fleurs-de-lis below.
?French, 15th century. No parallel traced.

<S187> Copper-alloy jetton
A<2670>, A[1]; -, - (1984 site clearance)
Diam 26mm, some wear: orb with cross in ornate border, flower VEAV(broken O)ME repeated three times around // haloed lion of St Mark with bible, crown GRVE:GLR(broken O)..IV(II):EV(broken O)MEN.. around.
Nuremberg nonsense-legend issue, c 1500–70. Cf Mitchiner 1988, 360, nos 1097ff. See also <S178>.

Weaponry

<S188> Iron arrowhead
A<3024>, A[3043]; period P1,
OA9
Corroded: socketed arrowhead, L
82mm, L of socket c 50mm, W at
barbs 55mm. A large, relatively
heavy arrow, probably suitable for
war and hunting.

Arrows are surprisingly common
finds at some religious house sites.

Miscellaneous items

<S189> Copper-alloy mount
(Fig 188)
A<501>, A[972]; period M9, B9
Copper alloy strip, with bevelled
sides and W 7mm, bent
approximately into circle Diam
c 60mm; broken off at constriction
at both ends where it is bent
outwards; central hole near one
end.

Presumably a mount of some
kind.

<S190> Lead trough (Fig 84)
A<545>, A[2349]; period P1,
OA12
Lead, D-shaped trough with flaring
rim, H 39mm, 52 x 35mm. Crude
decoration, on round side a shield
with lion rampant in reserve on
cross-hatching. Flanked along one
edge with triangles alternately
plain and cross-hatched, and on
straight side a shield with cross, all
areas being variously cross-hatched.
Trimmed with a blade on base and
at one point along mould seam
(possibly neatening following
casting). Part of the rim on the
straight side has been cut down.

A feeding trough for a caged
bird, several of these are known

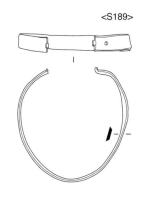

Fig 188 Copper-alloy mount <S189>
(from B9, period M9) (1:2)

from London, including an
example from the latest phase of
the religious house of St John
Clerkenwell (Sloane and Malcolm
2004, 360, <S107>).

<S191> Ivory object
A<957>, A[972]; period M9, B9
Fragment 16 x 7mm of flat,
neatly finished ivory object;
sections of one curved and one
straight side survive and parts
of two ?holes and an oblique
groove.

Dissolution and later period

Objects from Dissolution and immediately post-Dissolution
clearance and demolition contexts, presumed to be either from
the lifetime of the monastic house or from the Dissolution
phase, are included in the preceding section. The following
items come from Dissolution and later contexts, c 1538–c 1650
(period P1). A few are certainly post-Dissolution (beaker
<S193>, jetton <S200>). The others come from the area north of
the former chapel (B1), the former cemetery area; after the
Dissolution this became gardens (OA9 and OA10, period P1)
and formed part of Pope's mansion which occupied the site
(Chapter 5). These objects form an interesting group of
production items – pinners' bones, finished and unfinished pins,
wire, and a lead cloth seal – and occurred in various pit fills,
contexts with only small amounts of pot and thus limited
dating evidence: in Open Area 9 A[3033] fill (which also

contained window glass) of linear pit or depression A[3034]
over an earlier burial; two rectangular ?ash pits A[3059], with
pottery dated c 1480–c 1550; A[3873] fill of shallow amorphous
pit A[3874]; and in Open Area 10, A[3035] fill of a horticultural
trench, with pottery dated c 1550–c 1600 (Chapter 5.2). These
items probably derive from activities in the mid to later 16th
century, perhaps during the Dissolution and immediately post-
Dissolution phase, but may possibly date from the period of
monastic occupation.

GROOMING TOOL

<S192> Copper-alloy toothpick
(Fig 99)
A<847>, A[3035]; period P1,
OA10
L 78mm; twisted, two-ply wire
shaft, hammered into flat tab at one
end and hook at the other, where
there is also a loop for attachment;
tin coating. The hook, and possibly
the tab too, was probably for
cleaning the teeth.

A neater and better-made
version of <S156>. From a
horticultural trench fill, but
possibly of monastic date.

GLASS VESSEL

<S193> Glass beaker
A<1663>, A[1]; -, - (1984 site
clearance)
Fragment of vertical rim from
crystal-glass beaker with twisted
latticinio rods marvered in
vertically (the white threads
have largely decayed away on
the outside surface, making most
of the rods appear obliquely
hatched by transmitted light);
Diam c 70mm.

Late 16th century, probably a
London product.

PRODUCTION ITEMS

<S194> Lead cloth seal (Fig 189)
A<436>, A[3033]; period P1, OA9
Incomplete two-disc, quality-
control and tax-receipt lead seal for
a textile; Diam c 23mm // missing;
imprint from textile with five
threads per 5mm in one system and
much finer in the other. Crown
over portcullis (large grid of 3 x ?3
openings) (?no legend) // (on rivet)
part of arms of England, foliate
motif to side (the arms are well
engraved).

No certain parallel is known for
this alnage seal, which perhaps may
be a London issue (see Egan 1995b
for the use of lead seals in the
industrial regulation and royal
taxation of the cloth industry).
The seeming absence of any legend
is unusual.

<S195> Pinner's bone (Fig 116)
A<2288>, A[2613]; period P1,
OA9
Cattle metapodial, drilled
lengthways and cut off at proximal
end to L 80mm; the stump
trimmed into an irregular
pentagon, each facet having one or
two grooves lengthways.

<S196> Pinner's bone (Fig 116)
A<960>, A[3033]; period P1, OA9
Cattle metapodial, drilled lengthways
and cut off at proximal end to L
82mm; the stump trimmed into an
irregular hexagon, each facet having
a groove lengthways; stained green
at both ends from copper.

Ten pins, A<1094>, A<435> and
two pieces of wire, A<339>,
A<346> were recovered from the
same deposit.

<S197> Pinner's bone (Fig 116)
A<961>, A[3059]; period P1, OA9
Cattle metapodial, twice roughly
?drilled through lengthways (the
holes joining at the distal end) and
cut short at both ends to L 58mm;
both ends trimmed to irregular
polygons (less finished at proximal
end), the facets of which have
grooves lengthways; green staining
at both ends and in centre,
presumably from copper. Wire
<349> came from the same deposit.

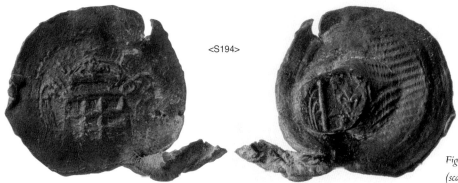

<S194>

Fig 189 Lead cloth seal <S194> (from OA9, period P1) (scale c 2:1)

<S198> Copper-alloy pins A<473>, A[3873]; period P1, OA9 Group of 29 pins, heads where present are of wire: 11 finished, L vary between 22mm and 31mm; one sharpened and with head but split at point, L 25mm; six apparently unsharpened shafts with heads, L all 27–28mm (one with head displaced on shaft); 11 headless and apparently unsharpened shafts and two fragments, L vary between 21mm and 39mm.

Presumably a manufacturing assemblage including uncompleted components, discarded misworkings and lost finished pins (cf Egan 1996, 90–1, fig 4C for the stages represented).

<S199> Copper-alloy pins A<342A–E>, A[3035]; period P1, OA10 Five pins: L 28mm, 32mm, 34mm, 42mm (head damaged) and 45mm (small head on relatively thick shank). From a horticultural trench fill, but possibly of monastic date.

JETTON

<S200> Copper-alloy jetton A<2675>, A[+]; -, - Diam 28mm. Bearded man casting accounts on an ornate-legged table, RECHEN MEISTER around top // alphabet, cinquefoil WVLF cinquefoil LAVFER cinquefoil IN cinquefoil NVRMBERG cinquefoil (R according to Mitchiner parallel), Wolf Laufer I (master maker 1544, d 1610; cf Mitchiner 1988, 473, no. 1671).

7.8   Animal bone

Alan Pipe and Kevin Rielly with Charlotte Ainsley

Methodology

For the hand-collected material well-preserved context groups containing at least 1.0kg of bone were selected for full recording. All selected hand-collected bone from the site was catalogued directly on to the MOLA database. The majority of the material was catalogued as individual bone records except when extreme fragmentation and/or poor condition prevented accurate identification of taxon and/or skeletal element. In such cases, fragments were assigned to approximate identification levels, for example 'sheep-sized mammal' and 'long bone fragment', and entered as multiple records. Whenever possible, however, all fragments were assigned to species and skeletal element using MOL reference collections together with external reference collections, for example that of the Natural History Museum, London, as required. Bone atlases, particularly Cannon (1987), Cohen and Serjeantson (1996) and Schmid (1972) were also used. Each identifiable fragment was recorded in terms of weight (g), skeletal element, handedness, degree of completeness, modification (eg butchery marks, working, pathological change, gnawing and burning). Pathological changes were described and interpreted following Baker and Brothwell (1980). Evidence for age-at-death was recorded in terms of epiphysial fusion (interpreted after Schmid 1972; Wilson et al 1982; Amorosi 1989), and dental characteristics (after Payne 1973; Grant 1982). The detailed data are available in the archive.

Fragments not identifiable to species level were assigned to the 'next best' taxonomic group, for example Gadidae (cod family), or an approximate identification based on size and wall thickness (eg 'cattle-sized' mammal, 'chicken-/duck-sized' bird). Whenever possible, sex was determined from skeletal morphology, for example of the head and innominate (mammals), from presence/absence of metatarsal spur in galliform birds and presence of medullary bone (adult female birds). Whenever justified in terms of surface condition and fragmentation, fully fused bones were measured to the nearest 0.1mm using manual Vernier calipers and following the sequences and techniques of von den Driesch (1976). Estimated withers ('shoulder') heights for the major mammalian domesticates were calculated using conversion factors summarised by von den Driesch and Boessneck (1974). Each bone was described in terms of completeness and fragmentation using the zonal method of Rackham (1986).

The bulk-sampled deposits were wet-sieved using a modified Siraf-type tank fitted with 1.0mm and 0.25mm meshes to retain the residue and 'flot' fractions respectively. The residues were air-dried and then visually sorted for faunal remains. When time allowed, the bones were catalogued on to the MOLA database as used for the hand-collected material. In the case of the very large sieved groups, for example the fish assemblage from A[972] (B9, period M9), subsamples were taken as a proportion of the total sample weight and the fragments identified in terms of species, skeletal element, weight and fragment count and used to provide an estimate of the size and composition of the complete assemblage. These data were then entered on to paper record sheets and are available for consultation on request. As with the hand-collected material, an effort was made to identify as much of the assemblage to species level as possible. Where this was impracticable for reasons of morphology or fragmentation, material was assigned to an approximate level of identification, for example ?plaice/flounder (Pleuronectidae).

Distribution of the material

The following discussion considers the period distribution of the animal bone and the detailed composition of the group from A[972], dumping in the reredorter (B9, period M9) (Table 18). Discussion of the medieval diet is given in Chapter 4.3 ('Diet and food preparation').

Period M2, c AD 850–1050

The greater quantity of bones was found within the quarry pits and the recut fills of the large east–west Late Saxon ditch (OA1; Chapter 2.5, 'Archaeological evidence'). The quarry pits assemblage was dominated by cattle bones but also produced a substantial quantity of pig fragments, 31.3% of the total quarry pit cattle/sheep/pig group, where cattle and sheep/goat respectively provided 55.7% and 13.0%. There is a minor representation of other species, including a single fragment of a game species, roe deer, from a quarry pit.

Samples were taken from a number of ditch fills, all of which provided relatively small quantities of bone. The

Table 18 The species representation by fragment count of the hand-collected fish, amphibian, bird and mammal bone by period, together with the hand-collected and wet-sieved data for A[972]

Period	M2	M4	M5	M6	M7	M9	PI	Total M2–PI	M9 except A[972]	M9 A[972]	M9 A[972]
Species Common name	(hand)	(hand)	(hand)	(hand)	(hand)	(hand)	(hand)	(hand)	(hand)	(hand)	(wet-sieved) {491} + {502} + {503}
Fish											
Sturgeon	0	0	0	0	0	4	0	4	0	4	0
Salmon family	0	0	0	0	0	3	0	3	0	3	0
Pike	0	0	0	0	0	12	0	12	0	12	0
Smelt	0	0	0	0	0	0	0	0	0	0	**176
Herring	0	0	0	5	0	0	0	5	0	0	**277
Conger eel	0	0	0	1	0	18	0	19	0	18	0
Plaice/flounder	0	0	0	7	0	83	0	90	0	83	0
Mackerel	0	0	0	0	0	7	0	7	0	7	0
Eel	0	0	0	0	0	10	0	10	1	9	0
Sole	0	0	0	0	0	11	0	11	0	11	0
Bream	0	0	0	0	0	3	0	3	0	3	0
Cod family	0	0	0	9	0	452	1	462	5	447	3
Carp family	0	0	0	0	0	29	0	29	0	29	0
Roach	0	0	0	0	0	3	0	3	1	2	0
Carp	0	0	0	0	0	2	0	2	0	2	0
Gurnard	0	0	0	0	0	39	0	39	0	39	0
Fish, unidentified	0	0	0	3	0	0	0	3	0	0	400
Amphibian											
Frog/toad	0	0	0	2	0	2	0	4	0	2	0
Birds											
Chicken	9	6	16	51	2	546	26	656	37	509	18
Chicken-sized bird	3	3	4	12	0	256	2	280	24	232	15
Goose, domestic	13	1	3	12	0	106	7	142	43	63	2
Goose-sized bird	3	0	0	0	0	29	1	33	0	29	1
Mallard/domestic duck	1	0	3	3	0	37	3	47	22	15	0
Pigeon, domestic	0	0	0	0	0	23	0	23	0	23	0
Partridge, grey	0	0	0	1	0	7	0	8	1	6	0
Wood pigeon	0	0	0	0	0	7	0	7	1	6	0
Swan*	0	0	0	0	0	1	0	1	0	1	0
Teal	0	0	1	3	0	5	3	12	0	5	0
Snipe	0	0	0	0	0	5	0	5	0	5	0
Woodcock	0	0	0	0	0	24	0	24	1	23	0
Thrush family (large)*	0	0	0	0	0	13	0	13	1	12	0
Thrush family (small)*	0	0	0	0	0	4	0	4	1	3	0
Wagtail/pipit	0	0	0	0	0	1	0	1	0	1	0
Passerine, small*	0	0	0	1	0	4	0	5	0	4	0
Jackdaw	0	0	0	0	0	7	0	7	1	6	0
Crow, carrion/hooded	0	0	0	0	0	4	1	5	1	3	0
Bird, unidentified	0	1	0	0	0	0	0	1	0	0	0

Table 18 (cont)

Period	M2	M4	M5	M6	M7	M9	P1	Total M2–P1	M9 except A[972]	M9 A[972]	M9 A[972]
Species Common name	(hand)	(hand)	(hand)	(hand)	(hand)	(hand)	(hand)	(hand)	(hand)	(hand)	(wet-sieved) {491} + {502} + {503}
Mammals											
Cattle	191	165	36	27	33	139	170	761	7	132	1
Horse	29	23	0	0	0	0	6	58	0	0	0
Cattle-sized mammal	296	200	79	107	45	436	191	1354	20	408	11
Sheep/goat	71	52	40	92	8	146	77	486	12	134	3
Sheep	22	14	10	17	2	32	30	127	2	30	1
Goat	1	0	0	0	0	0	0	1	0	0	0
Pig	109	123	22	129	20	177	64	644	9	168	11
Sheep-sized mammal	82	78	42	140	17	844	137	1340	26	818	103
Deer, red	2	0	0	3	0	0	0	5	0	0	0
Deer, fallow	0	0	0	3	0	1	2	6	0	1	3
Deer, roe	1	0	0	0	0	0	0	1	0	0	0
Deer, unidentified	0	0	0	1	0	0	0	1	0	0	0
Mammal, large, unidentified	4	10	0	35	0	600	28	677	0	600	0
Dog, domestic	1	0	0	0	0	14	1	16	0	14	0
Cat, domestic	1	0	1	9	0	19	1	31	0	19	0
Hare, brown	0	0	0	3	1	18	0	22	0	18	0
Rabbit	0	1	5	3	0	190	15	214	2	188	6
Mammal, small, unidentified	2	0	0	2	0	47	1	52	0	47	0
Rat, unidentified	0	0	0	0	0	6	0	6	0	6	1
Vole, unidentified	0	0	0	0	0	1	0	1	0	1	5
Mouse, wood	0	0	0	0	0	2	0	2	0	2	0
Porpoise	0	0	0	1	0	0	0	1	0	0	0
Total	841	677	262	682	128	4429	767	7786	226	4203	1037

* birds – swan identified from a vertebra, large thrush is blackbird size, small thrush is song-thrush size, small passerines are all smaller than thrush and probably include wagtails/pipits

** A[972] wet-sieved: herring and smelt from {502} only; cranial fragments, particularly auditory capsules, of herring indicate a minimum number of individuals in the sample of 36 (such calculations were not possible for smelt as this species was represented by post-cranial parts, particularly vertebrae, only)

east–west Late Saxon ditch was extensively sampled: amongst the ten samples taken from the use fills, four provided bone assemblages, and the combined collection from these is limited to a single identifiable ox fragment amongst a small number of 'cattle-size' and 'sheep-size' fragments. A sample from the first recut of this ditch provided a similarly poor bone group. A single sample from the north–south ditch (OA1) produced two fish bones, one identified as eel, and an unidentifiable fragment.

Other deposits from this period were dominated by the major mammalian domesticates, cattle, sheep/goat and pig, with minor representations of the domestic birds, particularly chicken and goose, plus again a single fragment from a game species, a roe deer metatarsal. There was also good recovery of horse bones, all of which may derive from the same carcass, which had been butchered. These were divided between A[1722], which provided the greater part of the ribcage and the articulated vertebral column, and A[1706] which produced a major proportion of the upper forelegs. Cat and dog are both present (one fragment apiece).

Period M4, *c* 1100–50

Bones from the ditch (D1) serving the first reredorter range (B8) followed the basic pattern of mammalian domesticate

dominance, with a small quantity of other species.

The east boundary ditch fill (A[1045] OA2; Chapter 3.2, 'Archaeological evidence') produced the following percentage representations of cattle, sheep/goat and pig: 46.7%, 13.3% and 40% (45 fragments) respectively. The ditch also produced four horse fragments, all from the lower hind legs of the same animal, comprising both tibias and one metatarsal. One of the tibias had been butchered at the distal end, which could conceivably represent a skinning cut but which is more likely to be the result of a dressing cut. Though no other marks were found, it can be conjectured that at least a proportion of this carcass had been prepared for meat removal and consumption.

A cemetery soil (A[2752] OA6; Chapter 3.2, 'Archaeological evidence'), which was heavily disturbed, produced a small quantity of bones chiefly belonging to the major mammalian domesticates, but also including a single rabbit fragment plus a partial horse skeleton. This latter individual comprised both jaws, a scapula, and a large part of the vertebral column. Two of the lumbar vertebrae, situated close to the sacrum, were fused together. This has been interpreted in modern riding and working horses as a pathological response to physical stress such as that imposed by load-bearing or traction (Baker and Brothwell 1980). One of the jaws was butchered, this showing a deep cut mark adjacent to the condylar process (mandible joint) on the medial side. Such a mark can be translated as resulting from an attempt to detach the lower jaw from the skull at the mandibular articulation which strongly suggests that the animal was used for its meat. Although an additional indication of a food use would be disarticulation, it is unfortunately unknown whether these bones were in an articulated state when found.

Period M5, c 1150–c 1200

The cesspit in the infirmary (B10; Chapter 3.3, 'Archaeological evidence'), provided a small assemblage, composed, with the exception of two chicken bones, of the major mammalian domesticates. Though the number of bones is small, it can be seen that the three main species are approximately equally represented (Table 18).

A silt fill within the stone-built drain (D2) provided a small quantity of bones, composed, with the exception of a single horse fragment, of the ubiquitous major mammalian domesticates. Two samples were taken from this deposit, revealing just one chicken bone amongst a small collection of unidentifiable fragments.

Period M6, c 1200–50

A large quantity of bones was analysed from the backfill of the construction trench for the chimney inserted against the south wall of the hall/lodgings (B8; Chapter 3.4, 'Archaeological evidence'). The assemblage was largely composed of unidentifiable fragments, showing a possibly high level of redeposition. Those that could be identified were predominantly sheep/goat and pig. The totals of the major domesticates from the assemblage in A[1122] (weight 3750g) were cattle 11.4%, sheep/goat 43.4% and pig 45.2%. Bones were also analysed from the fill A[1302] of a robber trench in the same building. Of interest is the absence of cattle, and 'cattle-sized' fragments from the robber cut assemblage. Both assemblages also produced low levels of domestic birds and game species. The game included teal, partridge, red and fallow deer, hare, and rabbit. In addition, the robber cut also produced a few fish bones. The great diversity of species found in these deposits, including a large number of game animals and birds, can be interpreted as the waste items from an obviously high-status diet.

Period M7, c 1250–c 1330

The small quantity of bones dating to this period was mainly taken from a make-up deposit A[1339] beneath the floor at the south end of the infirmary (B10). This collection featured the usual major mammalian domesticates as well as some chicken and a single hare fragment.

Period M9, c 1430–1538

Small hand-collected and sieved groups of bones were

recovered from a cess layer overlying the repaired floor of the (second) reredorter (B9). The sieved group includes a few unidentifiable fish fragments. Pits (OA6) dug between the chapter house (B4) and the chapel (B1) produced a large quantity of bone and oyster shell; this group of pits appears to have been part of the increasing use of the cemetery area for rubbish disposal.

A large bone assemblage was recovered from dumping in the reredorter (B9; Chapter 3.7, 'Archaeological evidence', 'Reredorter (B9)'). Within the hand-collected assemblage from A[972] there is a marked diversity of species, including the ubiquitous major mammalian domesticates which were in roughly equal abundance with cattle at 28.5%, sheep/goat 35.3% and pig at 36.2% (out of a total of 464 fragments) (Table 18). There were large quantities of domestic birds, mainly comprising chicken and goose, accompanied by wild duck and dove or feral pigeon; a wide range of game, largely comprising rabbit bones, but also with a few fallow deer, hare, partridge, wood pigeon, swan and teal, woodcock, snipe and various small passerine birds (possibly composed of thrushes and larks/wagtails/pipits). Fish were also well represented, comprising mainly gadids (cod family), but also including a range of marine, estuarine and freshwater species. Of some importance was the incidence of sturgeon, which combined with the deer and swan, are very clear indicators of a high-status diet. In addition to a large hand-collected assemblage, A[972] also provided the largest wet-sieved assemblage from the whole site. Of the three samples processed from this context two provided an equally wide range of species, while the third was entirely composed of herring and smelt.

Period P1, 1538–c 1650

A substantial assemblage was derived from various features within the garden area (OA11), in particular from the large pits. The collection is mainly composed of cattle, sheep/goat and pig bones, amongst quite a diverse array of food species. The wild component includes at least one high-status comestible, fallow deer.

7.9   Human remains

Brian Connell and William White

Introduction

No other Cluniac burial ground of any size has been excavated but comparisons with human skeletal remains from monastic institutions of different religious orders in England clearly are justified. Published comparative sites, therefore, are numerous. Analysis of the extremely large groups of skeletons excavated at two religious houses close to London – the Cistercian abbey of St Mary Stratford Langthorne (analysed sample of 647 individuals: White 2004) and Augustinian Merton Priory (664 individuals: Conheeney 2007) – was being performed concurrently with that of the priory and abbey of St Saviour Bermondsey, and certain comparisons could be made. Some large monastic sites remain only part-published and further demographic and pathological information is available in the LAARC. The skeletal material from all of the sites above (including Bermondsey) was among the 2240 skeletons which have been re-recorded as part of the Wellcome Osteological Research Database (White 2006, 107). The osteological data are available for comparative purposes via the MOL website (nd b): http://www.museumoflondon.org.uk/English/Collections/OnlineResources/CHB/Database/.

A discussion of the demography of the cemetery population and burial practices is given in Chapter 4.3 ('Demography and the health of the burial population').

The sample

Composition and representativeness of the sample

Excavations between 1984 and 1988 yielded 202 articulated burials and a number of charnel deposits. Of the former, 193 were available for inclusion in the analysis. There were in addition a large number of disarticulated bones, collected by the archaeologists as 'bone samples'. The latter and the charnel material were to be scanned for pathology only.

Any sample that exceeds 100 individuals ought to provide valid information about the population buried in the cemetery (Waldron 1994, 10–27). The 193 individuals should represent the monastic population reasonably well. However, the post-excavation assessment suggested that women were present among those buried, and documentary evidence attests to the burial of women in the priory, indicating a potentially, more or less, mixed, rather than solely 'monastic', population. On the other hand there was considerable evidence for the disturbance of burials (the 'bone samples'), including the collection of the disarticulated burials into pits. Of the 193 skeletons analysed only five are from the chapel (B1, period M4: 2; B1, period M6: 3) and the rest are from Open Area 6 (periods M4–M8). All cases discussed below refer to skeletons in Open Area 6 unless specified otherwise.

Preservation of bone

The physical condition of each skeleton was scored on a scale of 1 to 3 (good to poor); full descriptions of these categories are given in Connell and Rauxloh (2007). Using this grading the majority of the remains, 127 (65.8%), fell into the first category and provided the bulk of the potential information extractable from a skeleton, including an estimate of the stature of the living individual. A further 39 (20.2%) of the remains were in class 2, yielding a reasonable amount of osteological information for a more detailed analysis. A mere 28 (14.5%) were assessed as poor and likely to provide little data.

Of the burials, 29 (15.0%) had more than 80% of the

Table 19 *Completeness of the skeleton*

Integrity	<25%	26–50%	51–80%	>80%
No.	55	50	59	29
%	28.5	25.9	30.6	15.0

skeleton present and a further 59 (30.6%) had more than 50% present (Table 19). Although nearly half the burials (105) were not more than 50% complete these were usually represented by the lower part of the skeleton. Since this portion often contained the pelvis the number that could not be aged or sexed, therefore, was smaller than is indicated by this proportion.

Methods of analysis

Bone data were recorded on the MOLA ORACLE database. The condition of preservation of individual bones as a consequence of burial practices was noted and efficiency of recovery calculated by comparing the number of bones recovered with that expected from the total number of burials.

The age of any immature individuals was estimated using dental development and state of epiphyseal fusion (Brothwell 1981, 64–7; Bass 1995, 13–15) and diaphysial lengths (Ferembach et al 1980; Ubelaker 1984, 46–53). The age of adults was determined by tooth wear stages (Brothwell 1981, 71–2) and morphology of the pubic symphysis (Brooks and Suchey 1990). Sex was estimated using skull and pelvic dimorphism (Phenice 1969; Ferembach et al 1980; Brothwell 1981, 59–63). Complementary data for sex estimation were sought metrically (Bass 1995) but priority was given to the results of examination of the pelvis because this is regarded as the most reliable of the available techniques.

Conventional cranial and post-cranial measurements were taken following Bass (1995, 68–81) and Brothwell (1981, 79–87) and long bone lengths were employed in the estimation of stature using the regression equations established by Trotter and Gleser (1952, 1958). Non-metric traits were recorded (Berry and Berry 1967; Finnegan 1978) and where appropriate tested in the elucidation of family relationship.

The jaws were examined for non-metric traits, dental hygiene and pathology (Berry 1978; Hillson 1986). Information on general pathology was recorded (Ortner and Putschar 1985), as was the evidence for infectious disease (Rogers and Waldron 1989), joint disease (Rogers and Waldron 1995) and epidemiology (Waldron 1994).

Human variation

Age

A single individual A[2879] (period M7) was adolescent (aged 11–15 years, not sexed), the remainder (192) being adults (Table 20). Of the adults, 69 (35.9%) could not be aged with any degree of precision. A total of 23 (12.0%) were aged between 16

Table 20 The burial population: age and sex by period and land use

Period and land use	M3 OA2	M4 B1	M4 OA6	M5 OA6	M6 B1	M6 OA6	M7 OA6	M8 OA6	Unphased	Total no.
Total no. graves excavated	4	3	18	50	3	5	91	c 21	13+	208+
Total no. skeletons analysed	-	2	18	50	3	5	90	12	13	193
Male	-	2	12	29	1	5	53	7	9	118
11–15 years	0	0	0	0	0	0	0	0	0	0
16–25 years	0	0	2	2	0	1	9	2	3	19
26–45 years	0	2	4	12	0	2	27	4	4	55
≥46 years	0	0	4	9	0	2	13	0	1	29
adult	0	0	2	6	1	0	4	1	1	15
?Male	-	-	2	5	-	-	9	1	2	19
11–15 years	0	0	0	0	0	0	0	0	0	-
16–25 years	0	0	0	1	0	0	1	0	0	2
26–45 years	0	0	1	3	0	0	1	0	1	6
≥46 years	0	0	0	0	0	0	1	1	0	2
adult	0	0	1	1	0	0	6	0	1	9
Female	-	-	1	-	1	-	2	1	-	5
11–15 years	0	0	0	0	0	0	0	0	0	-
16–25 years	0	0	1	0	0	0	0	0	0	1
26–45 years	0	0	0	0	0	0	2	0	0	2
≥46 years	0	0	0	0	0	0	0	1	0	1
adult	0	0	0	0	1	0	0	0	0	1
?Female	-	-	-	1	-	-	2	-	-	3
11–15 years	0	0	0	0	0	0	0	0	0	-
16–25 years	0	0	0	0	0	0	1	0	0	1
26–45 years	0	0	0	0	0	0	0	0	0	1
≥46 years	0	0	0	1	0	0	0	0	0	1
adult	0	0	0	0	0	0	1	0	0	1
Indeterminate	-	-	3	15	1	-	24	3	2	48
11–15 years	0	0	0	0	0	0	1	0	0	1
16–25 years	0	0	0	0	0	0	1	0	0	1
26–45 years	0	0	0	0	0	0	1	0	0	1
≥46 years	0	0	1	0	0	0	1	0	0	2
adult	0	0	2	15	1	0	20	3	2	43

and 25 years (18.7% of ageable adults), 65 (33.9%) were aged between 26 and 45 years (52.8% of ageable adults), and 35 (18.2%) were aged ≥46 years (28.5% of ageable adults).

Sex

Of the 192 adults, 145 skeletons could be sexed: 137 (94.5%) were male or possibly male and only eight (5.5%) female or possibly female. This may be broken down further into 118 male (81.4%), 19 possibly male (13.1%), five female (3.4%) and three possibly female (2.1%) (Table 20). It is possible that the 47 (34.3%) adults of indeterminate sex included females but the evidence was lacking.

The overwhelming preponderance of males (and possible males) and the low proportion of females (and possible females) are in accordance with the character of a monastic house. The latter could potentially include a wide range of individuals – patrons and their family, corrodians and servants – whereas the former might embrace these civilians as well as the monks themselves. Seven of the eight females/possible females were buried in the external cemetery (OA6, periods M4–M8), and one within the chapel (B1, period M6).

The preponderance of males accords in particular with the location of the burials, given that the overwhelming majority of those analysed (188/193) were from the external, south-east or 'monastic' cemetery area (OA6), between the church (B3) and the chapel (B1). Five of the seven burials recovered from the chapel (B1) were analysed: the three males, one female and one of indeterminate sex were all adult; the earliest, buried in the chapel c 1100–50 (period M4), were two mature adult males (26–45 years).

Stature

In accordance with current recommendations stature was calculated using measurements made on the bones of the lower limb exclusively, since these are regarded as giving a more accurate result than using the arm bones (Stroud and Kemp 1993; Buikstra and Ubelaker 1994; Conheeney 1997). Thus, the calculated height for 68 men from the site ranged from 1.57m to 1.85m, with a mean 1.72m. This is c 30mm shorter than the modern British average height 1.75m (Department of Trade and Industry 1998). Plainly it can no longer be contended that people in the Middle Ages necessarily were very much shorter than their modern counterparts (Werner 1998). Stroud (1994, 436) cites 12 medieval cemetery sites with average male stature 1.70–1.74m. Meanwhile, average height for women at the same sites ranged from 1.57–1.61m. The data from other Cluniac establishments are sparse: 1.77m at Thetford Priory, based on five high-status men only (Wells 1957) and 1.72m for the 34 monks from Pontefract Priory (Hurst 1965). This is not to say that some groups (or subgroups) at medieval sites were not appreciably shorter than in the present day. Different ethnic groups or a disadvantaged minority might be distinguishable in the cemetery, by being at the lower extreme of stature. Examples include the Jews of York and Lincoln and the hospital inmates at St Mary Spital, London, for whom mean stature has been calculated as 1.67m and 1.69m respectively (Stroud 1994, 435–6; Conheeney 1997, 223).

Only one of the women from Bermondsey had leg bones sufficiently intact for stature calculation. She proved to have been exceptionally tall for a medieval woman at 1.72m (A[3262], period M7).

Handedness

In three of 18 pairs of upper limbs examined, the length of the left arm bones exceeded that of the right limb by 2–6mm. If the observed upper limb asymmetry is related to 'manual dominance' then these three (16.7%) were left-handed. In modern Britain about 10% of the population are left-handed. Was the sinistrous proportion of the medieval population higher than today or is there something in the monastic life that selects for left-handed men? Further research on London's monastic sites may help to resolve this question. The sample size, however, is admittedly small.

Cranial and post-cranial indices

Measurements made upon the skull, femur and tibia traditionally are used to produce indices which may appear to be of questionable significance but nonetheless remain of value for assessing variability within and between populations and for other comparative purposes (Stroud and Kemp 1993, 173–9; Stroud 1994, 437–9; Mays 1998, 96–100).

The calculated cranial index is a measure of the breadth of the cranium expressed as a proportion of its length. Thus, the cranial index for 50 men ranged from 74.9 (borderline dolichocranic, ie long-headed, cranial index ≥74.9) to 94.2 (hyperbrachycranic, very broad-headed, cranial index ≥85.0), with a mean of 83.1. The population, therefore, may be classified as brachycranic (broad-headed, cranial index 80.0–84.9), in common with other English medieval groups (Stroud 1994, 437). The people from the earlier City of London site of St Nicholas Shambles (11th–12th centuries) had a mean index 77.5 and, therefore, were mesocranic (middle-headed, cranial index 75.0–79.9; White 1988, 30). The same feature was also observed at Merton Priory, where Conheeney (2007, 268) noted a brachycranic population. At the abbey of

St Mary Stratford Langthorne, White (2004, 173) demonstrated a mean cranial index of 82.0, also a brachycranic population. This would suggest that for the most part brachycrany is the predominant cranial form in monastic houses in the London area.

The shaft indices for the leg bones have a bearing upon the physique of the community, even if the implications of the degree of flattening of the shafts are unknown (Wells 1964, 132–4; Andermann 1976). The femur shaft index for a sample of 89 men ranged from 98.3 (eumeric) to 64.2 (platymeric), with a mean 83.6 for the right side and for 86 men from 99.3 to 66.5, mean 83.1, for the left side. The population, therefore, was slightly platymeric (index 84.9). Similarly, 94 men ranged from 61.0 (platycnemic) to 92.3 (eurycnemic) (mean 73.3) for the right side and for 91 men from 60.2 to 94.9 (mean 72.8) for the left side. The population was classed as eurycnemic or normal.

Non-metric variation

Discontinuous or non-metric variation in the human skeleton has a heritable element and has been used in attempts to deduce the presence of family groupings in cemeteries. Such an approach, a priori, is unlikely to prove of great utility at a monastic site because of the nominal celibacy of the clergy and the unlikelihood of more than one son in any family entering the same monastic order. Thus father-and-child or sibling groupings in the monks' burial ground are unlikely, and hence any clustering of non-metric characters in the cemetery could be fortuitous. Accordingly, non-metric variation is recorded here as overall frequencies of characteristics for comparison with other populations.

The skeletons were examined for 36 cranial and 34 post-cranial characteristics and of these 30 different traits were found. The prevalence of the various cranial traits is summarised in Table 21. The only category of tooth missing congenitally other than third molars was the upper second premolar; this tooth was absent bilaterally in the upper jaw of one of the men A[3400] (period M7). Similarly, Carabelli cusps occurred bilaterally in the lower first molars of one mandible A[3905] (period M4).

An indication of the appearance of the people of the community could be obtained by subjective classification of the skull features (Dawes and Magilton 1980, 27–8). Subjectively, skulls were usually oval in shape, when viewed from the top of the head looking down: 19 out of 33 possible cases (57.6%). 'Pear-shaped' skulls amounted to a mere nine in number (27.3% of possible cases). The only other shape of consequence was 'round', of which there were five (15.2% of possible cases). Faces tended to be long and narrow (6/14 or 42.9% of possible cases), the remainder being divided into 'rectangular' or 'oval' (each 21.4% of possible cases). Chin shape was as likely to be round (11/22 or 50% of possible cases) as 'square'. There was a single instance of a bathrocranic skull, A[3905] (period M4), that is one with a protruding rounded bump at the back (Brothwell 1981, 169).

Table 21 Frequencies of cranial non-metric traits (unpaired and bilateral)

Cranial trait	No. observed	No. available	% of possible cases
Metopism	12	97	12.4
Lambdoid ossicle	4	97	4.1
Bregmatic ossicle	1	97	1.0
R asterionic ossicle	6	97	6.2
L asterionic ossicle	5	97	5.2
R epipteric ossicle	2	97	2.1
L epipteric ossicle	1	97	1.0
Coronal ossicle	2	97	2.1
R lambdoid ossicle	18	97	18.6
L lambdoid ossicle	17	97	17.5
R squamo-parietal ossicle	1	97	1.0
L squamo-parietal ossicle	1	97	1.0
R torus maxillaris	1	97	1.0
L torus maxillaris	2	97	2.1
Torus palatinus	10	97	10.3
R double occipital condyle	3	97	3.1
L double occipital condyle	4	97	4.1
R torus mandibularis	7	94	7.4
L torus mandibularis	7	94	7.4
R pterygoid spur	18	94	19.1
L pterygoid spur	18	94	19.1
Third molar absence	49	347	14.1

Table 22 Frequencies of post-cranial non-metric traits (unpaired and bilateral)

Post-cranial trait	No. observed	No. available	% of possible cases
Sternal foramen	2	48	4.2
R os acromiale	2	38	5.3
L os acromiale	3	38	7.9
R supra-scapular foramen	2	38	5.3
L supra-scapular foramen	2	38	5.3
R atlas posterior bridge	2	78	2.6
L atlas posterior bridge	5	78	6.4
R atlas lateral bridge	2	78	2.6
L atlas lateral bridge	2	78	2.6
R atlas double facet	8	78	10.3
L atlas double facet	8	78	10.3
R cervical rib	1	78	1.3
L cervical rib	1	78	1.3
R accessory sacral facets	4	106	3.8
L accessory sacral facets	2	106	1.9
Lumbosacralisation	3	71	4.2
Sacrolumbarisation	2	71	2.8
R acetabular crease	5	108	4.6
L acetabular crease	3	106	2.8
R septal aperture	1	86	1.2
L septal aperture	2	101	2.0
R supracondylar process	1	86	1.2
R 3rd trochanter	12	98	12.2
L 3rd trochanter	12	90	13.3
R Poirier's facet	8	98	8.2
L Poirier's facet	6	90	6.7
R Poirer's plaque	2	98	2.0
L Poirer's plaque	1	90	1.1
R squatting facet medial	3	95	3.2
L squatting facet medial	2	72	2.8
R squatting facet lateral	7	95	7.4
L squatting facet lateral	7	72	9.7
R calcaneal facet double	15	94	16.0
L calcaneal facet double	15	95	15.8
R talar facet double	11	91	12.1
L talar facet double	11	89	12.4
R talar squatting facet	5	91	5.5
L talar squatting facet	3	89	3.4
R os trigonium	1	91	1.1
L os trigonium	1	89	1.1

The prevalence of metopic sutures (12.4%) and third molar agenesis (14.1%) were broadly comparable to other medieval groups analysed (eg St Mary Stratford Langthorne, 7.3% and 13.7%: White 2004, 174, table 23). However, wormian bones (in every location on the cranial sutures; see ossicles Table 21) occurred at a lower frequency than at St Nicholas Shambles, City of London (White 1988, 34), or any of three sites in York (Dawes and Magilton 1980, 35, 41; Stroud and Kemp 1993, 185–8; Williamson 1994, 455). Similarly, auditory and palatine tori were present less commonly than at these other sites as was the maxillary torus (except at St Andrew Fishergate, York) and the mandibular torus, except at St Nicholas Shambles. However, such non-metric characteristics are generally more frequent at Bermondsey than at Stratford Langthorne where the prevalence of wormian bones and the cranial tori is markedly low (White 2004, 174, table 23).

A series of post-cranial traits were also recorded and the frequencies are given in Table 22. The most commonly seen traits were atlas double facets, femoral third trochanters and double facets in the calcaneum and talus.

One area where clusters of non-metric traits might have proved informative was the chapel (B1). However, of the seven burials excavated, only five were available for analysis and for one of these, A[3522], neither sex nor approximate adult age could be assigned. The remaining four were an adult female (A[3596], period M6) with limited preservation and three males (two males aged 26 to 45 years, A[3798], A[3817], period M4; and a headless adult male of unknown age, A[3522], period M6). None of the three males exhibited a pattern of non-metric traits such as could be used in the elucidation of possible family relationships.

Pathology

Trauma

One individual (A[3541], period M8) shows a small depressed fracture of the outer table of the left parietal. It is in the central area of the parietal and is quite small, measuring 10mm long by 4mm wide. It has not punctured the inner table, which is perhaps fortunate for this individual, as a perforating injury might have caused infection resulting in meningitis, which was usually fatal. The fracture has rounded edges and there is no evidence of an inflammatory response although these changes might have remodelled out over time.

The most common fractures in this burial group were those of the ribcage. Five individuals (A[2701], period M5; A[3723], A[3203], A[2967], A[3599], period M7) showed one or more broken ribs. Fractures to the ribs occurred on both left and right sides and were restricted to ribs in the upper and middle portions of the ribcage. All except two were well healed with no evidence of inflammation. Burial A[3723] has a fracture of the left first rib in its neck portion which has not united despite considerable callus formation around both broken ends, forming a pseudarthrosis. Fractures of first ribs are associated with severe trauma to the shoulder and thorax region and are particularly dangerous because of the rib's close association with major vascular structures such as the subclavian artery or aorta. A pseudarthrosis at this location, therefore, is quite unusual. The left clavicle from this individual is poorly preserved and incomplete so it is difficult to determine whether or not the first rib fracture was associated with fracture of the clavicle (which lies just above). A second individual A[3203] has two fractured ribs (right five and six) and both ribs have poor apposition and overlapping of the broken ends. The fractures are oblique and have resulted in slight angular deformity of about 5°. Healing is complete, but remodelling callus is patchy and irregular. The overall prevalence of broken ribs is 9/1964 or 0.5%.

Skeletons A[2898] and A[3236] (both period M7) have fractured right ulnae. In A[2898] the fracture is at midshaft level and the healing is good with no angular or rotational deformity. The callus is dense lamellar bone suggesting that the fracture occurred a considerable time before death. The second individual A[3236], shows a fracture of the distal end, transversely across the shaft. The union of the broken ends is good with slight callus formation that has remodelled into dense lamellar bone. Fractures of the shaft of the ulna are often referred to as 'parry fractures' as they are known to occur when an individual raises their arm to ward off a strike or blow; the subcutaneous edge of the ulna is exposed and takes the brunt of the force. This is a common interpretation, but ulnar fractures can equally be due to other causes. Prevalence of ulnar fractures is 2/160 or 1.3%. This is similar to the prevalence of 0.8% (4/471) seen at Stratford Langthorne (White 2004, 178).

Skeleton A[3607] (period M8) has a 'Pott's' fracture; three breaks had occurred in the right ankle (talo-crural) joint. Pott's fractures are named after Sir Percival Pott of St Bartholomew's hospital, London, who first described fracture of the distal fibula with displacement of the talus in 1769. In skeleton A[3607] both malleoli plus the posterior margin of the tibia are fractured. Eburnation and subchondral pitting on the talus also indicate secondary osteoarthritis. Fractures such as this are characteristic of a rotational injury, that is the foot being forcefully twisted to one side or the other. The fracture pattern seen in A[3607] is consistent with an external rotation injury of severe violence. This was probably the result of an accident, perhaps a particularly awkward fall.

The number of individuals buried at Bermondsey (priory and abbey) who had suffered fractures has been compared with fracture victims in other medieval populations. A total of 1023 long bones (humerus, radius, ulna, femur, tibia and fibula) from the cemetery were examined and a total of five had evidence of a fracture (0.5%). When ribs, crania and clavicles are considered also, the total number of individuals showing evidence of trauma in the form of fractures (healed and unhealed) is 13 out

of 193 adults (6.7%). Of these 13 adults, 12 could be confidently sexed as male. The overall fracture frequency, therefore, for males in this group is 12/137 or 8.8%. Comparison of fracture prevalence between the sexes was not possible because the sample had much lower numbers of females (8/193 or 4.2%). However, it is noted that males in other comparable sites suffer up to twice the amount of fractures than females (Grauer and Roberts 1996, 537).

Data given in Judd and Roberts (1998) and Grauer and Roberts (1996) demonstrate that fracture rates for males from five medieval urban sites ranged from 5.6% to 21.1% (St Helen-on-the-Walls, York, 7.3%; St Nicholas Shambles, London, 5.6%; Blackfriars Oxford, 8.1%; Whithorn (Wigtownshire), 5.7%; and Chichester, 21.1%). The fracture frequency for Bermondsey males (8.8%) falls within this range. The figure of 21.1% at Chichester is high because the cemetery is associated with a leper hospital: Judd and Roberts (1998) suggest that the increased fracture frequency at this site is due to the sensory impairment in leprosy infection. If one ignores this, biased, group then, the frequencies range from 5.6% to 8.1%, and Bermondsey is broadly comparable with this range at 8.8%. A slighter higher figure of 13% was observed at Merton Priory (Conheeney 2007, 269).

Soft tissue trauma

On some occasions, damage to soft tissues can result in tearing of ligaments and tendons, or a localised haematoma (blood clot). Under these circumstances a bone formative response is initiated, the proximity of blood clots to the periosteum can stimulate osteoblasts (Aufderheide and Rodriguez-Martin 1998). This results in a lesion known as myostitis ossificans. One possible case is seen in skeleton A[2722] (period M7), a young adult male, which shows small exostoses of dense lamellar bone up to 9mm long on the infraglenoid tubercle of the left scapula. This formation of new bone might have been initiated by avulsion or partial avulsion of the long head of the triceps.

Skeleton A[2898] (period M7) also has a dense nodule of bone on the posterior surface of the left lateral epicondyle of the humerus. It measures 21mm long and is 16mm at its widest point and is 7mm high. Inferiorly, the new bone extends as a flange and this might represent myostitis ossificans associated with the anconeus muscle. Skeleton A[2898] also has an ulnar fracture (above) and spondylolysis (below, 'Congenital and developmental disorders'). Three skeletons (A[2801] and A[3217], period M4; A[2823], period M5) also have deposits of sclerotic bone on the metatarsal shafts. Skeleton A[2801] (mature adult male) has new bone deposits on the lateral surfaces of left and right metatarsals two to four, with smaller circular deposits on the medial aspect of metatarsal four. Skeletons A[2823] and A[3217] also exhibit these bone deposits on the lateral surfaces of metatarsal three and four; skeleton A[2823] also shows smaller deposits on the medial surface of left metatarsal three. These bone deposits might represent myostitis ossificans due to repeated microtrauma to the dorsum of the foot.

Joint disease

Another frequently observed pathological change is joint disease, and changes to the joints can show up in several ways. Osteophytic (lipping) developments on the margins of joints are the most common. However, these on their own cannot be considered as evidence of osteoarthritis because they are also a product of the ageing process. Other changes such as subchondral pitting, contour alteration and eburnation in particular are indicative of cartilage failure and enable osteoarthritis to be identified more securely. There was no evidence of any erosive arthropathies amongst this burial group. The distribution of joints with evidence of osteoarthritis is summarised in Table 23.

The most frequently affected joints were the acromioclavicular joints in the shoulder. A total of 19 individuals (9.8%) showed degenerative changes in one or both shoulders. Another frequently affected joint was the knee, where 8.8% of individuals showed osteoarthritic changes. Within the knee joint itself the most common area affected was the anterior compartment or patellofemoral joint. Eleven of the 17 knee joints affected (65%) showed changes in this area, usually on one side only. Skeleton A[3613] (period M7), however, showed osteoarthritis in both of these joints. Of the 11 cases, eight could be aged, and six of these were in the older adult category (≥46 years). The same pattern of high prevalence of shoulder and knee changes was also seen in the males from St Mary Stratford Langthorne (White 2004, 177). Similarly, at Merton Priory the shoulder was the most commonly affected joint, where nearly half (100/222) of the skeletons showed joint changes (Conheeney 2007, 271). However, this was attributed to the age profile of the sample rather than to occupational factors (ibid, 272).

Table 23 Distribution of degenerative joint changes

Joint	Male	Female	Unsexed	Total no. of individuals	Total % of individuals affected
Temporo-mandibular	I	0	0	I	0.5
Shoulder	18	I	0	19	9.8
Elbow	6	0	0	6	3.1
Wrist	11	0	0	11	5.7
Hand	7	2	I	10	5.2
Hip	2	0	0	2	1.0
Knee	13	I	3	17	8.8
Ankle	2	0	0	2	1.0
Foot	3	0	I	4	2.1

Infectious disease

Infectious disease can be broken into two broad groups: specific infection and non-specific infection. Specific infection is where the changes observed (in this case in bone tissue) are characteristic of one type of pathogenic organism. Specific infections in palaeopathological contexts usually refer to

Treponemal disease (eg syphilis) or Mycobacterial disease (eg tuberculosis and leprosy). Non-specific infection refers to an infection where the bony changes observed are common to a wide range of pathogens (usually bacterial) and one particular species cannot be identified. At Bermondsey (priory and abbey), evidence of both specific and non-specific infection was found.

Specific infections

TUBERCULOSIS

Tuberculosis is caused by infection by one of two strains of the tuberculosis bacillus. The human type (*Mycobacterium tuberculosis*) is usually transmitted by droplets in the air and is primarily a lung infection. The bovine form (*Mycobacterium bovis*) can be caught by ingesting contaminated meat or dairy products and is primarily a gastrointestinal infection. Bone involvement in tuberculosis, therefore, is a metastatic phenomenon, that is bone becomes infected via spread from lesions in soft tissue. Areas in the skeleton such as the spine and long bones are predilicted sites of infection because of their rich vascular supply.

There is a probable case of tuberculosis in skeleton A[3231] (period M7), a young adult male. The lumbar vertebrae show changes characteristic of tuberculosis infection and these are as follows. Vertebra L3 shows two deep cavities on the anterior surface of the centrum that extend virtually the entire height of the vertebra. Both of these cavities have sharply demarcated margins and have walls composed of coarsely remodelled trabeculae. There is minimal bone formation except towards the inferior end plate where the trabeculae have become smoothed to form thin sheets of lamellar bone. The end plates are intact and unaffected. Vertebra L4 shows a central lytic focus within the body of the vertebra (c 17mm wide and 5mm high). The bone around this lytic focus consists of sclerotic trabeculae. A lytic lesion (scalloping) also exists on the anterior body of L4. The destruction caused by the central lytic focus has resulted in a crush fracture of L4 (the superior surface is inclined at an angle of approximately 10° transversely and 25° antero-posteriorly), which would have caused the spine to have become abnormally curved (kyphotic). Angular kyphosis (Pott's disease) has been described as the 'classic hallmark' of tuberculosis of the spine (Rogers and Waldron 1989, 614). Vertebra L5 also has scalloped lytic lesions that extend across the whole anterior surface. This lesion is not as clearly demarcated as those seen in L3 and L4, and has less distinct margins. The walls are composed of coarse trabecular tissue and the end plates are intact. The right L4/5 zygapophyseal joint is ankylosed, although this may have occurred as a result of the fracture rather than the infective process itself. The anterior surface of the sacrum is also affected by lytic lesions, S2 clearly shows the scalloping effect.

The key features of all these lesions are there is no apparent sinus formation, reactive bone formation is minimal (ie the lesions are primarily lytic in nature), the crush fracture at L4 and the scalloped anterior surfaces. The anterolateral scalloped lesions of the lumbar vertebral bodies, due to spread of infection beneath the anterior longitudinal ligament, are diagnostic of spinal tuberculosis (Rogers and Waldron 1989, 614; Stirland and Waldron 1990, 224).

In considering a differential diagnosis, other disease processes such as brucellosis, pyogenic osteomyelitis and mycotic (fungal) infection must be borne in mind. Brucellosis tends to present destructive and bone formative responses at the same time (Zimmerman and Kelley 1982, 92; Stirland and Waldron 1990, 225) and another common finding is that the intervertebral discs are affected, whereas in A[3231] they are normal. Osteomyelitis provokes marked proliferation of new bone (Stirland and Waldron 1990, 225) whereas in tuberculosis there is very little proliferation of new bone, sequestra are rare and no cloacae are formed (Rogers and Waldron 1989). Involvement of posterior elements is common in fungal infections affecting the spine (Aufderheide and Rodriguez-Martin 1998, 140).

Tuberculosis is often described as a population density dependent disease, and as Larsen (1997, 103) points out, the biocultural model and general pattern of skeletal involvement in the context of increasing population density and sedentism is well illustrated. The increase in population density in London during the medieval period (Keene 1989, 103) would have presented ideal conditions for increased prevalence of this disease. Tuberculosis in urban populations is usually the pulmonary type. However, Boylston and Roberts (1997) have found evidence of probable gastro-intestinal tuberculosis in the medieval population from the city of Lincoln. Cases of tuberculosis have been suggested at several monastic urban sites: Coventry Charterhouse (Warwickshire), Aberdeen Whitefriars (Aberdeenshire), SS James and Mary Magdalene Chichester and Jewbury York (Gilchrist and Sloane 2005, 211). Other possible cases of tuberculosis from medieval London include a 12-year-old child from St Mary Spital (13th century) (Conheeney 1997, 229). As bone involvement in tuberculosis is associated with advanced soft tissue disease it must have been apparent to the other inhabitants of Bermondsey Priory at that time (period M7) that the individual A[3231] was very sick. White (2004, 177) describes several instances of tuberculosis manifested in the vertebral column (Pott's disease) at the abbey of St Mary Stratford Langthorne. Tuberculosis was also seen in four individuals from Merton Priory (Conheeney 2007, 275), again suggesting that the disease was common in monastic establishments.

Non-specific infections

A common form of non-specific infection is periostitis. A low grade inflammation of the periosteum causes its osteogenic layer to lay down new bone on the cortex underneath. This usually results in striations of new bone being deposited, woven at first, coalescing into small areas of plaque-like new bone that will eventually be incorporated into the cortex. Periostitis is frequently seen in archaeological populations, particularly on tibiae and fibulae, especially tibiae. Periostitis may be the result of infection by common bacteria (eg *Staphylococcus* or *Streptococcus* spp) systemic disease or minor trauma. In the right

leg 27 out of 98 tibiae (27.6%) showed a periosteal bone formation on one or more surfaces. In four of these cases periostitis had also occurred on the fibula. The left leg showed a slightly higher prevalence with 26 out of 75 (34.6%) with periostitis on one or more surfaces. In eight of these cases periostitis had also occurred on the fibula. Overall, fibulae showed a lower prevalence with 11 out of 78 fibulae (14.1%) on both left and right sides.

Skeleton A[3555] (period M8), a young adult male, showed new bone formation on the anterior surface of the sacrum (S1–S3). On S1 the new bone consists of a lamellar plaque and on S2 there is a larger area of new bone, mostly on the left side consisting of spicules of lamellar bone. A trace of this new bone can also be seen on S3. This might have been caused by direct spread of bacteria from the colon or rectum.

Two mature adult males (A[2692], period M6; A[3515], period M7) have periosteal bone formative responses on the visceral surfaces of ribs. Skeleton A[2692] has fine woven bone deposits in the neck region of left ribs four and five. Skeleton A[3515] has three right ribs (right first and ?second and ?third) plus two left mid-section (five to eight) ribs with new bone deposits in the neck region of the visceral surface. The aetiology of periosteal rib lesions still remains uncertain. Pfeiffer (1991, 197), for example, suggests that rib lesions of this type are best interpreted as forms of non-specific inflammatory periostitis. However, Roberts et al (1994) found a strong association with these lesions in people who had died from tuberculosis. As this burial group already demonstrates clear evidence of tuberculosis (A[3231], period M7), the rib periostitis seen in A[2692] and A[3515] might represent further evidence for the presence of a chronic pulmonary stressor, such as tuberculosis. Conheeney (2007, 275) also describes the presence of these lesions in the skeletal population from Merton Priory.

Sinusitis

Sinusitis (or inflammation of the maxillary sinus) was found in four adult males (A[3490], unphased; A[3897] and A[3223], period M4; A[3914], period M5). The cause can be attributed to air pollution, but Lewis et al (1995) have noted other causes too. In skeletons A[3490] and A[3897] the inflammation was associated with dental abscesses of the first molar that had perforated the sinus. Skeleton A[3223] has bilateral sinusitis; the floors and antero-medial walls have spicules of new bone on their surfaces. Skeleton A[3914] has new bone formation (spicules of lamellar bone) on the floor of the sinus. These four cases of sinusitis are based on skulls with fragmentary maxillae and as such is a gross underestimation of the true prevalence because the sinus itself cannot be examined in intact skulls.

Circulatory disorders

Skeleton A[3458] (period M7) is an incomplete adult consisting only of the right femur, tibiae, fibulae and feet. The tibiae and fibulae show near perfect bilateral and symmetrical distribution of periosteal lesions. The tibiae and fibulae had new bone deposits at mid-shaft level consisting of well-remodelled striations of lamellar bone. The distal ends of the bones also have extensive new bone deposits consisting of coarse and porous new bone, suggesting a more recent formative process. The right femur of this individual also showed periostitis, plaques of lamellar bone on the shaft and porous new bone on the medial and anterior surfaces of the distal end. Although the skeleton is incomplete, the bilateral and symmetrical distribution of the lesions would suggest a systemic cause rather than trauma or infection.

The distribution of periostitis in the legs is possibly the early stages of hypertrophic osteoarthropathy, which consists of a strictly symmetrical periosteal bone deposition on the shafts of the long bones of the extremities (Ortner and Putschar 1985, 246; Fennell and Trinkaus 1997, 992). The incompleteness of this skeleton, however, limits the certainty of this. The bones most frequently involved are the forearms and lower legs, ankles (tibia and fibula) and the knee (Ortner and Putschar 1985, 246; Aufderheide and Rodriguez-Martin 1998, 91). Hypertrophic osteoarthropathy is a disease of considerable antiquity; Fennell and Trinkaus (1997) described a case dating from the Palaeolithic. The cause is unknown, although Aufderheide and Rodriguez-Martin (1998, 91) point out there is some evidence to suggest it represents a response to increased peripheral blood flow.

Diffuse idiopathic skeletal hyperostosis

Diffuse idiopathic skeletal hyperostosis (DISH) is a condition that has only become recognised relatively recently, both clinically and in palaeopathological contexts. The main manifestations of DISH are bony proliferations on the margins of the vertebral bodies that fuse together causing the spine to become rigid. Ossifications also occur elsewhere in the skeleton at sites of ligament and muscle attachment. DISH occurs in older individuals, usually over 50 years, and is far more common in males than in females (Resnick and Niwayama 1988). It is the vertebral changes that are most characteristic of DISH, blocks of ankylosed (fused) vertebrae have the appearance of melted candlewax dripped down the bodies (Fig 85). The exact cause is unknown, but it has an association with obesity and late-onset diabetes (Julkunen et al 1971; Waldron 1985).

The prevalence of DISH at Bermondsey is 15/193 (7.8%) when vertebrae and extra-spinal enthesopathies are considered together. For a comparison of the incidence of DISH to other medieval cemeteries see Chapter 4.3 ('Demography and health of the burial population').

Metabolic disease

Metabolic disease results from disturbances to the normal metabolic processes that occur during the growth and development of the body and can result from dietary deficiency or hormone imbalances. Bone changes of this type are often

Table 24 Skulls with cribra orbitalia (type follows Stuart-Macadam 1989)

Context	Sex	Age	Laterality	Type
A[3487]	male	mature adult	bilateral	3
A[3015]	not sexed	older adult	left	4
A[3220]	male	mature adult	bilateral	3
A[3558]	male	older adult	bilateral	3
A[3223]	male	young adult	bilateral	3

considered as 'stress indicators'. There is evidence of two types of metabolic disease or stressor in this population; cribra orbitalia and osteoporosis.

Cribra orbitalia can be recognised by porous bone lesions in the roof of the orbit (eye-socket). These lesions are considered to be suggestive of iron deficiency anaemia. However, that they could also represent an adaptive response to pathogen loads (Larsen 1997, 62) as a potential synergism with infection has also been suggested (Goodman et al 1988). Five skulls show evidence of cribra orbitalia (Table 24), the prevalence of this condition is 5/97 skulls with one or both orbits (5.2%).

Osteoporosis is a condition where bone is qualitatively normal but *quantitatively* deficient and is quite common in post-menopausal females. The loss of bone mass predisposes areas of the skeleton to fracture, such as the wrist, femoral neck or a crush fracture in the spine. One possible case of osteoporosis was seen in an older adult male skeleton A[3897] (period M4) which has a compression fracture of the first lumbar vertebra. Broken articular ends of long bones also show some degree of ante-mortem trabecular loss.

Congenital and developmental disorders

Congenital defects cover a range of abnormalities that are present at birth or manifest themselves later in life because of faulty development. Amongst the more common defects seen in the skeleton are minor variations in the number or form of vertebrae, particularly at the lumbo-sacral level.

Spondylolysis is a condition usually seen in lumbar vertebrae where the posterior section of the neural arch is separate at the junction with the pedicles at the *pars interarticularis*, either unilaterally or bilaterally. Spondylolysis is seen in up to 5% of modern populations (Dandy 1993), and it is usually twice as frequent in males than in females (Waldron 1992). The exact aetiology of this condition is still a matter of debate (Arriaza 1997; Aufderheide and Rodriguez-Martin 1998). Some authors suggest a congenital weakness (eg Roberts and Manchester 1995, 78) while some argue that spondylolysis can be caused by other than congenital factors (Pecina and Bojanic 1993). Three cases of spondylolysis were seen in the Bermondsey population, two in mature adult males (A[3817] from B1, period M4; A[3200], period M5) and one in an older adult male (A[2898], period M7). Skeleton A[3817] has bilateral spondylolysis at L5, but the other two cases (A[3200] and A[2898]) are slightly unusual because they are associated with other lumbo-sacral congenital defects.

In skeleton A[2898] there is bilateral spondylolysis of L4 in association with sacralisation of L5. Vertebra L4 has weakly developed transverse processes when compared to L3 or L5 that are inclined superiorly rather than perpendicular to the sagittal axis as in L1–L3. The detached segment of neural arch has come into direct contact with the left superior articular facet and both surfaces are eburnated at this point suggesting that the detached ossicle was capable of limited movement. Waldron (1992) also noted two cases of spondylolysis from St Mary Graces, London, where the detached segment became osteoarthritic.

Skeleton A[3200] shows bilateral spondylolysis at L5 associated with spina bifida occulta. Clinical studies have demonstrated that the proportion of individuals with spondylolysis in whom spina bifida occulta also occurs is usually 20–40%, although frequencies of up to 70% have been reported (Waldron 1993a, 55). An Anglo-Saxon example from Castle Mall, Norwich, has also been described (Anderson 1996, 15) but the spina bifida occulta only affected S1 and S2. In skeleton A[3200], the non-union in the midline seen between S1 and S5 also affects the separate posterior segment of L5 neural arch, that is it was in two halves not united in the midline, although one half of the ossicle has been lost post-mortem. The dysraphic defect extending to the L5 spondylolytic segment does appear, however, to be quite unusual.

Two individuals (A[3558], period M7; A[3200], period M5) have spina bifida occulta, where the posterior arches of the sacrum are open from S1 to S5. In A[3200], this was associated with spondylolysis (described above). Several other individuals had partial spina bifida occulta. Three sacra (A[2929], A[3099] and A[3251], period M5) had a non-union at S1 only; in A[3251] this was associated with a supernumary sixth lumbar vertebra. In A[2633] (period M5) non-union of S2–S5 was associated with a sixth lumbar vertebra. Five individuals also have the first coccygeal vertebra fused to the sacrum, three cases (A[3654], period M8; A[2643] and A[3294], period M7) were not associated with other lumbo-sacral congenital abnormality. Two other cases (A[3279], period M7; A[3914], period M5) were associated with lumbo-sacral congenital abnormality. There is one case of lumbarisation (A[3607], period M8) where S1 was separate from the sacrum and had a lumbar form. Skeleton A[2898] (period M7) had the reverse of this, where L5 had sacralised, that is had become incorporated into the sacrum. This was also associated with spondylolysis (above). Changes in rib segmentation had also occurred. Burial A[2812] for example showed a cranial shift in rib segmentation, C7 has cervical ribs and T12 has no rib facets and rudimentary transverse processes. Individual A[3613] (period M7) has no rib facets at T12.

Of a total of 14 individuals from the population as a whole with partial spina bifida occulta, five are from period M5; one of the two cases of spina bifida occulta is also from M5. There appears to be some spatial grouping of the six cases of spina bifida occulta and partial spina bifida occulta in period M5; the distribution of these cases in the cemetery (OA6) is shown in Fig 48 and discussed in Chapter 3.3 ('Archaeological evidence', 'Cemetery (OA6)').

Four individuals (A[2633] and A[3251], period M5; A[3268] and A[3279], period M7) had supernumerary lumbar vertebrae. The normal number of lumbar vertebrae is five, but these individuals had six. In two cases (A[2633] and A[3279]) the sixth vertebra was sacralised. Skeleton A[3251] was associated with dysraphism of S1. Chapman (1998, 47) describes four cases of sixth lumbar vertebrae dating from the medieval period, all of which were sacralised. In skeleton A[3501] (period M7) the posterior arch of the atlas is congenitally missing. Unfortunately, the skull is missing, so whether it was a separate bone or fused to the occipital must remain open to question. The embryological development of this area is complex and gives rise to a high incidence of congenital and acquired abnormalities (Black and Scheuer 1996, 189).

Five individuals had an absent third metacarpal styloid process. In two skeletons this was bilateral (A[3197], period M5; A[3015], period M7), but in the other three it was present in the right third metacarpal but the left was missing so it is impossible to tell if it was bilateral. In all five cases the styloid process was considerably reduced or absent and not present as a separate ossicle. In skeleton A[3200] (period M7) the hook of the right hamate is hypoplastic.

It can be seen that with many of the spinal congenital defects, one defect is found in association with another. Larger sample sizes will be needed to examine possible correlations in the prevalence of these defects.

Neoplastic disease

Neoplastic disease is an abnormal mass of tissue, commonly known as a tumour. It represents one of the rarer forms of disease seen in the archaeological record. However, there are some benign neoplasms that are seen more commonly. One example is dense outgrowths of bone from the outer table of the skull, often referred to as a 'button' or 'ivory' osteoma. These have no symptoms and are of little clinical significance. Two males (A[2640], period M7; A[3541], period M8) have solitary button osteomata on the right parietal bone, approximately 5mm in diameter. A third male A[3220] (period M7) had multiple osteomata; a total of nine were distributed all over the skull (four on the frontal, ranging from 4mm to 10mm in diameter, two on each parietal (10–20mm), one on the occipital (10mm) plus one on the lateral surface of the mandible below the right first molar (7mm). All were shallow protrusions not more than 2mm in height. Osteomata are usually solitary lesions, so the presence of one skull with nine is a little unusual. However, Stroud (Stroud and Kemp 1993, 223) describes a skull with over 20 from a medieval cemetery in York.

In addition to, and possibly related to, the multiple osteomata seen in skeleton A[3220] (period M7), is a solitary exostosis of bone in the same individual. The exostosis extends from the head of the fibula on to the posterior surface of the shaft, c 35mm in length, terminating in a small spike. This might represent an osteochondroma. The presence of both a benign osteogenic and chondrogenic neoplasm in the same individual might suggest that there is a relationship between the two and that they share the same aetiological factor. Alternatively, as both neoplasms are commonly occurring, their occurrence in the same individual could be due to chance.

Dental disease

Of the 193 individuals in this sample only 104 had the dentition present, either complete or incomplete. Of these 104 individuals, five could not be sexed and only three were female. As the number of females in this group is so low, this discussion relates to the presence of dental disease in the 94 males. Summaries of recorded dental pathology are given in Table 25. A total of 94 dentitions were assessed by tooth position for ante-mortem loss, non-eruption and abscesses, and by individual tooth for caries. Recovery of dentitions was good; out of a total of 3008 teeth (94 x 32 adult teeth) 2566 (85.3%) of the tooth positions were available for study. The amount of post-mortem tooth loss was low with only 8% lost altogether; single rooted teeth can drop out during the decay process and undoubtedly some will be lost during excavation.

Ante-mortem tooth loss

Severely diseased teeth such as those that have been partially destroyed by caries, or inflammation of the gums, will result in the disruption of the tooth socket and the tooth will drop out. The tooth socket (alveolus) will then remodel over with new

bone. In this group, the highest frequencies of ante-mortem tooth loss was seen in first and second molars. In the maxilla, the mean molar frequencies ranged from 15.3% to 19.6% compared to 2.6% to 3.7% in the anterior teeth. In the mandible, the mean frequency of ante-mortem molar loss ranged from 12.5% to 24.8% compared to 3% to 4% in the anterior teeth.

Abscesses

A dental abscess usually occurs when oral bacteria gain access to the tooth pulp cavity and the resulting infection then tracks down the root canal and causes a focal infection at the tip of the root in the surrounding bone. Accumulated quantities of pus will then extrude through the bone, leaving a hole in the alveolar bone. Abscesses in the maxilla can sometimes drain into the maxillary sinus creating an inflammation in the sinus (above, 'Infectious disease', 'Sinusitis'). Of a total of 1234 maxillary tooth positions, 41 (3.3%) showed an abscess (Table 25). Similarly, in the mandible, of 1332 positions, 34 (2.6%) showed an abscess. This frequency is similar to that seen at St Andrew Fishergate, York, where 1.6–4.1% of positions showed abscess cavity (Stroud and Kemp 1993, 201).

Caries

Oral bacteria ferment sugars found in the diet. A by-product of this is the production of acid, which in turn demineralises the

Table 25 Summary of dental pathology in maxilla and mandible (males only)

Maxillary dentition				Right								Left						
	M3	M2	MI	P4	P3	C	I2	I1	I1	I2	C	P3	P4	MI	M2	M3	Total
Tooth positions available	70	71	74	78	81	81	81	82	74	76	81	78	79	78	77	73	1234
Lost post-mortem	3	2	I	I	3	5	18	22	28	20	7	4	2	0	2	2	120
% lost post-mortem	4.3	2.8	1.4	1.3	3.7	6.2	22.2	26.8	37.8	26.3	8.6	5.1	2.5	-	2.6	2.7	9.7
Lost ante-mortem	9	10	14	3	5	I	2	4	2	2	I	2	3	19	17	9	103
% lost ante-mortem	12.9	14.1	18.9	3.8	6.2	1.2	2.5	4.9	2.7	2.6	1.2	2.6	3.8	24.4	22.1	12.3	8.3
Tooth unerupted	8	0	0	0	0	0	0	0	0	0	0	0	I	0	0	10	19
% unerupted	11.4	-	-	-	-	-	-	-	-	-	-	-	1.3	-	-	13.7	1.5
Positions with abscess cavity	I	5	6	2	2	3	I	0	I	I	2	3	3	6	4	I	41
% abscess cavities	1.4	7.0	8.1	2.6	2.5	3.7	1.2	-	1.4	1.3	2.5	3.8	3.8	7.7	5.2	1.4	3.3
Teeth	50	59	59	74	73	75	61	56	44	54	73	72	73	59	58	52	992
Caries cavity	5	6	12	11	7	3	2	I	I	2	2	5	2	10	9	8	86
% caries	10.0	10.2	20.3	14.9	9.6	4.0	3.3	1.8	2.3	3.7	2.7	6.9	2.7	16.9	15.5	15.4	8.7

Mandibular dentition				Right								Left						
	M3	M2	MI	P4	P3	C	I2	I1	I1	I2	C	P3	P4	MI	M2	M3	Total
Tooth positions available	83	83	81	81	82	84	84	84	83	83	83	84	82	85	85	85	1332
Lost post-mortem	I	I	I	4	5	7	10	14	14	10	6	4	3	I	3	I	85
% lost post-mortem	1.2	1.2	1.2	4.9	6.1	8.3	11.9	16.7	16.9	12.0	7.2	4.8	3.7	1.2	3.5	1.2	6.4
Lost ante-mortem	11	17	28	5	I	0	I	3	3	I	0	2	5	15	10	3	105
% lost ante-mortem	13.3	20.5	34.6	6.2	1.2	-	1.2	3.6	3.6	1.2	-	2.4	6.1	17.6	11.8	3.5	7.9
Unerupted	12	0	0	0	0	0	0	0	0	0	0	0	I	0	0	17	30
% unerupted	14.5	-	-	-	-	-	-	-	-	-	-	-	1.2	-	-	20.0	2.3
Positions with abscess cavity	0	3	8	I	I	I	2	3	3	0	I	2	0	8	0	I	34
% abscess cavities	-	3.6	9.9	1.2	1.2	1.2	2.4	3.6	3.6	-	1.2	2.4	-	9.4	-	1.2	2.6
Teeth	59	65	52	72	76	77	73	67	66	72	77	78	73	69	72	64	1112
Caries (one or more)	4	10	6	4	0	0	I	0	0	0	0	4	4	6	5	8	52
% caries	6.8	15.4	11.5	5.6	-	-	1.4	-	-	-	-	5.1	5.5	8.7	6.9	12.5	4.7

surface of the tooth. This causes a cavity to develop on the tooth enamel which progressively gets larger and penetrates through dentine into the pulp cavity of the tooth. The entire crown can be destroyed by such a process.

The caries frequency was calculated from the number of teeth rather than tooth positions. In the maxilla, 8.7% of teeth had at least one carious lesion, while in the mandible the overall frequency of caries was lower at 4.7% (Table 25). Caries was more common in the molar teeth with frequencies in the maxilla between 10.0% and 20.3% and in the mandible between 6.8% and 15.4%. The overall caries frequency at Bermondsey is 6.5% (138 lesions seen in 2104 teeth). This is similar to other medieval frequencies, for example that of St Nicholas Shambles was 5.5% (White 1988, 39). At Merton Priory 10.1% of teeth (in males) were affected by caries (Conheeney 2007, 274). At Stratford Langthorne, White (2004, 179) reports an overall caries frequency of 4.1% in males, suggesting that frequencies are in fact highly variable. This will depend much on the age profile as well.

Paget's disease

Paget's disease is a chronic disorder resulting from defective bone remodelling. The exact cause is not known, but it has a possible viral aetiology. Paget's disease usually affects people over 40 years and is more common in males than in females. The defective bone turnover usually involves a single bone or small groups of bones, but it rarely affects all bones in the body. Bones become thicker and more dense, in the early stages the bone becomes porotic followed by areas of sclerosis. In later stages there is thickening of the outer table of the skull, with loss of distinction between the inner and outer tables.

An isolated cranium A[1579] (unphased, and not counted in the sample) is noticeably heavier than is usual and the temporal bones are thickened. The frontal bone also has a thickened ridge in the sagittal plane. X-radiography shows enlarged cranial tables, up to 17mm thick, with obliteration of the diploic space. The grooves for the middle meningeal artery are also very clearly marked. These changes suggest that this individual suffered from Paget's disease.

Reported cases of Paget's disease in the palaeopathological record are rare (Stirland 1991; Roberts and Manchester 1995, 184). This might be due to the fact that it can only be recognised (macroscopically) in the later stages of the disease.

Pagetic changes might be detected in earlier stages if bones were routinely X-rayed. For example, Waldron (1993b) found four medieval cases of Paget's disease overall at the Royal Mint site, London (MIN86; Grainger et al 2008; Grainger and Phillpotts in prep), based on morphological features and confirmed by radiography. A further ten cases were found when radiography was carried out on bones x-rayed for other reasons. Waldron (1993b) found that the crude prevalence was 3.0% for males and 4.1% for females and that this was consistent with the prevalence found in modern populations, although here the women were more affected than the men.

Osteochondroses

In skeleton A[3220] (period M7) there are defects in the thoracic vertebrae. These defects consist of a failure of ossification on the anterior parts of the apophyseal rings on the inferior aspects of T4–T9. The T6–T8 section also displays a kyphotic defect (anterior slant of the spine). These changes might represent a possible case of Scheuermann's disease. Scheuermann's disease can be recognised by anterior wedging of thoracic vertebrae associated with localised bone destruction of the anterior margins of the vertebral end plates. The effect in the living individual produces a smooth rounded kyphosis or what may be termed a slight 'hunch-back' appearance. Scheuermann's disease usually affects adolescent males. The aetiology is not known (Lowe 1990), although Ortner and Putschar (1985) suggest the underlying cause is extrusion of nucleus pulposus (Schmorl's nodes) followed by anterior narrowing of the disc space and subsequent growth disturbance. Familial patterns, suggestive of a genetic aetiology, have been described although mechanical factors are gradually gaining credibility (Lowe 1990; Aufderheide and Rodriguez-Martin 1998).

Anderson and Carter (1994) note that Scheuermann's disease is rarely reported in the palaeopathological literature. One reason for this might be its confusion with intervertebral disc disease. Scheuermann's defects might also be masked by later age-related changes such as vertebral osteophytosis, although anterior wedging should indicate its presence. Clinical and radiological diagnostic criteria such as the presence of one or more vertebrae wedged for 5° or more and an increase in thoracic kyphosis of more than 40° have been suggested (Pecina and Bojanic 1993, 111–12) and this might be useful for archaeological material also.

FRENCH AND GERMAN SUMMARIES

Résumé

Elisabeth Lorans

Les fouilles conduites par MOLA (Museum of London Archaeology) sur le site du prieuré clunisien, plus tard érigé en abbaye, de Saint-Sauveur de Bermondsey, prirent place entre 1984 et 1995. Le site, autrefois dans le Surrey et maintenant intégré à la circonscription londonienne de Southwark, est protégé au titre des Monuments Historiques (GLSAM 165). Des travaux exécutés par W. F. Grimes en 1956 et 1962-1963 mirent au jour le côté nord du chevet de l'église abbatiale tandis que des fouilles récentes menées par PCA (Pre-Construct Archaeology Ltd) ont révélé des maçonneries dans la zone du bras sud du transept, de l'angle nord-est du cloître principal et de l'aile orientale (BYQ98 ; WBP07), des données qui ont été incluses dans cette publication. Des dessins et des observations effectués par l'antiquaire J. C. Buckler ont aussi été utilisés pour compléter et interpréter les éléments fournis par les travaux récents.

Les données archéologiques sont présentées par ordre chronologique (chapitres 2, 3 et 5) : un bref résumé de l'occupation préhistorique et romaine est suivi par ce qui concerne l'habitat de l'époque saxonne moyenne et tardive. Les premières constructions médiévales consistaient en une petite chapelle à abside, édifiée à la fin de l'époque saxonne ou au début de l'époque normande et entourée de fossés, et en des latrines en bois qui enjambaient le fossé au sud. Vers le milieu du XIIe siècle, la construction de l'église abbatiale et des principaux bâtiments monastiques avait bien progressé ; les réalisations incluaient les structures entourant le cloître principal doté d'un lavabo : l'aile orientale du dortoir, les latrines situées derrière lui et peut-être les bains, ainsi que le réfectoire. Le chevet de l'église prieurale fut reconstruit sous une forme asymétrique avec cinq chapelles échelonnées. Le cimetière monastique fut établi entre l'église et la chapelle primitive. Vers la fin du XIIe siècle, le sous-sol de l'aile orientale reçut une nouvelle voûte et un nouveau bâtiment de latrines fut édifié perpendiculairement à son extrémité méridionale. A l'est, la première infirmerie fut édifiée, avec son propre bâtiment de latrines et une grande salle ou des logements au sud. Un nouveau système de drainage fut également réalisé. Une chapelle à abside supplémentaire fut ajoutée au bas-côté nord de l'église prieurale, tandis que la chapelle saxo-normande fut conservée et agrandie. Un mur maçonné entoura la partie sud-ouest du monastère.

Dans la première moitié du XIIIe siècle, le second cloître, celui de l'infirmerie, fut étendu et le bâtiment à fonction de grande salle ou de logements reçut des cuisines et salle supplémentaires. La seconde moitié du XIIIe siècle et le début du XIVe siècle virent des changements majeurs apportés à l'infirmerie, avec l'abandon des latrines, l'ajout de structures et d'une cour à l'est et l'extension et la rénovation de la chapelle au nord de l'infirmerie. Au XIVe siècle (à partir de 1330 environ), l'église prieurale fut allongée par un chevet rectangulaire et un second bas-côté fut ajouté au nord. Le cloître principal et la salle capitulaire furent remodelés et une forte activité de construction fut entreprise en divers lieux : dans l'aile sud, autour du second cloître et sur son flanc oriental où une vaste cour et de nouveaux logements furent réalisés. Avant la Dissolution, cette zone est était déjà à l'abandon. La période de la Dissolution suggère un abandon rapide et un démantèlement systématique. Les données concernant le manoir d'époque Tudor édifié par Thomas Pope autour de l'ancien grand cloître sont présentées.

Certains aspects du prieuré médiéval sont traités de manière thématique (chapitre 4). Une section consacrée à la fondation aborde des questions complexes, y compris celle du *minster* anglo-saxon établi dans l'îlot de Bermondsey. La petite chapelle absidiale, une structure qui appartient à la période de transition, cruciale, qu'est la fin de l'époque saxonne et le début de l'époque normande, fait l'objet d'un intérêt particulier. Les plans restitués des phases du XIIe siècle et des environs de 1400 de l'église prieurale dédiée au Saint-Sauveur sont analysés à la lumière d'exemples contemporains en Angleterre et sur le continent. La topographie locale et le paysage précoce ainsi que leur impact sur le plan et les transformations du monastère et de la ferme associée sont examinés, en prenant en compte des bâtiments situés dans l'enclos et connus uniquement par les sources écrites. L'infirmerie et ses adaptations constantes tout au long de l'existence du prieuré sont analysées, avec une attention particulière portée à la ségrégation dans les premiers temps. Une section est consacrée aux occupants du monastère et tente de définir certains des processus sociaux les plus complexes à l'œuvre dans l'enclos : la démographie et l'état sanitaire des inhumés dans le cimetière monastique ainsi que les pratiques funéraires ; la culture matérielle et la diète ; la préparation culinaire, l'hygiène et l'approvisionnement en eau propre ; les fondements économiques du prieuré et les activités industrielles prenant place dans l'enclos. Un riche assemblage d'objets et de matériaux provenant des bâtiments conventuels est représenté et analysé.

Le chapitre 6 présente les résultats majeurs et les conclusions qui peuvent être tirées de l'étude du prieuré clunisien de Bermondsey et compare les objectifs premiers du projet de recherche aux résultats atteints pour établir la liste des questions restées en suspens. Les annexes des spécialistes (chapitre 7) incluent l'étude détaillée des informations livrées par les recherches conduites au XIXe siècle par John Chessel Buckler, celle des éléments architecturaux préservés, des autres matériaux de construction en pierre ou en céramique, des vitraux et de la poterie, le tout accompagné de catalogues et d'études complémentaires du mobilier. Enfin, elles comprennent aussi l'analyse des restes fauniques et celle des 193 individus inhumés sur place.

Zusammenfassung

Manuela Struck

An der Stelle des Cluniazenserpriorats und der späteren Abtei von St. Salvator in Bermondsey fanden zwischen 1984 und 1995 Ausgrabungen des Archäologischen Dienstes des Museum of London (MOLA) statt. Der Fundplatz, ehemals in der Grafschaft Surrey und heute Teil des Londoner Bezirks von Southwark, steht unter Denkmalschutz mit der Bezeichnung „Greater London Scheduled Ancient Monument (GLSAM) 165". Die von W. F. Grimes geleiteten Arbeiten legten 1956 und 1962–3 die Nordseite des Ostendes der Klosterkirche frei, während vor kurzem Ausgrabungen der Pre-Construct Archaeology Ltd (PCA) Mauerwerk im Gebiet des südlichen Querschiffs, der Nordostecke des Hauptkreuzganges und des Ostflügels zutage förderten (BYQ98; WBP07); Informationen dieser Kampagnen wurden in die vorliegende Publikation mit aufgenommen. Zeichnungen und die Bauaufnahme des Antiquars J. C. Buckler wurden ebenso genutzt, um die Ergebnisse der modernen Ausgrabungen zu ergänzen und zu erhellen.

Die archäologischen Befunde werden in chronologischer Reihenfolge (Kapitel 2, 3 und 5) beginnend mit einer kurzen Zusammenfassung der prähistorischen und römischen Aktivitäten im Untersuchungsgebiet, gefolgt von den Befunden für die mittel- und spätsächsische Besiedlung vorgestellt. Die ersten Gebäude am Fundplatz waren eine kleine Kapelle mit Apsis, die in der spätsächsischen oder frühnormannischen Zeit errichtet worden und von Gräben umgeben war, sowie eine Holzlatrine über dem südlichen Graben. Bis zur Mitte des 12. Jhs. schritt die Arbeit an der Prioratskirche und einigen der wichtigsten Konventgebäuden fort. Diese schlossen die Konstruktionen um den Hauptkreuzgang mit seinem freistehenden Waschbrunnen ein, nämlich den Schlafsaal im Ostflügel, die Latrine hinter dem Schlafsaal und ein mögliches Badehaus sowie das Refektorium. Das Ostende der Prioratskirche wird in Form von fünf parallel verlaufenden Apsiden in asymmetrischer Staffelstellung rekonstruiert. Der Klosterfriedhof entstand zwischen Kirche und früherer Kapelle. Im späteren 12. Jh. wurde das Untergeschoss des Ostflügels mit einem neuen Gewölbe versehen und eine neue Schlafsaallatrine in Stein über dem Südende des Ostflügels erbaut. Im Osten entstand der erste Krankenhauskomplex mit seiner eigenen Latrine und einer Halle oder Unterkünften im Süden. Eine weitere Neuheit war das Entwässerungssystem. Eine zusätzliche Kapelle mit Apsis wurde dem Nordschiff der Prioratskirche angefügt, während die spätsächsisch-normannische Kapelle beibehalten und vergrößert wurde. Eine Steinmauer umschloss nun den Südwestteil der Klosteranlage.

In der ersten Hälfte des 13. Jhs. wurde der zweite Kreuzgang mit dem Krankenhaus erweitert, und die Halle oder Unterkünfte erhielten eine neue Küche und Halle. Während der zweiten Hälfte des 13. und dem frühen 14. Jh. kam es zu größeren Umbauten für das Krankenhaus: Die Krankenhauslatrine wurde nicht mehr benutzt, neue Konstruktionen und ein weiterer Hof im Osten entstanden, und die Kapelle im Norden des Krankenhauses wurde vergrößert und renoviert. Im 14. Jh. (nach ca. 1330) wurde die Prioratskirche in ihrer Längsachse erweitert und mit einem rechteckigen Ostabschluß sowie einem zweiten Seitenschiff im Norden versehen. Gleichzeitig erhielten der Hauptkreuzgang und der Kapitelsaal eine neue Form. Auch andernorts wurde in großem Stil umgebaut, nämlich im Südflügel, um den zweiten

Kreuzgang herum und in seinem unmittelbaren Osten, wo ein großer Hof und neue Räume errichtet wurden. Schon in der Zeit vor der Säkularisierung wurde dieser östliche Bereich nicht mehr genutzt. Die Befunde aus der Periode der Säkularisierung sprechen für eine sofortige Aufgabe und eine systematische Demontage. Die Belege für das tudorzeitliche Herrenhaus, das von Thomas Pope um den ehemaligen Hauptkreuzgang errichtet wurde, werden abschließend beschrieben.

Kapitel 4 behandelt einzelne Aspekte des mittelalterlichen Priorats. Ein Abschnitt über die Gründung spricht einige komplizierte Umstände an, welche den Beginn des Priorats umgeben, inklusive das Verhältnis zur klosterähnlichen angelsächsischen Gründung (minster) auf der Flussinsel von Bermondsey. Die kleine apsidiale Kapelle, ein Gebäude aus den für die Problematik entscheidenden spätsächsisch-frühnormannischen Übergangsjahren, ist von großem Interesse. Die rekonstruierten Grundrisse der Bauphasen der dem Heiland geweihten Prioratskirche aus dem 12. Jh. und von ca. 1400 werden mit den zeitgleichen englischen und kontinentalen Beispielen verglichen. Die örtliche Topographie und frühe Landschaft sowie ihr Einfluss auf den folgenden Entwurf und die Entwicklung von Kloster und Gutshof des Klosters werden untersucht, wobei verschiedene Gebäude auf dem Klostergelände mit einbezogen werden, die wir lediglich aus den schriftlichen Quellen kennen. Beachtung erfährt auch das

Krankenhaus und sein andauernder Ausbau während des Bestehens des Priorats mit besonderem Augenmerk auf Hinweisen für Quarantäne in den frühen Phasen. Ein Abschnitt über die Klosterbewohner versucht einige komplexere soziale Themen anzusprechen, indem Demographie und Gesundheit der Bestatteten im klösterlichen Friedhof, Grabsitten, materielle Kultur und Ernährung der Population, Zubereitung des Essens, Hygiene und Versorgung des Hauses mit frischem Wasser, die wirtschaftliche Grundlage des Priorats und Belege für gewerbliche Aktivitäten innerhalb des Klosters untersucht werden; ein großer und auf einzigartige Weise informativer Fundkomplex, der Abfall von den Konventsgebäuden darstellt, wird in Abbildungen präsentiert und behandelt.

Kapitel 6 erwägt die Ergebnisse und Folgerungen aus den Untersuchungen des Cluniazenserklosters von Bermondsey und evaluiert, in wieweit die ursprünglichen Ziele des Forschungsprojektes erreicht wurden und welche Fragen noch zu beantworten sind. Die Anhänge der Spezialisten (Kapitel 7) beinhalten detaillierte Studien zu den Ergebnissen der Bauaufnahme von John Chessell Buckler aus dem 19. Jh. und der noch erhaltenen Architekturfragmente sowie des übrigen Stein- und keramischen Baumaterials, des Fensterglases und der Keramik. Sie umfassen außerdem Kataloge der Kleinfunde sowie die Analyse der Tierknochen und der Skelette von 193 hier bestatteten Menschen.

BIBLIOGRAPHY

Manuscript sources

British Library, London, manuscripts department (BL)

Add MS 24432 A and B history and description of the abbey of St Saviour Bermondsey and Sir Thomas Pope's mansion by John Chessell Buckler

Add MS 24433 plans and drawings of the abbey of St Saviour Bermondsey and Sir Thomas Pope's mansion by John Chessell Buckler, 1808–26

Add MS 36400A Buckler drawings vol XLV, Buckler's architectural drawings and descriptive notes of Reading Abbey

Cotton MS Claudius A.viii excerpts from the monastic charters of St Saviour Bermondsey

Conway Library, The Courtauld Institute of Art, University of London

Photographic collection of 12th-century monastic architecture and lapidary examples

The Cuming Museum, Southwark, London

The Cuming Collection archive

English Heritage, London Division, London

GLSMR Greater London Sites and Monuments Record
HB92 archive of works carried out within study area *c* 1902–22

London Metropolitan Archives (LMA)

(includes the former Guildhall Library's Print Room Collection, much of which is available online at COLLAGE: City of London Library and Art Gallery Electronic)

Pennant's London Collection volume including drawings by John Chessell Buckler:

p5359533 view of the abbey of St Saviour in Bermondsey, watercolour by J C Buckler, 1809, Pennant's London 6

p5369046 view of the pavilion at the north-east corner of Bermondsey House, wash by J C Buckler, 1816, Pennant's London 30

p5369520 view of the ruins of Bermondsey House, wash by J C Buckler, 1827, Pennant's London 33

p5368325 view of parts of the north wall in the garden of Bermondsey House, wash by J C Buckler, 1810, Pennant's London 36

p5369402 view of the north range and quadrangle of Bermondsey House, watercolour by J C Buckler, 1827, Pennant's London 37

Wakefield Collection:
p5367969 view of the remains of Thomas Pope's house, Mill Lane, Bermondsey, wash by J C Buckler, 1808, W.B2/MIL

The National Archives (TNA): Public Record Office (PRO)

CHANCERY
C2 court of Chancery
C66 patent rolls
C78 Chancery decree rolls
C81 warrants for the Great Seal, series I

EXCHEQUER CLASSES
E40 Treasury of receipt: ancient deeds, series A
E135 miscellaneous ecclesiastical documents
E178 special commissions of inquiry
E305 Court of Augmentations: deeds of purchase and exchange
E315 Court of Augmentations and predecessors and successors: miscellaneous books
E318 commissioners for the sale of crown lands: particulars for grants
E326 Augmentation office: ancient deeds

PREROGATIVE COURT OF CANTERBURY (PCC) WILLS
PROB 11/3 q 16 William Convers alias Kelshall, will dated 1428, proved 22 July 1432; PCC 16 Luffenham
PROB 11/3 q 19 Alice Kelshull [Kelshall], will dated 28 October 1433, proved 26 October 1435; PCC 19 Luffenham
PROB 11/6 q 12 Margaret de la Pole, will dated 17 May 1472; PCC 12 Wattys
PROB 11/11 q 14 Thomas Ashby, will dated 25 June 1487, proved 5 July 1497; PCC 14 Horne
PROB 11/11 q 23 Ann Lady Audley, will dated 11 November 1497, proved 24 June [14]98; PCC 23 Horne
PROB 11/14 q 18 fo 138 John Wippill clerk, will dated 24 Aug 1504, proved 15 Oct 1504; PCC 18 Holgrave
PROB 11/17 q 18 fo 139 Mathew Baker, will dated 26 May 5 Henry VIII [1513], proved 12 July 1513; PCC 18 Fettiplace
PROB 11/18 q 36 fo 287 Anne Baskerville, will dated 23 January 1513, 4 Henry VIII, proved 17 November 1517; PCC 36 Holder
PROB 11/25 q 7, fo 38 John Edgecumbe, will dated 28 October 25 Henry VIII [1533], proved 12 November 1533; PCC 7 Hogen

SPECIAL COLLECTIONS
SC1 ancient correspondence of the Chancery and the Exchequer
SC6 ministers' and receivers' accounts
SC8 ancient petitions

Natural History Museum, London

Collections, Library and Archive

Salisbury and South Wiltshire Museum, Salisbury

Medieval collection no. 270/1945 pinnacle from Old Sarum

Southwark Local History Library, London (SL)

Maps 174–5 (copied by Claudina Eastwall-Naijna *c* 1969) and PB 2804 and PB 2806 (photographs taken 1949 or 1950) 17th-century plans of the post-Dissolution Bermondsey House (PB 2804 dated ?1699; PB 2806 bird's eye view dated *c* 1650)

Printed and other secondary works

Aldrich, M, 1985 Gothic architecture illustrated: the drawings of Thomas Rickman in New York, *Antiq J* 65, 427–33

Alexander, J S, 1996 Masons' marks and stone bonding, in *The archaeology of cathedrals* (eds T Tatton-Brown and J Munby), Oxford Univ Comm Archaeol Monogr 42, 219–36, Oxford

Amorosi, T, 1989 *A postcranial guide to domestic neo-natal and juvenile mammals*, BAR Int Ser 533, Oxford

Andermann, S, 1976 The cnemic index: a critique, *American J Phys Anthropol* 44, 369–70

Anderson, S, 1996 The human skeletal remains from Farmer's Avenue, Castle Mall, Norwich, unpub Engl Heritage Ancient Monuments Lab rep 59/96

Anderson, T, and Carter, A R, 1994 A possible example of Scheuermann's disease from Iron Age Deal, Kent, *J Palaeopathol* 6(2), 57–62

Anfray, M, 1951 *L'Architecture religieuse du Nivernais au moyen age: les eglises romanes*, Paris

Anglo-Saxon Chron The Anglo-Saxon chronicle according to the several original authorities (ed and trans B Thorpe), Rolls Ser 23, 2 vols, 1861, London

Ann Monast Annales monastici: Vol 3, Annales monasterii de Bermundeseia, AD 1042–1432 (ed H R Luard), Rolls Ser, 5 vols, 1866, London

Archaeology Data Service, nd [Bermondsey Abbey archive], http://ads.ahds.ac.uk/catalogue/resources.html?stsaviour_eh_2009 (last accessed 11 September 2010)

Arriaza, B T, 1997 Spondylolysis in prehistoric human remains from Guam and its possible etiology, *American J Phys Anthropol* 104, 393–7

Askew, P, 1995 Land bounded by Long Walk, Tower Bridge Road and Grange Walk, London SE1, London Borough of Southwark: an archaeological watching brief (TWB94), unpub MOL rep

Astill, G G, 1993 *A medieval industrial complex and its landscape: the metalworking watermills and workshops of Bordesley Abbey. Bordesley Abbey: Vol 3*, CBA Res Rep 92, York

Astill, G, Hirst, S, and Wright, S M, 2004 The Bordesley Abbey Project reviewed, *Archaeol J* 161, 106–58

Aubertin, A, 1973 *Abbaye de Jumièges*, Jumièges

Aufderheide, A C, and Rodriguez-Martin, C, 1998 *The Cambridge encyclopedia of human palaeopathology*, Cambridge

Baker, J, and Brothwell, D, 1980 *Animal diseases in archaeology*, London

Bangs, C, 1995 *The Lear collection: a study of copper-alloy socket candlesticks AD 200–1700*, London

Barber, B, and Thomas, C, 2002 *The London Charterhouse*, MoLAS Monogr Ser 10, London

Barber, B, Chew, S, Dyson, T, and White, B, 2004 *The Cistercian abbey of St Mary Stratford Langthorne, Essex: archaeological excavations for the London Underground Limited Jubilee Line Extension Project*, MoLAS Mongr Ser 18, London

Barron, C, and Davies, M (eds), 2007 *The religious houses of London and Middlesex*, London

Barton, N J, 1994 (1992) *The lost rivers of London: a study of their effects upon London and Londoners, and the effects of London and Londoners upon them*, rev edn, London

Bass, W M, 1995 *Human osteology: a laboratory and field manual*, 4 edn, Missouri Archaeol Soc Spec Pap 2, Columbia, Miss

Beard, D, 1986 The infirmary of Bermondsey Priory, *London Archaeol* 5, 186–91

Bellamy, C V, 1965 *Pontefract Priory excavations 1957–61*, Publ Thoresby Soc 49, Leeds

Berry, A C, 1978 Anthropological and family studies in minor variants of the dental crown, in *Development, function and evolution of the teeth* (eds P M Butler and K A Joysey), 81–98, London

Berry, A C, and Berry, R J, 1967 Epigenetic variation in the human cranium, *J Anatomy* 101, 361–79

Besant, W, 1912 *London: south of the Thames*, Survey of London, London

Betts, I, 1998 Bermondsey Abbey (BA84): the building material, unpub MOL rep

Betts, I, 2007 Ceramic and stone building material, in Miller and Saxby 2007, 195–214

Betts, I M, 1990 Building materials, in Medieval buildings in the vicinity of Cheapside, London (eds J Schofield, P Allan and C Taylor), *Trans London Middlesex Archaeol Soc* 41, 220–9

Betts, I M, 1991 Building materials, Billingsgate Fish Market car park, Lower Thames Street, EC3, upub MOL rep

Betts, I M, 1995a Procuratorial tile stamps from London, *Britannia* 26, 207–29

Betts, I M, 1995b St Mary Clerkenwell nunnery, building materials, unpub MOL rep

Betts, I M, 1996 Glazed 11th-century wall tiles from London, *Medieval Ceram* 20, 19–24

Betts, I M, 1997 Building materials, in Excavations on the site of St Nicholas Shambles, Newgate Street, City of London, 1975–9 (ed J Schofield), *Trans London Middlesex Archaeol Soc* 48, 122–30

Betts, I M, 2002 *Medieval 'Westiminster' floor tiles*, MoLAS Monogr Ser 11, London

Betts, I M, 2007 Ceramic building material (and slate), in Bowsher, D, Dyson, T, Holder, N, and Howell, I, *The London Guildhall: an archaeological history of a neighbourhood from early medieval to modern times*, MoLAS Monogr Ser 36, 430–7, London

Betts, I M, Bateman, N, and Porter, G, 1995 Two late Anglo-Saxon tiles and the early history of St Lawrence, Jewry, London, *Medieval Archaeol* 39, 165–9

Biddle, M (ed), 1990 *Object and economy in medieval Winchester: artefacts from medieval Winchester*, Winchester Stud 7(2) (2 vols), Oxford

Bilson, J, 1909 The architecture of the Cistercians, *Archaeol J* 64, 185–280

Binski, P, and Massing, A (eds), with Sauerberg, M L, 2009 *The Westminster Retable: history, technique, conservation*, Painting and Practice 2, Cambridge

Black, S, and Scheuer, L, 1996 Occipitalisation of the atlas with reference to its embryological development, *Int J Osteoarchaeol* 6, 189–94

Blackmore, L, 1988 The pottery, in Cowie, R, and Whytehead, R L, with Blackmore, L, Two Middle Saxon occupation sites: excavations at Jubilee Hall and 21–22 Maiden Lane, *Trans London Middlesex Archaeol Soc* 39, 81–110

Blackmore, L, 1989 The pottery, in Whytehead, R L, and Cowie, R, with Blackmore, L, Excavations at the Peabody site, Chandos Place, and the National Gallery, *Trans London Middlesex Archaeol Soc* 40, 71–107

Blackmore, L, 1994 Pottery, the port and the populace: the imported pottery of London 1300–1600 (part 1), *Medieval Ceram* 18, 29–44

Blackmore, L, 1995 The Middle Saxon pottery, in Mills, P S, Excavations at the east range undercroft, Westminster Abbey, *Trans London and Middlesex Archaeol Soc* 46, 69–124

Blackmore, L, 2004 The pottery, in Sloane and Malcolm 2004, 331–55

Blackmore, L, 2008 The pottery, in Cowie and Blackmore 2008, 168–93

Blair, J, 1987 English monumental brasses before 1350: types, patterns and workshops, in *The earliest English brasses: patronage, style and workshops 1270–1350* (ed J Coales), Monumental Brass Soc, 133–75, London

Blair, J, 1991 *Early medieval Surrey: landholding, church and settlement before 1300*, Stroud

Blair, J, 1996 The minsters of the Thames, in *The cloister and the world: essays in medieval history in honour of Barbara Harvey* (eds J Blair and B Golding), 5–28, Oxford

Blair, J, 2005 *The church in Anglo-Saxon society*, Oxford

Blatherwick, S, and Bluer, R, 2009 *Great houses, moats and mills on the south bank of the Thames: medieval and Tudor Southwark and Rotherhithe*, MOLA Monogr Ser 47, London

Blows, J, 2001 A geological assessment of the architectural fragments, in Hicks and Hicks 2001, 183–6

Bond, J, 2001 Monastic water mangement in Great Britain: a review, in *Monastic archaeology: papers on the study of medieval monasteries* (eds G Keevill, M Aston and T Hall), 88–136, Oxford

Borg, A, 1967 The development of chevron ornament, *J Brit Archaeol Ass* 30, 3 ser, 122–40

Boylston, A, and Roberts, C A, 1997 Lincoln excavations 1972–87: report on the human skeletal remains, unpub Engl Heritage Ancient Monuments Lab rep 13/97

Bradley, S, and Pevsner, N, 2003 *The buildings of England London: Vol 6, Westminster*, London

Brayley, E W, 1850 *Topographical history of Surrey*, London

Brett, M, 1992 The annals of Bermondsey, Southwark and Merton, in *Church and city 1000–1500: essays in honour of Christopher Brooke* (eds D Abulafia, M Franklin and M Rubin), 279–310, Cambridge

Brodribb, G, 1987 *Roman brick and tile*, Gloucester

Brooks, S T, and Suchey, J M, 1990 Skeletal age determination based on the *os pubis*: comparison of the Acsàdi-Nemèskeri and Suchey-Brooks methods, *J Human Evol* 5, 227–38

Brothwell, D R, 1981 (1963) *Digging up bones: the excavation, treatment and study of human skeletal remains*, 3 edn, London

Brown, D, 1995 Iberian pottery excavated in medieval Southampton, in Gerrard, C M, Gutierrez, A, and Vince, A G, *Spanish medieval ceramics in Spain and the British Isles*, BAR Int Ser 610, 319–28, Oxford

Buckler, J C, 1828 *An historical and descriptive account of the royal palace at Eltham*, London

Buikstra, J E, and Ubelaker, D H (eds), 1994 *Standards for data collection from human skeletal remains*, Arkansas Archaeol Survey Res Ser 44, Fayetteville

Burton, J, 1994 *Monastic and religious orders in Britain, 1000–1300*, Cambridge

Cal Chart R Calendars of charter rolls (6 vols), 1903–27, London

Cal Close R Calendars of close rolls, 1892–1975, London

Cal Fine R Calendars of fine rolls (22 vols), 1911–62, London

Cal Husting Wills Calendar of wills proven and enrolled in the Court of Husting, London, 1258–1688 (ed R R Sharpe), 2 vols, 1889–90, London

Cal Inq Misc Calendar of inquisitions miscellaneous (Chancery), preserved in the Public Record Office (8 vols), 1916–2003, London

Cal Pat R Calendar of patent rolls preserved in the Public Record Office (65 vols, 1291–1509, 1547–63), 1893–1948, London

Cal Pat R Edw I Calendar of the patent rolls preserved in the Public Record Office: Edward I (4 vols, 1272–1307), 1993–71, London

Cal Pat R Eliz Calendar of the patent rolls preserved in the Public Record Office: Elizabeth: Vol 7, 1575–8, 1939–, London

Cal Pat R Hen III Calendar of the patent rolls preserved in the Public Record Office: Henry III (6 vols, 1216–72), 1901–13, London

Cal Plea and Mem R Calendar of plea and memoranda rolls preserved among the archives of the Corporation of the City of London: Vols 1–4, 1323–1437 (ed A H Thomas), 1926–43, Cambridge; *Vols 5–6, 1437–82* (ed P E Jones), 1953–61, London

Campbell, M, 1998 Medieval metalworking and Bury St Edmunds, in *Bury St Edmunds: medieval art, architecture, archaeology and economy* (ed A Gransden), Brit Archaeol Ass Conference Trans 20, 69–80, Leeds

Cannon, D Y, 1987 *Marine fish osteology: a manual for archaeologists*, Burnaby, Canada

Cart Holy Trinity The cartulary of Holy Trinity, Aldgate (ed G A J Hodgett), London Rec Soc Publ 7, 1971, Leicester

Cat Anc Deeds A descriptive catalogue of ancient deeds in the Public Record Office (6 vols), 1890–1915, London

CBA, 1987 Counc Brit Archaeol, *Recording worked stones: a practical guide*, CBA Practical Handbooks in Archaeology 1, London

Chapman, S, 1998 The incidence and effects of supernumeracy 6th lumbar vertebrae in two medieval human populations, in *Current and recent research in osteoarchaeology: proceedings of the third meeting of the Osteoarchaeological Research Group held in Leicester on 18 November 1995* (eds S Anderson and K Boyle), 47–9, Oxford

Cherry, J, 1991 Pottery and tile, in *English medieval industries: craftsmen, techniques, products* (eds J Blair and N Ramsay), 189–209, London

Cherry, J, 2001 Enamels, in *Salisbury and South Wiltshire museum medieval catalogue: Part 3* (ed P Saunders), 39–42, Salisbury

Chew, H M, and Weinbaum, M (eds), 1970 *The London eyre of 1244*, London Rec Soc 6, London

Chron Majora Matthaei Parisiensis, monachi Sancti Albani, chronica majora (ed H R Luard), Chronicles and memorials of Great Britain and Ireland during the Middle Ages (7 vols), 1872–80, London

Clapham, A W, 1934 *English Romanesque architecture: after the Conquest*, Oxford

Clark, J (ed), 1995 *The medieval horse and its equipment*, HMSO Medieval Finds Excav London 5, London

Clark, K, 1995 *The gothic revival*, London

Clarke, E T, 1901 *Bermondsey: its historic memories and associations*, London

Clay, P, 1981 The small finds: non-structural, in Mellor, J E, and Pearce, T, *The Austin Friars, Leicester*, CBA Res Rep 35, 130–45, London

Cluny Recueil des chartes de l'abbaye de Cluny: Vol 6, 1211–1300 (eds A Bernard and A Bruel), 1903, London

Coad, J G, 2003 *The battle of Hastings and the story of Battle Abbey*, London

Coad, J G, and Coppack, G, 1998 *Castle Acre castle and priory, Norfolk*, London

Cohen, A, and Serjeantson, D, 1996 (1986) *A manual for the identification of bird bones from archaeological sites*, rev edn, London

Colvin, H M (ed), 1963 *The history of the kings works: Vol 2, The Middle Ages*, 989–93, London

Conant, K J, 1959 *Carolingian and Romanesque architecture 800 to 1200*, Harmondsworth

Conant, K J, 1968 *Cluny: les églises et la maison du Chef d'Ordre*, Mediaeval Academy of America 77, Imprimerie Protat Frères, Mâcon

Conant, K J, 1987 (1959) *Carolingian and Romanesque architecture 800 to 1200*, 2 edn, London

Conheeney, J, 1997 The human bone, in Thomas et al 1997, 218–31

Conheeney, J, 2007 The human bone, in Miller and Saxby 2007, 255–77

Connell, B, and Rauxloh, P, 2007 A rapid method for recording human skeletal data, unpub MOL rep

Cook, G H, 1960 *The English cathedral through the centuries*, London

Coppack, G, 1990 *English Heritage book of abbeys and priories*, London

Coppack, G, 1991 *Mount Grace Priory*, London

Coppack, G, 1999 Free-standing cloister lavabos of the 12th and 13th centuries in England, their form, occurrence and water supply, in *Wasser-Lebensquelle und Bedeutungsträger: Wasserversorgung in Vergangenheit und Gegenwart: Regensburger Herbstsymposium zu Kunstgeschichte und Denkmalpflege* (eds H-E Paulus, H Reidel and P W Winkler), vol 4, 37–43, Regensburg

Coppack, G, 2006 *Abbeys and priories*, Stroud

Cornforth, J L, and Wall, C St Q, 1975 *Sudbury Hall, Derbyshire*, NT guidebook, no place

Cowan, C, Seeley, F, Wardle, A, Westman, A, and Wheeler, L, 2009 *Roman Southwark settlement and economy*, MOLA Monogr Ser 42, London

Cowgill, J, Neergaard, M de, and Griffiths, N, 1987 *Knives and scabbards*, HMSO Medieval Finds Excav London 1, London

Cowie, R, and Blackmore, L, 2008 *Early and Middle Saxon rural settlement in the London region*, MoLAS Monogr Ser 41, London

Cowie, R, and Corcoran, J, 2008 The prehistoric, Roman and later landscape between Watling Street and Bermondsey eyot: investigations at Rephidim Street and Hartley's jam factory, Bermondsey, *Surrey Archaeol Collect* 94, 159–79

Cronne, H A, and Davis, R H C, 1968 *Regesta regum Anglo-Normannorum, 1066–1154: Vol 3, 1135–54*, Oxford

Crowley, N, 1997 Ceramic building material, in Thomas et al 1997, 195–201

Dandy, D J, 1993 (1989) *Essential orthopaedics and trauma*, 2 edn, Edinburgh

Davis, H W C, and Whitwell, R J, 1913 *Regesta regum Anglo-Normannorum 1066–1154: Vol 1, 1066–1100*, Oxford

Davis, R H C, 1954 A catalogue of masons' marks, an aid to architectural history, *J Brit Archaeol Ass* 17, 3 ser, 43–76

Dawes, J D, and Magilton, J R, 1980 *The cemetery of St Helen-on-the-Walls, Aldwark*, The Archaeology of York 12/1, York

Dawson, G, 2002 What happened at Bermondsey at the Dissolution, *Southwark Lambeth Archaeol Soc Newslet* 92 (December), 4–7

Dawson, G, 2008 Letter to the editor: Bermondsey Abbey precinct, *London Archaeol* 12, 39

Dawson, G J, 1979 Excavations at Guy's Hospital, 1967, *Res Vol Surrey Archaeol Soc* 7, 27–65, Guildford

Degnan, S, and Seeley, D, 1988 Medieval and later floor tiles in Lambeth Palace chapel, *London Archaeol* 6, 11–18

Dennis, G, and Hinton, P, 1983 A medieval kiln group from Bankside, SE1, *London Archaeol* 4, 283–7

Department of the Environment, 1990 *Planning policy guidance note 16: archaeology and planning*, London

Department of Trade and Industry, 1998 *Adult data: handbook of adult anthropometric and strength measurements data for design safety*, Government Consumer Safety Research, London

Dickens, A G, 1967 (1964) *The English reformation*, rev edn, Glasgow

Divers, D, 1998 An archaeological evaluation at Bermondsey Square, London Borough of Southwark, unpub PCA rep

Dixon, P, and Lott, B, 1993 The courtyard and the tower: contexts and symbols in the development of late medieval great houses, *J Brit Archaeol Ass* 146, 93–101

Doggett, N, 2002 *Patterns of reuse: the transformation of former monastic buildings in post-Dissolution Hertfordshire, 1540–1600*, BAR Brit Ser 331, Oxford

Domingo, C de, 1994 The provenance of some building stones in St Mary Spital by geological methods, *London Archaeol* 7, 240–3

Driesch, A von den, 1976 *A guide to the measurement of animal bones from archaeological sites*, Peabody Mus Bull 1, Cambridge, Mass

Driesch, A von den, and Boessneck, J A, 1974 Kritische Anmerkungen zur Widerristhöhenberechnung aus Längenmassen vor- und frühgeschichtlicher Tierknochen, *Saugetierkundliche Mitteilungen* 22, 325–48

Duckett, G F (ed), 1888 *Charters and records among the archives of the ancient abbey of Cluny, from 1077 to 1534*, 2 vols, Lewes

Duckett, G F, 1890 *Visitations of English Cluniac foundations*, London

Duncombe, F, 1989 *The story of Caen* (trans A Moyon), Ouest-France

Dyer, C, 1989 *Standards of living in the later Middle Ages: social change in England c 1200–1520*, Cambridge

Eames, E S, 1980 *Catalogue of medieval lead-glazed earthenware tiles in the Department of Medieval and Later Antiquities, British Museum*, London

Eames, E S, 1982 The tile pavement, in Excavations at Eltham Palace, 1975–9 (ed H Wood), *Trans London Middlesex Archaeol Soc* 33, 238–44

Eames, E S, 1992 *English tilers*, London

Easton, T, 1986 The internal decorative treatment of 16th- and 17th-century brick in Suffolk, *Post-Medieval Archaeol* 20, 1–17

Egan, G, 1995a Buckles, hasps and strap hooks, in J Clark (ed) 1995, 55–61

Egan, G, 1995b (1994) *Lead cloth seals and related items in the British Museum*, Brit Mus Occas Pap 93, 2 edn, London

Egan, G, 1996 Some archaeological evidence for metalworking in London c 1050–c 1700, *Hist Metall* 30, 83–94

Egan, G, 1997 Non-ceramic finds, in Thomas et al 1997, 201–10

Egan, G, 1998a *The medieval household: daily living c 1150–c 1450*, HMSO Medieval Finds Excav London 6, London

Egan, G, 1998b Medieval opaque white glass from London, *J Glass Stud* 40, 182–5

Egan, G, 1999 Pilgrimage to Bermondsey, *Archaeology Matters* 5

Egan, G, 2005 *Material culture in London in an age of transition: Tudor and Stuart period finds c 1450–c 1700 from excavations at riverside sites in Southwark*, MoLAS Monogr Ser 19, London

Egan, G, 2007 The non-ceramic finds, in Miller and Saxby 2007, 219–35

Egan, G, and Forsyth, H, 1997 Wound wire and silver gilt, in Gaimster and Stamper (eds) 1997, 215–38

Egan, G, and Pritchard, F, 1991 *Dress accessories c 1150–c 1450*, HMSO Medieval Finds Excav London 3, London

Englefield, H C, 1782 Sir Henry Englefield on Reading Abbey, *Archaeologia* 6, 61–6

English Heritage, 1991 *Management of archaeological projects*, London

Evans, D, and Verhaeghe, F, 1998–9 Brickware objects of Low Countries origin in the collections of Hull Museums, *Medieval Ceram* 22–3, 93–112

Evans, J, 1938 *The Romanesque architecture of the Order of Cluny*, Cambridge

Evans, J, 1950 *Cluniac art of the Romanesque period*, Cambridge

Faithorne, W, and Newcourt, R, 1658 An exact delineation of the Cities of London and Westminster and the suburbs thereof together with the Borough of Southwark, reproduced in Margary, H, 1981 *A collection of early maps of London*, Margary in assoc Guildhall Library, Kent

Fennell, K J, and Trinkhaus, E, 1997 Bilateral femoral and tibial periostitis in the La Ferrassie 1 Neanderthal, *J Archaeol Sci* 24, 985–95

Ferembach, D, Schwidetzky, I, and Stloukal, M, 1980 Recommendations for age and sex diagnosis of skeletons, *J Human Evol* 9, 517–49

Fergusson, P, and Harrison, S, 1999 *Rievaulx Abbey: community, architecture, memory*, London

Fernie, E C, 1985 The Romanesque church of Waltham Abbey, *J Brit Archaeol Ass* 3 ser 138, 48–78

Fincham, H W, 1933 (1915) *The Order of the Hospital of St John of Jerusalem and its Grand Priory of England*, 2 edn, London

Finnegan, M, 1978 Non-metric variation of the infracranial skeleton, *J Anat* 125, 23–37

Firman, R J, and Firman, P E, 1967 A geological approach to the study of medieval bricks, *Mercian Geol* 2, 299–318

Fletcher, B, 1943 (1896) *A history of architecture on the comparative method for students, craftsmen and amateurs*, 11 edn, London

Gaimster, D R M, 1997 *German stoneware 1200–1900: archaeology and cultural history*, London

Gaimster, D R M, and Nenk, B, 1997 English households in transition *c* 1450–1550: the ceramic evidence, in Gaimster and Stamper (eds) 1997, 171–95

Gaimster, D R M, and Redknap, M (eds), 1992 *Everyday and exotic pottery in Europe c AD 650–1900*, Oxford

Gaimster, D R M, and Stamper, P (eds), 1997 *The age of transition: the archaeology of English culture 1400–1600*, Soc Medieval Archaeol Monogr Ser 15/Oxbow Monogr 98, Oxford

Gaimster, D R M, and Verhaeghe, F, 1992 Handles with face-masks: a cross-channel type of late medieval highly decorated basin, in Gaimster and Redknap (eds) 1992, 303–23

Gaimster, M, and O'Connor, K, with Sherlock, R, 2006 Southwark, in Medieval Britain and Ireland in 2005, *Medieval Archaeol* 50, 315–17

Geddes, J, 1985 Small finds, in *Battle Abbey: the eastern range and the excavations of 1978–80* (ed J N Hare), Archaeol Rep 2, 147–77, London

Gem, R, 1988 The English parish church in the 11th and early 12th centuries: a great rebuilding, in *Minsters and parish churches: the local church in transition 950–1200* (ed J Blair), Oxford Univ Comm Archaeol Monogr 17, 21–30, Oxford

Gem, R, 1990 The Romanesque architecture of old St Paul's cathedral and its late 11th-century context, in *Medieval art, architecture and archaeology in London* (ed L Grant), Brit Archaeol Ass Conference Trans 10, 47–63, London

Gentleman's Magazine, 1808a [article on the recording of Bermondsey Abbey by JC Buckler], 78(i) (June), 476–8

Gentleman's Magazine, 1808b [drawings of architectural fragments from Bermondsey Abbey], 78(ii) (August), 681, pl II

Gentleman's Magazine, 1808c [series of architectural details of Bermondsey Abbey], 78(ii) (November), 977

Gentleman's Magazine, 1810 [article by John Buckler, senior, including plates of the north-west corner of the mansion and architectural fragments drawn by John Chessell Buckler and

engraved by George Buckler (reprinted from 1808 issues)], 80(ii) (December), 513, 2 plates

Gervase Gervase of Canterbury, *The historical works of Gervase of Canterbury* (ed W Stubbs), Chronicles and Memorials of Great Britain and Ireland during the Middle Ages, 2 vols, 1879–80, London

Gilchrist, R, 1995 Sacred waters: the function and meaning of water in medieval monasticism, in *Water in archaeology* (eds G Barber and T Barnett), 42–53, Bristol

Gilchrist, R, 1998 Norwich Cathedral: a biography of the north transept, *J Brit Archaeol Ass* 151, 107–36

Gilchrist, R, and Mytum, H (eds), 1993 *Advances in monastic archaeology*, BAR Brit Ser 227, Oxford

Gilchrist, R, and Sloane, B, 2005 *Requiem: the medieval monastic cemetery in Britain*, London

Godfrey, W H, 1952 English cloister lavatories as independent structures, *Archaeol J* 106, supplement memorial volume to Sir Alfred Clapham, 91–7

Goffin, R, 2003 The loom weights, in Malcolm, G, and Bowsher, D, with Cowie, R, *Middle Saxon London: excavations at the Royal Opera House 1989–99*, MoLAS Monogr Ser 15, 216–22, London

Golding, B, 1981 The coming of the Cluniacs, in *Proceedings of the Battle conference on Anglo-Norman studies, 3, 1980* (ed R A Brown), 65–77, Woodbridge

Goodall, J A A, 2002 Henry VII's court and the construction of Eton College, in *Windsor: medieval archaeology, art and architecture of the Thames valley* (eds L Keen and E Scarff), Brit Archaeol Ass Conference Trans 25, 247–63, London

Goodman, A H, Thomas, R B, Swedlund, A C, and Armelagos, G J, 1988 Biocultural perspectives on stress in prehistoric, historical and contemporary population research, *Yearb Phys Anthropol* 31, 169–202

Graham, R, 1926 The priory of La Charité-sur-Loire and the monastery of Bermondsey, *J Brit Archaeol Ass* 32, 157–91

Graham, R, 1929 *English ecclesiastical studies*, London

Graham, R, 1937 The church of the Cluniac monastery of St Saviour at Bermondsey, *J Brit Archaeol Ass* 3 ser 2, 145–9

Grainger, I, and Phillpotts, C, in prep *The abbey of St Mary Graces, East Smithfield, London*, MOLA Monogr Ser

Grainger, I, Hawkins, D, Cowal, L, and Mikulski, R, 2008 *The Black Death cemetery, East Smithfield, London*, MoLAS Monogr 43, London

Grant, A, 1982 The use of toothwear as a guide to the age of domestic ungulates, in *Ageing and sexing animal bones from archaeological sites* (eds B Wilson, C Grigson and S Payne), BAR Brit Ser 109, 91–108, Oxford

Grauer, A L, and Roberts, C A, 1996 Palaeoepidemiology, healing and possible treatment of trauma in the medieval cemetery population of St Helen-on-the-Walls, York, England, *American J Phys Anthropol* 100, 531–44

Greene, J P, 1992 *Medieval monasteries*, Leicester

Griffiths, N, 1995 Harness pendants and other fittings, in J Clark (ed) 1995, 61–70

Grimes, W F, 1968 *The excavation of Roman and medieval London*, London

Harden, D B, 1956 Glass, in *Dark Age Britain* (ed D B Harden), 132–67, London

Harden, D B, 1978 Anglo-Saxon and later medieval glass in Britain: some recent developments, *Medieval Archaeol* 22, 1–24

Hare, J N, 1985 *Battle Abbey: the eastern range and the excavations of 1978–80*, Hist Build Monuments Comm Archaeol Rep 2, London

Harris, R B, 2008 The structural history of the White Tower, 1066–1200, in *The White Tower* (ed E Impey), 28–93, London

Harrison, S, 2000 *Cleeve Abbey, Somerset*, London

Harvey, B, 1993 *Living and dying in England 1100–1540: the monastic experience*, Oxford

Harvey, J H, 1978 *The Perpendicular style, 1330–1485*, London

Harvey, P D A, and McGuiness, A, 1996 *A guide to British medieval seals*, London

Hatcher, J, 1986 Mortality in the 15th century: some new evidence, *Econ Hist Rev* 2 ser 39, 19–38

Hayfield, C, 1984 A late medieval pottey group from Humberston Abbey, S Humberside, *Lincolnshire Hist Archaeol* 19, 107–10

Haynes, M, Baker, F, and Tipping, R, 1998 A still worm from excavations at Carrick Castle, Argyll, *Post-Medieval Archaeol* 32, 33–44

Hayward, P, Nelson-Smith, T, and Shields, C, 1996 *Sea shore of Britain and northern Europe*, London

Heard, K, 1996 The hinterland of Roman Southwark: Part 1, *London Archaeol* 8, 76–82

Heard, K, 1998 Vinegar Yard, 33 Tanner Street, Bermondsey, SE1: a post-excavation assessment (VIY97), unpub MOL rep

Heidinga, H A, and Smink, E H, 1982 Brick spit-supports in the Netherlands (13th–16th century), in *Rotterdam Papers: Vol 4, A contribution to medieval archaeology* (ed J G N Renaud), 63–82, Rotterdam

Henig, M, 1988 Small finds from 1960–5, in *Excavations at St Augustine's Abbey: reports on excavations, 1960–78* (eds D Sherlock and H Woods), Kent Archaeol Soc Monogr Ser 4, 177–87, Maidstone

Herrmann, C, 2005 Beobachtungen zur Verwendung des Backsteins in der mittelalterlichen Architektur des Preußenlands, in *Technik des Backsteinbaus im Europa des Mittelalters* (eds H Johannes and D Sack), 99–112, Petersberg

Hicks, M, and Hicks, A, 2001 *St Gregory's Priory, Northgate, Canterbury: excavations 1988–91*, The Archaeol Canterbury ns 2, Canterbury

Hillson, S, 1986 *Teeth*, Cambridge

Hinton, P, and Thomas, R, 1997 The Greater London publication programme, *Archaeol J* 154, 196–213

HMC, 1885 Historical Manuscripts Commission, *The manuscripts of the earl of Westmorland, Captain Steward, Lord Stafford, Lord Muncaster, and others: Tenth report, appendix part 4* (eds W O Hewlett et al), London

HMC, 1907 Roy Comm Hist Manuscripts, *Report on the manuscripts of the earl of Ancaster, preserved at Grimthorpe* (ed S C Lomas), Hist Manuscripts Comm 66, London

HMC, 1925 Roy Comm Hist Manuscripts, *Report on the manuscripts of Lord de I'Isle and Dudley preserved at Penshurst Place: Vol 1*, Hist Manuscripts Comm 77, London

Hodges, H, 1964 *Artefacts: an introduction to early materials and technology*, London

Hodges, R, 1981 *The Hamwih pottery: the local and imported wares from 30 years' excavations at Middle Saxon Southampton and their European context*, London

Hoey, L R, 1997 The articulation of rib vaults in the Romanesque parish churches of England and Normandy, *Antiq J* 77, 145–77

Hohler, C, 1942 Medieval paving tiles in Buckinghamshire, *Rec Buckinghamshire* 14, 1–49, 99–132

Horwood, R, 1813 'Plan of the Cities of London and Westminster, the Borough of Southwark', 3 edn, reproduced in Margary, H, 1985 *The A–Z of Regency London*, Margary in assoc Guildhall Library, Kent

Howard, F E, 1936 *The medieval styles of the English parish church*, London

Howard, M, 1987 *The early Tudor country house: architecture and politics 1490–1550*, London

Howard, M, 1997 Civic buildings and courtier houses: new techniques and materials for architectural ornament, in Gaimster and Stamper (eds) 1997, 105–13

Howard, M, 2003 Recycling the monastic fabric: beyond the act of dissolution, in *The archaeology of Reformation c 1480–1580* (eds D R M Gaimster and R Gilchrist), Soc Post-Medieval Archaeol Monogr 1, 221–34, Leeds

Hulme, F, 1899 (1892) *The history, principles and practice of symbolism in Christian art*, 3 edn, London

Hurst, J G, 1965 Excavations at Pontefract Priory, appendix G: coffins and interments, in Bellamy, C V, *Pontefract Priory excavations, 1957–61*, Publ Thoresby Soc 49, 127–32, Leeds

Hurst, J G, Neal, D S, and Beuningen, J H van, 1986 *Pottery produced and traded in north-west Europe 1350–1650*, Rotterdam Pap 6, Rotterdam

Jackson-Stops, G, 1978 *Knole, Kent*, London

Jenner, M A, and Vince, A G, 1983 A dated type-series of London medieval pottery: Part 3, A late medieval Hertfordshire glazed ware, *Trans London Middlesex Archaeol Soc* 34, 151–70

Johnson, C, and Cronne, H A (eds), 1956 *Regesta regum Anglo-Normannorum, 1066–1154: Vol 2, Regesta Henrici primi, 1100–35*, Oxford

Jones, H, 1993 An archaeological evaluation of land bounded by Long Walk, Tower Bridge Road and Grange Walk, Southwark, unpub MOL rep

Judd, M A, and Roberts, C A, 1998 Fracture patterns at the medieval leper hospital in Chichester, *American J Phys Anthropol* 105, 43–55

Julkunen, H, Heinonen, O P, and Pyörälä, K, 1971 Hyperostosis of the spine in an adult population, *Annals Rheumatic Diseases* 30, 605–12

Jurkowski, M, 2006 The archive of Bermondsey Abbey, *Monastic Res Bull* 12, 10–19

Jurkowski, M, 2007 Monastic archives in The National Archives, *Archives* 32(116), 1–18

Keary, C F, 1887 *A catalogue of English coins in the British Museum: Anglo-Saxon series I*, London

Keen, M H, 1973 *England in the later Middle Ages*, London

Keene, D, 1989 Medieval London and its region, *London J* 14, 99–111

Keily, J, 1990 274–306 Bishopsgate (BOS87) building materials archive report, unpub MOL rep

Keily, J, Pringle, S, and Smith, T P, 1998 Building materials assessment for all phases: Spital Square/Lamb Street/Nantes Passage/Folgate Street, Spitalfields residential, E1 (SQU94), unpub MOL rep

Kingsford, C L (ed), 1905 *Chronicles of London*, London

Knowles, D, and Hadcock, R N, 1953 *Medieval religious houses: England and Wales,* London

Knowles, D, and Hadcock, R N, 1974 (1953) *Medieval religious houses: England and Wales*, 2 edn, London

L and P Hen VIII Letters and papers, foreign and domestic, of Henry VIII (eds J S Brewer, J Gairdner and R H Brodie), 22 vols in 35, 1864–1932, London

Larsen, C S, 1997 *Bioarchaeology: interpreting behaviour from the human skeleton*, Cambridge

Lea, R, 1981 Medieval moulded stones from Harp Lane, unpub MOL rep

Lever, C, 1977 *The naturalised animals of the British Isles*, London

Lewis, M E, Roberts, C A, and Manchester, K, 1995 Comparative study of the prevalence of maxillary sinusitis in later medieval urban and rural populations in northern England, *American J Phys Anthropol* 98, 497–506

Liber Albus Liber albus: the white book of the City of London (comp J Carpenter, trans H T Riley), 1861, London

Lilley, J M, Stroud, G, Brothwell, D R, and Williamson, M H, 1994 *The Jewish burial ground at Jewbury*, The Archaeology of York 12/3, York

Lloyd, N, 1983 (1925) *A history of English brickwork*, repr, Woodbridge

Locker, A, 1997 The fish bones, in Thomas et al 1997, 234–5

Lockett, R B, 1971 A catalogue of Romanesque sculpture from the Cluniac houses of England, *J Brit Archaeol Ass* 34, 43–61

London Possessory Assizes London possessory assizes: a calendar (ed H M Chew), London Rec Soc 1, 1965, London

Lowe, T G, 1990 Current concepts review: Scheuermann's disease, *J Bone Joint Surgery* 72, 940–5

Lyne, M A B, 1997 *Lewes Priory: excavations by Richard Lewis 1969–82*, Lewes

MacGregor, A, 1985 *Bone, antler, ivory and horn: the technology of skeletal materials since the Roman period*, London

Mackinder, A, in prep A medieval drain at 161 Grange Road, Bermondsey, *London Archaeol*

Manning, O, and Bray, W, 1804–14 *History and antiquities of the county of Surrey*, 3 vols, London

Margeson, S M, 1993 *Norwich households: the medieval and post-medieval finds from Norwich survey excavations 1977–8*, E Anglian Archaeol Rep 58, Norwich

Marks, R, 1993 *Stained glass in England during the Middle Ages*, London

Marshall, C J, 1924 A medieval pottery kiln discovered at Cheam, Surrey, *Surrey Archaeol Collect* 35, 79–94

Martin, A R, 1926 On the topography of the Cluniac abbey of St Saviour at Bermondsey, *J Brit Archaeol Ass* 32, 192–228

Mayhew, N J, 1983 *Sterling imitations of Edwardian type*, Roy Numis Soc Spec Publ 14, London

Mays, S, 1998 *The archaeology of human bones*, London

McDonnell, K, 1978 *Medieval London suburbs*, London

McKisack, M, 1959 *The 14th century, 1307–99*, Oxford Hist Engl 5, Oxford

Mellor, M, 1994 A synthesis of Middle and Late Saxon, medieval and early post-medieval pottery in the Oxford region, *Oxoniensia* 59, 17–217

Mercer, E, 1962 *English art 1553–1625*, Oxford Hist Art 2, Oxford

Millénaire de Cluny, 1910 Congrès d'histoire et d'archéologie tenu à Cluny, les 10, 11, 12 sept., 1910, Académie de Mâcon, 2 vols, Mâcon

Miller, P, and Saxby, D, 2007 *The Augustinian priory of St Mary Merton, Surrey: excavations 1976–90*, MoLAS Monogr Ser 34, London

Mills, A D, 2001 *A dictionary of London place-names*, Oxford

Mitchiner, M, 1988 *Jetons, medalets and tokens: Vol 1, The medieval period and Nuremberg*, London

Mon Angl Dugdale, W, 1817–30 *Monasticon anglicanum* (eds R Dodsworth, J Stevens, J Caley, H Ellis, B Badinel and R C Taylor), 6 vols in 8 pts, London

Moore, N J, 1991 Brick, in *English medieval industries: craftsmen, techniques, products* (eds J Blair and N Ramsay), 211–36, London

Moorhouse, S, 1972 Medieval distilling-apparatus of glass and pottery, *Medieval Archaeol* 16, 79–121

Moorhouse, S, 1993 Pottery and glass in the medieval monastery, in Gilchrist and Mytum (eds) 1993, 127–48

Morley, B M, 1990 *Wenlock Priory*, London

Morris, R K, 1978 The development of later Gothic mouldings in England, *Architect Hist* 21, 18–57

Morris, R K, 1979 The development of later Gothic mouldings in England, *Architect Hist* 22, 1–48

Morris, R K, 1990 The gothic mouldings of the Latin and Lady chapels, in *Saint Frideswide's monastery, at Oxford* (ed J Blair), 169–83, Gloucester

Morris, R K, 1992 An English glossary of medieval mouldings, *Architect Hist* 35, 1–16

MPRG, 1998 Medieval Pottery Res Group, *A guide to the classification of medieval ceramic forms*, Medieval Pottery Res Group Occas Pap 1, London

Museum of London, nd a [website home page], www.museumoflondonarchaeology.org.uk/english (last accessed 11 September 2010)

Museum of London, nd b [osteological data], http://www.museumoflondon.org.uk/English/Collections/OnlineResources/CHB/Database/ (last accessed 11 September 2010)

Nelson, S, 1981 A group of pottery waster material from Kingston, *London Archaeol* 4, 96–102

Nenk, B, 1992 Ceramic culinary moulds, in Gaimster and

Redknap (eds) 1992, 290–302

Newton, R, 1976 The effects of medieval glass paint, *Stained Glass* 71, 226–30

Noël Hume, I, 1957 Medieval bottles from London, *The Connoisseur* March, 104–8

North, J J, 1975 *English hammered coinage*, 2 vols, London

Norton, C, 1993 The export of decorated floor tiles from Normandy, in *Medieval art, architecture and archaeology at Rouen* (ed J Stratford), Brit Archaeol Ass Conference Trans 12, 81–97, Leeds

Observances *The observances in use at the Augustinian priory of S Giles and S Andrew at Barnwell, Cambridgeshire* (ed, trans and glossary J W Clark), 1897, Cambridge, http://www.archive.org/details/observancesinuse00stgi (last accessed 11 September 2010)

O'Neill, J P (ed), 1996 *Enamels of Limoges 1100–1350*, Metropolitan Museum of Art, New York

Orton, C R, 1988 Post-Roman pottery, in *Excavations in Southwark 1973–6, Lambeth 1973–9* (ed P Hinton), London Middlesex Archaeol Soc/Surrey Archaeol Soc Joint Publ 3, 295–364, London

Orton, C R, and Pearce, J E, 1984 The pottery, in Excavations at Aldgate 1974 (eds A Thompson, F Grew and J Schofield), *Post-Medieval Archaeol* 18, 34–68

Ortner, D J, and Putschar, W G J, 1985 *Identification of pathological conditions in human skeletal remains*, Washington, DC

Oxford DNB Oxford Dictionary of National Biography, www.oxforddnb.com/articles/3/3863-article.thml?back= (last accessed 17 August 2010)

Paris, *Flores* Paris, M, *Flores historiarum* (ed H R Luard), 3 vols, 1890, London

Parsons, D (ed), 1990 *Stone quarrying and building in England: AD 43–1525*, Chichester

Paul, R W, 1912 The plan of the church and monastery of St Augustine, Bristol, *Archaeologia* 63, 231–50

Payne, S, 1973 Kill-off patterns in sheep and goats: the mandibles from Asvan Kale, *Anatolian Studies* 23, 281–303

Pearce, J E, 1992 *Post-medieval pottery in London, 1500–1700, border wares*, Norwich

Pearce, J E, 1997a Evidence for the early 16th-century Surrey-Hampshire border industry from the City of London, *Medieval Ceram* 21, 43–60

Pearce, J E, 1997b Post-Roman pottery from Hibernia Wharf (HIB79), unpub MOL rep

Pearce, J E, 1998 Hanging lamps – ceramic, in Egan 1998a, 127–9

Pearce, J E, 2001 Post-Roman pottery from the City ditch (WFG18), in Milne, G, with Cohen, N, *Excavations at medieval Cripplegate, London: archaeology after the Blitz, 1946–8*, 21–4, Swindon

Pearce, J E, 2002 The 13th- to 15th-century pottery, in Howe, E, *Roman defences and medieval industry: excavations at Baltic House, City of London*, MoLAS Monogr Ser 7, 70–4, London

Pearce, J E, in prep Post-Roman pottery from Bull Wharf (BUF90), unpub MOL rep

Pearce, J E, and Vince, A, 1988 *A dated type-series of London medieval pottery: Part 4, Surrey whitewares*, Trans London Middlesex Archaeol Soc Spec Pap 10, London

Pearce, J E, Vince, A, and White, R, 1982 A dated type-series of London medieval pottery: Part 1, Mill Green ware, *Trans London Middlesex Archaeol Soc* 33, 266–98

Pearce, J E, Vince, A G, and Jenner, M A, 1985 *A dated type-series of London medieval pottery: Part 2, London-type ware*, Trans London Middlesex Archaeol Soc Spec Pap 6, London

Pecina, M M, and Bojanic, I, 1993 *Overuse injuries of the musculo-skeletal system*, Boca Raton, Fla

Pedes finium Pedes finium: or, fines relating to the county of Surrey, levied in the king's court, from the seventh year of Richard I, to the end of the reign of Henry VII (ed F B Lewis), Surrey Archaeol Collect extra vol 1, 1894, Guildford

Peers, C, 1957 *Kirby Muxloe Castle, Leicestershire*, Department of the Environment guidebook, London

Pennant, T, 1790 *Of London*, London

Pfeiffer, S, 1991 Rib lesions and New World tuberculosis, *Int J Osteoarchaeol* 1, 191–8

Phenice, T W, 1969 A newly developed visual method of sexing the *os pubis*, *American J Phys Anthropol* 30, 297–302

Phillipe, A, 1905 L'Église de la Charité-sur-Loire, *Bulletin Monumental* 69, 469–500

Philp, B J, 1968 *Excavations at Faversham, 1965: the royal abbey, Roman villa and Belgic farmstead*, Kent Archaeol Res Group Coun Res Rep 1, Maidstone

Pinnell, J, 1999 *Wenlock Priory*, London

Pinto de Matos, M A, and Monteiro, J P, 1994 *Oriental influence on 17th-century Portuguese ceramics*, Lisbon

Pipe, A, 1990 The faunal remains from Tower of London postern gate, unpub MOL rep

Pipe, A, 1997 The animal bones, in Thomas et al 1997, 231–4

Platt, C, 1981 *The parish churches of medieval England*, London

Poole, A L, 1955 *From Domesday book to Magna Carta, 1087–1216*, 2 edn, Oxford Hist Engl, Oxford

Poole, H, 2000 *Lewes Priory: the site and its history*, Lewes

Poulton, R, 1988 *Archaeological investigations on the site of Chertsey Abbey*, Surrey Archaeol Soc Res Vol 11, Guildford

Poulton, R, and Woods, R, 1984 *Excavations on the site of the Dominican friary at Guildford in 1974 and 1978*, Surrey Archaeol Soc Res Vol 9, Guildford

Pritchard, F, 1986 Ornamental stonework from Roman London, *Britannia* 17, 169–89

Pritchard, F, 1991 The small finds, in Vince (ed) 1991a, 120–278

Pryor, S, and Blockley, K, 1978 A 17th-century kiln site at Woolwich, *Post-Medieval Archaeol* 12, 30–85

Raby, F J E, and Reynolds, P K B, 1979 *Thetford Priory, Norfolk*, London

Raby, F J E, and Reynolds, P K B, 1983 (1952) *Castle Acre Priory*, 2 edn, London

Rackham, D J, 1986 Assessing the relative frequency of species by the application of a stochastic model to a zooarchaeological database, in *Database management and zooarchaeology. Journal of the European study group of physical, chemical, biological and mathematical techniques applied to archaeology* (ed L H van Wijngaarden-Bakker), Res Vol 40, 185–92, Amsterdam

Raleigh Radford, C A, 2006 (1995) *Crossraguel Abbey*, rev edn, Edinburgh

RCHM(E), 1921 Roy Comm Hist Monuments (Engl), *An inventory of the historical monuments in Essex: Vol 2, Central and south-west*, London

RCHM(E), 1924 Roy Comm Hist Monuments (Engl), *An inventory of the historical monuments in London: Vol 1, Westminster Abbey*, London

Redknap, M, 1991 The Saxon pottery from Barking Abbey: Part 1, Local wares, *London Archaeol* 6, 353–60

Redknap, M, 1992 The Saxon pottery from Barking Abbey: Part 2, The Continental imports, *London Archaeol* 6, 378–81

Reed, I, 1992 Oil pot or what? *Medieval Ceram* 16, 71–2

Reg Edington The register of William Edington, Bishop of Winchester 1346–66 (ed S F Hockey), Hampshire Rec Ser 7 pt i, 1986; 8 pt ii, 1987, Winchester

Reg Pontissara Register of John de Pontissara, Bishop of Winchester, 1282–1304 (ed C Deedes), Surrey Rec Soc Ser 1, 6 (2 vols), London

Reg Woodlock Registrum Henrici Woodlock diocesis Wintoniensis 1305–16 (ed A W Goodman), Canterbury York Ser 43–4, 1940–1, Oxford

Reilly, K, 2006 Vertebrate remains, in Seeley et al 2006, 130–42

Resnick, D, and Niwayama, G, 1988 (1981) *Diagnosis of bone and joint disorders*, 6 vols, 2 edn, Philadelphia

Richards, J D, 1993 *The Bedern foundry*, The Archaeology of York 10/3, York

Rickman, T, 1817 *An attempt to discriminate the styles of English architecture, from the Conquest to the Reformation*, London

Rigold, S, 1977 Romanesque bases in and south-east of the limestone belt, in *Ancient monuments and their interpretation. Essays presented to A J Taylor* (eds M Apted, R Gilyard-Beer and A D Saunders), 99–137, London

Riley, H T (trans), 1863 *Chronicles of the mayors and sheriffs of London, AD 1188–1274*, London

Rinaldi, M, 1989 *Kraak porcelain: a moment in the history of trade*, London

Roberts, C A, and Manchester, K, 1995 (1983) *The archaeology of disease*, 2 edn, Stroud

Roberts, C A, Lucy, D, and Manchester, K, 1994 Inflammatory lesions of ribs: an analysis of the Terry collection, *American J Phys Anthropol* 95, 169–82

Rocque, J, 1746 'Exact survey of the City of London Westminster and Southwark and the country 10 miles round', reproduced in Margary, H, 1971 *'Exact survey of the City of London Westminster and Southwark and the country 10 miles round' by John Rocque, 1746*, Margary in assoc Guildhall Library, Kent

Rogers, J, and Waldron, T, 1989 Infections in palaeopathology: the basis of classification according to most probable cause, *J Archaeol Sci* 16, 611–25

Rogers, J, and Waldron, T, 1995 *A field guide to joint diseases in archaeology*, Chichester

Rot Parlt Rotuli parliamentorum: ut et petitiones, et placita in parliament (ed J Strachey), 6 vols, 1783–1832, London

Ruempol, A P E, and Dongen, A G A van, 1991 *Pre-industrial utensils 1150–1800*, Rotterdam

Russell, R, 1979 *Guide to British topographical prints*, Newton Abbot

Ryan, P, 1996 *Brick in Essex*, London

Samuel, M W, 1997 Moulded stone, in Thomas et al 1997, 186–95

Samuel, M W, 1999 The use and significance of the mason's marks: how these and other technical features throw light on the craft traditions of the waterfront masons, in Thurley, S, *Whitehall Palace: an architectural history of the royal apartments 1290–1698*, 164–8, London

Samuel, M W, 2001 The architectural fragments, in Hicks and Hicks 2001, 151–82

Samuel, M W, 2007 The moulded stone, in Miller and Saxby 2007, 176–95

Samuel, M W, 2009 Reconstructing the north range and tower/gatehouse; and Architectural fragments from Rotherhithe, in Blatherwick and Bluer 2009, 27–31; 159–65

Saxby, D, 1997 12–23 Jacob's Island, bounded by Mill Street, George Row, Jacob Street and Bermondsey Wall West, London SE1 (JAC96), unpub MOL rep

Schmid, E, 1972 *An atlas of animal bones for prehistorians, archaeologists, and Quaternary geologists*, London

Schofield, J, 1984 *The building of London from the Conquest to the Great Fire*, London

Schofield, J, 1993 (1984) *The building of London from the Conquest to the Great Fire*, rev edn, London

Schofield, J, 1994 *Medieval London houses*, London

Schofield, J (ed), with Maloney, C, 1998 *Archaeology in the City of London 1907–91: a guide to records of excavations by the Museum of London and its predecessors*, MoLAS Archaeol Gazetteer Ser 1, London

Schofield, J, 2009 The question of a court style, in Blatherwick and Bluer 2009, 154–5

Schofield, J, and Lea, R, 2005 *Holy Trinity Priory, Aldgate, City of London: an archaeological reconstruction and history*, MoLAS Monogr Ser 24, London

Scott, M, 1980 *Late Gothic Europe 1400–1500*, Hist Dress Ser, London

Seeley, D, Phillpotts, C, and Samuel, M, 2006 *Winchester Palace: excavations at the Southwark residence of the bishops of Winchester*, MoLAS Monogr Ser 31, London

Service, A, 1982 *The buildings of Britain, Anglo-Saxon and Norman, a guide and gazetteer*, Buildings of Britain Ser, London

Sewart, R, 1996 The distillation vessels, in Hutchinson, M, Edward IV's bulwark: excavations at Tower Hill, London, 1985, *Trans London Middlesex Archaeol Soc* 47, 130–1

Sherlock, R L, 1960 (1947) *British regional geology: London and Thames valley*, 3 edn, London

Sidell, J, Cotton, J, Rayner, L, and Wheeler, L, 2002 *The prehistory and topography of Southwark and Lambeth*, MoLAS Monogr Ser 14, London

Slade, C F, 1976 Excavation at Reading Abbey 1971–3, *Berkshire Archaeol J* 68, 29–70

Sloane, B, in prep *The Augustinian nunnery of St Mary Clerkenwell, London*, MOLA Monogr Ser

Sloane, B, and Malcolm, G, 2004 *Excavations at the priory of the*

Order of the Hospital of St John of Jerusalem, Clerkenwell, London, MoLAS Monogr Ser 20, London

Smith, T P, 1975 Rye House, Hertfordshire, and aspects of early brickwork in England, *Archaeol J* 132, 111–50

Smith, T P, 1985 *The medieval brickmaking industry in England 1400–50*, BAR Brit Ser 138, Oxford

Smith, T P, 1990 The Roper Gateway, St Dunstan's Street, Canterbury, *Archaeol Cantiana* 108, 163–82

Smith, T P, 1992 The diaper work at Queens College, Cambridge, *Brit Brick Soc Information* 55, 20–3

Smith, T P, 1997 The brickwork of Goltho chapel, Lincolnshire, *Brit Brick Soc Information* 71, 7–11

Smith, T P, with Betts, I, 2004a Ceramic building material, in Barber et al 2004, 138–46

Smith, T P, 2004b The late medieval bricks and brickwork of London Wall in Saint Alphage Garden, EC2, *London Archaeol* 10, 255–63

Spencer, B, 1984 Medieval seal dies recently found at London, *Antiq J* 64, 376–82

Spencer, B, 1998 *Pilgrim souvenirs and secular badges*, Medieval Finds Excav London 7, London

Stalley, R, 1987 *The Cistercian monasteries of Ireland*, London

Stamp, L D, 1969 *Nature conservation in Britain*, London

Steele, A, and Sloane, B, 1997 Monastery of St Saviour, Bermondsey SE1, London Borough of Southwark, English Heritage project 29: an archaeological assessment of excavations 1956–95 and updated project design, unpub rep

Stephenson, R, 1991 Post-medieval ceramic birdpots from excavations in Greater London, *London Archaeol* 6, 320–1

Stephenson, R, 2007 The pottery, in Miller and Saxby 2007, 214–19

Stephenson, R, and Miller, P, 1996 Interim statement on the excavation of a medieval kiln site at Eden Street, Kingston upon Thames, *Medieval Ceram* 20, 71–3

Stewart, I, 1984 The early English denarial coinage, *c* 680–*c* 750, in *Sceattas in England and on the Continent: the 7th Oxford symposium on coinage and monetary history* (eds D Hill and D M Metcalf), BAR Brit Ser 128, 5–26, Oxford

Stirland, A, 1991 Paget's disease (osteitis deformans): a classic case? *Int J Osteoarchaeol* 1, 173–7

Stirland, A, and Waldron, T, 1990 The earliest cases of tuberculosis in Britain, *J Archaeol Sci* 17, 221–30

Stocker, D, 1993 Recording worked stone, in Gilchrist and Mytum (eds) 1993, 19–27

Stopford, J, and Wright, S M, 1998 A group of late medieval inscribed tiles from Bordesley Abbey, *Antiq J* 78, 307–22

Stott, P, 1991 Saxon and Norman coins from London, in Vince (ed) 1991a, 279–325

Stow, J, 1603 *A survey of London* (ed C L Kingsford), 2 vols, 1908 repr 1971, Oxford

Stroud, G, 1994 The population, in Lilley et al 1994, 424–49

Stroud, G, and Kemp, R L, 1993 *Cemeteries of the church and priory of St Andrew, Fishergate*, The Archaeology of York 12/2, York

Stuart-Macadam, P L, 1989 Nutritional deficiency diseases: a survey of scurvy, rickets and iron-deficiency anaemia, in

Reconstruction of life from the skeleton (eds M Y Iscan and K A R Kennedy), 201–22, New York

Summerson, J, 1991 *Architecture in Britain: 1530–1830*, Harmondsworth

Surrey feet of fines Abstracts of Surrey feet of fines, 1509–58 (ed C A F Meekings), Surrey Rec Soc Ser 19, 1946, London

Tatton-Brown, T, 1980 The use of Quarr stone in London and east Kent, *Medieval Archaeol* 24, 213–15

Tatton-Brown, T, 1984 St John's Hospital, Canterbury 1084–1984 [information leaflet], Canterbury

Tatton-Brown, T, 1990 Building stone in Canterbury, in Parsons (ed) 1990, 70–82

Taxatio Taxatio ecclesiastica Angliae et Walliae auctoritate P Nicholai IV (eds T Astle, S Ayscough and J Caley), Rec Comm, 1802, London

Taylor, J, 2008 Medieval and post-medieval buildings along Bermondsey Street, *London Archaeol* 12, 9–14

Taylor, H M, and Taylor, J, 1978 *Anglo-Saxon architecture: Vol 3*, Cambridge

Theuerkauff-Liederwald, A-E, 1988 *Mittelalterliche Bronze- und Messinggefässe: Eimer, Kannen, Lavabokessel*, Bronzegeräte des Mittelalters 4, Berlin

Thoby, P, 1953 *Les Croix Limosins de la fin du 12e siécle au debut du 14e siécle*, Paris

Thomas, C, Sloane, B, and Phillpott, C, 1997 *Excavations at the priory and hospital of St Mary Spital, London*, MoLAS Monogr Ser 1, London

Thomas, G, 2003 *Late Anglo-Saxon and Viking-Age strapends 750–1100: Part 1*, Finds Res Group AD 700–1700 Datasheet 32, no place

Thurlby, M, 1995 The Lady chapel of Glastonbury Abbey, *Antiq J* 75, 107–70

Thurley, S, 1993 *The royal palaces of Tudor England*, London

Thurley, S, 2003 *Hampton Court: a social and architectural history*, London

Timby, J R, 1988 The Middle Saxon pottery, in *The coins and pottery from Hamwic* (ed P Andrews), 73–122, Southampton

Trotter, M, and Gleser, G C, 1952 Estimation of stature from long bones of American whites and Negroes, *American J Phys Anthropol* 10, 463–514

Trotter, M, and Gleser, G C, 1958 A re-evaluation of estimation of stature based on measurements of stature taken during life and long bones after death, *American J Phys Anthropol* 16, 79–123

Turner-Rugg, A, 1995 Medieval pottery from St Albans, *Medieval Ceram* 19, 45–66

Tyler, K, Stephenson, R, and Betts, I M, 2008 *London's delftware industry: the tin-glazed pottery industries of Southwark and Lambeth*, MoLAS Monogr Ser 40, London

Ubelaker, D H, 1984 *Human skeletal remains: excavation, analysis, interpretation*, Washington, DC

Val Eccl Valor Ecclesiasticus, tempore Henrici VIII, auctoritate regia institutus (eds J Caley and J Hunter), Rec Comm, 6 vols, 1810–34, London

VCH, 1902 *The Victoria history of the county of Surrey: Vol 1*, London

VCH, 1906 *The Victoria history of the county of Norfolk: Vol 2*, London

VCH, 1907 *The Victoria history of the county of Derbyshire: Vol 2*, London

VCH, 1909 *The Victoria history of London: Vol 1* (ed W Page), London

VCH, 1912 *The Victoria history of the county of Surrey: Vol 4*, London

VCH, 1967 (1902–14) *The Victoria history of the county of Surrey: Vol 2*, 4 vols, London

VCH, 1973 *The Victoria history of the county of Sussex: Vol 2*, London

Vince, A, 1985 Saxon and medieval pottery in London: a review, *Medieval Archaeol* 29, 25–93

Vince, A, 1990 *Saxon London: an archaeological investigation*, London

Vince, A (ed), 1991a *Aspects of Saxo-Norman London: Part 2, Finds and environmental evidence*, London Middlesex Archaeol Soc Spec Pap 12, London

Vince, A, 1991b Early medieval London: refining the chronology, *London Archaeol* 6, 263–71

Vince, A G, and Jenner, A, 1991 The Saxon and early medieval pottery of London, in Vince (ed) 1991a, 19–119

Virey, J, 1910 Un ancien plan de Cluny, in *Millénaire de Cluny* 1910, ii, 231–47 and pl XI

Waldron, T, 1985 DISH at Merton Priory: evidence for a 'new' occupational disease, *Brit Medical J* 291, 1762–4

Waldron, T, 1992 Unilateral spondylolysis, *Int J Osteoarchaeol* 2, 177–81

Waldron, T, 1993a A case referent study of spondylolysis and spina bifida and transitional vertebrae in human skeletal remains, *Int J Osteoarchaeol* 3, 55–7

Waldron, T, 1993b The human remains from the Royal Mint site (MIN86), unpub MOL rep

Waldron, T, 1994 *Counting the dead: the epidemiology of skeletal populations*, Chichester

Walton Rogers, P, 1997 *Textile production at 16–22 Coppergate*, The Archaeology of York 17/11, York

Ward Perkins, J D, 1940 *London Museum medieval catalogue*, London

Watson, B, Brigham, T, and Dyson, T, 2001 *London bridge: 2000 years of a river crossing*, MoLAS Monogr Ser 8, London

Weinbaum, M (ed), 1976 *The London eyre of 1276*, London Rec Soc 12, Leicester

Wells, C, 1957 The medieval burials, in Robertson-Mackay, R, Recent excavations at the Cluniac priory of St Mary, Thetford, Norfolk, *Medieval Archaeol* 1, 99–103

Wells, C, 1964 *Bones, bodies and disease: evidence of disease and abnormality in early man*, London

Werner, A, 1998 *London bodies: the changing shape of Londoners from prehistoric times to the present day*, London

West, J, 1993 The priory church of St Bartholomew the Great: the 12th-century building and its context, in *'The Guild of Rahere' Annual Rep*, 19–30, London

White, E, 1993 The measure of meat: monastic diet in medieval England, in *Food for the community: special diets for special groups* (ed C A Wilson), 5–42, Edinburgh

White, W, 1988 *Skeletal remains from the cemetery of St Nicholas Shambles, City of London*, London Middlesex Archaeol Soc Spec Pap 9, London

White, W, 2004 The human bone, in Barber et al 2004, 158–79

White, W, 2006 The Museum of London's Wellcome Osteological research database, in Lohman, J, and Goodnow, K, *Human remains and museum practice*, 106–10, London

Wight, J A, 1972 *Brick building in England from the Middle Ages to 1550*, London

Wilcox, R, 1989 Thetford Cluniac Priory excavations 1971–4, *Norfolk Archaeol* 40, 1–18

Wilkinson, R, 1819 *Londina illustrata: Vol 1*, London (no pagination)

Williamson, M H, 1994 Multivariate studies, in Lilley et al 1994, 450–5

Wilson, B, Grigson, C, and Payne, S, 1982 *Ageing and sexing animal bones from archaeological sites*, BAR Brit Ser 109, Oxford

Wilson, C, 1984 Sculpture, in *English Romanesque art 1066–1200* (eds G Zarnecki, R Gem and C Brooke), 204–6, London

Wilson, C A, 1973 *Food and drink in Britain from the Stone Age to recent times*, London

Wood, M E, 1965 *The English medieval house*, London

Wooldridge, K, 2003 The archaeology of 151–153 Bermondsey Street, Southwark, *Surrey Archaeol Collect* 90, 181–210

Wright, S M, 2008 (2010) London's religious houses: a review of ongoing research, *Church Archaeol* 12, 49–63

Zimmerman, M R, and Kelley, M A, 1982 *Atlas of human palaeopathology*, New York

Compiled by Susan Vaughan

Page numbers in **bold** indicate illustrations and maps
All street names and locations are in London unless specified otherwise
County names within parentheses refer to historic counties